The Social Origins of Language

Oxford Studies in the Evolution of Language

General Editors
Kathleen R. Gibson, *University of Texas at Houston,*
and Maggie Tallerman, *Newcastle University*

RECENTLY PUBLISHED

See the end of the book for a complete list of titles published
and in preparation for the series.

The Social Origins of Language

Edited by
DANIEL DOR, CHRIS KNIGHT,
AND JEROME LEWIS

OXFORD
UNIVERSITY PRESS

OXFORD
UNIVERSITY PRESS

Great Clarendon Street, Oxford, OX2 6DP,
United Kingdom

Oxford University Press is a department of the University of Oxford.
It furthers the University's objective of excellence in research, scholarship,
and education by publishing worldwide. Oxford is a registered trade mark of
Oxford University Press in the UK and in certain other countries

First Edition published in 2014

Impression: 1

Published in the United States of America by Oxford University Press
198 Madison Avenue, New York, NY 10016, United States of America

British Library Cataloguing in Publication Data
Data available

Library of Congress Control Number: 2013953434

ISBN 978–0–19–966532–7 (hbk)
      978–0–19–966533–4 (pbk)

As printed and bound by
CPI Group (UK) Ltd, Croydon, CR0 4YY

Contents

Part III. Apes and People, Past and Present

Part IV. Social Theories of Language Evolution

Part V. The Journey Thereafter

Acknowledgements

This volume began life in a small but intensive workshop—'The Social Origins of Language'—held at the Department of Anthropology, University College London. Feeling that the social aspects of language were the key to a more profound understanding of language's evolution, the editors invited an international group of scholars from a wide range of disciplines to come and discuss these issues for five days in London. Rather than dictate themes, the editors asked each invitee to propose the titles and lengths of the interventions they wished to contribute, and we organized the proceedings with as much time for discussion as exposition to ensure a more discursive and exploratory workshop. The results, laid out here, exceeded our expectations. The range of ideas, research, and debate synthesized are remarkable for their breadth, erudition, and depth, marking a significant step toward understanding how language first evolved.

The editors would like to thank the Department of Anthropology at UCL for the generous support given to the workshop and later in preparing the manuscript. Susanne Kuechler, Martin O'Conner, Sorin Gogg, Chris Hagisavva, and Keiko Homewood were especially supportive and we thank them very much. The good will of the contributors to peer-review each other's work, to contribute to an online debate to continue the conversation beyond the conference, and to provide materials on time is much appreciated. Cathryn Townsend deserves special thanks for her hard work in the editorial process. John Davey, Julia Steer, and the series editors Maggie Tallerman and Kathleen Gibson at OUP have been especially supportive and engaged facilitators whose long term critical and perceptive encouragement has been immensely valuable to the success of this project.

List of Figures

List of Tables

Notes on the Contributors

Zanna Clay is a Post-Doctoral Research Fellow, currently at Emory University, working on empathy and communication in bonobos. She completed her Ph.D. in Psychology at the University of St Andrews, focusing on bonobo vocal communication, social behaviour, and their links to language evolution. Using the comparative approach, Zanna Clay's research concerns comparative models of language evolution and primate vocal communication as well as primate social behaviour, socio-cognitive development, empathy, and emotion processes.

Dan Dediu is a Senior Investigator in the Language and Genetics Department, the Max Planck Institute for Psycholinguistics, Nijmegen, and his main interests concern the genetic bases of language and speech and their influence on language origins, evolution, and diversity. He is currently investigating the effects that genetic biases influencing vocal tract anatomy and physiology might have on phonetic and phonological diversity. In his work, he uses a variety of advanced quantitative methods, computer simulations, and experimental approaches.

Jean-Louis Dessalles is Associate Professor at Telecom ParisTech. His research interests include the study of relevance and of the stability of honest communication, using Simplicity Theory and Game Theory as modelling tools. He authored *Why We Talk* (Oxford University Press 2007). www.dessalles.fr

Daniel Dor has a Ph.D. in Linguistics from Stanford University, and is Senior Lecturer in Communication at Tel Aviv University. His main interest lies in the development of a theory of language as a communication technology. Together with Eva Jablonka, he has written extensively on the evolution of language. In a different (but related) domain, Dor has published books and articles on the role of the media, and its language, in the construction of political hegemony. His *Intifada Hits the Headlines* was chosen as book of the year 2004 in communication by Choice Magazine.

N. J. Enfield is Professor of Ethnolinguistics at Radboud University Nijmegen and Senior staff scientist at the Max Planck Institute for Psycholinguistics. He is leader of the European Research Council project 'Human Sociality and Systems of Language Use' (2010–2014). His latest book *Relationship Thinking* was published in 2013.

Simona Ginsburg is a neurobiologist at the Open University of Israel also engaged in philosophy of biology. She studied the function of ionic channels in the presynaptic nerve terminal and the kinetic and stochastic properties of channels in general. In the past decade her work has focused on early nervous systems and the evolution of experiencing.

EVA JABLONKA has an M.Sc. in Microbiology from Ben-Gurion University, Israel and a Ph.D. in Genetics from the Hebrew University, Jerusalem, Israel. Her post doctoral studies were in the Philosophy of Science and in Developmental Genetics. She is a professor in the Cohn Institute for the History and Philosophy of Science and Ideas, Tel-Aviv. Her main interest is the understanding of evolution, especially evolution that is driven by non-genetic hereditary variations, and the evolution of nervous systems and consciousness.

SVERKER JOHANSSON is Director of the Education and Research Office at Dalarna University, Sweden. After an initial research career in particle physics and neutrino astronomy, he switched to evolutionary linguistics, where his main focus is synthesis of evidence across the multiple disciplines involved.

ADAM KENDON studied biological sciences and experimental psychology at Cambridge (BA 1955) and Oxford (D.Phil. 1963). He has worked at universities in the United States, Australia, and Italy. His books include *Sign Languages of Aboriginal Australia* (1988), *Conducting Interaction* (1990), *Gesture: Visible Action as Utterance* (2004), and *Gesture in Naples and Gesture in Classical Antiquity* (2000), a translation of Andrea de Jorio's treatise on Neapolitan gesture of 1832. He is Editor of *Gesture*.

CHRIS KNIGHT lectures for the Radical Anthropology Group and was for many years Professor of Anthropology at the University of East London. Best known for his 1991 book *Blood Relations: Menstruation and the Origins of Culture,* he co-founded with Jim Hurford the Evolution of Language (EVOLANG) series of international conferences and has published widely on the evolutionary emergence of language and culture.

EHUD LAMM is a philosopher and historian of biology at the Cohn Institute for the History and Philosophy of Science and Ideas at Tel Aviv University. He holds a degree in Computer Science and taught Computer Science academically and is the co-author with Ron Unger of a textbook on Biological Computation. His work focuses on genetics and the theory of evolution. His current research interests are the evolution of the genome, evolution of language, modelling, and evolutionary narratives.

STEPHEN C. LEVINSON's research focuses on language diversity and its implications for theories of human cognition. Language is the only animal communication system that differs radically in form and meaning across social groups of the same species, a fact that has been neglected in the cognitive sciences. His work attempts both to grasp what this diversity is all about, and to exploit it as a way of discovering the role that language plays in our everyday cognition.

JEROME LEWIS lectures in Anthropology at University College London and co-directs the Extreme Citizen Science Research Group and UCL's Environment Institute. His research focuses on Pygmy hunter-gatherers and former hunter-gatherers in Central Africa. Current research focuses include communication and cultural transmission in an egalitarian context among Mbendjele Pygmies in Congo-Brazzaville, and hunter-gatherers more widely.

SIMONE PIKA is the head of the Humboldt Research Group on 'Comparative Gestural Signalling' at the Max Planck Institute for Ornithology in Seewiesen, Germany. Her Ph.D. at the Max Planck Institute for Evolutionary Anthropology in Leipzig, Germany, focused on gestural complexity and underlying cognitive skills of great apes. She held research fellowships at the University of Alberta, Canada, and the University of St Andrews, Scotland, and a post as Assistant Professor at the University of Manchester, UK.

CAMILLA POWER is Senior Lecturer in Anthropology at the University of East London. She specializes in Darwinian models for the emergence of the symbolic domain including ritual, art, and language. Her fieldwork with the Hadza investigates the importance of ritual for women's solidarity. She has published widely on African hunter-gatherer gender ritual and cosmology.

JACK SIDNELL is an Associate Professor of Anthropology at the University of Toronto with a cross-appointment to the Department of Linguistics. He is the author of *Conversation Analysis: An Introduction* (2010), the editor of *Conversation Analysis: Comparative Perspectives* (2009), co-editor (with Makoto Hayashi and Geoffrey Raymond) of *Conversational Repair and Human Understanding* (2013) and (with Tanya Stivers) *The Handbook of Conversation Analysis* (2012).

CHRIS SINHA is Distinguished Professor of Cognitive Science at the College of Foreign Languages and International Studies, Hunan University. His central research interest is in the relations between language, cognition, and culture, and his research aims to integrate cognitive linguistic with socio-cultural approaches to language and communication. He has been President of the UK and International Cognitive Linguistics Associations, and is General Editor of the journal *Language and Cognition*.

LUC STEELS is currently ICREA research professor at the University of Pompeu Fabra (Barcelona). He combines a background in linguistics and computer science to develop agent-based computational models of the cognitive mechanisms and cultural processes that underlie the origins and evolution of language. A recent overview publication is *Experiments in Cultural Language Evolution* published by John Benjamins in 2012.

IAN WATTS has been investigating the early archaeological record of earth pigment use in southern Africa for twenty years. His initial research used multi-site Middle Stone Age data to establish a symbolic tradition of pigment use prior to initial migrations of modern humans beyond Africa. Subsequently, he was part of the team reporting a tradition of geometric engraving of ochre at Blombos Cave extending back 100,000 years, while at the nearby site of Pinnacle Point, he showed preferential use of the reddest materials extending back ~164,000 years. He is currently working as an independent researcher on still earlier (Fauresmith) pigment use in the Northern Cape. He has also published (with Camilla Power) on African hunter-gatherer gender construction through initiation ritual, and on lunar aspects of Bushman cosmology, ritual, and economic practice.

CHARLES WHITEHEAD was creative director of an advertising agency for twenty years before gaining his Ph.D. in anthropology and neuroscience (UCL 2003). He taught anthropology at the University of Westminster for seven years but is now an independent researcher investigating brain functions supporting social displays. He also aims to promote greater collaboration between academic disciplines with a view to resolving their conceptual differences concerning what makes us human and the place of consciousness in reality.

EMILY WYMAN is a Research Fellow in the School of Economics, University of Nottingham. Her research focuses on the psychology and development of children's cooperation; their understanding of social conventions and norms; and evolutionary perspectives on human uniqueness.

JORDAN ZLATEV is Professor of General Linguistics at Lund University, where he is one of the research directors of the transdisciplinary Centre for Cognitive Semiotics (CCS) established in 2009. His research focuses on language as a predominantly conventional-normative semiotic system for communication and thought, and especially on its biocultural evolution and development in children. This implies careful investigations of its relation to other semiotic resources such as gesture, and its dialectical relationship with cognition and consciousness. He is the author of *Situated Embodiment: Studies in the Emergence of Spatial Meaning* (1997), and over 50 articles in peer-reviewed journals and books.

KLAUS ZUBERBÜHLER is a Professor in Biology at the University of Neuchatel in Switzerland. His research interests are in comparative cognition and communication. The current focus is on how human language has evolved from more basic vocal and gestural communication. To this end, he carries out field research with various primate species in their natural habitats, using both observational and experimental techniques.

1

Introduction: a social perspective on how language began

DANIEL DOR, CHRIS KNIGHT, AND JEROME LEWIS

There are moments in science when the challenge is to imagine new questions in order to find better answers. Such occasions provoke us to examine with fresh eyes our previous findings, arguments, and assumptions. For the interdisciplinary community attempting to reconstruct how language first evolved, such a moment is documented in the diverse contributions to this volume.

The modern discourse on language origins is today one of the most vibrant in the human sciences. Much of the excitement stems from the intrinsic interest of the topic for understanding who we are, and the wider problem of reconstructing human origins. As a component of this problem, the emergence of language has proved bafflingly difficult—to the point where, today, some scholars view it as 'the hardest problem in science' (Christiansen and Kirby 2003). Part of the difficulty is, of course, the absence of direct evidence, compelling us to proceed much as if we were a detective looking for circumstantial evidence or a cosmologist relying on theoretical means to detect echoes of the origins of the universe. But while the difficulties are immense, so too are the potential rewards. Accounting for the origins of language in an elegant, persuasive way brings us closer to the unification of the natural and human sciences, enabling us at last to see ourselves as one curiously gifted, self-aware species with challenging responsibilities for the only known living planet.

Over recent decades, the linguistic sciences have become increasingly fragmented. With the rise of a multitude of new sub-disciplines, specialized journals, and conferences, and with the gradual decline of the Chomskian paradigm as a unifying framework, more and more of what we learn about language remains confined to specialized professional circles. However, to understand the origin of language requires a move in the opposite direction—a large-scale, collective interdisciplinary effort at theoretical synthesis. The detective-like analysis of circumstantial evidence knows no disciplinary borders. Everything counts. For this reason the topic has provided a meeting place for linguists of all convictions, psychologists (cognitive, social, and developmental), sociologists and anthropologists, biologists and geneticists, neuroscientists and philosophers, paleontologists and archeologists, ethologists and primatologists, evolutionists, and computer scientists. The present volume is an interdisciplinary synthesis in this spirit.

1.1 Questioning dominant assumptions

In the first years of its emergence, the modern study of the origins of language focused largely on the formative question of the human genetic endowment for language: if language is encoded in our genes, as Chomsky claimed, we must figure out how this happened. The idea that social dynamics must have played a role in the evolutionary process was rarely explicitly denied, but the overall contribution of these dynamics was taken to be secondary, peripheral to the drama of the genes. With time, the picture has changed considerably. Much evidence from different disciplines, presented here together for the first time, has accumulated to show that changes in society and culture must have played a central role in the entire process. Two insights are central here. The first is that human evolution is better understood as being prompted or driven by behavioural changes that lead to genetic changes; secondly, since language has only evolved in our species, there must be specific barriers to its evolution that our ancestors overcame.

The gene-centred approach to language's evolutionary emergence relies on an outdated conception of evolution. Current research in evolutionary biology highlights the fact that major changes in behaviour and cognition can take place without any changes in the genes. In many cases it is behavioural change that comes first, subsequently determining genetic change (Dor and Jablonka, Chapter 2). This understanding opens up the possibility that linguistic capacities may have preceded genetic accommodation for language. This, together with the indisputable fact that much of our behaviour and cognition is socially constructed implies that social and cultural dynamics need to be positioned centre-stage in any explanation for the emergence of *Homo sapiens*.

Since the publication of *Syntactic Structures* in 1957, Chomsky and his colleagues have relentlessly insisted that linguistics is a branch of natural science, not social, cultural, or historical science. Language, from this standpoint, was exclusively 'internal-' or 'I-language', defined as an object located in the individual mind/brain. The previous tradition of focusing on communally shared, historically determined 'external-' or 'E-languages' was now deemed unscientific, even though notions such as 'French' or 'Swahili' remained unavoidable in ordinary conversation. For linguistic theory, according to Chomsky (1986, 2005, 2012), only 'I-language' exists.

Whereas Chomsky views language as an internal faculty fitted to the requirements of private thought, we view it as designed essentially for communication between two or more speakers. In language, we formulate our thoughts for others and hence for ourselves. It's a system for publicly expressing our thoughts to help others imaginatively reconstruct them (see Dor, Chapter 9; Whitehead, Chapter 12). This communication technology is used by all human societies despite manifesting remarkable variability in technical design. It resides and develops at the level of the community, and is acquired by individuals as part of their socialization. Investigating the evolution of our individual cognitive and linguistic abilities as if they operate in social isolation ignores this central component of language. As we attempt to show throughout the volume, focusing on language in context allows for a new understanding of its origins, since it places social and cultural relationships centre-stage. It suggests that our pre-linguistic ancestors may have already had significant linguistic potential, but remained blocked from collaboratively constructing actual languages (Tomasello 2003a; see Dor and Jablonka, Chapter 2) owing to conflict-ridden, mistrustful social conditions. If this was the problem, language's evolutionary emergence would have required profound social and political change, more trusting, stable relationships enhancing the chances of cultural innovations being preserved and transmitted (Whiten 1999; Henrich and Gil-White 2001), leading eventually to the cumulative construction, grammaticalization, and historical diversification of stable linguistic traditions as we know them today.

Regardless of precise definition, 'language' in the sense meant by linguists has emerged in only one biological species, suggesting a profound and recurrent obstacle to its evolution. What could this obstacle be? Linguists in the tradition of Chomsky would expect a genetic limit on computational capacity, with the implication that an account of language origins must explain how this deficiency was overcome. Theorists in this tradition tend to deny that social conditions could possibly have been relevant to how language evolved. After all, humans everywhere speak to one another in equally creative, grammatically complex ways—regardless of technological level or social arrangements. Since social factors make no difference, the underlying faculty must surely be 'a distinct piece of the biological make-up of our brains' (Pinker 1994: 18), much like stereoscopic vision. No one would suggest that seeing things in 3-D depends on politics or culture.

In this book, we accept part of that argument. Yes, human nature is different from ape or monkey nature. And, yes, linguistic production and comprehension presupposes specific computational capacities. Where we differ from Chomsky and his colleagues, however, is in insisting that language is not like stereoscopy. Unlike perception in 3-D, it presupposes engagement with other minds. To be 'language-ready' (Arbib 2006a), the brain must be social to an unusual degree; and for the human brain to be that social, human society must have gone through an unusual evolutionary dynamic.

At first sight, human social and cultural arrangements may seem limitlessly varied. But the illusion falls away when we expand our field of view to include nonhuman primates. In contrast to those of apes and monkeys, all human societies rest on moral rules governing sex and many other aspects of life. No hunter-gatherer community would tolerate its members seeking dominance simply by throwing their weight around, physically assaulting or threatening others in the group. Everyone must *earn* social standing or prestige among their peers, this being freely conferred by neighbours and kin according to their perceived contribution to the common good (Henrich and Gil-White 2001).

Needless to say, humans are capable of violence, just as apes and monkeys are. In certain contexts, violence pays. But in the case of many nonhuman primates, dominance asserted through violence or threat is the *internal principle* of social organization, a situation which humans would find psychologically intolerable. Within a human speech community, physical violence or threat between speaker and listener can easily destroy mutual trust. Where public trust collapses, people cease to be 'on speaking terms'. Such conditions are not conducive to linguistic creativity. Since there are good theoretical reasons for this, several of our contributors infer that, for as long as this type of primate-style social dynamics prevailed, evolving humans would have been unable to realize their linguistic potential in the delicate joint enterprise of constructing, preserving, innovating, and transmitting actual languages historically across generations.

On one point, we are all agreed: languages began evolving as a consequence not of one social factor but multiple interacting ones. This, then, is our overall thesis. Unprecedented levels of collective co-operation favoured genetic capacities for intersubjective sensitivity and understanding. Pre-linguistic innovations most probably included shared childcare, the control of fire and cooking, projectile weapons, big game hunting, increasingly equal power relations between the sexes, emotional bonding through music, dance and other forms of ritual—and, as a consequence of increased trust within relatively stable coalitions, steadily increasing chances for cultural innovations to be preserved and transmitted to future generations. All this drove selection pressures favouring novel capacities for mimetic, gestural, and vocal communication, culminating finally in levels of trust sufficient for linguistic innovations to be preserved and for self-organized grammatical structures (products of 'grammaticalization'—see Steels, Chapter 24) to emerge.

1.2 Theoretical foundations

The first three chapters place language origins within the context of current evolutionary thinking. In Chapter 2, Daniel Dor and Eva Jablonka present some of the major evolutionary considerations behind their move from gene-culture co-evolution to culturally driven co-evolution. The framework of Evolutionary-Developmental Theory (evo-devo) reverses the traditional view of the causal relationships between genes, cognition, behaviour, and culture. As a result, the evolution of language should be seen as a development in which collective processes of cultural exploration, based on cultural and cognitive plasticity, led to new behavioural strategies which in turn ultimately changed individual cognition in ways that were genetically accommodated, at least partially. Language is a collectively built communications technology that must have emerged through a process of collective, interactive innovation. Dor and Jablonka suggest that the major feature separating us from the apes is our special social capacity for collective exploration and invention.

As Chris Sinha argues in Chapter 3, none of this implies that the social and biological explanations 'are fated to eternal opposition'. On the contrary, the new paradigm highlights the 'dual ontology' of language—the fact that it exists both in society and in the mind. Language constitutes a 'biocultural niche', embedded within the entire human 'semiosphere'—everything in human culture, material and non-material, that is symbolic in nature. Sinha thus identifies the origins of language in the transition from signals of the kind used by other animals to influence one another's behaviour—what might be termed body language—to something entirely new. Humans began to interact 'intersubjectively', each viewing their own mental states and intentions as if through the other's eyes. Against this background, our ancestors accomplished the momentous transition to mutually agreed symbols, used by humans to influence not the world, but how others understand that world.

In Chapter 4, Camilla Power argues that if we are to explore how signals evolve in the animal world, the appropriate body of theory to turn to is Signal Evolution Theory (Maynard Smith and Harper 2003). According to Zahavi's (1975) 'handicap principle', animal signals evolve as intrinsically reliable demonstrations of the quality of the signaller, since they impose a cost rendering them either 'difficult' or 'impossible' to fake. Language seems to be the only known system whose component signals are digital, cheap, efficient—and intrinsically unreliable. Analysing various clues, such as the dynamics of hominin encephalization, the parallel changes in life history, mothering and alloparenting, Power (see also Chapter 15) focuses on the trend towards counter-dominance and egalitarianism highlighted by the co-operative eye hypothesis and deep social mind. Counter-dominance in Power's view culminates in reverse dominance established through a uniquely human social revolution—inaugurating a hunter-gatherer tradition of ritual action in which primate-style dominance is periodically overthrown and then restored up to a point, only to be overthrown and restored again and again.

'If we are to develop a new overall perspective on the evolution of language', writes Sverker Johansson in Chapter 5, 'we need to ground such a perspective firmly with empirical evidence.' Johansson reviews four types of indirect evidence available for this task: animal communication and social life; language and language use today; neurobiology of the human language capacity and social capacity today; and, finally, the fossil and archaeological record. He shows how different types of data may be used to derive testable predictions from hypotheses, constrain and falsify evolutionary scenarios, and open the way towards new questions.

1.3 Language as a collective object

This section addresses a basic question: what exactly is this 'language' whose origin we are seeking to explain? In Chapter 6, Adam Kendon stresses that spoken language is not just vocal but poly-modal. When interacting face-to-face, speakers gesture with their hands, faces, and bodies. These gestural signals are 'neither supplements nor add-ons' but an integral part of each communicative act. To ask how language evolved, then, is to ask how humans evolved their unique capacity for poly-modalic communication.

Speech and gesture, according to Kendon, must have evolved as modified versions of practical actions for mothering, grooming, mating, fighting, and/or obtaining food. One conclusion is that 'language', as the isolated component that is spoken, must have gradually developed through a process of specialization and differentiation.

In Chapter 7, Jerome Lewis explores further the theme of poly-modality, drawing on his long-term fieldwork among forest hunter-gatherers in the Congo Basin. For the BaYaka Pygmies, communication is an unbroken language–music continuum. In addition to speaking, it embraces yodelling, dancing, drumming, gesturing, signing, whistling, mimicking animal sounds, and imitating the sounds of neighbouring languages. These activities are deeply gendered, with men and women speaking and singing in quite different ways. So men mimic to attract game in the forest while women mimic in order to direct bursts of derisive laughter against antisocial behaviour within the group. Lewis argues that it makes little sense to speculate about the origins of language without ethnographically constraining those speculations to hunter-gatherer social organization—in particular, without understanding in detail how speaking is bound up with the many other ways in which humans and nearby sentient beings send messages, listen attentively, and echo back one another's signals in a hunter-gatherer context.

For Nick Enfield and Jack Sidnell (Chapter 8), an understanding of language as a social-interactional system involves taking account of the dynamics of natural conversation. What is it that individuals really do as they talk to one another? They review some results from the relatively new discipline of Conversational Analysis, showing how a step-by-step analysis of conversation exposes an entire infrastructure for social interaction, with procedures and markers that are collectively used by participants for the management of the conversation. This infrastructure, Enfield and Sidnell argue, should be understood as a crucial link between language as a formal system and the world of human sociality.

In the final contribution to this section, Chapter 9, Daniel Dor presents a new theoretical characterization of the functional uniqueness of language as a communication technology. All the other intentional communication systems, whether used by humans or by other animals, work with what Dor calls the 'experiential strategy': they turn the communicator's intention into an object for direct experiencing. Language is the only system that employs a radically different strategy, the 'instructive strategy': the communicator provides the interlocutor with a skeletal list of the basic co-ordinates of the intended meaning, actively instructing the interlocutor in the process of *imagining* what the communicator wanted to mean. As Dor shows, this view of the functional specificity of language allows for a new type of approach to the dynamics of the origins and further evolution of language—one which identifies the instructive strategy itself as the driving force behind the entire process.

1.4 Apes and people, past and present

The first two chapters in this section deal with ape social communication. In Chapter 10, Simone Pika discusses gestural communication in chimpanzees. She begins with an overview of the field, arguing that chimpanzee gestures are complex, intentional, flexible, and socially learned. Gestures, often accompanied by special vocalizations, play a crucial role in the maintenance of the all-important social activity of grooming. They are used to solicit a grooming session, to negotiate roles during the session, to direct the grooming individuals to other parts of the body, and so on. According to Pika, these gestures in many ways prefigure key features of language conceived as a tool of social interaction; we should take them into account in any attempt to understand how human language evolved.

Unlike apes' gestures, their vocalizations have traditionally been viewed as genetically hardwired, involuntary expressions of emotional states. If this were so, we could hardly view them as precursors of human spoken language. In Chapter 11, Zanna Clay and Klaus Zuberbühler argue strongly against this widespread perception. They show that vocalizations play a major role in the social lives of chimpanzees and bonobos, some being produced with the intention to inform other individuals. For example, the copulation calls made by female bonobos are indicative of the dominance rank of the male partner. Many calls also show audience effects: they can be modified according to who might be listening. Taking issue with Pika's argument that language must initially have been gestural, Clay and Zuberbühler insist that primate vocalizations can tell us a great deal about the social and communicative preconditions for the emergence of spoken language in humans.

This leads us to ask why humans evolved language whereas our ape cousins did not. In Chapter 12, Charles Whitehead reviews the web of similarities and differences between ourselves and other primates; in doing so, he highlights our own species' unique capacity for complex social displays, a capacity supporting special levels of social awareness and allowing for the establishment of hunter-gatherer-style mimetic culture and ritually structured life. Surveying the developmental literature, he shows that the ways in which children play and display develop in tandem with their capacity for intersubjectivity—suggesting that a similar spiral dynamic characterized human evolution.

Emily Wyman, in Chapter 13, agrees that play—in particular, pretend play—is crucial. Complex pretend play from the age of four seems to be a universal phenomenon. This is important, because the adult world, including language, is founded on rules and norms, regulative and constitutive, and a set of 'shared fictions' or 'institutional facts' (a modern example being money) which emerge at the intersubjective level through collective consent. Wyman shows that in pretend games, children gain experience in establishing collective consent over invented events and entities, learning the basic structure of rules and practising normative behaviour. This means that, unless we can first explain how humans began inhabiting the necessary cognitive environment—a world of ritually structured let's pretend—there can be no hope of explaining the origins of language.

In Chapter 14, Dan Dediu and Stephen Levinson argue against the recently popular 'saltation' view of language evolution, according to which language emerged during the European Upper Palaeolithic revolution around 40 thousand years ago. They analyse evidence from archaeology, paleontology, and linguistics to show that even prior to the evolution of modern humans, the emergence and development of language was already underway. Dediu and Levinson suggest that language and speech emerged some time between 1.5 million and 0.6 million years ago—crucially, before the branching of modern humans and Neandertals from their common ancestor, most probably *Homo heidelbergensis*. Opposing a common view, they argue that Neandertals produced culture and technology comparable to that of modern humans, and may have had language resembling that of the modern humans of their time. If the roots of language are that ancient, it would shed new light on the inferred social dynamics of the whole evolutionary process.

The following three contributions focus on the evolution of ritual as critical to the social preconditions for language to emerge. In Chapter 15, Camilla Power connects the emergence of ritual with a uniquely human social revolution, a revolution against primate-like male dominance based on physical power. Ritual is the primary tool of counter-dominance enabling coalitions of weaker individuals to resist dominance; during the course of human evolution, counter-dominance culminated in reverse-dominance—in which the community as a whole dominates to the exclusion of sectional interests or individuals. Power examines ritualization processes of sexual selection as the likely source for generating new forms of communication. Ritual, she claims, emerged when female coalitions began to use cosmetics to display their quality, to attract probing males, in competition with rival female coalitions. From this ritual order, language emerged as a collective, symbolic, and normative system.

Ian Watts, in Chapter 16, provides an in-depth review of the archaeological and fossil evidence for early ritual and symbolic culture, arguing that it supports a two-stage scenario of human evolution. During the first stage, from at least half a million years ago, archaeological data shows signs of the emergence of ritual, most importantly the use of red ochre for the social display of fertility by female coalitions. Although its beginnings are early, this novel strategy becomes evolutionarily stable only much later, around the time of our speciation between 150 and 200 thousand years ago, the culmination (in Africa) of a final phase of brain-size increase. Watts agrees with Dediu and Levinson that language did not have to wait until the European Upper Palaeolithic so-called 'revolution' at forty thousand years ago. But whereas Dediu and Levinson focus on fossil evidence for complex vocal and auditory capacities for spoken language—innate capacities which they argue emerged with *Homo erectus*—Watts is working within a theoretical framework which distinguishes capacity from performance. Examining the interrelationship between language and the rest of symbolic culture, Watts is looking for potential archaeological correlates of ritual as a communal bonding mechanism and, on that basis, attempting to date the establishment of the trust system necessary for language to work. Watts therefore locates the key transition significantly later than Dediu and Levinson, identifying it with the time of modern human speciation in the African Middle Stone Age.

Chris Knight wraps up the section in Chapter 17, with an attempt to synthesize the ideas and findings discussed so far into an overall solution to the problem of the emergence of symbolic culture, language (in his view) being an internal component of this. Positioning sex and ritual at the centre of the drama, he critically connects threads from the debates over cheap versus costly signalling, the significance of red ochre, the nature of co-operation, the emergence of alloparenting, the reliance of language on accepted falsities, counter-dominance and intersubjectivity, hunter-gatherer ethnography, mimesis, ritual, and play. Taken together, all these begin to draw a vivid picture of the evolution of everything social, within which the evolution of language is but a particular aspect. Our prospects of comprehending how language evolved, Knight argues, are all too often hindered by the institutional fragmentation and conceptual atomization of Western science. Following Lewis (Chapter 7), Knight suggests that the more integrated perspectives of hunter-gatherers may enable us to connect up the dots more effectively, concluding: 'It may be that everything is simpler than we thought.'

1.5 The social origins of language

In the opening chapter of this section, Chapter 18, Jordan Zlatev goes back to the paradox of co-operation and sharing in language: if biological evolution is based on the natural selection of individuals, sharing remains an anomaly. Zlatev reviews a series of theoretical attempts to resolve the paradox, and shows that they converge

rather than contradict each other. All indicate that the solution to the paradox lies in the co-evolution of language together with two other human anomalies: intersubjectivity and morality. This co-evolutionary explanation requires a 'multi-level selection' theory of evolution, according to which evolution operates at the very least on the levels of the gene, the cell, the organism, and, crucially, the group. Significantly, the co-evolutionary dynamic involved an arms race between 'selfish' individual selected traits and 'altruistic' group-level selected traits.

In Chapter 19, Ehud Lamm proposes a co-evolutionary explanation involving language and normativity. Not just language and social norms, but language and the intrinsic motivation that humans have to commit themselves to norms, behave according to them, and use them to justify their behaviour. Lamm presents developmental evidence showing that children co-develop their language and their normative capacity, and describes the basic properties of the parallel co-evolutionary scenario. In both ontogeny and phylogeny, he identifies the normative rules of pragmatics as a major link between normativity and language.

Jean-Louis Dessalles, in Chapter 20, begins with his characterization of linguistic communication as competitive signalling, correlating the emergence of language with the advent of weapons. For the first time, weapons enabled the easy killing of dominant individuals by their subordinates. In this new social reality, 'the only valid life insurance is to have friends'. The dominance game becomes a competition over potential friends, and language is used by individuals to demonstrate their qualities. The capacity for story-telling, for example, proves that the teller understands the social situation and is sensitive to novelty. Dessalles presents a formal model to show that this scenario turns language into an evolutionarily stable strategy, and discusses some of its implications.

In Chapter 21, Chris Knight and Jerome Lewis argue that nonhuman primates are profoundly constrained in their vocal signalling because listeners demand reliability, not creativity. In the human case, vocal flexibility evolved thanks to the highly unusual, species-specific strategies through which men deployed vocal mimicry to deceive animals in the course of hunting, while women engaged in choral singing to scare away predators. Deployed in the first instance to deceive outsiders, vocal mimicry within gender-based coalitions began serving additional internal functions: choral singing harmonized emotions and built trust within the group. With trusting listeners prepared to find communicative relevance in one another's patent fictions, signals were no longer under pressure to incorporate costly handicaps as demonstrations of reliability. Once this age-old constraint had been removed, humans could vocalize creatively with volitional movements of the tongue and other articulators. Knight and Lewis hypothesize that resistance to alpha male dominance turned the world upside down, with laughter, dance, and playful adult games establishing the conditions for linguistic potential to flower.

1.6 The journey thereafter

The last three chapters attempt to deal with the dynamics of the cultural evolution of language, from its initial emergence to eventual stabilization and diversification. In Chapter 22, Simona Ginsburg and Eva Jablonka adopt Dor's characterization of language as an imagination-instructing technology, and show how its evolution must have been entangled with the evolution of the capacities involved in imagination, most importantly the capacity for memory. The beginnings of instructive communication, within a multi-levelled context of social practices and cognitive-emotional capacities, allowed for the evolution of a new type of memory-encoding and recall, word-based episodic recall. Episodic recall became free of its experiential cues and allowed for imagination—the reconstructing and recombining of representations from past experiences to generate novel ones—on the basis of the speaker's words. The fact that humans could begin to recall and recombine their episodic memories, and thus to communicate about them, gave them new insights into their own minds as well as into those of others.

Nick Enfield, in Chapter 23, moves on to suggest an explanatory framework for the cultural evolution of language, based on an analysis of cultural epidemiology. The fate of a cultural innovation—whether it spreads in a population or is resisted, whether it changes in the course of diffusion or not—is determined by the cumulative effect of a range of biases, which serve as accelerants or decelerants in the competition between different cultural practices. Enfield characterizes every step of language change as a four-stage dynamic, from exposure to representation, then to reproduction, and finally to its material instantiation. Each of these stages implies a particular set of biases.

In Chapter 24, Luc Steels wraps up the volume with his discussion of a central problem: the initial emergence of formal linguistic structure. He goes back to the foundational debate between Formalism and Functionalism: if the structures of language are formally arbitrary, the fact that they change can only be explained in terms of random drift; if they are functional, they can be explained as the result of selection. Steels shows how agent-based models—computer simulations in which agents interact in language games—confirm the functionalist-selectionist view. Formal properties of language—such as parts of speech, agreement, hierarchical structure, and case grammar—are adopted by agents because they enhance communicative efficiency.

But how does this whole process of selection for communicative efficiency get off the ground in the first place? Steels concurs with the many contributors to this volume who see uniquely human levels of co-operation and trust as the necessary prerequisite.

When a theoretical problem repeatedly defies the best minds in science, a point may be reached when the question itself becomes suspect. Could it be that the whole idea of a 'theory of the origins of language' is somehow misconceived? What we can say is that science is unlikely to stumble upon a 'magic ingredient X' solution to the puzzle—for reasons that Steels (this volume) nicely explains. The idea is unrealistic, if only because language is *not* like stereoscopy or echolocation. It is *not* a self-sufficient, individually beneficial biological adaptation.

For the language faculty to be of any use, each of us needs others. For speakers to 'do things with words' (Austin 1962), a very wide spectrum of entangled conditions is required—cultural, social, political, cognitive, and emotional. In other words, language is an internal component of a much wider continuum: social intercourse and culture in distinctively human form. This, then, is why the problem is so difficult: to explain language, we seem to need nothing short of 'a theory of everything'—everything distinctive about human consciousness, life, and culture taken as a whole. Our 23 contributions, from leading researchers in a wide array of fields, take up different parts of this daunting intellectual challenge. Disagreements abound—life would be dull without these! But we broadly converge on a shared scientific understanding of the co-evolutionary dynamics that must have characterized this 'major transition in evolution' (Maynard Smith and Szathmáry 1995). Instead of explaining the language faculty as an outcome of genetic change, all of us picture the biological faculty evolving incrementally on the basis of capacities already in existence, genetic change occurring as previous adaptations were recruited and fine-tuned to serve novel communicative ends (Dor and Jablonka, Chapter 2; Steels, Chapter 24). The major transition, all of us agree, must have been the establishment within social groups of unprecedentedly co-operative, trusting relationships. Only then could language, as we recognize it today, begin to evolve.

Part I

Theoretical Foundations

2

Why we need to move from gene-culture co-evolution to culturally driven co-evolution

DANIEL DOR AND EVA JABLONKA

2.1 Introduction

The question of the origin and evolution of human language was born as a mystery: in 1866, the Paris Linguistic Society decreed that papers dealing with the topic could not be read in its meetings. More than a hundred year later, Noam Chomsky still wrote that 'it seems rather pointless... to speculate about the evolution of human language from simpler systems—perhaps as absurd as it would be to speculate about the "evolution" of atoms from clouds of elementary particles' (Chomsky 1968: 61). Then, when the question began to be thought of more seriously, it was formulated as a question about the origin and evolution of the individual, genetically based capacity for language: *what happened to the human brain/mind that allowed for language to emerge?* As Pinker and Bloom put it in their foundational paper, 'the ability to use a natural language belongs more to the study of human biology than human culture; it is a topic like echolocation in bats or stereopsis in monkeys, not like writing or the wheel' (Pinker and Bloom 1990: 708). Pinker and Bloom did not deny that cultural dynamics may have had a role to play in the evolution of the human capacity for language, and they explicitly discussed the possibility of gene-culture co-evolutionary dynamics—as did many authors later on (see Deacon 1992b, 1997; Tomasello 1999, 2008; Pinker 2003; Levinson and Jaisson 2006; Evans and Levinson 2009; Hurford 2007, 2011; Richerson and Boyd 2005). Throughout the entire discourse, however, the original premise (in its most general formulation) has been kept intact: the emergence of language can and should be explained on the basis of a prior advance (or a series of advances) in individual human cognition. Early humans must have reached a certain level of cognitive capacity (general or language-specific) before language (and languages) began to evolve at the social level, and possibly began to influence the evolution of human cognition further along the way.

In Dor and Jablonka (2000, 2001, 2004, 2010), we have suggested that this original premise should be reversed: language began exactly like writing or the wheel—or the newly discovered ability to use echolocation by blind human individuals (Thaler et al. 2011), to which we shall come back later. Language emerged as a collectively developed *communication technology* (see Dor, Chapter 9), before individuals acquired the capacity to handle it efficiently. It was the product of a process of *collective exploration*, which created a new realm of communication, and then dragged individual cognitions and genes into a co-evolutionary dynamic that eventually produced the languages, and language-compatible minds, that we now have. Thus, innovative practices of communication gradually, cumulatively, and partially shaped something that resembles echolocation in bats or stereopsis in monkeys. *First we invented language, then language changed us.* There is obviously something counter-intuitive about this claim: after all, how could we invent language and use it if we didn't have the capacity for it already there? In this paper, we would like to address this issue from several directions, and try to show why this is not only possible—but in a very real sense the only viable option.

It goes without saying that the process of gene-culture co-evolution in the human species began to spiral a very long time before language came into being. The process of collective exploration that brought language about was probably made possible (among many other things) by individual capacities that had to have already evolved before—most importantly, the capacities involved in *intersubjectivity*, the ability to understand others' mental states, share experiences with them, and empathize with them, and the enhanced human *plasticity*, the ability to explore and innovate. These capacities, in their turn, co-evolved with prior projects of cultural exploration: the emergence of alloparenting, (the sharing of responsibility for the young by individuals other than the mother), the manufacture of tools, the invention of cooking, and so on: the process goes a long way back. The issue, however, is not just of temporal precedence. It is mainly an issue of explanation, because there are two questions involved in this story: (1) What made the emergence and further development of language *possible*?, and (2) What made the emergence and further development of language *happen the particular way that it did*? The process was made possible by a wide range of preconditions—social, cultural, and also, undoubtedly, cognitive. It was determined, however, along with the particular properties of its product, by the actual dynamics of exploration and innovation, as they took place within a particular cultural context. The process was culturally *driven*.

Our claim, then, amounts to a reversal of the causal relationship between genes, individual cognition, individual behaviour, and the cultural world. The evolution of language was not a process in which genetic change drove a change in individual cognition, which in its turn produced new behaviours that shaped a changing cultural world. It was a process in which collective processes of cultural exploration produced new behaviours, which in their turn changed individual cognition in ways that were eventually partially genetically accommodated.

In Section 2.2, we concentrate on the relationship between innovative behaviour, cognitive capacity, and genetics at the level of the individual. As the growing literature within the framework of Evolutionary-Developmental Biology (evo-devo) makes clear, genuinely new behavioural patterns emerge from exploratory processes made possible by brain plasticity. They are gradually shaped by experience to approximate their functions, become objects of learning, mould capacities in their shape, and eventually, if the selection pressure remains, drive a process of genetic accommodation. Adaptation thus begins at the level of phenotype: capacity emerges from behaviour, not the other way around. Genes are followers in evolution.

All this is true of all innovative behaviours, but with language, it is accentuated by the fact that it is a collective innovation—which means that it must have emerged from a process of *interactive exploration*. In Section 2.3, we characterize language as a product of interactive exploration in two related senses. First, it is a product of a dynamic of cultural accumulation, in which many different individuals, with different capacities and interests, building on prior achievements and dealing with emergent communicative needs, made different, partial and local contributions to the developmental process. Second, the local contributions themselves emerge as answers to communicative needs, and should thus be accepted by the different participants in the conversation, with their different positions and interests. In both senses, then, the innovative effort and its results cannot be explained on the basis of the dynamics of any individual brain or even individual exploration.

As we then claim in Section 2.4, the realization that full-blown language does not require the specific capacities suggested by the generative paradigm should not mask the simple fact that language does require quite a few capacities that are specific enough, and thus different enough from their pre-adaptations. The explanation of these language adaptations is only possible if we assume that these capacities emerged *for* language—which means, again, that the linguistic challenges must have been there before the capacities. We thus suggest that the co-evolutionary spiral that eventually produced both the languages and the speakers of today must have been driven, from the very beginning and all through, by the collective process of cultural exploration. Our proposal, however, *does not* address the specific selection regimes that may have driven this uniquely hominin co-evolutionary dynamics. Selection scenarios highlighting the importance of particular social practices are discussed in many of the chapters of this volume.

We conclude with the suggestion that the major capacity that separates us from the apes is the social capacity of collective invention. When introduced to a language already invented by humans, Kanzi managed to acquire and use it effectively for communication, showing a level of comprehension (but not production) of a two and a half-year-old child (Savage-Rumbaugh and Lewin 1994). As far as we know, the apes have never invented a comparable, first prototype of language in the wild—not because they lack the individual cognitive capacities, but because they lack this capacity for collective exploration and innovation.

2.2 Plasticity and the emergence of evolutionary novelties: genes as followers

The relationship between ontogenetic and evolutionary adaptation has been central to biological thinking since the dawn of evolutionary studies at the beginning of the 19th century. The Lamarckians regarded hereditary transmission as a continuous, direct aspect of development: they assumed that ontogenetically acquired adaptations, when repeated for long enough, inevitably become evolutionary adaptations. Hence, the thick skin on the sole of the feet with which a human baby is born was interpreted as the cumulative result of many generations of bipedal locomotion followed by sole abrasion, which eventually led to the development of thick skin even before the feet were used for walking. The loss of eyes in cave animals, and the lack of fear in animals on isolated oceanic islands were interpreted, respectively, as the cumulative effect of disuse of sight and persistent lack of fearful stimuli. Use and disuse, learning and unlearning, were seen as directly leading to evolutionary adaptations. This position was shared by Darwin, although he always stressed the role of natural selection of both acquired and accidental variations in the shaping of complex adaptations (Darwin 1868, 1871, 1872).

With the rise of neo-Darwinism at the end of the 19th century, the relationship between ontogenetic and evolutionary adaptations was seen as indirect. The neo-Darwinians rejected the assumption that ontogenetic adaptations were directly stamped upon the individual's hereditary physiology and suggested instead that developmental adaptations altered the way selection operated. Focusing on the evolution of instinctive behaviours, Lloyd Morgan, J.M. Baldwin, and Fairfield Osborne suggested that when facing a new challenge many individuals in a population adapt by learning (Avital and Jablonka 2000). The learned adaptation enables the members of the population to survive until new mutations that enable an inborn response appear, in a process that came to be known as the 'Baldwin effect' (Simpson 1953).

A neo-Darwinian explanation for the inheritance of learned (and more generally developmentally induced) responses was independently suggested by Conrad Waddington in Great Britain, and by Ivan Schmalhausen in the Soviet Union in the mid 20th century. They suggested that selection for the genetic basis of the developmental capacity to respond adaptively to a new environmental stimulus (developmental plasticity) has reinforcing effects, leading to the construction of a genetic constitution that facilitates or stabilizes the development of such an adaptation. The process is based on sexual reshuffling of Mendelian genes, and depends on several assumptions: (i) individuals are plastic, and can respond to new challenges by learning; (ii) individuals in the unchallenged population vary genetically, and much of the genetic variation is cryptic: it does not have phenotypic effect in the original environment, and is thus selectively neutral; (iii) some of the cryptic genetic variations affect the responsiveness to the new challenge and become manifest and selectable when the challenge occurs; (iv) the individuals who respond to new inducing or learning conditions in a more 'inborn' manner have a selective advantage.

If these very general and commonly encountered assumptions hold, then, over time, individuals in the population would come to respond more and more readily to the challenge, until, in some cases, a threshold would be crossed, and the trait that was originally induced or learned would appear without any external induction or learning. Waddington termed this process of induction-selection *genetic assimilation* and Schmalhausen called it *stabilizing selection* (for discussion see Jablonka and Lamb 2005: chs 2 and 8). As Waddington and Schmalhausen stressed, *full* genetic assimilation is not necessary. In many cases, assimilation will be partial, leading to less dependence on a process of induction or learning, but some induction or learning would still be required. In other words, predispositions rather than full-blown instincts will evolve.

Waddington experimentally demonstrated processes of full genetic assimilation in the fruit fly *Drosophila melanogaster*. In one of his experiments, he exposed early embryos of the fruit fly *Drosophila melanogaster* to ether vapour. As a result, a proportion of the exposed flies developed four wings instead of the two that flies normally have. Waddington selected the 'responsive' four-winged flies as parents for twenty generations, and produced a strain in which a high proportion of the flies developed four wings *even in the absence of ether vapour*. The explanation he gave for this and for similar experimental results was that the new conditions destabilized development and therefore exposed previously cryptic heritable variation. He suggested that the ability to respond to the stimulus (ether) by developing the new phenotype (four wings) was the result of particular interacting combinations of alleles of several genes. After the sexual reshuffling of genes and selection for responsiveness, initially rare 'responsive' alleles became more common, until eventually a regulatory network was constructed that made induction unnecessary—the response became constitutive (Waddington 1957). Table 2.1 (based on Avital and Jablonka 2000; Jablonka and Lamb 2005) provides a simple hypothetical model of such assimilation (in the real world there are many genes with two or more alleles each that form the genetic network leading to the production of wings).

TABLE 2.1. Interactions between genetic loci and selection for an environment-insensitive (genetically assimilated) trait

Gametes	A^1B^1	A^1B^2	A^2B^1	A^2B^2
A^1B^1	$A^1A^1B^1B^1$	$A^1A^1B^1B^2$	$A^1A^2B^1B^1$	$A^1A^2B^1B^2$
A^1B^2	$A^1A^1B^2B^1$	$A^1A^1B^2B^2$	$A^1A^2B^1B^2$	$A^1A^2B^2B^2$
A^2B^1	$A^2A^1B^1B^1$	$A^2A^1B^2B^1$	$A^2A^2B^1B^1$	$A^2A^2B^1B^2$
A^2B^2	$A^2A^1B^2B^1$	$A^2A^1B^2B^2$	$A^2A^2B^2B^1$	$A^2A^2B^2B^2$

Two genetic loci, A and B affect the expression of a trait (4-wing development). Assume: (i) each locus has two alleles: at locus A, A^1 and A^2; at locus B, B^1 and B^2. (ii) p, the frequency of A2 and B2 alleles (type 2 alleles), is 0.1; q, the frequency of A^1 and B^1 (type 1 alleles) is 0.9. (iii) Induction by ether during a sensitive developmental stage leads to development of a 4-wing phenotype in individuals with two or more type-2 alleles (all shades of grey). (iv) Only individuals with four type-2 alleles (darkest grey) develop the changed trait without induction; they are constitutive with respect to the phenotype and their frequency in our example is p^4, 1 in 10,000 or 0.01 per cent. Following induction or learning, over 5 per cent of the population will exhibit the novel trait (the overall frequency of genotypes with two or more type-2 alleles, the frequency of the grey-shaded boxes, is given assumption (i)–(iii): $6p^2q^2 + 4p^3q + p^4 = 0.0523$, or over 5 per cent). Induction followed by selection of inducible individuals would lead to rapid increase in type-2 alleles, and, if selection is persistent, the constitutive genotype will become fixed in the population.

Following Waddington's suggestion, and realizing that a simple explanation scheme such as the one described in Table 2.1 can be applied to the evolution of behaviour, eminent biologists such as J.B.S. Haldane, R.F. Ewer, and Alister Hardy applied the idea of learning-dependent, 'phenotype-first' process to explain the evolution of behavioural biases and instincts (see Avital and Jablonka 2000: ch. 9 for a comprehensive discussion).

For many years, however, genetic assimilation was neglected by evolutionists. Since the mid 20th century, most evolutionary neo-Darwinian biologists saw evolution in terms of chance genetic variations, which happened to lead to beneficial variations and were then selected. The double role of the environment, as both a selecting and an inducing agent, was disregarded. Then, interest in the interaction between environmental conditions affecting gene expression and the selection of genes was reawakened with the advent of evo-devo, when the relation between ontogeny and phylogeny became a central topic of research (Bateson and Gluckman 2011). The most general and broad analysis was presented by Mary-Jane West-Eberhard (2003). She proposed that adaptive evolution of novelties starts with a plastic, phenotypic response to a new input, which is either a new mutation, or, more commonly, a changed environment. Such challenge makes the plastic organism adjust to this new input and reorganize its development. Following the reoccurrence of the input, a subpopulation of organisms that are able to respond to it is selected. Selection is for adaptive variation in the regulation, form, or side effects of the plastic trait, leading to *genetic accommodation* (West-Eberhard 2003: 140). From this more general perspective, Waddington's genetic assimilation, which leads to a transition from a more conditional response to a constitutive stimulus-independent response, is a special case of genetic accommodation. Genetic accommodation can also lead to enhanced plasticity, to an increase in the range of responses the organism can make, rendering them more dependent on the environmental context, and it may also lead to the amelioration of any deleterious side effects that the new challenge induced. Comparative studies show that the 'phenotype-first' mode of evolution may be quite common (e.g. Palmer 2009), and new experimental studies have shown genetic accommodation of both decreased and increased plasticity following new environmental challenges (Suzuki and Nijhout 2006; Gilbert and Epel 2009). As West-Eberhard (2003: 20) put it, 'genes are followers, not leaders, in evolution'.

This view of adaptive evolution seems to be particularly relevant when considering the evolution of new behaviours in animals. The behavioural plasticity of neural animals is based on open-ended plasticity, manifest for example in Hebbian learning. Novel associations can be made, and new neural connections can be formed when animals adapt behaviourally to new conditions. These behavioural-neural associations are novel: they were not part of the set of behaviours ever manifested in the past by members of the lineage. Since the solution to a new challenge that an animal finds by learning is based on multiple, simultaneous, and often novel changes in the nervous system, the chances of finding a single mutational solution that could simulate the learned solution is small. Adaptation by genetic accommodation, on the other hand, can readily lead to improved learning. By uncovering previously cryptic variations in the several genes that affect the new type of learning, the process leads to the construction of a new gene-network that makes the animals depend on fewer learning trials.

As we pointed out in earlier publications (Avital and Jablonka 2000; Dor and Jablonka 2000), genetic assimilation can lead not only to a more ready and efficient response but also to the emergence of 'rules' of behaviour, to the emergence of new sensory modalities, and to the lengthening of behavioural chains. We call this latter process the 'assimilate-stretch' principle: it is based on the idea that genetically assimilating some previously learned units of behaviour in a behavioural sequence (making them more automatic) 'frees' the individual to add additional units to the sequence, without extending the limits set by its learning capacity. If an animal originally needed to learn four consecutive acts, for example, then following the assimilation of one or more behavioural elements, additional elements can be learned with the same cognitive resources. These elements can be added to the existing sequence, thus leading to the sophistication of the observed behaviour. This process, which involves the *assimilation* of a part of the behavioural sequence, and the resulting *stretching* of the sequence by learning, may underlie adaptations such as nest building in birds and some insects. Partial genetic assimilation can also lead to the emergence of learning predispositions based on some *general* features of the stimulus, thus forming new behaviour-organizing rules or *categories* (Avital and Jablonka 2000). Finally, a change in the environment can lead to alteration in the way sensory information is used, and, in some cases, can lead to modifications in the usage of sensory modalities. For example, a change in the habitat in the Palestine mole rat, which started living in underground burrows, led to the recruitment of the visual areas of the moles' brain for auditory functions. In this case, as in many other cases of altered behaviour, the new way of life (i.e. burrowing underground) also led to a change in the environment in which the animal and its descendants are selected; the animals construct their niche and this results in rapid and directional evolutionary change (Dor and Jablonka 2000, 2010; Avital and Jablonka 2000; Jablonka and Lamb 2005; Odling-Smee et al. 2003). The activity of the animal, as it adapts to its new conditions, and the central role of developmental plasticity in the processes of ontogenetic and (eventually) genetic adaptation, are central to our evolutionary view. In all cases, the developmental and the evolutionary potential of the animal *can only be appreciated a posteriori.*

To make this point clearer, let us try the following thought experiment. Pinker and Bloom (1990) argue that human language is more like bat echolocation than like reading and writing. Let us, then, try and evolve bat-like echolocation in humans. Until recently, the suggestion that humans could evolve echolocation would have been considered impossible, on a par with the suggestion that pigs could fly. However, recent data shows that blind people can learn to echolocate by making clicking sounds (Thaler et al. 2011). This echolocation ability was discovered independently by several blind people, but Daniel Kish, who became blind at the age of 13 months and who began to practise echolocation from a very early age, has made it known to the general public as well as to scientists. This echolocation ability, which depends on learning and exercise, enables Daniel Kish and other blind people who practise it to identify distant objects, cross busy streets, and ride bicycles in the mountains. Recent fMRI studies shed some light on what happens in the brains of early and late blind echolocators: there is recruitment of the unused visual area in the cortex by the auditory areas (Thaler et al. 2011). This can be the basis of an imaginary, but not impossible, evolutionary scenario. Imagine a group of genetically blind humans who become isolated, then discover echolocation by clicks and spread the invention among them. There would then be selection for the best echolocators, and in time the ability would be genetically accommodated—it would improve and become more refined, appear earlier in ontogeny, involve new physiological and cognitive adaptations for emitting efficient clicks and for receiving and interpreting them, and so on. And although, initially, this innovation-first scenario may not involve cumulative cultural evolution, it is not difficult to imagine how echolocation through clicking would affect these people's norms of behaviour, lead to assortative mating (among best echolocators), alter the education of young children, affect the choice of materials and the methods of building artefacts, and make people increasingly dependent on the new sensory modality. The new echolocation-niche constructed by our imaginary humans would affect their cultural and biological evolution, including the genetic evolution of their echolocation abilities. Although we do not suggest that the evolution of echolocation in bats involved such cumulative cultural evolution, it is quite likely that phenotypic individual adaptations preceded genotypic ones even in bats.

All 'phenotype-first' adaptive scenarios are based on the universally valid assumption that biological organisms are highly plastic. The range and boundaries of plasticity are not fixed, however, and in some cases plasticity itself can be plastic. This is especially clear in the case of complex behaviours. For example, the cultural technologies of reading and writing seem to have extended human memory, enabled abstract chains of reasoning, and guided new ways of scanning visual items, thus making human even more cognitively plastic (Goody 1997; Donald 1991). Material tools extended human capacities, and the ability to make a tool for the production of other tools led to a qualitative leap in capacities and expanded behavioural and cognitive plasticity. Hence, it is only *a posteriori*, once behaviours are invented and learned, developed and refined, that their effects on other behaviours and on their own plastic development can be appreciated. Only then can we estimate how plastic the organism was, and we need to update these estimations when new capacities evolve. Crucially, in both ontogeny and phylogeny, the *mature capacity* is the product of the process of innovation and practice.

2.3 Collaborative innovation: interaction as the engine of language evolution

Even at the level of individual cognition, then, language-related evolution was a phenotype-first adaptation process. This, however, is only half of the story, because language (just like reading and writing) is a communication technology, which means that it most probably emerged and further developed at the level of the group—as the product of collective explorations during social interactions. It is thus not just impossible to predict the emergence of language from the capacities of the individual mind/brain, it is also impossible to predict it from the exploratory behaviour of any single human individual.

There are two issues here, and the first is well-established: languages as we know them are the products of long cumulative processes, in which numerous contributions, large and small, were made by many different individuals, and groups of individuals, all along the way. As Tomasello puts it, 'the actual creation of the linguistic conventions and constructions that people use to structure their linguistic interactions with one another in particular languages are due both to cultural-historical processes that transcend individuals and to psychological processes during ontogeny of social learning, joint attention, analogy, and so forth' (2008: 308). For Tomasello, the psychological preconditions are given as a constant foundation for the entire process, while we have tried to show that these very capacities were themselves entangled from the very beginning with the actual cultural-historical process. It seems quite clear that the actual steps along the way, the local dynamics of innovation, stabilization, propagation, and acceptance, were heavily determined by the social and cultural conditions. Innovations appeared from exploratory processes as answers to specific communicative needs, and were thus structured mainly by the needs that had to be met, and by the general culture of communication. Whether they were accepted, modified, and propagated, and to what extent, was also heavily determined by the social and cultural context. Individual brains/minds were involved, of course, but each of them was only exposed to a very local temporal segment of the process. Throughout the entire dynamics, language was a much larger phenomenon than whatever could be detected at the level of the individual.

The second issue is this: language is not just a collective innovation in the sense that the burden of innovation was spread across many generations of speakers, each building on the achievements of the former. It is also collective in the sense that every particular innovation, in a certain locale at a certain time, must have appeared in a moment of *communicative exploration*. Linguistic innovations appear as answers to communicative needs, and these, by their very definition, involve several individuals in the conversation—certainly more than one person at a time. For a linguistic innovation to work, for example, it must be mutually identified and normatively accepted by both speaker and hearer. As these very often have different interests in the conversation and face different constraints (ambiguity, for instance, presents the listener with a challenge that the speaker may not even notice), linguistic innovations emerge and make their way towards stabilization and acceptance through implicit *social negotiation*. This is clearly evidenced in currently investigated processes of language change (e.g. Eckert 2012), and language emergence (Senghas et al. 2005; Kisch 2008). In such dynamics of negotiation, the creative process involves all the participants, and thus transcends every one of them.

The growing literature on the collective nature of human inventiveness may help us take a first step towards an answer to the question. Following a half-century in which the discourse on creativity centred on the decontextualized individual cognition of the *lone genius*, much of the field has gradually moved towards a socio-cultural approach, inspired, among others, by Vygotsky and Winnicott. Within this new approach, 'emphasis is put on mutuality, sharing, negotiation of a joint perspective or shared meaning, coordination, intersubjectivity' (Grossen 2008: 248). As Glaveanu (2011: 486) puts it, creativity is seen as a process that 'takes place in a *representational space*...a space of intersubjectivity and mediation between self and other, self and community, self and culture' (emphasis in the original). In situations of collaborative creativity, different individuals, with their unique perspectives on the problem, build a common representational space between them, in which they 'come to realize other ways of understanding or doing things'. The emergent solution is new, because 'the solution or creative idea (or ideas) are dissimilar to the current knowledge of the participants'.

The important point, for our purposes, is the fact that such processes do not always succeed. As a matter of fact, they very often fail. As it turns out, success depends on a long set of conditions. To begin with, there seem to be interesting conditions regarding individual variability between members of the group. On the one hand, members have to be *different enough* from each other, in terms of their experiences, their worldviews and their perspectives on the problem to be solved. The entire process relies on the sharing of differences: if all the members of the group see the world in the same way, nothing would happen. (Note that co-operation as such, in the sense of doing things together towards a common goal, does not require this level of individual variability.) On the other hand, members of the group cannot be *too* different, because that would destroy the sense of group identification necessary for collaboration (Mannix and Neale 2005). Second, the members of the group probably have to accumulate some experience in working together before creative results are shown, which is why real-life teams have been found to be more creative than arbitrarily formed teams in laboratory conditions (Milliken et al. 2003). Third, the emotional dynamics of the group have to be right to allow for free exchange under conditions of trust, motivation, and group identification. Under these conditions, if the members engage in intensive, motivated, and trustful communication, the group may reach what Sawyer (2007) calls *group genius*, 'a peak experience' where the group as a whole performs 'at its top level of ability'. It is interesting to note that Sawyer begins his discussion with his own experiences as a jazz musician:

My years of playing piano in jazz ensembles convinced me that what happened in any one person's mind could never explain what made one night's performance shine and another dud. At any second during a performance, an almost invisible musical exchange could take the piece in a new direction; later, no one could remember who was responsible for what. In jazz, the group has the ideas, not the individual musicians. (2007: x)

Social play among human children displays similar dynamics, since the play's unfolding depends on mutual negotiation among the participants and ongoing, interactive fine tuning. Gray (2009) argued that social play moulds egalitarian relationships in hunter-gatherer societies, and Ginsburg and Jablonka (Chapter 22) suggest that social play in human children—in particular pretend-play—co-evolved with episodic memory and analogical thinking that were crucial for the evolution of language.

This understanding of the conditions under which collaborative creativity produces successful innovations suggests that, if the original emergence of the first prototype of language was made possible by the maturation of pre-linguistic human societies as sites of collaborative creativity, all the conditions for success mentioned above must have already been met. Members of the group must have been able to bring different perspectives and capacities into the process, but still maintain a strong sense of group identification; they must have already been experienced in collective exploration, working within an emotional climate of trust—and they must have already had the capacity, *still without language*, to efficiently communicate their perspectives to each other to an extent that eventually allowed for the emergence of language. We therefore move beyond the 'individual phenotype-first' evolutionary dynamics that we described in the previous section. It is a 'cultural-phenotype-first' process that drives changes in individual cognitions, and eventually changes in the gene pool.

Moreover, it is important to realize that language itself, once it was there, immediately enhanced the group's capacity for further collective exploration, because it provided a revolutionary new tool for the construction of the common representational space. As Tylen et al. (2010: 3) indicate in a comprehensive review article, experimental evidence clearly shows that language facilitates social interaction in four ways, all of which are crucial for collaborative exploration: 'Language dramatically extends the possibility-space for interaction, facilitates the profiling and navigation of joint attentional scenes, enables the sharing of situation models and action plans, and mediates the cultural shaping of interacting minds.' Galantucci (2005: 3), for example, created experimental settings in which pairs of participants had to negotiate a new language from scratch in order to solve a co-operative game that could not be solved otherwise: 'Despite great differences in speed (under twenty minutes to nearly three hours), most pairs eventually managed to jointly develop stable systems of symbols, which turned a nearly impossible task into a trivial one' (Tylen et al. 2010: 7). Language, then, may have been entangled from the very beginning in a co-evolutionary spiral with the human capacity for collaborative creativity—first as a product, *within* the common representational space, then (immediately) as a tool *for* the further construction of the common space.

2.4 Language requires unique cognitive capacities: we evolved *for* language

Throughout this culturally driven process, the cognitive challenges that individual minds/brains had to face evolved together with language itself. As the challenges increased, and as they became more specific, patterns of variability between different individuals began to be exposed: some turned out to be better at handling the revolutionary technology than the others. Eventually, individuals began to be selected for their linguistic capacities. Because of that, modern humans do have innate capacities for language, but these capacities are *derivative, emergent, variable,* and *partial*—not constitutive, foundational, universal, and complete (Dor and Jablonka 2010). Innateness is *a posteriori*, not a priori. And it is not only cognitive: the deepest indication that we have evolved *for* language is not the fact that we can do it—but the fact that we need it; our minds are language-*craving*.

The discourse on the innateness and specificity of the capacities required by language has developed in an interesting way in the last half-century. In the beginning, the discourse worked with the premise that language the way we know it requires unique and specific capacities of a certain formal type. Coupled with the assumption that these capacities should have already been there before language, this working hypothesis raised a foundational problem: Why would such capacities evolve in the first place? Then, gradually, much of the discourse moved on to adopt the Function-alist/Cognitivist contention that language is based on general cognition. This was a positive and highly productive move, but it also threw out the baby together with the bath water: language does require capacities that are specific and unique, and this, *as such*, has never really been denied in the literature. What has been denied (and rightfully so) was, first, the claim that language is founded on a set of innate capacities of the specific formal type suggested in the Generative literature; and, second, that uniqueness is an *absolute* term. Jackendoff and Pinker (2005: 214), for example, distinguish between two interpretations of the claim that 'a trait' is 'unique to language' or 'unique to humans':

It can be interpreted in absolute, categorical, all-or-none terms: a 'unique' trait is sui generis, with nothing remotely similar in the rest of the mind or the rest of the animal kingdom, and appearing out of the blue in the course of evolution. Or the claim can be interpreted in graded terms: that the trait has been modified in the course of human evolution to such a degree that it is different in significant aspects from its evolutionary precursors.

Jackendoff and Pinker adopt the second interpretation, and we agree: it is a fact that competent speakers of full-fledged languages are required to perform highly specific computations at all the relevant levels, and these are not transparently reducible to general cognition. The computations of auditory phonetics cannot be explained as simple manifestations of the human hearing ability; the machinery of lexical memory is not the same as that of general memory; semantics cannot be reduced to general world knowledge; and, as we will show later on in this volume, language challenges the human capacity of *imagination* in ways that are unparalleled anywhere else.

So, the question remains: How and why did these unique capacities emerge? Jackendoff and Pinker (2005: 214) suggest that they emerged from different evolutionary precursors, 'presumably as a result of adaptation to a new function that the trait was selected to serve'. Again, we agree. The question, however, is this: Where did the new function come from? What was it that provided the *attractor* for the adaptation process? The only possible candidate for such an attractor seems to be language itself, which means, quite simply, that it should have already been there before the language-adapted cognitive evolutionary process began.

Putting cultural evolution first, then, allows for a major reformulation of the relationship between general cognition and language-specific capacities. It is true that language-specific capacities could not have emerged before language itself, but that does not mean that there are no such capacities *today*. There are capacities that are unique to language (unique in the weak sense proposed above), and these emerged because human individuals began to be selected for their ability to survive in a new cultural environment, with the technology of language at its centre. Every capacity that proved useful was selected for, including much that is generally cognitive. As the technology itself became more complex and more specific, however, individuals had to find ways to cope with more specific challenges. These initiated processes of exploration, both individual and collective, that were specific to language, and these eventually produced novel behaviours, novel capacities, and then, very partially, novel genetic makeups. Today, we are predisposed to learn language before we are born, not in the sense that we have innate knowledge of language, but in the sense that we are born with minds that evolved *for* language, and thus have a unique propensity for language acquisition and usage.

2.5 Apes can learn protolanguage, but apparently do not invent it by themselves

Most of the discourse about the origin of language begins with a negatively formulated question: Why *don't* the apes have language? The negative formulation of the question has forced us to take a very close look at the apes and their capacities, and what we now know is that the apes already have what is required at the cognitive level for the acquisition and use of a first viable prototype of language—what Tallerman (2012) calls 'protolanguage'. The answer to the question—why don't the apes have protolanguage—is *not* a matter of individual cognition. For a long while, it has been assumed that the apes do not have a *theory of mind*—therefore they have no language. It turns out that they do understand others' intentions, therefore have at least a rudimentary theory of mind (see review by Gibson in Tallerman and Gibson 2012). For a long while, it has been assumed that the apes cannot *learn* language. What Kanzi (and his sister Panbanisha) managed to learn in Sue Savage-Rumbaugh's lab (Savage-Rumbaugh and Lewin 1994; Segerdahl et al. 2005) proves that they can learn to use referential gestures and lexigrams sufficiently well to qualify as possessing protolanguage capacities. It is sometimes claimed that Kanzi's linguistic behaviour actually shows that the apes *cannot* acquire human language the way we know it. His capacity does not reach that of a three-year-old. This is true, but it is also totally beside the point. The crucial fact is that the apes in the wild not only lack fully developed languages—they lack what Kanzi managed to learn in the lab as well. The negatively formulated question should thus read: Why don't the apes in the wild have protolanguage *at the level* that Kanzi managed to learn? And the answer to this question cannot have anything to do with the capacities that allow humans to go beyond Kanzi's level. What Kanzi and other apes, observed in the wild and experimented with in the different labs, actually demonstrate is only this: ape cognition is sufficient for the learning and use of a first functioning prototype of language as a tool of communication. When an intelligent ape is provided with a protolanguage already invented and stabilized by *others*, the ape is perfectly capable of learning it to a level that allows for efficient communication. It stands to reason, then, that the problem lies elsewhere: in the invention of even a rudimentary system of protolanguage.

Crucially, apes do invent (McGrew 1992; Whiten et al. 1999; Yamamoto et al. 2008), and they certainly do things together, as a group, although the jury is out on the question of whether they co-operate (see, e.g., the Tomasello–Boesch debate over collective hunting in chimpanzees in Tomasello et al. 2005). The invention of a system such as language, however, requires more than individual innovation or co-operation. It requires a collective capacity for *collaborative creativity*, which the apes, not as individuals, but as collectivities, seem to lack. The only observations we could find that could hint at collaborative innovation—as opposed to individual innovation—appear in Menzel (1972) among captive apes, and in Russon et al. (2010). In Russon's study of water-related innovation in a group of orang-utans in Indonesia, they found that '"innovators" rates of close association with other innovators were disproportionately high and between non-innovators they were disproportionately low' (2010: 21). Such close associations must have played a central role in the evolution of the human capacity for full-scale collaborative innovation. Looking for the origin of language in individual cognition thus misses out on the essential uniqueness of the human species: the answer is not there.

To sum up, four lines of argumentation indicate that the emergence of language can and should be explained as a culturally driven process that entangled individual minds/brains in a process of evolution *for* language: (1) capacities and their genetic accommodation emerge from exploration and innovation, not the other way around;

(2) the emergence of language as a communication technology must have required collaborative exploration and innovation; (3) language requires relatively specific capacities, which can only be explained through a process of accommodation for the specificities of language as a technology; (4) the apes can learn a first prototype of language, but cannot, as far as we know, invent it by themselves.

The emergent picture, then, positions the bottleneck of the evolution of language on the other side of the capacity–behaviour–culture continuum, in the cultural and social conditions that allowed for such processes of collective creative exploration to take place in the first place. The original question should thus be reformulated as follows: *What happened to human cultures that allowed for the process of collective exploration that brought about first protolanguage and then language—eventually changing us in the process?* As we see it, the picture of early human societies that emerges from this volume—with its divisions of labour, material expertise, social relationships, play, mimesis, music, and ritual—takes us a major step forward towards an answer.

3

Niche construction and semiosis: biocultural and social dynamics

CHRIS SINHA

3.1 Introduction: paradox and problematic in human evolution

Our focus in this volume could be construed as a theoretical counterblast to the predominance of biologically based theorizing in recent approaches to language evolution. This construal has some validity, inasmuch as the hypothesis, until recently widely entertained, that evolutionarily modern language emerged as a result of a single genetic mutation, is now considered inconsistent with the archaeological evidence for human evolution in Africa (Botha and Knight 2009). It would, however, be a mistake to suppose that social and biological explanatory frames are fated to eternal opposition in our quest for the understanding of language origins and evolution. Ever since the question of language origins was first debated by Enlightenment theorists such as Descartes and Condillac, language and the language capacity have indeed been conceptualized as part of *either* uniquely human nature (nativism) *or* uniquely human culture (environmentalism). This opposition, however, has been effectively superseded as a result of recent advances in the biological and behavioural sciences—advances that confront us with a striking and challenging paradox.

The paradox is one of discontinuity in continuity. On the one hand, the biological characteristics of the human species display no dramatic discontinuities with those of other species; yet, on the other, human cognitive capacities and cultural constructions appear from our current vantage point to be as exceptional in the living world as they did to Descartes. It can, of course, be argued that the cognitive and cultural discontinuity reflects merely a gap in the available evidence—there are, after all, no other living representatives of the human lineage since it diverged from the ancestors of our closest living primate relatives. If there were, the discontinuity might prove to be an illusion. Even so, it is hard to resist the conviction that, however extended the event or sequence of events in evolutionary time, something happened involving language that radically transformed the evolving human mind. This transformation poses a profound and complex problem for both biological and social theory.

To begin with continuity: Darwin's refutation of the idea that the human species is essentially different, in biological constitution and evolutionary history, from other species, received, in the closing years of the last century, strong confirmation in two very different domains. Succinctly stated, neither genes nor culture, singly, can account for what, if anything, makes humans different from other species. There is no evidence of dramatic genetic discontinuity between humans and their closest primate relatives, chimpanzees. The two species share, even on the most conservative estimate, about 95 per cent of their genetic material (Britten 2002). Taken together with the results of the human genome project, this suggests that whatever cognitive capacities distinguish the human species from other closely related species are unlikely to be attributable to dedicated genetic material available for directly coding such capacities. This does not mean that there is no genetic component of specifically human capacities. It does mean that the ascription of differences between the cognitive capacities of humans and those of non-humans to interspecies genetic differences alone is likely to be false. This is bad news for nativist modularity theories.

The news for those who would argue that what is unique about humans is the capacity for culture, a favoured hypothesis for generations past of social anthropologists, is hardly better. Culture can minimally be defined as the existence of intra-species group differences in behavioural patterns and repertoires, which are not directly determined by ecological circumstances (such as the availability of particular resources employed in the differing behavioural repertoires), and which are learned and transmitted across generations. On this definition, there is ample evidence of cultural differences in foraging strategies, tool use, and social behaviours in chimpanzees (Whiten et al. 1999; de Waal 2001). Such a definition will also qualify, for example, epigenetically learned intra-species dialect differences between songbird communities as cultural and culturally transmitted behaviour (Marler and Peters 1982). Again, this does not mean that there is no cultural foundation for uniquely human cognitive capacities; rather, it suggests that human culture, from an evolutionary and developmental point of view, must be treated as *explicandum* as much as *explicans*.

What is needed, it seems, is a theoretical apparatus capable of integrating culture and biology. One version of such integration, in which culture is analysed as quasi-heritable units ('memes' or 'culturgens') has been argued for by theorists such as Richard Dawkins (1976) and Edward O. Wilson (1998). Such accounts, however, have often been criticized for their reductionism, and more recent evolutionary theory suggests that the relation between biology and culture is much more of a two-way street than was ever envisaged by socio-biology. Far from eliminating culture by absorbing it into the genotype, some biologists are increasingly acknowledging the role of culture in shaping the evolutionary process at the genetic level, by the construction of new selective environments. Current developments in theoretical biology, among which niche construction theory (Laland et al. 2000; Odling-Smee et al. 2003) is particularly salient, significantly depart from the neo-Darwinian synthesis that dominated 20th-century biology, by incorporating an ecological dimension that, I shall argue, proves to be particularly important for understanding human linguistic and cognitive evolution.

3.2 Neo-Darwinism and its discontents

I begin by outlining the premises of, and the outstanding problems with, the neo-Darwinian synthesis unifying Darwin's theory of natural and sexual selection with modern population genetics. In the neo-Darwinian synthesis, the unit of selection (*what* is selected) is the gene, or more specifically alternative variants (alleles) of the 'same' genes. The *agent* of selection (what *does* the selecting) is the extra-organismic environment, including (a) the inanimate surround, (b) other species ((a) and (b) together being the basis of natural selection), and (c) (subpopulations of) genes of the same species (the basis of sexual and kin selection). The relevant *attribute* upon which selection works (what is selected *for*) is any genetically transmitted trait. The mechanism of selection determines the differential reproductive success of the gene (allele) within the population of interacting genes, and thus the frequency distributions of genes and traits in the population. This model, when appropriately formalized, can be extended, as we shall see, by including cultural traits in the environment, that act as 'amplifiers' on the selection of genetic variation: this is known as the theory of gene-culture co-evolution (Lumsden and Wilson 1981).

The core issues at the heart of the problems besetting the neo-Darwinian synthesis can be briefly summarized. First, genes do not come singly, but as combinations (genotypes), packaged in organisms (phenotypes). It is this distinction that Dawkins (1976) recasts as a distinction between the 'replicator' (that which is copied), and the 'vehicle' (that which embodies the genotypic collection of replicators, and interacts with the environment). For Dawkins, it is only the gene that is actually copied, and therefore he identifies the gene (unit of selection) as the replicator, and the phenotype as a mere 'vehicle' for the replicator.

However, it is organisms, not genes, that are subject to direct selection pressures in terms of those traits conferring fitness. The organism level of biological organization receives scant attention in population genetics but, even granted that the gene is the unit of selection, it is the organism that must be considered as the site of selection. Organisms, in most (though not all) cases, can be regarded as morphological individuals. However, the actual process of selection by an 'agent' occurs in relation to the functioning, behaving organism. It was for this reason that Jean Piaget upheld the leading role of behaviour in evolution (Piaget 1979). In the light of this, it may be (and frequently has been) questioned to what extent it remains legitimate to identify the 'replicator' with the genetic unit of selection.

Ecologists emphasize that animals, through their behaviour, shape, as well as are shaped by, their niches. Organismic behaviours may eventuate in significant trans-formations of the very environment to which the organism must adapt. A simple example (from Sinha 1988: 136) is the following: 'A "path" may ... be an unintended consequence of locomotion from one place to another, but it is, nevertheless, a useful one ... such shaping ... can [however] introduce distal consequences—food shortage, erosion, pollution, competition with other species—which are outside the initial circuit of adaptation' (see also Costall 2004). In many cases, however, a process of positive feedback will occur in which organism and environment are in a comple-mentary relationship, each shaping the other. An oft-cited example is the hoof of the horse and its adaptation to the grassland steppe whose ecological characteristics the horse, through its own motion through the landscape, reproduces. The horse is an agent in the evolution and reproduction of the steppe, just as the steppe is an agent in the reproduction and selection of the horse, and it is behaviour that is the link between these agentive processes. Even if the DNA-based biochemical replicator, then, is the gene, the evolutionary dynamic of replication-plus-selection should, it can be argued, more profitably be identified with the entire complex of the site of selection, which is the active, behaving organism in its ecological niche.

In an important subset of cases, the niche resulting from behaviour can be seen not merely as a contingent consequence of behaviour, but as an animal artefact, inas-much as phenotypic individuals are genetically, morphologically, and behaviourally adapted to the production of specific niches which are integral to the survival and/or reproduction strategy of the species. Examples of such artefactual niches are the nests of bower birds and the dams of beavers. The male bower bird builds and decorates an elaborate nest (bower) to attract females, using attractive objects such as flowers, shells, and leaves. The bower forms an integral part of the male's mating display, and sexual selection by the female is based upon the bower as much as upon the behavioural display of the male. Beavers construct, through co-ordinated and col-laborative behaviour, dams that serve both as a defence against predators and as a means to enhance the availability of food. The dams of beavers not only serve as a constructed, artefactual niche for beavers themselves, but also reproduce the wetland ecology in which many other species thrive. As a final example of the significance of animal artefacts, we can mention the termite mound, whose material structure is not only integral to the reproductive strategy of this species of social insect, but also constitutes the morphological structure of the colony as a 'group organism'.

Animal-made artefactual niches are just as much heritable as genes, and behav-ioural adaptations to artefactual niches are subject to natural and sexual selection just as much as any other behaviours. Furthermore, such behavioural adaptations are, in a very real sense, what artefactual niches are 'made for'. In the ecological psychology of James J. Gibson (1979), a key role is played by affordances, properties of the ecological niche affording or supporting specific kinds of action made possible by the motor system and morphology of the animal. Such actions are both species-typical (though not necessarily species-unique) and adaptive. Because affordances, Gibson maintained, are directly perceived, the phenomenal world of the animal is meaningful, in that it potentiates the activation of perception–action circuits: objects present themselves as edible, climb-able, graspable, and so forth. Gibson neglected, however, to note the crucial importance of the fact that some affordances, in the case of artefactual niches, are constructed by the animal itself. Artefactual niches are adaptive precisely because of the behaviours and strategies that they afford—nests are for nesting, and burrows are for burrowing. In such cases, the site of selection is no longer just the organism, but the organism in its self-constructed niche: the organism/niche coupling or organism plus artefact.

What are the implications of this for the neo-Darwinian synthesis, and for theories of gene-culture co-evolution? A conservative reading would be that the only modification required is that the phenotype, or 'vehicle', be extended to incorporate the artefactual niche. This is, indeed, the interpretation favoured by Dawkins (1982), who employs the terminology of the 'extended phenotype'. Under this interpretation, the 'replicator' remains the gene, and only the gene. However, it is not only the gene that is copied or replicated. In fact, the artefactual niche too is both reproduced across generations and serves as a fundamental precondition for genetic replication. The artefactual niche is thus both a consequence of and an agent in natural and/or sexual selection, and must then be seen as a key ingredient of the evolution of the species-typical genotype.

It seems, therefore, that the integration of ecological considerations into evolutionary theory, and specifically the existence of animal artefactual niches, further undermines the hard and fast distinction between germ-line and soma, genotype and phenotype, 'replicator' and 'vehicle'. In fact, it makes better sense to say that, even granted that the unit of Darwinian selection remains the gene (allele), the 'replicator' includes both the artefactual niche and the niche-adaptive behavioural repertoire of the animal. Such considerations lead us back to Piaget's more general proposition that behaviour is the leading edge and motor of evolution, reinforcing the conclusion that the identification by Dawkins of the 'replicator' with the unit of selection (the gene, or its hypothesized cultural analogue, the 'meme' (Dawkins 1976)) is deeply flawed, and that replication can as well or better be considered as a property of the entire site of selection.

At this point, it is useful to make a brief critical detour to re-examine neo-Darwinist theories of gene-culture co-evolution, such as that of Lumsden and Wilson (1981), as applied to human culture and society. Such accounts presuppose a functional parallelism between units of biological replication and units of cultural replication—memes, or 'culturgens' as they were termed by Lumsden and Wilson;

and treat memes as human behavioural variants analogous to gene alleles. In this perspective, ethnographic variation is analysable in terms of aggregate properties of human populations. The Lumsden–Wilson theory thus presupposes both an ontological distinction, and a functional parallelism, between gene and meme, nature and culture, without explaining either the ontological distinction, or the functional parallelism, that is supposed to exist between the units of selection in the domains of biology and culture. The Lumsden–Wilson theory has also been criticized for making 'the reductionist assumption that the characteristics of a society can be understood as simply the sum of the characteristics of the individuals of that society' (Alpert and Lange 1981: 3976), and for having no place for emergent properties of societies. Alpert and Lange's critique did not specify what these emergent properties are, but we are now in a position to do so: the emergent properties of human societies are those that are specific to human biocultural niches, and that cannot be reduced to the properties of the artefactual niche of any other species.

3.3 Niche construction: language as a biocultural niche

The critical considerations outlined above have led to a more radical formulation of human gene-culture co-evolution, advanced by Laland et al. (2000) and Odling-Smee et al. (2003), in which a key role is played by genotype/phenotype combinations or 'phenogenotypes'. Odling-Smee et al. (2003: 365–6) write that 'a phenogenotype can be thought of as a human with a package of genes and package of experiences', adding that this concept 're-establishes the organism as the central unit of human evolution, not as vehicle but as replicator. In fact, what is really replicated is a biocultural complex, with a composite array of semantic information...and inherited resources.' The concept of phenogenotype is not restricted, however, either to human evolution or to the experiences of a single individual, since it encompasses also the ecological niche constructed by, and adapted to, the species and its subgroups.

In the cases discussed above, the behavioural repertoire of the species includes behaviours that are specifically adapted to the making of the quasi-artefactual niche, and these behaviours in turn support wider repertoires of behavioural strategies exploiting the niche. Artefactual niches are adaptive precisely *because of* the behaviours and strategies that they afford—nests are for nesting, and burrows are for burrowing. The artefactual niche in many cases can be regarded as an extension of either a behavioural repertoire (e.g. male mating display) or of the organism's morphology (e.g. the bower bird's bower as functionally equivalent, as an indicator of fitness, to the tail of the peacock). Indeed, we can further ask if it might be fruitful to consider certain species-specific behavioural repertoires, such as birdsong, also to be kinds of animal quasi-artefacts, inasmuch the song of the adults provides a niche within which the singing behaviour is epigenetically learned (Marler and Peters 1982; Sinha 2004).

Laland et al. (2000: 132) criticize the 'human-centred' perspective of previous accounts of gene-culture co-evolution, emphasizing that many *non*-human species behaviourally co-direct genetic evolution through niche construction. This point is important, because it situates the role of culture and language in human evolution within the wider class of processes involving adaptation to artefactual niches such as nests, dams, mounds, and burrows. Laland's et al. niche construction model, then, is a general one, not confined to human culture and evolution. They acknowledge, however, that humans are 'unique in their extraordinary capacity for culture' (Laland et al. 2000: 133). I interpret this to mean primarily that human cultures are unique in some fundamental respect, that is they are different (and irreducibly, discontinuously so) from the cultures of other species; and, secondarily, that the capacity for creating, acquiring, and transmitting cultural forms is uniquely developed (though clearly not unique) in humans.

One evident discontinuity between human and non-human cultures is that human cultures are linguistic, and the capacity for human cultural acquisition and trans-mission is mediated by the unique human language capacity. The nativist modularist account of this capacity proposes its inscription in the human genotype, a hypothesis vulnerable to many objections, including the difficulty stated above of locating this profound discontinuity in the continuous landscape of the primate genome. The alternative account that I outline above views the human language capacity as phenogenotypic. Language, in this account, is a quasi-artefactual biocultural niche, and the capacity to acquire and use it involves the evolution and replication of a phenogenotypic biocultural complex (Laland et al. 2000: 144). In a nutshell, then, I propose that although non-human species may properly be said to display behav-iours that can be regarded as both cultural and culturally transmitted (Whiten et al. 1999), human culture is distinguished by the predominant place occupied in it by language as a biocultural niche (Sinha 2009a).

It might be argued that the designation of 'artefact', even modified as 'quasi-artefact', should be reserved for more or less enduring constructed material struc-tures. Pinker (1994), in keeping with his nativist and modularist view of the language capacity, denies that language is an artefact: he regards it as a part of the natural world, the capacity being part of human nature. Rather than responding with an equal and opposite view—conceptualizing evolutionarily modern languages as cul-tural artefacts *tout court*—we may regard them as the biocultural ground for what is unique about human symbolic culture. Culturally transmitted, specialized behav-ioural repertoires constitute not merely biological, but biocultural artefacts/niches that are functionally analogous to animal artefacts. If this argument is accepted, it follows that human natural languages can also be viewed as quasi-artefacts and species-specific biocultural niches.

Treating language as a biocultural niche yields a new perspective both on the human language capacity and on the evolution of this capacity. First, it unifies, in a non-reductionist fashion, the evolutionary dynamics of human material culture and symbolic culture. As Boivin (2008: 190) has pointed out, '[t]ools, technologies, and other aspects of the material world of humans and their predecessors have largely been seen as the outcome of evolutionary developments, and little attempt has been made to investigate their potential role as selection forces during the course of human evolution.' The same can be said of the biocultural niche of language, which is not separate from the other material and symbolic components or niche-structures that make up the human biocultural complex. The biocultural niche of language is culturally situated, that is, it is dynamically embedded within the entire semiotic biocultural complex that includes other symbolic and non-symbolic artefacts.[1] It is crucial to appreciate, in this context, that the human biocultural complex, like other animal artefactual niches, is not merely part of what is reproduced, but is also fundamental to the process of its reproduction and transmission, since it constitutes a self-made environment for adaptive selection.

Second, treating language as a biocultural niche means that theories of language learning no longer require, as do generative linguistic accounts, the organism to possess an innate Universal Grammar to account for language acquisition, any more than the building of a nest requires an innate abstract model of the nest. The grammar of the language is in the language, just as the structure of the nest is in the nest.

There are many documented similarities between the known languages of the world, but recent comparative research also highlights dimensions of variation that have in the past received insufficient attention, and which cast doubt on whether there are any true language universals at all (Evans and Levinson 2009). Common properties of languages take the form of constraints on variation rather than putative universals, and can be hypothesized to be accounted for by common properties of the human cognitive system, in concert with the transculturally shared communicative intentions of language users. This does not mean that human languages are not dramatically different from the communicative signals and signal systems that are ubiquitous in the animal world. They are, but this difference is a consequence of the fact that only human languages systematically employ symbols rather than signals (Sinha 2004). As regards the relations between language properties and language acquisition, the capacity to acquire language is a transcultural and species-specific

---

[1] Whiten and Erdal (2012) use the term 'human socio-cognitive niche' to refer (on one reading) to what I am calling (after Laland et al. 2000) the 'biocultural complex'; in both cases, a more general or transcultural meaning is implied than in many other usages of terms like 'cognitive niche' (see also Clark 2006; Magnani 2009). An alternative reading of Whiten and Erdal's notion of 'socio-cognitive niche' would be more equivalent to Laland's et al. 'phenogenotype'.

human cognitive capacity, but as I argue below, this is an evolutionary outcome consequent on epigenetic plasticity in human infant and child development.

The capacity for constructing a language is, from this perspective, a cognitive-behavioural relationship between language user and the constituents of language, just as the capacity for building a nest is a cognitive-behavioural relationship between the builder and the constituents of the nest; and it is this relationship that, in each case, has been selected for in evolution. This biocultural niche account of language and language learning is thus compatible with usage-based, cognitive functional theories of language and language acquisition (Tomasello 1998, 2003a).

Because of its pre-eminence in mediating both cultural reproduction and individual cognitive processes, language is the primary and most distinctive constituent of what the Russian semiotician Yuri Lotman called the 'semiosphere' (e.g. Lotman 1990): the universe of signs, or the semiotic dimension of the human biocultural complex. The self-constructed human biocultural complex both favoured the emergence and elaboration of language, as proposed by Odling-Smee and Laland (2009: 120); and, because language is co-constitutive of that niche itself, the biocultural complex was fundamentally transformed by language into a symbolic biocultural niche or semiosphere continuous with what we might call the material-artefactual technosphere. The class of organisms with the language capacity (normally developing humans) can thus be theorized as a phenogenotypic replicator, systemically associated with a wider biocultural complex of symbolic and praxic-constructive cognitive capacities, also of a phenogenotypic nature; and individual language acquisition and use are situated in the contexts of actuation of these interrelated capacities. This account accords with the view that what makes humans unique is not an innate language acquisition device plus a variety of other species-specific innate cognitive modules, but a generalized semiotic or symbolic capacity, epigenetically developed from a suite of cognitive capacities largely shared with other species, but attaining higher levels of organization in humans (Piaget 1945; Deacon 1997; Sinha 1988, 2004). This capacity is not inscribed in the human genome, but distributed across the practices and systems co-constituting (with the epigenetically developed human organism) the human phenogenotype.

3.4 Phenogenotype, semiosis and the epigenesis of symbolization

Epigenesis and epigenetics are terms referring to inheritance processes and mechanisms, at different levels ranging from the molecular to the organismic, that are controlled or modulated by factors other than those inscribed in the genome (Jablonka and Lamb 2005). Epigenesis occupies a central position in Piaget's later work, which was strongly influenced by the theoretical biology of C.H. Waddington (e.g. Waddington 1953), as well as in more recent 'evo-devo' approaches integrating human evolution and development (see Dor and Jablonka, Chapter 2). Piaget considered epigenesis to provide a third way between nativism and environmental-ism, and to underpin his constructivist genetic epistemology. Sinha (1988) further argued that epigenetic processes provide an integrative bridge between biological and social processes in evolution and development, introducing the notion of epigenetic socio-naturalism. In this section, I outline the integrative relations between niche construction and epigenetic processes in human ontogenesis and its evolution, proposing that this dynamic coupling grounded the emergence of symbolic behaviours.

Epigenetic developmental processes in ontogenetic behavioural development are those in which the developmental trajectory and final form of the developing behaviour are a consequence as much of the environmental information as of the genetically encoded information. A genetically specified initial behavioural repertoire is subsequently elaborated through experience of a relevant environment, yielding an envelope of potential trajectories and outcomes. The process of elabor-ation is directional, and once it has taken place the initial plasticity of the embryonic, or unelaborated, repertoire is largely (though not necessarily wholly) lost. In other words, epigenesis involves a developmental transition from relative organismic plasticity and informational openness, to relative rigidity and informa-tional closure.

Augmented epigenesis is therefore advantageous for organisms in which pheno-genotypic organism–niche couplings are both frequent and variable, which is an appropriate general description of the human cultural organism. Regulatory genes augmenting epigenetic openness can therefore be expected to have been phenogen-otypically selected for in the human genome, permitting further adaptive selection for domain-specific learning in the biocultural complex, in particular for language. As yet, we know too little to accept or reject hypotheses regarding the innateness of a specifically syntactic component of the human language capacity. I certainly would not wish to reject the possibility that the epigenetic processes selected in the evolution of the human biocultural complex include a predisposition for learning syntax, but this does not necessarily imply that any such predisposition is or was dedicated from the start exclusively to language. Furthermore, innate adaptations of the perception–action system facilitating the epigenetic learning of languages do not imply the innate specification of putative language universals. In an epigenetic perspective, any adaptive developmental predisposition for learning language is unlikely either to involve direct coding of, or to be dedicated exclusively to, linguistic structure (Mueller 1996). Rather, we may hypothesize that epigenetically governed adaptations initially evolved in response to proto-linguistic socio-communicative and symbolic processes, later capturing and re-canalizing behavioural adaptations (such as serial and hierarchical constructive praxis) initially targeted to other developmental and cognitive domains.

3.4.1 *The transition from signal to symbol*

Sensitivity to signals is as basic a property of life as the ability to reproduce. All organisms are able to detect signals indexing the presence of conditions hospitable to survival and reproduction. The more complex the organism, the greater the range of signals to which it is sensitive, and the more complex its behaviours both in response to, and in the active search for, life-relevant signals. Signals, in social animals, may also be used to communicate. Communicative signals are not conventional, although (as in the case of the vervet monkey alarm calls studied by Cheney and Seyfarth (1981)) they may involve systematic encoding: that is, the same communicative modality may support a variety of coded instructions, and it is even possible for them to support a simple 'code-syntax' (Ouattara et al. 2009b). The social exchange of signals does not, however, depend upon a socially shared world of joint reference, and there is no shared convention of a sign 'standing for' a referent or class of referents. The mechanism underpinning the social exchange of signals is neither intersubjectivity nor social convention, but co-ordination of individual organismic behaviour.

Symbols, by contrast, are conventional, depending upon shared understanding that the symbol is a token representing some referential class, and that the particular token represents a particular (aspect of) a shared universe of reference and, ultimately, of discourse. Conventional symbol systems are grounded in an intersubjective meaning-field in which speakers represent, through symbolic action, some segment or aspect of reality for hearers. This representational function is unique to symbolization, and is ultimately what distinguishes a symbol from a signal. A signal can be regarded as a (possibly coded) instruction to behave in a certain way. A symbol, on the other hand, directs and guides not the behaviour of the organism(s) receiving the signal, but their understanding (construal) or (minimally) their attention, with respect to a shared referential situation.

The centrality of reference as a criterion for symbolization has been pointed out by several authors, including by John Searle in his famous 'Chinese room' thought experiment (Searle 1980). Reference, however, is only the first of two criteria for fully developed, or 'true', symbolization. Joint reference is the criterial basis for the emergence of symbolization, while the second criterion, which I shall call, following Langacker (1987), construal, constitutes the set of cognitive operations which underpin the elaboration of proto-symbolic joint reference into linguistic conceptualization proper (Sinha 2004).

It is possible to envisage an evolutionary scenario for the phylogenetic emergence of symbolic communication from signal communication involving the following steps:

(1) The receiver comes to pay attention to the sender as the source of communicative signals.

(2) The sender comes to pay attention to the receiver as a recipient of communicative signals.

(3) The receiver comes to pay attention to the evidential reliability of the sender's communicative signals as a source of information, by checking what the sender is paying attention to, or doing.

(4) The sender comes to pay attention to the receiver's readiness to reliably act upon the information communicated, by paying attention to what the receiver is paying attention to, or doing.

The first two steps of this sequence do not involve intersubjective sharing by the communicating organisms of a referential world, but they do require orientation towards, or social referencing, of a communication partner either as a source of information or as an actor whose behaviour can be influenced. This level of communicative capacity is probably widespread among mammals, underpinning complex signal-mediated social behaviours. Not only communication between conspecifics, but also communication between humans and domesticated or working animals, often seems to involve an understanding on the part of the animal that the human can both send and receive signals. Communication, with the achievement of Steps (1) and (2), remains signal-based, but it implies the establishment of a first or primary level of intersubjectivity, consisting of a recognition by each communication partner of the other *as* a communication partner, and the recognition by each partner of the other as an agent capable of acting as initiator or mediator of goal-directed action.

Primary intersubjectivity appears to be innate in human infants. Caretakers (usually mothers) and infants engage from a very early age in episodes of communication in which the bodily movements, facial expressions, and vocalizations of the two participants provide the signals necessary for the maintenance of the communicative channel or intersubjective 'we' formed by the dyad. The real-time temporal meshing by the mother of her actions with those of the baby is of fundamental importance to the maintenance of intersubjectivity (Trevarthen and Hubley 1978), indicating the emergence of a psychologically real 'ontology of the social'.

In taking Steps (3) and (4), the sender and/or receiver develop the further capacity to understand that a signal indexes an intention, rather than the action intended. With this, the possibility is opened for deception and suspicion regarding intentions. The most basic level of understanding of the communicative partner not just as a potential agent, but as an experiential subject within the intersubjective field, is the ability to follow gaze, as evidenced by human infants from about six months of age (Butterworth and Jarrett 1991) and by a number of other species. From around nine or ten months of age, human infants:

begin to engage with adults in relatively extended bouts of joint attention to objects.... In these triadic interactions infants actively co-ordinate their visual attention to person and object, for example by looking to an adult periodically as the two of them play together with a toy, or by following the adult's gaze. Infants also become capable at this age of intentionally communicating to adults their desire to obtain an object or to share attention to an object, usually through non-linguistic gestures such as pointing or showing, often accompanied by gaze alternation between object and person. (Tomasello 1996: 310)

The achievement of joint reference in human infancy establishes the 'referential triangle' referred to as 'secondary intersubjectivity' (Trevarthen and Hubley 1978).

The emergence of the referential triangle marks the emergence of the first criterion for symbol usage, namely reference in an intersubjective field. From this point until about 14 months of age, infants increasingly mediate the manipulation of the field of joint attention by manipulating objects in give-and-take routines, and early in the second year of life they begin to demonstrate active mastery of the conventional usage of objects in play situations, their usage of such objects being dominated by objects' canonical functions until well into the third year of life (Sinha and Rodríguez 2008). It seems to be a well-founded conclusion that, by early in the second year of life, the basic foundations of symbolization in intersubjectivity and in an understanding of conventionality have been laid. The elaboration of symbolization into grammar involves the mastery of natural language subsystems that functionally permit flexible construal (Sinha 2004; Tomasello 2003a).

3.4.2 *Infancy, evolution, and culture*

There is a common developmental logic to the phylogenetic and ontogenetic development of symbolization. The logic is one of process, from signals to the emergence and elaboration of symbols. The logic involves the following sub-processes, which significantly temporally overlap but which emerge in the order of mention below:

(1) Intentionality and intersubjectivity.
(2) Conventionalizaton based in intersubjectivity.
(3) Structural elaboration yielding flexible construal.

This shared developmental logic does not, however, imply that 'ontogenesis recapitulates phylogenesis'. Instead, I suggest that ontogenesis—and in particular the biocultural niche of human infancy—played a crucial role in the evolutionary development of the human symbolic capacity and, therefore, of the biocultural niche of language within which infancy itself is embedded. Human infants, as has often been pointed out, are extraordinarily well adapted to the demands of enculturation and the acquisition of symbolic communication. This is because, once established, the emergent social ontology of intersubjectivity and conventionalization set up new parameters for the selection of context-sensitive and socially situated learning processes. This phenogenotypic account differs significantly from hypotheses focusing on the evolutionary selection of innate, content-dedicated cognitive mechanisms, including a putative innate Universal Grammar or 'language instinct'.

3.5 Conclusion

The account outlined above revolves around the proposition that the epigenetic stabilization of the phenogenotypic semiosphere introduced the evolutionary discontinuity characterizing human culture and human cognition. Signs are both transformative cognitive tools and constitutive of specifically human cultural ecologies. The semiotic capacity is hypothesized to have triggered transformative effects across all or most cognitive domains, thereby potentiating human symbolic cultures, which constitute the biocultural complexes in which human cultural innovation and transmission occur. The semiotic capacity is the explanatory link binding what is unique to human cognition with what is unique to human culture. In conclusion, I offer the following reflections on the role of the human semiotic capacity in integrating development, evolution, language, and cognition.

(1) Understanding the transformative role of signs presupposes understanding the evolutionary logic of the sign itself, and in particular the distinction between signals (ubiquitous in non-human communication systems) and symbols, icons, and other signs possessing referential value in an intersubjective field, the capacity to use which is strictly limited in non-human species. Pavlov's insight that human cognition was distinguished by a 'second signal system' can only be further developed by recognizing that the human symbolic capacity is an evolutionary and developmental acquisition which builds upon, but is fundamentally different from, the capacity to exploit signalling.

(2) The proposition, derived by extension from Laland et al. (2000), that signs and sign systems are artefacts/niches can be complemented by the proposition that *all* human artefacts (that is, material as well as symbolic cultural products) are situated, and can be re-situated, in semiotic fields, and are thus to be considered as having semiotic value (Sinha 1988, 2005; Sinha and Rodríguez 2008). A particular case is that of the material anchoring of cognitive processes dependent upon symbolic notations in instrumental artefacts (Hutchins 2005). Frequently, the human body itself serves as such a material anchor (Enfield 2005); to this extent, the body itself can be viewed as an artefact with semiotic value, that is, as *embodying* semiotically mediated cognition (as well as aesthetic value).

(3) It is increasingly recognized, in theories of distributed cognition, that human cognitive processes extend 'beyond the skin', involving intersubjectively shared mental states and cultural-cognitive technologies. This presents a

conceptual problem not only for psychology, with its traditionally individualist assumptions, but also for biology, which assumes by default that the organism as a behavioural and morphological individual is identical to the organism as bearer of genetic material. It is this general problem that the notion of 'phenogenotype' (Laland et al. 2000) is designed to address and resolve.

(4) However, a further step, specific to human evolution and development, can and should be taken. The human organism, by virtue of the semiotic status of the body and the normative shaping of its activities in a cultural field, has a dual ontology, both culturally constituted as a constituent of the semiosphere and, at a purely biological level, a genetic individual. The body is part of the system which extends beyond the body, as well as being the originating *sine qua non* of that system. While non-human organisms are simplex, the human organism is duplex, and its phenogenotypic coupling with constructed niches involves a developmental process of auto-construction. Language has a dual ontology, as part of biological human species-being—what it means to be human—and as a foundational social institution in the Durkheimian sense (Durkheim 1895).

(5) This dual ontology of the human body (individual-biological and socio-cultural) is, in modern humans, incorporated in the genotype, and expressed, in the very early stages of post-natal epigenetic development, in the responsiveness of the human infant to the communicative actions of caretakers in the primary intersubjective semiotic circuit (Trevarthen 1998). More generally, ontogenesis, and the niches of infancy and childhood, played a crucial role in the evolutionary development of the human semiotic capacity. Human infants and young children, as has often been pointed out, are extraordinarily well adapted to the demands of enculturation and the acquisition of symbolic communication (Tomasello 1999). Once established, the emergent social ontology of intersubjectivity and normativity set up new parameters for the selection of context-sensitive and socially situated learning processes. The species-specific cognitive capacities of young humans are often conceptualized in terms of mind reading or 'theory of mind'. Such an internalist-mentalist perspective can be criticized for neglecting the epigenetically constitutive role of the semiosphere, and of material culture, in the development of this capacity (Sinha 2009b). Internalist theories also pay insufficient attention to the emergent social-ontological property of *normativity* (Itkonen 1983), which characterizes human artefacts and institutions at both micro and macro levels.

(6) The characterization of language as a biocultural niche emphasizes the biological continuity of the human semiosphere with the constructed niches that we find in many other species. Language is also, however, following the logic of dual ontology, a normative social institution (Sinha 2009a), and as such

emergently discontinuous with non-human constructive niches. Although frequentist strategies may play a role in the learning of specific norms, the norms themselves, being in principle negotiable, are irreducible to frequency of occurrence. The evolutionary emergence of normativity was fundamental in the construction of the human semiosphere, which encompasses ethical and aesthetic, as well as cognitive, values. Norms and conventions, governing the use of both symbolic and material artefactual resources, were fundamental to the social origins of language.

(7) The account of the social origins of language that I have offered in this chapter is consistent with that of the previous chapter by Dor and Jablonka, drawing on many of the same theoretical and empirical sources. I completely concur with their assertion that '[w]e evolved *for* language', as well as with the slogan coined by Arbib (2012: ix) that '[o]nly the human brain is *language ready*'. Niche construction theory, in which language is viewed as a biocultural artefact/niche, is the theoretical articulation of the dialectical and dynamic unity of these two apparently opposing propositions. I have emphasized process dynamics in this chapter, leaving unanswered the key question: When, then, did language emerge in the course of human evolution? There is no compelling reason, however, to suppose that evolutionarily modern languages co-emerged with the speciation event giving birth to a biologically modern human population. I offer the following tentative and revisable timetable. Multi-modal protolanguage (holophrastic speech + gesture + mime) very likely has a time depth of 1–2 mya. It was almost certainly possessed by *H. erectus*, given that species' dispersal range. Early language (Heine and Kuteva 2007), involving lexically based constructions and differentiated participant roles, can be hypothesized to have emerged as the first original biocultural semiotic artefact of the language-ready brain 200–100 kya. I concur with Arbib (2012) that evolutionarily modern languages (grammaticalized, morphosyntactically more complex, and with elaborated functional differentiation) probably date from 100 kya to 60 kya. Their emergence can be hypothesized to be associated with social and kinship differentiation (clan/moiety structure) and with the emergence of mythic and collective narratives, expressed also in other semiotic media, including rock art, song, and dance.

4

Signal evolution and the social brain

CAMILLA POWER

Signal evolution theory deals with the emergence, function, and design of animal signals. Maynard Smith and Harper (2003: 3) define a 'signal' as 'an act or structure which alters the behaviour of other organisms, which evolved because of that effect, and which is effective because the receiver's response has also evolved'. This means that it must, on average, pay the receiver to behave in a way favourable to the signaller; for this to work, the signal must carry information of interest to the receiver. That information must be accurate often enough for selection to act on the receiver's response.

Signal evolution theory is the main body of theory applied to animal communication. So it is axiomatic that any scientific study of the evolution of language adopts this theoretical approach as starting point. To argue that the evolution of language is a special case to which signalling theory does not apply, we have to explain why not, within that theory's terms.

Signal evolution theory focuses on social interaction and behaviour in the world, and is quintessentially political in its approach. Central debates have concerned honesty and reliability of signals (Zahavi and Zahavi 1997), manipulation and mind-reading (Krebs and Dawkins 1984), and effects of shared versus conflicting interest in outcomes (Maynard Smith and Harper 2003). Among primates generally, tactical use of deception is predicted by neocortex volume (Byrne and Corp 2004), a finding consistent with the Machiavellian intelligence hypothesis—the idea that intelligence evolves under pressure to deal with social challenges. Humans—the only species known to have evolved language—are clearly Machiavellian in terms of political alliance formation and ability for deception. Therefore, these questions must be central to language origins.

Zahavi's Handicap principle (1975) states that all animal signals evolve as intrinsically reliable demonstrations of the quality of the signaller, since they impose a cost rendering them either 'hard' or 'impossible' to fake (sometimes distinguished as handicaps and indices). There have been numerous attempts to refute this hard-line position. Where signaller and receiver share common interest in the same rank order of possible outcomes, minimal-cost signals—that is, signals whose reliability does not depend on high costs, which can be made by any member of the population—may evolve (Maynard Smith and Harper 2003: 37). Zahavi responds that no two individuals ever share interests completely, and in reality, signal costs will always tend to be driven upward to secure reliability. We can reconcile these positions by proposing that the cost threshold for ensuring reliability will vary according to degree of shared or conflicting interest between individuals. This is similar to the manipulation model of Krebs and Dawkins (1984) where signal costs vary according to whether signallers are likely to encounter 'sales resistance', owing to conflicting interests, or whether there is strongly shared interest between signaller and receiver, enabling the evolution of 'conspiratorial whispering'.

Even where signaller and receiver rank outcomes in a different order, there are alternative models for the evolution of minimal-cost signals. Where the pair share overriding common interest in coordinating activity but there is low-level immediate conflict over the next move—the so-called Battle of the Sexes game (Farrell and Rabin 1996)—low-cost signals could stabilize. A further example can occur where the pair interact repeatedly, though there may be no strong interest in coordination. This has been effectively modelled as a Prisoner's Dilemma game by Silk et al. (2000) who also provide empirical examples of high-rank macaque females using low-cost grunts to honestly signal benign intent to low-rank mothers when approaching to handle infants. However, these soft calls potentially are indices of mood, attitude, and temper—a tensed animal with aggressive intentions may not be able to produce the quiet signal that would reassure the mother. In that case, this would not be an example of a minimal-cost signal.

Zahavi's reponse to arguments about cooperation (or low-cost signals) evolving through mechanisms of reciprocity is to point to the cost of policing defection (Zahavi and Zahavi 1997: 132–3). This does appear to constrain the evolution of real examples of reciprocal altruism in non-humans. The other context for minimal-cost signals being evolutionarily stable proposed by Maynard Smith and Harper is where dishonest signals are punished. Again, the problem with this is the difficulty of evolving punishment if it is costly (2003: 37) and there are few, if any, convincing non-human examples (see Maynard Smith and Harper 2003: 99–100).

Overall, Zahavi's position that animal signals are handicaps—investments which intrinsically demonstrate quality—appears valid. This is what makes language such a theoretical anomaly. Knight (1998, 1999) compared the features of speech with ritual in terms of conspiratorial whispering versus sales advertising (compare Krebs and Dawkins 1984). Across human cultures, ritual displays the hallmarks of costly signals: indexical, analogue, repetitive, energetic, multimedia, and emotional in effect. Speech, by contrast, is conventional, digital, low-cost, and dispassionate. Whereas, in ritual, the receiver's focus will be on performance, in speech, the focus shifts to underlying intention: what is the speaker meaning to say?

The cost of a signal can be divided into a component of 'efficacy' cost (Guilford and Dawkins 1991)—what is needed to ensure the information can be perceived—and 'strategic' cost—the extra handicap which ensures honesty (Grafen 1990a, 1990b, after Zahavi 1975). In the case of speech, extraordinarily, all the costs appear to fall into the efficacy component; the efforts of both speaker and listener are channelled into distinguishing between contrastive phonemes, combined and recombined on a second digital level where semantic meaning emerges. Honesty is not assessed by extra costs; in fact, uniquely in the case of language, honesty has entered a negative space. The digitally processed, sound sequences of language are by Zahavian stand-ards 'fakes'. All human conceptual thought is metaphorical (Lakoff and Johnson 1980), a metaphor being literally false. As metaphors become increasingly familiar through repeated use, they tend to be abbreviated and conventionalized. Pressures to economize on time and energy lead eventually to the formation of lexical items, grammatical markers, and constructions (Deutscher 2005; Heine et al. 1991). Humans have evolved a disposition to attend to these shorthand residues of what were originally imaginative fictions, probing beneath them for truth on another level. Wild-living animals have not evolved to expend time or energy on patent fakes.

Lachmann et al. (2001) model the evolution of cost-free signal systems in conflict-ridden animal groups. They contrast the paradigmatic example of reliable and costly signalling—the peacock—with sparrows. Various 'bibs' and patches of plumage on the throat or forehead may be reliable indicators of a bird's fighting ability. A sparrow which sports an artificially large bib is liable to be attacked by birds with naturally larger badges. This case is claimed as an example of conventional signalling in that signal costs may be low, with costs being incurred only when a 'wrong' signal is punished (but see Maynard Smith and Harper 2003: 100, for alternative interpret-ations). Here, the signalling sparrow has low efficacy costs; strategic costs only arise if a receiver responds by punishing a wrong signal. Lachmann and colleagues propose cost-free human language would evolve through such mechanisms, with socially imposed sanctions against 'liars'. A non-human primate case is found among rhesus macaques: an animal which omits a food call and is subsequently discovered feeding may be attacked (Hauser and Marler 1993). Here, punishment is for failure to call rather than for giving a wrong or misleading call. In general, flexibility of primate vocal communication appears profoundly constrained (Zuberbühler 2012: 72, 75), an observation consistent with selection for intrinsic reliability.

Accounting for this constraint on primate vocal communication, Knight (1998) describes Machiavellian apes as 'too clever for words'. The difficulty for Lachmann and colleagues is to explain how, in the human case, vocal communication was emancipated from such constraints. How and why could strategic costs, incurred fully by the producer in ancestral ape vocalization, be offloaded completely onto the receiver who now has the onus of verifying zero-cost signals? No non-human primate takes on these costs: verification is inbuilt in the emotional affect of the signal combined with context. Suppose for a moment that hominin listeners did take on such costs in monitoring. Is that in fact the way language works? Do people listen to the sound sequences of speech checking veracity phoneme by phoneme or even word by word? Emphatically not. While it is true that we judge others' reliability in potential interactions, and we may listen to the judgements of those we trust about third parties, when it comes to conversational speech, we tend to give one another the benefit of the doubt—seeking to reconstruct honest communicative intentions behind streams of patent fakes (Knight 2008a). We are not systematically monitoring for lies or liars. Indeed, language is in a sense built from components which are 'lies'—figures of speech whose 'truth' emerges only on a higher combinatorial level. We operate on Gricean principles, probing for relevance and communicative intent (Grice 1975; Sperber and Wilson 1986). Rather than punishing wrong information, humans reward originality when they perceive it as relevant (Dessalles 1998).

4.1 Navigating a virtual world

Language, then, reverses the usual logic of signal evolution in reversing the relative costs of efficacy compared with strategic components; and in removing the focus from analogue performance to the level of pure intention. Where all non-human signals evolve to alter behaviour in the real world, and are affected by factors of Darwinian behavioural competition for food and mates, language is designed instead to alter what is inside a listener's mind, operating in that sense in a virtual world. Steklis and Harnad (1976: 450) proposed an 'allegory of the rooms' to illustrate 'the kind of cognitive capacity which we feel is unique to language'. In their thought experiment, two organisms are out of sight from one another in two rooms with identical contents, identically located, consisting of more or less familiar objects. A third party enters one of the rooms and displaces one of the objects. The task of the observing organism is to signal to his counterpart in the other room what has been done, so that the counterpart can do the same. This cannot be done iconically, via imitation, but only by tapping out on the wall what was moved with reference to some conventionally shared, coordinate system. Such an imagined and constructed space can only be navigated with shared attention by speaker and listener digitally.

Because that space is removed from the immediate behavioural competition for sex and resources of the material world, trust in signals can be infinite (Knight 2008a). Strategic costs tend to zero, leaving only efficacy costs. In addressing how linguistic signals could evolve in such a novel direction, we need to ask why and how human ancestors engaged in mutual mindreading concerning their virtual worlds—those closed-off rooms, imperceptible to the senses.

4.2 Contexts for mindreading: counter-dominance

Chimpanzees and bonobos, our closest relatives, are extremely intelligent, but it is debated to what extent they have theory of mind—the ability to infer mental states in others from direction of gaze, facial expression, etc. In humans, this is highly developed. The differences may lie in contrasting levels of cooperation. Suppose two individuals try to reconstruct each other's thoughts. Either they compete or they cooperate. If competing, each tries to block the other's mindreading efforts while promoting its own. Only where both cooperate will Darwinian selection favour what psychologists term intersubjectivity—the mutual interpenetration of minds.

Chimps appear able to read intentions and understand what other chimps see in certain competitive contexts (Call et al. 2004; Tomasello et al. 2003). But they seem to fail to understand communicative or cooperative intentions, and so do not try to share attention with conspecifics by pointing, showing, or offering intentional communicative signals (Call and Tomasello 2005; but see Crockford et al. 2012). The Cooperative Eye hypothesis posits that humans evolved their unique eye morphology of almond shape with white sclera background (Kobayashi and Kohshima 2001) to enable following of eye direction as the basic mechanism supporting shared attention and cooperative mutualistic social interaction (Tomasello et al. 2007). Where chimpanzees are concerned, gaze following via head direction appears a distinctly one-way activity.

Whiten's idea of 'deep social mind' (1999) where he argued a necessary coevolution of mutual mindreading with cultural transmission and egalitarianism anticipated this political view of the emergence of specifically human cognition. The nine-month ontogenetic 'revolution' enabling the human infant to participate in intersubjectivity and shared intention (Tomasello and Rakoczy 2003) must be based in a phylogenetic revolution of certain species of *Homo* where Machiavellian strategies of counter-dominance (Erdal and Whiten 1994, 1996) and reverse dominance (Boehm 1999) became more successful than primate dominance. Whiten and Erdal (2012) emphasize the socio-cognitive complex of cooperation, egalitarianism, and mindreading alongside language and cultural transmission in the evolution of humans as successful hunter-gatherers. On the basis of similar life history variables (Robson and Wood 2008)—length of lifespan, inter-birth intervals, onset of childhood, and late maturation—candidate species for sharing in this overthrow of primate dominance leading to cooperative cultural cognition are *H. neanderthalensis* and possibly *H. heidelbergensis*, ancestor of ourselves and the Neanderthals from half a million years ago (Opie and Power 2008; Stringer 2012). Evolutionary shifts in life history supported by grandmothering (Hawkes et al. 1998) and other cooperative breeding strategies (Hrdy 2009) may have got underway with *H. erectus*—that is, individuals other than the mother became willing and able to take charge of her infant, and *she trusted them to do so*. It is tempting to speculate on the eye morphology of *H. erectus* beginning to develop in modern human directions. Zuberbühler (2012) links the evolution of vocal flexibility to the needs of infants competing for attention in a cooperative breeding system.

For such revolutionary strategies to prevail in a Darwinian world, individuals attempting to maintain physical dominance and monopoly over resources or mates would lose out in terms of eventual reproductive success compared with those more willing to collaborate in shared goals. Social prestige and ultimately sexual rewards would go to those willing to settle for rough equality, and contribute resources or childcare cooperatively. Hrdy's (2009) outline of our evolutionary heritage of cooperative breeding in genus *Homo* as the matrix for shared intentionality can be linked to Whiten's deep social mind. Whiten (1999: 180) sketches a 'U-shape' curve (derived from Knauft 1991), bottoming out with a lengthy egalitarian phase of human hunter-gatherer evolution, before a sharp switch back into hierarchical societies with the advent of farming and pastoralism over recent historic time.

The Machiavellian Intelligence or Social Brain hypothesis argues that the neocortex expanded as hominin groups and social networks became larger and more complex. Across monkeys and apes, neocortex volume, measured as size of neocortex relative to total brain size, is shown to relate to specifically female group size, and not to male group size, suggesting that female social demands have driven the evolution of intelligence (Lindenfors 2005). Given cooperative breeding strategies, it is reasonable to argue that *Homo* males were selected to be more like females in their abilities to track social interactions. Coevolving with increased social complexity—and increased costs for mothers—was the capacity for tactical deception (Byrne and Corp 2004)—and hence for manipulation of 'fictions'; while dominant individuals were less and less able to maintain reproductive dominance against Machiavellian allies (Pawlowski et al. 1998). Increased non-visual neocortex size relative to the rest of the brain also correlates with extension of the juvenile period of life history, implicated in play and social learning (Joffe 1997).

4.3 Egalitarianism, encephalization, and cultural intelligence selection: female costs, female-driven solutions

While we do not know the exact timescale of Knauft's hierarchy curve, it can be redrawn schematically as a mirror of the curve of brain volume (Figure 4.1).

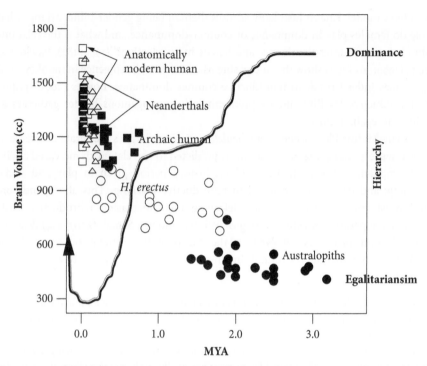

FIGURE 4.1 A hypothesized trajectory of change in 'dominance' relations in human evolution reflecting change in brain size. (Chart adapted from Dunbar 2010 and Whiten 1999, after Knauft 1991)

A strong hypothesis is that as brains maximize in size, towards the end of the Middle Pleistocene in early *Homo sapiens*, societies become most egalitarian. An initial reduction of primate-style dominance hierarchies can be associated with cooperative breeding in *H. erectus*, along with the first major increase in brain and body size *c.* 2 million years ago. Further reduction of dominance hierarchy would associate with renewed increase of brain size in *H. heidelbergensis*. If encephalization reflects Machiavellian intelligence escalation producing counter-dominance, it must also mobilize female strategies for alleviating reproductive stress. Erdal and Whiten focus largely on economic equality in food-sharing, assuming that reduction of risk in accessing unpredictable resources is the main adaptive cause (1996: 147). But from an evolutionary perspective, the most important type of levelling is equality in reproductive fitness. Without concomitant reduction of reproductive variance, counter-dominance could not be a stable strategy. In his comment on Erdal and

Whiten's model, Knauft justifiably accuses them of being gender-blind, asking 'what role do females play in dominance or counter-dominance, and what is the relationship between counter-dominance and female mate selection?' (1994: 182). Pawlowski et al. (1998: 361 fig. 1) show that increasing Machiavellian intelligence in monkeys and apes does indeed result in reproductive counter-dominance. Bowles (2006) points to reproductive levelling among predominantly monogamous hunter-gatherers as critical to egalitarianism.

As late Middle Pleistocene *Homo heidelbergensis* undergoes accelerated increase in brain size, especially after 300 kya, this is predicted to correlate with increased ability to manipulate fictions; an increased life-history period given to play and social learning; and egalitarianism based in reproductive levelling. This all depends on, and must coevolve with, females defraying their increasing reproductive costs through cooperative breeding strategies. Whiten and van Schaik (2007: 614) describe the selection processes involved in the Machiavellian Intelligence Hypothesis, and the complementary Cultural Intelligence Hypothesis and behavioural drive hypotheses:

The central idea in all of these proposals is that whatever the cause of an initial rise in social intelligence, the fact that this is manifested in social interactions means that an increase in intelligence in any one individual selects for increases in others, and so on in spiralling, positive-feedback fashion. As in the case of sexual selection, this is potentially a runaway process. Of course some additional factor must eventually apply a brake, where the costs (for example, of manufacturing and maintaining expensive brain tissue) outweigh benefits in the current ecological niche.

Such a feedback process characterizes the period of accelerated encephalization associated with selection for social and cultural intelligence in *Homo heidelbergensis*. During that time (approximately 700–200 kya), mothers break through a 'grey ceiling' of constraints on *Homo* brain size. The problems which mothers particularly had to solve can be summarized as follows: a) because of pressure on time budgets, females need an efficient mechanism, such as gossip, for maintaining alliances; b) with larger group sizes, females suffer more risk of freeriding by philandering males who have more opportunities for mate desertion; c) females must negotiate with other female coalition partners, especially cycling females who are potential rivals for male investment.

In Chapter 15 (this volume), I apply signal evolution theory to outline the evolution of ritual as a process of sexual selection, with female ritual coalitions mobilizing the economic effort of males. This Machiavellian counter-dominance strategy directly undermines reproductive variance in males, favouring investor males against would-be dominant philanderers. In line with the ritual/speech coevolution model (Knight 1998; Power 1998, 2000), high-cost ritual performance creates coalitions bonded by trust within which low-cost communicative signals can stabilize—for instance, gossip about reputation (Dunbar 1996b). Ritual may institutionalize punishment for defectors through sanctions and taboo. According to Durkheim (1964) and Rappaport (1999), ritual alone can establish such collective representation and contractual understanding. Ritual is the generator of that shared, virtual world which is the subject of all our conversations.

5

How can a social theory of language evolution be grounded in evidence?

SVERKER JOHANSSON

A social origin of language makes eminent intuitive sense, not least because human communication today is so dominated by cooperative social interactions. But the history of science is littered with theories that made eminent sense but turned out to be empirically wrong. The history of the science of language evolution is furthermore littered with theories that made intuitive sense to their proponents, but simply did not connect with any evidence, rendering them into untestable, uninteresting just-so stories (see Knight, Chapter 17). Thus, if we are to study the social origins of language, and develop a new overall perspective on the evolution of language that is actually testable and is not mere words, we need to ground such a perspective firmly in empirical evidence. In this chapter, I will consider what kinds of evidence may be available for this grounding.

Testability also requires that theories are constructed so that they actually yield predictions that can be confronted with the evidence. Too many candidate theories are either too vague, or make predictions that fall outside the available evidence. In contrast, a good example in this regard is set by the Female Cosmetic Coalitions Model (Power 2009: 273–4; Power, Chapter 15; Watts, Chapter 16), which does provide specific testable predictions.

We also need to consider how direct the inference from the evidence we invoke is. Pretty much all the evidence available concerning social origins of language is indirect, and requires a chain of inferences, first to sociality, and then from the aspect of sociality inferred to language evolution. What bridging theories (Botha 2000, 2008) do we need to invoke in making these inferences?

Evidence pertinent to the social origins of language may come from four main areas:

- Animal communication and sociality
- Language and language use today

- Neurobiology of the human language capacity and 'social capacity' today
- Fossil and archaeological evidence

I will review the first three areas very briefly, just going through what types of relevant evidence are available without going into any detail, and how they may be fruitfully applied to the study of the social origins of language. I will go somewhat deeper into the fossil and archaeological evidence, but doing so with the perspective of a devil's advocate, deliberately looking for places where reasonable doubt may exist concerning the sociality of our fossil relatives.

5.1 Animal communication and sociality

The comparative study of communication and sociality in non-human animals (Hauser 1997; McGregor 2005; Oller and Griebel 2008) provides invaluable background data for inquiry into language origins. From data on other primates (e.g. Clay and Zuberbühler, Chapter 11; Cheney and Seyfarth 2010; Pika et al. 2005a; Pika, Chapter 10), reasonable inferences can be made about communication and sociality in the last common ancestor of us and other apes, as a starting point for both social evolution and language evolution along the human lineage. This provides evidence bearing on what is to be explained in language origins—which features in human language and sociality are actually uniquely human, and which are a shared ape heritage. Recent reviews of pertinent evidence can be found e.g. in the various chapters in Kappeler and Silk (2009) and in Tallerman and Gibson (2012).

Wider comparative samples give insights into the full spectrum of social systems and communication systems among extant animals. Especially valuable here are data points from species which share features with us that we do not share with chimps, indicating parallel evolution from which inferences, for example about selection pressures, can be made. Vocal learning and imitation is one interesting area here, which a few groups of mammals and birds (but *not* non-human primates; Hauser 2011a) share with humans. Especially in birds, extensive studies have been made of the neurological and genetic bases of vocal learning (Jarvis 2007). It is intriguing to note that the homolog of the *FOXP2* gene implicated in human language (see Section 5.3) is involved also in the genetic basis of vocal learning in birds (Haesler et al. 2004).

Valuable are also data sets covering several closely related species with a firm phylogeny, so that we can trace the order and context of appearance of social and communicative features.

The biological evolution of any kind of animal communication requires both that sending increases the fitness of the sender, and that receiving increases the fitness of the receiver (Krebs and Dawkins 1984); this is the basis for signal evolution theory (see Power, Chapter 4). As noted, for example, by Knight (Chapter 17), the evolution of human language is puzzling in this respect, as it appears to deviate strongly from the costly signalling that signal evolution theory predicts in most circumstances, and which is commonly observed in animal communication. Any language evolution theory needs to take this issue seriously.

Animal data can also be used to constrain and falsify scenarios for language origins that e.g. postulate starting points inconsistent with the inferred common ancestor, or that violate the 'chimp test' (factors invoked to explain language origins should *not* be operative in chimps).

5.2 Language, language use, and sociality today

Human language today is predominantly used for social purposes in social contexts, which would appear to be *prima facie* evidence in favour of social origins of language (e.g. Givón 2009). But this conclusion is not entirely self-evident—language is also used non-socially, as a medium for thought inside our heads, and it remains a defensible (or at least defended) hypothesis that this may have been what language originally evolved for (Chomsky 2002; Newmeyer 2003; Berwick 2010; Piattelli-Palmarini 2010; Hauser 2011b). Even if language, as seems most plausible, did evolve for external communicative purposes, a very wide diversity of hypotheses has been proposed for the original purpose of language, as reviewed in Johansson (2005), and far from all of them have social evolution at the centre of the story.

One possible form of evidence would be to look for which quirks and design features of language and sociality are expected under different hypotheses, and which ones are actually present in modern language (see Dessalles, Chapter 20):

- What features does social theory X, Y, Z of language origins predict?
- What features does non-social theory A, B, C of language origins predict?
- What features do modern language and sociality actually have?

This exercise would be easier if linguists actually agreed on the features of language (Zuidema 2005; Számadó et al. 2009), and sociologists on the features of sociality. Meanwhile, it is imprudent to base language-origins scenarios on features that are strongly dependent on specific theoretical assumptions.

The focus in language evolution studies has often been on the origins of the core structures of language, notably syntax and the lexicon, with less input from those branches of linguistics that study language in its social context. Rectifying this imbalance, with more attention paid to evidence, for example from sociolinguistics and pragmatics (see Lamm, Chapter 19; Enfield, Chapter 23), would benefit the study of the social origins of language.

It should also be kept in mind that what actually evolves are not the adult features; what evolves are the ontogenetic processes that lead to the adult features

(West-Eberhard 2003). In other words, evidence from language acquisition and socialization and how they interact is likely vital (see Wyman, Chapter 13).

It has been argued, for example by Bickerton (2009), that 'restricted linguistic systems' today (pidgins, child language, early L2, Basic Variety, etc.) may be informative about language origins (see Botha and de Swart 2009). This possibility is worth looking into, but mainly as 'proof of principle' for the existence and functionality of languages different from normal adult modern human language, not as any kind of direct evidence of features of protolanguage.

Similarly, it has been argued that present-day hunter-gatherer societies may be informative about early human sociality (e.g. Knight 1991; Hrdy 2009). This argument definitely has some merit for inferences about early *Homo sapiens*, but not necessarily for pre-*sapiens* hominins.

5.3 Neurobiology and genetics of the human language capacity and 'social capacity' today

The human language capacity can be roughly defined as all the biological stuff in our bodies and brains that we use for linguistic purposes, and that enables us as language users. One could similarly define a 'social capacity', which may be useful in the present context. Pertinent evidence here would likely come mainly from the relation between components of the social capacity and the language capacity, especially from dissociability or lack of it. Through studies of e.g. lesions, and in recent years also various brain-imaging methods, we have a substantial, if unstructured, body of data concerning the language capacity in the human brain (e.g. Ben Shalom and Poeppel 2008; Fedor et al. 2009).

Studies of the social capacity lag far behind, however (Whitehead 2008). Tricomi et al. (2010), with their study of neural mechanisms associated with inequality aversion, is one of the rare exceptions. Inequality aversion in humans is fairly well studied at the behavioural level, and has been observed also in non-human primates, but with an interesting difference: humans are averse to inequity also when it benefits themselves, but this has not been found in non-humans (Lakshminarayanan and Santos 2010). Further studies in this direction may be highly informative of the roots of human sociality. Our growing understanding of the biological basis of autism spectrum disorders (State and Šestan 2012) may also provide clues; while autism is a highly complex phenomenon, it is clear that social capacity problems play a central role.

As the genetic and developmental basis for the two capacities is gradually unravelled, this may also provide clues to the origins of the two capacities. As with neurobiology, more progress has been made with the genetics of language (reviewed in Stromswold 2010) than with the genetics of sociality, though studies of the genetics of autism may be pertinent for the latter. The gene *FOXP2* is a case in point. Hailed by the media, though not by most biologists or linguists, as a 'language gene', *FOXP2* is a gene regulating synaptic plasticity that is involved in vocalization circuits in a wide variety of species (Lieberman 2009). Attempts have been made to estimate the time of origin of the human-specific mutations in *FOXP2* (Enard et al. 2002), but such estimates are fraught with pitfalls (Diller and Cann 2009, 2012). More interesting is that Neanderthals apparently had the derived human form of *FOXP2* (Krause et al. 2007; compare Dediu and Levinson, Chapter 14; Dediu and Levinson 2013).

5.4 Fossil and archaeological evidence

In order to determine, or at least constrain, the time frame and palaeoanthropological context of the social origins of language, fossil and archaeological evidence are essential. Concerning language, the time constraints that can be inferred from the available evidence are reviewed in Johansson (2011) and Dediu and Levinson (Chapter 14); see Watts (Chapter 16) for an alternative perspective. In brief, there is no convincing upper limit to the time of language origins, but the lower limit is rather more constraining. Language in some form (not necessarily full modern human language) is unlikely to be younger than the last common ancestor of *Homo sapiens* and Neanderthals, more than half a million years ago, and language origins more recently than the last common ancestor of all living humans can be firmly excluded. The latter limit excludes all theories connecting language origins with the supposed cognitive revolution marking the beginning of the Upper Palaeolithic in Europe (Johansson 2011).

But for investigating the social origins of language, a time frame is not enough. We also want data on the evolution of human social systems concurrent with language emergence. As all African apes are social, it is of course highly likely that our last common ancestor was a social creature as well. But the various ape social systems are different both from each other and from human sociality, which limits the inferences that can be made about ancestral sociality using the comparative method. And even if the ancestral social system were known in detail, the path and timing of social evolution along the human lineage would still have to be inferred from fossil and archaeological evidence. It cannot be taken for granted that human social evolution was a linear progression towards more and more human-like sociality.

Inferring sociality from fossil evidence is, however, quite difficult. Just like language, social relations do not fossilize. Even for a species with a very rich fossil and archaeological record, like Neanderthals, the evidence of sociality at all, while present, is quite limited (Davies and Underdown 2006), though genetic evidence from fossil DNA may provide clues. Solid conclusions about detailed social patterns in prehistory require data sets like that of Lalueza-Fox et al. (2011) for Neanderthals, or

Haak et al. (2008) for *Homo sapiens*, which are simply not available for earlier hominins, before the Middle Palaeolithic.

Or consider a case a bit further removed from us: lions and tigers. Lions are social animals who live in prides, whereas tigers are solitary, rarely interacting with each other. Yet their skeletons look very much the same, and are indistinguishable to non-experts. If we only knew tigers and lions from fossils, how could we know that one is social and the other is not? Absent jackpot fossils like an entire pride killed and fossilized together (e.g. by a flash flood), or fossil footprints showing the coordinated movements of a group, the short answer is that we couldn't. And even the jackpot fossils could only be positive evidence of the presence of sociality—its absence would be essentially impossible to infer from fossils.

There are statistical patterns, supported by reasoning from behavioural ecology, that connect sociality with observable anatomy, notably brain size (Dunbar 1998; Pérez-Barberia et al. 2007). But these are statistical patterns only, with a substantial spread, not reliable for inferring sociality in individual cases—in the case of lions vs. tigers, for example, the more social lions have *smaller* brains relative to body size than tigers, bucking the statistical trend (Yamaguchi et al. 2009)—and there are also numerous methodological pitfalls even for living species (Healy and Rowe 2007). Among our closer relatives, it can be noted that there is no significant difference in relative brain size between *Pan* (chimpanzees) and *Pongo* (orang-utans), despite major differences in sociality. Making inferences directly from endocranial volume to sociality in individual fossil species is not warranted.

Some aspects of mating systems can sometimes be inferred from fossils showing sexual dimorphism (Plavcan 2001). But there are several caveats even here—for one thing, it is not trivial to tell if a collection of fossils comes from a single dimorphic species, or from two separate species. Circularity also needs to be avoided—if the fossils are assigned to sex purely on the basis of, for example, canine size, then it is perilous to use the thus divided sample as evidence of canine size dimorphism. Furthermore, inferences from dimorphism to mating system to social system in general can be ambiguous—the same degree of dimorphism may be found in living species with very different social systems. Notably, the degree of dimorphism is quite similar in modern humans and chimpanzees, despite radically different mating systems. During the course of human evolution, there is some evidence for a larger size dimorphism among australopithecines (Harmon 2006; Gordon et al. 2008; but see also Reno et al. 2003) but not within the genus *Homo* (Robson and Wood 2008; but see also Spoor et al. 2007). The canine dimorphism that is ubiquitous among other primates pretty much disappeared early in our history (Suwa et al. 2009), which is difficult to interpret and remains a datum that any theory of our social evolution should be compatible with.

Life history evolution is another area that may provide inferences about past sociality. Notably, the modern human pattern, with offspring that are both highly encephalized and highly dependent for much longer than typical interbirth intervals, entails such a heavy childcare burden that extensive allocare is effectively obligatory. This cooperative breeding requires a social system with a much higher degree of cooperation and trust than is found among other great apes, and may be a key human feature influencing our evolution (Hrdy 2009; van Schaik and Burkart 2010). Data are lacking concerning when interbirth timing was decreased in the human lineage. We do have some data on developmental rates that may be relevant (reviewed by Zollikofer and Ponce de Léon 2010), but there is no consensus on their interpretation, especially for *Homo ergaster/erectus*, with for example Coqueugniot et al. (2004) and Leigh (2006) reaching opposite conclusions. Robson and Wood (2008) conclude in their review that a modern life history is present from *Homo heidelbergensis* onwards, but not in *erectus*.

Our major increases in relative brain size, however, are well documented (see Whitehead, Chapter 12; Watts, Chapter 16; Power, Chapter 4). The relative brain size increase itself may be sufficient to infer the necessity of allocare, with concomitant implications for sociality, either beginning already at the transition ending with *Homo erectus* (Aiello and Key 2002), or at the latest in connection with the additional relative brain size increase taking place during the Middle Pleistocene.

There are also a few fossils of hominins who apparently lived for a considerable span of time after becoming crippled in different ways (Trinkaus and Shipman 1993; Lebel et al. 2001). It may be inferred that these individuals lived in a social setting where they received help and support, as it might be argued that it is difficult for a solitary cripple to survive in nature. Similarly crippled apes have, however, been found surviving in the wild (Hublin 2009a). We also have the fossil find known as 'The First Family', or more formally A.L.-333, remains of numerous *Australopithecus afarensis* individuals found together (Johanson et al. 1982). If they also died together, which is often assumed but for which there is no evidence (Behrensmeyer 2008), then this indicates that at least some australopithecines did live in groups not smaller (but possibly larger) than the number of individuals killed (from 9 to 17), but tells us little about their social system beyond that.

In the case of hominins, we do have more than just fossils; there is also an archaeological record to consider. But this record is not very informative about sociality until fairly recent times. In the case of australopithecines, we have some evidence of possible tool use (McPherron et al. 2010; Semaw et al. 2003; Backwell and d'Errico 2001; Shipman 2001), but this does not tell us anything useful about their social life, unless one makes the bridging assumption that tool making is impossible without some postulated degree of sociality, cooperation, or mutual trust.

Within the genus *Homo* the direct evidence for sociality is still scarce for the first million years or so. Even in the few cases where several early *Homo* fossils were found in the same place, for example at Dmanisi in Georgia (Gabunia et al. 2000; Vekua et al. 2002; Rightmire et al. 2006), we still do not know whether these people actually lived together, or just died at the same place at widely separated times. It is not until the late Acheulean that, for example, Stiner and colleagues (2009a, 2011) find evidence of organized living spaces and cooperative hunting and meat sharing in Middle Pleistocene Israel, which would imply a fair degree of sociality.

We have abundant hand axes and other Acheulean and Oldowan stone tools from earlier periods, but the social context of their production is difficult to ascertain (see Grove and Coward 2008 for some ideas). Wynn (2002), Bayly (2010), Hodgson (2011), McNabb (2012), and others have discussed the possibility that at least some Acheulean hand axes were intended for display purposes rather than, or in addition to, their practical function as tools, based both on their symmetry properties and on the dysfunctionally large size of some specimens, which would have social implications. Machin (2009) finds that no single factor can account for the full diversity of hand axes, but that there is some evidence for social cooperation in their production.

In summary, it is normally taken for granted that early *Homo* did live in groups, and while I do not dispute this, I do wish to emphasize that this is based more on parsimony and indirect inference than on solid fossil evidence. The indirect evidence for some kind of sociality is compelling enough, which is unsurprising given the comparative evidence from other apes, but little is known of early *Homo* social structures beyond that.

For Neanderthals and other Middle Palaeolithic people, as noted above, there is some evidence of sociality, but it is neither abundant nor easy to interpret. On a general level, many aspects of what is called 'behavioural modernity' are observed in the MP/MSA record in Africa, Europe, and the Middle East (d'Errico 2003). The whole modernity package reasonably entails modern human levels of sociality as well, but care should be taken in making inferences concerning sociality from single 'modern' behaviours.

There is some evidence of ceremonial burial of (and presumably by) Neanderthals (Trinkaus and Shipman 1993; d'Errico et al. 2003), which would imply a human level of awareness of self and others, as well as a social community that cared about dead members; Gargett (1999) and Davidson (2003) argue against the burial interpretation, but Hovers et al. (2000), Riel-Salvatore and Clark (2001), and d'Errico (2003) defend it against Gargett's arguments.

Opinions are sharply divided concerning Neanderthal camp organization, so no firm conclusions can be drawn about the details (Davies and Underdown 2006), but at least it is well established that they had camp sites of some kind, as shown, for example, by widespread evidence of fire management (Roebroeks and Villa 2011). There is also evidence that some Neanderthal populations engaged in long-range (200 km) trading of stone, which may indicate extended social networks, but signs of this are rare (Feblot-Augustins 1993). Similarly, evidence of Neanderthal symbolic culture exists (e.g. Langley et al. 2008; Zilhão 2007; Zilhão et al. 2010; Watts, Chapter 16; Peresani et al. 2011; Morin and Laroulandie 2012), but it is neither abundant nor uncontested (Higham et al. 2010; Mellars 2010). But some recent finds, notably the painted shells of Zilhão et al. (2010), are unaffected by this critique, as their context is more secure and they predate the arrival of *Homo sapiens* by a fair margin; see also Caron et al. (2011) for a specific response to Higham et al. (2010). Pigment use by Neanderthals likewise goes back at least 200,000 years (d'Errico et al. 2009; see also Watts, Chapter 16). Estimates of Neanderthal group size and other aspects of sociality vary drastically, with sometimes contradictory conclusions from different authors (Davies and Underdown 2006). The recent results of Lalueza-Fox et al. (2011), however, do provide some solid evidence of Neanderthal social structure based on fossil DNA, indicating that the group studied had a patrilocal mating system, with all the adult males in the group, but not the adult females, being maternally related.

For modern humans, of course, we have abundant evidence of sociality. But if we look at the archaeological record, the evidence is quite uneven. Some hunter-gatherer populations, like the Upper Palaeolithic people in Europe with their cave paintings and other artefacts, have left a record amply documenting that they had a rich social life. But other hunter-gatherers have a material culture dominated by perishable materials, in which clues to sociality and symbolic culture would be less archaeologically visible. Notably, Brumm and Moore (2005) and Roebroeks and Verpoorte (2009) report that some Australian tribes have left a record not notably different from that of Neanderthals. Do we conclude that, for example, Tasmanians were not fully modern humans, with a human degree of sociality? Of course not!

5.5 Conclusions

The evidence pertaining to the social origins of language remains indirect, and various bridging theories are needed to connect theory with evidence. The evidentiary basis of these bridging theories is itself of highly variable quality, and needs to be kept in mind.

The primary evidence for the social origins of language remains within archaeology, palaeoanthropology, and primatology. But I wish to draw attention to some additional areas that have received less attention:

- Evidence from sociolinguistics, pragmatics, and other social aspects of language use.
- The neural and genetic basis of sociality.
- Parallel evolution of analogies of human features in unrelated lineages.
- Comparing archaeology with ethnography may help us discriminate between absence of evidence and evidence of absence in the fossil and archaeological record.

Part II

Language as a Collective Object

6

The 'poly-modalic' nature of utterances and its relevance for inquiring into language origins

ADAM KENDON

6.1 Speaking and extra-oral bodily action

When speakers speak, there is always a mobilization of bodily action beyond the confines of the anatomical apparatus needed for speaking. This extra-oral action, which can be quite variable in its extent, may involve the muscles of the face and the eyes, the muscles of the neck effecting head movements, the upper body and trunk, the forelimbs, and much else besides. It is *patterned* with the activity of speaking in complex ways.

The ebb and flow of visible bodily movement in a speaker is rhythmically organized in relation to the ebb and flow of speech. At the same time, these visible bodily actions are usually recognized as having meanings of various sorts, meanings commonly deemed to be coherent with what is being expressed in speech.

From this point of view, the meanings of speech and the meanings of visible bodily action unfold in time in a co-ordinated relationship and if the meanings of speech and the meanings of these bodily movements are taken together, a richer and more complex expression may be appreciated than if either words or extra-oral actions are considered separately. For example, the head is often moved when a person speaks. The amplitude of these movements tends to be co-ordinated with variations in loudness in speech, so that they may be more conspicuous in association with points of linguistic stress, as if emphasis can be both vocal and kinesic. However, Ray L. Birdwhistell (a pioneer in the study of body motion in relation to speech and one of very few investigators to study head movements in this way), who made these observations, went on to observe, studying American English speakers, that such movements of the head, when made in relation to stressed pronouns, tend to show a directional patterning. It was as if the head was pointing in one direction or another to the items referred to pronominally, as if these items were disposed differentially in space (Birdwhistell 1963, 1966, 1970: 110–43, 163–5).

Facial actions are also related to speech, as Birdwhistell also described. For example, different brow positions and movements can mark points of linguistic stress, and they can be used to bracket different segments of discourse, marking interrogative or subordinate clauses (Birdwhistell 1970; see also Ekman 1979). Hand movements in speakers, which have received far more attention than either head movements or facial actions (but little studied by Birdwhistell, oddly enough), have also been shown to be organized as patterns of movement co-ordinated with prosodic features of speech production (for early accounts, see Kendon 1972, 1980. See also McNeill 1992 and, especially, Kendon 2004: 108–26).

At the same time, these movements are also deemed as meaningful and as being related to meanings expressed in speech (see Kendon 2004 for one extended account). For example, speakers may use their hands to provide diagrammatic or pantomimic representations of what is being talked about; to point to things; or they can use them to engage in actions which operate on what is being said (as in gestures of negation or affirmation), in actions which display the kind of speech act or interactional move that the speaker's utterance accomplishes (as in gestures of offer or refusal, hesitation, request, and many others), or in actions which function in relation to the regulation of behaviour within the interaction (as in gestures of greeting, gestures that request a turn at talk, and the like). Extra-oral visible bodily action, in short, is deployed by speakers in ways that serve a great diversity of semantic functions but which yet, if done while the person is speaking, are so closely co-ordinated with this activity that it is to be understood as an integrated component of it.

6.2 Neurological foundations

This integration of extra-oral bodily action and vocal-oral action appears to be present from infancy. When babies vocalize they also move their bodies in a co-ordinate fashion (Trevarthen 1977; Iverson and Fagan 2004). Before the emergence of linguistically recognizable vocalizations, but after the development of what has been called 'canonical babbling', hand movements may be observed that are co-ordinated in a detailed fashion with the syllabic organization of babbling (Ejiri and Masataka 2001). These hand movements, like the vocalizations they accompany, although they have no recognizable meaning, nevertheless may appear to be patterned and spatially organized in ways rather similar to how an adult may gesticulate. It seems clear that the neuromuscular mechanisms that underlie speech–hand co-ordination are already in place. Probably they begin developing from an early stage. Although adult speakers may show a good deal of flexibility and higher order control over how and when they deploy hand movements in relation to speaking (see e.g. Kendon 2004: chs 8–10), it seems clear that they are making use of existing co-ordination mechanisms. Hand–mouth co-ordination in speakers is not something that is learned later, but is made possible by a developmentally established neuro-anatomy.

Neurological studies of various kinds confirm, in several different ways, that there are intimate relationships between the systems controlling manual actions, oral-facial actions, and the systems involved in speaking. Doreen Kimura (1973a, 1973b) observed that speakers who gestured when speaking were more likely to use their dominant hand to do so, in contrast with hand movements unconnected with speech, such as self-touching actions. This already suggested that the control centres for speech-related manual movements and those for speaking are linked and are both located in the same hemisphere (usually the left hemisphere). Kimura's observations have been confirmed by others (Dalby et al. 1980; Saucier and Elias 2001), and they also receive support from the long series of studies of hand–mouth co-ordination in speaking undertaken by Gentilucci and colleagues (2007). These they interpret to mean that, to quote the title of one of their papers (Gentilucci and Dalla Volta 2008): 'Spoken language and arm gestures are controlled by the same motor control system'. Studies of brain activity, using various imaging techniques, have also contributed a wide range of observations that show that regions of the brain, such as Broca's area, long thought of as involved in the control of speaking, are also involved in the control of hand movements as well as movements of the expressive muscles of the face (see e.g. Meister 2003; Willems et al. 2007; Aboitiz and García 2009; and Aboitiz 2012 include discussions of this in their reviews).

All this diverse work leads one to suppose that we should think in terms of facial-expressive, oral-expressive, oral-vocal-articulatory, and manual-expressive systems developing together, as an ensemble. That is, these different expressive systems develop in co-ordination with one another. Although the components of this ensemble may be employed in relation to one another in different ways, according to the occasions of social interaction in which they are used, and, in consequence, they are thus shaped by social processes of various kinds, the apparatus that permits this integration develops from the beginning, and must have a very long evolutionary history. As Aboitiz (2012: 8) remarks, the evidence regarding the intimate relationship between hand, face, and speaking actions supports the view that 'the early steps of language evolution also consisted of multi-modal signals, instead of being predominantly hand-based or vocalization based'.

6.3 Accounting for the integration

How is this to be accounted for? Why should there be this kind of integration? Much of the work done on the study of visible action in relation to speech—much of it passing under the label of 'gesture studies'—concentrates on issues of communicative, linguistic, or cognitive *function*. There has been a good deal of concern with whether and to what extent manual activity associated with speech contributes to the communicative import of utterances (Kendon 1994; Hostetter 2011). Studies have also been carried out to investigate the question of whether, and how, these manual movements play a role in the processes of speech production. The point of view generally taken is that these movements must somehow be *auxiliary* to the process of speech production. For example, they seek to establish a role for these movements in lexical retrieval (Krauss et al. 2000), in facilitating how speakers organize what they wish to express so it suits verbal expression (Kita 2000), in serving as an alternative means of representing relationships between ideas, thus helping in the development of problem solving discourse (Goldin-Meadow 2003), or in serving as a means by which imagistic aspects of thought may be given expression (McNeill 1992, 2005).

One can agree that these manual movements probably do have all of these functions, but none of these can be taken as explanations as to why they should be undertaken in the first place, nor why they should be so closely interrelated with the activity of speaking as to appear to be a part of it. None of these functional explanations can be used to account for why, in pre-linguistic babies, we may see well-organized hand–babble coordination, nor can they be invoked for an evolutionary account. Such an account has to find the origins of the gesture–speech relationship in something other than the functions that it may serve today.

6.4 The 'Gesture First' account and its difficulties

One evolutionary explanation for the gesture–speech relationship is that linguistic expression first developed as gesture, and the use of gestures by modern speakers is explained as a persistence of an older form of communication (see Hewes 1973; Corballis 2002; Tomasello 2008; Arbib 2005). Various arguments and observations have been put forward to support this idea. Thus it is suggested that because vocalizations of modern apes are too constrained in the circumstances of their production, are not articulated, and are limited in the degree to which they are under voluntary control, they cannot be regarded as a starting point for human language. The flexible inventiveness of gesturing in modern apes, on the other hand, seems to make this more attractive as a form of action that could get a language started (Pika, Chapter 10).

The relative success in teaching human-raised apes to use manual actions symbolically seems to suggest that the gesture-route to the production of semantically significant actions is an easier one. In any case, it implies that the capacity for symbolic communication by means of visible action would already have been present in the Last Common Ancestor of apes and humans. The capacity of modern humans to create languages entirely in the kinesic medium, as in sign languages, is also regarded as supporting a 'Gesture First' position. Tomasello (2008: 328), for example, has argued that this capacity would be 'almost inexplicable' if humans were adapted only for vocal language. If they had adapted to a gesture language first, then the 'gestural inventions' of sign language could be 'much more readily explained' (Tomasello 2008: 328). Further support is adduced from studies which suggest that the first language-like actions in infants are gestures, not spoken words. The neurological work referred to above, showing the intimate relationships between the control of speaking actions with manual and oral–facial actions, is also cited as support. (A useful survey of much of the work we have mentioned is in Meguerditchian et al. 2011.)

Great importance has also been attached to the discovery of mirror neurons which, in the macaque, were first discovered in respect to grasping actions. This has led Arbib, especially, to see in mirror neurons a basis for the way in which conspecifics are able to recognize each other's actions and also as providing a basis for imitation, essential components of any kind of language-like communication (Rizzolatti and Arbib 1998; Arbib 2005, 2006b, 2008, 2012).

A critical study of all this evidence and of the way it has been used to support a 'Gesture First' view of language origins, although lending plausibility to the idea, is far from conclusive (Kendon 2011a). None of the current 'Gesture First' theories, furthermore, offer any convincing explanation as to why speech is, in modern humans, the dominant vehicle for language (see e.g. Burling 2005; MacNeilage 1998a, 2008). On the other hand, those who reject the 'Gesture First' view, and who look for ways in which language could have arisen just in the vocal modality, tend to play down discussion of the role of visible bodily action. MacNeilage (2008: 283–5), who does mention gesture, nevertheless remains puzzled by it. Yet, as we have seen, extra-oral bodily action, although variable in its extent and amplitude, is always observed when a person speaks. Any theory of the evolutionary origins of language needs to take this into account.

6.5 An alternative approach

MacNeilage (1998b, 2008) has suggested that the complex oral actions that form the basis of speech have their origins in the oral manipulatory actions that are involved in the management of food intake. Here we propose to extend this idea to actions of other parts of the body also involved in feeding. If an animal is to masticate its food, food has to be brought into the mouth in some way. Leroi-Gourhan (1993 [1964–65]) pointed out that an animal may do this by moving its whole body close enough to foodstuffs so that it can grasp them with its mouth directly. Animals that do this tend to be herbivores, and all four of their limbs are specialized for body support and locomotion. They acquire food by grazing or cropping. On the other hand, many animals, for example squirrels and racoons, grasp and manipulate foodstuffs with their hands, which they also use to carry food to the mouth. Such animals tend to be carnivores or omnivores, and their forelimbs are equipped as instruments of manipulation, each with five mobile digits. In mammals of this sort, a system of forelimb–mouth co-ordination becomes established. This development is particularly marked in primates, of course, who, perhaps, in adopting an arboreal style of life, have developed forelimbs that can serve in environmental manipulation as well as in body support and locomotion. This sets the stage for the development of oral-forelimb manipulatory action systems, and this may explain the origin of co-involvement of hand and mouth in utterance production (see Gentilucci and Corballis 2006).

We suggest here (and see also Kendon 2009) that the actions involved in *speaking* and in *gesturing* are mobilizations of the oral-manual environmental manipulatory systems employed in practical actions, now transferred to function as actions in social interaction. That is, the actions of speaking and gesturing do not derive just from earlier forms of expressive actions but are re-dedications, as it were, of manipulatory actions now performed in the service of communicative action. We may expect, accordingly, that there will be components of the executive systems involved in speech that will be closely related to those involved in forelimb action and that these will be different from those components of oral and laryngeal action that are part of the vocal-expression system.

This view receives some support in the neuroscience literature, where it is reported that the actions of the tongue and lips by which the oral articulatory gestures of speech are achieved, controlled as they are in the pre-motor and motor cortex, can be separated from actions involved in exhalation and in the activation of the larynx, which produce vocalization. The control circuits for these actions involve sub-cortical structures, instead. However, in normal speech, the oral gestures of speech articulation are combined with vocal expression, which provides the affective and motivational components of speaking (see e.g. Ploog 2002).

6.6 Remarks on speech

If we are to understand the actions involved in *speaking* and in *gesturing* as a re-dedication to communicative action of the oral-manual environmental manipulatory system, we still must understand how these manipulatory systems became linked to vocalization and its voluntary control. While there is, as yet, no complete answer to this question, there are some things that it may be useful to take into consideration in thinking about this.

First of all, contrary to the widely repeated view already mentioned, that non-human primate vocalizations are involuntary and inarticulate, there is reason to think that, at least among some species, voluntary mouth actions producing articulated vocalizations do play a role in communicative vocalizations. For example, this is suggested by R.J. Andrew's (1976) work on baboon grunts, Green's (1975) work on

Japanese macaques, or Richman's (1976) studies of vocal activity among gelada baboons. From this it is evident that these creatures are capable of complex sequences of articulated vocalizations. This means that evolutionary steps towards voluntary control of articulated vocalizations must have already begun among primates a very long time ago (compare Jurgens and Alipour 2002). Furthermore, the ability of geladas to participate in chorusing and to adapt their vocal patterns to each other (Richman 1978), also observed in many other species of monkey (such as pygmy marmosets and guenons—see Lemasson 2011 for references), strongly suggests a good deal of voluntary control. In the light of the recent work of Zuberbühler and colleagues on chimpanzees (Zuberbühler et al. 2011; Clay and Zuberbühler, Chapter 11), and also by Hopkins et al. (2011), it seems we must modify the commonly accepted view of ape vocalizations in this direction, as well. Evidently, some of the important capacities for the oral-vocal actions required for speech can be found quite widely in various non-human primate species, suggesting a long evolutionary history. If MacNeilage (2008) is right that the voluntary actions of the mouth used in speech derive, ultimately, from the manipulatory actions of the mouth in feeding, the ability to use them in non-feeding contexts and to do so concurrently with phonation must have been arrived at a quite early stage in primate evolution.

What might have encouraged this development? Changes in social life, with the development of sustained personal friendships between individuals, and expansion of group size, and perhaps the exploitation of dense, forested environments are among the factors that might encourage an elaboration in the complexity of vocal signalling and could encourage the use of oral actions in creating more complex repertoires of calls. Comparative studies on modern primates, especially among monkeys, indicate that changes in complexity and variety of social interactions may well be related to the complexification of vocalizations. For example, McComb and Semple (2005) undertook a comparative study of vocal repertoire size, group size, and time spent grooming in over 40 species of non-human primates, and found that there was a link between the amount of time individuals spent grooming and the size of vocal repertoire, suggesting that the more complex and sociable social relations are, the more complex is vocal communication. In a study by Mastripieri (1999), in which he compared three species of macaque, ranging from the rhesus, with a high-dominance or 'despotic' social organization, to the more egalitarian and flexible kinds of organization found in stump-tail and, especially, pig-tail macaques, it was found that the macaque species with the most complex gestural repertoire was also the species with the most egalitarian and fluid social organization. Although Mastripieri did not have data available to do a similar comparison regarding the vocal repertoires of these species, he was able to quote some separate studies that noted the richness of the vocal repertoire in the stump-tail macaque and concludes, tentatively, 'that it seems likely that differences in vocal communication among macaque species are parallel rather than complementary to those found for their gestural communication' (1999: 73). These studies are consistent with the widely cited proposal of Dunbar (1993), who suggested that because, as group size increased, it becomes more difficult to sustain social bonds between individuals through physical grooming, vocal communication elaborated as a kind of substitute. In general, we may say that complexification of social interaction goes hand in hand with complexification of communication conduct, including the elaboration of and diversification of vocal action. Accordingly, any scenario that we might develop to account for the emergence of voluntarily controlled articulated vocalization, perhaps first elaborated in social play, and which became the basis for speech (once this activity acquired semantic functions), requires an understanding of the evolution of social interaction at quite intimate levels of detail.

Looking at vocalization in apes, however, which seems appropriate, given humans' close phylogenetic relationship with them, notwithstanding the recent work of Zuberbühler and Hopkins, mentioned above, we are rather far from any sort of persuasive model from which to extrapolate to something like human speech. However, humans are not descended from modern apes, but from some ancestral form once shared with the ancestors of apes. Accordingly, there is no reason to suppose that the vocal systems of contemporary apes should show much in common with what is found in humans.

Clearly, part of what was involved in the differentiation of the line leading to humans, that began at least five million years ago, was an elaboration of voluntary control over vocalization and the ability to combine this with voluntary articulations in the mouth so that something that could become speech could emerge. In the light of what is suggested by the comparative studies just mentioned, we need to look for developments in group size and social organization that could encourage the complexification in vocal signalling that would certainly be achieved if oral actions of tongue and lips could be combined with vocalizing. It is our hypothesis that, quite early in the hominin line, capacities for articulated vocalization developed which were exploited in the management and maintenance of complex social relations. This capacity, along with others, such as bipedalism, loss of body hair, changes in structure and size of the brain, and so on, is a part of the complex of features in terms of which the hominins diverged from the other members of the Homininae.

Eventually, of course, articulated vocalizations acquired semantic significances, and became speech. The process by which this happened is not understood. One suggestion is that it did so as a part of the way by which, within social interactions, past events were recalled through re-enactments. Vocal patterns could become established as components of repeated types of interaction events or exchanges and could then be used as a way of evoking these (a process that recalls a suggestion made by Jespersen 1922). In such a scenario, the integration of manual manipulatory action would be maintained because patterns of articulated vocalization would always be components of social action.

6.7 Implications for language origins inquiries

In the view advanced in this chapter, the gestures that are so often a part of speaking are neither supplements nor add-ons. They are integral to speaking. They are so because they are derived from practical manipulatory actions from which speaking itself is also derived. Looked at in this way, we can better understand why it is that visible bodily action is mobilized when speakers speak and why, more generally, when language is used in co-present interaction it always involves *poly-modalic* forms of action.

If we take this approach, the kinds of questions we might wish to pursue in seeking an evolutionary account of language origins may be extended and reframed. For example, we might wish to incorporate into our investigations an inquiry into the roles of extra-oral action in the process of language formation, not just as this is relevant for the question of how expressive actions become symbolic or representational, but also for understanding how the interactional conditions necessary for the emergence of shared referentiality can come about. Tomasello (2008) has emphasized the importance of the establishment of a shared attentional focus for this.

As has become clear from work on the organization of co-present interaction among humans (see, especially, Goffman 1963, 1971, 1974), it is through delicate co-ordinations between the movements and orientations of participants that shared co-operative intentions can be established among them. For example, the spatial-orientational systems that participants in focused interaction can enter into and co-operatively sustain play an important role in the means by which the shared attentional frame necessary for shared reference comes to be established. This, it appears, is accomplished through reciprocally sustained spatial and orientational manoeuvres (see Kendon 1990: 239–62). Accordingly, once we see that intelligible linguistic exchanges presuppose and depend upon the setting up of such joint attunements of attention, it becomes clear that the very activity of uttering linguistic acts of some sort requires an understanding of how shared 'participation frameworks' are established.

There are now a number of good descriptions of this for human interaction. Studies of great ape interaction that take a comparable approach would be extremely useful. A beginning has been made in the work of Simone Pika (Pika and Mitani 2009; Pika, Chapter 10) with chimpanzees, the work of Joanne Tanner on gorillas (Tanner 2004), and see also the book by Barbara King *The Dynamic Dance* (King 2004). Such work will allow us to compare how occasions of interaction between species are organized, going beyond the approach that has been common hitherto, in which vocal and gestural signals produced as discrete units of action are compared (as in Call and Tomasello 2007; see Kendon 2008 for commentary; see also Tanner 2004 for a study of gorillas using an interactional approach). This will greatly enrich our understanding of how joint referentiality of actions, in whatever modality, might have been enabled.

Secondly, as we have argued above, the 'natural' state of spoken language is a *speech-kinesis ensemble*. This means that 'language', when it is considered purely in its spoken (or written) form (as it so often is in language origin discussions), is to be understood as the outcome of processes of specialization and differentiation. Accounts of language origins can then be recast to become accounts of these processes of progressive specialization and diversification, accounts which show that these emerged and emerging systems are shaped through an evolution that involves social interaction as much as biology.

7

BaYaka Pygmy multi-modal and mimetic communication traditions

JEROME LEWIS

7.1 Introduction

Anthropological analyses of Central African hunter-gatherer ethnography reveal a set of similarities shared by Pygmy groups across the Congo Basin that, together with genetic evidence, suggest that they are remnants of an ancient hunter-gatherer culture. These hunter-gatherers share a particular mimetic language style, polyphonic music, forest hunting and gathering, an egalitarian social and economic organization, and genetic distinctiveness from non-Pygmy local populations.

A focus on the BaYaka Pygmies' communicative practice—composed of signing, whistles, animal sounds, signs made with plants, words from other peoples' languages, percussion, singing and dancing, and re-enactments—serves as a reminder of the range of modalities that humans use to communicate. By placing these gendered practices in the social context of a hunter-gatherer society we gain insight into the social conditions in which language evolved. BaYaka have developed this range of communicative practices in order to address appropriately different audiences: from human groups to animal species and the forest. They explain that in order to be able to speak (*pfofa*) in the 'language' (*djoki*) or speech (*pfofedi*) of others, whether neighbouring farmers, monkeys, or other camp members, one must mimic their sounds back to them.

7.2 The comparative ethnography of hunter-gatherer societies

The ethnography of hunter-gatherer sociality and language-use throws light on some of the potential conditions facing our hominin ancestors, notably in social and economic organization, but also on the situation of being both predator and prey. The responses of contemporary hunter-gatherers to these conditions are suggestive of how some human communicative abilities may have emerged and influenced the diversity of languages and musical styles evident today.

In the late 1970s, James Woodburn developed his comparative analysis of the ethnography of hunter-gatherers to show that they could be divided into 'immediate-return' or 'delayed-return' societies (1982). Although taking economic activity as the starting point, the implications of the difference between immediate- and delayed-return societies go well beyond economics to determine key aspects of social structure and political organization.

In summary, members of immediate-return societies consume most of their food on the day that they produce it, do not depend on specific others for access to land, resources, or tools, and have an economy based on 'demand sharing'. They do not invest in long-term production strategies. By contrast, people in delayed-return societies invest labour over long periods before a yield is obtained. Typical examples include farming, herding, or capitalist systems, but also certain hunter-gatherer societies that invest labour over time or store yields (such as the Kwakiutl and Inuit, and most Amazonian farmer-foragers). The requirement to manage labour during the period in which the yield is being produced results in relations of dependence and authority developing between people to assure that labour is put in at the right times and that those who contribute are recompensed when the yield is obtained, and so willingly provide their labour again. Control over the distribution of vital resources promotes political inequality and hierarchy through the emergence of elites. Whereas delayed-return societies are by necessity hierarchically organized with inequalities between peers, seniors and juniors, and gender groups, immediate-return societies are politically and economically egalitarian. While both delayed- and immediate-return societies exist among hunter-gatherers, only delayed-return societies exist among non-hunter-gatherers.

In immediate-return societies, relations are economically egalitarian through procedures that impose sharing on anyone with more than they can immediately consume, and so prevent saving and accumulation. A range of mechanisms, such as demand sharing, gambling, ritual, or gifting ensure that valued goods circulate without making people dependent on one another. People are systematically disengaged from property, and therefore from the potential for property to be used to create dependency. Each member of such a society has direct individual access to the resources on which they depend for survival, to the means of coercion, and to freely move where they want. Such societies are politically egalitarian, since no one can coerce others to do their will. People who brag or try to assert their wishes or views on others are mercilessly teased, avoided, and if they persist even exiled. Such societies are indeed rare today, but include some Pygmy groups in Central Africa (Aka, Baka, Bayaka, Biaka, Efe, Mbendjele, Mbuti), Hadza in Tanzania; some San groups in Namibia and Botswana; several groups in India, such as the Jarawa Andamanese,

Hill Pandaram, and Nayaka; and in south-east Asia, the Agta, Batek, Maniq, Penan, and others.

Though numerically insignificant, these societies are hugely significant for anthropology since their immediate-return orientation represents such a radically different mode of social organization to the numerous hierarchically organized delayed-return systems that currently dominate human societies. The distribution of these immediate-return traits across the world suggests that these are such successful human adaptations to life as a hunter-gatherer that they are likely to have great antiquity.

In reviewing how his typology had stood up to the evidence from 30 years of new ethnography, Woodburn (2005) noted that immediate-return societies have shown remarkable resilience over time. Despite the combined forces of government sedentarization and assimilationist policies, agricultural expansion, industrial exploitation, and fortress conservation all putting huge pressures on these societies, they tenaciously cling to their immediate-return lifestyle. Immediate-return societies have shown themselves to be stable, enduring, and resilient systems, internally coherent and meaningful to those who live in them, and resistant to change even when under intense pressure, such as experienced by Rwanda's Twa Pygmies (Lewis and Knight 1995; Lewis 2000).

While societies organized around delayed-return economies dominate today's world, it is likely that during the period in which the language capacity evolved, there would have been a far greater variety of immediate-return societies, and possibly a dominance of such societies since,

immediate-return systems though not simple in form, are intrinsically simpler than delayed-return systems and it seems plausible to argue that there will have been a time when all societies had immediate return systems (Woodburn 2005: 20).

Given the commonalities between immediate-return hunter-gatherers distributed across the globe, these modern forms of more ancient structures and practices provide important clues to guide our understanding of past human societies and key aspects of the social relations and conditions during language evolution.

Just as archaeologists who seek to relearn old skills such as flint-knapping (e.g. Stout and Chaminade 2007) must understand the physical constraints and cognitive needs for performing such tasks skilfully, anthropologists may observe the constraints and affordances facing people living by hunting and gathering for indications of those that faced our evolving ancestors. In previous work on language origins (Lewis 2009), I focused on some of the constraints and practical issues posed if spear hunting large, clever, and dangerous animals such as elephants, or herd animals. The solutions that contemporary spear-hunters have developed to safely kill such dangerous animals, and their implications on other areas of social life, provide us with insight into key constraints and possible solutions employed by ancestral populations. In this chapter, I will explore these insights to consider whether language has its origins in certain key contexts of immediate-return hunter-gatherer social life.

7.3 African hunter-gatherers and the Pygmies of Central Africa

Africa has the greatest range and variety of hunter-gatherers in the world. Within the borders of almost every sub-Saharan state live hunter-gatherers and former hunter-gatherers ranging from extremely egalitarian, immediate-return groups such as the Hadza of Tanzania to more hierarchically organized delayed-return groups such as the Okiek of Kenya. The greatest number of contemporary hunter-gatherers in the world live in the forests of the Congo Basin and estimates of their overall numbers range from 100,000 to 500,000. While there is great diversity among the many Pygmy groups of the Congo Basin there are also some remarkable similarities.

The BaYaka groups I will be focusing on here occupy forest west of the Ubangi River, in Central African Republic (CAR), Congo-Brazzaville (Congo), Cameroon, and Gabon. They are made up of 60,000 Aka-Mbendjele (Bahuchet 2012: 25) and 45,000–60,000 Baka, and several smaller groups such as the Mikaya, Luma, Kola, Gyeli, Bongo, and others (maybe around 10,000–15,000). Many still largely depend on hunting and gathering in an immediate-return society, though others, such as the Bongo, Kola, Gyeli, Luma, and increasingly Baka too, are engaged in increasingly diversified economies. The term 'BaYaka' is contracted to different extents and used by Aka, Baka, Luma, Mbendjele, and Mikaya, typically as *bayaka*, *baaka*, or *baka*.[1] I shall use BaYaka to encompass all these western groups, but use their individual ethnonyms when providing specific examples.

In addition to a past or actual forest hunter-gatherer way of life, ethnographers of Pygmy groups across the Congo Basin remark on certain shared practices that serve to reproduce a particularly effective forest hunter-gatherer adaptation. One striking similarity between groups living very far apart is their unusual singing style, which is a highly integrated, non-hierarchic choral yodelled polyphony (alternating between chest and head voice) composed of multiple overlapping melodies—see Arom 1978, 1981, 1985 (on western Pygmies); Demolin 1993 (on the eastern Pygmies); Fürniss 1993, 1999, 2006, 2007 (western Pygmies); Fürniss and Bahuchet 1995 (western Pygmies); Fürniss and Olivier 1997 (on the differences between Bushman and Pygmy polyphony); Grauer 2009 (on the similarities between Bushman and Pygmy polyphony); Kazadi 1981 (on similarities across Tua or Twa Pygmy groups in DRC); Lewis 2013 (on BaYaka music and society); Lomax 1962 (on an overall Pygmy-Bushman musical style); Merriam 1980 (on similarities in DRC); Oloa Biloa 2011

---

[1] Since the Baka are Ubangian language group speakers, whereas the Aka and Mbendjele are Bantu language group speakers, I write the ethnonym as BaYaka to emphasize this dual classification. Bahuchet (1992) uses *Baakaa* to designate their ancestral population.

(on polyphony among Bagyeli Pygmies in Cameroon); Rouget 2004 (on the Pygmy musical style); Hewlett 1996 (on ritual similarities); and others. Becker et al. (2010: 19) recently formulated it thus: 'In Central Africa, cultural criteria, such as the way of life, identity with forest, language, music, or social interactions, are often used to distinguish Pygmies from non-Pygmies.'

Bahuchet (1996: 109, table 5.1) tabulates his observations of cultural similarities and differences between Kola, Bongo, Baka, Aka, Twa, Asua, Mbuti, and Efe Pygmies stretching from west to east across the Congo Basin. Across the region, yodel and polyphony together are consistently associated with forest mobility, camps made of leaf and liana huts, woven-handled axes, and an egalitarian political and economic social order. Before exploring the causal links behind these associations more explicitly, it is useful to note that the greater the degree of acculturation to farmer and village lifestyles the less frequent is yodelled polyphonic music. Those groups Bahuchet identifies as no longer singing polyphonies (Kola and Bongo) are those that Verdu et al. (2009: fig. S3) show to be the most influenced by outsiders' genes. Since Bahuchet compiled his table, new research has described polyphony among the Gyeli/Kola (Oloa-Biloa 2011), and I have heard Bongo in Congo performing polyphony in 2005. Therefore the common characteristic of all the groups listed is that they all have a recent forest-dependent hunter-gatherer lifestyle and they still participate in polyphonic music, despite significant differences in the types, amount, and varieties performed. These differences are loosely proportional to the differences in their degree of acculturation to a sedentary agricultural lifestyle.

By combining linguistic, material culture, and genetic evidence with paleoecology of the Congo Basin, Bahuchet (1996, 2012) hypothesizes that the region was populated by the ancestors of today's Pygmies 40,000–30,000 years ago during a period of forest expansion (1996: 112). As the forests regressed again between 30,000–12,000 years ago, these groups became isolated in forest refuges, developing the degree of genetic and linguistic diversity observed between them today (Cavalli-Sforza 1986). As the forest grew again from 12,000 years ago to the present, the isolated Pygmy groups moved out from the forest refuges to populate the regions we find them in today. Verdu et al. (2009) further argue that the arrival of agricultural peoples from 5,000 years ago, but particularly from 2,800 years ago, created a second period of isolation between Pygmy groups that led to the genetic diversity of western Pygmy groups in Cameroon and Gabon.

Those still engaged in forest-oriented lifestyles and dependent on forest resources share similar cultural traits. These traits can still be found in partial ways among those 'Pygmy' groups no longer living in the forest, or who have become dependent on agriculture. Different Pygmy groups have been isolated from one another for long enough to have developed different languages, genes, technologies, and techniques for exploiting forest resources, while still being acknowledged as the 'first people' of the region. They share underlying structural similarities in music and ritual styles, demand sharing economies, non-hierarchical politics, gender roles based on blood (Lewis 2008), and a predatory engagement with their environment and neighbouring cultures. These similarities suggest that their shared traits are likely to be remnants of a more ancient Pygmy culture dating back to an ancestral population whose diversification is described above.

Verdu et al. (2009) suggest that the population ancestral to both Pygmy groups and Bantu-speaking agriculturalists separated sometime between 54,000 and 90,000 years ago, though the date is presumed to fall towards the later period since the Bongo genetic sample was exceptionally mixed due to more recent interactions. Genetic research by Chen et al. (2000) further shows that today's Pygmy populations are related to today's San Bushman populations and once formed a single ancestral population. Victor Grauer (2007) compares this work to ethnomusical analyses to make the strong claim that:

Biaka Pygmies ... could represent one of the oldest human populations ... (and that) the Kung exhibited a set of related haplotypes that were positioned closest to the root of the human mtDNA phylogeny, suggesting that they too, represent one of the most ancient African populations ... [therefore] the almost indistinguishable musical practices of the two groups may well date to at least the time of their divergence from the same population—a period that could ... date to at least 76,000 years ago, but possibly as much as 102,000 years ago (Chen et al. 2000: 1371, quoted in Grauer 2007: 6).

Grauer uses this genetic evidence to support an earlier analysis by Alan Lomax (1962) based on the metrics he had selected to compare folk music from around the world (the cantometric database) to show that San and Pygmy music represent a distinctive and unique polyphonic musical style in their world sample. By combining Colin Turnbull's early recordings and ethnography (e.g. 1966) of the Mbuti with cantometric analysis, Lomax (1962: 435) sought to illuminate the relationship between music, performance, and social structure:

There is a difference in kind between the main performance structure of Western European folk song, where a lone voice dominates a group of passive listeners ... and the situation in which every member of a group participates, not only in the rhythm and the counter-point of a performance, but in recreating the melody, as in the Pygmy hocketing style. . . . A comparison of the structure of inter-personal relationships and of role-taking in the two societies shows the same order of contrast, strongly hinting that musical structure mirrors social structure or that, perhaps, both structures are a reflection of deeper patterning motives of which we are only dimly aware.

These insights may go some way to explaining why the more sedentarized and agricultural the Pygmy group today, the less they perform polyphony and the less they use yodelling in singing the polyphony.

The evidence from these studies suggests that yodelled polyphonic singing is directly proportional to adherence to a particular immediate-return hunter-gatherer lifestyle, since, as this lifestyle is abandoned, so too are the songs and forms of musical participation that support it. Applying this logic in the opposite direction suggests that those groups still practising polyphonic yodelling and a forest hunter-gatherer lifestyle represent modern vestiges of an extraordinarily resilient cultural system.

This seemed self-evident to my Mbendjele friends in Congo-Brazzaville when, in 2010, they heard recordings of Mbuti music made by Colin Turnbull in the late 1950s over a thousand miles to the east. Almost immediately they exclaimed that, '[t]hey must be Bayaka to sing like this!' Bahuchet (1996: 109) and Cavalli-Sforza (1986) agree with them, but point out that the two groups demonstrate such genetic difference that they have been isolated from one another for a very long time.

In sum, while location, language, ecology, technologies, and genes have changed, musical performance and a forest hunter-gatherer economy have remained remarkably consistently associated. Even if the specific dates or scenarios suggested by these different authors are inaccurate, there appears to be a convergence of evidence for the association of a forest hunter-gatherer lifestyle with a particular egalitarian or immediate-return form of social and economic organization, a gendered division of labour based on blood, particularly mimetic language styles, and a distinctive musical style. These elements, while too specific to emerge from convergent evolution and with genetic evidence proving a shared past, appear to be key components of a highly resilient and effective adaptation to forest hunting and gathering. Using the Mbendjele BaYaka as a modern example of these shared traits as they relate to the range of activities BaYaka describe as communicative, I seek to provide insight into the social origins of language.

7.4 Forest hunter-gatherers and gendered language styles

The equatorial forests of Central Africa are home to great floral and faunal diversity. Among the many mammals are large, dangerous ones, such as forest elephant, buffalo, leopard, chimpanzee, and gorilla. BaYaka women are especially fearful of being attacked by these dangerous animals. This fear is culturally elaborated into a complex of associations and taboos collectively referred to as *ekila* (Lewis 2008) that organize and naturalize the gendered division of labour by keeping different types of blood apart: that of killing animals from that of human fertility, as exemplified by menstruation.

One result of this is that men and women behave differently in the forest. Women move in large noisy groups, accompanied by children, and often yodel loudly as they walk in order to frighten game. The daily communalism of women's lives results in strong solidarity between them that they readily use to resist men and assert their influence in conflicts and decision-making. Women's speech is more song-like than men's, and they accompany each other's utterances with sung expletives that contribute to increasing the volume and distinctive melodiousness of their conversations.

Men also accompany speech, but in a subdued manner by comparison with women. When out hunting men explicitly value quietness in speech and movement. If passing through dense noisy undergrowth men sit down to be quiet and scout with their ears. They discuss in signs and whispers the sounds around. Listening so intently to the forest, one learns the subtle particularities distinguishing pig grunts or the direction of bees' flight from the forest soundscape, or whether a 'crack' is an old branch falling from a tree or buffalo treading on a branch nearby. Recognizing these distinctions accurately can determine whether there is meat for dinner, honey for dessert, or whether you must run for your life!

The importance of correctly interpreting sound leads BaYaka to pay careful attention to the sounds of key events. When people tell stories, they draw on a standard stock of these conventionalized accompanying sounds I refer to as 'sound signatures' (Lewis 2009). When recounting lived experience, narrators also pay careful attention to precise sound mimicry of the event described, sometimes without offering any additional verbal explanation. Indeed, they take pride in perfectly mimicking such key sounds when recounting events, often dropping lexical descriptions altogether. These sounds tell the forest educated listener all they need to know as well as reminding or educating others about what different sounds signify and what one should do in response. Lewis provides more detail (2009, 2013).

Mixing lexical description with sonic mimesis results in a distinctive style of storytelling common to all western forest-orientated Pygmies and eastern Ituri Pygmies. Among BaYaka, it is cultivated most elaborately by men in secret locations called *njanga* to which only the initiated are allowed. Here, men re-enact great hunting moments, mimicking the sounds and typical postures and movements of themselves and the prey animal perfectly. This is an important apprenticeship for young men in disguised communication, hunting techniques, and animal behaviour. Group hunting techniques, for instance, rely on sign language and hunters disguising their speech as bird calls to co-ordinate and manage the group as they encircle the prey and co-ordinate the attack.

A striking use of such disguised modes of communication by men is to fake animal calls to lure in prey. These techniques work so well because people can fake sounds that the animals concerned do not fake, making them successful time and again. This is a common hunting technique among other human groups too; European and North American hunters use a wide range of commercially available lures for different prey—from ducks and wildfowl to deer and moose; many Amazonian Indians call monkeys out of high trees. Many Central African hunters, like BaYaka men, fake duiker, monkey, pig, crocodile, or buffalo calls to draw these animals out of undergrowth or high trees and into range so as to spear or shoot them. In dense forest this is an important contributor to hunting success. A strategy related to that of mimicking animals' 'speech' to better hunt them is also applied to extract desirable goods from their villager neighbours. Like the Mbuti Pygmies described by Turnbull in *Wayward Servants*, BaYaka contrive to extract with minimal effort and danger what they want from farmers by speaking in the villagers' tongue, claiming pity, and by playing up to the villagers' claims to 'own' BaYaka (Köhler and Lewis 2002).

BaYaka use their voices so as to make their speech an open, expansive medium for communication that imitates any other languages or meaningful sounds and actions that work to communicate with the significant others with whom they wish to maintain social relations. These include duikers, pigs, crocodiles, and monkeys, as well as other BaYaka and villagers from many different language groups. To achieve this range of communicative possibility BaYaka actively cultivate their skills as mimics. But men and women do so in different ways.

Women's chat (*besime ya baito*) often uses mimicry. A typical situation might be when a group of women sit down by the sides of a path to rest from their heavy baskets to chat. In more focused moments, called *moadjo* (re-enactment), one or two may rise and re-enact a recent event of note. Poor sharing or hoarding, or abusive, violent, stupid, or outrageous behaviour inspire comical mimicry of those involved. The audience works out who it is but doesn't mention names. Instead, a humorous but critical commentary shares key values through their negation during the re-enactment. *Moadjo* often focus on men's behaviour. Only widows and elder women are tolerated to shame others publicly, and have power in society as a consequence.

Egalitarian gender relations do not mean that everyone is the same, but rather that each gender group has strengths or qualities that are different from the other, but socially they are equally valued. Women's social value is rooted in their ability to bear life, in the communalism of their daily activities and the solidarity this entails, and in their use of mimicry to mock behaviour that goes against the norms of society. This contrasts with men's social value which derives from taking life and providing meat to grow and sustain human bodies, from their physical strength and toughness, and from using mimicry of animal and non-BaYaka sounds and actions to ensure safe access to dangerous but desired products such as wild animals, forest spirits, or farmers' goods.

Mbendjele and other Pygmy groups' multi-modal communicative strategies targeting different audiences remind us of the environmentally embedded context of language use likely to have dominated in the past. BaYaka seek to speak as many 'languages' (*djoki*) as they can. Their speech is incorporative, open, encompassing, and inclusive. It is a skilful multi-modal deployment of a range of capacities inherent to human bodies that serve to establish relationships with as many creatures as possible. By contrast, most language users today think of languages as conceptually fixed to a distinctive vocabulary, grammar, and speech style, facilitating interaction between members of a particular human group, and as being political by being selective, exclusive, and oppositional.

7.5 Music and language as alternative communication modes adapted to different audiences and purposes

In the BaYaka's large corpus of fables (*gano*), humans often interact with animals that speak and have personalities and intelligence similar to human persons. Similarly, BaYaka communicative strategies serve to maintain multi-species and multi-cultural relationships that reinforce the BaYaka view of themselves not as subjects in a society outside nature, but rather as a society of nature. Just as a society of people implies communication and transaction between them, so a society of nature implies communication and transaction between its members. This is typical of an 'animist' cosmology (Bird-David 1999; Ingold 2000), where sentience can be a property of many natural kinds, from other animals to trees, rocks, and even landscapes such as valleys, mountains, or forests. Concerned with maintaining relationships, animist people 'communicate' and transact with natural kinds in many ways—from hunting, gathering, and sharing them, to more abstract interaction such as Inuit animal carving, masked spirit dancers or shamanic ceremony.

While all people are exquisitely attuned to their environment, BaYaka, like other animist people, have explicitly developed techniques to communicate with many non-human sentient beings around them. When you understand the noises being made by other sentient beings, the forest's sound can be experienced as an inter-species conversation. To Mbendjele, the forest is 'talking' to them all the time: elephant is over there; monkeys have seen pigs; bees are going home (i.e. go home too); frogs invite you to drink, etc. Inter-species communication is more common and important than many realize. So duikers drawn to fruiting trees by colobus calls eat what the monkeys let fall from their mouths as they greedily shove in the fruit, while knowing that they will be warned of an approaching leopard by the monkeys' alarm calls.

By sharing such meaningful sounds, relationships are efficiently established with a wide range of sentient beings in the forest from whom Mbendjele want things. To ensure the sounds are appropriate to the sentient being concerned, and therefore meaningful, Mbendjele mimic the sounds used by these sentient beings back to them. Mimic duikers, crocodiles, pigs, and monkeys if you want to catch them more easily, or mimic farmers' languages and ape their stereotypes of you if you want to get things safely from them. And so it is with the forest as a whole.

Mbendjele say that the forest likes to hear 'good' sounds coming from people: polyphonic song, story-telling, laughter, happy conversations, and the calls of children playing. Such sounds please the forest so that it 'opens the camp for food' and all the things people need for a good life are easily available. In the same way that Mbendjele listen to the forest to know about it, so they say the forest is listening to them in order to know about them.

Since the forest's 'song' is a polyphony of animal, insect, and bird melodies and sound-making, it is unsurprising that people so adept at environmental mimicry will 'speak' back to the forest by singing polyphonically.[2] Such communication with forest has been elaborated into a wide range of rituals that call forest spirits (who are said to 'eat' song) into the camp using yodelled polyphonic singing. These rituals are generically called 'spirit plays' (*mokondi massana*) by Mbendjele (Lewis 2002, 2013), and called '*me*' by Baka (Tsuru 1998). Spirit plays are communicative technologies explicitly developed to 'soften' (charm) the forest and those that hear it. So *Malobe*, *Bula*, and *Yeli* spirit plays demand specific game animals; *Ejengi* celebrates abundance; and so on.

Spirit plays are the major social arena for learning key forest skills, co-operation, and group co-ordination skills that are crucial to the success of hunting and gathering (Lewis 2002). Musical performances, such as spirit plays, involve a wide range of potential meanings and functions—from the sound and structure of the music itself to the social and political relationships established between performers in order to produce it, or the way it signifies culture-specific concepts or identity, and organizes time. In other work (Lewis 2013) I analyse this style of singing as a 'foundational cultural schema' (Shore 1996). Through the performance of spirit plays key cultural models that are non-linguistically organized and which cross-cut diverse cultural realms, such as economics, politics, history, and cosmology, are re-experienced and learnt by each generation.

During spirit play performances the whole camp assembles in the central space sitting closely together, resting limbs on each other, and touching. As their bodies intertwine, so too do their voices singing out different melodic lines that overlay each other to constitute the polyphonic song. It is easy to lose oneself in this physical and acoustic mass and experience profound *communitas*. Singers seek to co-ordinate excellently just because it is beautiful, and the more beautiful it becomes the more you lose your sense of self and enter the ɛseŋgo (joy). The arrival of the forest spirits among the singers symbolizes the achievement of *communitas* with the forest.

To achieve this, Mbendjele explicitly work to establish a certain quality of relations between participants: no arguing, shouting, or chatting, and all should share what they have by contributing as best they can. In conjunction with a musical education, there is a social and political one. There is no hierarchy during musical performances; although one may begin a song, anyone else can stop it and start a new one; everyone is free to join whichever part of the polyphony they wish. To contribute appropriately one must not drown out one's neighbours, or sing the same melody as they do. Listening is as important as singing. If too many sing in unison, participants

---

[2] Like Fela Kuti's sonic mimicry of the sounds of Lagos traffic in his music, environmental mimicry has often inspired music.

immediately and instinctively diverge by choosing alternative melodic modules to maintain the polyphony.

Regularly singing like this instils certain ways of co-ordinating and structuring group activities that are applied outside spirit play performances. For instance, the instinctive way that singers avoid unison has economic implications. In an egalitarian society, daily hunting and gathering activities are intuitively co-ordinated without the need for anyone to tell others what to do. If too many do the same thing, there may be nothing to eat, so being musically primed to do something different but complementary to others improves the chances that the camp will eat well. Similarly, knowing a sufficient range of melodic modules and when to insert them into the song structurally resembles the way environmental knowledge is employed to identify and extract resources from the forest efficiently. Musical participation in spirit plays is the main avenue through which BaYaka learn these unspoken grammars of daily interaction (Lewis 2013). This resembles what Nick Enfield calls a 'diagram', in the technical sense. Here, relations between participants in musical performance are iconic for their relations in the social organization (Enfield 2005, 2009b).

When considering the range of communicative objectives that Mbendjele sound-use achieves, Ian Cross's (2005) suggestion that music and language are part of a human communicative continuum is useful. Mbendjele have adapted each to different purposes: language to express individual intentions and needs, and to organize and negotiate interpersonal relationships and activities; music to structure groups and enable them to 'speak' to other groups as collectives rather than as individuals.

When Mbendjele group together in ritualized ways to sing and dance, they speak as one. If only one spoke for them all, it would imply leadership. If each talked at once nothing would be understood. But when all sing, the message is reinforced and repetition strengthens the point rather than tiring listeners. Crucially, a singing group can say things that no individual in the group could say without fearing repercussions. Strong, provocative, insulting, or political statements can be made without giving the intended recipients any space to respond or interrupt. This enables the full statement to be made and allows tensions to be expressed and acknowledged even if they cannot be resolved.

Widely distributed spirit plays such as Ejengi and Yeli are found among BaYaka groups speaking different languages and living in different countries (Aka—Central African Republic; Baka—Gabon, Congo, Cameroon; Mbendjele, Mikaya, and Luma in Congo) suggesting that they are ancient. Ejengi, in particular, establishes a special arena in which living people connect with the ancestors by re-enacting mythical narratives. In the Mbendjele case, the initiation ceremony reforges the ancient pact between men's and women's groups that established society as we find it today (Lewis 2002: 173–95, ch. 24).

The analysis of BaYaka communicative practices shows the importance of mimetic practices to drive their creative spoken and sung engagement with humans, animals, and the forest. Learning to sing polyphonically and participating appropriately when it is performed inculcate particular cultural dispositions and patterns of behaviour central to reproducing BaYaka hunter-gatherer culture and society. The association noted earlier between forest hunting and gathering and yodelled polyphonic singing explains why Mbendjele and other BaYaka groups hold up musical form, ritual practice, and forest skill rather than language as the key indicators for judging the extent to which other people are forest hunter-gatherers 'like themselves' (Lewis 2002: 54–70). The wide distribution across Central Africa of this unusual musical style suggests that it is of some considerable antiquity, and therefore that the cultural dispositions it primes participants towards are probably refractions of a much more ancient culture.

Genetic and socio-cultural evidence supports this emic perception and my interpretation, but in reverse. Comparative work, such as that of Bahuchet (1996) and Verdu et al. (2009) cited earlier, demonstrates that the more sedentarized and genetically mixed the Pygmy population is, the less egalitarian they are, the less they participate in the yodelled polyphonic singing characteristic of spirit plays, and the less they depend on forest hunting and gathering.

7.6 Some considerations for the social origins of language

From a BaYaka perspective, following in the ancestors' path produces a distinct socio-cultural aesthetic that includes particular speech, singing, and performance styles, a particular oral tradition, a taste for forest foods above all other food, and a love for the cool, shady forest over the hot open spaces of rivers, fields, and villages.

Here, language in a formal sense is manifestly not synonymous with culture. Many BaYaka groups have adopted grammatical structures and extensive vocabulary, even a new language in the Baka case, from non-BaYaka groups without losing their distinctive cultural identity. Mbendjele and Baka, for instance, see each other as sharing the same origins and culture, despite Mbendjele speaking a Bantu language and Baka an Ubangian one. They contrast their BaYaka lifestyles and values to those of their villager neighbours, even when they speak the same language as the villagers.

They identify performance styles rather than vocabulary; speech protocols (see Lewis 2009) such as the *mosambo* (public speaking) rather than grammatical form; the habit of dropping consonants and otherwise disguising speech; of perfectly mimicking animal sounds and people's languages; of excellence at singing and dancing, and the art of calling forest spirits into camp; of teasing, joking, and clowning. It is not what repertoire people are singing but the polyphonic yodelling singing style they use, not which dances they dance or which spirits they call but the ritual structures they follow when doing so, not the language they speak but how it is spoken. The perception of what it means to be BaYaka is based on an aesthetic quality in which structure or 'style' matters more than content.

This chapter has described a range of communicative techniques, including language, used by present-day hunter-gatherers to establish fruitful social relations between people and with their environment. These techniques are such an effective adaptation, ensuring the efficiency and safety of production and reproduction, and for maintaining an egalitarian polity, that they persist with striking similarities among groups of hunter-gatherers who have been separated for many thousands of years.

A striking characteristic of their communicative practices is the impressive role of mimesis; ranging from literal to stylized, costly to deceptive, physical to acoustic, aimed at corporate communication and sung, or aimed at individual interaction and spoken. The extent and range of these mimetic practices offer important clues to help us understand some likely evolutionary pathways by which arbitrary sounds became accepted as conventionalized signifiers. Knight and Lewis (Chapter 21) develop this to propose a general theory of how language evolved.

The BaYaka ethnography shows how gendered mimicry can drive both lexicon and normativity; from men that mimic animals or farmers' languages, to women who use mimicry to humble antagonists and enforce social norms. This suggests that the gendered use of mimicry by early hominids could have first developed as a means to deceive animals, and only later became a means to communicate between people— this seems to accord with the two-stage hypotheses presented by Whitehead, Power, and Watts and in their respective contributions to this volume. For arbitrary signs to communicate meaning, people must agree to adopt linguistic conventions and categories, and play the language game honestly (Knight 2009; Lamm, Chapter 19). Mimicry BaYaka-style facilitates both these processes.

The central role of mimicry in the evolution of language is further hinted at by Brent Berlin's demonstration of the role of onomatopoeia and sound synaesthesia (phonoaesthesia) in determining suitable names for things (especially 2005, 2006). This work suggests that 'non-arbitrary sound-symbolic, phono-mimetic reference must have had enormous adaptive significance for our hominid ancestors . . . that the intuitively plausible and metaphorically motivated principles of phonoaesthesia served to drive lexicon in general' (2006: 49). Ramachandran and Hubbard (2001) show that phonoaesthesia appears to be based on cross-sensual mimicry. In the context of lexicon this occurs from the inputs received by the senses to movements of the tongue on the palate (Ramachandran and Hubbard 2001:19). Mimicry pervades the human language faculty.

Just as each sex employs different reproductive and productive strategies, so too do they differ in their use of similar propensities for mimicry. Based on insight from Mbendjele, women's mimicry is aimed outwards to ward off dangerous animals, and inwards against individuals who don't respect the moral order. Women's mimicry depends on their solidarity for its success: in the case of keeping dangerous animals away, they group together and mimic the forest and each other to produce overlapping sounds that deceive animals about the size of the group. In the second case, they use mimicry to collectively shame those who have behaved in socially unacceptable ways and so impose a normative order on society. The first is an example of what Power and Knight discuss in this volume as 'counter-dominance'— here the singers' alliance works to resist domination by a potential predator; the second is an example of 'reverse dominance'—the collective domination of an individual not respecting social norms (Boehm 1999).

Both these uses of mimicry enable high levels of trust to be generated and maintained between members of the social group. This enables deceptive signals normally aimed at outsiders to be redeployed for social reasons within the trusting group. So men returning from the hunt could use acoustic and gestural animal mimicry to share their experiences—for instance in describing an accident to non-participants back at camp—and with repetition, establish early lexicon.

8

Language presupposes an enchronic infrastructure for social interaction

N. J. ENFIELD AND JACK SIDNELL

8.1 Introduction

While some approaches to language evolution have been thoroughly linguistic yet without becoming particularly social, others have had the opposite problem. Coming out of an ethological tradition of research on primate social systems, Robin Dunbar hypothesized that language arose in our species as a way of managing or servicing social relationships, in a way analogous to physical grooming in apes and monkeys (Dunbar 1993, 1996b). The approach is grounded in research on the maintenance of social relations in complex social groups, but it has failed to gain traction in linguistics because, linguists say, the argument 'does not say anything about the intricate grammatical structures of human languages' (Hurford 1999: 182). 'While language is used for social "grooming" purposes,' says Hurford, 'this emphasis fails to account for the impressive and subtle referential power of language' (1999: 186). The sentiment points to a deep disconnect between the social and the linguistic in current research of relevance to language evolution. Either the researcher is handling the technicalities of language without really grasping what is going on socially, or vice versa. In this chapter, we want to draw attention to a sorely needed solution to this problem, taking as a starting point the behaviour of social interaction from a technical point of view, and seeing what language looks like from there.

8.2 Language in social interaction

Suppose that in order to get at the social origins of language we would begin by looking at language as it is employed in social interaction rather than looking at language as linguists traditionally view it. We might expect that these patterns of social interaction vary radically across cultures without significant constraint. Inuit song duels, Wolof greetings, Iatmul Naven are just a few of the anthropologically more famous forms that human social interaction takes (Eckert and Newmark 1980; Irvine 1974; Bateson 1936). When seen in comparison with more familiar forms such as found in English courtrooms, American presidential press-conferences, and French family dinners, we may be impressed by apparently limitless diversity. However, research on the basic structures of social interaction, which serve as a chassis for linguistic behaviour, has shown that beneath such diversity is a robust, universal, generic infrastructure that exploits a range of species-specific cognitive abilities and prosocial motivations (Enfield and Levinson 2006; Levinson 2006; Schegloff 2006; Sidnell 2007; Tomasello 2008). This infrastructure is not some kind of conversational equivalent of the mental module or device that has been proposed to account for putative underlying commonalities among the grammars of the world's languages. The infrastructure being described here emerges from a combination of evolved cognitive capacities in the domain of sociality (in part specifically human, though not specific to language) and the structural patterning that emerges when social moves are made and counter-made, in the form of the kinds of few-second chunks of behaviour we call utterances (see Enfield 2013: chs 3 and 6). The precise nature of this emergence is a major topic for research. The hypothesis is that there is a universal underlying infrastructure for the use of language in interaction, even when basic styles of human interaction seem to differ radically across groups— compare, for example, norms of interaction in Japan versus Anglo America (Lebra 1976; Lebra and Lebra 1986; Wierzbicka 1991: 72ff). The technical properties of this infrastructure cannot be discovered by applying existing research tools of linguistics.

If research on the social origins of language is to be properly informed about the object of study, then what is needed, as a complement to approaches to language within the discipline of linguistics, are approaches that focus on (a) those aspects of language that are unique to multi-unit sequences produced not by a single person but by multiple people in a social interaction, i.e. conversation; and (b) those aspects of cognition-for-language that are unique to the management of social relations rather than to the conceptual management of information per se. Fortunately, these needs are already met. There are established research traditions that provide resources for studying language and cognition in just these ways. To date, however, they have tended not to be well connected with linguistics, or cognitive science more generally, partly for reasons of disciplinary affiliation: they exist as branches of anthropology and sociology. They take an enchronic perspective on language, which is to say that they look at language in the move-by-move flow of interaction, as opposed to the (also invaluable) perspectives of diachronic versus synchronic, and ontogenetic versus phylogenetic (on enchrony, see Enfield 2009a: 10, 2011: 285–91, and 2013). To review these lines of research at any length would go beyond our present scope (see e.g. Heritage and Atkinson 1984; Duranti and Goodwin 1992; Duranti 1997; Schegloff

2006, 2007; Sidnell 2010; Sidnell and Enfield 2012; Sidnell and Stivers 2012; Enfield et al. 2014). Here we merely want to point in their direction.

Current thinking about face-to-face interaction from an enchronic perspective has been influenced by a variety of lines of research including linguistic pragmatics, Peircean semiotics, as well as research in anthropology, psychology, and other disciplines (see Enfield 2013, and many references therein). Here we want to highlight an approach to interaction that emerged in the work of Harvey Sacks, Emanuel Schegloff, and Gail Jefferson and that has come to be known as conversation analysis (Sacks 1992; Sacks et al. 1974; Sidnell 2010; Sidnell and Stivers 2012). Both Sacks and Schegloff were students of Erving Goffman, a transdisciplinary scholar who, although trained as a sociologist, had a major impact upon, and indeed was himself strongly inspired by, anthropology (see especially Goffman 1964, 1967, and 1971). Goffman was perhaps the first, and certainly the most eloquent, defender of the view that face-to-face interaction constituted its own phenomenon, that it had properties which were *sui generis* and not reducible to individual psychology or broader social processes (Goffman 1964). Sacks, Schegloff, and Jefferson incorporated this idea, and it may be understood as the first pillar of conversation analysis (see especially Schegloff 1968).

When Sacks and Schegloff were studying with Goffman at Berkeley, they were influenced by the highly original studies of Harold Garfinkel and the approach he developed known as ethnomethodology (Garfinkel 1967). The goal of Garfinkel's early studies was to uncover the underlying practices of reasoning which members of a society use in accomplishing everyday activities and which ultimately make society possible. A major part of Garfinkel's investigations was taken up with the question of how a person makes sense of another's conduct including their talk. This concern was incorporated into conversation analysis, as a kind of second pillar: the idea that participants in social interaction engage in practical reasoning both to produce their own talk and to understand the talk of others (see Heritage 1984). Both Goffman and Garfinkel thus provided inspiration for a new and distinctive approach to the study of ordinary social interaction. Others were left with the task of inventing a method by which ordinary social interaction might be systematically studied.

Sacks, Schegloff, and Jefferson took up this challenge. They studied social interaction by listening to audio recordings of telephone calls as well as co-present interaction, and there they found a locus of intricate order. Early studies showed that an interaction can be analysed into parts and that these parts consist of definable practices of speaking which have systematic effects and which together form orderly sequences of action in interaction (Schegloff 1968; see also Schegloff 2006). This order is not the product of statistical regularities or of categorical imperatives but rather of a persistent and pervasive orientation by the participants to a set of structures or norms. Like any set of norms in this sense, the norms that organize social interaction do not determine conduct but rather provide a framework through which it is intelligible and through which it is evaluated (see Heritage 1984; Stivers et al. 2011). Membership in any particular social group (e.g. German, Surgeon, Skateboarder) requires that one be aware of, and unable to plausibly deny the existence of, a certain set of norms, and thus to be accountable to those norms at every step. Participants in interaction can then be seen—not only by analysts but, in the first place, by other participants—as following a rule, deviating from it, attempting but failing to follow it, or simply violating it flat out. These alternatives generate further informative inferences about what that participant intends or means by behaving in that way (Sidnell 2010). The orderliness of interaction then is an endogenous product that is achieved by participants in interaction in each and every one of its local instantiations through the application of regular practices of reasoning.

Since the establishment of conversation analysis as a field of empirically based research on the structures of social action, a significant literature has been produced. The recent *Handbook of Conversation Analysis* (Sidnell and Stivers 2012) has a list of some 2,000 bibliographical references. But from the point of view of linguistics and other branches of cognitive science it is as if there were a hermetic seal around this literature. In even the most sympathetic work in linguistics, there is little if any connection to what is empirically known about the structure of human interaction, nor to the social cognition that underlies it nor the situated use of language as a cooperative activity. There are a few notable exceptions, for example in psycholinguistics (e.g. Clark 1996) and linguistic anthropology (e.g. Moerman 1988; Sidnell 2005), but surprisingly, in the language evolution literature that begins with the social-relational functions of language (e.g. Dunbar 1996b; Dessalles 2009) this large and directly relevant field of research is overlooked.

8.3 Linguistic structures in social interaction

When we look at language in the context of its functions and distributions in social interaction, the phenomenon takes on a new light. Over the last 20 years or so, a group of linguists with functionalist affiliations have begun to yield new insights by incorporating analytic concepts developed in conversation analysis, particularly those of turn-taking and conversational sequence, in the analysis of traditional linguistic topics. For example, Ford (1993) examines the grammatical structures known as sentence-final adverbial clauses in English and shows ways in which their structure and distribution are not arbitrary but may be 'interactionally generated' (Ford 1993: 108 and *passim*). In the following example (1) the speaker S poses a question, and when no uptake is forthcoming from the recipient R in the subsequent line, S then adds the increment (in line 3), which in turn elicits the uptake from R (in line 4) that lets S know they are being understood.

(1) 1 S: Y'know when it– (.) came from the:: I think (a) air conditioning system, it
            drips on the front of the ca:rs?
     2   (0.1 second pause)
     3 S: if you park in a certain place?
     4 R: mm-hm

The increment produced in line 3 is grammatically fitted to what came before it in line
1, but clearly lines 1 and 3 were not produced as a whole unit, such as they might appear
to have been if cleaned up and written down on the page (. . . *it drips on the front of the
cars if you park in a certain place?*). Rather, we see that in the real-time context of the
dyadic interaction, at line 2 some sort of confirmation of understanding appears to
have been due from R, but there was silence instead. By then producing the increment
in line 3, S can continue as if the turn was not yet finished, thus getting another
opportunity to elicit a confirmation of understanding, which indeed comes from R in
line 4 (see also Sidnell 2012). This type of study complements linguistic research on
grammatical structures by giving us a sense of the functions that such structures can
have in the enchronic social context of the speech event, as distinct from their
referential or representational relations to the event being narrated or described.

    Another area is the study of the 'procedural resources' that languages provide for
managing talk (see Blakemore 1987, 2002; Schiffrin 1988; Clark 1996). All languages
have various kinds of 'feedback markers' (*mm, uh-huh*), 'discourse markers' (*oh, so,
well*, etc.), 'trouble markers' (*um, uh*), 'editing expressions' (*I mean* etc.), 'repair
initiators' (*what? huh?*), etc. Despite their ubiquity and importance in regulating the
flow of interaction, these kinds of items are seldom studied in typological or cognitive
scientific approaches to language, where the tendency is to focus on the referential
functions of language. Upon inspection of data from conversation, it can be shown that
these types of items have distinct distributional properties in relation to formal patterns
of language use. For example, with regard to so-called 'newsmarks' in English (such as
Really?), Jefferson (cited in Heritage 1984: 340) shows that there are definable and
recurrent multi-turn sequences like the following: (Move 1) announcement of some
piece of new information by Speaker A (e.g. that she didn't smoke any cigarettes);
(Move 2) *Oh really?* by Speaker B; (Move 3) reconfirmation by A; and finally (Move 4)
an evaluation or 'assessment' by B (e.g. *Very good*). This kind of pattern is not a
construction in any standard linguistic sense, but it clearly points to a kind of
interactional grammar associated with these procedural linguistic elements.

    In some research, procedural items are not considered to be linguistic at all. Levelt
(1989: 484) looks at *er* as a marker of disfluency (similar to *um, uh*, etc.), and while he
shows that *er* has a specifiable function—signalling that 'at the moment when trouble
is detected, the source of trouble is still actual or quite recent'—he concludes that it is
'a symptom, not a sign'. By contrast, Jefferson (1974: 184) suggests that *uh* perhaps has
'the status of a word in the English language'. The same has been argued by Clark and

Fox Tree (2002), who found in a corpus study that *um* and *uh* show different functional distributions in English. In addition, a quick look across languages reveals that the precise form of such items is locally conventionalized: English has *um* while Lao has '*un*' (Enfield 2007: 314). These kinds of procedural items do not have the referential functions that linguists tend to privilege, but they are no less linguistic for that.

In the sorts of approaches we have just reviewed, the researcher is either looking at a familiar grammatical structure in the unfamiliar light of conversational sequence, or is looking at a well-known but oft-marginalized element that can hardly be studied at all without consulting conversational data. Then there are domains of structure that are off the linguistic map altogether. These possibly universal and arguably generic underlying components of the infrastructure for interaction, already alluded to above, are organized into partially independent or semi-autonomous domains or systems. We now want to draw attention to two of the most central of these systems, which will need to be properly defined and handled by any natural approach to language as a form of social behaviour.

8.4 Turn-taking and sequence organization in conversation

An organized system of *turn-taking* provides for the orderly distribution of opportunities to participate in talk-in-interaction. Sacks et al. (1974) define the system as having two components. A turn constructional component defines the units out of which a possible turn can be constructed and by extension allow participants in interaction to anticipate the possible/probable extent and shape of any actual unit and thus to project or predict its completion. A turn allocation component specifies an organized set of practices by which transition from a current speaker to a next speaker is managed. Together, these two components and the rules that organize the relation between them, provide for the orderly or systematic nature of turn-taking in interaction. Sometimes the system operates in such a way that we see seamless transitions between speakers in a sequence. The following example from a telephone call shows tight temporal alignment in 'floor transition' between the two speakers:

(2) (Rahman corpus A:1:VM:(4); transcription slightly simplified; transition measurements in secs from de Ruiter et al. 2006)
     (Begin call)

     Mat: 'lo Redcah five o'six one?,
     Ver: [+0.15s] Hello Matthew is yer mum there love.
     Mat: [+0.13s] Uh no she's, gone (up) t' town
     Ver: [+0.24s] Al:right uh will yih tell'er Antie Vera rang then.
     Mat: [−0.03s] Yeh.
     Ver: [+0.13s] Okay. She's alright is she.

> Mat: [+0.10s] Yeh
> Ver: [+0.07s] Okay. Right. Bye bye luv,
> Mat: [+0.02s] Tara,
> (End call)

The turn-taking model suggests that people in a conversation will actively minimize the amount of overlap in speech (i.e. they will avoid having two or more people speaking simultaneously), and at the same time they will actively minimize the amount of silence between turns in a sequence, as we have just seen. But having such imperatives or 'rules' does not entail that all conversation actually proceeds one speaker at a time. Overlaps and gaps occur constantly (Sacks et al. 1974; see also Schegloff 2000: 47–8, n. 1), and these exceptions can have functional effects, arising from the very fact that people perceive them as exceptions. It is sometimes suggested that in this or that culture or social setting, a completely different system applies, or that there is no system at all (for instance, 'In Language/Culture X, people all talk at the same time'; see Stivers et al. 2009: 10587). However, there are to date no systematic empirical studies of informal conversation that provide counterexamples to the claim of a one-speaker-at-a-time normative design for the regulation of conversational turn-taking (Schegloff 2000: 2). As in many domains of linguistic analysis, impressions and intuitions turn out not to be supported by empirical data (see de Ruiter et al. 2006; Stivers et al. 2009). Sidnell (2001) tested Reisman's (1974) claim that everyday conversation in Antigua follows a 'contrapuntal' style, and found that in fact the data are compatible with a one-speaker-at-a-time model.

It is common to observe overlapping speech in conversation, but rather than constituting exceptions to the turn-taking rules, such cases usually provide evidence in support of it. When people self-select as speakers of next turns, the system dictates that they should begin speaking at a point where the previous speaker's turn is possibly complete and where transition to a new speaker is pragmatically relevant. In example (3) below, left square brackets mark the onset of overlapping talk. Our focus is on what happens at lines 4 and 5. After Old Man says 'The funfair changed it', this is a point of possible completion of his utterance, and it is a point where transition to a new speaker would be relevant. Parky twice attempts to begin his turn 'That changed it' (before it is eventually produced in full at line 6), yet finds himself in overlap on both occasions (line 5). Notice the split-second timing here with Parky attempting to come in at just those points where Old Man has reached possible (though obviously not actual) completion of his current turn. Clearly, in order to come in at just these points, Parky must have anticipated where Old Man would reach possible completion of his current turn.

(3) Parky
     1 Tourist: Has the park changed much,
     2 Parky: Oh yes,

3   (1.0)
4 Old man: Th' *Fun*fair changed it'n [awful lot [didn'it.
5 Parky: [Th-   [That-
6 Parky: That changed it,
(example from Sacks et al. 1974; transcription slightly simplified)

An important and widely underappreciated point is that this turn-taking system operates independently of whatever social actions are being accomplished in and through the talk it organizes—that is, whether people are requesting, inviting, questioning, answering, agreeing, disagreeing, complaining, excusing, insulting, or whatever else they do in turns-at-talk constructed and distributed through the turn-taking system. All of this supports the idea that the turn-taking system is part of an infrastructure that operates 'underneath', and independent from, the goal-directed social behaviour that people are effecting with their context-situated usage of language.

The arrangement of linguistically conducted social actions into *sequences* represents a distinct domain of organization in interaction, yet it presupposes an underlying turn-taking mechanism (Schegloff 1968, 2007). Many social actions that are carried out through the use of language come in pairs, for example request and granting (or rejection), invitation and acceptance (or refusal), complaint and excuse (or denial), and so on. These pairs are linked together by a relation of conditional relevance whereby, to paraphrase Schegloff, given a first action (such as a request, invitation, or complaint), a second action is made expectable. Upon the occurrence of a second it can be seen to be a second item to the first (rather than an independent turn) and upon its non-occurrence it can be seen to be absent (where an infinite number of other things did not occur but are not absent in the same way; Schegloff 1968). Conditional relevance thus establishes a relation between a first and second action that has both a prospective and a retrospective dimension. The prospective dimension ensures that the doing of a first action will activate a norm making the doing of the second action relevant and noticeably absent if not produced. This norm draws on a cooperative assumption in social interaction. The retrospective dimension allows the speaker of the first to see if, and how, she was understood. For example, if someone produces a responsive utterance that is recognizable as an *excuse*, this will reveal to the first speaker that she was apparently heard to be complaining or accusing, whether that was her intention or not. Thus the production of actions within sequences constitutes an architecture of intersubjectivity by which understandings are publically displayed and ratified incarnately, *en passant* in the course of whatever business the talk is occupied with (Heritage 1984; Clark 1996).

Episodes of talk-in-interaction can, typically, be described in terms of base sequences (often adjacency pairs) and their frequently multiple pre-, insert-, and post-expansions (Schegloff 2007). Such expansions are also made up of sequences and these may be the loci of their own expansions. Thus a maximally simple ordering of utterances into adjacency pairs can nevertheless result in sequences of considerable complexity, again implying a kind of structured grammar of interaction, of clear importance to the social origins of language and yet unknown to the science of linguistics.

If we take the elements of the turn-taking system and the action sequences that ride upon it and incorporate them into our understanding of language structure, this can give us new insights into the function and distribution of the kinds of lexico-grammatical structures that linguists normally want to explain. One of the central features of conversational sequences, as just described, is the notion that utterances are not just produced as conversational moves in a flat string, but rather are related to each other in specific ways. Most important among such inter-move relations is the relation between *initiating* utterances and *responsive* utterances. A simple example of an initiating utterance is a question: it initiates one person's local project (e.g. it is a means to achieve a person's goal to get a piece of information that they need prior to some next action, such as when I ask you the time so I can know whether I need to run for the train or not), and obliges another person to join this local project and, if possible, cooperate by providing the required information (see example (3), Q = 'Has the park changed much,' A = 'Oh yes,'). Many other kinds of two-turn sequences have this kind of structure, where the first move puts an obligation on another person to provide a next move of a certain type (see discussion above).

Linguists seldom invoke turn or sequence structure in carrying out core linguistic research, but recent attempts to do just this have yielded good results. Gipper (2011) examines a set of grammatical markers of evidentiality in Yurakaré (a language isolate of Central Bolivia), of the kind that have proven notoriously difficult to pin down in semantic and pragmatic analysis. Gipper draws on data from Yurakaré conversation, which allows her to use sequential position as a factor in the analysis. She distinguishes cases in which a certain evidential is used in an initiating type of turn in a conversational sequence from cases in which it is used in a responding type of turn. She finds that the different effects or meanings of evidential markers can be defined in terms of the conversational position (and, relatedly, the action type) they occur in.

Earlier research used these pair–part asymmetries of conversational sequence as a way to account for the distribution of certain kinds of lexical and grammatical structures, while bringing in more explicit reference to the social elements of speakers' rights and duties in producing different kinds of utterances. Pomerantz (1984) discovered some ways in which an utterance can set up a *preference* structure that constrains the ways in which another person can respond (Pomerantz and Heritage 2012). For example, when a person issues an invitation, the linguistic structure of the response will be different depending on whether it is an acceptance or a rejection. In the case of accepting, which we can regard as the socially preferred, cooperative response to an invitation, the response normally comes without delay and in simple form, as shown in example (4a). By contrast, in the case of declining, which we can regard as the relatively non-cooperative, socially marked response to an invitation, the response has a set of formal properties that are not observed in the acceptance, namely delay, prefacing with 'discourse markers' like *well*, markers of disfluency or hesitation, and the provision of accounts or reasons for the declination, as shown in example (4b):

(4) (a) i. Do you want to go for a drink?
         ii. Sounds good!

     (b) i. Do you want to go for a drink?
         ii. (pause) Um, well, I kinda still have work to do, so maybe um. . . .

A series of studies have subsequently examined these issues of preference, where the social-interactional factors at play at a given moment in the interaction can account for why a particular grammatical structure has been selected at all, accounting thus for both the specific function and distribution of a grammatical device which might otherwise go unexplained (Pomerantz 1984; Pomerantz and Heritage 2012; Heritage and Raymond 2005; Sidnell and Enfield 2012, among many others). These kinds of features of preference structure have two important properties that put them outside the scope of most linguistic research. Firstly, they are explained in terms of inherently social-interactional factors such as the degree to which an utterance constitutes a cooperative action, as opposed to an action that resists the trajectory that another person has set out on. Secondly, they are inherently enchronic, being defined in terms of specific positions in conversational sequence—initiating versus responsive—which cannot be studied without looking at data from conversation. Conversation is a type of data that is seldom studied in linguistics, including the kinds of linguistics that have currency in research on language evolution.

8.5 Repair

A second system of practices for the use of language in interaction is the system for *repair* (Schegloff et al. 1977). In using language in human interaction, there is always the possibility that troubles will arise in speaking, hearing, and understanding (Levelt 1983; Clark 1996; Schegloff 2006; Hayashi et al. 2013). An organized set of practices of repair constitutes a natural, interactive system by which such troubles may be addressed at or near the point where they occur, and may be potentially resolved more or less immediately before there is intolerable divergence of the participants' intersubjective understandings of what is going on in the interaction. Research on the practices of repair have shown it to be a structured and systematic domain, as if repair had a grammar all its own; though again, this system has remained outside of the usual purview of linguistics.

The analysis of repair in interaction makes reference to several kinds of distinguishing structural features. Firstly, there are distinctions in the *components* of the repair sequence, listed in (5):

(5)   Components of a repair sequence
      A. **Trouble source or repairable** = some element of an utterance that constitutes a source of trouble, for any of a range of reasons including problems of production, word choice, hearing, and appropriateness, relevance, among other possible problems.
      B. **Signal of trouble** = a sign that there is a source of trouble, including the manifest nature of the trouble itself as well as techniques for drawing attention to the trouble.
      C. **Initiation of repair** = a sign that the trouble will be, or should be, fixed; often is formulated in such a way as to identify and/or characterize the trouble source.
      D. **Repair** = a correction or redoing of the trouble in (A).

Secondly, there are distinctions in the *personnel* involved in the repair sequence. The speaker of the trouble source turn is often referred to as 'self' (e.g. in the term *self-repair*), though this person may or may not be the one to produce some other component of the sequence; for instance, a major class of repair sequences is called *other-initiation of repair*. This refers to cases in which a problem in one person's utterance is signalled by another person in a subsequent turn, and is subsequently repaired by the original speaker, as shown in the following example:

(6)   Other-initiation of repair in a 3-turn sequence
      Trouble source   B: Oh Sibbie's sistuh had a baby boy
      Initiation of repair   A: Who?
      Repair   B: Sibbie's sister.
      (example from Schegloff et al. 1977: 376–8; transcription slightly simplified)

Thirdly, there are distinctions in the possible *positions* in a 'repair opportunity space' at which the different components can be observed, and where different personnel can be involved:

(7)   Positions in the repair opportunity space: '3 turns long', 4 main positions
      A. **Same turn** = within the turn that includes the 'trouble source' (T1)
      B. **Transition space** = at completion of T1, when turn transition is relevant/possible
      C. **Next turn** = in the turn that follows T1 (T2)
      D. **Third turn/position** = in the turn that follows next turn (with complexities left aside here)

Together, these three sets of distinctions—the components, personnel, and positions of a repair sequence—define a possibility space for how any repair sequence might emerge or be generated in a given stretch of social interaction. A solid literature has begun to make inroads into mapping out the many possible structures and functions of repair sequences, mostly with a focus on English. Much more work needs to be done, not only on continuing to describe the grammar of repair and determine the extent to which it constitutes a system, but also to carry out the necessary cross-linguistic comparative work (see Hayashi et al. 2013, and references therein, for steps in this direction).

8.6 Conclusion

We have introduced a couple of the most important contributions of pioneering research on talk-in-interaction over the last 30 years or so. A key feature of this line of work is that it has effectively taken an ethological approach to the use of language in human behaviour, but has not suffered from one of the central problems of human ethology, namely the problem of proceeding as if our possession of language doesn't make enough of a difference that we should study people any differently from how we study animals. We are of course animals, and we are not excused from being studied as such (Tiger and Fox 1966). But let's face it, language changes things a lot. We have argued that to get a direct view of how language works in social terms, an enchronic perspective is required, a causal frame in which the moves we build from bits of language (and much else) are embedded in trajectories of joint activity that necessarily involve multiple parties and that necessarily have social causes and consequences. Technically defined systems for interaction such as turn-taking and repair seem to transcend language, and yet they are so closely bound up with it that we might ultimately expect some kind of a co-evolutionary account. That said, to have been able to get language up and running as we know it today, it seems to us that the fundamentals of the infrastructure for interaction would have to have been in place first. This implies, as many have suggested (e.g. Tomasello 2006), that if our closest relatives lack certain key capacities for the shared intentionality that enables the most basic sequences of human interaction, this would account for why they also don't have language, and can't get it. It seems clear that in the realm of vocal communication (see Clay and Zuberbühler, Chapter 11), other apes do not show anything like the responsive, contingent turn-taking behaviour so characteristic of human interaction (Arcadi 2000); though we note that in the realm of visible bodily behaviours such as ritualized gestures, there are patterns of behaviour that do more closely resemble the kernels of adjacency–pair sequences (Rossano, F. 2012). So what's now needed is more empirical research. The first pass that conversation analysis has carried out over recent decades was an important initial step toward developing a rigorous account of the enchronic infrastructure for interaction. By determining the systems or domains out of which talk-in-interaction is composed, and upon which language usage rides, this work has uncovered some fundamental areas upon which entire research programmes can now be based.

Subsequent research will have to explore implications for language evolution of the idea that language *presupposes* an enchronic infrastructure for social interaction. If language is not possible without such an infrastructure, then the question of language evolution turns to the evolutionary origins of the infrastructure itself. An important issue for subsequent work will be to test the extent of human diversity in the basic structures of interaction. Recent work from an anthropological and cross-linguistic perspective has begun to ask whether the particular language being spoken has consequences for the organization of interaction as described here (see Sidnell 2009; Dingemanse and Floyd 2014). That research is in its infancy but initial results suggest that the underlying, generic structures of interaction may be inflected or torqued by the particular semiotic structures through which interaction is accomplished, as well as the local circumstances within which it operates. Sidnell and Enfield (2012) explore the idea that the distinct lexico-syntactic resources of a language can have distinct *collateral effects* on the ways in which certain types of social action can play out in sequences of conversation.

Our goal in this chapter has been to draw attention to some aspects of language that inhabit the divide between the established reference-oriented, sentence-based interests of linguistics, on the one hand, and the social-relational concerns of research on human sociality, on the other. Linguistics has achieved an enormous amount, yet it still struggles to connect with social cognition and social behaviour in ways that other disciplines can apprehend and apply. We submit that this problem can be readily solved in research on the social origins of language, thanks to the existence of a significant body of literature that provides the much-needed link between language and human sociality.

8.7 Acknowledgements

We are extremely grateful to Daniel Dor, Chris Knight, Maggie Tallerman, and Kathleen Gibson for comments on drafts of this chapter. Some sections draw on parts of the chapter 'Face-to-Face Interaction' by Jack Sidnell (2012, in *Encyclopedia of Theory in Social and Cultural Anthropology*; Sage Publications) and a section from p. 516 of de Ruiter, Mitterer, and Enfield (2006). We thank members of the audience at Social Origins of Language conference at UCL (London, February 2011) and the Linguistic Society of America Institute Workshop 'Interactional Foundations of Language' (Boulder CO, 18 July 2011) for their input. This work is supported by European Research Council (ERC Project 'Human Sociality and Systems of Language Use', 2010–2014), and the Max Planck Institute for Psycholinguistics, Nijmegen.

9

The instruction of imagination: language and its evolution as a communication technology

DANIEL DOR

9.1 Introduction

The general hypothesis, that human language emerged as a new collective innovation from within the rich cultural and communicative context of pre-linguistic hominin society, is founded on a conception of language itself as a socially constructed tool, or technology, of communication. This view of language has informed much of the linguistic discourse in the first half of the 20th century (de Saussure 1915 [1983]; Sapir 1921; Meillet 1921; Gardiner 1932; and others), has been argued for in the philosophy of language (Wittgenstein 1953; Lewis 1969; Davidson 1994), and has been taken as given in most of the disciplines interested in language, in sociology, anthropology, semiotics, communication studies, literature studies, critical studies, and so on. In the last two decades, it has made a comeback in the linguistic sciences, and is now promoted by a very wide array of scholars, coming from different disciplines (Tomasello 2008; Itkonen 2003; Zlatev and Sinha 2008; Croft 2000; Dor 2011; Dor and Jablonka 2000; Levinson and Evans 2010; Everett 2012; Mufwene 2013; and all the chapters in this volume). Taken as literally as possible, as I think it should be, this perspective positions language, together with other communication technologies, such as the writing system, the telephone, and the Internet, in the social realm—between speakers, not in them. It takes the universal human fact, Language with a capital L, to be the technology type itself, like the Book or the Fax. Specific languages and dialects are variants of the technology, and the cognitive capacities required for the acquisition and usage of the technology are just that: emergent answers to the cognitive challenge of handling the technology. In the most general terms, the perspective thus investigates the idea that language was invented and further developed, like all the other technology types, in the course of the ongoing human effort to improve social communication. This could have happened in a single community or simultaneously in many. Then, unlike the others, it spread its variations all across the human world, and has already had a deep influence on our cognitions, emotions, and genetic makeup, because it changed the environments within which individuals were selected.

This perspective, then, raises a foundational question: if language is indeed just another component of the human *semiosphere* (Sinha, Chapter 3), how should we capture its *functional uniqueness*? What does language do for us as a communication technology that no other system is capable of? One promising direction to look at is the fact that language allows for what Hockett (1960) calls *displacement*:

> Man is apparently almost unique in being able to talk about things that are remote in space or time (or both) from where the talking goes on. This feature—'displacement'—seems to be definitely lacking in the vocal signaling of man's closest relatives, though it does occur in bee-dancing.

The idea that displacement is the key to the essence of language has lately been adopted by Bickerton (2009) and Mufwene (2013). The problem, however, is that the function of displacement, as such, is not unique to language. We can also communicate about remote things with paintings and sculptures, photographs and films, ritual display, dance and pantomime. What we need, then, is a closer grasp on the specific functional strategy that language employs in order to allow for displacement. In Dor (2011), I propose a new characterization of the functional specificity of language, which captures the distinction between language and the other systems, and allows for the unified treatment of a wide range of empirical and theoretical issues currently discussed in functional and structural analysis, lexical semantics, conversational analysis, pragmatics, sociolinguistics and the sociology of language, linguistic relativity and language acquisition. In a nutshell: all the other systems work with what I call the *experiential* strategy. They provide materials for the interlocutors to experience with their senses. Language, on the other hand, works with a radically different strategy: it is dedicated to the systematic *instruction of imagination*. It allows speakers to intentionally and systematically instruct their interlocutors in the process of imagining the intended experience, as opposed to directly experiencing it. Speakers provide interlocutors with a code, a skeletal list of the basic co-ordinates of the experience. Following the code, the interlocutors raise past experiences from their memories, and then reconstruct and recombine them to produce novel, imagined experiences.

In this chapter, then, I would like to do two things. In Sections 9.2–9.4, I will present a skeletal and informal description of this functional conception of language, say a few words about the way it is fulfilled, and show how and why it has opened new horizons for human communication. In Sections 9.5–9.7, I will claim that my proposed characterization, together with the culturally driven conception of the co-evolution of language and its speakers (Dor and Jablonka 2000, 2010; and see Dor and Jablonka, Chapter 2), allows for the construction of a new *type* of dynamic and gradualist approach to the question of the origins and evolution of language—as a question of technological evolution. The approach takes the characterization of language as a technology quite literally, and suggests that it must have evolved like other technologies do (Arthur 2007). It thus proposes a strictly gradualist narration of the process, while at the same time allowing for revolutionary moments, in which the accumulation of small changes results in the radical transformation of both the technology and the dynamics of its evolution. In line with Arthur (2007), it takes the notion of *invention* to refer to a complex emergent process, which does not necessarily imply a conscious intention to invent, but does imply a constant need to explore new solutions to pressing problems.[1] It identifies the exploratory emergence of the functional strategy itself, the instruction of imagination, as the engine driving the entire process, which means that it implies a high level of *developmental determinism*: language emerged for the instruction of imagination, and further evolved to make it gradually more efficient.

9.2 The functional specificity of language and the experiential gap

To understand the functional specificity of language, I suggest that we have to re-position language in the overall context within which it operates—the context of *experience*. The process of experiencing is the foundation of our lives as mental creatures. Like all the other animals with a nervous system, we live in experience. Experiencing includes everything that we call feeling, thinking, understanding, seeing, hearing, imagining, wishing, and so on—but also, importantly, everything that happens in our nervous system when we do, move, touch, react, try, succeed, and fail. As our experiences accumulate in our minds, we detect similarities and analogies between them, and construct generalized, perceptual categorizations—modal, analogue, holistic, fuzzy, and context-dependent—which then colour, shape, and sometimes determine the way we further experience.[2] This is how we learn. All this does not deny the possibility that our nervous systems might be innately biased, in different ways, towards certain ways of experiencing and accumulating experiences (Rupert 2009; Elman et al. 1996). What it does deny, and very strongly so, is the idea that our general cognition can be described—let alone explained—in terms of formal

---

[1] What Arthur (2007) does in effect is show that the evolution of material technologies, which Keller (1994) calls 'phenomena of the second type', is actually not very different from the evolution of 'phenomena of the third type', which emerge without prior intentional planning, like 'the paths beaten across fields by many separate people' (Hurford 2011: 139). Invention is always emergent.

[2] Barsalou (1999) terms these analogue categorizations 'perceptual symbols'. I accept much of his analysis of these entities, but I find the term itself quite problematic. The categorizations are indeed perceptual, but they are not symbolic.

computational operations on abstract symbol-like entities. It thus denies the existence of a Fodorian *language of thought* (Fodor 1975) and the existence of *conceptual
structure* as a level of cognitive representation (Jackendoff 1990). The theoretical
move from abstract representationalism to experiencing (very often under the title of
situated cognition) has been inspired, among others, by some of the major works of
the late 19th and early 20th centuries in Philosophy and Psychology (Dewey 1938;
Heiddeger 1962 [1927]; Merleau-Ponty 2012 [1945]; Wittgenstein 1953; James 1990
[1890]; Vygotsky 1986 [1934])—and has been substantially argued for in the last two
decades on philosophical, cognitive, computational, experimental, phenomenological, biological, and evolutionary grounds. I will not attempt to review the literature here (see Robbins and Aydede 2009 for an extensive overview). The important
point for our purposes is only this: the assumption of abstract representationalism
has kept us away from the essence of language, because it created an illusion of
sameness between the way we *know* and the way we *speak*, between the categorizations of our experiences and the categorizations of our languages. This illusion of
sameness masks the foundational problem that language, as a communication
technology, has to overcome, and thus misses out on its functional specificity.

Three properties of experiencing, then, are crucial for our purposes here. First,
experiencing is *private*. We experience on our own, within ourselves, even when we
experience together. It is important to see that this does *not* deny that important
things happen at the intersubjective level when we experience together (Gallagher
2008). It only insists that, even then, we still experience intersubjectivity from our
own private perspective. Current discourse on human experiencing tends to ignore
the privacy of experience for a very good theoretical reason: much of the discourse
has emerged as a counter-reaction to the solipsistic view of human experiences based
on Cartesian philosophy, and has thus systematically highlighted the intersubjective
nature of human experiencing—the primacy of the interpersonal over the intraper-
sonal. Much of the discourse thus concentrates on the human facts of experience-
sharing, social learning, mimesis and imitation, mind-reading, joint attention and
empathy, and on the consequent human capacity for co-operation, collective
thought, and cultural production. All these are undisputable and extremely important. I agree with Clark (1996), Tomasello (1999, 2008), Donald (1991), Zlatev and
Sinha (2008), and many of the authors in this volume, that language and intersubjectivity are very closely interrelated, and that early humans must have gone through
an entire stage of evolutionary development, *before* language, that resulted in the
emergence of a co-operative, mimetic, intersubjective species. I will also try to show,
later on, how this pre-linguistic development eventually allowed for the emergence of
language. I do not agree, however, with the implicit assumption that the evolution of
human experiencing into the intersubjective dimension somehow erased whatever
was there before. The unparalleled human capacity for intersubjectivity evolved
from an experiential foundation much closer to solipsism, and this foundation

is still there, at the very core of our experiential lives: intersubjectivity, like everything else, is always eventually grounded in private experiencing (Hurford 2007, 2011).[3] Failing to see this leads to another illusion of sameness between the experiences of different individuals, which, again, masks the challenge that language has to overcome. Language is indeed made possible by intersubjectivity, both ontogenetic- ally and philogenetically, but what it *does* goes beyond intersubjectivity. To under- stand what language does, we have to begin with human individuals as private experiencers.

The private essence of experience implies that every human individual, each of us, experiences the world in different ways. This is the second property of human experiencing, its *variability*. Every individual looks at the world from his or her own egocentric perspective; every one carries a different baggage of memories, different private histories of interaction with different worlds. Every individual comes to rely on different strategies for understanding the world; each is by nature (and by instruction) more deeply attuned to certain aspects of the world than to others. Every human individual lives in a different experiential world (which, again, does *not* deny that there are similarities). The third property is this: we are forever separated from each other by *experiential gaps*. Even with intersubjectivity, human individuals have no direct access to the experiential processes taking place inside the others' minds.

In order to understand language, then, I suggest that we have to abandon both the Kantian dictum, the foundational presupposition of the cognitive sciences, that all human experiences comply with a universal interpretative scheme, and the neo- Kantian conviction, the foundational presupposition of most of the social sciences, that the members of every culture and sub-culture experience the world in the same ways. We have to begin with the acknowledgement that each human individual lives in a private, experiential world which is different from that of the others, and is inaccessible to them. This is a foundational fact about our cognitive nature, and it is the foundational *obstacle* to communication which language, as a social invention, set out to circumvent. Human cognition participates in the story of language not just as part of the origin, but also, more importantly for our purposes here, as the *original problem* that had to be solved by a social technology.

---

[3] A referee suggests that 'if you and I are intersubjectively engaged, then by definition we have managed to achieve perspective reversal—such that I am viewing my own mental states "through your eyes" and you through mine.' I disagree: when we are intersubjectively engaged, we *try* to get as close as we can to perspective reversal, but I always view my mental states (and you mine) through *my interpretation of* your viewpoint, and this interpretation is eventually determined by my own private perspective. The intersub- jective achievement is always partial.

9.3 Other systems of communication allow for the sharing of experience

The above understanding of experience allows for an explicit demarcation between the specific function of language and the functions of all the other active systems of communication used by humans and other animals—those that allow for displacement and those that do not. All the other systems (with the possible exception of the dancing rituals of the bees) allow for the *sharing* of experience. I will call the sharing of experience *experiential communication*. Systems of experiential communication do *not* attempt to bridge the experiential gap between the two sides: they only become functional where the gap itself is reduced. There are two types of systems of experiential communication: the great majority are what I call *presentational*. These allow the communicator to behave in a way that is, at the very same time, determined by his or her experience and made available for experiencing by the receiver. A cry of pain, a frowning expression, a smile, a hug, a kick, a threatening posture, demonstrations of physical strength, different forms of mimesis (and teaching through mimesis), manual gestures, grunts and screams, music and dance—all these employ the strategy of presentation. Many other systems of communication, invented and used only by humans, employ a different but related strategy: they are *re-presentational*. They allow for displacement of the experiential type. In such systems—drawings, paintings, maps, musical recordings, photographs, and movies— the sender's experience is recorded, frozen in time, delivered from the here-and-now of the sender's experience into the receiver's here-and-now, where it is 'melted back', so to speak, brought back to life (always only partially) in his or her mind. The products of re-presentational communication are iconic: they provide their receivers with echoes, or silhouettes, of what they would perceive had the original experience been directly presented to them. Just like presentational systems, re-presentational systems do not attempt to bridge the experiential gap between the sender and the receiver. They use various technical means to allow for the displacement *without* actually bridging the experiential gap.

9.4 Language bridges the experiential gap through the instruction of imagination

Language is the only tool of communication that goes beyond the experiential strategy, and works with what I call the *instructive strategy*. Instead of presenting or re-presenting his or her experience to the interlocutor, the communicator provides the interlocutor with a skeletal list of the basic co-ordinates of the experience—and thus actively *instructs* the interlocutor in the process of *imagining* the communicated experience. The imagined experience is supposed to reflect the original experience not because it is perceptually based on it, but because it is (approximately) of the same *type*. In experiential communication (presentational and re-presentational), the sender communicates: '*This* is my experience'. In instructive communication, the sender communicates: 'My experience is of *this type*—try to *imagine*'.

This way, language actually allows for communication *across* the experiential gap: with language, speakers can make the others imagine things without presenting them with any perceptual material for experiencing. This allows for displacement, and also for the communication of inner experiences that are very difficult to communicate in experiential ways: interpretations of reality, causal generalizations, plans for action.[4] This, I suggest, is the specific function of language, and it is the essence of the linguistic revolution in the evolution of humankind. Language is still, today, the only technology that is capable of doing this. As I will claim later on, it is also the key to the evolutionary dynamics that brought language about.[5]

Within my model, language consists of two components: the *symbolic landscape* and the *communication protocol*. The symbolic landscape is what we usually think of as the lexicon, but it is much more than just a list of words and constructions. It is a huge semantic web, a radically simplified *model* of the world of experience, which reflects the entire history of negotiation and struggle, within the linguistic community, over what should be properly thought of as a *normative* worldview. The communication protocol is a set of socially negotiated, prescriptive procedures for the process of linguistic communication. Just like the signs of the symbolic landscape, the procedures emerge from the struggle over norms—this time, the norms of communication. The two components allow speakers to channel, *through the symbolic landscape*, skeletal descriptions of their private experiences—which the listeners then imagine into experiential interpretations.

---

[4] It is important to remember that the question here is one of communication, not of mental representation. The question is: which types of experiences can be communicated experientially, and which are only communicable with language? The distinction thus only partially correlates with Gärdenfors' (1995) distinction between *cued* and *detached* representations. For Gärdenfors, cued representations are directly connected to what the individual perceives at the moment, while detached representations make up the 'inner environment' of the individual—a 'small-scale model' of the external world that frees the individual from dangerous trial-and-error behaviour. Two points are important: cued representations are not always communicable in any way, and detached representations are sometimes easily communicable with experiential means. I thank an anonymous referee for discussing this point with me.

[5] It might be important to note at this point that *unintentional* activation of an interlocutor's imagination may also occur as a result of experiential communication. Zuberbühler (2003), for example, shows that Diana monkeys retain a representation of an alarm call's semantic content for at least five minutes, which means that they might be imagining the predator throughout this time (this, of course, is not a necessary implication of Zuberbühler's experiment). There is, however, no indication that the callers intend to make this happen. Callers are not interested in the location of their interlocutors vis-à-vis the detected predator: some of the interlocutors do not have to construct an inner representation, because they raise their heads and actually see the predator; other may have to imagine; but nothing hinges on that as far as the calling is concerned. If such calls do indeed involve unintentional activation of the imagination, this may be another early precursor for the emergence of language. The difference between all this and language, however, is clear: as a technology, it is specifically designed (by cultural evolution) for the intentional and systematic instruction of the interlocutors' imaginations.

The key to this unique communication strategy lies in the fact that it requires a huge amount of collective effort to make it work, prior to actual communication—the effort of *mutual identification*. As individuals whose private experiential worlds are different, speakers have to work together to create a model of the world that they can tentatively agree on, and thus use as a channel for instructive communication. They also have to agree on sets of norms for the usage of the technology, to make sure that the listener interprets the instructions in a way that is similar enough to that intended by the speaker. It is precisely in this sense that language is a technology: it has to be built before it can be used.

In instructive communication, the listener is not invited to share an experience with the speaker, but to create an independent experience, on the basis of the skeletal formulation of the message, within his or her own experiential world—which is both different from and isolated from the experiential world of the speaker. In the creative activity of imagination, the listener may imagine in a wide variety of ways, all of which would always follow the analogue complexities of his or her own experiential world, never that of the speaker. The message should thus be able to instruct the listener in a process in which he or she not only has to create a more or less focused image (an object of imagination, not necessarily a visual representation)—but also a focused image that more or less corresponds to the original experience of the speaker: an image of the same type. This is a very ambitious goal. The strategy of instructive communication does this through the co-ordinated investment of enormous social energies in the never-ending process of careful mapping and marking of those points in experience, and those ways of speaking, which the different speakers within the community may, more or less reliably, count on in the process: 'When I use *this* word, imagine a thing of *this* type (not *that*)'; 'when I use this word together with *this* one, imagine *this* type of experiential relationship (not *that*)'; 'when I arrange the words in my sentence *this way*, imagine you look at the experience from *this* perspective (not *that*)'.

Crucially, the process of mutual identification does not result in the replacement of private experience with the shared model of the world. It creates another level of meaning—a digital level of semantics—that is represented in our minds side by side with the level of experience. The two levels of meaning are only partially correlated with each other: one is based on the private process of experiencing; the other on the social process of mutual identification. They also influence each other in a variety of dialectical ways. In the course of linguistic communication, we translate back and forth between the two levels, always engaging in a process of meaning approximation between the private and the social. This has far-reaching implications for the study of lexical semantics, the relativity problem, and other topics, that I will not discuss here. As I claim below, the emergence of the separation (and then dialectic entanglement) of the new level of meaning from (and with) the ancient level of private experience lies at the heart of the drama of language evolution.

This understanding of the instructive strategy allows for a new conception of linguistic communication as a process of *iterative conversion*. In conversion processes, inputs of one type are transformed into outputs of another. In the telephone, for example, sound waves are converted into electrical signals in the microphone, and the signals are converted back into sound waves in the earphone. The important point for us is that the telephone performs its function with a *single* conversion on each side of the communication event: sound to electricity on the speaker's side, electricity to sound on the side of the listener. In this sense, experiential communication of the presentational type is similar to the telephone. It performs a single conversion on each side: from private experience to perceptible behaviour, and then from perceived behaviour to private experience. Systems of re-presentational communication also require a single conversion, but of a very different type. Consider painting, for example: it converts one type of visual percept, the view as it was privately experienced by the painter, into another type of visual percept, the painting, that is then presented for perception to the viewers. The essence of re-presentation lies exactly in this fact, that it remains in the domain of perception, that it allows for displacement by converting perceived material into perceived material.

What about language, then? According to the generally accepted view, the uniqueness of language lies in the fact that it performs *two* conversions instead of one. The communicative intent is not converted directly into perceptible behaviour. There is another level in between, a level of *formal structure*. When we produce an utterance, we begin by converting our intended meaning into a formal configuration of words, morphemes, and other types of constructions, which is then converted into perceptible behaviour when we actually speak. The same happens on the listener's side. Perceived behaviour (the stream of speech) is converted into a formal structure: the words and their formal relations are extracted from the stream of speech, isolated, recognized and registered. Then, the formal configuration is converted again, to produce a meaningful interpretation.

In Dor (2011), I suggest that this picture requires a serious update. The secret of language, the trick that allows for instructive communication, is the fact that language performs *three* conversions, not just two. Crucially, the first conversion is not from meaning to form. It is from meaning to *meaning*: from the communicative intent to instructions for imagination. From private meaning to *collective* meaning. From experiential meaning to *semantics*. The production process begins, as in all the other types of intentional communication, with an experiential intent in the mind of the speaker: something that is, for that particular speaker, at that particular time, the mental object of the intention to communicate. The intent is experiential and private, and is thus, crucially, *prior* to language. It is the original material that the technology receives from the outside, the material that it has to process. In the first conversion, then, the normative rules of the communication protocol guide the speaker, step by step, in the conversion of the experiential intent into an ordered set of instructions for imagination.[6] I use the term *message* to refer to this ordered set. In the first conversion, then, the intent is converted into a message. The building blocks of the message are the inherent meanings (the *signifieds*) of the words and constructions, chosen by the speaker on the basis of the intent. The first conversion, then, transfers meaning from the realm of the private to the realm of the social. By doing this, it makes it communicable: it turns something that is privately experienced into instructions that the others can understand.

It is the message, then, the ordered set of instructions for imagination, that provides the input for the next conversion, which is indeed the conversion to formal structure. The message is converted into a formal configuration consisting of the perceptible structures of the words and constructions (their *signifiers*), and the phonological, morphological and syntactic relationships between them. I call this configuration the *utterance*. Finally, in the third stage, the utterance is converted into perceptible behaviour—actual speech. Sound waves (or visible motions) are produced for the interlocutor (listener or viewer) to experience.

The process is governed throughout by the normative rules of the protocol, which also govern the process as it takes place, in the opposite direction, on the side of the interlocutor. As in all other types of intentional communication, the comprehension process begins with the perception of behaviour: we listen to the stream of speech, or view a stream of visible motion, and take them in. The perceived material is then converted into a mental representation of the utterance. The stream is phonetically, phonologically, morphologically, and syntactically analysed, and the signifiers and their structural relations are identified. The utterance is then converted into the message, the ordered set of instructions for imagination constructed by the speaker. Finally, and most importantly, the message then activates the interlocutor's imagination and instructs it to retrieve from memory certain types of experiences, and arrange them together in a particular way, in order to create a private imaginary experience. Not *the* experience of the speaker, but an experience of the same *type*. This imaginary experience, I call the *interpretation*. The entire process, then, is depicted in Figure 9.1.

What is important to see in this flow chart is the fact that it redefines the relationship between the *mental* and the *social*. What happens inside the mind of the speaker is the socialization of the private intent. What takes place inside the listener's mind is the privatization of the social message. Language mediates between private experience and the social world. This is what it does as a social technology. This is how it bridges the gap.

---

[6] Acquiring the normative rules, the speaker thus learns to *think for speaking* (Slobin 1996).

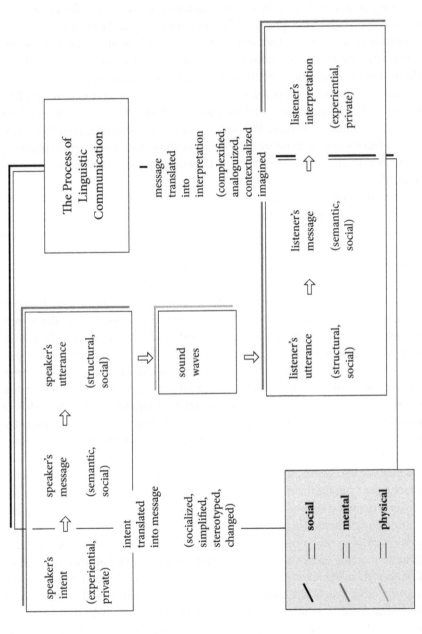

FIGURE 9.1 The Process of Instructive Communication

9.5 The emergence of the instructive strategy

The above characterization of the unique functionality of language allows for a new principled approach to the question of its *moment of origin*. The issue is no longer the appearance of a new system, different from everything that was there before, but the appearance of an innovative, exploratory communicative function—performed in the beginning with the already existing tools of experiential-mimetic communication, and only then, in the ensuing dynamics of exploration, stabilization, and further development, sparking a process in which the autonomous system of language gradually emerged. Not 'First there was no language, then there was'; but 'First there was only experiential communication, then there were exploratory beginnings of instructive communication, then language to serve the function more efficiently'.

Much of this volume is dedicated to the hypothetical description of pre-linguistic human societies. With systematic pointing and eye connection, bodily and vocal mimesis, manual demonstration, bodily movement and posture, facial expression and uniquely human social emotions, individuals in these societies co-operated in unprecedented ways, taught each other and learned from each other, negotiated complex social relations and divisions of labour, and led highly sophisticated lives—with increasingly higher rates of collective innovation, stabilization and retention (the ratchet effect, Tomasello 1999), alloparenting (Hrdy 2009), music, dance, pretend play, ritual, and so on. A major component of all this was the stabilization of mutual identification as such—the ability to synchronize perception (always partially)—within the here-and-now of communication events. These societies, then, have developed experiential communication to its functional limit: communicators could systematically and reliably direct their interlocutors to a very wide variety of experiences—provided that they could be made (within a very short time range) to experience them by themselves. Handling situations in which the thing to experience was outside the experiencing range of the receiver, however, lay beyond the functional limits of the system as such. This was the Rubicon. To us, it may not seem like much of a river, but for them it must have been. Like all other animals, they were still totally experiential creatures. Everything they achieved with mimesis, pointing, and teaching, allowed them to experience much more—*you see, you point, then I see what I hadn't noticed myself*—but this only deepened their capacity for experiencing. In their understanding of the world, they still only knew how to follow their own senses.

Consider, then, the following scenario: individual A points at something *x* (a prey, a predator, other people, fire), and produces a certain mimetic sound associated with *x*; individual B sees A pointing, hears the mimetic sound, and looks in the direction pointed at. If B manages to identify *x*, the communicative act ends with success. But if *x* is positioned outside B's field of vision, the act *fails*. What is required for it to succeed lies beyond the scope of the functional envelope of experiential communication. To make this bit of communication work, B would have to go through a revolutionary change of attitude. He or she would have to understand the call in a totally different way—not as an invitation to experience, but as an invitation to *imagine*. B would have to understand (without words): 'A is intentionally attempting to turn my attention to something by pointing. His or her vocalization indicates that it is of the type *x*. As for myself, I cannot see anything there. I will, however, choose to go against my own experiential judgement, *believe* A's experiential judgement, *imagine there is something there of the type* x, and act upon my imagination.' To imagine what you cannot see with your own eyes, simply because you believe somebody else, this is the Rubicon. If B could manage to do it, the entire interaction would count as a genuine instructive exchange. If A and B, and then the others, could manage to stabilize this new understanding, and begin to use it systematically, the Rubicon would be crossed. The signal used for experiential communication would turn into a linguistic sign, still holistic and analogue, but already performing the task of instruction. Language would then emerge, not yet as a system, but as a new communicative strategy.

What is required, then, for this type of exploratory revolution to begin? First, it is clear that such explorations into instructive communication could have only begun following a major rise in *trust* within the community. As the literature clearly shows (Knight 2008b; Tomasello 1999), this was indeed the case. Importantly, the rise in trust was entangled with all the different developments in social co-operation, and with the stabilization of the more advanced systems of experiential-mimetic communication. Receivers gradually learned, for example, in regular events of pointing and mimesis, that they could trust the senders for their experiential judgement. Time and again, they heard a call that referred to something, looked at the direction of the pointing—and there it was, within their experiential range.

Trust, however, could not be enough. Innovative exploration is motivated by necessity, and I would like to suggest two types of necessity that may have pushed interlocutors across the Rubicon. First, at the practical level, interlocutors would be forced to experiment with instructive communication under a condition that I would like to call *epistemic dependency*: in such conditions, one individual, A, experiences something that calls for action, but he or she cannot act on the basis of the experience; another individual, B, is in a position to act, but he or she does not experience the thing that actually calls for action; and the survival of *both* depends on A's capacity to get B to do what is required. The challenge of epistemic dependency can only be met if A and B manage to engage in exploratory instructive communication. In such states of affairs, the exploratory events would essentially be attempts to get the others to do things outside of their here-and-now: The first prototypes of orders and requests. As Bickerton (2007) suggests, for example, individuals had to be able to provide information to the others about resources found on the way.[7] Second, at the social level, a new type of necessity may have emerged with the full stabilization of the sophisticated divisions of labour of pre-linguistic societies. The divisions of labour changed the overall makeup of life in two complementary ways: on the one hand, individuals came to depend much more on the performance of others. Gatherers, hunters, tool-makers, cooks, fire experts, parents, and alloparents—all of them depended for their survival on the others doing their part. On the other hand, the divisions of labour must have *widened* the experiential gaps between different professional sub-groups. Members of different sub-groups developed different ways of looking at the world, different interpretations of the same scenery, different understanding of what needs to be done, and how. This must have threatened the sense of shared experience that provided the basis for group identity at the societal level—and thus threatened the very basis of co-operation and trust. In such a state of affairs, there would be a shared interest in any way of communication that could give people a sense of the experiences of the others. This was probably already done, before language, with ritual, dance, and mimicry—but these, advanced as they may be, are still modes of experiential communication. They only convey what they can present to the audience's senses. The innovative explorations into instructive communication, added as another layer on top of the existing experiential systems, could thus be first attempts to add to the *story* meanings that could not be presented.

Three points, then, are crucial: first, when we look at things this way, it becomes evident that both the necessity and the set of capacities that brought the explorations about could only have emerged *after* the full stabilization of mimetic communication and everything that it allowed for (see Zlatev, Chapter 18). Humans had to reach the limits of experiential communication, and build communities complex enough, dependent enough on communication, and sophisticated enough in terms of collective innovation (Dor and Jablonka, Chapter 2) to begin the exploratory search for means of communication that could bridge the experiential gaps between the communities' members. This, in line with everything else in this volume, explains the apparent fact that the apes never invented a language for themselves in the wild. Second, the above definition of the moment of origin requires nothing beyond what we already know about pre-linguistic societies and their members, no additional stipulations at the social, cultural, behavioural, communicative, cognitive, or genetic level. The new exploratory function could be performed with the old tools, by individuals accommodated to experiential-mimetic communication, but nothing more than that. What this means is that at the very beginning, there was nothing visibly or auditorily different about the exploratory events. This, as such, seems to be a very welcome result: other things being equal, a gradualist account of evolutionary

---

[7] See Marwick (2003) for an analysis of the changes in distances of raw material transportation as an index to the capacity of early hominid groups to pool information about the environment.

change is always preferable to stipulations of abrupt saltations. Third, the fact that we identify the origin of language with the emergence of the revolutionary function of instructive communication, not with the emergence of language as a system, allows for a new dynamic hypothesis concerning the entire evolutionary development of language: throughout the entire process, *the function itself served as the driving force*. Language as an autonomous system gradually emerged in an iterative collective effort to maximize the efficiency of instructive communication. As Arthur (2007: 274) shows with respect to modern technologies, this is exactly how technology very often evolves:

Invention is a process of linking some purpose or need with an effect that can be exploited to satisfy it. It may begin with a purpose or need for which existing methods are not satisfactory; this forces the seeking of a new principle (the idea of an effect in action). Or it may begin with a phenomenon or effect itself—usually a freshly discovered one—for which some associated principle of use suggests itself. Either way, translating this base principle into physical reality requires the creation of suitable working parts and supporting technologies. These raise their own challenges or problems, the solution of which may raise further challenges. As a result, invention is a recursive process: it repeats until each challenge or problem (and subproblem, and sub-subproblem) resolves itself into one that can be physically dealt with.

In the remainder of this chapter, then, I would like to present a skeletal narrative of the evolution of language as a process of technological evolution, the way it is described above. Like all such narratives, what I attempt to suggest here is a speculation: we will never know what actually happened. My goal, however, is just to demonstrate how the constant pressure for higher levels of success in events of instructive communication could have isolated language, in a gradual manner, from everything else around it, and how it could have dragged human societies, human cognitions (and emotions), and human genes, into a co-evolutionary spiral that brought us to where we are now.

9.6 How the instructive function could push language to autonomy

Let us, then, begin our journey with a group of hominins, co-operative, and trusting to a sufficient degree, efficiently using experiential-mimetic communication, who manage to stabilize their first exploratory attempts, and are now using a small number of signs—still holistic and analogue, no different from the ways they sound and look in their regular, experiential usage—to instruct each other's imaginations.[8] In the process of the stabilization of the new function, the lives of our

---

[8] As opposed to the suggestions made by Arbib (2002, 2005) and Wray (1998, 2002), and in line with the critiques of Tallerman (2007, 2008), Bickerton (2003), and Hurford (2011), I do not see how these holistic and analogue signals could be long and complex enough to allow for their fractionation, later on, into morphemes. The entire point of my proposed narrative is that the inventors of language began with a set of signals that stabilized for the purposes of experiential-mimetic communication, within the here and now of the communication event, and these would not need to be multisyllabic in the first place. For the same reason, the signals would not need to be phonetic, and could not be arbitrary.

innovative individuals would begin to change in a revolutionary way: their epistemic reach would begin to expand beyond their own experiential envelope. More and more elements of the world would penetrate their worlds from the outside: things they did not experience by themselves, but were told about. If there ever was a Copernican revolution in the history of humankind, this was it: almost all the animals on the planet experience; apes know how to follow the experiences of the others in order to learn about the world; pre-linguistic hominins learned how to direct the experiences of the others, and let the others direct theirs—but with language, hominins could finally begin to experience *for the others*, and let others experience *for them*.

This epistemic revolution would not just be extremely useful in terms of the entire set of challenges, both practical and social, facing the innovators' communities: it would begin to change the very essence of social and communicative life, with new levels of information exchange and co-operation, new types of opportunities for coalition formation and social struggle, new social relationships, identities and roles, new communicative stances, even a new set of social emotions (and new ways to manipulate them): *truth-related* emotions. As we show in Jablonka et al. (2012), experiential communication is founded on the interlocutor's capacity to verify the communicated meaning at the time of the communication event. Instructive communication, on the other hand, brings with it a totally new question, the question of truth and falsity: is the communicator *right*? Because of this, instructive exchanges would probably be accompanied, from the very beginning, by new feelings of suspicion and doubt, certainty and belief.

All this would obviously develop very slowly, but from very early on, it would present the innovative developers with three novel challenges. First, to increase the efficiency of their emerging technology, they would have to sophisticate their instructions for imagination in terms of their *meanings* (their signifieds). This would provide the impetus for the further invention and mutual identification of additional signs, the gradual *dissection* of experiences already mutually identified into more discrete components (each of which would receive its own sign), and the gradual categorization of mutually identified experiences into general types. Importantly, these processes would not be required in experiential-mimetic communication, where the entire goal is to direct the attention of the interlocutors to something they could then perceive by themselves. For instructive communication, however, it would be vital: every advancement would provide speakers and interlocutors with more precise tools to work with. It stands to reason, then, that following the language's initial stabilization, speakers would begin to spend more collective energy on the ongoing process of experiential mutual identification, dissection, and categorization. More and more types of experiences would be isolated from the continuum of private experience, and highlighted by social agreement. Importantly, certain domains of experience, that were never of interest for experiential communication,

would enter the realm of communication for the first time. In experiential communication, for example, the physical terrain is always given as part of the context.
Everything in it can be pointed at. To instruct the interlocutors' imagination in a way
that would help them find a place they have never been to, on the other hand,
requires a project of classification, eventually the creation of a new semantic field.
Gradually, then, the symbolic landscape would begin to emerge and develop.

Second, the first exploratory attempts would begin to change the dynamics of
communicative interactions. A strategy that allows its users, for example, to let the
others know that there is a certain entity, out of sight, in a certain direction, is bound
to produce communicative events in which the interlocutors express disagreement
about the right direction to look at, signal their understanding or confusion, or
actually try to ask (in the most rudimentary way, with combinations of gestures,
pointings, and signs): is it here or there? Is it this or that?

Third, instructive success would depend not just on the mutual identification of
experiences, and the development of new ways of communicating, but also on the
mutual identification of the *vocalizations* (and/or gestures) associated with them. On
the analogue continuum of experiential communication (both at the mimetic and the
pre-mimetic level), vocalic and emotional variability between individuals plays a
central part in the exchange. It is functional. The instructive strategy, however, would
require speakers and listeners to abstract away from all this (very partially in the
beginning, and then very gradually), and learn to produce and identify the *same*
vocalizations or gestures across the continuum. In this state of affairs, every change in
the arsenal of vocalization and gestures that would produce higher levels of *perceptual distinctiveness* would be adopted (to the extent that it could be repeated and
learned), and the small changes would eventually accumulate to produce a categorical and combinatorial phonetic system (Zuidema and de Boer 2009). Zuidema and
de Boer define perceptual distinctiveness in terms of the probability of *confusion*,
which captures the collective nature of the proposed process. Interestingly, they show
that the process requires a certain significant level of noise. When noise is very low,
the signals remain holistic regardless of any small changes that occur in their
production. This seems to capture a crucial point: throughout the entire process,
the exploratory attempts to implement the instructive strategy would be embedded
within a social world already suffused with experiential-mimetic communication,
where small changes in production are either immaterial, or actually functional for
communication. To raise their levels of success in instructive communication, our
speaker would have to *isolate* their emergent phonetic system from within the
continuum of experiential vocalization. What this means, if the premises are
accepted, is that language would gradually begin to *sound* differently. *Phonetics*
would gradually emerge.

The same thing, then, would begin to happen at all three levels: the specific
function of instructive communication would force speakers gradually to isolate

language from everything else that was already part of their experiential worlds. Their experiences of linguistic sound would be gradually demarcated from their experiences of experiential vocalizations; their experiences of linguistic communication would gradually be demarcated from their experiences of experiential communication (mimetic and pre-mimetic); and the socially constructed worldview of their symbolic landscape would gradually demarcate itself, in their minds, from their worlds of private (and collective) experiencing. Language would be making its first steps towards autonomy.

At some moment, it stands to reason that innovative speakers would begin to experiment with the *concatenation* of sounds into longer and longer strings. Some of the literature (e.g. Jackendoff 1999; Bickerton 2009) takes this to be a rather trivial development, still far away from the emergence of combinatorial syntax. Looked at from the point of view of the instructive strategy, however, it actually reveals itself as a revolutionary change, in two complementary ways. First, the speakers experimenting with concatenation would actually be presenting their interlocutors with a radically new challenge: they would no longer just be required to bring up from their memories clusters of experiences that were associated with mutually identified sounds. They would be asked to imagine the experiences associated with the sounds, and then *calculate the intersection* between them: concentrate on chasing-experiences, and on rabbit-experiences, and then calculate the experience of rabbit-chasing. This would be revolutionary for many different reasons, but most importantly because, to the extent that it worked, it would allow for communication about the intersected cluster of experiences (the cluster of rabbit-chasing) *without* the prior mutual identification of the cluster itself. The members of the language community could from now on communicate not just about the experiences they mutually identified, but also about different combinations of these experiences. (Which means, among other things, that they could communicate about entities that they themselves would build up, in their imaginations, from pieces of experiences. The cultural consequences would be enormous.) All this would thus imply a great leap forward in the expressive power of the technology: the function from the number of signs to the number of messages, which was up to now a linear one, would turn into an exponential function, and this would imply much higher dividends on the mutual identification of new signs. With time, as each sign would come to be concatenated, again and again, only with certain signs but not with others, a network of *semantic* connections between signs would begin to emerge. Very gradually, the socially constructed worldview of the symbolic landscape, which up to now included sets of isolated experiences, would begin to turn into a categorized system.

Second, concatenation implies *linearization*. Speakers would have to pronounce their signs one after the other, which would immediately allocate dividends to those who could produce longer strings (while maintaining the clarity and coherence of their instructions) and do it *faster*. With the rise in speed, as signs would come to be pronounced closer and closer together, phonological relations at the utterance level could begin to emerge, to allow for the swift move along the string of sounds. The listeners, on their side, would have to find ways to interpret the longer strings, calculate the intersections between larger sets of experiences, and also do it faster, to keep pace with the speakers. The emergence of concatenation, then, which would only become functional with the invention of the instructive strategy, would gradually force the emergence of *internal complexity* in the evolving technology. From the symbolic landscape and the phonetic system that had already begun to evolve, semantic and phonological structures would begin to emerge.

Every small improvement in all of the above, that could be mutually identified by both speakers and listeners, would enhance the overall efficiency of the technology. From a certain moment, however, new problems would begin to appear, among them new types of *miscommunication*. The speakers would be gradually producing longer and longer utterances, and these, for the interlocutors, would be more and more difficult to interpret. They would be increasingly *ambiguous*: the signs could be re-arranged in different ways to produce different messages, and thus different inter-pretations. And they would be increasingly *opaque*: the signs would still be mutually identified as such, but the intersections, growing in complexity, would not. This, together with other problems, would gradually require a collective effort of a new type—the stabilization of sets of mutually identified, normative rules to regulate the actual process of linguistic communication. This would be the beginning of the *protocol*. Speakers, in their constant attempts to understand and be understood, would begin to explore different options: norms of *linear order*, for example, *adjacency* and *iconicity*. For Bickerton (2009), this would not yet take language beyond the 'lawless' combination of signs. 'Lawful' combinations would have to wait for the emergence of hierarchical phrase structure. From the point of view developed here, however, which thinks about the law in social terms, such innovations would allow for the first genuine examples of lawful combinations. They would begin to reduce the levels of misinterpretation, and thus spark a new dynamic of collective explor-ation and stabilization of exceedingly *formalized* variations on the topic of the normative regulation of linguistic communication (where the notion of formalization is, again, taken in its social sense, as the collective stabilization of standard forms for communication). This dynamic still manifests itself today in the process of gram-maticalization (Heine and Kuteva 2002, 2007).

How all this brought about the grammatical systems of modern languages depends, of course, on the way one thinks about these systems. In terms of the constructionist perspective (Goldberg 2006; Croft 2001), where grammar is analysed as an inventory of form–meaning pairs of different sizes and shapes, nothing seems to be required beyond the further cultural invention (and then iterated learning and further development) of more sophisticated, mutually identified forms for instructive communication, through grammaticalization, construction, categorization, and other such processes. This, of course, is Tomasello's (2003a) view, and it seems to be supported by current computer simulations (Smith et al. 2003; Steels 2012; Steels, Chapter 24). If one thinks in terms of the generative perspective, the dynamic would involve a more serious change at the genetic level, maybe the exaptation of capacities from other cognitive domains, such as vocal control or spatial reasoning (Fitch 2011a). Whether such exaptation was indeed required is an open question, but it goes without saying, to the extent that we accept the general premises of evolutionary-development biology (Dor and Jablonka 2012; Dor and Jablonka, Chapter 2), that each and every step in the cultural development of the technology added to challenge facing individual speakers, changed developmental pathways in language acquiring children, exposed new levels of hidden genetic variability between individuals, and, to the extent that the pressure for more efficient instructive communication remained intense, drove a process of genetic accommodation, which resulted in speakers more adapted to the technology.

Within this functionally driven conception of the origin and evolution of language, moreover, the fact the languages of the world today manifest the complex typological patterns of variability and similarity that they do (Evans and Levinson 2009; Levinson and Evans 2010) emerges as a natural outcome. All languages are socially constructed technologies for the instruction of imagination, but the actual dynamics of exploration and stabilization in each and every language could be as variable as their communities, their histories, their particular communicative needs, their collective capacities, and the private experiential worlds of their speakers. Some of the technological problems must have appeared in all languages: it is impossible to develop concatenation without eventually confronting the problem of ambiguity. Other problems were probably more variably distributed. By the same token, many of the more fundamental solutions emerged in language after language—not necessarily for the same problems—whereas other solutions were only developed here and there.

9.7 Conclusion

The characterization of language as a socially constructed technology, dedicated to the bridging of the experiential gaps between its users through the instruction of imagination, allows for a new conception of its evolution—as a process sparked by first exploratory attempts to achieve the instruction of imagination with the old tools of experiential-mimetic communication, and then pushed forward by the constant need to raise the levels of instructive success. The first explorations could only begin with the full stabilization of the entire set of social, cultural, and communicative deployments of pre-linguistic human societies, most importantly the systematic collective capacity for experiential mutual identification. The gradual stabilization of the instructive strategy, and the fact that it opened totally new horizons for human societies, dictated a constant flow of innovative changes and developments, in the properties of the old tools themselves, in the communicative environment, and in the cognitive and emotional lives of individuals. Some of the changes, most importantly the emergence of concatenation, paved the way towards technological revolutions, which in their turn dictated entire sets of new gradual dynamics on all fronts. Technological problems that appeared on the way required mutually identified solutions, and drove the development of sets of normative rules for the regulation of instructive communication. Importantly, this functionally driven narration implies a high level of *developmental determinism* along the entire process, and for me, this is a welcome result: if we agree to position the foundational function of language at the very beginning of the story, and then let languages and speakers evolve to fulfil this function at higher and higher levels of success, we find that much of the way languages are today was already in the cards at the moment of origin.

Part III

Apes and People, Past and Present

10

Chimpanzee grooming gestures and sounds: what might they tell us about how language evolved?

SIMONE PIKA

> Language is a tool. We use it to do things.
>
> (Bates 1976: 1)

10.1 Introduction

Human language depends crucially on linguistic symbols—which are, in their essence, individually learned and intersubjectively shared social conventions (Pika et al. 2005a). The ability to speak, unprecedented elsewhere in the biological world, has often been used to define what it means to be human. Language's origin has puzzled scientists for centuries (Condillac 1746; Darwin 1871; Diderot 1904 [1751]; McNeill 2012).

In the 19th century, the Société de Linguistique de Paris (1865) and the Philological Society of London (1873) instituted a ban on discussions about the evolution of language that lasted for more than a century. Papers on language origins became respectable once again in the middle of the 20th century, when anthropologists, palaeontologists, primatologists, and linguists began working together on this topic. One of the first outcomes of these interdisciplinary exchanges was a volume entitled *Language Origins* (Wescott et al. 1974), which suggested that the evolutionary precursors of language are more likely to be found in the gestural rather than in the vocal domain of our ape-like ancestors. Since then, a considerable amount of research attention has focused on the gestural abilities of our closest living relatives.

In this chapter, I will provide an overview of the current state of the art with particular reference to features critical to human language such as intentionality, flexibility, and acquisition. I will then discuss my recent work on communicative signalling of chimpanzees (*Pan troglodytes*) in the wild during grooming. Grooming is a distinct behavioural context that (i) permeates virtually every aspect of chimpanzee social life (Goodall 1986); (ii) represents the prime medium for servicing and maintaining relationships; and (iii) is a prolific medium for the development of highly sophisticated gestures (Pika 2009). Dunbar (1993, 1996b)[1] even argues that grooming represents the evolutionary precursor of speech.

10.2 State of the art

Although the gestural domain has long been neglected by comparative researchers, in 1935, a Russian psychologist, Ladygina-Kohts (1935), provided the first detailed comparison between the expressive behaviour of a juvenile chimpanzee and a human child. Ladygina-Kohts made two crucial observations that are important to this chapter: (1) human children go through a gestural phase before they use their first spoken words; and (2) the initial language of the human child incorporates gestures and facial expressions quite similar to those of the chimpanzee.

Joni the chimpanzee, for instance, produced gestures such as EXTENDING ONE HAND FORWARD[2] as a sign of request; EXTENDING BOTH HANDS as an expression of enhanced request or entreaty often accompanied by groaning and even crying sounds; EXTENDING ONE HAND and POINTING at something; and SHAKING his HEAD or TURNING his FACE away from something to reject unwelcome food (Ladygina-Kohts 1935). Similarly, when Ladygina-Kohts' nine-month-old son, Roody, wanted to change his position from lying to sitting, he EXTENDED his HANDS FORWARD, BENT his BACK, and made SHAKING movements with his HANDS. When he wanted to get an object that was out of his reach, he BENT his HEAD and his entire BODY in that direction and used his index finger to POINT at the object, 'groaning' intensely. To reject unpleasant food, Roody TURNED his HEAD to the side, SHOOK his HEAD, and COVERED his FACE with his hands.

Turning to comprehension, Ladygina-Kohts observed that Joni understood when she used a POINTING gesture to communicate a distinct direction she wanted him to go. In addition, Joni recognized referential relationships between gestures and a third entity such as an object. Ladygina-Kohts (1935: 195) wrote:

Once, Joni was near the ceiling of the cage, and there was a mug from which he usually drank. I needed this mug and said, 'Joni, give me the mug!' But, he did not understand what I wanted and only looked attentively at me and around him. Then, I took another mug in my hand; Joni understood immediately, took the first mug, and handed it to me.

---

[1] Although Dunbar suggested that precursors of human speech evolved in the context of grooming, he strongly supports the hypothesis that speech originated in vocalizations rather than in gestures.

[2] Gestures and grooming sounds will be depicted in SMALL CAPITALS from this point on.

This study therefore suggested that gestural production/comprehension is very similar in chimpanzees and pre-linguistic human children. In addition, the study noted the use of the POINTING gesture, an observation that became significant only in light of subsequent findings showing that POINTING marks a pivotal change in the communicative competence of human infants and is thought to be the foundation on which symbolically mediated conversation is then built (Bates et al. 1979; Bruner 1975a). Since chimpanzees and other great ape species in the wild (but see Vea and Sabater-Pi 1998) do not use POINTING gestures to communicate with conspecifics (Goodall 1986; Nishida et al. 1999), Ladygina-Kohts' study provided the first evidence that chimpanzees are able to learn gestures that are not triggered as their communicative abilities develop naturally.

In the 1940s, Hoyt (1941) raised a gorilla (*Gorilla gorilla*) orphan, Toto, in her own home from infancy to the age of nine years. She also described how Toto used the POINTING gesture to request desired food and drinks (see also Yerkes 1943). However, Toto also performed this and other gestures in a hiding game, in which she would hide keys under her arm, for instance, and would then POINT to and show parts of her body where the keys were *not* hidden; for example POINTING to her elbow, OPENING both HANDS, or SHOWING the soles of her FEET. Thus, these early observations suggested that a gorilla was able to use a single distinct gesture intentionally and flexibly across different contexts and to communicate different messages.

Since attempts to teach human speech to chimpanzees had failed (Hayes 1951; Kellog and Kellog 1933), Gardner and Gardner (1969; see also Gardner et al. 1989) investigated gestural production and comprehension of chimpanzees based on *signs* used in American Sign Language. They successfully taught a female chimpanzee, Washoe, over 300 manual *signs* and provided the first evidence that chimpanzees have a very high degree of manual flexibility and are able to use symbols to communicate. Washoe was not only able to use distinct, single gestures to meaningfully communicate with her caretakers and other language-trained chimpanzees, she was also able to combine them in spontaneous sequences (Fouts 1989; Fouts 1974). This approach was equally successful with a gorilla, Koko (Patterson 1978), and an orang-utan, Chantek (Miles 1986, 1990). Furthermore, Premack and Premack (1972), Rumbaugh (1977), and Savage-Rumbaugh and colleagues (1986, 1993) demonstrated that chimpanzees and bonobos are able to use three-dimensional plastic pieces and two-dimensional geometric designs to represent words or ideas.

In addition, pioneers such as Schaller (1963, 1964), Van Lawick-Goodall (1968a, 1968b), van Hooff (1967, 1973), and Kummer (1968) studied and described the behaviour of some great ape and monkey species in natural interactions with their conspecifics. They created so-called ethograms, which consist of many of the communicative gestures that have been observed in subsequent studies in the wild and captivity and have inspired several generations of researchers to develop new questions and research domains (for a recent overview, see Pika and Liebal 2012a).

Plooij (1978, 1979) for instance, fascinated by the debate on chimpanzee 'language' (Gardner and Gardner 1969; Premack and Premack 1972; Rumbaugh et al. 1973), investigated whether any precursor of human language might be manifested under natural conditions. Setting out from the philosopher John Austin's distinction between perlocutionary and illocutionary acts, Plooij sought to apply Speech Act theory (Austin 1962) to the ontogeny of communication among chimpanzees in the Gombe Stream National Park, Tanzania. This theory centres around performative utterances, or performatives for short. The word 'performative' is derived from the verb perform with the noun action and indicates that the issuing of the utterance is the performing of an action. Since performatives and actions in general can be performed unintentionally or intentionally, Austin further differentiated between perlocutionary and illocutionary acts. Perlocutionary acts are defined as behaviours in which communication occurs only because the receiver is adept at interpreting the behaviour of the 'sender' (e.g. fear, excitement, curiosity, etc.). By contrast, illocutionary acts, being immaterial, cannot arise from the behaviour of any one individual impacting on another. Rather, illocutionary force presupposes joint attention and collusion between two or more minds as, together, they establish or negotiate a shared perspective on the world (Austin 1962; see also Bates et al. 1979; Wyman, Chapter 13). To exert illocutionary force is to secure a shift in perspective, irrespective of any subsequent causal (psychological, emotional, behavioural, etc.) effects. Based on this approach, Plooij (1978, 1979) suggested that, similar to human children, chimpanzees between approximately nine and twelve months of age undergo a developmental shift from perlocutionary to illocutionary acts. In addition, he argued that that they use highly sophisticated gestures—characterized by a flexible relationship between means and ends—for the purpose of attracting and redirecting attention. Means–ends dissociation suggests that individuals are able to use (i) synonymous signals/gestures to achieve a certain outcome/goal, and (ii) ambiguous gestures for different outcomes/goals (Pika and Liebal 2012b). For example, gestures such as TOUCHING and REACH OUT ARM are used by chimpanzee infants to communicate to their mothers that they want to be picked up and thus carry the same message (Smith 1965).[3] In contrast, the gesture ARM RAISE can be used to solicit grooming but also to calm and appease an anxious conspecific (Plooij 1979); it thus communicates and embodies different messages in different contexts. Plooij (1978: 127) remarked: 'This indicates the ability to understand and to produce new meanings,

[3] Smith (1965) introduced three distinct concepts to animal signalling: message, meaning, and context. The message of a signal may refer, among other things, to a generalized anxiety or an emotional state such as aggression or fear and does not necessarily imply the intention of a sender to communicate. The meaning is identified as the response selected by the recipient from all of the responses open to it, and the context refers to anything that can be thought of as accompanying a signal.

and this suggests openness, which is one of the most characteristic design features of human language.'

Subsequently, Tomasello, Call, Liebal, and Pika continued and expanded this cognitive approach to gestural signalling of all great ape species along with one species of small ape (for an overview see Call and Tomasello 2007). These studies were carried out over more than a decade and resulted in the first comprehensive database on ape gestural abilities and underlying cognitive complexity.

We showed that apes:

- use open-ended, multifaceted gestural repertoires, including *species-distinctive* and *species-indistinctive* gestures, whose meaning and use must be learned (Call and Tomasello 2007; Pika et al. 2003);
- develop group-specific gestural traditions (Pika et al. 2003, 2005b), implying underlying social learning processes involved; and
- utilize gestures as flexibly produced intentional strategies, based on key characteristics drawn from studies of intentional communication in human children. These include: (i) recipient specificity; (ii) persistence to the goal (e.g. repetition of a gesture or use of a different one until the goal has been achieved); (iii) means–ends dissociation; and (iv) adjustment to audience effects, for example by (a) adapting the signal category to the attentional state of the recipient and/or (b) moving in the recipient's visual field before producing a gesture (Call and Tomasello 2007; Liebal et al. 2004a, 2004b; Pika et al. 2005a, 2005b).

Tomasello (2008: 55) has emphasized the impact of these findings on scenarios of language evolution:

In all, I personally do not see how anyone can doubt that ape gestures—in all of their flexibility and sensitivity to the attention of the other—and not ape vocalizations—in all of their inflexibility and ignoring of others—are the original font from which the richness and complexities of human communication and language have flowed.

Surprisingly, although the first studies on gestural behaviour in apes were carried out in their natural environments (Fossey 1983; Goodall 1986; Schaller 1963), gestural research over the last two decades has been biased towards investigations of captive apes (e.g. Call and Tomasello 2007; Cartmill and Byrne 2007; Pollick and de Waal 2007; Schneider et al. 2012; Tanner 2004). Recently, researchers have realized that to acquire a full understanding of ape gestural abilities, we must study them in their natural environments under active selection pressures (e.g. Pika and Mitani 2006; see also Boesch 2007). To date, we still lack systematic investigations on the gestural skills of bonobos and orang-utans in their natural environments. Concerning gorillas, however, Parnell and Buchanan-Smith (2001) reported that silverbacks at *Mbeli Bai*, Nouabalé-Ndoki National Park, Republic of Congo, use SPLASH DISPLAYS to intimidate potential rivals. Fay (1989) observed that female gorillas from several different groups in Southwestern Central African Republic HAND-CLAP when they are nervous and 'wish' to alert the silverback to danger. The most comprehensive study of gorilla gestural complexity to date is by Genty and colleagues (Genty et al. 2009), who observed wild gorillas at *Mbeli Bai*, Nouabalé-Ndoki National Park, Republic of Congo, with a special emphasis on intentionality and underlying learning processes. They confirmed that, like captive gorillas (Pika et al. 2003), those in the wild use gestures intentionally and flexibly across a range of contexts, adjusting them to the attentional states of recipients. Surprisingly, however, and contrary to several studies emphasizing gorillas' sophisticated manual gestural skills (Byrne and Tanner 2006; Patterson 1978; Pika et al. 2003), Genty and colleagues (2009) suggested that gorillas' impressive gestural performance can be explained simply as a consequence of their very large innate repertoire of species-specific signals. In a subsequent project, the same research group came to the same conclusion for chimpanzee gestural production, based on data on the gestural behaviour of chimpanzees from the *Sonso* community, Budongo Forest Reserve, Uganda, and behavioural ethograms of the chimpanzee populations at Gombe and Mahale (Goodall 1986; Nishida et al. 1999). Therefore, according to this view (Genty et al. 2009; Hobaiter and Byrne 2011), gestural production is not so different from the production of displays and *fixed action patterns* found in many other animal species (e.g. Lorenz 1943; Tinbergen 1959; van Hooff 1967), except that they can be used also as intentional strategies.

In my view, it is fruitless to dwell on the outdated and naïve question of whether individuals acquire all or most of their characteristic behaviour from *nature* or *nurture* (Ridley 2003; Laland and Janik 2006). Studies of both captive and wild-living primates have shown that many species seem equipped to communicate via truly learned gestural signals (see Figure 10.1 for an idiosyncratic gesture observed by a chimpanzee from the *Ngogo* community, Kibale National Park, Uganda). To the extent that the evidence for this is convincing, contemporary studies should focus on why, under conditions in the wild, these same animals mainly choose to rely on large, yet still relatively limited, gesture sets without creatively expanding on them.

In addition, if we apply similar methods and describe the gestural repertoires of pre-linguistic children, we would also come up with a distinct species-typical set of frequently used movements showing considerable commonality of gesture across the whole family of great apes (gestures such as ARM RAISE, GRAB, POKE, MOVE OBJECT, SHAKE, TAP, TOUCH, etc.). Like its chimpanzee counterpart, when a human infant is within reaching distance of its mother, it will use the most obvious and least costly movement to communicate: a movement of the hand(s) and arm(s) toward the mother that results in contact—a TOUCH. However, since human infants develop much more slowly than great ape infants and have lost the ability to cling, they might RAISE their ARMS to be picked up while chimpanzee infants will instead REACH OUT or TOUCH their mother so that she lowers her back and they can cling and climb up. These differences in gestural expressions for the same function have been shaped through

FIGURE 10.1 Idiosyncratic gesture used by a single adult male (second), Dolphy, over a period of five consecutive years at *Ngogo*, Kibale National Park, Uganda. © K. Langergraber

phylogenetic and ontogenetic factors to enable the most efficient and least costly communication transfer. In addition, they are directly linked to:

(i) anatomical features and movement constraints of a given species;
(ii) the communicative scenario (e.g. short-distance communication versus long-term communication, communicative contexts); and
(iii) *recipient-affordances* (location, posture, and distance to recipient; attentional propensity of recipient).

Interestingly, Wilkinson and colleagues (2012) recently introduced a new tool to the scientific study of gestural communication and language evolution by combining methods of comparative research with a micro-analytic approach in the form of conversation analysis (ten Have 2007; see Enfield and Sidnell, Chapter 8). By analysing active sharing episodes of chimpanzees from the *Ngogo* community, Kibale National Park, Uganda, with a particular focus on gestures used to request meat, they describe the interactive process by which requests may not be acceded to and how a further request may then be produced. This method of examining chimpanzee communicative interactions sheds new light on (i) how particular gestural signals emerged within particular contexts; and (ii) how, at the same time, that signalling behaviour might itself constitute a context which others will subsequently act within (compare Heritage 1989).

10.3 Communicative signalling during grooming

Since 2005, I have been investigating communicative signalling of chimpanzees at the *Ngogo* community, Kibale National Park, Uganda (for details of the study area see Butynski 1990; Struhsacker 1997), with a special focus on cognitive components required for language to evolve. One of the crucial behavioural contexts in which chimpanzees mainly rely on short-distance signals, such as gestures and low-amplitude sounds, is the grooming context. Grooming is defined as brushing and picking through the fur with fingers, mouth, and toes (Van Lawick-Goodall 1968a) and can vary from self-grooming to dyadic interactions and grooming chains involving several individuals (Goodall 1986). Although grooming has received much research attention in chimpanzees (e.g. Mitani and Amsler 2003; Nakamura 2000; Sugiyama 1988; Watts 2000) and other nonhuman primate species in relation to its function (e.g. Barrett and Henzi 2001; Dunbar 1991; Keverne et al. 1989; Seyfarth and Cheney 1984; Wittig et al. 2008), relatively little is known about the communicative signals involved or their underlying cognitive complexity.

10.3.1 *Solicitation of grooming and response*
Intriguingly, chimpanzees use a distinct set of behaviours to solicit grooming. These range from simply approaching and starting to groom to using gestures, combinations of two gestures, and multi-modal signals (see Table 10.1).

A chimpanzee soliciting grooming usually either (i) stands or sits in front of his chosen partner and uses gestures such as DIRECTED SCRATCHES or PRESENTS those PARTS of his BODY that he cannot easily access himself; or (ii) starts scratching in the distance while waiting for a possible grooming partner to approach. In response to such solicitations, the recipient responds in one of four ways: by grooming, by counter soliciting through gesturing himself, by ignoring the request, or by moving away.

10.3.2 *Grooming gestures*
The chimpanzees from the *Ngogo* community use an impressive set of gestures during grooming sessions (see Table 10.1). These gestures convey different messages

TABLE 10.1. **Signals used during grooming**

Signal category	Functional category	Signal description
Gestures	*Solicitation gestures*	DIRECTED SCRATCH: An individual makes a relatively loud and exaggerated scratching movement on a part of his body. EMBRACE HALF: An individual wraps one arm around the passing or nearby recipient and maintains physical contact. PRESENT BODY PART: An individual offers a body part such as the arm, armpit, back, genital region, leg, or rump to the recipient. REACH ARM: An individual extends the outstretched arm in the direction of the recipient. RAISE ARM: An individual lifts the outstretched arm in the air more or less perpendicular to the ground.
	Negotiation gestures	DIRECTED SCRATCH: See detailed description above. PRESENT BODY PART: See detailed description above.
	Directional gestures	HAND ON: An individual puts the hand on a body part of the recipient and leaves it there for more than two seconds. LIFT: An individual touches a body part of the recipient to apply a lifting, but short and mechanically ineffective, movement. NUDGE: An individual taps lightly, sometimes repetitively, upon a body part of another animal with the palm(s) or knuckle(s). PULL: An individual applies subtle pressure against the recipient's body with a short, mechanically ineffective movement of the hands towards himself. PUSH: An individual applies subtle pressure against the recipient's body with a short, mechanically ineffective movement of the hands away from himself. TOUCH: An individual puts the hand gently and briefly ($\leq$ two seconds) on any body part of the recipient.
	Referential gestures	DIRECTED SCRATCH: See detailed description above. PRESENT BODY PART: See detailed description above.
Sounds		LIP-BOB: An individual opens and closes the mouth repeatedly with lips subtly touching while producing a soft round sound. LIP-SMACK: An individual opens and closes the mouth rapidly and repeatedly with lips touching and uses the tongue to produce a smacking sound. RASPBERRY: An individual produces a spluttering sound while pressing air and sometimes saliva through the lips. TEETH-CLACKING: An individual makes clicking sounds with the teeth by rapidly moving the upper and lower jaw against each other in small movements.

(continued)

TABLE 10.1. Continued

Signal category	Functional category	Signal description
Gesture combinations		DIRECTED SCRATCH on the PRESENTED BODY PART; PRESENT BODY PART and TOUCH a distinct spot; PRESENT BODY PART and LOOK AT it; REACH ARM and using a DIRECTED SCRATCH; RAISING ARM and using a DIRECTED SCRATCH.

and meanings in relation to the stage of the grooming session and the underlying function. They are used to (i) solicit a grooming session (e.g. EMBRACE HALF, REACH ARM, RAISE ARM); (ii) negotiate roles during a grooming session and keep the session going (e.g. DIRECTED SCRATCH, PRESENT BODY PART); (iii) direct the recipient, thereby gaining access to additional body areas (e.g. LIFT, NUDGE, PULL, TOUCH); and (iv) refer to distinct body parts to be groomed (e.g. DIRECTED SCRATCHES, Pika and Mitani 2006, 2009). Chimpanzees also use combinations of two gestures (e.g. PRESENT BODY PART and DIRECTED SCRATCH) as well as multi-modal combinations (e.g. RASPBERRY sound and DIRECTED SCRATCH) to reinforce the communicated message. In addition, recipients of these gestures understand the conveyed message and respond to it in appropriate ways, such as moving an extremity in the indicated direction after a directional TOUCH, or grooming the indicated spot after a DIRECTED SCRATCH (Pika and Mitani 2006, 2009).

In sum, chimpanzees use their gestures as highly flexible communicative strategies to intentionally influence the behaviour and mental states of recipients. Gestural usage during grooming thereby shows many parallel characteristics to human speech, including (i) intentionality; (ii) directionality; (iii) flexibility; (iv) reference; (v) negotiation of roles; and (vi) role reversal.

10.3.3 *Grooming sounds*

The chimpanzees of the *Ngogo* community utter four distinct sounds when grooming: LIP-BOBBING, LIP-SMACKING, RASPBERRY (also known as 'Bronx cheer', 'splutter': Hopkins et al. 2007; or 'sputtering': Nishida et al. 2004), and TEETH-CLACKING (for detailed descriptions see Table 10.1). The most interesting sound with regard to precursors of speech is the RASPBERRY sound. Although Nishida and colleagues (2004) suggested that RASPBERRY is only performed by individuals of low rank, additional data showed that this sound is used by individuals of all sex and rank classes and that there were variations based on individual preferences.

The RASPBERRY sound can be characterized by several unique features:

(i) it is common in chimpanzees living in captivity (Hopkins et al. 2007), but has been described as 'abnormal' (Walsh et al. 1982) and 'species-atypical' (Hopkins et al. 2007) behaviour;

(ii) it has so far only been observed as a frequent occurrence at *Ngogo* and not at any other well-studied chimpanzee communities, such as *Kanyawara* (Wrangham, personal communication), only 10 km north-west of *Ngogo*, or *Gombe* and *Mahale* in Tanzania (Nishida et al. 2004; but see, for orang-utans, Van Schaik et al. 2003);

(iii) is used in several contexts: in captivity it is performed during grooming or to attract the attention of a human caretaker or another chimpanzee (Hopkins et al. 2007; Russell et al. 2005); at *Ngogo* it is used at the beginning of or during a grooming session, but also (contrary to LIP-BOBBING, LIP-SMACKING, and TEETH-CLACKING) to solicit grooming; and

(iv) can be utilized as a multi-modal signal, in combination with gestures such as DIRECTED SCRATCHES.

The RASPBERRY sound therefore represents a unique and flexible signal, which is used in different contexts to convey different messages. Since its absence at *Kanyawara* cannot be explained in terms of ecological differences between the two study sites, the RASPBERRY sound may represent a socially transmitted and enhanced behaviour (Whiten et al. 1999). Furthermore, its production may involve a volitional component (Hopkins et al. 2007), and its usage in combination with gestures may therefore offer an evolutionary scenario explaining the shift from gestural symbols to voluntarily produced sounds and vocalizations.

10.4 Conclusion

Theories of language origins must take account of the relatively short time available for the evolution of this highly sophisticated behaviour—probably no more than 1.8 million years (Diller and Cann 2009). Regardless of which date we choose, the time available seems insufficient for the evolution of the entire cognitive apparatus required. I support an alternative perspective, according to which 'there is a great Borrowing going on, in which language is viewed as a parasitic system that builds its structures by raiding the software packages of prior or parallel cognitive capacities' (Bates et al. 1979: 6).

To pinpoint the cognitive structures on which language depends, most comparative studies have focused on vocal communication in nonhuman primates (for an overview, see Arbib et al. 2008). Unlike human linguistic signs, however, which are used to influence what others know, think, believe, or desire (Grice 1957), the vocalization types studied thus far do not intentionally provide conspecifics with information (Seyfarth and Cheney 2003; however, see recent studies by Crockford et al. 2012 and Schel et al. 2013 for likely cases of intentional vocalization).[4] For signals which are referential, intentional, and used to influence others' mental states, we must turn to the salient gestures and sounds that chimpanzees produce during grooming. They show many striking parallels to crucial features of human language and also fulfil one of its most important functions: 'Language is a tool. We use it to do things' (Bates 1976: 1).

10.5 Acknowledgements

I thank the Uganda Wildlife Authority, the Uganda National Council for Science and Technology and Makerere University for permission to work at the Makerere University Biological Field Station. I am grateful to A. Tumusiime, A. Twineomujuni, L. Ndagizi, G. Mbabazi, and A. Magoba for invaluable assistance in the field. I am indebted to J. C. Mitani and D. P. Watts, who encouraged me to study gestural behaviour of chimpanzees at the *Ngogo* community and shared their tremendous knowledge on chimpanzee behaviour and field skills as well as their data. A big thanks to K. Langergraber for the permission to work at *Ngogo* and for sharing his wonderful pictures with me, and to C. Rowney for constructive criticism and help with editing the chapter.

The research was supported by a Sofja Kovalevskaja Award of the Alexander von Humboldt Foundation.

---

[4] However, a recent study by Crockford and colleagues (2012) suggests that chimpanzees are able to intentionally produce and adjust a distinct alarm call, the 'alert hoo'. This is a relatively quiet call, used to communicate information to recipients in close proximity. These findings imply that nonhuman primate vocal complexity may have been underestimated and that future studies should focus in much greater detail on the cognitive complexity underlying low-amplitude calls used in short-distance communication.

11

Vocal communication and social awareness in chimpanzees and bonobos

ZANNA CLAY AND KLAUS ZUBERBÜHLER

11.1 Introduction

Part of what it means to be human is the capacity to understand and interact with others using language. For centuries, language has been a topic of intense scientific interest, yet how it might have evolved has remained relatively obscure. What is uncontested is that the capacity for language must have emerged from earlier forms of communication and cognition, but what exactly these forms were is the topic of much ongoing research. Language is based on capacities of representational thought, co-operation, social learning, culture, vocal tract control, and, perhaps most crucially, specialized social skills in recognizing, understanding, and manipulating the mental states of others. These different components may have their own and independent evolutionary histories, suggesting that a reasonable way of studying language evolution is to investigate the evolutionary origins of these components separately.

A core principle of Darwinian evolutionary theory is that complex traits evolve gradually, usually as elaborations of pre-existing simpler traits, rather than appearing suddenly and spontaneously. This principle is visible in the fossil record, but it is less evident in behavioural or mental capacities. One way of obtaining an understanding of behavioural and cognitive evolution is through the comparative approach. By exploring the cognitive and communicative abilities of our closest living relatives, the non-human primates, it is possible to make inferences about the likely capacities of extinct common ancestors. This is because the physiological apparatus responsible for cognitive capacities and motivational propensities is partially inherited. For this reason, the comparative approach is commonly invoked when studying the evolution of behavioural traits. For complex behaviours, such as language, it allows assessments about which components of language are uniquely human and which ones are phylogenetically older, having emerged earlier in the primate lineage.

In this chapter, we review recent research on non-human primate communication that is relevant for questions about the social origins of language, specifically, the interaction between social awareness and vocal production. One key problem is to know what inferences primates are able to make about their social world through hearing each other's vocalizations. Are signallers able to control, modify, and target their vocalizations depending on the nearby audience? What role does the social system play in the evolution of communication?

When addressing these points, our attention will be on our two closest living relatives, the chimpanzees and bonobos (*Pan troglodytes* and *P. paniscus*), by exploring the relation between their communication behaviour and underlying social awareness. Humans share a common ancestor with the *Panins* (bonobos and chimpanzees) around 7–8 million years ago (Won and Hey 2005; Langergraber et al. 2012). Bonobos and chimpanzees share a common ancestor around a million years ago, a time period that has been sufficient to evolve a number of considerable behavioural differences (Stanford 1998; Wrangham 1993; Hare and Tan 2011; Hare et al. 2012). Like all great apes, both species are typical forest dwellers, occupying dense forest habitats throughout the African rainforest belt. They live in large multi-male, multi-female fission-fusion groups with male philopatry (Boesch et al. 2002). As both are equally closely related to humans, models of human evolution and identification of uniquely human features, such as language, will necessarily require information from both species (e.g. de Waal 1997).

Here, our focus will be on experimental and observational work on communicative behaviour provided that it reveals something of the nature of underlying social cognition and awareness in these species. To date, ape communication has more thoroughly been studied in the gestural domain, partly on the grounds that individuals have more volitional control over their limbs than their vocal tracts, and partly due to an influential school of thought that locates the origins of human language in the gestural domain (Corballis 1999). As a result, research on ape vocal behaviour has not received much attention, and our goal here is to address this imbalance by highlighting recent advances in ape vocal research.

11.2 Evolutionary approach to social communication

Before exploring the relationship between social awareness and vocal communication in chimpanzees and bonobos, it is relevant to first briefly think about some theoretical approaches to social communication in animals.

One way of conceptualizing the evolution of social communication is to assume that animal signals have evolved as ritualized abbreviations of more basic behavioural or physiological processes. It may be less costly for an individual to advertise some of its behavioural propensities, rather than executing them directly, suggesting that natural selection will favour such ritualizations. A key variable in this process probably is the psychological predispositions of receivers, which will determine which signal types receivers are likely to attend to and remember (Guilford and Dawkins 1991).

It is interesting in this context that dishonest signals are relatively rare, at least in intra-species animal communication. One explanation for this finding is Zahavi and Zahavi's (1997) 'handicap principle'. According to this theory, receivers will only attend to signals that are physically difficult to produce and hard to fake by low-quality or poorly motivated individuals, something that is particularly important in competitive interactions.

Another explanation is that in some species, receivers and signallers know each other and often pursue shared goals, so that they gain little from deceiving each other. Primates and possibly other groups of animals can learn to ignore unreliable signallers (Cheney and Seyfarth 1988), suggesting that 'reputation' acts as a safeguard against dishonest signalling in groups where members know each other individually (Silk et al. 2000).

11.3 Vocal communication in chimpanzees and bonobos: a neglected field

Chimpanzees are one of the most researched non-human primates, both in the wild and in captivity (Goodall 1986; Tomasello and Herrmann 2010), and much of their behaviour, ecology, and cognition is now thoroughly described. It is therefore particularly perplexing that chimpanzee vocal communication has never really been thoroughly investigated, beyond qualitative descriptions (e.g. Goodall 1986; Mitani 1996). The evidence is even more limited for bonobos, the least understood of the great apes. Bonobos have largely remained in the shadow of their cousins, the chimpanzees, although studies exploring their social and cognitive behaviour are now starting to emerge (e.g. Hare and Tan 2011). Despite such efforts, bonobo communication, particularly in the vocal domain, is still extremely under-researched.

Compared to humans, non-human primates have less control of their vocal production and are unable to modify vocal output in the manner humans and some animals capable of vocal learning can do. Some scholars have thus taken the view that primate vocalizations are genetically hardwired, involuntary expressions of emotions, which lack flexibility, are not subject to learning and are broadcast indiscriminately without taking into account their audience (Lancaster 1975; Lieberman 1968, 1998). Ape vocal behaviour, in other words, has been judged to be cognitively uninteresting.

In contrast, primate gestures have been posited as more language-like and thus more relevant for investigations into how language has evolved. A key argument has been that ape gestures, unlike vocalizations, exhibit three essential features that characterize human language: learning, flexibility, and intention (Call and Tomasello 2007; Genty et al. 2009). Many ape gestures are used in a range of social contexts, often intentionally towards specific recipients and by taking into account their attention state (e.g. Call and Tomasello 2007). It has also been argued that gestures may be learned from others or even invented, although the evidence for these claims is controversial (Hobaiter and Byrne 2011). Nevertheless, it is nowadays widely argued that gestures, not vocalizations, are the evolutionary foundations of language (Arbib et al. 2008; Corballis 2002).

A growing body of research indicates that the traditional picture of vocal communication as cognitively uninteresting and of little relevance to capacities associated with language may be inaccurate. This is especially so when taking the perspective of the receiver. In various monkey species, recipients are able to use each other's vocal signals to make fairly complex assessments of what exactly the signaller has experienced, a finding that is somewhat at odds with the notion of hardwired, inflexible signalling. When taking the receiver's perspective, vocal communication shows great levels of sophistication and flexibility, beyond what has long been assumed (e.g. Seyfarth et al. 2010). If monkeys have such capacities, then it is very likely that chimpanzees and bonobos have them as well. Our basic question thus is how these two species express their social awareness during communication and how they use vocalizations to navigate their social worlds.

Another reason for the relative neglect of systematic empirical work on ape vocal behaviour has been of a mere technical nature. Both chimpanzee and bonobo vocalizations are highly graded, which makes them notoriously difficult to analyse. Gradation in an animal vocal system is usually defined in terms of the scaling of acoustic similarity between call types. A graded vocal system lies at one end of a continuum, with discretely organized call types at the other. Graded vocal repertoires have been identified in a number of primate species, including rhesus macaques (Rowell and Hinde 1962), Japanese macaques (Green 1975), red colobus monkeys (Marler 1970), chimpanzees (Marler 1976), and bonobos (de Waal 1988). In contrast, many forest monkey species have more discrete vocal systems, which enable researchers to classify calls more easily by ear, without complicated acoustic and statistical analysis techniques. Although more difficult to describe, graded signals have the potential to convey rich information, perhaps more so than discrete signals, provided there is a sufficiently tight relationship between signal structure and context (Marler 1977) and provided receivers are able to perceive acoustic differences among them, which they can then link to signal meaning (Hauser 1998).

While primate vocal systems are typically classified as either graded or discrete (e.g Evans and Marler 1995), recent evidence is now indicting that this assumed dichotomy may not be valid. For instance, there is now good evidence that even within vocal systems that have been interpreted as discrete, such as those of many forest guenons, there is considerable acoustic gradation within different call types and, in several cases, this has proven to convey relevant information for recipients (e.g. Ouattara et al. 2009a, 2009c).

Within the vocal systems of both chimpanzees and bonobos, extensive variation in gradation both within and between call types has been well documented. For instance, the chimpanzee 'waa-bark' is highly graded, whereas their laughter is a more discrete call type (Marler 1976). However, even for more discrete calls, such as laughter, it is likely that subtle gradation also exists, which can also be discriminated by receivers. In both ape species, gradation is particularly apparent in their screams and barks, which creates the potential for social information to be conveyed via subtle changes in acoustic structure. For instance, acoustically variable chimpanzee screams communicate an array of social information, including caller identity, the caller's social role in the fight and the intensity of attack (Slocombe and Zuberbühler 2007, 2009).

Although bonobo vocalizations are generally higher in pitch than chimpanzees' (e.g. Mitani and Gros-Louis 1995), there are numerous parallels between the two *Panins* in both acoustic form and contextual usage of calls. This is perhaps unsurprising considering their recent shared phylogenetic history (Won and Hey 2005). Chimpanzees have a fixed vocal repertoire consisting of around a dozen call types, mainly different variants of screams, hoots, barks, grunts, pants, and squeaks (Marler and Tenaza 1977; Slocombe and Zuberbühler 2010). The bonobo vocal repertoire has also been estimated to consist of a similar number of main call types, which include varieties of hoots, peeps, barks, grunts, pant laughs, pout moans, and screams (de Waal 1988). Most likely, these basic call types are not an accurate description of vocal capacity because there is much variation within each call category in both species (chimpanzees: Goodall 1968; bonobos: Bermejo and Omedes 1999; de Waal 1988). At the moment, no formal comparison has been made between the repertoires of the two species, although a number of homologies are clearly evident. In bonobos, for example, pant laughs, pout moans, low hoots, and 'wieew' barks showed considerable overlap with similar calls produced by chimpanzees in both their acoustic structure and contextual usage.

11.4 Long-distance communication in chimpanzee and bonobos

For long-distance communication, bonobo 'high hoot' calls show contextual similarity with chimpanzee 'pant-hoot' calls (Figure 11.1). Bonobos, like chimpanzees, use these vocalizations for long-distance communication with unseen individuals, as well as in response to food discovery and other relevant events or disturbances (de Waal 1988; Marler and Tenaza 1977; van Hooff 1973; Hohmann and Fruth 1994).

a. Bonobo high hoot

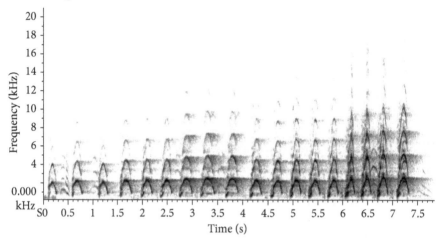

b. Chimpanzee pant-hoot

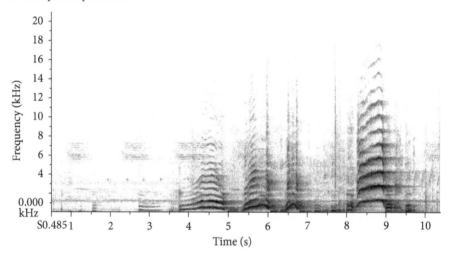

FIGURE 11.1 Spectrograms showing representative examples of bonobo high hoots and chimpanzee pant-hoots. These individually distinct and partially socially learned call types are used in long-distance communication in both species.

Studies of pant-hoots have dominated the early vocal research in chimpanzees (e.g. Mitani and Nishida 1993; Mitani and Gros-Louis 1996; Arcadi 1996; Marshall et al. 1999). The pant-hoot is a composite vocalization composed of four distinct phases: an introduction, build-up, climax, and downward phase. In the low-visibility, dense forest habitats in which most wild chimpanzees live, group members are often separated from each other over large distances when they travel and forage. Pant-hoots give individuals some control over their social environment, by communicating with group members that are out of sight. Pant-hoots are not given indiscriminately, but seem to be used in socially structured ways (e.g. Mitani and Nishida 1993). One line of evidence for this is that males, in both the wild and in captivity, have a tendency to converge on pant-hoots that are acoustically similar to those of other males with whom they associate frequently (Mitani and Brandt 1994; Marshall et al. 1999). Equally relevant is the finding that, during pant-hoot choruses, males converge on pant-hoots that are more acoustically similar to each other, compared to when vocalizing alone (Mitani and Gros-Louis 1998). This process is probably also responsible for the finding that chimpanzees have group-specific pant-hoot 'dialects' (Crockford et al. 2004). In this study, four communities in the Taï forest, Ivory Coast, produced community-specific pant-hoots, regardless of a number of ecological variables or genetic similarities, indicating that vocalizations were shaped by a history of social interactions. This finding is also relevant in relation to the hypothesis that primate vocal behaviour is genetically fixed and inflexible. Although the production mechanisms underlying this acoustic flexibility are only poorly understood, they highlight the importance of social variables on shaping vocal communication processes.

In contrast, very little is known about 'high hoots', the vocal signal used for long-distance communication in bonobos. In the wild, patterns of call convergence and synchronization between group members have been observed, similar to those found in chimpanzees (Hohmann and Fruth 1994). This preliminary study found high degrees of behavioural synchronization between vocalizers, with individuals producing high hoots in distinct alternating sequences with out-of-sight group members. Furthermore, individuals shifted the pitch of their high hoots to correspond with those of responding group members. This surprising degree of vocal flexibility and synchronization with vocal partners suggested that bonobos are equally able to control and modify this vocal signal in response to social variables. More research is urgently needed to better understand the dynamic interaction between social life and call production in both chimpanzees and bonobos.

11.5 Call combinations: flexibility within a constrained vocal system

There is relatively good evidence that some monkey species combine different calls in context-specific ways that are meaningful to recipients (e.g. Arnold and Zuberbühler 2006, 2008). This type of communication behaviour has been interpreted as a way of escaping the limitations of poor vocal control and limited vocal repertoires in primates. For chimpanzees, Crockford and Boesch (2005) have demonstrated prolific use of call combinations across a multitude of contexts, but whether recipients are able to make inferences about the caller's experience, simply by listening to different call combinations, has yet to be investigated. Relevant questions here are whether

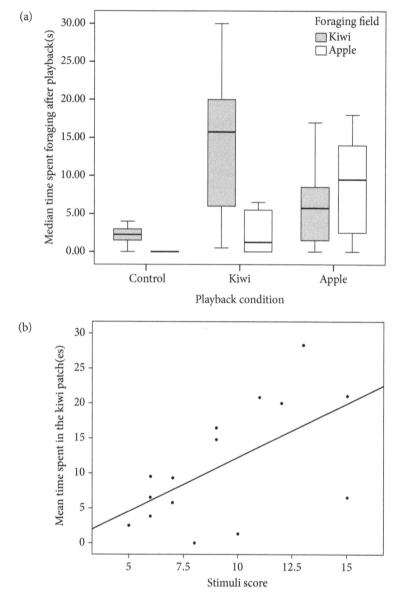

FIGURE 11.2 Results from a playback study testing whether food-associated call combinations convey information about food quality to listeners. (a) Time spent visiting high-quality (i.e. kiwi) and low-quality (i.e. apple) food patches, after hearing playbacks of high- or low-quality food-call sequences. (b) Relationship between composition of call sequences (the cumulative value of the stimuli sequence) and measured response strength, suggesting that recipients integrate information across call sequences.

Source: Clay & Zuberbuhler, 2011a.

component calls have their own independent meanings and, if so, whether they are combined in an additive or combinatorial way, to generate meanings beyond those of component calls. Ultimately, playback experiments will be needed to explore whether the way calls are combined is meaningful to receivers.

Call combinations have also been reported in bonobos (de Waal 1988). In a field study, Bermejo and Omedes (1999) identified 19 different vocal sequences, though the authors indicated that many more were likely to be found. These sequences were used in a range of contexts, and produced in varied and flexible ways. For example, one sequence contained a large number of peeps, peep-yelps, and barks and was observed in a range of contexts, including during feeding, agonistic interactions and displays.

We followed up on these preliminary observations by conducting a series of studies examining food-associated calling sequences in bonobos, taking into account both the producers' and receivers' perspectives. We found that, during feeding, bonobos produced an array of acoustically distinct food-calls and combined these into sequences, whose composition related to the quality of food encountered in a probabilistic way (Clay and Zuberbühler 2009). In a subsequent playback study, receivers were able to extract meaning regarding the food quality encountered by the caller by attending to these call combinations (Clay and Zuberbühler 2011a). We interpreted these results as an ability of receivers to integrate information across call sequences. Overall, the results provide empirical support for the hypothesis, which suggested that call combinations play an important role in bonobo communication (Figure 11.2).

It is important to note that the manner in which bonobos, as well as other animals, communicate using sequences of calls is unlike the hierarchical organization and complexity seen in human syntax. Nevertheless, bonobos were able to extract specific information, the type and location of food encountered by the caller, by attending to combinations of four different call types. This suggests that some of the cognitive processes required for the comprehension of syntactic structures are present in the natural communication of apes, pointing to shared ancestry. More research is needed on call combinations in bonobos, but it is highly likely that call combinations play an integral role in how bonobos communicate about their environment and during social interactions.

11.6 Drawing inferences about the social world: tracing conflicts through screams

There is currently good evidence that primates can draw inferences about events in the external world by attending to vocalizations of others (e.g. Seyfarth and Cheney 2003; Seyfarth et al. 2010). Most examples are in terms of ecologically relevant external events, such as encountering a predator or finding a new food source. However, a number of studies also suggest that individuals can draw inferences about features of their social worlds via vocalizations.

Social conflict represents one of the most relevant events for any socially living animal. Attending to the vocalizations emitted during such conflicts allows individuals to track interactions and the associated changes in social relations. This is especially relevant for forest-dwelling primates, who live in dense habitats with limited visibility.

Various studies have shown that primates are highly sensitive to vocalizations given during agonistic interactions and can draw inferences about resulting social relationships (e.g. Bergman et al. 2003; Paxton et al. 2010). In rhesus macaques, agonistic screams communicate an array of information about the nature of the encounter, such as the intensity of aggression and the social role of the opponents (Gouzoules et al. 1984). In baboons, playback experiments have shown that individuals have some understanding of the consequences of dominance rank changes during within- and between-family conflicts, a demonstration that their knowledge of kin and rank-based relationships includes an appreciation of the invisible hierarchical organization of their social groups (Bergman et al. 2003).

In chimpanzees, screams change acoustically as a function of the social role of the caller (victim or aggressor; Slocombe and Zuberbühler 2005). A subsequent playback study has demonstrated that chimpanzees hearing different scream variants are able to infer something about the social roles of the conflicting individuals and the direction of aggression between them (Slocombe et al. 2010a). In the experiment, subjects were exposed to playbacks that simulated aggressive interactions between three familiar group members that either did or did not conform to their expectations of dominance relations. Looking time measures indicated that subjects took more interest when the direction of the interaction was incongruent to the existing hierarchy (i.e. a lower-ranked individual makes an aggressor scream followed by a victim scream of a higher-ranked individual), compared to a congruent interaction (i.e. high-rank aggressor screams followed by low-ranking victim scream).

Chimpanzee screams have also been shown to convey acoustic information relating to the intensity of the aggression encountered by a victim of aggression (Slocombe and Zuberbühler 2007). A playback study conducted in the wild demonstrated that listeners distinguished between screams given during mild to severe aggression on the one hand, and tantrum screams on the other (Slocombe et al. 2009). To date, no comparable work has been carried out with bonobos.

These studies are important for several reasons. First, the manner in which individuals produce and respond to vocalizations provides a useful window into the underlying cognitive mechanisms and social awareness of the individuals involved, which can generate important insights into the evolution of complex social cognition (Seyfarth and Cheney 2003). Second, they highlight the integral role of vocalizations in the social lives of primates, with vocalizations enabling individuals to both express and understand the dynamics of their social relationships, both with others and between others. Social conflicts can have serious consequences for the broader social structure, dominance hierarchies, and group stability. Being able to track and infer the outcomes of third-party interactions, often occurring out of sight, has clear benefits to listeners, because it enables them to predict others' social interactions and to better manage their own social relationships.

11.7 The impact of social life on communication: insights from copulation calls

Like humans and some monkey species, female chimpanzees and bonobos produce acoustically distinct vocalizations during sexual interactions, known as 'copulation calls'. The adaptive significance of these signals is considered to be in promoting the caller's direct reproductive success, which may be via a number of mechanisms (see Pradhan et al. 2006). In Barbary macaques and yellow baboons, for example, female copulation calls have been shown to convey information about caller identity (Deputte and Goustard 1980; Semple 2001), sexual swelling size (an approximate cue to fertility status, e.g. Nunn 1999; Semple and McComb 2000; Semple et al. 2002), and, for yellow baboons, the rank of the male partner (Semple et al. 2002). By advertising sexual activity, females can attract potential mates and so incite male–male competition and increase the quality or number of sexual partners. The acoustic structure of Barbary macaque copulation calls co-varies with the occurrence of ejaculation (Pfefferle et al. 2008a), allowing listening males to discriminate ejaculatory from non-ejaculatory copulation calls and adjust their subsequent mating decisions (Pfefferle et al. 2008b). By providing honest information about successful copulations and the rank of the male partner, other males can more efficiently pursue their own mating strategy (Semple et al. 2002).

Copulation calls by female chimpanzees and bonobos share a number of similarities. For example, both species produce individually distinct calls that provide cues to the identity of the caller and the rank of their partner (Townsend et al. 2011; Clay et al. 2011). Although playback studies will eventually be required, it is likely that by attending to these calls, receivers are able to make inferences about the ongoing sexual interaction, which may subsequently serve to influence their own social behaviours or reproductive decisions.

There is also good evidence showing that chimpanzee and bonobo copulation calls are subject to audience effects, which suggests that females have some control over call production and may be aware, to some extent, of the effect of their vocalizations on others. In wild chimpanzees, females inhibit copulation call production when in the presence of high-ranking females, which is possibly part of a strategy to reduce female mating competition, which can be severe in this species (Townsend et al. 2008). There is evidence of female-led infanticides and severe lethal aggression among females (Townsend et al. 2007). By inhibiting copulation calls in the presence of the most likely perpetrators of infanticide, the high-ranking females, females may seek to reduce the risks of provoking aggression from other females towards their own offspring.

While there are similarities in copulation calling behaviour of the two *Pan* species, there are also some important differences (Figure 11.3). Compared to chimpanzees and other primates, bonobos exhibit a notably heightened sexuality, which is frequently divorced from reproduction, with females commonly engaging in sexual interactions in all age and sex combinations (Kano 1992; de Waal 1987; Hohmann and Fruth 2000). In bonobos, sex thus also serves as a social tool for expressing, establishing, consolidating, and repairing relationships. It also appears especially important in facilitating the integration of young females into their new community and their subsequently peaceful co-existence and affiliation with non-related group members (e.g. Kano 1992; Furuichi 1989; de Waal 1987; Hohmann and Fruth 2000). Sexual interactions between bonobo females are known as 'genital contacts', whereby individuals embrace ventro-ventrally and swing their hips laterally, while keeping their vulvae in contact (Kuroda 1980).

During same-sex interactions, female bonobos sometimes produce 'copulation calls', as when mating with males (Thompson-Handler et al. 1984). Despite the differences in the physical nature of the interaction, calls produced while interacting with male and female partners have the same acoustic morphology and cannot be statistically discriminated (Clay and Zuberbühler 2011b). However, the calls contain strong cues of caller identity, while subtle differences in call delivery are indicative of partner sex and the dominance rank of male, but not female, partners. Although females are more likely to call with males than females, females are significantly more likely to call with high- than low-ranking partners, regardless of their sex (Clay et al. 2011). Taken together, these results highlight the social significance of copulation calls in bonobos and suggest that, similar to their sexual behaviour, calling has become functionally detached from its original reproductive function to be used socially.

It is interesting that in previous studies, rank effects in copulation calling have been explained as reproductive strategies, such as to promote mate guarding (Pradhan et al. 2006), but this hypothesis has no obvious relevance for bonobos during same-sex interactions. Instead, rank effects highlight the social aspect of copulation calling, something that has not received much attention so far.

In a recent study, we investigated some of the other factors that may influence calling during female-female genital contacts (Clay and Zuberbühler 2012). Here we found that calling was not driven by physical stimulation alone, as genital contact duration and spatial position had no effects, while social variables had considerable explanatory power. Females demonstrated awareness of dyadic dominance ranks during sex, with low-ranking females more likely to vocalize when engaged in sex with a high-ranking female. Callers were also sensitive to who initiated the

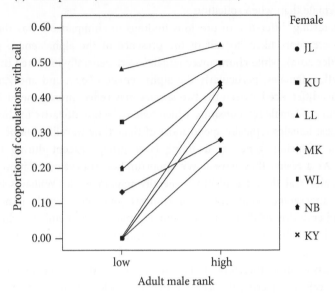

(a) Chimpanzee (sexual interactions with males)

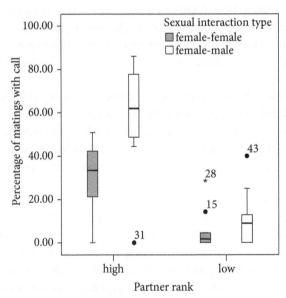

(b) Bonobo (sexual interactions with females and males)

FIGURE 11.3 Effects of social dominance and partner sex on copulation calling behaviour in (a) female chimpanzees and (b) bonobos.

Source: Townsend et al. 2008; Clay et al. 2011.

interaction, with females more likely to call when invited to have sex by a high-ranking female than when soliciting.

An interesting difference to previous findings in chimpanzees was that bonobo females were more likely to call in the presence of the alpha female (Clay and Zuberbühler 2012), while chimpanzee females were generally inhibited by the presence of other females, particularly the alpha female (Townsend and Zuberbühler 2009). This difference between the two species may reflect more general differences in the nature of female relationships, which tend to be less affiliative in chimpanzees. Chimpanzee females typically spend most of their time travelling alone with their dependent offspring, generally avoiding large groups except during periods of oestrous. As a result, they have fewer opportunities to develop relationships with other females and their friendships generally remain weak (Williams et al. 2002; but see Langergraber et al. 2009). In contrast, unrelated female bonobos form strong and enduring relationships with other female group members, which enables them to form alliances and achieve considerable social power (Stanford 1998; Furuichi 2009).

One interpretation therefore is that, in bonobos, low-ranked females produce copulation calls to advertise the fact that they been selected for sex by an established female within the social group—a sign of social recognition. Developing affiliations with dominant group members is very critical to a female's own social position, thus having been chosen by a higher-ranking partner may enhance a female's general social standing in a group, which would also explain why females are particularly likely to call when the alpha female is nearby. This hypothesis requires further testing, and it is also unclear whether it has functional relevance for other primate species.

In conclusion, research on several primate species, including chimpanzees and bonobos, has indicated that copulation calls can convey a considerable amount of social information to listeners, which can influence subsequent mating and other social behaviour. A key finding is that females can be selective in their calling, suggesting that they may have some control over call production in possibly strategic ways.

How exactly the recent findings on ape copulation calls compare to similar behaviour in humans is not so clear. It may well be that the production of copulation calls by human females is susceptible to similar social factors, that is, that calling functions to advertise something about the mating partner and that this is influenced by the composition of the nearby audience. Whether in humans or non-humans, in any event, such vocalizations are susceptible to cognitive assessments of the surrounding social situation and their likely impact in advertising ongoing mating behaviour to others. Much of this may not be governed by conscious decisions but may be part of a more general subconscious ability to maximize social and reproductive success.

11.8 Is *Pan* communication intentional?

One frequently cited objection to the idea that language could have evolved directly from primate vocalizations is that the latter are not thought to be intentional signals. This is often contrasted with ape gestural signals, which are sometimes used in intentional and flexible ways towards specific targets (see Pika, Chapter 10). However, the question of whether vocalizations qualify as intentional signals has rarely been directly addressed.

Some recent studies challenge the assumption of inflexibility. For example, in a recent field experiment, wild chimpanzees produced more alarm calls to a model snake when in the company of ignorant group members, suggesting that they took into account the recipients' state of knowledge (Crockford et al. 2012). Rather than alarm calling indiscriminately, it was found that chimpanzees that were aware of the danger behaved as if they intended to vocally inform naïve recipients, as opposed to recipients already aware of the danger. This study is important as it suggests that producers take into account the knowledge state of a recipient and can use their vocalizations to inform or change the knowledge state of recipients. More generally, this finding raises the possibility that some aspects of chimpanzee vocal production may be intentional and driven by a motivation to inform others.

In a related study, wild chimpanzees encountering a new food source behaved as if they took into account the composition of the nearby audience in a manner that suggested that their vocal production was modified by considerable social awareness (Slocombe et al. 2010b). When finding food, chimpanzees produce acoustically distinct 'rough grunts' whose production was shown to vary as a function of audience composition: males finding food called more in the presence of long-term allies and they recommenced calling upon the arrival of an ally at the feeding tree. This directed form of vocal behaviour appears to function in strengthening affiliative ties between coalition partners.

In summary, while studies of ape gestures have repeatedly demonstrated that individuals can use communication signals in intentional and flexible ways, for example to re-engage a reluctant partner during a social game (Pika and Zuberbühler 2008), more recent research shows that the same cognitive processes underlying gestural communication may also drive part of the vocal behaviour.

11.9 Summary

There are striking similarities but also crucial differences in the vocal behaviour of bonobos and chimpanzees, painting what is overall a complex picture of how social awareness and communication interact. Although more research is needed, the currently available studies highlight that much of vocal behaviour is driven by social awareness. Although much remains uncertain, it is clear that apes do not produce vocalizations in indiscriminate, inflexible ways, but that individuals are considerably influenced by their social environment and knowledge, both as vocal receivers and producers. As producers, they modify vocal behaviour in response to different audiences (e.g. Clay and Zuberbühler 2012; Slocombe and Zuberbühler 2007), may sometimes modify signal meanings by using call combinations assembled in context-dependent ways (e.g. Clay and Zuberbühler 2009)—and may sometimes even vocalize intentionally to inform naïve recipients (Crockford et al. 2012). As receivers, they can form inferences by listening to vocalizations, sometimes in combination with contextual information (Slocombe et al. 2010a; Clay and Zuberbühler 2011a). Based on these findings, we conclude that insight from studies of primate vocal communication and underlying social awareness is crucial for a balanced and satisfactory account of the social origins of language.

11.10 Concluding remarks: a comparative approach to language evolution

Darwin (1871) argued that, in their mental faculties, there was no fundamental difference between man and the higher mammals. Over the decades, this claim has received increasing support from empirical evidence. One mental faculty, however, the faculty of language, has remained relatively enigmatic. Although primates have little control over their articulators, they are able to encode information using discrete and graded signals, sometimes composed into more complex sequences, but this is still very different from the enormous flexibility seen in human signal production. One challenge will be to understand how humans acquired this unusual ability after splitting off from the ape lineage. Another is to improve our understanding of the kinds of meaning receivers can extract from signals and signal sequences, and how they integrate signal structure and sequential composition with pragmatic context and signaller intention. A third challenge is to study the biological origins of common ground, including audience awareness and co-operative motivation during acts of communication. Primate social cognition and communication are intimately intertwined; any attempt to shed light on this crucial intersection should lead to a deeper understanding of the primate origins of the human language faculty.

11.11 Acknowledgments

This chapter emerged from 'The Social Origins of Language' workshop held at University College London, organized by Chris Knight, Jerome Lewis, and Daniel Dor. We are grateful to the organizers for being invited to participate in this discussion. Much of the empirical research reviewed in this chapter has been funded with grants by the Leverhulme Trust, the BBSRC, and the European Commission (FP6). We thank the Royal Zoological Society of Scotland for providing core funding to the Budongo Conservation Field Station.

12

Why humans and not apes: the social preconditions for the emergence of language

CHARLES WHITEHEAD

12.1 Introduction

In this chapter, I aim to show that the preconditions for the emergence of language are both social and uniquely human, using a theory that I think fits what we know about human behaviour better than its more popular rivals.[1, 2] Social mirror theory arose at the end of the 19th century as an explanation of self-consciousness (Dilthey 1883–1911; Baldwin 1894). It holds that 'mirrors in the mind depend on mirrors in society' (Whitehead 2001)—that is, social displays (such as facial expressions, music, pictures, and language) make thoughts and experiences public, so that, during childhood, they make us aware of thoughts and experiences in our own minds and in the minds of others. In this way, we become self-aware and other-aware at the same time, and self/other awareness is a single, indivisible phenomenon (henceforth 'social awareness' or 'intersubjectivity').

Social mirror theory complements a second theory, originally proposed by Émile Durkheim (1964 [1912]), that the emergence of language depended on ritual. This idea has been extended to become 'ritual/speech co-evolution theory' (Knight 1998). The theory further maintains that any attempt to explain language as an isolated trait is akin to explaining the emergence of the credit card without considering the preconditions on which credit cards depend—including commerce, money, banking, the digital computer, and the means to detect and punish fraud.

---

[1] All Whitehead references cited in this chapter (except 1995 and 2004) can be downloaded in draft or final form at www.socialmirrors.org. Go to 'About Charles Whitehead'.

[2] The main theories are reviewed at www.socialmirrors.org. Go to 'Self/Other Consciousness' and click link to section 2 (at foot of page).

According to these two theories, in order to explain the origins of language, we must first explain the whole package of social displays and social awareness on which human ritual depends. In what follows, I will discuss the unique nature of human social displays, social awareness, and culture, and present a 'play-and-display' hypothesis to explain the evolution of human sociality and our 'culture-ready brain', without which language would not be possible.

12.2 The human difference

12.2.1 *Social displays and social awareness*

We humans have a formidable armamentarium of social displays. According to social mirror theory, these displays account for our exceptional social awareness. Although all apes have a rich repertoire of displays, I submit that humans have a broader range of displays—some unique to our species, and some which are more greatly elaborated than those of other apes.

Note that, in the context of social mirror theory, a social display is any kind of shared behaviour which makes thoughts, intentions, or experiences public. Hence it includes behaviours such as grooming and play, in addition to those more commonly regarded as 'signals'. In animals with mirror neurones (neurones which fire when an individual performs an action *and* when the individual sees another perform the same action), even pragmatic actions—such as grasping a nut to eat it—can function as social displays which, according to most theories of social awareness, would generate a basic level of insight into desires and intentions.

We humans have three distinct kinds of social display—communication, play, and performance—which serve quite different functions (Whitehead 2001, 2003). Communication is generally goal-directed and aimed at influencing others (Krebs and Dawkins 1984). Play is quite different. It serves exploratory and developmental functions, but has no goal—it is pursued 'just for fun'. Performance is different again. It is both communicative and playful, and can serve the additional functions of social grooming and entrainment,[3] enabling two or more 'selfish' individuals to behave like one much bigger selfish individual.

Our three types of display come in at least three modes—implicit, mimetic, and conventional—which sustain different levels of social awareness (Burling 1993; Mitchell 1994). Implicit displays deal with emotions (e.g. laughter) and autonomic states (e.g. yawning). Mimetic displays, on the other hand, deal with perceptions, representing concrete things, actions, and actors by resemblance (Donald 1990). Conventional displays are culturally transmitted and their meanings rarely depend on resemblance to their referents. Mimetic and conventional modes, being voluntary

---

[3] 'Entrainment' implies coordination of thought, mood, and/or behaviour between individuals.

TABLE 12.1. **Illustrative examples of social display**

		Communication	Play	Performance
Implicit		Affective gesture-calls (e.g. laughing, crying)	Embodied play (e.g. contingent mirror play)	Grooming Song-and-dance display Mark-making
Mimetic	*Projective*	Iconic gesture-calls (e.g. 'drawing pictures in the air')	Projective pretend play (using toys to represent real things, persons, etc.)	Representational image-making
	Introjective	Miming praxic actions	Role-play (using oneself to represent animals, persons, etc.)	Pantomime Hypnotic trance
Conventional	*Implicit*	Implicit signals (e.g. speech prosody, some conventional gestures)	Collecting behaviour	Musical arts Architecture, design, etc. Wealth displays (material, moral, aesthetic, cultural, spiritual, etc.)
	Mimetic	Mimetic codes (e.g. musical scores, pictographic writing, computer icons)	Iconic gaming pieces	Ritual/ceremony Theatre 'Fine art'
	Unprecedented	Cryptic codes (e.g. language, writing, mathematical denotations)	Play scripts	Myth Literary arts
		Economico-moral codes	Games-with-rules	Socio-economic *personae* (role)

After Whitehead 2001: based on Huizinga 1955; Bourdieu 1972; Winnicott 1974; Jennings 1990; Burling 1993.

and intentional, can be used to lie, and their utility depends on sufficient levels of social trust. Table 12.1 shows the nine types of display with some illustrative examples which hopefully make these distinctions clear (for further explanation, see Whitehead 2001, 2010a, 2012).

Many animals have highly elaborated displays, but these are usually of a single type and in the implicit mode. Only humans have multiple sophisticated displays of all three types in all three modes, and all nine are uniquely developed in humans, including many displays which have no obvious precedent in other species. Even implicit gesture-calls are greatly elaborated in humans—for example, 'the eloquence of the human face' involves considerably more facial muscles than are found in other primates (Young 1992).

12.2.2 *Cultural displays and cultural awareness*

Claude Lévi-Strauss (1969) noted that human societies—in contrast to animal societies—are governed by culturally variable *rules* (involving a social contract, on which the utility of language depends: Austin 1962; Grice 1969; Searle 1969). Human rules are of two types—regulatory and *constitutive*, where the latter serve to establish institutional forms of social order (Rawles 1955; Searle 1995). Two fundamental institutions which structure all known human societies are formal systems of inflated kinship and extended reciprocity. Kinship and reciprocity are familiar terms to biologists—used to explain the evolution of altruism—yet biologists seldom consider cultural institutions when attempting to explain 'strong reciprocity' in humans. A case could be made for 'strong empathy' in humans, based on role-play and hypnotic suggestibility, but large-scale co-operation and out-group reciprocity surely depend on cultural systems.

Of course, you cannot have rules without social displays (such as stories, images, and ritual performances) to transmit them from generation to generation. But social displays are more fundamentally important than that—they are virtually constitutive of human culture. Although post-industrial societies have an elaborate material culture with obvious or supposed instrumental utility, even utilitarian objects usually have some aspect of *design* or *display* which is intended to influence people or say something about the owners or users of such artefacts. Émile Durkheim (1964 [1912]) coined the term 'collective representations' to refer to the shared displays through which human communities define their identity and assert their moral authority. Many of our assumptions about the human condition and the reality we inhabit— those which are passed down from our ancestors, and are so commonsensically taken for granted that they are seldom questioned even by scientists (Bourdieu 1972)—are 'collective representations'. Human infants appear to show a spontaneous interest in cultural displays (Trevarthen 1995) and there can be little doubt that collective representations have profound influences on psychological factors such as personality, self/other-awareness, and visual perception, with concomitant effects on functional brain anatomy (Chiao et al. 2008; Turner and Whitehead 2008).

One point that many behavioural scientists miss is the *theatrical* nature of enculturated human behaviour—first noted by G.H. Mead (1934) and elaborated by Erving Goffman (1959), Victor Turner (1982), and others. Role-play and theatre are the most fundamental displays on which human cultures are founded. Today, people who spend 35 hours a week role-playing managers, lawyers, employees, etc. may then spend as many hours of vicarious role-play watching television. We live in a make-believe world, wholly believing in our pretence. Wholly-believed-in role-play is a widely accepted definition of the hypnotic state—hence Charles Tart's (2009) notion of the *consensual trance*. Constitutive rules, institutions, and theatrical fictions implicate a relatively large role for invention in the emergence of human culture.

12.3 The developmental spiral

Infant development supports two predictions of social mirror theory: first, that social displays and social awareness (self/other-awareness and intersubjectivity) develop in tandem; and second, the development of displays in one mode precedes major transitions in social awareness, accompanied by the emergence of displays in higher modes.

In what follows I rely mainly on research by performative psychologists, because they specifically investigate intersubjectivity and social displays. Colwyn Trevarthen spent 40 years studying human babies and infants in various cultural settings, including video and audio recording of social interactions especially between infants and mothers, and detailed analyses of what he called 'proto-conversational exchanges' which prepare for language acquisition and enculturation (Trevarthen 1974). He concluded that infants are born with a 'virtual other' representation, and are innately motivated to seek, mirror, and interact with the motives and expressions of sympathetic others (Trevarthen 1998). Repudiating the copy-cat view of 'simulation theory' (as embraced by the Parma team who discovered mirror neurones), performative psychologists have shown that human infants are pro-active in their own socialization and enculturation. The input → processing → output model derived from computing simply cannot accommodate this pro-active creativity. 'Cognitive science', Trevarthen writes, 'restricting the role of motives and emotions, puts childhood play and imagination behind bars' (personal communication).

Infant interactions are playful, jocular, and often musical (Gratier and Trevarthen 2008). Contingent mirror play is the first in a long series of self-motivated (i.e. playful) activities. By three months, babies express melodic vocalizations coordinated with balletic limb movements ('song-and-dance display'); and around six months use indexical gestures and engage in preverbal 'clowning, tricks, and jokes' (Dunn 1991; Trevarthen 1995; Reddy 2001). At nine months, infants begin to make marks on any surface—including their own bodies—whether with paint, jam, or faeces (Jennings 1990).

These developments in display are followed, at around nine months, by the first of two developmental watersheds which have no apparent parallel in apes. Simon Baron-Cohen (1995) calls this the onset of the 'shared attention monitoring mechanism', whereas Trevarthen (1995) calls it the perception of 'the self as participant'. The child becomes aware of herself as a social player and realizes that she and mother can share awareness of an object of interest. Trevarthen (1995) observed that the child—unlike the scientist—strives to understand the world 'in active negotiation of creative imaginings that are valued for their *human-made unreality*' (emphasis added). He notes that babies are born 'hungry for culture' and it would seem that they are pre-programmed to live in a cultural world of fantasy and fiction.

Three months later children begin to engage in projective pretend play (playing with representational toys), use iconic gestures, and utter the first words (Trevarthen 1995). Pretend play precedes the emergence, at around 18 months, of the self-conscious ability of children to recognize themselves in mirrors (Gallup 1994), when they may show embarrassment or coyness at their reflection (Parker et al. 1994). Soon afterwards, they begin to use the pronouns 'me' and 'mine' (Lewis 1994).

At 24 months occurs the second distinctive watershed—the beginning of the 'terrible twos' (Lewis 1994) and a new sense of self perceived in terms of social value. Until this age, infants are relatively passive, allowing parents to dress, wash, or change them as they wish. But the terrible two-year-old asserts her newly discovered autonomy and self-worth by rebellion.

This is also the age of the 'verbal explosion' and the beginning of role-play. Around the same time, mark-making behaviour develops into swirling 'mandalas' and geometric designs (Jennings 1990). By 30 months, language rules are understood, the 'mandalas' turn into faces, and children begin to draw ideographic pictures, especially of people. Six months later, children can experience new emotions (and recognize them in others), notably those associated with self-value: shame, guilt, pride, contempt, and hubris (Parker et al. 1994). By four years (or earlier: Dunn 1991) normal children have acquired explicit 'theory of mind' (ToM)—the ability to infer epistemic mental states (knowing, thinking, believing, etc.) in themselves and in others (Baron-Cohen 1995). At this age it becomes possible to hypnotize children (Bliss 1986). Hypnosis involves mind influencing mind and may well depend on reflective ToM. It seems logical that early attempts to explore personhood and agency—through role-play and picture-making—should precede the emergence of these abilities.

By the age of six, enculturation has progressed to the point where children understand consensual morality (Parker et al. 1994), and are ready to play competitive 'games-with-rules' (Parker and Milbraith 1994). Hypnotic ability peaks a year later and thereafter declines, at least in westerners (Brown 1991). At this age, role-play can occasionally achieve hallucinatory force, and lonely children may create imaginary companions (dissociated autonomous *personae*: Bliss 1986). I infer that 'theatre of mind' (the ability to imagine social scenarios with 'toy people' who behave as though they have minds of their own) must be established at this age.

Around the time of puberty, children can experience stage-fright at the thought of performing in front of any audience, and not merely when ridiculed (Mitchell 1994). It takes the whole of childhood to develop principled morality (Parker et al. 1994) and perhaps longer to create full-blown *economico-moral personae*—the social roles we play in adult life.

Table 12.2 summarizes the above, showing the spiral relationship between social displays and social awareness. Major transitions are marked by diagonal arrows. Note the build-up of social displays prior to each major shift in social awareness, and the way major shifts coincide with transitions to higher modes of display. Language, however, seems to follow a precocious schedule, suggesting some hard-wired basis. In Section 12.4, I will argue that social displays and social awareness co-evolved in a similar spiral manner.

TABLE 12.2. **Co-development of social displays and social awareness**

		Social awareness	Social displays
Weeks	0	Innate ⟶	***Implicit***
			Contingent mirror play/Embodied play
			Affective and autonomic gesture-calls
	6–8		Proto-conversational exchanges
Months	3		Song-and-dance
	6		Clowning, tricks, and jokes
	9	Self as participant ⟶	***Projective mimetic***
			Making marks
	12		Iconic gesture-calls/Pretend play
			First words
	18	(Mirror self-recognition)	Coyness, embarrassment
	20		Personal pronouns
	24	Self as value ⟶	***Introjective mimetic***
			Role-play
			Verbal explosion
	30		Making pictures
			Language rules
	36		Expressions of self-value (pride, guilt)
Years	4	Theory of mind ⟶	***Increasingly conventionalized***
			Hypnotic ability
			Expressions of surprise
	6	(Theatre of mind)	Dressing up/Complex joint role-play
			Games-with-rules
	7		Peak in hypnotic ability
	11	Economico-moral *personae* ⟶	***Fully enculturated***
			Conventional roles
			Collective representations
			Wealth displays
			Collective deceptions

12.4 The evolutionary spiral

If we consider the types and modes of social displays illustrated in Table 12.1, it is clear that they cannot all have emerged simultaneously, and must have evolved in a logical order (Whitehead 2003). Communication has to come first because, in contrast to play and performance, it is a universal feature of all living organisms. All animals that play also communicate, and social play would be impossible without communication. If performance is a playful extension of communication, it follows that communication must be older than play, and play than performance. A similar argument applies to our modes of display—implicit signals are universal in higher animals, mimesis is rare, and both have to be in place before they can be conventionalized to generate modern human culture, including language.

The argument goes further if we assume that performance in one mode scaffolds the emergence of communication in a higher mode. Thus, song-and-dance generates the levels of social trust and social insight—the ability to put ourselves in others' shoes—required for the later emergence of informative mimesis (Whitehead 2003). It also appears that dance may have pre-adapted the brain for advanced mimesis, since dance engages a subset of the brain areas involved in pretend play (Whitehead 2010b).

This parallels Durkheim's (1964 [1912]) theory that ritual pantomime (mimetic performance) is essential to the emergence of language (conventional communication). What distinguishes language from animal communication, Durkheim reasoned, is displaced reference—the ability to refer to things not present in the here and now, but only in the mind of the speaker. How can we encrypt an intangible, he asked, unless it is first made public by ritual pantomime—a conventionalized drama that everyone understands, and that is 'sacred' in the sense that it carries the consensual authority of an entire community?

Building on Durkheim, proponents of ritual/speech co-evolution theory (Gellner 1989; Knight 1998; Rappaport 1999) have advanced a second argument which points to the same conclusion. Words are cheap and it is too easy to lie. If language could not be trusted, they argue, it would simply be ignored. Hence language depends on a 'social contract' and, in societies without police or judiciary, this can only be implemented through ritual and ritually constructed supernatural beliefs.

There is a third argument which also points to a ritual origin for language, though this was denied by its eccentric author, who deemed ritual unworthy of scientific interest. Lévi-Strauss (1950) was greatly intrigued by the curious fact that, in animistic societies, words such as *mana*, *wakan*, and *orenda*—commonly translated as 'medicine' or 'sacred power'—also function as empty referents. That is, like 'something' in English, they can be used to denote anything new, strange, or for which no other word can be found. He inferred a single big-bang origin for both language and religion. In that primal creative moment, 'the entire universe all at once became *significant*' (Lévi-Strauss 1950: 60). In his view, the first utterance would refer to this cosmic significance and then, as later words were differentiated from this mother-of-all-words, the residual signifier would continue to refer to the prime mover in creation *and* everything not yet included in our referential system of meanings.

Anyone familiar with religious experience research, as pioneered by William James (1985 [1902]) and Alister Hardy (1979), will recognize this 'entire universe all at once became significant' as a classic feature of spiritual experience. While 40 per cent of westerners have such experiences, perhaps once in their lifetimes, they are much more widespread and frequent in foraging communities (Bourguignon 1973). Indeed, it is difficult to see how words like *mana*, *wakan*, and *orenda* could have acquired their significance in any other way. It should not surprise us if the first utterance that others interpreted in a language-like way (Burling 1999; Tinbergen 1952) did originate in an 'altered state'.[4] Such states are an inevitable consequence of human dissociative or hypnotic abilities and, among hunter-gatherers, virtually all innovations derive from dreams, visions, ritual trances, or divine visitations (review: Whitehead 2011). Foraging communities accept innovations only because they are regarded as gifts from the supernatural realm.

Durkheim's argument regarding the ritual origins of language has never, to my knowledge, been effectively countered, and it has been widely influential in social anthropology. If my extension of his argument is accepted—that performance in one mode scaffolds the emergence of communication in a higher mode—then we have the evolutionary spiral shown in Table 12.3. This predicts at least three major transitions during human evolution. The first would be the emergence of song-and-dance display; the second a major expansion of mimetic and pretend play abilities culminating in ritual pantomime; and this in turn would trigger the third—the emergence of modern culture, with the development of social rules, language, religion, and all the cultural arts.

According to the 'play-and-display' hypothesis (Whitehead 2003), the proliferation of social displays—especially play and performance—was a major factor in human brain expansion, generating a 'culture ready brain' capable of performing the first ritual pantomime and maintaining culture of modern type (Whitehead 2010b). Social displays must make demands on the brains of performers and observers alike. All forms of play and performance require multi-modal integration, and performance can involve high levels of acquired skill. Song-and-dance in particular demands fine timing precision (in gelada choral displays, voices are synchronized to within a

---

[4] This idea was first proposed in my M.Sc. dissertation (Whitehead 1995) and is based on Turner's (1969) theory of anti-structure, and the observation that the transformative power of ritual depends on collapse or inversion of everyday categorical distinctions. Such anti-structure is equally characteristic of altered states of consciousness, including ritual trance. Parallel ideas occur in psychological theories of creativity which invoke playful as opposed to instrumental thought, e.g. 'creative chaos' (Cooley 1902) and 'cognitive synergies' (Apter 2008).

TABLE 12.3. **Hypothetical evolutionary sequence of social displays (from Whitehead 2003)**

	Communication	*Play*	*Performance*
Implicit			
Mimetic			
Conventional			

millisecond: Richman 1978). Finally, role-play requires a brain that can run at least two minds in parallel. In our dreams and daydreams, there may be several *dramatis personae* who apparently do have minds of their own—capable of saying and doing things which 'we' do not expect.

Accordingly, the first two postulated transitions would initiate phases of brain expansion. The third transition—the emergence of modern culture—would not be expected to lead to further expansion, because social cohesion maintained 'from the outside' by rule-bound formal systems would, if anything, reduce the selection pressure for individual playful and performative capacities.

Ontogenesis would not be expected to exactly recapitulate phylogenesis. However, if new levels of self-consciousness require the prior development of appropriate displays in human infancy, it seems unlikely that our ancestors evolved a different way of doing this. So the play-and-display hypothesis would further imply that song-and-dance display would generate a level of social awareness akin to the 'self as participant' in human infancy, projective mimesis would lead to self-value, and introjective mimesis to 'theory of mind'. Finally, the emergence of culture with regulatory and constitutive rules would necessarily produce economico-moral personae.

I do not have space here to review the archaeological and fossil evidence relevant to changes in hominin behaviour and the brain. I have done so elsewhere (Whitehead 2003, 2008, 2010b) though further work needs to be done. I claim only that it is not inconsistent with the play-and-display hypothesis, though other hypotheses cannot be ruled out. However, in the next section, I review neuroimaging evidence that appears to support the evolutionary sequence proposed here.

12.5 The culture-ready brain

With a few exceptions, social displays have been relatively neglected in neuroscience. For example, following the discovery of mirror neurones in grasping cortex, there have been more than forty brain imaging studies of grasping, hand-object manipulation, and tool use (Grèzes and Decety 2001). In contrast, there have been only four such studies of dance (Calvo-Merino et al. 2005, 2006; Cross et al. 2006; Brown et al. 2006), three of pretence (German et al. 2004; Whitehead et al. 2009; Smith et al. 2013), and only one of role-play (Whitehead 2003). Nevertheless, what we have learned about the brain basis of social interaction and displays is highly suggestive (for fuller detail and references see Whitehead 2010b, 2012).

12.5.1 *Body movement and empathy*

Figure 12.1 shows the presumed human motor mirroring system, based on the many studies of tool-use, object manipulation, etc. The figure shows the right hemisphere only. Praxic actions such as tool-use activate this system mainly in the left hemisphere, whereas expressive gestures recruit more bilateral activity. Two main areas are involved. The superior parietal lobule is a navigational area that maps space in body-centred coordinates, while the left frontal operculum includes Broca's area, classically associated with motor sequencing for speech. However, the operculum is clearly involved in all kinds of motor actions including movements of all body parts. Just below this area—in the cleft dividing the frontal from the temporal lobe—lies the insula. The anterior insula and anterior cingulate cortex have been associated with a mirror system for facial expressions and empathy (review: Rizzolatti et al. 2006).

12.5.2 *Dance*

The mirror system for body movement, as one would expect, is activated by dance. Dance also activates lateral and medial areas in the parietal and temporal lobes (Figure 12.2). The inferior parietal lobule is a multi-modal integration area in a pivotal position—surrounded on all sides by visual, auditory, somatosensory, and motor cortices. The temporal pole is likewise a multi-modal area.

   Curiously, auditory cortex is activated even when people are watching silent videos of dance—perhaps reflecting imagined music. This is the only primary sensory cortex which is expanded in human relative to chimp brains (Deacon 1992a).

12.5.3 *Projective pretence*

Studies of observing pretence showed activity in the main areas associated with dance, plus orbito-medial prefrontal cortices and the superior temporal sulcus (Figure 12.3). The medial prefrontal cortices include the anterior cingulate (associated with a mirror system for facial expressions) and other areas of major social

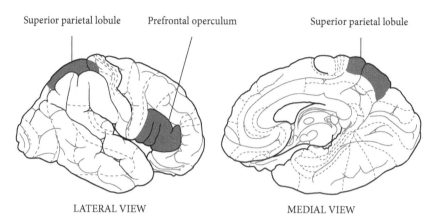

FIGURE 12.1 Right cerebral hemisphere showing motor mirroring areas.

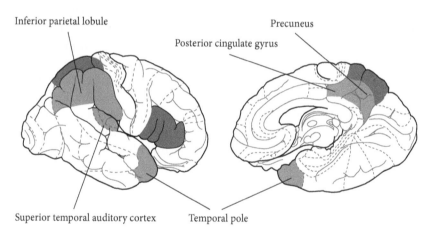

FIGURE 12.2 Major cortical areas in which activation loci were associated with dance.

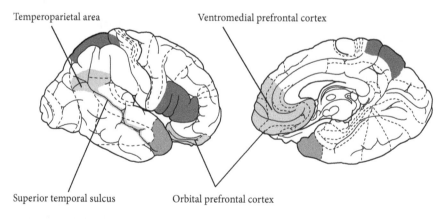

FIGURE 12.3 Major cortical areas in which activation loci were associated with projective pretence.

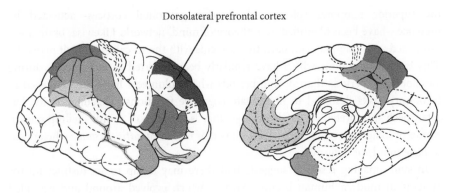

Dorsolateral prefrontal cortex

FIGURE 12.4 Major cortical areas in which activation loci were associated with narrative and role-play. (Source: Whitehead 2010b, 2012)

importance. Note that four major language areas—Broca's area, Wernicke's area, the temporal pole, and the superior temporal sulcus—are all activated by pretend play. Three of those areas are also activated by dance, whereas only one is associated with body movements more generally.

12.5.4 *Introjective pretence*

The same expansive trend is apparent in studies of introjective pretence (role-play) and narrative (mental role-play) (Figure 12.4), implicating all previously mentioned areas with the addition of dorsolateral prefrontal cortex (Whitehead 2003; Mar 2004). Numerous authors assume functional continuity between role-play, narrative, and daydreaming (Mar 2004)—which are all 'story-telling' activities of one kind or another.

12.5.5 *Discussion*

It has not been established that all the cortices shown in these figures include mirror neurones, though one would expect them to be fundamentally important for social displays. In the light of Arbib's (2002) suggestion that human brain enlargement involved the expansion and reduplication of mirror systems, with new systems then adapting to new functions, the figures do suggest a build-up of display systems, with more recently evolved displays 'piggy-backing' on and extending beyond older systems. The overlaps between dance, pretend play, and classical speech areas, might indicate that earlier forms of display likewise pre-adapted the brain for language.

The data further supports a link between displays and social awareness. The mirror system for facial expressions has obvious implications for empathy. The tempero-parietal areas and temporal poles—common to dance and pretence—together with the superior temporal sulcus and anterior prefrontal cortices—activated by pretence—have been identified as a 'theory of mind' network. Likewise, brain areas associated with role-play and narrative coincide with the so-called 'default network'. This is a set of regions which have regularly been reported as more active during baseline 'rest' periods than during periods when volunteers have been engaged in laboratory tasks designed to investigate cognitive functions. 'Default activity' has often been interpreted as daydreaming—that is, 'theatre of mind'—telling oneself stories or imagining social scenarios with two or more *dramatis personae* who appear to have minds of their own.

In sum, imaging research suggests that there may be up to six distinct mirror systems in modern human brains—each of which evolved around and extended beyond phylogenetically older ones. The first two systems, which we share with monkeys, would be those for reading body actions and affective signals. A possible third would be a song-and-dance system, a fourth a mimetic and pretend play system, a fifth a role-play system, and a sixth a language system.

12.6 Conclusion

I set out to show that the preconditions for the emergence of language are both social and uniquely human. Invoking social mirror theory, I argued that there are profound discontinuities between human and animal behaviour, social awareness, and culture. At the heart of these discontinuities lies our formidable armamentarium of social displays, which sustain our high levels of social awareness, are preconditions for the emergence of language, and are virtually constitutive of modern human culture. Our three types and three modes of display do have animal parallels, but we are unique in having all nine, and in having multiple displays in all nine—most of which are more sophisticated than any animal equivalents, and many of which (including language) are uniquely human.

The evidence I have presented is at least consistent with social mirror theory and its corollary, the play-and-display hypothesis. There is strong evidence of a spiral relationship between social displays and intersubjectivity during human development, and I have suggested that a similar spiral is likely to have occurred during hominin evolution. Finally, the presumed evolutionary sequence of displays is supported by brain imaging research.

13

Language and collective fiction: from children's pretence to social institutions

EMILY WYMAN

13.1 Introduction

Traditional theories of linguistic communication have investigated how language arbitrarily encodes thought into utterances for communication (see Saussure 1983 [1915]). Explorations in the field of pragmatics, however, have focused on the paradox that linguistic utterances contain scant information relative to the wealth of what is actually understood by a listener (Sperber and Wilson 1986). To take a simple illustration, on hearing the statement 'looks like it might rain', a listener may understand that the speaker wishes to postpone going for a walk and prefers to stay at home by the fire, despite the fact that none of this is encoded in the actual words themselves. Pragmatics theorists, therefore, see linguistic utterances not merely as units of encoded information, but as conventional tools that enable individuals to communicate their broader intentions to each other. Language, on this account, is not a system for encoding and decoding information, but a medium of social action (Austin 1962; Searle 1969).

Acts of communication or 'speech acts' conceptualized in this way enable illocutors to either describe or to change the world according to their desires (Searle 1969). So, for instance, the assertion 'the sky is blue' aims to describe, and the imperative 'go away' attempts to bring about a change in the environment. However, a curious type of speech act known as a 'performative' neither describes nor brings about change in the world, but creates altogether new institutional states of affairs, or 'institutional facts', within it (Searle 1995). When uttered in a particular context, for example, statements such as 'we hereby name this child John Brown', 'I pronounce this couple man and wife', and 'war is now declared' make it the case that the child's name is

Brown, the couple are now of married status, and that some group is now at war. Our capacity to create institutional facts using performative speech acts such as these, however, lies not in the words themselves, but in the way in which they are understood to bestow rights and obligations upon the individuals involved. In fact, one and the same individual will typically find him or herself embedded in a whole matrix of institutional rights and obligations conferred this way, with profound consequences for their conduct. For example, the individual will likely be held responsible for actions conducted in their name, may enjoy the rights associated with married life, and even find themselves obliged to participate in warfare on behalf of their social group.

The mechanism by which institutional facts are generated through the production of performative speech acts, has been described in terms of a 'constitutive rule' with the underlying structure 'X counts as Y in Context C' (Searle 1995). This rule assigns non-physical functions or 'status functions' to people, actions, and objects by collective agreement. For example, 'these words constitute officially naming a child in our community' or 'consecrating a marriage within our culture' describe the underlying structures of the institutions of naming and marriage. Subsequently, 'this child's name is John Brown' and 'this couple are married' describe facts that the institutions generate, and with normative consequences for social interaction: when a child is officially named or a couple is deemed married they now ought to act in culturally prescribed ways and we, as the community, ought to treat them appropriately, lest we face penalties (Gilbert 1989).

Performative speech acts thus function as efficient tools for publically assigning institutional status that guides our social interactions in specified ways. The curious feature of this process relates to the fact that there is nothing physically intrinsic to the couple, child, or group etc. (the 'X term') that specifies their new status (the 'Y term') or the rights and obligations that derive from it. The existence of this status, and the efficacy of performative speech acts in assigning it, rests on our community-wide recognition that it exists, and agreement—even if implicit—to treat them as having it. Without this, the utterances that assign, for example, the institutional status of being married would remain, literally, 'just words' (Searle 1969). But this social agreement, in turn, depends on a community of individuals being cognitively equipped to understand performative utterances, status assignment, and the normative consequences this has for action. Thus, the emergence of this communicative function in language must have depended directly on the prior or co-evolution of a social-cognitive apparatus that enabled it to be used to institutional ends. It is the social-cognitive foundation that enables performative speech acts to have institutional consequences with which this chapter is concerned. In fact, the way in which this foundation develops in children will be explored in order to investigate the specific social-cognitive skills required, and to highlight the lessons of this developmental picture for the evolution of language and human sociality.

Most centrally, the way in which performatives confer status functions that have no physical or material ontology (existing, rather, in virtue of collective consent) has led to their being characterized as 'shared fictions' (Castoriadis 1998) or 'prescribed imaginings' (Walton 1990). Section 13.2 will, therefore, explore how speech acts and the notion of collective consent operate in fiction, and how children's pretend play activities may introduce them to this. Section 13.3 will investigate the process by which children's pretending may transition from play into serious institutional practice, with specific reference to cross-cultural variation in children's pretence. Section 13.4 will explore the idea that children's pretend dramatizations of institutional practices may later support a dual-level understanding in adulthood that, although institutional facts are treated as having objective ontological status, their existence is, in fact, rooted in social consent. In conclusion, the implications of all this for human linguistic and social evolution will be explored.

13.2 Fiction and intersubjective standards of validity

One prominent proposal for how children come to understand performative speech acts, and the institutional facts that they create, is through games of pretend play. In such games, pretend status is commonly assigned through language, or by what may be termed 'proto-performative' speech acts. These emerge initially as implicit status assignments such as 'this block is now our apple' or 'now you be the mummy' in younger children, and over time come to include explicit statements of pretend status such as 'let's pretend you are the dragon and I am the prince' (see e.g. Garvey and Kramer 1989; Lloyd and Goodwin 1995). This pretend status assignment occurs by collective intention (it is by our agreement that 'this block counts as an apple in our game'), and with normative consequences (so it ought to be 'eaten' and not used to build with). For these reasons, pretend play has been described as a 'developmental cradle' in which the structure of proto-institutional facts are learned (Rakoczy 2006; Rakoczy and Tomasello 2007).

However, another lesson that children may learn in pretence (that will later be essential for their institutional understanding) is that both types of activity generate facts or propositions whose validity may only be evaluated by reference to social consensus. With regard to institutional facts, there is no naturally occurring, objective standard in the world by which a fact such as 'this couple are married' may be evaluated. But neither is the fact that the couple are married a matter of subjective, personal opinion. As succinctly put by Kalish and Sabbagh (2007: 2) 'conventional knowledge sits in a kind of "middle ground" between objective and subjective knowledge about the world ... it is neither strictly objective, nor subjective—it is intersubjective'.

To see how this works in the case of pretence requires a short detour into how fiction may relate to non-fiction generally. One approach to this question is to examine both adult fictional discourse and children's pretence in terms of pretended speech acts (Searle 1975). In making a serious speech act such as an assertion, one undertakes a series of commitments that include licensing others' belief in the truth of the assertion, licensing them to draw further inferences from it, and being able to justify it under certain conditions (Brandom 1980; Searle 1969). But when a pretend assertion, such as 'this block is our apple', is made, a question arises as to how the act remains an assertion, but the conditions governing the relevant commitments of the act are suspended (Searle 1975).

One solution may be that the conditions that define, for example, a serious assertion are not simply suspended in fiction, but are replaced by directly analogous, intersubjectively defined variants. This would mean that those engaged in fiction are not committed to the truth of the proposition 'the block is an apple', but are committed to its intersubjective 'truth' (i.e. truth by mutual consent); they are not committed to being able to justify the proposition with objective evidence, but with evidence considered valid intersubjectively (e.g. 'watch, I can "cut" the apple') and, importantly, they do not license further inferences that follow objectively, but those that follow logically within the intersubjective frame (e.g. 'now the apple has been cut, I can go ahead and "eat" it'). So, fictional play may offer children early experience of how the validity of some facts (later, those in institutional domains) is assessed by reference to intersubjectively defined standards, rooted in social consensus.

Research with children suggests that, within their games of pretend play, they grasp the rudimentary building blocks of institutional practice by way of performative speech acts, the basic structure of constitutive rules, and intersubjective standards of validity. This understanding presents itself most clearly in the types of inferences they make in pretence, and their normative enforcement of the internal logic of pretence games. From around three years of age, children demonstrate a basic understanding of the context-relativity of pretend status assignment. When a stick, for instance, is assigned a pretend identity in one context (e.g. 'toothbrush'), but a different identity in a second context (e.g. 'carrot'), children pretend appropriately when switching back and forth between these contexts (Wyman et al. 2009b). Thus through their pretend actions, they show an implicit understanding of the basic structure of constitutive rules ('X counts as Y in context C').

They also appear to understand that the validity of the inferences they make in such games is judged intersubjectively. For instance, when children from around age two (in some cultures, see Section 13.3) observe an adult put pretend 'toothpaste' on their pretend 'toothbrush' (e.g. a stick), they inferentially elaborate the pretend stipulation by pretending to 'brush teddy's teeth' with the stick (Harris and Kavanaugh 1993). Importantly, these inferences only make sense against a background of intersubjectively defined standards: in inferring what action is appropriate to extend the adult's pretend stipulation, the child does not refer to objective standards of validity ('what are you doing, that's just a stick!'), nor to subjective standards ('I prefer to pretend it's a pen'), but rather those that follow from the intersubjective agreement ('since you put toothpaste on, I'll brush').

Lastly, children see these joint fictions as having normative force. Not only do they act in accordance with jointly assigned pretend status, they police third-party violations of that status. So, if a stick is assigned the pretend status of 'toothbrush', and a puppet enters and pretends to 'eat' it (e.g. claiming it is a 'carrot') children protest 'No that's our toothbrush!' (Rakoczy 2008). And this norm enforcement operates relative to context: if the puppet performs exactly the same action without first joining the pretend game, or joining a different pretend game beforehand, children see his action as unproblematic (Wyman et al. 2009a).

In all, children's pretend games appear to constitute an early microcosm of institutional practice. The experience that children gain in these games with proto-performative speech acts, proto-constitutive rules, the normative consequences that these have, and the way in which pretence operates against a background of inter-subjectively defined standards may cognitively enable them to later partake in serious adult institutions (see also Ginsburg and Jablonka, Chapter 22; Knight and Lewis, Chapter 21). The next question, then, is how to deal with the cross-cultural variation that is observed in children's pretence development. Interestingly, this investigation may point to a mechanism by which children's pretence supports their initiation into the actual institutional practices of their culture.

13.3 From developmental 'cradle' to 'gateway': a cross-cultural approach

If pretence acts as an early, localized context for the development of children's institutional understanding, a number of questions follow: how do children from cultural groups who pretend less, or perhaps differently from others, develop an understanding of institutional facts and practices? Also, once children come to grasp the collective intentional assignment of status functions, how is this translated into an understanding of serious institutional practice? Pretending in Euroamerican children seems to emerge towards the end of children's second year, when they produce simple pretend actions (e.g. pretending to 'wipe up' milk that has been 'spilled': Harris and Kavanaugh 1993). It occurs mainly in the context of infant–caregiver interactions and is centred around object play, particularly with toy replicas (Haight and Miller 1992). However, cross-cultural observation and experiment suggests that this picture may be somewhat atypical of children's pretence in general. Pretence understanding appears to emerge much later in other cultures (e.g. Callaghan et al. 2011), occur at much lower frequencies, and occur in groups of peers, rather than with adults (Gaskins 2000; Göncü et al. 2000).

Differences also exist by way of content, such that non-Euroamerican children's pretence appears more focused on real-life social scripts rather than the fantasy dramatizations of Euroamerican children (Haight et al. 1999). There may be various factors that contribute to this variation, particularly relating to parental attitudes towards the importance of play (Gaskins 2000; Gaskins et al. 2007; Pan 1994), and the wealth and availability of material culture across different communities (Göncü et al. 2000; Haight et al. 1999). But if pretence provides young children with early experience of proto-institutional structures, how and when might children in non-middle-class, non-Euroamerican cultures develop this understanding?

One possibility is that the types of pretend play that children engage in during early and later childhood represent two functionally distinct stages in the development of their institutional understanding. And these stages may be differentially cultivated and thus elaborated differently in development across cultures. It may be, for instance, that pretence in early childhood enables children to gain initial cognitive, but relatively rudimentary grip on the basic idea that fictional status can be assigned by joint intention, with normative consequences for action. But this has yet to be recruited over development into more complex forms of pretence that act as a 'developmental gateway' for their entry into their own culturally specific institutional practices.

Despite the apparent discrepancy in how often and how supported young children's pretence is between cultures, other forms of pretence appear more universally: older children (from around 4 years of age) engage in collaborative pretence in mixed-age peer groups in the dramatization and re-enactment of actual social roles and scripts that they see adults perform. These scripts include the playful imitation of, for example, food processing activities in which children use sticks to pretend they are grinding food, as adults do (Lancy 1996). But they go on to include more detailed scripts such as 'hunting' and 'driving to town to sell produce' by Mayan children (Gaskins 2000), and 'birthday party' scripts in American children (Edwards 2000). And, at the more complex end of the spectrum, they can entail the re-enactment of symbolic, institutional scripts such as 'shopping with money' by middle-class American children, church scenes by lower-class American children (Göncü et al. 2007), as well as court scenes and detailed interactions between figures of different professional status by Kpelle children in Liberia (Lancy 1980, 1996).

This suggests one way of making sense of the cross-cultural variation observed in children's pretence. Variations in the frequency or the particular character of early childhood pretence may not fundamentally affect its elaboration, or cultural contextualization during later stages. Indeed, the high rates of pretence exhibited by Euroamerican children in early childhood may represent a historically novel or atypical case in which the parents of urban Western children have superfluous time resources to invest in scaffolding children's imaginative play, and are philosophically inclined to do so (seeing it as producing some cognitive benefit: Haight and Miller 1992). Conversely, older children in these groups may be in the culturally unusual position of not having routine observational access to many of the institutional practices of adults due to, for example, the cultural focus on formal schooling in which they are separated from general adult activities for much of their day. Indeed, this may also explain why later pretence in Euroamerican children has been noted to be fairly fantasy-oriented (with themes borrowed from television, for instance), while in other cultures more reality-oriented (see Gaskins et al. 2007).

The pretend dramatizations of older children, may act as a functionally important arena for their developing institutional understanding across all cultures. While children may not be necessarily 'practising' these roles for later deployment (Lancy 1980 points out that those playing the role of 'judge' or 'blacksmith' will not necessarily later turn out to be judges or blacksmiths), at least two other possibilities present themselves. One is that the integration of basic institutional scenes into pretence may provide children with the general insight that many actual, serious, adult activities operate within a 'special' framework, that of intersubjectively governed normative constraints. The idea here would be that when they are later initiated into some adult practice, such as a religious or economic exchange scenario, they would still need to learn the roles, objects involved, the details of the practice etc. But they would already bring a general understanding that certain activities are guided not by physical or objective constraints, but by conventional rules rooted in in-group consent.

Another possibility is that when children re-enact adult scenes in pretence, they additionally gain familiarity with the rudimentary structure of culturally specific, institutional scripts. When they are later initiated into a serious practice such as a shopping activity, they will not only understand that much of the interaction is governed by social rules, but also roughly grasp the roles and sequences that might occur. For example, they may intuit that there will be an individual who wants to gain possession of some good, another party who is in control of this good, and there will be a transfer of some type of currency that will enable the main transaction. On this account, children's pretend games are becoming culturally contextualized to some degree over ontogeny. Their actual initiation into adult practices will entail increasing understanding of the details of the scripts and the rules governing adherence to them (for which there is some developmental evidence outside the domain of pretence, see Nelson 1978).

Whichever of these may be the case, the idea that children in some sense 'pretend into' institutional practice may have interesting consequences. The first is that pretence may operate as a kind of internalization mechanism: adult practices are initially re-enacted with a general play attitude, and children's actual understanding of the specific conventions and norms governing them lies in the background. Initiations into real adult practices may then entail a progressive de-emphasis of the play attitude, and an increasing grasp of the details and norms governing such interactions, that gradually conceals the way in which they are governed by social-conventional rules. Indeed, Vygotsky perceptively described the development of children's play as a progression from 'an overt imaginary situation and covert rules, to games with overt rules, and a covert imaginary situation' (1978: 98).

Finally, this process may leave its traces psychologically in a lingering sense for children that, although institutional facts are perceived and treated as ontologically objective, they ultimately derive their force from social consensus. This dual-level understanding may persist—though subtly—into adulthood, and may be under-pinned by a cognitive assessment system that supports conceptualization at both levels. This is to be discussed next.

13.4 The paradox of 'real fictions'

It is probably fair to say that most people—academics and political revolutionaries aside—do not routinely contemplate the ontological basis of their institutional realities. Assumptions of objectivity that, for instance, paper is money and couples are married seem to be deeply ingrained, and for good reason. A number of social processes suggest to us that institutional facts have objective status, so they conse-quently appear to exist as part of our natural worlds. Most obviously, the historical sequence by which an institution has emerged remains hidden to those who enter the institutional practices at a later point. Especially in the case of children, for example, the social-institutional world is first encountered as, in a sense, 'un-authored' (Berger and Luckmann 1966) and, indeed, it does exist independently of children's intentions, at least initially. Further, because by the nature of constitutive rules there is nothing in the X term that physically denotes the Y term, this must be conventionally represented, and often is so in the form of material objects (Searle 1995). For instance, the transfer of rights and obligations central to some exchange practices are represented in the form of bank notes. These then serve to publicly objectify the institution itself. In this way, institutions and institutionalized relations are reified through material representation (Searle 1995). But such institutions are addition-ally legitimated (particularly by those who benefit from the institution) by further 'social imaginaries', or public discourses that justify, in particular, the moral and historical reasons for their existence (Castoriadis 1998). And perhaps most concretely, the regulation, legalization, and policing of social institutions is unquestionably real (Plotkin 2003). Disobeying the authority of those held in high social status will likely result in punishment, and failing to acquire the linguistic institutions of one's community will necessarily result in some degree of social exclusion.

However, while these processes may, in some sense, serve to 'conceal' the social foundations of institutions, other processes may have the opposite effect. Particularly important sources of information may be instances in which there is a change of status within an institution, for example when one currency is superseded by another, or when a political leader is stripped of power and succeeded by a new one.

But yet other situations may highlight the way in which the existence of whole institutions depends on collective consent, for instance when a monarch falls, or when particular languages or religious practices die out. It seems important that in all these cases there may be a shared sense that such changes have come about through collective decision (either the decision of some authority, or a series of decisions by the practitioners of the institution to abandon it), rather than by nature's forces.

It may be partly in virtue of these divergent social processes that adults and older children have varying intuitions about the properties and ontologies of different types of fact. For instance, when comparing natural laws and social rules (e.g. 'little boys can't touch the sky' vs. 'little boys can't get in the bath with their clothes on'), both children and adults state that natural laws cannot be violated, regardless of whether an individual knows about the law, or intends to violate it. Social rules, it is claimed, may potentially be violated either by intention or by ignorance of the rule (Kalish 1998). In addition, the justifications provided for the possibility or impossibility of violation differ between the two types of situation. Natural laws, it is claimed, cannot be violated because physical constraints govern such laws; social rules, by contrast, are open to violation because they rest on notions of social permission and obligation (Kalish 1998).

Even more relevant, however, are situations in which adults and children (in later childhood) claim that changes in conventional status produce changes in what is deemed 'true'. So, for example, if an object is given away or renamed, they state that it is now true that it belongs to someone else, and truly has a new name. But, if it is only within a pretend game that these events occur, the original owner and the original name remain the true ones (see Kalish et al. 2000). What this provisionally suggests is that both adults and older children grasp the way in which some form of intersubjective truth or 'truth by social consent' may be established by collective decision or agreement.

This raises the problem of how we psychologically reconcile the apparent objective ontology of institutional facts with an understanding of their social foundations. Here it seems relevant that in other domains, similar paradoxes in our conceptualizations of various phenomena appear to exist, which also hinge on this question of ontological status. One, for example, centres on the question of how it is that adults and children, who well understand the difference between fiction and reality, respond to fictional materials such as film, theatre, or pretend games with genuine emotion (e.g. fear or sadness, see Harris 2000; Harris et al. 1991). The basic proposal is that we are equipped with a cognitive assessment system comprised of two dedicated components (Harris 2000). The primary appraisal system perceives events in the environment, appraises them for elements of relevance to the individual, and generates an emotional response (e.g. on witnessing a person find a snake and scream, the appraisal system might register 'scream', 'snake', and 'danger', and so produce fear in the observer). This appraisal system does not register the ontological status of events, so the observer responds with genuine emotion, even if the image is fictional. Where necessary, however, an independent 'evaluation system' can be intentionally recruited. This evaluates the ontological status of an event, designating it as 'real' or 'fictional' (producing a conclusion, for instance, that 'it is only a film'), and the emotional response is attenuated accordingly.

One possibility, then, is that our cognitive processing of conventional and institutional phenomena may follow a somewhat similar pattern, though with important differences that will need qualification. This analysis will try to deal with the fact that the way in which we consider institutional facts (e.g. 'this couple are married') to be objective is quite different to the sense in which we consider natural facts (e.g. 'Mount Everest is the highest mountain on earth') to be objective. And it shows up most clearly in our sense that we can collectively intend to create, change, or nullify institutional facts, but not natural laws. It will also try to account for the fact that we do not consider institutional facts to be ontologically subjective in any standard sense. This is most obvious in the instinctive knowledge that we cannot create, change, or nullify such facts, simply by changing our personal opinions about them (I cannot decide that you are 'no longer married', for instance).

The first qualification to be made is that in making ontological evaluations, the individual may, crucially, not be restricted to the traditional dichotomy of objective vs. subjective. Rather than contemplating whether an institutional fact exists independently of human intention, or dependently upon personal opinion, they may also refer to a third category of facts that exist intersubjectively, in virtue of collective consensus. The second qualification is that, unlike in the case of, for instance, emotional reactions to films in which a person's evaluation may result in a verbalizable statement about ontological status (e.g. 'the film is not real'), in the case of institutional facts, the conclusion may be rather in the form of a judgement: the persons themselves can be instrumental in the manipulation or invalidation of the fact (perhaps diagnostic of its non-objectivity), and any such act will depend on acquiring additional social consent (perhaps a telling sign of its non-subjectivity).

In more concrete terms, this means that when an individual encounters a situation in which institutional information is encoded, he or she will first automatically appraise the scene for information of general relevance to themselves. The default treatment of such information will be to treat it as part of the objective environment. Thus, the individual acts according to the institutional facts without ontological evaluation. But under certain circumstances, they may intentionally evaluate and distinguish the ontological status of varying aspects of the scene, judging a certain category of facts within it to exist by intersubjective agreement or consent.

An example may help. Mr Jones returns home one night to a standard scene, permeated with institutional structure: he drives home in the company car, at a particular time, to his jointly owned house, to three individuals he knows to be his two children and wife. However, he returns his wedding ring to Mrs Jones and declares his intention to file for divorce and sell the house. Mr Jones knows that there are certain 'natural' aspects of this scene that exist independently of his intent, and other institutional aspects that depend on his continued consent that they exist. While he may not think he can spontaneously nullify the institutions of marriage or ownership, he does understand that he can, by intention, nullify the institutional facts that he is married and jointly owns a house. And he knows that the way to do this will be to obtain additional consent from various other social bodies.

However, there are other instances in which we may intuit that we can, by collective intention, abolish whole institutional structures (though we may be less often inclined to do so). If we organize a plot to bring down the monarchy and institute a republic in its place, we intend to abolish the institution of monarchy. If we organize to ban a particular religion or religious practice, we intend to negate the existence of whole institutions, not just the institutional facts that they generate. So, although we may rarely contemplate the fact that our institutional reality rests on collectively agreed status assignments that are normatively governed (though it seems significant that this too is possible in the human case), human social and political action indicates some grasp of the role of collective consent in maintaining it.

So what can be said of how we conceptualize the institutions and institutional facts that govern our lives? One possibility (after Searle 1995) is to suggest that we understand the way in which institutional facts depend for their existence on social agreement, but that we can nevertheless make statements about them that are objectively true. For instance, we may grasp that the institutional fact that a couple is married depends on collective agreement. But we sense also that a statement that 'the couple is married' is true, irrespective of our consent or lack thereof. Another possibility is to emphasize that the categories that humans recruit in making sense of the world are, in general, not restricted to the traditional ontological dichotomy of objective vs. subjective. They also include categories of fact that may be termed 'ontologically intersubjective', in that they exist in virtue of group consensus. Indeed, it may be precisely because such facts elude objective or subjective categorization that we recognize their intersubjective foundations, and with no reduction in their normative force. As Plotkin incisively observes, it is simply that for many human affairs, 'the law is grounded in the group' (2003: 209).

13.5 Conclusion

Human social life has become institutionalized over the course of evolution. Our closest living relatives, the chimpanzees, demonstrate impressive cultural capacities (Whiten et al. 1999). But in no case do these take on the conventional or institutionalized character of human practice, in which social codes of conduct are mediated by status functions, and regulated according to collective consent (see Wyman and Rakoczy 2011, for details of the phylogenetic comparison). Performative speech acts function centrally here, as tools for the public assignment of institutional status to people, actions, and objects. And through our common consent and collective imagination, it is this status that specifies the rights, obligations, and norms that guide institutionalized social interaction.

The developmental home of an ability to collectively imagine together with others appears to be children's pretend play activities. In their pretence games, children gain familiarity with proto-performative speech acts and constitutive rules, jointly imagining with play partners that, for example, 'we are mummy and daddy', and 'now we are going shopping'. This may provide them with early insight into the way in which, within certain contexts, social interaction is guided by social rules so that the appropriateness of actions within this context will be evaluated by reference to intersubjectively established standards of validity. With an initial grasp of the basics of institutional practice, older children's collaborative, pretend re-enactments of adult practices may culturally contextualize their pretence, and provide a critical gateway or arena for transition into institutional life. These games may, for instance, provide them with a background understanding that social-normative constraints shape specific practices, and perhaps even some of the rudimentary contents of the practices themselves. The way in which children 'pretend into' their institutional realities may also leave them with an intuition that, although institutional facts must be respected as objective features of their social environment, their existence is essentially rooted in intersubjective consensus.

That the efficacy of performatives in creating institutional facts lies in such a rich foundation of collective imagination and consensus suggests that this linguistic function could not have emerged in human evolution independently of these cognitive and social competencies. Here, it seems significant that although nowadays our primary mode of status assignment is linguistic, it need not be in any strict sense. For instance, written status representation in the form of ownership and employment contracts, birth certificates and passports has replaced the spoken performative in many cases. But the use of symbolic marking, for example, in the case of tribal tattooing and scarification practices, or the transfer of symbolic objects in which wedding rings are exchanged or a royal crown is inherited also mark the creation and transfer of institutional status. Similarly, symbolic *actions* such as those involved in a Christian baptism, or the accolade in a British knighthood, perform like functions to the performative speech act (now rendering a person Christian or a member of the knighthood).

These cases point to a scenario in which the first performative devices to emerge in human evolution were not linguistic but, rather, action-based. For example, whereas group membership is commonly designated today by performative speech acts in which children are assigned family names, it is likely that this was formerly achieved through public initiation by way of symbolic body marking. Similarly, the union represented by the performative words spoken at a wedding likely had predecessors in the form of symbolic marking of the newlyweds themselves, and gift exchange between families. This is partly indicated by the tight association that still exists between performative speech acts and their ritual contexts: the situations in which linguistic performatives are uttered remain couched in rich, symbolic action sequences such as those entailed in christenings and wedding ceremonies. However, it is also pointed to logically: the force of linguistic performatives depends on their being uttered in the appropriate ritual context (for instance, at a wedding, or by an appropriate official), whereas the efficacy of ritual performatives does not depend on their being represented in language (for example, in the case of symbolic body-marking of group membership). On this account, the evolution of the spoken performative essentially points to the prior emergence of not only a rich set of cognitive capacities, but an equally critical foundation of symbolic, ritual practices (Knight 1999). Performative speech acts, then, appear to have come to complement and partially replace symbolic actions as devices for achieving status assignment in a particularly effective manner.

More generally, that humans use language and symbolic action to coordinate their private imaginings into shared, public fictions that have normative force is profoundly revealing with regard to our social evolution. In addition to sophisticated behavioural coordination strategies (shared with many other species of the animal kingdom) humans have, in addition, evolved modes of coordinating cognitively. The ability to jointly imagine and subscribe to a set of fictional statuses that we subsequently use to guide our interactions in normative terms is qualitatively different from anything observed outside our own species (see Wyman and Rakoczy 2011). Indeed, the whole framework of collective intentionality, in which we share attention to aspects of the environment, share goals and plans for collaborating together (Tomasello et al. 2005), and subscribe to shared fictions that then further govern our interactions, indicates an evolutionary environment in which the threats of competition and social exploitation became outweighed by the necessities of cooperation and trust (see also Wyman and Tomasello 2007).

It thus seems highly relevant that significant phases of human evolution appear to have been characterized by distinctly egalitarian socio-political organization (Knauft 1991; Power, Chapter 4). These centrally involve anti- or reverse-dominance mechanisms that punish individuals who try to establish superior social status over others, continually blocking the development of social hierarchy (e.g. Boehm 1999; Erdal and Whiten 1994; Knight, Chapter 17). A socio-political climate such as this may have been pivotal in attenuating competition levels in hominin communities, such that collective imagination, status functions and institutions, and the performative devices that enable us to negotiate these could emerge in human evolution.

14

The time frame of the emergence of modern language and its implications

DAN DEDIU AND STEPHEN C. LEVINSON

14.1 Social origins and the time frame of language evolution

Language is social in origin in at least two main senses: its primary function, acquisition, and main usage are in face-to-face social interaction (where it conveys *inter alia* social and cultural information); secondly, the great bulk of the structure of languages (the sound structure, the morphology, the syntax, and the lexicon) is a product of cultural evolution. Most of this book is concerned with these matters, and with the emergence of the social cognition that made these systems possible. This chapter is rather different—it is about the time frame of the emergence of languages of a modern type. It argues that, firstly, this time frame is much greater than most researchers in the language sciences imagine—essentially, humans of half a million years ago probably had languages structurally very similar to those on the planet today. Language as we know it emerged in the million years prior to that point. Secondly, this much greater time frame has consequences for both kinds of social origin, which we will allude to here, and pick up below. The intensive face-to-face communication with its turn-taking which typifies human communication and is absent among the other great apes is probably of much greater antiquity than complex language or speech, which has come to fit a niche it is in some ways ill-designed for. But the longer time-frame has fundamental importance for how we should think about the depth of cultural evolution that lies behind languages, as we will make clear.

14.2 The myth of the 'modern human revolution'

Not so long ago, the European archaeological record[1] seemed to show an abrupt transition about 40 thousand years ago (kya) between two species of humans, with

---

[1] It must be noted, however, that this seemed not to be limited to Europe, but thought at the time to apply also to Africa and even the apparently contemporaneous colonization of Australia was taken to support this view.

the more archaic Neandertals[2] being replaced by fully modern humans, an anatomical transition coinciding with a cultural one, witnessing the sudden emergence of the 'hallmarks' of modern human behaviours, such as art and personal ornaments, cave paintings, large-scale exchange networks, and projectile weapons (Henshilwood and Marean 2003; McBrearty and Brooks 2000; Mellars 2005; Roebroeks and Verpoorte 2009; Stringer 2002). Therefore, numerous ideas have been proposed to explain this 'revolution', such as externalized memory, integration of cognitive modules, representational redescription, large social groups, economic networks, symbolic behaviour, and, most of all, *language* (e.g. Bickerton 2002; Donald 1991, 2001; Dunbar 1996b; Gabora 2003; Mithen 1996). Some concluded that this was the result of an evolutionary *saltation*, a sudden unique genetic mutation giving rise to the full 'modern package', with a concrete proposal being, for example, Crow's (2008) *protocadherinXY* gene, and a specific cognitive one being promoted by Chomsky (2010: 59): '...a rewiring of the brain took place in some individual, call him Prometheus, yielding the operation of unbounded Merge, applying to concepts with intricate (and little understood) properties...'.

However, when we 'zoom out' of Europe, properly seen as a 'remote cul de sac' of human evolution (McBrearty and Brooks 2000: 454), this 'revolution' turns out to be an illusion, caused by the migration of an intrusive population coming from Africa, bringing both a new anatomy and culture. In Africa, the emergence of modernity was *gradual*, a process of piecemeal accretion, both behaviourally and morphologically, across hundreds of thousands of years and continent-scale geographical distances, and thus far from a linear progression through time in a single direction from 'archaic' towards 'modern' (Henshilwood and Marean 2003; Klein 2009; McBrearty and Brooks 2000; Mellars 2005; Roebroeks and Verpoorte 2009; Stringer 2002). Thus, the view of a sudden and concerted irruption of modernity—biological, cultural, and linguistic—has been dealt a fatal blow by refocusing on the larger-scale evolutionary history in Africa (McBrearty and Brooks 2000).

Another blow to the saltation view comes from the recent discoveries and reassessment of those 'archaics', the Neandertals in particular, for example in what had been thought to be their limited cultural capacities. Far from being simple,[3] the Neandertal stone tool technology (the Mousterian, and the Levallois technique in particular) was in fact complex, showed many variants and elaborations (see Klein 2009: 485ff), and required considerable skill and training, involving hierarchical (recursive) planning and execution to strike flakes off a highly prepared core (Stout

---

[2] We will prefer the newer 'Neandertal' over the original spelling, 'Neanderthal', throughout this Chapter.
[3] The following brief overview of selected features of the Neandertal archaeological record does not imply that these features were present throughout their whole history and geographical range, but we are forced to gloss over these complexities.

et al. 2008). Patterns of wear on these stone tools suggest they were primarily used to produce yet further tools of wood, pointing to a rich material culture that has not preserved, a conjecture spectacularly confirmed by the discovery in Germany of carefully shaped javelins ~400 kya old (Thieme 1997). The Neandertals managed to adapt to a very harsh, sub-Arctic climate by controlling fire, possibly making sewn skin and footgear as inferred from energy-use considerations (Sørensen 2009), and hunting a range of large animals (Conard and Niven 2001; Villa and Lenoir 2009). They took care of sick and infirm individuals, with fossils showing healed or permanent injuries (e.g. Spikins et al. 2010), probably buried their dead with grave offerings (Grün and Stringer 2000; Klein 2009), and used pigment and personal ornaments (d'Errico and Soressi 2002; d'Errico and Vanhaeren 2009; Watts 2009). Moreover, when in contact with modern humans, they borrowed the latest cultural innovations, as shown by the Arcy Châtelperronian (e.g. Floss 2003), showing that there was nothing that prevented their ability to use, integrate, and transmit modern technology.

On the other side of the coin, there have been groups of indubitably modern humans possessing the full capacity for modern culture and language but who have left archaeological records considerably simpler than the Neandertals (Roebroeks and Verpoorte 2009). Such well-known examples include the Tasmanians (Richerson et al. 2009), who lacked bone tools, clothing, spear throwers, fishing gear, hafted tools, and probably the ability to make fire (Henrich 2004); the North American early Archaic (Speth 2004); and the Yaghans of Tierra del Fuego (Darwin 1845). Thus, we cannot infer from a relatively simple technology that a particular group of humans lack the capacity for modern culture or language (Speth 2004). Demography seems to play a crucial role in cultural and especially technological complexity. Like the Tasmanians, Neandertals had very low population densities, and suffered repeated local extinctions and recolonizations due to climate shifts (Dennell et al. 2011; Hublin and Roebroeks 2009), processes that would have adversely affected the accumulation and persistence of complex culture (Habgood and Franklin 2008; Kline and Boyd 2010; Powell et al. 2009; Richerson et al. 2009). Cultural elaboration is cumulative, so it can itself play a major causal role in further elaboration and development. Given a set of conditions, such as time free from subsistence activities, health, moderate peer competition, parental investment in the young, ecological wealth, etc., culture will ratchet up through incremental cultural transmission.

Thus, the relationship between modern anatomy, cognition, culture, and language is a complex one, and cannot be captured by a single saltationary event, let alone by a single 'gene' acquired at a specific moment in our evolutionary history, leaving unambiguous traces in the fossil or archaeological record. This myth of a 'modern human revolution' is now totally rejected by paleoanthropologists and archaeologists, but it is disturbing to see it persisting—explicitly or implicitly—in discussions of language and cultural evolution (e.g. Chomsky 2010; Crow 2008).

14.3 Neandertal capacity for speech and language

Related to the myth of the modern human revolution, there is a lingering idea that recognizably modern speech and language (as opposed to the protolanguages of many recent proposals) are a very recent phenomenon, more or less coinciding with the emergence of modern humans. What we mean by recognizably modern speech and language encompasses a continuum of verbal communication systems which would look familiar to a present-day linguist. More specifically, such linguistic systems would use a similar range of phonemes and phonetic features such as tone, vowel quality, contrastive voicing, etc., making use of the same principles such as duality of patterning and limited recursion as most modern languages today. They would have a sizable vocabulary, complex syntax, and variable morphology, as well as pragmatics as intricate as found in all present-day natural languages. It is hard to specify more exactly what a capacity for modern languages would look like for a range of reasons worth spelling out.

First and foremost, it is far from clear if there is any single universally valid definition of what a modern language is. Hockett's (1960) 'design features' can be taken as rough guides, but systematic searches for linguistic universals have failed to find detailed properties common to all (Evans and Levinson 2009; Levinson and Evans 2010). Thus, it is perhaps best to visualize 'modern language' as a fuzzy cloud in the space of all possible communication systems, a cloud defined as much by the intrinsic requirements of communication, the constraints and biases of the human brain (Christiansen and Chater 2008; Dediu 2011), and the properties of the vocal apparatus and the auditory system, as by the contingencies of evolution, both cultural and biological. Secondly, because nearly all normal humans end up speaking (or signing) a complex language, we have swallowed a myth of the uniformity of linguistic competence. Actually, like any other biological substrate, there will be the inevitable variation in the population without which evolution cannot occur (Levinson and Gray 2012). There is thus almost certainly a large amount of variation in the genetic bases of speech among normal present-day humans (Dediu 2011) as shown by numerous heritability studies (e.g. Bishop 2009; Stromswold 2001) and the ongoing identification of the genes and molecular mechanisms involved (Bates et al. 2011; Bishop 2009; Fisher and Scharff 2009; Newbury and Monaco 2010; Vernes et al. 2008). While this variation is mostly hidden when looking at the phenotype of language behaviour since nearly all humans acquire highly functional versions of their own native language(s), there are probably cases where these differences do matter: such genetic biases can shape the synchronic linguistic diversity, and influence the diachronic trajectory of language change and evolution (Dediu 2011; Dediu and Ladd 2007; Ladd et al. 2008). Thus, even living people seem to differ slightly in the biological machinery supporting language, and the degree of differences between us and the long-gone individuals living hundreds and tens of thousands of years ago would have probably been somewhat greater. Third, we want to argue here that the current archaeological and genetic data strongly suggest that languages very similar to modern ones were in use about half a million years ago. We do this by invoking evolutionary parsimony: humans living around that time had very modern-looking vocal and auditory characteristics adapted for speech; their behavioural and cultural remains suggest the use of a complex language; the few known genes related to speech and language in modern humans are also present in almost identical forms in them; and (according to our view) they were biologically the same species with us. Ergo, they most probably had speech and language very similar to ours—that is, their languages would have fallen within or close to the range exhibited by linguistic diversity today.

The Neandertals are a sister group to modern humans and we shared a common ancestor about half a million years ago (660 ± 140 kya for mitochondrial DNA, Hublin 2009b; 270–440 kya based on the whole genome, Green et al. 2010).[4] That common ancestor is normally identified as *Homo heidelbergensis*, best exemplified by extensive remains found at Atapuerca in Spain.[5] Their descendants in one branch, the Neandertals, had a series of diagnostic morphological features such as the shape of the cranium and face and generally robust body build (Hublin 2009b). The body proportions result probably from adaptation to the cold climate they inhabited, while the cranial shape was due mostly to random genetic drift (Weaver et al. 2007; Weaver 2009). They inhabited western Eurasia, and their habitat expanded and contracted following the severe climatic fluctuations of the period, mostly by the extinction of local groups and repeated recolonization from surviving populations (Dennell et al. 2011; Hublin and Roebroeks 2009). The extraction and analysis of Neandertal DNA (Green et al. 2010) shows that they were extremely similar to us, as expected, given the very recent date of separation between our lineages, and reveals that modern humans and Neandertals interbred sometime after our lineage left Africa about 70 kya.[6] Due to this interbreeding, modern humans outside Africa have, on average, 1–4 per cent Neandertal DNA, but this proportion is probably much higher for those genes that conferred an adaptive advantage in the different non-African climates (Hawks and Cochran 2006), such as the immune system (Abi-Rached et al. 2011). This supports earlier findings of fossils interpreted by some paleoanthropologists as

---

[4] Since the discovery of the Denisovans, a sister clade to Neandertals, who shared the same crucial genetic variants like the modern alleles of *FOXP2*, this date might need to be pushed back to their common ancestor at *c.* 800 kya. We will work with the conservative figure of half a million years, but this is a *terminus ante quem*.

[5] The exact place of the Atapuerca fossils in human phylogeny is disputed; they may have been a side-shoot distinct from the main line from *H. heidelbergensis* to Neandertals, but if so they were nevertheless close.

[6] Earlier interactions, at around 100 kya, have been noted in the Levant.

hybrids between modern humans and Neandertals, such as the fossils from Abrigo do Lagar Velho (Bayle et al. 2010; Duarte et al. 1999), Peştera cu Oase (Rougier et al. 2007; Trinkaus et al. 2003), Peştera Muierii (Soficaru et al. 2006) and Mladeč (Teschler-Nicola 2006). It also explains genetic markers with a history that did not match a recent origin of modern humans in Africa (Evans et al. 2006; Garrigan et al. 2005a, 2005b; Yu et al. 2002; Ziętkiewicz et al. 2003). The few genetic differences between Neandertals and modern humans are intriguing as they concern skin pigmentation (*TRPM1*), metabolism (*THADA*), skeletal morphology (*RUNX2*), and possibly cognition (*DYRK1A, NRG3, AUTS2, CADPS2*). Neandertals disappeared from the fossil record about 30 kya after cohabiting with modern humans for several tens of thousands of years; the reasons for this disappearance are hotly debated but little understood.

The analysis of fossilized parts of the vocal tract and the auditory system, combined with data from living humans and models seems to suggest that modern speech is an old characteristic of our lineage, although some researchers express scepticism about what that means for language (Fitch 2009). On the perception side, human audiograms have a very specific shape with high sensitivity in the 1–6 kHz range as opposed to chimpanzees, which show a low sensitivity in this region. Reconstructions of the external and middle ears of *H. heidelbergensis* fossils from Sima de los Huesos, Spain (Martínez et al. 2004, 2008) show that they had a modern auditory system, suggesting that their hearing could support modern speech (but see Fitch 2010: 325). The Neandertal ear ossicles from Qafzeh and Amud (Quam and Rak 2008) fall within the range of modern variation, further suggesting that, very probably, modern hearing tuned to the bandwidth of speech predates our last common ancestor with the Neandertals. On the production side, Lieberman and Crelin's (1971) early and influential interpretation of the high position of the larynx in the Neandertals and their resulting incapacity for speech is largely falsified by recent data. A wealth of findings shows that the Neandertal hyoid bone is essentially modern (Arensburg et al. 1989, 1990; Martínez et al. 2008; Rodríguez et al. 2003), in contrast to the archaic characteristics of *Homo erectus* (Capasso et al. 2008) and of *Australopithecus afarensis* (Alemseged et al. 2006). This modern morphology of the hyoid bone in Neandertals suggests that air sacs—cavities filled with air and connected to the vocal tract, present in many primate species (de Boer 2009; Hewitt et al. 2002)— have been lost since at least our common ancestor *Homo heidelbergensis*. It has been suggested that the presence of air sacs reduces the range of distinctive speech sounds which can be produced (de Boer 2009), linking their absence to the presence of modern speech in the last ancestor of modern humans and Neandertals. The Neandertal larynx was most probably low in the vocal tract (DuBrul 1977; Falk 1975; Fitch 2009; Houghton 1993; Le May 1975), but the significance of its position for modern speech is probably more modest than usually assumed (Fitch 2000, 2009). Also on the production side, the size of the hypoglossal canal (indicative of tongue control) in modern humans and other apes overlaps substantially (DeGusta et al. 1999; Jungers et al. 2003), being of limited value in assessing fossil humans. The thoracic vertebral canal could be important for breathing control and voluntary speech production (MacLarnon and Hewitt 1999, 2004) and it seems to be enlarged in Neandertals, but also as early as the Dmanisi *Homo erectus* (Meyer 2005), suggesting that it might be of limited value as well. Genetically, the modern form of *FOXP2*, a transcription factor crucial for the fine motor control necessary for speech (Fisher and Scharff 2009; Lai et al. 2001), is shared between modern humans and Neandertals (Krause et al. 2007) but is different from the variant present in the other primates (Enard et al. 2002), suggesting that probably our common ancestor also had this modern variant (Trinkaus 2007). It has been suggested (following Darwin 1871) that all these adaptations for speech could have been motivated by something other than language, for example music (compare Mithen's 2005 'singing Neandertal'; Fitch 2009), but in our view this hypothesis has little likelihood given the tuning of hearing for speech rather than music, the dissociations between music and language (Peretz 2006), and the existence of fundamental differences between the two, such as different structural organization, categorical bases, and propositional meaning (Patel 2008).

The Neandertals' brain size was comparable to that of modern humans even after correcting for body size (Klein 2009), but there might have been slight structural differences (such as the 'occipital bun' suggesting a greater development of visual areas). They almost certainly had a similar neocortex size to modern humans, which suggests group sizes and social complexity in the range of modern human hunter-gatherers (Dunbar 1993). The birth process in Neandertals was very similar to that in modern humans, an inference based on the reconstruction of the birth canal (Weaver and Hublin 2009) and the neonate head size (de León et al. 2008) indicating that birthing was as difficult as in modern humans, requiring 'obligate midwifery and all of the attendant social implications' (Franciscus 2009: 9126). In fact, Weaver and Hublin conclude, reviewing the Tabun Neandertal pelvis, that despite some small differences 'a human-sized neonate would have been able to pass through Tabun's birth canal' (2009: 8154). The developmental trajectory was also probably very similar but not identical (Gunz et al. 2010), as shown by, for example, the analysis of the pattern of dental eruption in *Homo antecessor* (de Castro et al. 1999, 2010) and a suggested three-year interval between births, similar to the modern hunter-gatherers (Lalueza-Fox et al. 2011). Thus, Neandertal infants most probably benefited from the slow development and prolonged dependency crucial for the transmission of culture and language in modern humans.

As discussed above, Neandertal culture and technology, far from being the simple product of primitive minds, is directly comparable with that of modern humans in similar climatic and demographic contexts, and we find it hard to imagine how such cultural complexity could be transferred without language. While recognizing that language does not fossilize, putting together all the genetic, paleontological, and archaeological data as briefly reviewed above, the overwhelming probability seems to be that Neandertals possessed recognizably modern languages and cultures, well within the range of the ethnographic record for modern humans.

14.4 The antiquity of language has implications for languages as cultural artefacts

Recognizably modern language and speech and the capacity for complex culture are thus old characteristics of our genus, *Homo*, predating the last common ancestor of modern humans and Neandertals, over half a million years ago. We have a fairly good overview of the linguistic diversity in modern humans (Haspelmath et al. 2005; Lewis 2009) and we begin to understand the evolutionary processes that shaped it (Greenhill et al. 2010; Levinson and Gray 2012; Pagel 2009), but what happened to the languages developed by the other lineages of humans such as the Neandertals?

It was believed for a long time that, after their expansion from Africa, modern humans completely replaced the existing archaic populations inhabiting the world without significant genetic and cultural exchanges (Stringer and Andrews 1988), but we now know that there was significant exchange of both genetic and cultural material, as discussed above: modern humans interbred with Neandertals on exiting Africa *c.* 70 kya (so all humans today—except in Africa—share Neandertal genes), and they interbred with Denisovans as they went through SE Asia on the way to Australasia *c.* 60 kya (present-day Papuans and Australians carry their genes). We know that there were further archaic hominins in SE Asia, as shown by late fossils of *H. erectus* in Java and the 'hobbits' of Flores (descended from *H. erectus* or some earlier form of hominin). In Africa, there was also extensive morphological variation, with hominins showing archaic features living as recently as 13 kya and pointing to deep population substructure (as shown by the Iwo Eleru fossils from Nigeria: Harvati et al. 2011a). Our suggestion has been that at least the Neandertals and Denisovans (with essentially modern DNA) were language-bearing fellow races of our species just like the modern humans recently out of Africa. They interacted as shown by the genetic exchanges. All three varieties had small demographies (e.g. there may have been under 10,000 Neandertals; Sørensen 2011) and would have interacted perhaps only occasionally, but sufficiently intimately to borrow major technological innovations. The technology may have gone mostly one way (although since Neandertal technology may have been largely in wood, we can't be sure), but Neandertal genetic and especially cultural adaptation to the Eurasian climate and ecology must have been valuable transferable assets, the latter best acquired through language.

So what happened to the languages of our archaic cousins? Several scenarios are imaginable, such as (1) *language shift* (modern humans lost their own and adopted the archaics' languages), (2) *language extinction* (almost complete extinction of the archaic languages), (3) *pidginization* between modern and archaic languages, and (4) *sustained low intensity contact* resulting in linguistic and cultural exchanges. Scenarios (1) and (3) seem improbable, given the evidence from the fossil record, the outcomes of historical contact between human groups, and the lack of a clear linguistic and cultural discontinuity between Africa and the rest of the world (Cysouw and Comrie 2009). Scenario (2) is compatible with the older Out-of-Africa with replacement model (Stringer and Andrews 1988) and is not incompatible with genetic exchanges (as we know from recent and historical cases that cultural and genetic contact can accompany language loss), but we think that a much more probable scenario is (4). Although genetic transfer may imply only cursory contact, cultural exchange of the kind reflected in the Châtelperronian technology must reflect more extensive contact.[7] Just as the colonists of the European colonial period adopted subsidence technologies and cultivars from the colonized (compare the origin of tomatoes, tobacco, rice, bananas), so it is likely that the archaic humans who had lived for hundreds of thousands of years outside Africa must have discovered many cultural tricks useful for modern humans entering these new environments. Neandertals may have overlapped with modern humans for 10,000 years in Northern Europe (currently controversial), but for even longer elsewhere like the Levant.

If we assume low-intensity but sustained contact between archaic and modern humans, perhaps throughout Eurasia, then present-day linguistic diversity may still preserve traces of these events. In fact such a scenario may help to explain a puzzle raised by current linguistic diversity, namely that it is hard to imagine how it could have all been generated from an initial exodus out of Africa a mere 70 kya. To put this in perspective, consider that this is just seven times deeper than the plausible reconstructed depth of the Indo-European family. Consider too that recent work on structural change inside language families, including Indo-European, shows that structural features of language change on average at a glacial pace, of the order of one major change in tens or even hundreds of thousands of years (Dunn et al. 2011).[8] Some major language families like Dravidian or Bantu show relatively little structural change at all in their reconstructed histories. But if the small numbers of modern humans arriving in Eurasia blended their native languages with the greater and more widespread diversity developed by the pre-existing populations of archaic humans, there would have been a significant reservoir of diversity to draw on.

---

[7] The bone adornment material from these sites is disputed, but the technological innovations of the later Neandertals are not (Mellars 2010).

[8] These dates are computed by seeing how many times in all the parallel lineages inside a large family a change occurs—Indo-European can thus harbour a couple of hundred thousand years of independent developments.

There are similar speculations, for example by David Gil (2011) who suggests that the 'Mekong-Mamberamo' linguistic area (extending from mainland SE Asia through most of Indonesia and into the western half of New Guinea) could be a remnant of contact with Denisovans, itself an extension of McWhorter's (2008) suggestion that contact with *H. floresiensis* (Flores man) led to the simplification of the Austronesian languages on the island of Flores.

These speculations could be firmed up by further examination of the patterning of linguistic diversity within Africa vs. outside Africa, and by a comparison between Eurasian vs. Papuan and Australian languages, looking for subtle structural differences compatible with influences from a non-African substrate. If such influences can be detected, then present-day linguistic diversity has drawn on a much deeper pool of variation, six or seven times more ancient than the latest African exodus. Thus, just as for genetics, Neandertals and Denisovans (and likely further archaic cousins) might be extinct as human lineages but continue to live in us through their genes and perhaps speak through us as well. The much deeper time frame for cultural evolution thus envisaged makes a fundamental difference to how we perhaps should think about languages as cultural artefacts—they have been honed over geological time, and have adapted less to the particular cultures and societies we now find them in, and more to the underlying sociality of the species and the ecologies we have inhabited for long periods of time.

14.5 The social origins of language

We have argued, contrary to the saltation theories popular in linguistics, that language is an ancient development. We have also argued that the languages we now have are the result of cultural evolution and enhancement over more than half a million years—in that sense their complexity, expressiveness, and richness is perhaps largely a product of ratcheting social transmission. The origins of complex linguistic communication therefore lie much further back. What the fossils suggest is that modern speech capacities were not present 1.8 mya (at the time of *H. erectus*), but probably were present by 0.5 mya, and very likely 600 kya. So speech must have emerged in that interval, but it is currently unclear what the actual trajectory of this process was during this enormous time span.

Can we say anything about that process and its beginnings? There are some clues in the social context, the interactional niche that language occupies. Casual language usage is characterized by rapid turn-taking, with very short gaps of 100–200 ms (Stivers et al. 2009). A puzzle about this system is that it beats our fastest reaction times—it takes at least 600 ms to find a word and say it (Levelt 1989). We solve the puzzle the same way we play tennis—by predicting where the ball or the words will be. In tennis, the prediction is done by the visual system and the reaction by the motor system; in contrast, in predicting what will be said and pre-formulating our response we are using the very same language system—breaking yet another barrier, the mind's bottleneck on complex central parallel processing (Sigman and Dehaene 2005). From a design perspective this is a mad system; it is simply too intensive computationally, and must be at the very limits of human performance.

How did such a mad system arise? There are clues in human ontogeny: by about four months old, infants can take vocal (non-linguistic) turns with latencies around 700 ms—pretty fast, considering their still developing nervous systems. This fast turn-taking collapses as infants learn language and produce their first multi-word utterances. By three years, toddler turn-taking is painfully slow, with latencies of 1.5 seconds or more, slowly speeding up through middle childhood. What this suggests is that, unlike in the other great apes, there is a deep instinct for vocal alternation, and that it takes years of acquired linguistic skill to pack complex linguistic clauses into the short turns characteristic of mature human language usage. The other apes produce a single sound (with some modulation perhaps) on a breath, in contrast to our extraordinary vocal choreography. This suggests that the rhythm of our turn-taking goes back to a period when a single simple sound exhausted a turn, and that language has had to adapt to the timing constraints of this ancient system. It may well be, then, that the basic parameters of our interactional infrastructure (the 'interaction engine' of Levinson 2006), including the timing, the multi-modality, the intense face-to-face mode of communication, and its roots in 'mind reading', are much more ancient than language and can be traced back to the emergence of the complex culture expressed in early tool assemblages.

Finally, we should correct a possible misreading of what we have outlined here. We have suggested that modern language is half a million years old. Yet we have also emphasized the role the last half million years of cultural evolution have played in linguistic complexity, through language contact and linguistic change. Of course, evolution, whether cultural or genetic, is never in abeyance, and the raw fuel for evolution is variance in the population. That variance is still visible today in language, cognition, and the genes that support them, although linguists and cognitive scientists have tended to idealize that variance away. The origins of language lie in a gradual, incremental co-evolutionary process between genes and culture. Genetic differences relevant to communication were probably as widespread in ancient humans as they are today and they both enabled, and in turn have been selected by, more complex cultural communication systems, leading to a spiralling co-evolutionary race leading in tandem to language, speech, and to their anatomical, physiological, and neuro-cognitive bases. Building language and speech involved, and still does, the construction of the language cultural niche as well as it own biological and cultural supports. This co-evolutionary process generated—and continues to generate—strong selective pressures on the biological bases of our cognition, language, and speech, explaining the continued, and in some cases the accelerated, evolution of modern humans. The most basic ingredients probably were the *co-operative instincts* (Tomasello 2008) and the *interaction engine* (Levinson 2006) that allowed the emergence of cultural transmission. Probably essential was the intention recognition system with its neuro-cognitive instantiation (Noordzij et al. 2010). On these bases were later built the more complex aspects of language (phonology, syntax, and lexicon) and the speech system.

14.6 Acknowledgements

We wish to thank the Editors for their invitation, and an anonymous reviewer for their comments and suggestions.

15

The evolution of ritual as a process of sexual selection

CAMILLA POWER

Back in 1960, social anthropologist Marshall Sahlins contrasted typical primate dominance with human relations mediated by symbolic kinship: 'Dominance is at its nadir among primitive hunters and gatherers,' he wrote. 'Culture is the oldest "equaliser". Among animals capable of symbolic communication, the weak can always collectively connive to overthrow the strong' (1960: 83).

Victor Turner, one of the greatest experts on ritual, adopted Iowan Lewis's phrase 'the powers of the weak' in his thesis on sacredness (1969: 85). Aspects of the sacred are liminality, the state of being betwixt and between, marked by juxtaposition of phenomena counter to perceptible reality (Turner 1967: 105), and communitas, the assertion of equality through stripping away all difference of rank. A true Durkheimian, Turner rooted symbolism in ritual action, and gave ritual primacy as generator of linguistic concepts. If the weak can temporarily take power from the strong, it is because symbols summon the force of their ritual coalition in action—collective intentionality in John Searle's (1995) terms. Turner's idea of ritual symbols as a force—direct action in a field of social drama—suggests the causality of Sahlins' formulation should be reversed: because among Machiavellian humans the weak can connive to overthrow the strong, we are animals capable of symbolic communication.

Only given social forces of counter-dominance—where individuals with allies can resist being dominated—and reverse dominance—where the collective dominates any would-be dominant individual—is language likely to emerge. The strong have no need of it; they have more direct, physical means of persuasion. Any tendency towards helping others to read one's mind will be suppressed to the extent physical dominance holds sway. No one exposes what they are thinking to bullies. Although vulnerable to being hijacked by the politically powerful, sacred traditions the world over invoke manifestations of reverse dominance as the collective moral sanction, the alliance of the weak against unrestrained physical dominance. Without a model for counter-dominance ameliorating basic economic, social, and sexual inequalities, no speech community can be viable. In David Erdal and Andrew Whiten's (1994) view, such counter-dominance arises as part of the evolutionary process of selection for Machiavellian intelligence and encephalization. While they address economic and political competition, no Darwinian model can be adequate without incorporating factors of sexual competition. Female proto-symbolic strategies (Power and Aiello 1997) of coalitionary action introduce that component and must be seen as integral to Machiavellian intelligence models of gossip (Dunbar 1996b; Power 1998) and counter-dominance (Erdal and Whiten 1994). Within symbolic culture, this becomes fully expressed as reverse dominance (Boehm 1999) implementing collective intentionality.

If we accept the hypothesis that we can have no language without the evolution of ritual performance (Durkheim 1964 [1912]; Knight 1998; Maynard Smith and Szathmáry 1995; Power 1998; Rappaport 1999; Watts 2009), this is good news for students of the evolution of language. A coevolution model means material archaeological evidence and the possibility of testing predictions. Models for the evolution of ritual also offer more prospect of direct analogy with non-human animal behaviour, as Turner acknowledged when he engaged in a conference organized by Julian Huxley on 'Ritualization of behaviour in animals and man' in 1965. Such continuity implies we can ask concretely what circumstances in *Homo* evolution would lead animal ritualized behaviour to be spread into signalling coalitions (rather than signaller–receiver dyads), and to engage with 'the other world'—imaginary space and time beyond the here and now.

15.1 A ritualization process

Pursuing my arguments in Chapter 4, I apply signal evolution theory to model the evolution of ritual behaviour in *Homo*. Zahavi and Zahavi (1997) incorporate interactions between prey and predator or parents and offspring within signal selection in addition to sexually selected display. However, when considering the evolution of elaborate signalling systems among hominins, the most promising arena is communicative interaction between the sexes. With both conflict and cooperation endemic in complex multi-male, multi-female social groups, costly signalling between potential mates may especially arise where there is strategic conflict over levels of investment in offspring. In circumstances where both sexes participate in extensive parental care, and either sex stands to lose badly from defection by the other, Møller (1997: 44–5) suggests that sexual evolutionary conflict will generate elaborate signal evolution and adapted psychologies—a 'breeding ground for extreme abilities of mind-reading'.

Discussing the earliest contexts for symbolic communication, Deacon (1997) asks what selection pressures would favour such a 'radical shift in communicative strategy' among hominins, and considers the general circumstances which 'produce significant evolutionary changes in communication in other species . . . the context of intense sexual selection' (1997: 379–80). Such sexual selection models may be considered as the evolutionary motor of more general and abstract 'social selection' models (compare Nesse 2009). Hunter-gatherer social groups operate with marked gender-solidarity, such that coalitionary allies are liable to be same-sex. Having social partners of your own sex is probably an important factor in being attractive as a mate. This implies that processes of social selection will be implicated in sexual selection, and that individuals may advertise themselves as potential mates within contexts of their coalitions. There are two strong reasons for narrowing the model to sexual selection specifically. Firstly, the story of hominin evolution in our ancestry is one of solving the matter of investment in increasingly large-brained, costly offspring, therefore of parental investment and sexual selection (Trivers 1972). Secondly, this focus produces specific predictions, enabling testability.

In his account of the emergence of symbolic communication, Deacon (1997: 379–84) invokes a sexual selection process of ritualization arising from the problem of maintaining pair-bonds in complex multi-male, multi-female evolving human groups. Huxley (1914) coined the term 'ritualization' for the process by which movements that serve as signals are derived from movements that originally served some other function. For example, the preening activity of grebes, through formalization and stereotypical exaggeration, develops into elaborate courtship sequences. Once displaced from its original function, the ritualized behaviour is only useful for communicative display.

Ritualization is fundamentally driven by the observer—an individual interested in evaluating the behaviour of some other individual, whether that be prey, offspring, a mate, or a rival. The observer tries to detect some cue anticipating the likely actions of the animal observed, perhaps some movement that conveys information without being performed for that reason. This Krebs and Dawkins (1984) term 'mind-reading'. Once observers have evolved to pick up certain cues, then it may pay observed individuals to exaggerate those movements to make sure they are seen. At this point, as exaggeration evolves in ways designed to convey information to receptive observers, the movement becomes a signal. There is a cost to the signaller, in that the movement may lose its original intrinsic usefulness, but the benefit comes through energy saved by accurately conveyed information regarding the quality of the signaller. The signal may be highly energetically costly—as, for instance, the stotting of a gazelle, or roaring of red deer—yet still save net energy if it convinces the observing predator or rival *not* to chase or fight that particular individual. The signal must provide some accurate measure of the quality the observer is interested in. So, it remains a symptom or index—that is, the form taken by the signal is intrinsically linked to its content. But, with ritualized movements in this way displaced from original functions, in a sense their meaning has changed. What once was preening of feathers in the grebe now signifies courtship. Even though real information is being conveyed about intentions, at a certain level the meaning of the movement is deceptive or illusory. Receiver and signaller share mutual benefit in engaging with and probing behind that 'illusion', for instance that apparent feather-preening is really a courtship display.

In processes of ritualization, therefore, we find some collusion between a signaller and receiver that one thing, X (directly perceptible, the original behavioural cue), stands for something else, Y (intangible or inferred, the quality reliably demonstrated by the display)—a process that mirrors the key aspect of symbolism: displaced reference. Ritualization in non-humans generally involves signals between individual signallers and receivers; rarely is such collusion in the significance of display shared among a collective as in human ritual, although there may be examples of coalitionary ritualized behaviours in hunting dogs, flamingos, dolphins, and possibly chimps (Maynard Smith and Harper 2003: 127–8). Certainly, among non-humans we find no references to another world; all signals are necessarily indexical, intrinsically linked to the real world in ways that indicate the quality of the signaller. But something resembling human ritual could emerge through ritualization involving coalitions of signallers in costly display, who engage collectively in some illusion—'things that don't exist' outside a symbolic context. This would yield an evolutionary model for the emergence of the symbolic domain through a process driven by observers probing the display for signals of quality.

15.2 Two possible scenarios

Each sex pursues differential strategies of investment in offspring, giving rise to conflict both within and between the sexes. This suggests two basic possible scenarios for a ritualization process that could yield symbolic culture—and only two. The first is of male coalitions performing ritualized displays of quality to probing females, in competition with rival males. This follows the standard animal model of male–male competition and female choice in sexually selected display. The reverse possibility is of female–female competition and male choice. In this, female coalitions display their quality to attract probing males in competition with rival female coalitions. Each scenario offers different predictions about the specific signalling that would emerge (Power 2009: 266, 273, table 12.1).

The first, and standard, model is of hominin male ritual coalitions as primary. Individual members might be expected to demonstrate qualities of strength, agility, throwing skills, and weaponry among a large, impressively coordinated group. The signals and performance should be indexical of these qualities—real numbers, real muscles, real handaxes. For this reason, although it is easy to believe such ritualized activity occurred from early stages in *Homo* evolution, it is harder to see how collective representations of the 'other world' emerged. Males as members of coalitions are predicted to advertise their sexual availability and maturity, rather than establish any sexual taboo. Nor should they signal as anything else but male, anatomically speaking. They might use cosmetics for amplification of physical attributes, but, in the case of blood, only the real thing will prove bravery and endurance. Cosmetic or fake blood won't do. There could be elements of Machiavellian counter-dominance, for instance if a coalition of males strategically opposes a would-be dominant male. But there is no definite source of counter-reality in this model. Even if, as is possible for later *H. erectus*, male coalitions performed ritualized displays before joining a hunt, this remains similar to behaviour of African hunting dogs, using ritualized actions to synchronize and harmonize a group. It could function as evidence of each member's commitment to a group, but such a signal does not necessitate construction of another world beyond the here and now. The signature of the 'liminal'—juxtaposing phenomena counter to perceptible reality—is not generated by this model.

15.3 Why we need reverse sexual selection

This leads us to consider the reverse model, that collective female display drove the emergence of a ritually generated symbolic domain—the sacred, the liminal, counter to reality. What is the justification for reversing the normal direction of sexual selection? To answer that, we need to consider life history and reproductive energetics.

Evolving hominin females incurred major shifts of energetic costs of reproduction at two particular stages. The first around 2 million years ago (Aiello and Key 2002) involved significant body and brain size increase; in the past million years, we see evidence of larger brains, with some body mass increase, in the early Middle Pleistocene (*c.* 800–600 kya) (Rightmire 2009) leading to rapid encephalization (brain sizes increase but body mass remains stable) from 300 kya in both Eurasian and African lineages (see Watts, Chapter 16, table 16.1). Brain tissue is ten times more expensive than the average metabolic cost of body tissue. The larger the brain of the baby, the more slowly the child matures, the more burdensome to the mother who must find more energy to support her through breast-feeding. Mothers could not have afforded such increases of reproductive costs without organizing allocare and coalitionary support.

Hrdy (2009: 233) observes that only human mothers among great apes are willing to let another individual take hold of their own babies; further, we are routinely willing to let others babysit. She identifies lack of trust as the major factor preventing chimp, bonobo, or gorilla mothers from doing the same: 'If ape mothers insist on carrying their babies everywhere . . . it is because the available alternatives are not safe enough' (Hrdy 2009: 235). The fundamental problem is that ape mothers (unlike monkey mothers who may often babysit) do not have female relatives nearby. The strong implication is that, in the course of *Homo* evolution, allocare could develop because *Homo* mothers *did* have female kin close by—in the first place, most reliably, their own mothers (Hawkes et al. 1998). Extending the Grandmother hypothesis, Hrdy argues that evolving *Homo erectus* females necessarily relied on female kin initially; this novel situation in ape evolution of mother, infant, and mother's mother as allocarer provided the evolutionary ground for the emergence of intersubjectivity. She relates this onset of 'cooperative breeding in an ape' to shifts in life history and slower child development, linked to the change in brain and body size from the 2 million year mark (Hrdy 2009: 277–80).

If cooperative breeding in the first place is based on intergenerational cooperation between females (compare Key and Aiello 1999), how do males fit in? Opie and Power (2008) argue that grandmother support, by reducing mother's interbirth intervals, would also significantly promote mating effort by males, since a mother with a supportive mother herself is more likely to be fertile sooner. Male support to a mother who enjoys her own mother's support will help reduce infant mortality, enabling selection for longer lifespans with delayed sexual maturity. This combination of female kin support with male mating effort could provide the cooperative breeding framework for the early Pleistocene, accounting for female costs in the first major body/brain size increase. Note that male mating effort can be supportive in a multi-male/multi-female context, with increased hominin group sizes, without necessarily implying exclusive pair-bonds. Some form of partible paternity strategy (Beckerman and Valentine 2002), whereby mothers mate more than one male, could bring extra investment and insurance against infanticide risk, if one mate deserted. Large neo-cortices characterize monogamous species in mammals and birds, whether or not biparental care is involved (Schulz and Dunbar 2007). Dunbar (2010: 165) suggests that the evolution of pair-bonding 'is dependent on having a large brain to manage the relationships involved, rather than pair-bonding having evolved to facilitate the rearing of large-brained offspring'. Human pair-bonding then is an outcome of having the cooperative breeding network in place to support larger-brained offspring.

The accelerated encephalization in *Homo heidelbergensis*, both in Africa and Eurasia, from 700 kya, and especially from 300 kya (see Watts, Chapter 16), suggests a runaway feedback process of selection for social intelligence (Whiten and van Schaik 2007). Coordination of emergent pair-bonds against a background of increasing group size in the Middle to Late Pleistocene could be a contributing factor to this feedback loop (Dunbar 2010: 166). As males invest more reliably and regularly in female partners, in a context of Middle Palaeolithic/Middle Stone Age hunting economies, they should, under classic parental investment and sexual selection theory (Trivers 1972), become more discriminating about which particular female they invest in. Hence *Homo heidelbergensis* females come under increased pressure of sexual selection—that is the reverse of the usual direction.

It is in the process of securing male-female pair-bonds against the background of multi-male/multi-female large group sizes that collective ritual action arises. The

Female Cosmetic Coalition model (Power 2009) predicts the signalling involved. Which females do males choose? Those who are cycling as against those who are visibly pregnant or lactating. Menstruation is a significant cue for males; therefore they are interested in and observant of the cue. This implies individual females may exaggerate that cue to give information about imminent fertility to males. Once females draw attention to menstruation through some cosmetic or amplification effect this becomes a signal. But such a signal is a threat to non-cycling females who stand to lose attention and investment from their own partners, attracted to cycling females. The proto-symbolic strategy is for non-cycling females to take control over the signal of any cycling female, by joining collectively in exaggeration and amplification of the 'blood' or 'fertility' signal in order to attract new outsider males and labour to the signalling coalition.

Why should male observers sexually select cosmetically decorated females, if the blood is fake or symbolic? The argument is not that males are likely to be fooled by the signal, but that the collective performance using cosmetics is an honest indication of something would-be male investors will be interested to gauge. Suppose a young female starts to menstruate, prompting a network of female kin and neighbours to stage cosmetic ritual. Cosmetic ritual performance demonstrates in ways that are hard-to-fake the solidarity and extent of this particular female's kin support network. Effectively, she is signalling through the coalitionary body-paint display: 'Invest in me because I have extensive kin support and my babies will have it too!' Would-be philanderer males, aiming to target and separate menstrual/cycling females from kin, will be deterred by the solidarity of this decorated female coalition, while investor males who are prepared to hunt and perform bride-service will be attracted. Hence, the ritual action can be described as countering the would-be reproductive dominance of philanderers in favour of investors.

This then is a ritualization process that engages coalitions of early humans in some form of shared pretence or imaginary construct. In earlier stages of this process, proto-ritual display may be effectively indexical, occurring as and when a local female in fact menstruates, principally to deter philanderers. But as brain sizes increase and females suffer greater costs of reproduction, this may drive a regular routine of performance, potentially linking lunar phase and menstrual cycles (Knight 1991; Watts 2005). This earliest ritual tradition would institutionalize an economic division of labour and forms of social cooperation between the sexes and kin groups, embedding pair-bonds into relations with 'in-laws' involving bride-service obligations.

15.4 Why symbolism?

Whereas in the case of male ritualized coalitions there is no necessity for symbolism to arise, it is an intrinsic part of the process in the case of female coalitions. The cause of this is the need for collective resistance to dominance, which naturally arises in the case of female coalitions signalling to would-be dominant males, but not the other way round (males displaying for females). Furthermore, males as kin to females will be involved in this ritualized signalling, whereas, given a male ritual model, it is not clear why there would be female involvement in performance. What, then, are the predicted signals?

Where deceptive displays occur only because a local female actually menstruates, these signals, however elaborated, remain indexical and embedded in perceptible reality. But it is easy to see how a female coalition would be pushed into signalling shared fictions. Males attracted by cosmetic displays may be reluctant to leave the vicinity; they may instead be inclined to mate-guard imminently fertile females, or even attempt to abduct them. In those circumstances, female coalitions drawing on male kin support would have to respond with louder, clearer signals of resistance. Knight et al. (1995: 84) argue that the way female coalitions would construct their 'No' signal is by reversing the settings of the species mate-recognition system. Where female animals in courtship normally display 'right species/right sex/right time', systematic reversal by a defiant female coalition yields '"wrong species"—we are animals, not humans; "wrong sex"—we are males, not females; and "wrong time"— we are not fertile right now (but soon we will be)'. However absurd it seems to turn the world upside down in this way, this is the predicted signature of ritual power, establishing the inviolable, taboo, or sacred state of menstrual or body-painted females. Transmission of such signals counter to perceptible reality and counter to normal relations of dominance (Boehm 1999; Erdal and Whiten 1994) would require energetically expensive, repetitive, iconographic pantomime—high-cost ritual signals sustaining fictitious gods (Durkheim 1964 [1912]).

The need for quality dependence of signals—males really have to show they are ready for fighting or hunting—constrains male ritualized coalitions to refer only to perceptible reality. But in the case of female coalitions, representations of counter-reality become quality-dependent. The more improbable the panto-mime of wrong species/wrong sex, the more solid and committed the coalition must be to perform convincingly. It provides an accurate measure of coalition-ary solidarity through exaggeration of the counter-dominance signal. Further, only a high-quality female coalition confident of males returning could risk signalling 'No' to outsider males.

Female coalitionary display readily produces a repertoire of shared fictions. The motive for coalitionary action is economic—the need for bride-service. The signal-ling system delineates a boundary of kinship between groups: male kin act defen-sively in support of female relatives who display to outgroup males. This first symbolic strategy is also the first moral strategy, since non-cycling females exert collective pressure to obstruct sexual access to cycling females. All the dimensions of economics, kinship, and morality emerge together in the first symbolic ritual performance. Rights to food, rights in sex partners, and allocation to social group of kinship and gender are all now decided collectively, hence signalled digitally and categorically.

15.5 Are cosmetics necessarily symbolic?

The Female Cosmetic Coalition model generates a range of predictions across a wide field of disciplines and is potentially testable against evidence from the archaeological record, the fossil record, and the ethnographic record of hunter-gatherer myth and ritual (Power 2009: 273, table 12.2). The main archaeological prediction is that the first symbolic evidence will be found in a cosmetics industry focused on blood-red pigment (see Watts 2009, Chapter 16). The FCC model also leads us to expect that the Neanderthals would develop cosmetic traditions, since Neanderthal mothers would have had at least equally heavy reproductive costs as moderns. In the Neanderthal case, though, Eurasian conditions during glaciations probably constrained Neanderthal reproduction seasonally. This has the effect that Neanderthal pair-bonds may have been more stable during cold climatic periods, leading to differing outcomes in terms of the pigment record between African and Eurasian lineages (see Power 2009: 276–80; Power et al. 2013).

The African pigment record extends over 300,000 years, and becomes regular from the time of emergence of modern *Homo sapiens* around 200,000–160,000 years ago (Watts 2009; Watts, Chapter 16). Geometric engraved pieces of haematite are found from *c.* 100 kya (Henshilwood et al. 2002, 2009). Accompanying them are necklaces of marine shell beads, found in the southern and northern edges of Africa, and the Near East (Bouzouggar et al. 2007; d'Errico et al. 2005; d'Errico and Vanhaeren 2009; Vanhaeren et al. 2006), some appearing to be stained with red ochre used as body paint.

Some archaeologists have contrasted the ochre record to that of jewellery and engraved pieces, arguing that pigment use alone does not imply fully modern cognition. Kuhn and Stiner (2007: 51) suggest that 'pigment-only decorative systems' provided a 'form of individual display...rather than a medium for communicating about more constant, institutionalized relationships among individuals or groups of individuals'. It is easy to forget that, before mirrors, self-decoration must be public and social: a person needs friends and allies to help her decorate. In traditional societies where cosmetics underpin ritual, successful cosmetic display is an indexical signal of the care taken of you by friends and relatives.

Henshilwood and Dubreuil (2009: 52–3) argue that 'wearing of beads suggests that one person can understand how she looks from the point of view of another person'. This, they say, would need the second level of perspective-taking, as when a child of four can fully represent the point of view of others, and is able to reconstruct how an object looks from another's perspective. They propose a shift of cognitive capacity during the African Middle Stone Age equivalent to the shift between level-1 perspective-taking, effectively Tomasello and Rakoczy's shared intentionality (2003: 133–4), to level-2, effectively collective intentionality or 'theory of mind'. Pettitt (2011) proposes an even more complicated scheme based in Dunbar's gradualist, incremental levels of intentionality model.

I argue that the ornamented body immediately lies at the base of symbolic culture and consciousness. While female proto-ritual is purely indexical—happening only in relation to actual menstruation—this corresponds to shared intentionality. But as soon as there is any need to signal resistance to non-cooperative males, the repertoire of shared fictions—wrong species/wrong sex—comes into being. Adding the ideal to the real, the individual is no longer just herself. In constructing a playful shared fiction of identity, an individual experiences herself as others see her. In asking 'Who am I?' and 'How do I look to others?', she grows aware of her own thinking through the thoughts of others (compare Whitehead, Chapter 12). Human consciousness and identity entail locating the individual within the social cosmos. This is an interactive feedback of individual and collective: self-decoration is display of the individual in relation to the enduring social group to which she belongs. Cosmetic display, through ritual performance and collective intention, constitutes the social group. A ritual collective engaged with the 'other world' cannot go part of the way. This Durkheimian ritual context of cosmetics use is both necessary and sufficient for generating collective consciousness, intentionality, and representation of stable moral constructs—effectively Searle's institutional facts. As Watts (2009: 82) notes, 'it is almost inconceivable that the MSA occupants of Blombos were engraving such [abstract] designs onto pieces of ochre while not doing similar things with ground ochre powder on their bodies ...'.

Further predictions of the FCC model concern traditions of magico-religious symbolism (Power 2009: 274). A 'time-resistant' syntax of ritual power, which boils down to WRONG + RED (with either cosmetic or real blood), is expected to be the conservative, archaic signal at base of all religious ritual evolving from that point. Such ritual is neither exclusively male nor female, but should encompass initiation of both sexes, with boys predicted to mimic girls. Only from this starting point is it possible to explain the observations of anthropologists like Turner of reversal of sexual signals among male initiates, sometimes with explicit reference to male circumcision as 'male menstruation' (e.g. Calame-Griaule 1986: 159, 182; Turner 1967: 96). Secret male initiation practice has developed costly and far-fetched ways of mimicking menstruation, involving traumas such as circumcision and subincision. From a Darwinian perspective of young males advertising sexual maturity, this is highly counter-intuitive, yet it is a regular finding in ethnography of initiation (Power 2001). The improbability of these predictions renders the model more easily falsified.

15.6 Conclusion: adults at play

The 'ratchet' effect (Tomasello et al. 1993) implies transmission of cultural traditions down the generations, so that what one generation knows is not lost to the next. In the case of human evolution this was embedded in a feedback process of cultural intelligence selection (Whiten and van Schaik 2007), with capacities of social learning producing multiple cultural traditions, selecting in turn for enhanced social learning, increased smartness, and ability to innovate. The associated encephalization, in the ancestry of moderns and Neanderthals, would be linked to an increase in the length of juvenile period supporting social learning (Joffe 1997; van Schaik et al. 1999), that is, to the period spent 'at play' (Ginsburg and Jablonka, Chapter 22; Knight and Lewis, Chapter 21).

Whiten and van Schaik (2007, following Donald 1991) propose that storage requirements of culturally acquired knowledge may drive encephalization. Another approach is to understand the body itself through an individual's life history as a site for ontogenetic construction of knowledge (compare Robertson 1996). Lewis (2008) highlights autonomous, self-organized pedagogic mechanisms such as the concept of *ekila* among the BaMbendjele. The *ekila* collection of beliefs—governing menstruation, blood, food, sex, hunting, and exchange practices—is encountered by each person in accordance with their own natural curiosity as they grow up, and so exerts 'an anonymous but pervasive pedagogic action' (Lewis 2008: 305). *Massana*, the collaborative arena for ritual and play based in complementary gender groups, provides the 'major avenue for transmission of cultural and gendered skills' where juniors learn by observation and imitation of slightly older children. Intergenerational teaching is rare among the BaMbendjele since it would offend against the egalitarian spirit. This example meets expectations of Whiten's 'deep social mind' hypothesis, where cultural transmission and two-way intersubjective mindreading thrive in egalitarian circumstances.

Among apes, humans and bonobos—where female–female alliances notably prevail—can maintain childlike, relatively egalitarian, playful relationships even past puberty. For hunter-gatherers, initiation ritual provides the chief conduit for inculcating core cultural representations. As Turner had it (1967), this is a realm of 'primitive hypothesis', where the novice enters a liminal world, filled with masks, emblems and designs counter to perceptible reality, where all engage in communitas, a reversal of normal worldly hierarchy. Among the Hadza, the liminal phase of *Mai-to-ko*, the girls' initiation, is played out as a ritualized battle of the sexes, with girls reversing sexual characteristics, dressed up as 'hunters' and 'hunting' boys (Figure 15.1). Shared experience of traumatic bloodshed during the first part of *Mai-to-ko* forms the crucial occasion for securing solidarity among women's coalitions.

FIGURE 15.1 Hadza girls' initiation played out ritually and mythically as a battle of the sexes. (Photo: Camilla Power)

Typically, hunter-gatherer coalitions among the Hadza, Mbuti, or Mbendjele, are gender-based, deploying their solidarity in playful opposition (Finnegan 2009). If our evolutionary models of ritualized sexual selection can account for such gendered coalitions, we can predict the ratchet effect working where sexual selection motors male choice for ritually playful females, and mutually female choice for ritually playful males. Through the record of persistent pigment use, we can trace in the archaeological record where and when the ratchet effect takes hold, both for our ancestors and potentially also for Neanderthal populations.

16

The red thread: pigment use and the evolution of collective ritual

IAN WATTS

16.1 Introduction

Was language fully established half a million years ago, everything since then being just 'history'? This idea (Zilhão 2007: 41, 2011: 127; Goren-Inbar 2011; Dediu and Levinson, Chapter 14) seems attractive on several grounds:

- Language is an aspect of symbolic culture, evidently possessed by African *Homo sapiens* throughout the Late Pleistocene (beginning 128 kya) (d'Errico and Stringer 2011; Henshilwood et al. 2011; see also Coulson et al. 2011) and seemingly also by Neanderthals from at least ~50 kya (Zilhão et al. 2010). Therefore, the most recent common ancestor, around ~400 kya (Endicott et al. 2010; Stringer 2012), may already have possessed the basic preconditions.
- With brain size considered to fall within the modern human range at ~600 kya (Barham and Mitchell 2008: 24, 200) or ~400 kya (Cartmill and Smith 2009: 292), the necessary cognitive hardware for language might be assumed (Barham and Mitchell 2008: 219; Deacon 1997; Zilhão 2007).[1]
- Between ~500 kya and ~300 kya, there was a reconfiguration of hominin social organization, with a major technological transition, more effective and logistically organized hunting, and repeated evidence for campsites and controlled use of fire (see Section 16.4).
- The reason material residues of symbolic behaviours took so long to achieve fixation may be simply demographic. Innovations of any kind rarely get fixed under conditions of small group size, low population density, and little inter-connectivity (Zilhão 2011: 125, citing Shennan 2001; Powell et al. 2009).

---

[1] Earlier versions of this argument underpinned the notion of 'archaic *Homo sapiens*', lumping together all post-*erectus* and pre-'*Homo sapiens sapiens*' fossils by virtue of cranial capacities typically exceeding 1200 cm^3 (see Tattersall 1986 for an early critique).

16.2 The argument

Against this view, I will argue that symbolic culture—including language as we know it—can only safely be inferred from around the time of our speciation (between 200 and 150 kya) and considerably later in the case of Neanderthals. I don't doubt that critical aspects of language and its interactional infrastructure were in place half a million years ago, but I have serious reservations about calling this 'modern language' (Dediu and Levinson, Chapter 14). I suspect that the different interpretations ultimately concern the distinction between communication about 'brute facts' and communication framed by and about 'institutional facts' (Searle 1995; Knight, Chapter 17; Wyman, Chapter 13), an issue not touched on by Dediu and Levinson. Two more concrete areas of disagreement likely to bear on this topic are: (1) how we interpret brain size increase in the latter stages of hominin evolution, and (2) whether or not collective ritual is theoretically integrated into our respective scenarios. The first issue can initially be posed as a naïve question; the second requires some discussion.

If 'modern language' was already established half a million years ago, why does the steepest rise in cranial capacities occur within the last 300,000 years (e.g. de Miguel and Hennerberg 2001: fig. 1; Lee and Wolpoff 2003: fig. 2)? Any increase in relative brain size imposes high energetic costs, ontogenetically experienced as maternal energy budget costs. In the final stages of *Homo*'s evolution, there's the additional—life-threatening cost—of trying to get still larger brained offspring through the pelvic canal (Weaver and Hublin 2009). Regardless of whether the selection pressure for larger brains was domain specific (the frontrunner being the Machiavellian social intelligence hypothesis, see Byrne and Whiten 1988; Dunbar 1998) or domain general (the 'cultural intelligence' hypothesis, see van Schaik et al. 2012), significant encephalization after the evolution of 'modern language' seems counterintuitive, requiring careful explanation. 'Modern language' should, like good computer software, make life simpler. The unprecedented levels of trust involved imply greatly improved problem-solving abilities, which should result in reduced or neutral selection for further encephalization. This paradox cannot simply be abolished by declaring that encephalization had effectively ceased around half a million years ago.

The authors cited in my opening scarcely mention ritual. The omission is odd, particularly for Dediu and Levinson, who claim to be addressing language origins from a social perspective. Other contributions to this volume (e.g. Power, Chapter 15) take seriously the Durkheimian proposition (Deacon 1997; Durkheim 1964 [1912]; Knight 1998; Rappaport 1999; Sosis and Alcorta 2003) that, in the absence of ritual, it would be impossible to establish sufficient community-wide *trust* or confidence in *institutional facts* (Searle 1995; see also Lukes 2007) for language to evolve. Communal ritual, according to this body of theory, provides a framework of highly redundant, costly, and correspondingly *reliable* associations between markers of abstract relationships, making it possible to abandon reliance on cause-and-effect associations in favour of an implicit, higher-order logic of associations between phenomena in a 'virtual' world (see Deacon 1997: fig. 3.3, 99, 405). Institutional facts (i.e. social fictions) presuppose aligned perspectives (Steels, Chapter 24; Wyman, Chapter 13). Conceptual and linguistic alignment leads to self-organization, massively accelerating cultural evolution (Steels 2012). Ritualized games—involving rapid turn-taking, prediction, and role-play—are crucial in securing the necessary joint attention for alignment to occur (Kaplan and Hafner 2006; Wyman, Chapter 13). Knight and Lewis (Chapter 21) emphasize that children's ritualized play and community-wide ritual are points along a continuum.

From an archaeological perspective, the great attraction of ritual is its characteristic costliness, redundancy, and stereotypy; once durable materials are involved, it's liable to leave an archaeological signature, one likely to be biased towards eye-catching materials. Where is the archaeological evidence for ritual at 500 kya, and when can *habitual* collective ritual be inferred?

In this chapter, I begin by briefly reviewing brain size increase and behavioural change in the Middle Pleistocene (780–130 kya). On the basis of the brain size review, I infer two stages of Middle Pleistocene encephalization, the first marking the speciation of *Homo heidelbergensis* at the beginning of the epoch, the second marking the speciation of *Homo sapiens* towards the end (in Europe, this second stage is delayed, occurring in the Late Pleistocene). Different explanatory models may be required for these two stages. Relating the brain-size story to the environmental and behavioural reviews, the first stage is best regarded as a refinement to the adaptive niche of *Homo ergaster/erectus* as an open-landscape generalist, responding to the demands of greatly increased climate variability during the Mid-Pleistocene Transition. The second stage is unique, both in comparison to the initial evolution of the genus *Homo* and the speciation of *H. heidelbergensis*, having no allometric component and being unrelated to major climate change. Between these two stages, archaeologists identify much of the evidence for the protracted evolution of central-place foraging, a 'campsite'-focused form of social organization. Among the various strands of evidence is the earliest evidence consistent with ritual performance, but it is not until the last phase of brain size increase that such evidence ceases to consist only of unique observations, allowing us to infer habitual behaviour.

In developing this last part of the argument, I focus on the record of earth pigment use, testing predictions derived from the Female Cosmetic Coalitions model of the evolution of symbolic culture (Knight et al. 1995; Power and Aiello 1997), refined by the 'seasonality thermostat' sub-hypothesis (Power et al. 2013). Given that I'm closely associated both with this model and the study of early pigment use, I should say that I'd be happy to test the predictions of any rival *theoretical* approach to the ochre record if one existed.

To avoid repetition, let me assume familiarity with the basic outlines of the model (see Power, Chapter 15). If FCC is correct, archaeological evidence for the use of cosmetics should track the later stages of encephalization, as females sought to mobilize ever more reliable levels of male investment to meet maternal energy budgets, a goal that entailed reducing inter-male reproductive variance and placing cooperative breeding on a new footing—underwritten by morally authoritative constructs. Two detailed predictions should be easy to falsify if the model is wrong:

(i) in Africa, use of red ochre should become regular and ubiquitous as *Homo sapiens* cranial capacities stabilize;

(ii) in Europe, before classic Neanderthal cranial capacities stabilize, use of red ochre should correlate with periods of reduced birth seasonality.

16.3 Brain size

Table 16.1 presents estimates of cranial capacity for Middle Pleistocene and earlier Late Pleistocene western Eurasian and African fossils. Within Africa, there are two pronounced periods of increase:

(1) Across the Lower/Middle Pleistocene transition, cranial capacities increase from a range of 700–1000 cm^3 for late *H. ergaster* (1.2 mya to 800 kya, Anton 2003: table 3; Potts et al. 2004), to >1200 cm^3 for early *H. heidelbergensis* (780 kya to 600 kya).[2]

(2) In the late Middle Pleistocene, values increase from a mean of 1288 cm^3 (s.d. 67 cm^3, n=6) in the period 300–200 kya, to a mean of 1445 cm^3 with early *H. sapiens* (195–130 kya), with no overlap in standard deviations.

Encephalization is inferred for the speciation of *H. heidelbergensis* (Rightmire 2004, 2009), but it's associated with increased body mass (Churchill et al. 2012: 337; Rightmire 1996: table 1;[3] Robson and Wood 2008) and dramatic climate change (Donges et al. 2011). The Mid-Pleistocene Transition (broadly defined as 1.2 mya to 500 kya, narrowly defined as 940–650 kya) saw increased aridification and a shift from low amplitude 41,000 year glacial cycles to high amplitude 100,000 year cycles (Head and Gibbard 2005). According to the 'variability selection' hypothesis (Potts 1998; see also Donges et al. 2011),[4] selection for greater flexibility in responding to rapid environmental change drove the speciation of both *H. ergaster* and *H. heidelbergensis*.

---

[2] A lower range will undoubtedly obtain if early Middle Pleistocene female fossils are recovered, but this is unlikely to diminish the impression of a grade shift.

[3] The relevant observations in Rightmire's (1996) table 1 are Bodo's orbit height and breadth, in comparison to Early Pleistocene KNM-ER 3733, these measures providing good proxies of body mass (Spoctor and Manger 2007).

[4] More flexible social organization would be a critical component of general flexibility, so the variability selection hypothesis need not contradict social intelligence or cultural intelligence as the selection pressure for larger brains.

TABLE 16.1. Middle Pleistocene and earlier Late Pleistocene cranial capacities in Africa and Western Eurasia. (Adapted from de Miguel and Henneburg 2001)

Sample	Fossil	Date estimate (kya)	Cranial volume (cubic cm)	Sources for revisions and additions
African pre-Homo-sapiens	Ternifine[a]	750	1300?	
	Saldanha	700	1217	Klein et al. 2007
	Bodo	600	1275	
	Salé	400	930	
	Ndutu	400	1100	Bräuer 2008
	Kabwe	300?	1320	Stringer 2011
	Ileret	270	1400	
	Florisbad	260	1280	
	Ngaloba	250	1284	Manega 1993: 123
	Eliye Springs	200	1210	Bräuer et al. 2004
	Eyasi 1	250	1235	Trinkaus 2004
	sample mean		**1232**	
	s.d.		**125**	
African Middle Pleistocene Homo-sapiens	Omo 1	195	1400	McDougall et al. 2005
	Omo 2[b]	195	1430	McDougall et al. 2005
	Jebel Irhoud 1	160	1426	
	Jebel Irhoud 2	160	1378	
	Herto	160	1450	White et al. 2003
	Singa	150	1550	
	Border Cave 1[c]	150	1478	Grün & Beaumont 2001
	sample mean		**1445**	
	s.d.		**57**	
Levantine Early Late Pleistocene Homo-sapiens	Skhul 1	115	1450	Wood 2011
	Skhul 2	115	1300	
	Skhul 4	100	1555	
	Skhul 5	115	1499	
	Skhul 9	110	1587	
	Qafzeh 6	90	1561	
	Qafzeh 9	90	1531	
	Qafzeh 11	90	1280	
	sample mean		**1470**	
	s.d.		**119**	
Eurasian Middle Pleistocene >200 kya	Atapuerca 4	400	1390	Stringer 2012[d]
	Atapuerca 5	400	1125	Stringer 2012[d]
	Atapuerca 6	400	1153	Stringer 2012[d]
	Ceprano	400	1185	Manzi et al. 2010
	Arago	400	1139	
	Swanscombe	400	1305	

	Petralona	300	1266	
	Reilingen	300	1432	
	Steinheim 1	300	1140	
	Ehringsdorf	203	1450	
	sample mean		1259	
	s.d.		129	
Eurasian MIS 6	Vertesszollos 2	186	1335	
& MIS 5	Biache	178	1200	
	Krapina D	130	1450	
	Krapina C	130	1200	
	Apidima 2	130	1454	Harvati et al. 2011b
	Saccopastore 1	120	1234	
	Saccopastore 2	120	1295	
	Tabun C	120	1270	
	Gánovce	120	1320	Kneblová 1958
	sample mean		1306	
	s.d.		95	

[a] Ternifine cc estimate based only on a parietal, Wolpoff 1996–97.

[b] Omo 2 is included as *H. sapiens* on dating grounds and growing appreciation of the potential morphological variation among early *H.sapiens* (Harvati et al. 2011a).

[c] Border Cave 1 is treated as Middle Pleistocene as a 5BS derivation is just as plausible as 4BS at ~82 kya (Grün and Beaumont 2001: 478).

[d] A periodization of Sima de los Huesos between ~350 and 400 kya on genetic and morphological grounds (Stringer 2012) is favoured here over current radiometric estimates of ~600 kya (>530 kya) (Bischoff et al. 2007).

There is little evidence for brain size increase during the middle portion of the Middle Pleistocene, beyond what would be predicted of populations occupying higher latitudes (Bergmann's rule). Later Middle Pleistocene encephalization (extending into the earlier Late Pleistocene in Europe) is unique in having no allometric component and not correlating with a major period of climate instability (as distinct from glacial/interglacial cyclicity). Body mass estimates from at least 500 kya until ~20 kya are essentially stable (Rosenberg et al. 2006; Ruff et al. 1997). The claim that brain size increase had effectively ceased by 500 kya is often justified by comparing early Middle Pleistocene fossils (thought to be male) with the mean for living populations (~1350 cc, both sexes). However, significantly reduced body mass over the last 20,000 years, with concomitant (allometric) reductions in cranial capacity (Ruff et al. 1997; Ruff 2002: 216), implies that the modern average is not the most appropriate comparison when evaluating the evolutionary trajectory over the Middle and early Late Pleistocene.

Western Eurasian fossils predating 200 kya provide a mean of 1259 cm^3, comparable to their African counterpart. Fossils <200 kya and >100 kya, effectively from Marine Isotope Stage (MIS) 6 (the penultimate glacial) and MIS 5.5 (the last interglacial *sensu stricto*), show a moderate increase to 1306 cm^3—well below the contemporary African average. The very large cranial capacities of classic Neanderthals, ~1500 cm^3 (Ruff et al. 1997: table 1), are only known from ~70 kya onwards; these capacities are indistinguishable from early Upper Palaeolithic European *Homo sapiens* (Ruff et al. 1997: table 1) (for whom Bergmann's rule can be invoked relative to earlier *H. sapiens* samples). This implies that the last stage of Neanderthal encephalization was delayed in comparison to our lineage, occurring in MIS 5–4 rather than MIS 7. Given that the glacial of MIS 6 (190–130 kya) was much more severe than that of MIS 8 (300–242 kya) (Scott and Ashton 2011 with refs.), the simplest explanation would be an environmental constraint.

In sum, it's misleading to say that cranial capacities in the earlier Middle Pleistocene already fall within the modern human range, and the idea that brain size increase was essentially complete by 600 kya (Barham and Mitchell 2008: 24, 200, 219), ~500 kya (Zilhão 2011), or ~400 kya (Zilhão 2007)—is simply wrong.

16.4 Behaviour

A suite of behavioural adaptations are seen during the Mid-Pleistocene Transition:

- Occasional transport of animal parts to protected locations, evidenced at Gran Dolina (Spain) (Villa and Lenoir 2009) and Wonderwerk (South Africa) (Klein 1988, see Chazan et al. 2008 for dating).
- Range expansion to cool temperate habitats at ~900 ka (Parfitt et al. 2010).
- The earliest good evidence for controlled use of fire, at Wonderwerk Cave ~1 mya (Berna et al. 2012), and at Gesher Benot Ya'aqov (GBY, Israel) in the early Middle Pleistocene (Alperson-Afil et al. 2007).[5]
- From ~1.1 mya, the innovation of prepared core techniques—producing large flake blanks of pre-determined form for manufacturing bifaces (Barham and Mitchell 2008: 194 with references). Between ~800 and 700 kya, the innovation of soft-hammer percussion in finishing bifaces (Barham and Mitchell 2008: 190 with references). Both developments are considered economizing behaviours contributing to greater flexibility in foraging adaptations (Barham and Mitchell 2008: 200).

---

[5] The excavators consider the relevant archaeology at GBY to be nearly 790 kya (Goren-Inbar et al. 2004), but combined U-Th/ESR assays indicate an age between 681 and 623 kya (Rink and Schwarcz 2005; see also Herries 2011: 17–18).

The overall impression is of significant evolution of behavioural flexibility relative to early *H. ergaster*, consistent with the presumption of improved cognitive abilities based on brain size and the inferred speciation during this period. However, despite the important findings from Wonderwerk and GBY, it does not appear that a form of social organization focused on campsites became widely established. In Europe, evidence for controlled use of fire is non-existent prior to ~400 kya (Roebroeks and Villa 2011). Long after this, Neanderthals were not habitual fire users (Sandgathe et al. 2011). In the Levant, following GBY, the next well-documented occurrence is at ~380 kya (Karkanas et al. 2007). There seem to have been significant obstacles to establishing a form of social organization that allowed some individuals to remain at a home base, indefinitely maintaining captured wildfire. Speculatively, these may have concerned an absence of mechanisms of punishment and reward to enforce cooperation between strangers, a prerequisite of 'institutional facts'.

Habitual cooking would have had major evolutionary consequences (Aiello and Wheeler 1995: 210; Wrangham and Conklin-Brittain 2003; Carmody et al. 2011), including allowing further encephalization without increasing basal metabolic costs. Wrangham and colleagues (1999) proposed that this might explain the evolutionary changes associated with early *Homo ergaster*. Wonderwerk and GBY notwithstanding, the European and Levantine evidence suggests that cooking associates more closely with late Middle Pleistocene encephalization (extending into the Late Pleistocene in Europe).

Qesem Cave (Israel), in addition to providing repeated ash layers between ~380 and 200 kya (Karkanas et al. 2007), provides evidence for hunting focused on prime-age animals and the transport of high-quality parts, implying delayed consumption and food sharing (Stiner et al. 2009). Intriguingly, cut-marks on bone are more abundant and randomly oriented than in later Levantine contexts, suggesting that more individuals were involved, with little or no formal apportioning of meat (Stiner et al. 2009). This might be read as another indication of an absence or weak development of institutional facts.

The stronger evidence for campsites in the second half of the Middle Pleistocene coincides with one of the most important technological changes, the augmentation and eventual replacement of handaxes by blades and/or points. In Africa, this begins between ~550 and 500 kya (Johnson and McBrearty 2010; Wilkins and Chazan 2012), in Europe at ~300 kya (Santonja and Villa 2006; White et al. 2011). There's no doubt that the new technology greatly facilitated more logistically organized foraging (e.g. Scott and Ashton 2011), but it provides no stronger basis for inferring language (let alone 'modern language') than Goren-Inbar's (2011) analogical ethnographic argument for language-based teaching of prepared-core biface manufacture. In the interior of southern Africa, the transition is represented by the Fauresmith industry (but see Underhill 2011). At Kathu Pan (Northern Cape), with dating estimates of ~500 kya (Porat et al. 2010), analysis of the points showed they were spear tips, the earliest documented hunting technology (Wilkins et al. 2012). With early Middle Stone Age (MSA) assemblages in the region providing dating estimates of ~280 kya and ~290 kya (albeit with wide error margins, Grün et al. 1996; Porat et al. 2010), the Fauresmith probably spans the period from ~300 kya to at least ~500 kya. The contrast with preceding Acheulean adaptations is nicely illustrated at Wonderwerk Cave (Northern Cape)—extending 140 m straight into a hillside. Acheulean and Oldowan assemblages are at the front of the cave, but artefact densities are so low that, despite the use of fire, occupation seems ephemeral, more like an extension of the surrounding landscape than a campsite (Chazan and Horwitz 2009). Fauresmith occupations (poorly dated at Wonderwerk) are documented right at the back of the cave, where it's so gloomy that—without firelight—all you can see is the distant entrance. There seems to be no functional reason for repeated use of this part of the cave.

16.5 Non-subsistence-related behaviours

There is a longstanding suggestion that the refinement, symmetry, and size of some (Middle Pleistocene) handaxes indicates an 'aesthetic appreciation of form' (Clark 1975: 190). Invoking costly signalling theory, Kohn and Mithen (1999; Kohn 1999) proposed that the visible effort of making these impressive examples came under sexual selection, providing females with a hard-to-fake index of individual male quality. Although Nowell and Chang (2009) have critiqued this idea, most scholars agree that the largest and/or most symmetrical handaxes served a display role (Machin 2009; Currie 2011; Hodgson 2011; McNabb 2012). Visual display of a fundamentally self-referential character is regarded by some Acheulean specialists as setting the bounds to the complexity and depth of information transmission (McNabb 2012). In Europe, most—possibly all—Acheulean assemblages post-date the posited establishment of 'modern language' by 500 kya (Santonja and Villa 2006; Jiménez-Arenas et al. 2011).

A variety of unique occurrences suggest novel signalling behaviours in the second half of the Middle Pleistocene (e.g. Oakley 1973; Steguweit 1999; d'Errico and Nowell 2000; Chazan and Horwitz 2009). Chazan and Horwitz (2009) report what appear to be unusual Fauresmith manuports at the back of Wonderwerk Cave—quartz crystals, pretty pebbles, and possible deliberate incisions on ironstone slabs (see also Bednarik and Beaumont 2010: figs. 8–10; but see Tryon 2010; Jacobson et al. 2013). To this list may now be added more compelling evidence: scraped specularite (a glittery form of haematite) and scraped red ochre (personal observation, research ongoing). While some utilitarian uses of red ochre are arguably demonstrable in much later contexts (e.g. use in hafting mastics, Lombard 2007; Wadley et al. 2009), and others—such as hide preservation—are plausible (Rifkin 2011), they seem most implausible in this context.[6]

---

[6] For lack of space and because no one seriously proposes they could provide a general account of early 'pigment' use, these hypotheses are not discussed here.

The Wonderwerk pigments strongly suggest collective ritual dating back to 300–500 kya, with fire-lit 'song-and-dance' performances, the dancers glowing red and glittering.

16.6 The red thread

What kind of rituals might have been occurring at the back of Wonderwerk Cave during the Fauresmith? Was it the kind of egocentric display suggested for some Late Acheulian handaxes and that some authors have proposed for early pigment use (Kuhn and Stiner 2007: 51; Mithen 1999: 154)? A simple consideration suggests otherwise. Individuals make handaxes, but anything but the crudest body-painting requires a colleague to apply the design, implying a rudimentary coalition.

To proceed further, we need an explicit evolutionary model. We offered one in the 1990s (Knight et al. 1995; Power and Aiello 1997; Power and Watts 1996), and made the following predictions:

(1) Initial use of ochre should not predate the onset of Middle Pleistocene encephalization (then placed at ~500 kya).
(2) There should be a selective focus on red rather than white, black, or yellow.
(3) Initially, exclusively local raw materials should be used.
(4) There should be a shift from irregular to regular use by the time modern brain size had stabilized. Since we modelled this as a runaway process of sexual selection, we predicted an abrupt rather than gradual change.
(5) The competitive dynamic between female coalitions should result in:
  (a) pronounced selective bias for the reddest and most saturated raw materials (Watts 2010; Hodgskiss 2012);
  (b) where these were locally unavailable, considerable costs should be incurred to procure them (Salomon et al. 2012; Watts 2009).

Our model explained cosmetic display as a female response to the challenges of encephalization. Since Neanderthal and *Homo sapiens* lineages underwent similar encephalization, it was inherently a multi-species approach. Power (2009; Power et al. 2103) has since refined the model, making this multi-species (or multi-lineage) aspect more explicit, with distinct predictions relating to the Neanderthal pigment record:

(6) In regions or periods of pronounced birth seasonality, there should be fewer opportunities for male philandering. This should make pair bonds more stable, reducing pressure to resort to ritual mechanisms to secure male investment. It follows that, in Europe, prior to any long-term habitual use, red ochre should be largely restricted to periods of reduced seasonal variation—interglacials and interstadials.

After briefly considering prediction (1) for its bearing on the antiquity of collective ritual, I focus on predictions (4) and (6), these being the ones which seem most vulnerable to falsification.

16.6.1 *Prediction (1)*

With the revision to the onset of Middle Pleistocene encephalization, from ~500 kya to the early Middle Pleistocene (<780 kya), the prediction concerning initial use alters accordingly. Two places where this might be tested are Wonderwerk Cave and Hunsgi (India). At Wonderwerk, 'haematite' collection is reported as extending back to ~1 mya (Beaumont and Vogel 2006: 222). Preliminary investigation has not supported the claim but work is ongoing. Hunsgi Locality 5 is an Early Acheulean assemblage associated with ground haematite (Paddayya 1976). A minimum age for similar contexts in the region is ~300 kya (Mishra 1995), but the Early Acheulean in southern India extends back ≥1.07 Mya (Pappu et al. 2011).

The assessment that pigment use probably extends back ~500 kya (Watts 2009: 74, 2010: 393) can be put on a firmer footing. I can confirm Beaumont's (1990a) report of Fauresmith pigments at Kathu Pan 1 (Stratum 4a), at ~500 kya (Porat et al. 2010), having identified scraped specularite and probably ground red ochre (paper in preparation). Together with the use of both materials in Fauresmith horizons at Wonderwerk (Section 16.5), ground haematite at Nooitgedacht 2 (Beaumont 1990b: fig. 4; see also Underhill 2012: 165), and specularite associated with a probable Fauresmith horizon at Canteen Koppie (McNabb and Beaumont 2011: 53), it seems that pigment use in the Northern Cape was well established prior to ~300 kya. It should be noted that specularite, the most visually arresting form of haematite, outcrops quite widely in this region (Beaumont 1973).

16.6.2 *Prediction (4)*

We predicted that regular use—generalized across sites—should be established by the time modern cranial volumes were stabilized. For Neanderthals, pigment use became fairly widespread from ~60 kya (Soressi and d'Errico 2007: 303), broadly synchronous with maximal cranial capacities. For *Homo sapiens*, the earlier summary of encephalization implies that pigment use should be regular and ubiquitous by ~200 kya or shortly thereafter.

In MSA research, southern Africa (south of the Limpopo) remains the most intensively investigated portion of the continent. Throughout the Late Pleistocene, habitual and ubiquitous use of red ochre in caves/rockshelters (locations almost invariably used as campsites) was demonstrated some time ago (Watts 1999).[7] Seven shelter sites in the region are known or believed to contain Middle Pleistocene MSA assemblages,[8] relevant details for six of these are provided in Table 16.2.

---

[7] Ubiquity was inferred where pigments were present in ≥80% of excavation aggregates assigned to one of Volman's (1981) informally defined techno-typological MSA stages.

[8] An eighth site, Elands Bay Cave (Western Cape), is disregarded as the excavator suggests it primarily served as a quarry during initial (MSA 1) use (Parkington 1992).

TABLE 16.2. Pigment counts and relative frequency in Middle Pleistocene and early Late Pleistocene South African MSA shelter sequences

Site	Excavation Aggregate	Industry	Age	Lithics [n]	Pigments [n]	Pigment [%a]	Refs	Exc. Area[b]
Cave of Hearths	Bed 4	Early Pietersburg	>200 kya?	4000	0	0.00	Mason 1988	9
	Bed 5	Middle Pietersburg	?	3319	0	0.00		9
	Beds 6–9	Late Pietersburg	Late Pleistocene	2827	5	0.18	Mason 1962: 273	9
Mwulu's Cave	Bed I	Middle Pietersburg	MIS 6?	1345	1	0.07	Watts 1998: fig. 3.2	10
	Bed II	Middle Pietersburg?	?	474	7	1.48	Watts 1998: Site App. 2.4-3	13
	Bed III	Late Pietersburg	Late Pleistocene	661	5	0.76		13
Border Cave	6BS	Middle Pietersburg?	>227 kya	9914	1	0.01	Watts 1998: table 3.2	18
	5WA	Middle Pietersburg	174 +/-9 kya, 227 +/-11 kya	10537	3	0.03	Watts 1998: Site App. 2.14.9	17
	5BS	Middle Pietersburg?	166 +/-6 kya, 147 +/-6 kya[c]	16925	30	0.18	Grün and Beaumont 2001	14
	4WA	Late Pietersburg	116 kya	21972	35	0.16		8
	4BS	Late Pietersburg	82 kya	2484	4	0.16		13
Bushman Rock Shelter[d]	Levels 63–39	Pietersburg	MIS 7–6?	4332	1	0.02	Watts 1998: table 3.5	
	Level 36	Pietersburg	MIS 6?	2118	1	0.05	Watts 1998: Site App. 2.3.5	6
	35	Pietersburg	MIS 6?	346	0	0.00		6
	34	Pietersburg	MIS 6?	1067	0	0.00		6

(continued)

TABLE 16.2. Continued

Site	Excavation Aggregate	Industry	Age	Lithics [n]	Pigments [n]	Pigment [%a]	Refs	Exc. Area b
	33	Pietersburg	MIS 6?	2415	0	0.00		6
	32	Pietersburg	MIS 6?	3154	1	0.03		6
	31	Pietersburg	MIS 6?	5323	6	0.11		6
	30	Pietersburg	MIS 5?	6047	8	0.13		6
	29	Pietersburg	MIS 5?	1353	3	0.22		4
Peers Cave	Trench 2 Lwr	MSA 1	>200 kya?	1013	0	0.00	Volman 1981: table 30	3
	Trench 2 Up	MSA 1	?	9310	0	0.00	Volman 1981: table 29	2
Pinnacle Point e	LC-MSA Lwr		164 kya	1508	29	1.89	Thompson et al. 2010	0.75
	SBS/URS		94 kya	1615	36	2.18	Watts 2010: SOM	6.25

a Pigment % = (Lithics + Pigments/Pigments) x 100.
b Excavated area, square metres or square yards.
c 5BS ESR estimates were stratigraphically inverted.
d BRS pigment counts exclude 'shaley mudstone', see Watts 2002: 6.
e PP13B lithic and pigment counts are plotted and 10mm screened material, excludes 3mm screening.

Regular use extends back to MIS 6 in at least two sequences, Pinnacle Point (Western Cape) (Marean et al. 2007) and Border Cave (KwaZulu-Natal) (Watts 2009: fig. 4.1). The same can probably be said of two other sequences. At Wonderwerk Cave, pigments (including specularite) are reported as a general feature of the MSA (Beaumont and Vogel 2006: 222); their presence in the underlying Fauresmith (see Section 16.5) suggests this applies to Middle Pleistocene (MIS 6) and Late Pleistocene MSA deposits (Vogel 2001 for dating assays, but see Herries 2011). At Bushman Rock Shelter (BRS) (Mpumulanga Province), regular use can be inferred from level 32 or 31, levels 31–37 being tentatively correlated to MIS 6 on geomorphological grounds (Volman 1981: 96, citing Butzer and Vogel 1979).

Three sequences show shifts from irregular to regular use. At Border Cave, this occurred within MIS 6. At BRS, levels 41–32 show irregular use, largely or wholly falling within MIS 6 on the foregoing geomorphological inference. At Mwulu's Cave (Limpopo Province) (Tobias 1949), a single pigment was recovered from Bed I, with multiple pieces associated with the smaller lithic samples from overlying Beds II–III.[9] Bed I lithics are comparable to Cave of Hearth Bed 5 (Mason 1957: 135; Sampson 1972: 99), in turn compared (not on the basis of detailed analysis) to dated late Middle Pleistocene assemblages from Border Cave (Beaumont and Vogel 2006: 224).

Three sequences provided no pigment in the earliest MSA levels. At Cave of Hearths (Limpopo Province), Mason (1957: 135; 1962: 273) contrasted pigment's absence in the Early and Middle Pietersburg[10] (Beds 4 and 5) with its presence in the smaller Late Pietersburg samples (Beds 6–9). Volman (1984: 203) suggested that Beds 4–5 were Middle Pleistocene, largely on the basis of the heavy-duty tool component, a common feature of earliest MSA industries across Africa (see Barham and Mitchell 2008). Cave of Hearths Bed 4 is probably >200 kya (Barham and Mitchell 2008: 231). The heavy-duty tool component in Anthony's Trench II at Peers Cave (Western Cape) leads me to suspect that some or all of this deposit also predates MIS 6. Volman (1981: table 30) reported no pigment from the small basal sample, nor in the much larger—technologically comparable—sample from the rest of Trench II (1981: table 29, but see Andreassen 2010: 75). Ochre is common in the Late Pleistocene MSA deposits excavated by Bertie Peers (pers. obs., Iziko South African Museum). At BRS, no pigments were encountered in levels 63–42. Partial examination of underlying levels (down to basal level 107) also suggested an absence.

---

[9] Mason (1962: 273) reported ten pigments from Bed II and none from Bed III. I identified seven pieces assigned to Bed II and five pieces with catalogue numbers but no square/spit designations. The catalogue numbers of these pieces largely fell within the range of numbers for Bed III grindstones and retouched lithics (Watts 1998: Site App. 2.4.1). Tobias (2005: 47) confirms the presence of pigments in Bed III.

[10] The Pietersburg (see Goodwin 1929) was raised to the status of a 'culture' showing temporal change on the basis of Border Cave excavations (Cooke et al. 1945). These changes were more formally defined by Mason (1957).

The proposed MIS 6 age of levels 31–37, and comparison with Border Cave, suggests that levels below 41 are probably >170 kya.

In sum, setting Cave of Hearths Bed 5 aside, there are reasonable grounds for thinking that those portions of the sequences from Cave of Hearths, BRS, and Peers Cave with no pigment, predate ~170 kya. The proposed chronologies are conjectural but testable.[11] The pattern identified by Mason (based on Cave of Hearths, Mwulu's Cave, Olieboompoort), of pigment use becoming habitual in the course of the Pietersburg, was overlooked in subsequent MSA research, but subsequently excavated or re-excavated Pietersburg sequences (BRS and BC) confirm the pattern. Together with the observations from Wonderwerk, Peers Cave, and Pinnacle Point, several tentative conclusions can be drawn:

- Pigment use in southern Africa became regular and ubiquitous to shelter occupations during MIS 6 (with dated sequences suggesting this had occurred by ~170 kya).
- It was not regular and ubiquitous in earlier phases of the MSA (MIS 7–8).
- Even if the earlier cluster of Northern Cape Fauresmith occurrences indicate regular use, and even if direct continuity to MSA aggregates in that region were to be shown, this remained a localized phenomenon.
- Where documented (Border Cave, BRS, Mwulu's Cave), the shift from irregular to regular use appears fairly abrupt.

More generally, in terms of the current resolution of fossil and genetic studies, this shift appears to correlate with our speciation.

16.6.3 Prediction (6)

The prediction of the 'seasonality thermostat' (ST) hypothesis was that—prior to anything approaching widespread and regular pigment use—Neanderthal use of red ochre should correlate with milder climatic conditions. This is the most apparently improbable—hence testable—of the model's pigment predictions.

The earliest claims (de Lumley 1966: 50; Howell 1966: 129; Cremaschi and Peretto 1988) concerning red ochre at Terra Amata, Ambrona, and Isernia, remain questionable (Butzer 1980; Wreschner 1983, 1985). Should de Lumley's claim for abrasion be confirmed, then pigment use extends back to the interglacial of either MIS 9.3 (~322–335 kya) or MIS 11.3 (~400–425 kya) (Falguères et al. 1991; Valensi 2001 with refs.). Ambrona also probably dates to MIS 11 (Soto et al. 2001; Falguères et al. 2006). Isernia, at ~610 kya (Coltorti et al. 2005), also provided proxies of interglacial conditions. The pigment status of the remaining European Middle Pleistocene occurrences is generally less controversial, with ground red ochre reported from Achenheim

---

[11] BRS has an exposed, well-preserved section profile that should be dateable. At Peers Cave, in principal one could re-excavate back-fill to locate a section profile of Anthony's Trench II for dating. At Mwulu's Cave, Tobias left half the deposit intact.

(Wernert 1957: 211), Bečov I (Fridrich 1976; Marshack 1981), and Combe Grenal layer 58 (Demars 1992). A pigment status for the haematite at Maastricht-Belvédère also seems probable (Roebroeks et al. 2012). Few details are available for the red ochre at Ehrings-dorf (Svoboda et al. 1996: 96, citing Behm-Blancke 1960).

Maastricht-Belvédère may date to the interglacial of MIS 9 or MIS 7 (Roebroeks et al. 2012), but Achenheim, Bečov, and Ehringsdorf are all believed to date to MIS 7.[12] With the exception of Combe Grenal layer 58 (probably late MIS 6, Delpeche and Prat 1995), all Middle Pleistocene occurrences are from interglacial contexts, with use as red pigment beyond reasonable doubt in MIS 7.

Archaeological visibility for the late Middle Pleistocene in continental NW Europe (the most intensively studied region) is relatively good: only the pleniglacial portions of MIS 8 and MIS 6 indicate abandonment or regional population extinction (Roebroeks et al. 2011; Scott and Ashton 2011); interglacial maxima show low arch-aeological visibility, while peak population densities are inferred for periods charac-terized by cool and open conditions (Scott and Ashton 2011). Combe Grenal aside, the absence of pigments during MIS 8 and MIS 6 also applies to southern Europe, where abandonment/extinction is not an issue (Turq 1999; Moncell 2011). The temporal patterning to the European Middle Pleistocene pigment record doesn't seem to be attributable to an interglacial bias in the archaeology (although the absence of MIS 7 occurrences in southern Europe should be noted).

The shift to very warm interglacial conditions of substage MIS 5.5 (the Last Interglacial *sensu stricto*, 128–116 kya) should have triggered some cultural cosmetic activity, as it seems to have done in northern Europe during MIS 7, but no pigments are documented from this sub-stage. However, sites dated to MIS 5.5, particularly campsites, are sparsely represented across the continent (Gaudzinski-Windheuser and Roebroeks 2011; Slimak et al. 2010; Wenzel 2007: fig. 12.1), so the absence of pigment may be a sampling issue. Later in MIS 5, there is the polished and red-ochred section of mammoth molar from Tata (Vértes 1959); a dating estimate of ~100 kya (Hausmann and Brunnacker 1988) suggests a correlation with the mild conditions of sub-stage MIS 5.3.

The long Mousterian sequences of Pech de l'Azé IV and Combe Grenal, with temperate and cold period occupations, provide an opportunity to correlate Late Pleistocene Neanderthal pigment use with palaeoclimate at a finer level of resolution. At Pech IV, the earliest pigments (red ochre) were in Bordes' level J3b (Demars 1992), equivalent to level 6a of recent excavations (Dibble and McPherron 2006), probably dating to the final mild sub-stage of MIS 5 (5.1), centred on ~80 kya (Sandgathe et al. 2011: 221–2). In overlying layers (5–4 of the recent excavations, Bordes' J1–I1), dating to the glacial of MIS 4, manganese predominates, although red ochre is present in

---

[12] For dating and/or proxies of interglacial conditions: Achenheim, see Packman and Grün 1992; Heim et al. 1982; Bečov see Svoboda et al. 1996: table 4.1; Ehringsdorf, see Blackwell and Schwarcz 1986.

layer I2. The greatest concentration of ochre, in the youngest Mousterian of Acheulean Tradition (MAT) horizon, is associated with temperate conditions within MIS 3 (Richter et al. 2013). At Combe Grenal, again using Demars' (1992) pigment inventory, red ochre was encountered in levels 21, 14, 12, and 7, with pollens indicating short-lived episodes of milder climate in levels 22–20, 13–11, and 8–7 (Mellars 1996: 40). Intriguingly, as at Pech IV, black manganese (first encountered in level 35, with high frequencies in levels 25–23) correlates with cold conditions (Mellars 1996: 39).

For MIS 6 and MIS 5, the contrast between the Neanderthal and *Homo sapiens* pigment records is probably the most striking behavioural difference between the two lineages. Current data is sufficiently congruent with the prediction of the ST hypothesis to suggest that it offers a plausible explanation for temporal patterning to the Neanderthal ochre record prior to ~60 ka. Most Neanderthal pigments are from younger contexts (Demars 1992; Soressi and d'Errico 2007; Langley et al. 2008: fig. 2). While falling short of the ubiquity seen in southern Africa from ~170 kya, fixation of the trait is implied. Most occurrences are red ochre, but manganese is common in the MAT of the Perigord. The frequent use of manganese by classic Neanderthals of SW France—from ~70 kya onwards—remains unexplained. The logic of the 'seasonality thermostat' hypothesis might suggest that, in MIS 4 at least (74–60 kya), an aversion to using red, quasi-menstrual signals when pair-bonds were relatively stable, tipped cultural traditions towards manganese use.

16.7 Discussion and conclusions

Archaeologists have been criticized (Botha 2009) for inferring 'modern language' on the basis of widely agreed evidence for symbolism. It's an inherently riskier enterprise to make such an inference on the basis of non-representational activities such as central-place foraging or prepared-core biface manufacture. Yet this, together with the mantra that early Middle Pleistocene crania fall within the modern human range, plays a crucial role in underpinning recent claims that 'modern language' was already in place at least half a million years ago (e.g. Zilhão 2007, 2011; Barham and Mitchell 2008; Goren-Inbar 2011; Dediu and Levinson, Chapter 14). This is theoretically indistinguishable from the extreme gradualism prevailing 30 years ago, when a hunter-gatherer way of life (including language and a sex-based division of labour) was extrapolated back almost two million years. It is ironic, therefore, that Deacon (1997: 379–410), presenting the most sophisticated defence of extreme gradualism (after its demise), considered the resolution of conflicting reproductive interests by ritual means to be the key mechanism by which symbolic reference came to be established. Such considerations are absent from current gradualist scenarios.

Let's be clear about the implications of this scenario. 'Modern language' slightly predates evidence for the stabilization of campsites and any compelling evidence for ritual. To square such an account with Durkheimian propositions about ritual's role in establishing institutional facts, one would have to invoke archaeologically invisible rituals at an earlier date—along the lines of Deacon's (1997) imagined wedding ceremonies for early *Homo*. The last phase of brain size increase would remain unaccounted for (presumably having nothing to do with language or with the cognitive demands of conflicting reproductive interests), as would the subsequent—archaeologically supported—evolution of costly, community-wide ritual (a spandrel of language?). The simplest way to avoid such conundrums would be to assume that, while volitional vocalization must have been evolving over the previous million years (as part of the evolution of social/cultural intelligence and more specifically of cooperative breeding: Burkart et al. 2009), at 500 kya this still fell short of 'modern language'. Such an assumption would be consistent with the results of initial attempts to identify the time (and place) of origin of modern languages on the basis of linguistic criteria (Perreault and Mathew 2012; but see Atkinson 2012 and refs).

Moving from the known towards the unknown, symbolic culture was well established across Africa by 130 kya. I have argued that regular and ubiquitous use of red ochre provides a proxy for habitual collective ritual, transcending here-and-now contexts, with ritual performers across vast landscapes participating in shared fictions. Although not addressed in this chapter, the model used posits a unitary shared fiction concerning 'blood' symbolism, establishing the community's 'Ultimate Sacred Postulate' (Rappaport 1999). I consider this aspect of the ochre record, where identified, to be no less compelling evidence for symbolic culture than the isolated finds of beads, engravings, and burials in the early Late Pleistocene. Accordingly, in southern Africa, symbolic culture extends back ~170 kya. But this isn't simply a minimum inferred date; I'm suggesting there was a pronounced, fairly abrupt change from a mosaic pattern of no use, irregular use, or highly localized regular use, to regular and ubiquitous use. In terms of the current resolution of palaeontological and genetic studies, this is effectively simultaneous with our speciation. Earlier than this, and both claims (geographic ubiquity and regularity within sequences) tend to break down. This reading of the archaeological record was not empirically driven, but arose from an attempt to test predictions derived from the FCC model, premised on Darwinian behavioural ecology. Material residues of ritual performance can be traced back ~500 kya (and may yet go back 700–800 kya). The cluster of Northern Cape Fauresmith occurrences, probably predating ~300 kya, includes the most compelling circumstantial evidence for fire-lit, body-painted, song-and-dance performance archaeologists could reasonably wish for (Wonderwerk). At face value, the ochre record suggests the evolution of communal ritual, especially as it seems to be a trait shared by all *Homo heidelbergensis* lineages and coincides with the development of campsites. The question arising is why, if the basics were already established ~500 kya, the novel strategy only became an evolutionarily stable one ~170 kya?

Is it simply a matter of demographics, as suggested by Zilhão? While ecologically framed demographic constraints are certainly important, two considerations suggest they're insufficient to address the issue. In the earlier part of this interval (~500 kya to ~300 kya), other behavioural innovations—indefinite maintenance of fire, cooking, and point/blade manufacture—did achieve some degree of fixation, so why not body-painted ritual display? In the later part of the interval, some DNA studies indicate a *Homo sapiens* population bottleneck during MIS 6 (e.g. Fagundes et al. 2007), when aridity probably led to isolation of sub-populations (Marean 2011), a scenario supported by other genetic studies (Behar et al. 2008). Such conditions are the opposite to those conducive to fixation of novelty under the demographic model.

It seems more parsimonious to look at the most significant anatomical change over the same period: the increase in African average cranial capacities from 1288 cm^3 to 1445 cm^3 either side of our speciation in the final Middle Pleistocene. Whatever the selection pressures for larger brains and whatever the benefits, how did mothers meet the corresponding reproductive costs? Cooking doubtless played an important role, but seems unlikely to account for this final spurt in encephalization. Perhaps a more revealing clue lies with the Neanderthal pigment record. We interpret the near absence of red pigments from the glacial cycles of MIS 4, 6, and 8 as reflecting the relative stability of pair bonds when birth seasonality is pronounced—with females under no pressure to resort to cosmetic ritual to regulate access to food and sex (Power 2009; Power et al. 2013). Conversely, occasional resort to ritual may have occurred in MIS 11 and MIS 9, more definitely in MIS 7, in post-interglacial but mild sub-phases of MIS 5, becoming widespread in MIS 3. Seen in this light, the patchiness of regular use in Africa prior to ~170 kya is less perplexing. Granting that behavioural change can drive speciation (Mayr 1982: 612; Dor and Jablonka, Chapter 2), habitual collective ritual may have been causally implicated in our speciation, in which case we would expect regular pigment use at a few sites earlier than ~200 kya (McBrearty and Brooks 2000: 528; Barham 2002; this chapter).

What does it matter if symbolic culture emerged closer to 200 kya than 500 kya, initially with one of the three probable daughter allo-taxa of *Homo heidelbergensis* (*sapiens*, *neanderthalensis*, and Denisovians) rather than with the stem species (see Stringer 2012)? It matters if we're interested in the content of symbolic culture. The FCC model goes on to make very specific, non-trivial predictions about a universal syntax to the mobilization of ritual power, testable in the light of archaeological, rock-art (Power 2004; Sims 2006), and mythico-ritual data (Knight 1987, 1991, 1997; Power and Watts 1997, 1999; Watts 2005). High-fidelity transmission of traditions is consistent with a recent migration of *Homo sapiens* populations out of Africa, carrying with them a template of symbolic culture forged in our speciation; it's inherently less plausible with a multi-lineage scenario going back half a million years.

16.8 Acknowledgements

I thank Michael Chazan for making it possible to examine material from Wonderwerk and Kathu Pan, and for allowing me to refer to preliminary findings ahead of scientific publication. Thanks also to David Morris (McGregor Museum, Kimberley) for access to these collections. For an earlier stage of the research, thanks to Peter Beaumont for access to the Border Cave collections, Lyn Wadley for access to Bushman Rock Shelter and Mwulu's Cave collections, and to the British Academy, the University of London Central Research Fund, and the L.S.B. Leakey Trust for financial support. The financial support of Marina Kanta is also gratefully acknowledged.

17

Language and symbolic culture: an outcome of hunter-gatherer reverse dominance

CHRIS KNIGHT

> Symbolic culture . . . requires the invention of a whole new kind of things, things that have no existence in the 'real' world but exist entirely in the symbolic realm. Examples are concepts such as good and evil, mythical inventions such as gods and underworlds, and social constructs such as promises and football games.
>
> Philip Chase (1994: 628)

From a Darwinian standpoint, 'symbolic culture' is an unsettling notion. Modern science became established in opposition to the idea that culturally accepted fictions can be equated with facts. Yet the concept of symbolic culture requires us to grasp just that paradoxical possibility. Long before the late-twentieth-century invention of the Internet, evolution allowed humans to flit between two realms: reality on the one hand, virtual reality on the other. Symbolic culture is an environment of objective facts—whose existence depends entirely on collective belief. To use language is to navigate within that imagined world.

17.1 Two kinds of fact

'Brute facts', in the terminology of John Searle (1995: 27), are facts which are true anyway, regardless of human belief. Suppose you don't believe in gravity: jump off a cliff and you'll still fall. Natural science is the study of facts of this kind. 'Institutional facts' are fictions accorded factual status within human social institutions (see Wyman, Chapter 13). Monetary facts are fictions of this kind. The complexities of today's global currency system are facts only while we believe in them: suspend the belief and the facts correspondingly dissolve. Yet although institutional facts rest on human belief, that doesn't make them mere distortions or hallucinations. Take my confidence that these two five-pound banknotes in my pocket amount to ten pounds. That's not merely my subjective belief: it's an objective, indisputable fact. But now imagine a collapse of public confidence in the currency system. Suddenly, the realities in my pocket dissolve.

For scholars familiar with Rousseau, Marx, or Durkheim, none of this is especially surprising or difficult to grasp. Some facts are true anyway, irrespective of human belief. Others subsist in a virtual realm of hallucination or faith. For Saussure (1983 [1915]: 8), it was the parallel between linguistic meanings and currency values—all in some sense hallucinatory—which made a scientific linguistics so problematical:

Other sciences are provided with objects of study given in advance, which are then examined from different points of view. Nothing like this is the case in linguistics...The object is not given in advance of the viewpoint: far from it. Rather, one might say that it is the viewpoint adopted which creates the object.

It was in rebellion against such troubling notions that Noam Chomsky (2000: 106–33) redefined 'language and similar phenomena' as 'elements of the natural world, to be studied by ordinary methods of empirical enquiry'. Linguistics, within Chomsky's new paradigm, ceases to be social and becomes natural instead. Ideologically hostile to Marx, Durkheim, and what they termed 'Standard Social Science', a generation of Darwinians (Tooby and Cosmides 1992, 1995; Pinker 1994) embraced Chomsky's 'cognitive revolution'. Somehow, language had now to be explained as an innate cognitive module without biological precedent, emerging suddenly and without reference to anything social (e.g. Hauser et al. 2002; Fitch et al. 2005). The consequence of all this was to render language's very existence an insoluble mystery (Knight 2004, 2009). Far from yielding to Darwinian explanation, the evolutionary emergence of language is nowadays increasingly considered 'the hardest problem in science' (Christiansen and Kirby 2003). Is it theoretically possible that the difficulties stem largely from our own culture-specific assumptions? If so, it might be a good idea to try abandoning them as a preliminary intellectual step. Among other things, I think we must abandon Chomsky's foundational insistence that language is a biological entity located in the head.

17.2 Four positions on the origins of symbolic culture

Within the past two decades, archaeological revelations from the African Middle Stone Age have transformed our picture of the timing of symbolic culture's emergence. Until the early nineties, the prevailing view of the 'human revolution' (Mellars and Stringer 1989) was unfortunately Eurocentric, focused as it was on the Upper Palaeolithic Revolution conceived as humanity's 'Great Leap Forward'. Recent discoveries from Africa have at least doubled the time-depth of probable or at least possible evidence for symbolic activity. This has left us with four main archaeological positions:

17.2.1 *Francesco D'Errico*

Multispecies transition across Africa and Eurasia. Symbolic capacities already in place with *Homo heidelbergensis* 300,000–400,000 years ago. Sporadic behavioural expressions of symbolism occurring simultaneously among ancestors of both Neanderthals and ourselves (D'Errico 2003).

17.2.2 *Sally McBrearty and Alison Brooks*

Down with the revolution! African ancestors of modern humans undergo gradual, sporadic build-up of modern cognition and behaviour spanning 300,000 years. Symbolism presents no special theoretical difficulties, emerging as part of the package of modern, flexible, creative behaviours within Africa. What archaeologists once termed the 'human revolution' in Europe had nothing to do with the origin of symbolism. It was the collision of two species, one of which (modern humans originating from Africa) had gradually developed symbolism prior to reaching Europe, while the other (Neanderthals in Eurasia) produced little evidence of symbolism (McBrearty and Brooks 2000; McBrearty 2007).

17.2.3 *Christopher Henshilwood and Ian Watts*

There was a human revolution but it occurred well before the Upper Palaeolithic in Europe, being inseparable from the process of modern human speciation in Africa (Mellars et al. 2007). Evidence in the form of cosmetics and personal ornamentation is the archaeological signature of this African Middle Stone Age transition. Emerging at this time, symbolic culture was not an optional extra; life following the transition was fundamentally organized through symbols (Henshilwood and Dubreuil 2009; Watts 2009; Watts, Chapter 16).

17.2.4 *Richard Klein*

Recent interpretations of the African Middle Stone Age record are wrong; the original 'human revolution' theory remains correct. Middle Stone Age humans evolving in Africa may appear anatomically modern, but did not become cognitively modern until the Late Stone Age/Upper Palaeolithic. Language and symbolic culture emerged no more than 50,000 years ago, caused by 'a fortuitous mutation that promoted the fully modern brain' (Klein 2008: 271).

17.3 The archaeological evidence

In the African archaeological record, the earliest persuasive evidence for symbolic culture includes certain engraved pieces of ochre (Henshilwood et al. 2002) associated with marine pierced shells (Henshilwood et al. 2004; d'Errico et al. 2005). Dated to around 70,000 years ago, these were recovered from Middle Stone Age levels at

Blombos Cave, South Africa. Mounting evidence for symbolic behaviour at still earlier dates includes a South African coastal site (Pinnacle Point) yielding mollusc remains, bladelets, and red ochre pigments dating to 164,000 years ago (Marean et al. 2007). Use of ochre pigments extends back between 250–300 kya at some sites in the tropics; regular and ubiquitous use in South African rockshelters dates back to the time of modern speciation (Watts 2009, Chapter 16).

Most archaeologists now accept that the Blombos and other shells and pigments were used for personal ornamentation. Often, the shells were strung together to form a necklace. Traces of red pigment have been found on a set of 82,000-year-old perforated shells from the Grotte des Pigeons in North Africa, suggesting that the wearer's body may already have been ochred (d'Errico and Vanhaeren 2009: plate 2). Traces of red ochre pigment have similarly been found on some shells from Blombos in South Africa (d'Errico et al. 2004). Several modified pieces of ochre from the same site have a sharp bevelled edge, as if designed to produce a clear outline of colour on a surface (Watts 2009: plate 4). Ochres yielding the most saturated dark reds—especially 'blood' reds—were subjected to the greatest intensity of grinding and use (Watts 2009). Pinnacle Point nearby yields similar 'crayons' dated to c. 164,000 kya (Marean et al. 2007). Geometric engravings found on Blombos pieces (Henshilwood et al. 2002) add to the suggestion that many of these delicately shaped 'crayons' were used to produce blood-red abstract designs, presumably on the human body (Watts 2009). This cultural tradition can be traced back to at least a hundred thousand years ago (Henshilwood et al. 2009). Such evidence suggests that cultural traditions involving body painting were already being established with the speciation of *Homo sapiens*.

17.4 Explanatory scenarios

To Christopher Henshilwood and Benoit Dubreuil (2009), the cosmetic evidence indicates that Middle Stone Age people were capable of symbolic communication. For individuals to wear cosmetics or a necklace, they must care about how they look. To adorn yourself appropriately, you must imagine your appearance from the standpoint of others. The requisite capacities for multiple perspective taking are distinctively 'modern' and underlie all symbolic communication including language. Henshilwood and his colleagues on that basis conclude that the producers of the Blombos pigments and ornaments had language-ready minds.

Ian Watts (2009; Watts, Chapter 16) arrives at similar conclusions concerning language, but on different theoretical grounds. Since my own theoretical position converges closely with that of Watts, and since we both support Camilla Power's Female Cosmetic Coalitions model (see Power, Chapter 15), I will avoid repetition at this point and turn directly to Richard Klein, who is the main archaeological opponent of the idea that African Middle Stone Age findings from sites such as Blombos have anything to do with symbolism.

As noted above, Richard Klein (1999, 2008; Klein and Edgar 2002: 271–2) argues that a single mutation installed a language organ some 50,000 years ago, triggering a symbolic and cultural explosion in Africa, the Middle East, and Europe. Although Chomsky (2005, 2012: 43) still supports this once-popular idea, it has little to recommend it. We should be suspicious when a puzzle regarding our own species is addressed using 'special' methods—methods without parallel elsewhere in evolutionary science. No biologist studying, say, elephants or social insects would invoke a single fortuitous mutation as sufficient explanation for an entire complex adaptation. Neither would a behavioural ecologist explain an animal species' behavioural or other adaptations by invoking fixed properties of its 'mind' or 'mind/brain'. Mental capacities themselves have to be explained, and this is done by reference to a wider context of reproductive, social, foraging, and other behavioural strategies conceived as adaptations to changing conditions. We need a theory of the evolution of *Homo sapiens* faithful to the methods of behavioural ecology which have proved so successful elsewhere in the living world.

It might be thought that by now we would have a number of theoretical attempts in this direction. Sadly, this is not the case. If we restrict ourselves to hypotheses which are (a) based on tried-and-tested methods of behavioural ecology; (b) focused on the emergence of symbolism; and (c) testable in the light of archaeological data, the range is strikingly limited. Camilla Power's Female Cosmetic Coalitions model (see discussion in Sections 17.9–17.11) meets all three conditions. But before evaluating it, I will survey a range of models which meet at least some of these basic preconditions.

17.5 Costly versus cheap signals: co-operation between strangers

17.5.1 *Philip Chase: Symbolism enforces co-operation between strangers*

During the later phases of human evolution, humans began to invent entities lacking any existence in the real world—intangibles such as underworlds, promises, and totems. Symbolic culture arose because its coercive rituals and associated belief systems provided the only mechanisms of punishment and reward capable of enforcing co-operation between strangers, in turn a prerequisite for the establishment of institutional facts. The term 'co-operation between strangers' means co-operation on a scale transcending the limits of Darwinian kin-selection or reciprocal altruism (Chase 1994, 1999).

17.5.2 *Richard Sosis: Costly ritual enforces co-operation between strangers*

Religious communities are networks of 'strangers' held together by costly ritual. The supernatural entities that help to inspire allegiance don't spontaneously replicate in human brains: they must be coercively installed. Painful ordeals such as initiation rites perform this function. The only way to reliably demonstrate religious commitment is to undergo rituals so demanding of personal sacrifice that the benefits of subsequent defection are likely to be outweighed by the costs (Sosis 2003).

17.5.3 Merlin Donald: Mimesis

Symbolic culture became established as *Homo erectus* came under communicative pressure to exercise cognitive control over previously hard-to-fake, emotionally expressive body language. Mimetic culture emerged as learned, culturally transmitted, simulated versions of previously instinctive responses. Through dance, song, pantomime, and ritual, evolving humans bonded with one another more and more closely, becoming correspondingly adept at expressing in public their emotional and cognitive states (Donald 1991, 2001).

17.5.4 Dan Sperber: To qualify as symbolic, an expression must be false

To determine whether a signal or statement is 'symbolic', a simple rule can be applied. Is it patently false? If not, symbolism is absent. Expressions are symbolic, according to Sperber, to the extent that they are literal falsehoods serving as guides to communicative intentions. Metaphor, irony, sarcasm, and much verbal humour illustrate the principle—'saying' one thing while 'meaning' another. This communicative strategy relies on listeners' inferential and imaginative abilities; it is central to all linguistic communication. Language in some form must have begun evolving from the moment when, for whatever reason, our ancestors first began deploying and decoding patent falsehoods in communicatively helpful ways (Sperber 1975, 2005; Sperber and Wilson 1986).

17.5.5 Roy Rappaport: In the beginning was the Word

Words are cheap and therefore unreliable. Communal investment in repetitive and invariant (purposefully 'inefficient') ritual is the solution to this problem. At the apex of any congregation's hierarchy of symbols is its 'ultimate sacred postulate'—that article of faith which lies beyond possible denial. Without the community's confidence in that symbol of itself, faith in the entire system of interconnected symbols would collapse. During the evolution of humanity, therefore, the crucial step was the establishment of community-wide rituals capable of upholding the levels of public faith necessary for low-cost verbal communication to work (Rappaport 1999).

17.5.6 Jerome Lewis: Hunting, mimicry, and play

Since they are incapable of mimicry, the various antelopes, monkeys, and other animals hunted by Central African forest people trust their own species-specific calls, treating them as intrinsically reliable. Forest hunter-gatherers routinely exploit such gullibility, faking animal cries to lure their targets within range. When these same hunters subsequently recall a particular hunting episode, they act out the story drawing on the same sophisticated capacities for faking, mimicry, and pantomime. Story-telling, ritual, play, and religious symbolism in such societies are the in-group, co-operative, and correspondingly honest redeployment of capacities for deception initially deployed in the forest. This converges with the people's indigenous view: they conceptualize their signs, songs, and rituals as echoes of the forest's own voices and spirits (Lewis 2009, Chapter 7; Knight and Lewis, Chapter 21).

17.6 Symbolism: puzzles and paradoxes

Turning now to a review of these ideas, archaeologist Philip Chase asserts that Darwinism alone cannot explain co-operation between strangers. He also reminds us that symbolic culture enforces just this kind of co-operation. But how did symbolic culture itself emerge? Having posed the question with admirable clarity, he leaves the evolutionary emergence of symbolic culture unexplained.

Behavioural ecologist Richard Sosis does offer a Darwinian model in which individual strategies of alliance-building enforce co-operation between strangers. To explain the mechanisms at work, Sosis relies on costly signalling theory (Zahavi 1975; Zahavi and Zahavi 1997). Religious communities hold themselves together by insisting that each individual member pay admission and continued membership costs so heavy as to deter freeriding. The threshold of costs will be set by the probability of social defection. This explains why rituals of initiation are so often painful, and potentially why there should be variability in costliness. A ritual involving no hardship or sacrifice cannot signal commitment: it would allow freeriders to flourish. Sosis has done his main studies on contemporary or recent historic religious communities, who are already immersed in symbolic culture. In principle, however, the model can apply to the evolutionary emergence of ritual and religion. Indeed Alcorta and Sosis (2005) discuss the African Middle Stone Age archaeological record, mainly the ochre evidence, in relation to this model. The value of this work is that it suggests a bridge between animal signalling and symbolic cultural display: the same body of theory can be applied in both domains. But why exactly must hard-to-fake ritual generate what Chase (1994) terms 'things that have no existence in the "real" world'? Hunter-gatherer ritual and religious landscapes are populated by animal spirits, tricksters, and other such fictional entities. What is the connection between these two apparently incompatible properties of ritual—its intrinsic reliability on the one hand and its reliance on trickery on the other?

In stark opposition to the hard-to-fake costly signal model stand Merlin Donald and Dan Sperber. For symbolism to evolve, if we accept their positions, evolving humans had to stop probing signals for their reliability and instead collude with patent fakes. At first sight, this seems wholly incompatible with Sosis' argument that symbolically constituted communities hold themselves together by resorting to signals whose reliability is underwritten by their costs. If Donald and Sperber are correct, symbolism seems to presuppose signals which are not just unreliable but patently false. But perhaps the cheap signals and the costly ones perform distinct functions, operating on quite different levels?

This is essentially the argument of Roy Rappaport (1999), the distinguished social anthropologist who rejected modern selfish-gene Darwinism but independently discovered the costly signalling idea. Social acceptance of symbols presupposes high levels of trust already in place. Sosis follows Rappaport's argument that costly ritual is designed to generate trust where none existed before. Integrating these lines of reasoning, we might conclude that ritual is needed to cement bonds sufficiently trusting to permit communication on the basis of cheap fakes such as words.

Let me put this another way. A distinction can be drawn between signalling costs of two kinds (Grafen 1990a; Guilford and Dawkins 1991). Either the signaller must generate trust on a signal-by-signal basis, or sufficient trust can be assumed already in advance. In the first case, the relatively low costs involved in minimizing perceptual ambiguity won't suffice: added costs must be incurred to ensure reliability as well. A strong case can be made that all animal signals without exception involve costs of both kinds—'efficacy costs' plus 'strategic costs'. The reason for this is that animal signals must always carry at least some of the burden of generating the trust necessary for communication to work.

Now to the second case. What if the signaller doesn't have to generate trust at all? Trust could be assumed already in advance, leaving the signaller free to concentrate on perceptual discriminability. Suppose no strategic costs whatever need be incurred. All signalling effort can now be poured into efficacy. Carried to its conclusion, this should permit reduction to digital alternatives—enabling communication of the cheapest, most efficient kind theoretically possible. We know that human language is in fact digital in fundamental ways, both phonological and semantic, this being one of its most remarkable, biologically unprecedented characteristics (Jakobson 1938; Burling 2005: 25-7, 53-5; Chomsky 1991: 50).

As an evolutionarily stable strategy, digital encoding under Darwinian social conditions is ruled out for the same reason that reliance on patent falsehoods is ruled out. Costly signals, by definition, are signals designed to demonstrate reliability. Regardless of receiver psychology, they can't be decoded in either/or (i.e. 'digital') terms. If all primate vocal repertoires are ultimately graded rather than discrete (Clay and Zuberbühler, Chapter 11), the reason is simple: signallers and receivers have conflicting interests, preventing them from carving up the cost continuum into conventionally agreed categories. As meanings are contested, the gradations are infinite, leaving receivers with no choice but to evaluate performance on an analogue scale (Zahavi and Zahavi 1997: 57-8).

Putting all this together, it seems that language is digital for the same reason that it isn't real. Its field of operation is exclusively the imagination. Its zero-cost features can prove socially acceptable and evolve only under highly unusual conditions—namely, those internal to a ritually bonded community whose members cannot benefit from lying.

Combining the insights of Chase, Sosis, Donald, Sperber, and Rappaport, we might summarize by defining symbolic culture as a domain of transparent falsehoods whose social acceptance depends on levels of trust generated through the performance of costly ritual. We might add that once the relevant fictions are socially accepted, they qualify automatically as 'institutional facts' (Searle 1995; see Wyman, Chapter 13). Whether in language or elsewhere, institutional facts are digitally contrastive by logical necessity. You cannot be more or less someone's wife, more or less a knight in chess. X either does have status Y or it doesn't: there are no shades of grey. Since they depend on communal agreement, facts of this special kind presuppose the uniquely human phenomenon of 'co-operation between strangers'. While such co-operation must have evolved, it remains to be explained how and why.

Following Maynard Smith and Harper (2003: 3), we may define a 'signal' as any act or structure which alters the behaviour of other organisms, which evolved because of that effect, and which is effective because the receiver's response has also evolved. If one animal pushes away another, that's not a signal. If one animal makes another retreat by baring its teeth, that action is a signal because the response depends on evolved properties of the receiver's psychology and sense organs. The signal must carry information of interest to the receiver. While this needn't always be correct, it must be correct sufficiently often for receivers to be selected to respond appropriately. Against this background, Krebs and Dawkins (1984) conceptualized signal evolution as an arms race between signallers as manipulators and receivers as mind-readers. Zahavi (1975; Zahavi and Zahavi 1997) proposed 'the handicap principle' to explain why signal selection in the animal world favours extravagance and apparent wastefulness, not utilitarian efficiency. Receivers on guard against deception force signallers to compete in producing signals so costly that they cannot be fakes.

The problem is that by these standards, fast, efficient, digital communication on the model of language appears to be theoretically impossible, a point which is explicitly made by Zahavi (1993). As Steels (Chapter 24) explains, communicative efficiency—not wasteful extravagance—is the engine driving grammaticalization in human languages. But how, during human evolution, did the shift from wastefulness to efficiency come about? Machiavellian primates can produce tactical deceptions, but these are frequency-dependent: they work only if most signals are honest. To explain the emergence of human cultural symbolism, we need a theory which addresses this difficulty: How can we imagine falsehoods so prevalent and so valued as to be embraced by all? How can we imagine Machiavellian evolving humans, by definition resistant to deception, opting to immerse themselves in infinite realms of fiction?

Here is a possible solution. Is this or that signal deceptive or reliable, costly or cheap, analogue or digital? It depends on who is doing the evaluating and from what standpoint. Imagine a coalition of individuals co-operatively aiming deceptive signals at an external target. Viewed from inside the coalition, those patent deceptions will have positive value. Instead of being resisted, they should be celebrated and embraced. But that's only when viewed from the inside; viewed from an external perspective, everything will seem quite different. To quote Saussure (1983 [1915]: 8) once again: 'The object is not given in advance of the viewpoint: far from it. Rather, one might say that it is the viewpoint adopted which creates the object.'

Drawing on his work with the Mbendjele forest people of Central Africa, Jerome Lewis (2009, Chapter 7) offers a proposal along similar lines, viewing distinctively human capacities for vocal mimicry and deception as adaptations to the hunter-gatherer lifestyle. Human volitional control over vocal signalling, he suggests, did not evolve initially in contexts of human social interaction. Instead, it was used initially to deceive prey animals who would prove vulnerable again and again to such fakes. Humans co-operating with one another to deceive external targets wouldn't be predicted to resist one another's deceptions. On the contrary, they should echo and amplify them. In Lewis' account, vocal simulations redeployed internally within the community laid the basis for vocal humour, children's games, choral singing, narrative fiction, metaphor, religion, and so forth. Humans successfully 'deceived' the forest and then constructed the symbolic domain as that forest's own echo, now directed back into the human social world.

We now need to consider how hunter-gatherer strategies of this kind might have beome established in the evolutionary past.

17.7 Counter-dominance, egalitarianism, and collective intentionality

17.7.1 *Michael Tomasello: The cultural origins of human cognition*

Cultural evolution can proceed rapidly, helping to explain the accelerated pace of evolution since the emergence of *Homo sapiens*. Cultural advance presupposes the 'ratchet effect', in which innovations are preserved and accumulated intergenerationally. This would have been fostered by co-operative strategies in which individuals subordinated their private purposes to collective future goals. Apes are not capable of this kind of co-operation, which explains why they don't even point—or, at least, don't point things out to one another when interacting under natural conditions in the wild. Declarative pointing presupposes 'we'-intentionality: a shared subjectivity rendering things interesting or relevant 'for us'. It involves a triadic structure of representation in which signaller and receiver share the same focus of attention. If the cognition of apes is poorly adapted to such tasks, the explanation is ultimately that in the wild, their way of life makes them just too competitive (Tomasello 1999, 2006).

17.7.2 *Andrew Whiten: The evolution of deep social mind*

Primate Machiavellian cognition reflects the fact that reproductive success is likely to be secured by deception and trickery as much as by honesty and co-operation. In humans, strikingly novel cognitive developments reflect novel strategies of co-operation whose roots lie in 'counter-dominance'—resistance to being physically dominated by others. Within increasingly stable coalitions, internal status began to be earned in novel ways, social rewards accruing to those perceived by their peers as especially co-operative and self-aware. Selection pressures favoured such psychological innovations as imaginative empathy, joint attention, moral judgement, project-oriented collaboration, and the ability to evaluate one's own behaviour from the standpoint of others. Underpinning enhanced probabilities of cultural transmission and cumulative cultural evolution, these developments led to the establishment of hunter-gatherer-style egalitarianism in association with minds which were now 'deeply social' (Whiten 1999).

17.7.3 *Christopher Boehm: From counter-dominance to reverse dominance*

During the later stages of human evolution, counter-dominance tipped over into 'reverse dominance'. Humans became so resistant to being dominated by others that they remained constantly on guard, ready at any moment to band together in countering perceived threats (see Dessalles, Chapter 20). As coalitions organized in this way regularly defeated all opposition, they established themselves collectively as the dominant force. Society became 'moral' when everyone was embraced within the same coalition, evaluating the behaviour of its individual members from this new collective standpoint (Boehm 1999, 2012).

17.7.4 *Robin Dunbar: Social brain, gossip, and grooming*

Seeking safety in numbers, evolving humans favoured life in larger groups. Among primates, the larger the group, the more intense are the likely levels of internal competition presenting individuals with increased prospects of harassment and associated stress. Social success in larger groups also selects for a larger neocortex, hence increased childcare burdens, placing females in particular under more reproductive stress. Dunbar proposes a strategy for cutting the costs of time budgets. Females and other subordinates buffer themselves by forming defensive alliances, maintaining friendships through manual grooming. As alliances become progressively larger, pressure mounts to find a cheaper, more efficient way of maintaining social bonds. There is a solution: switch to vocal grooming. By using vocal sounds in place of fingers, evolving humans discover that they can service multiple allies at once while leaving their hands free for practical tasks. Although the idea has been heavily criticized (Power 1998), Dunbar (1996b) claims that 'gossip' has its origins here.

17.8 Dominance and reverse dominance

Psychologist Michael Tomasello studies the cognitive interface between humans and other primates. The special thing about humans, in his account, is co-operation in pursuit of a future goal held jointly in mind. An element of contractual understanding is involved, since commitment would collapse without confidence that promised gains will be shared. Resource sharing is in this way bound up with an orientation toward the future. There has to be a dream or vision, those sharing it committing themselves to whatever forms of collaboration are needed to secure its practical implementation.

So how and why did *Homo sapiens* begin collaborating in this special way? The fact that wild-living apes don't even point things out to one another shifts attention from cognitive mechanisms to competitive and co-operative strategies. Declarative pointing presupposes individuals so trusting and co-operative that they are willing to decide collaboratively on the perspective to be adopted toward the world. Humans during the course of evolution established such 'we'-intentionality. Linguistic rules and symbols—complex elaborations on the simple theme of pointing—are, in Tomasello's view, culturally inherited patterns which evolved and became transmitted from the moment when this development occurred. As to why it occurred, Tomasello once remarked—with refreshing candour—'I really have no idea' (Tomasello 2003b: 108–9). Pressed for an answer, he now invokes an early stage of obligatory collaborative foraging followed by the development of group-on-group social conflict and competition (Tomasello et al. 2012).

Without giving it special emphasis, Tomasello also considers a third possibility: collective resistance to being dominated by 'individuals who attempted to hog all of the food' (Tomasello et al. 2012: 676). The struggle to resist dominance ('counter-dominance') has an inherent tendency to bring together unrelated individuals who might not previously have been allies. Andrew Whiten (1999) invokes this idea to explain why human hunter-gatherers evolved to be so insistently egalitarian. In Whiten's model, humans retain their primate heritage of 'Machiavellian' strategic intelligence, initially without undergoing any psychological rupture or break. But as they developed increasingly effective strategies of resistance, the benefits of imposing dominance on others became matched by the associated costs. Eventually a stalemate was reached: instead of everyone competing to find someone else to dominate, the winning strategy was 'don't mess with me'—a generalized refusal to be dominated. As this strategy became evolutionarily stable, it altered the trajectory of cognitive and cultural evolution, leading to the emergence of distinctively modern human psychology.

Whiten avoids the conundrums and paradoxes associated with the topic of symbolism. Boehm does little better, barely mentioning ritual, religion, or language.

Yet Boehm takes one notable step in the necessary direction. Tomasello, as we have seen, links the evolution of symbolism with collaboration in pursuit of a shared vision or goal. Boehm in this context offers a concrete proposal. The vision which mattered was a *political* one. There was an effort to take hold of primate-style dominance and turn it upside down. No longer should physical violence or threat be allowed to determine access to resources or status within the group. Humanity's first moral community was committed to the ideal of an egalitarian order turning dominance on its head.

According to Boehm, the strategy of resisting dominance leads eventually to full-scale revolution. But how exactly did this happen? Boehm asks us to envisage a coalition expanding until it eventually includes everyone. This is an unrealistic concept: a coalition by definition presupposes a boundary between insiders and outsiders. Given that primate dominance is always in some sense sexual, it would follow that a model of counter-dominance culminating in reverse dominance should take account of this. Could male-versus-female conflict and co-operation lead to a coalition embracing everyone? Boehm (1999) does consider distinctively female strategies, but only when dealing with chimpanzees. As he turns to consider the emergence of human hunter-gatherer egalitarianism, sex surprisingly disappears.

If we are to consider counter- and reverse dominance in human evolution, the most critical issue becomes reproductive counter-dominance. How do these models deal with the question of reproductive inequality or 'skew' among males—that is, with the degree to which any dominant male can monopolize reproductive success? Bowles (2006) points to reproductive levelling among predominantly monogamous hunter-gatherers as critical to egalitarianism. To explore the evolutionary establishment of egalitarianism on this reproductive level, we must ask questions about the strategies of females.

According to the Social Brain hypothesis (Dunbar 1996a, 1998, 2003), the factor driving increase in neocortex size in hominin ancestors was increasing group size. In the case of early *Homo*, as climate dried towards the end of the Pliocene, groups needed to be bigger for protection in more open environments. In the case of later *Homo*, during the Pleistocene, the main danger of predation was likely to have been from other human groups. Under pressure to live in larger groups, *Homo* was selected for increased Machiavellian intelligence to negotiate increasing social complexity. Pawlowski et al. (1998) show that as neocortex size increases in primates, the correlation of male rank with mating success is progressively undermined. Selection for increased social intelligence therefore goes hand in hand with greater reproductive levelling.

Larger brain sizes in later *Homo*, along with larger bodies, led to increased costs of reproduction for females. It is now time to consider how the extra energetic requirements of mothers of large-brained offspring were met. We turn to models for sexual strategies and investment.

17.9 Female coalitionary strategies

17.9.1 *Sarah Hrdy: The origins of mutual understanding*

Ape mothers are insufficiently trusting to allow others to hold their babies. *Homo erectus* mothers, facing increasingly heavy childcare burdens, enhanced their fitness by getting trustworthy kin—especially female kin—to help. However, according to Hrdy, this was only possible if mothers and daughters could stay close together (see Hawkes, Section 17.9.2). Distinctively human cognition evolved in this female kin-coalition context, as mothers probed potential allocarers for their co-operative intentions. Infants monitoring the intentions and feelings of mothers and others became adept at perspective-taking and integrating multiple perspectives. Offspring more skilled in reading the intentions of others and eliciting their help were better nourished and more likely to survive. Female strategies of co-operative childcare can explain how and why humans became cognitively and emotionally 'modern' (Hrdy 2009).

17.9.2 *Kristen Hawkes: Grandmothering and show-off hunting in human evolution*

Hawkes and colleagues, James O'Connell and Nick Blurton Jones, offer two key arguments for investment in offspring at different stages of human evolution. The 'grandmother' hypothesis (Hawkes et al. 1998; O'Connell 1999) argues for the beginnings of humanlike life history in early *H. erectus*. Burdened with increasingly heavy childcare costs, evolving *Homo* mothers sought help from the most reliable source—female kin and especially their own mothers. Post-reproductive lifespans extended as older females came under selection pressure to invest in the offspring of their daughters. As the climate became drier in the Early Pleistocene, increasing the scarcity of accessible foods for weanlings, older females stepped in, providing gathered foods such as tubers to these young offspring. In terms of life history, this selected for relatively early weaning (hence shorter interbirth intervals) along with longer childhood dependency on adult provisioning, with correspondingly delayed sexual maturity and longer lifespans. Males were intermittently or unreliably involved in supporting offspring at this early stage, but during the Middle Pleistocene (associating to *Homo heidelbergensis*), hunting strategies become more effective and reliable. Males were motivated to hunt big game to gain prestige in female eyes. Rather than hunt small to medium game for their own genetic offspring alone, they demonstrated quality by generously providing big game to the whole camp (Hawkes and Bliege Bird 2002). In short: females gained male investment by stimulating mating effort rather than by attempting to keep males monogamously faithful and paternal.

17.9.3 *Camilla Power: Female cosmetic coalitions*

The evolution of concealed ovulation, extended receptivity, and increased reproductive synchrony in the human female forced males to spend more time in female company. Potential philanderers were deprived of the information they needed to successfully rove from one female to the next, picking and choosing on the basis of current fertility cues. However, one signal—menstruation—was unavoidably left salient, giving away this potentially dangerous kind of information. As an indicator of imminent fertility, menstruation will trigger conflict both between males, who may compete for the cycling female, and between females, who may compete for male investment. In the absence of countermeasures, mothers who are pregnant or lactating may be at risk of losing male investment to the cycling female. The rapid increase in neocortex size characteristic of human evolution over the last half million years meant that mothers—now burdened with correspondingly heavier childcare costs—could no longer tolerate rampant philandering; it was in their individual fitness interest to prioritize future economic security over short-term sexual favour-seeking. Counter-dominant female coalitions on this basis responded by 'painting up' with false signals representing all members of the coalition as uniformly 'fertile'. Investor males—whose offspring might have better chances of survival—had a fitness interest in colluding with the corresponding fictions. The evolutionary stability of female strategies of cosmetic bonding and adornment culminated in the transition to symbolic ritual, and—as a consequence of dramatically increased levels of in-group trust—the earliest beginnings of language-like communication (Power and Aiello 1997; Power 1999, 2009, Chapter 15; Power et al. 2013).

17.10 On co-operative breeding

Sarah Hrdy effectively combines the 'grandmother' model with Tomasello's arguments for intersubjectivity as the basis for human culture and cognition. Pregnancy and postnatal childcare in *Homo* were exceptionally heavy burdens, offering for that reason the most convincing context for the development of novel co-operative strategies. Alone of the great apes, we became co-operative breeders. Hrdy's arguments about the effects of alloparenting on human cognitive evolution are persuasive. Her focus on changing female strategies and on consequences for infant psychology are necessary and welcome. Demographically flexible co-operative breeding networks could act as a safety net for mothers, compensating for extreme variability in levels of male commitment.

Neither Hrdy nor Kristen Hawkes, whose model Hrdy acknowledges as the initial steps into co-operative breeding, aim to deal with symbolic culture. Both models also keep males as investors in the margins, with female kin getting on with the job, not expecting regular investment from males. Males enter the picture only late, becoming more reliable hunters as female sexual choice drives them to intensified mating effort. There is no clear argument from Hawkes as to what causes the shift in male behaviour and productivity between *Homo erectus* and subsequent encephalized humans. In fact, in her life history models she does not take much account of increasing brain size, even though this must have been critical in adding to female costs. Among Hadza bow-and-arrow hunters, to this day, males are only intermittently successful, an observation which led Hawkes to doubt the validity of the model of 'man the hunter' provisioning exclusively his own genetic offspring.

Camilla Power concurs with Hrdy's and Hawkes' initial position of female kin-related social structures among *Homo erectus*. Because female fertility is affected by the grandmother strategy—mothers with allocare support tending to have shorter interbirth intervals and be fertile more often—this must affect male behaviour. More dominant males might attempt to target fertile females opportunistically, moving from one to another, while less dominant males could pursue a strategy of hanging around more reliably, offering provisioning and protective support to a particular female and her kin. As interbirth intervals shortened, one consequence would be that investor males who waited around instead of competing for additional mates should gain reproductive benefits. Such a picture of variability in male commitment fits Hrdy's observations of stark differences between modern human fathers.

Power argues that while such variability may have been tolerable for less encephalized early *Homo erectus*, as brains rapidly expanded during the Late Middle Pleistocene (from *c.* 500,000 to 150,000 kya), female fitness would have been increasingly affected by whether or not males were providing help. In these conditions among *Homo heidelbergensis*, sporadically in Eurasia, and increasingly regularly in Africa, females resorted to the cosmetic strategy from *c.* 300,000 kya. This had the effect of rejecting dominant male philanderers reluctant to work and invest—in favour of more co-operative males competing to impress females with their hunting skills and generosity (Power et al. 2013).

An advantage of Power's model is that the emergence of symbolism is intrinsic to the strategy. Symbols are socially accepted fakes; that means, in the first instance, cosmetics. But were pigments necessarily used by women alone? Evolving human males had little Darwinian reason to alter or transform their biologically perceptible identity. With females, matters had always been more complex. The evolving human female had good reason to conceal external signs of ovulation, since philanderer males might use the information to their advantage. The use of blood-red cosmetics to scramble menstrual signals was in that sense nothing new. Power's model does not exclude males from using cosmetics; but, she argues, it's hard to think of a good Darwinian reason why males should take the lead in 'faking' their biological appearance using cosmetics (see Power, Chapter 15). At present, the Female Cosmetic Coalitions (FCC) model is the only Darwinian explanation as to why processed, curated, distinctively *blood-red* ochre is so prominent at Blombos and other Middle Stone Age sites.

The FCC model posits counter-dominance leading to reverse dominance. Unlike in Boehm's version of reverse dominance, however, in Power's FCC scenario both the initial dominance and its subsequent reversal are gendered. The model applies a standard behavioural ecological approach (one distinguishing sexual strategies and male and female trade-offs) to the suggestions of Whiten and Boehm. Females concealing ovulation and extending sexual receptivity are already promoting 'counter-dominance' on a sexual level, since the strategy discriminates against dominant males in favour of subordinates more likely to invest time and energy. When the scrambling of reproductive signals is extended to menstruation, the effect is to tip 'counter-dominance' into 'reverse dominance'. When a female begins to menstruate, her senior female kin have every interest in surrounding her, identifying with her attractions and 'painting up' to spread those attractions around. But they also have every interest in barring male access to her except on their terms (compare Knight 1991; Knight et al. 1995).

Hawkes' model of male hunting as a 'show-off' strategy needs to be placed in this wider sexual and political context. After all, there are many different ways in which males might show off, not all of them conducive to symbolic culture. Males could resort to physical force, 'showing off' through violence and aggression (see Dessalles, Chapter 20). An advantage of the Female Cosmetic Coalitions model is that it explains how males might have been corralled into showing off helpfully rather than destructively.

17.11 Sex and symbolism

Whereas Chase argues that symbolic culture emerges in order to enforce co-operation between strangers, Power sets out from selfish-gene theory and stays with it throughout. 'There is no reason to believe that symbolic culture was ever essential to survival', writes Chase (1994: 626–8). But in that case, why invest so much energy in the necessary rituals? Chase has contributed to the conceptual definition of symbolic culture, but in the absence of any evolutionary theory he lacks specific predictions about exactly what taboos, laws or rules would be collectively enforced. By contrast, Power offers an array of specific predictions testable against the archaeological, fossil, and ethnographic records (Power 2009: 273, table 14.2; for detailed ethnographic tests, see especially Watts 2005).

But how exactly does the model generate such detailed predictions? In pursuing their direct reproductive interests, women 'gang up' on anyone in their ranks who might constitute a weak link in the chain. A female who has just begun cycling comes potentially into that category: in view of her evident fertility—hence special attractiveness to males—she might be tempted to break ranks. Abandoning his current partner, we would expect any would-be philanderer to be on the look-out for such an opportunity. To gain his attention, we would expect the favour-seeking female to indicate that she is of the same species as the dominant male, of the opposite sex, and currently or imminently fertile. This immediately gives us the predicted signature of reverse dominance. The defiant, cosmetically adorned coalition must bond tightly with the female concerned. Reversing her perceived biological identity, they must signal collectively: 'Wrong species, wrong sex, wrong time!'

Note that we now have a coalition which might in principle extend to embrace everybody, as Boehm's argument demands. On the one hand, the entire female community has an interest in joining up, irrespective of kinship or previous friendship or familiarity—all should benefit over the long term by making philandering an unplayable game. But the coalition of females should also expect male support. Brothers and sons might be expected to defend female kin. Investor males should have an interest in ganging up against dominant philanderers threatening to impregnate their long-term mates. On all these grounds, we might expect the 'reverse dominance/reverse reality' coalition to succeed in imposing its message.

There is cognitive hardship in believing in counter-reality. It is not easy to accept that reality as perceived can be so completely reversed—that the categories of human versus animal, female versus male, menstrual blood versus hunting blood can be so radically interchanged and confounded. But such tricks—the stuff of mythology the world over—are not arbitrary cultural inventions. Reverse dominance generates them by conceptual necessity. The message which results is patently false. The biological female undergoing her initiatory ordeal (her incorporation into the coalition) is not a male, not an animal, and not wounded. But if everyone accepts the fiction, it's an institutional fact. And not just any such fact. If Power's argument is accepted, reverse sexual dominance by its own internal logic generates a characteristically hunter-gatherer version of Rappaport's Ultimate Sacred Postulate—a paradoxical truth serving to underpin all others.

17.12 Conclusion

In this chapter, I have tried to show how the problem of the emergence of symbolic culture might be solved. In revisiting a set of currently prominent models—all of which offer insights—I have asked how we might parsimoniously fit them together.

My aim has not been to set up the Female Cosmetic Coalitions (FCC) model in opposition to the others considered here. Chase is correct to view symbolic culture as a means of enforcing co-operation between strangers. But we require more than a statement: we need a Darwinian explanation. Rappaport and Sosis are surely right about the importance of ritual, but for a model of ritual origins to be testable, we need sufficient detail: which rituals, serving whose purposes, when, where, how, why? Donald is persuasive in his arguments about mimesis. But mimesis is 'faking it': if everyone is just acting, why should anyone believe? Similar theoretical difficulties afflict Sperber: how, when, where, and on what basis could patent falsehoods have been trusted by evolving humans as valid intellectual currency? Whiten's model is persuasive but unfortunately avoids the topic of sex, as does Boehm's. Whiten and Boehm correctly address politics, but skate over the nuts and bolts. What specific political purposes might have been sufficiently constant and unifying to give rise to 'deep social mind'? Tomasello posits commitment to shared future goals as a condition for language's evolutionary emergence. Can we specify whose goals? Hrdy reminds us that half the human population is female, and that mothers caring for infants are most likely to have driven the emergence of new strategies of social cognition and co-operation. But why stop short of the emergence of symbolism, given the increasing reproductive costs of encephalization following the evolution of *Homo erectus*? Why not explain the relatively late emergence of symbolism in terms consistent with the previous logic of allocare? Hawkes brings male mating effort back into the picture, but without explaining why symbolism had anything to do with it.

Lewis comes into a rather different category. Instead of proposing yet another cultural origins theory, he invites us to open our minds to the insights of hunter-gatherers. The Mbendjele forest people who inspire Lewis' vision challenge the conceptual distinctions central to Western evolutionary and social science. Language, play, ritual, and cosmology are all cut from the same cloth. Religion is not a different thing from childhood pretend-play: it's pretend-play taken seriously and continued into adult life. Hunting or gathering is not necessarily unconnected with speaking or singing: from a Mbendjele perspective, it involves pleasing the forest by echoing back its own sounds. Lewis argues persuasively that such interconnections should be borne in mind by those of us struggling to explain the evolutionary emergence of human language and symbolic culture. It may be that everything is simpler than we thought.

Part IV

Social Theories of Language Evolution

18

The co-evolution of human intersubjectivity, morality, and language

JORDAN ZLATEV

18.1 Introduction

Language crucially involves two kinds of *sharing* between the members of a community: (a) of lexical meanings, grammatical rules, and conventions of use, all of which are necessary for successful symbolic communication; and (b) using these for honestly communicating factual knowledge and for constructing fictive beliefs. Due to (a), human languages can conveniently be defined as 'socially shared symbolic systems' (Nelson and Shaw 2002) and due to (b), *cooperation* is a central property of language use, and is furthermore essential for the conventions of (a) to be established (Clark 1996). If evolution is fundamentally based on the natural selection of individuals, or of their genes (Dawkins 1976), the evolution of both kinds of sharing appears anomalous. On the basis of such assumptions, Fitch (2010: 417) concludes: 'The cooperative sharing of information thus remains a central puzzle in language evolution'.

The proposal of this chapter is that a solution to this puzzle can be found by linking the evolution of language to that of two other (interconnected) features of human sociality, which likewise have appeared as anomalous for a gene-centred perspective on evolution. This first is *intersubjectivity*, a suite of capacities such as joint attention, joint actions, and empathy involving 'the sharing of affective, perceptual and reflective experiences between two or more subjects' (Zlatev 2008: 215). The second is *morality*, understood as 'a sense of right and wrong that is born out of group-wide systems of conflict management based on shared values' (Flack and de Waal 2000: 69). While intersubjectivity is essentially a dyadic, subject-to-subject relation and does not presuppose a group-wide system of shared values, morality is clearly normative. Neither of the two is equivalent to *altruism*, either in the evolutionary sense of involving a fitness cost to the donor and a fitness benefit for a recipient, or in the psychological sense of a genuine, 'other-oriented, altruistic motivation' (Eisenberg 2000: 677); intersubjectivity can also be used 'selfishly' for the purpose of manipulating others, and morality (commonly) involves the punishment of those who transgress the moral precepts. Still, both intersubjectivity and morality are essentially super-individual phenomena, involving at least in part a degree of psychological altruism. Hence, unsurprisingly, both have been difficult to reconcile with individual-fitness accounts of evolution, assuming that we need 'to teach generosity and altruism, since we are born selfish' (Dawkins 1976: 2).

Here, I argue that the co-evolution of intersubjectivity, language, and morality in human beings requires a *multi-level selection* (MLS) theory of evolution (Sober and Wilson 1998, 2000a; O'Gorman et al. 2008), according to which evolution operates on the levels of genes, cells, organisms, and groups, implying a trade-off between 'selfish' individual-selected traits, and 'altruistic' group-level selected traits. Further, I show that MLS coheres with the theory of *cultural group selection* (Richerson and Boyd 2005), and gene-culture co-evolution, providing together a basic framework for addressing the co-evolutionary thesis in the title of the chapter. I proceed by focusing on four currently influential theories of the evolution of human sociality, comparing and evaluating them. Since they show complementary strong and weak points, this opens the possibility for a composite account, which is suggested at the end.

18.2 Beyond ape intersubjectivity and morality

Since Darwin (1871), in attempting to uncover what is special about us as a species, it has become necessary to compare human traits with analogous (or homologous) ones in other species, and in particular with species with which we are most closely related. De Waal and colleagues (e.g. de Waal 1996, 2007; Preston and de Waal 2002) have persuasively argued that intersubjectivity should be viewed phylogenetically and ontogenetically as consisting of several layers or levels, with mammalian roots in basic processes of maternal care and emotional contagion. More cognitively demanding processes of 'feeling into' (*Einfühlung*) another's mental state—and on occasions acting sympathetically—are testified by numerous cases of targeted helping and consolation behaviour in chimpanzees and other great apes, but not in monkeys. Yet, chimpanzees succeed in understanding the perspectives, goals, and knowledge states of another conspecific or human partner mostly in *competitive* contexts, i.e. in order to maximize their own profits (Hare et al. 2000, 2001, 2006; Melis et al. 2006; Kaminski et al. 2008). This suggests strongly that at least one extra layer of intersubjectivity has been selected for after the last common ancestor of our species, four to five million years ago.

With respect to morality, Flack and de Waal (2000: 3) argue that non-human primates, and especially apes, 'have similar methods for resolving, managing, and preventing conflicts of interest within their groups. Such methods, which include reciprocity and food sharing, reconciliation, consolation, conflict intervention, and mediation, are the very building blocks of moral systems.' However, capacities such as these 'building blocks' are rather to be viewed as precursors or pre-adaptations of true moral systems (e.g. Boehm 1999; Knauft 2000; Thierry 2000). The latter require collectively shared norms, which in all human societies are reflected, if not explicitly expressed, by language. In the often quoted words of Goodall (1982), chimpanzee societies are characterized by 'order without law', i.e. not just lack of legal systems (which are absent in many traditional societies), but lack of shared moral ones too, as shown by an observation of in-group cannibalism, occurring when the victims were unprotected by close relatives or allies, without this leading to group sanctions to the perpetrators.

In sum, while current comparative psychological and evolutionary research has done much to counteract age-old asymmetrical dualisms such as human vs. animal, culture vs. nature, reason vs. emotion, human beings remain a very 'peculiar' kind of social animal. As Flack and de Waal (2000: 22, table 1) admit: 'It is particularly in these areas—empathy, internalization of rules, sense of justice, and community concern—that humans seem to have gone considerably further than most other animals.' But how and why has this happened? The simple answer 'language' will not suffice since we are brought back to the question of why and how language evolved, and since language is fundamentally a socially shared phenomenon, it requires the evolution of sociality in the first place. Thus, in attempting to tackle the evolution of human sociality and language, we are led to a chicken-and-egg problem (Zlatev 2008). This in itself suggests the venue of addressing it: a co-evolutionary account, based on the common denominator of language, intersubjectivity, and morality: *sharing*. But sharing presupposes at least a degree of (psychological) altruism, running against the stream of mainstream evolutionary reasoning.

Darwin (1871) was aware of the limits of individual-level natural selection to account for cases of altruism, such as the risks taken by group members to defend other members, and proposed *group selection*, with competition between rather than within groups, as the mechanism though which altruistic traits evolved. Since the 1960s, when the notion of group selection fell out of favour in evolutionary biology due to arguments that it is non-parsimonious and inefficient compared to individual-level selection (Maynard Smith 1964; Hamilton 1964), there have been repeated attempts to account for the evolution of apparently altruistic behaviour through gene-level and individual-level selection. The most straightforward is *mutualism*: the actor/donor gains a fitness benefit by teaming up with the recipient, for example for obtaining food, or minimizing the risk of predation. Cases of such mutualism can easily be found in the animal kingdom, but are of course not a matter of altruism but of co-selfishness. Hamilton (1964) proposed the influential notion of *kin selection*, also known as 'inclusive fitness', and the famous rule for the conditions for the evolution of altruistic behaviour: $rB > C$ ('Hamilton's Rule'), i.e. if the cost for donor C is smaller than the benefit B for a recipient, standing in degree of genetic relatedness r, then such behaviour would be optimizing fitness on the genetic level. Kin selection would thus appear to explain phenomena such as parental care, or even self-sacrifice for close relatives, and nepotism more generally, but cannot be extended to cooperation between the members of large social groups, many of which are not closely related.

In another influential paper, Trivers (1971) proposed *reciprocal altruism* as an essential component in the evolution of cooperation: the donor takes on a cost for performing an action that benefits a recipient, assuming that the recipient will reciprocate in the future. This functions in small groups, where reciprocating ultimately gives benefits to each member, but in larger groups the system is vulnerable to 'free-riders' who reap the benefits of others' altruistic acts, but do not reciprocate. A sizable literature has been devoted to various mechanisms of *indirect reciprocity* that may curtail the negative effect of free-riders. Two of these are *image scoring*, according to which so-called bystanders (third-party observers of the interaction) elevate the social reputation of individuals who help a needy recipient and decrease the social reputation of individuals who do not (Nowak and Sigmund 1998) and *social standing*, where bystanders decrease the social reputation only of individuals who fail to help a recipient in good social standing (Leimar and Hammerstein 2001). Such models have been applied to empirical cases of cooperation in animal species such as sticklebacks (*Gasterosteus aculeatus*) and guppies (*Poecilia reticulata*) where two or more animals leave the larger social group to gain information about an approaching predator (Dugatkin 2008). If the inspecting fish cooperate by keeping a similar distance to the predator, the strategy is most efficient. At the same time, by observing their behaviour bystanders can judge their reputations. This process has been suggested to affect future willingness to cooperate and to mate. Such explanations rely heavily on notions of individually remembered reputations and collectively shared 'social standings'—which imply fairly advanced memory and communication. Ecologically, they require rather small and/or compact groups: 'The payoff for exhibiting cooperative behaviour . . . will be realized only if bystanders are present in sufficient numbers to ensure that added benefits are available to balance the extra investment' (Early 2010: 2680). The combination of these conditions is questionable for any animal species, and especially for primates.

A final factor that appears necessary for extensive cooperation are *sanctions*, punishing free-riders in one way or another. But if such punishment is to be enforced by individual members there is the problem of 'second-order free-riders', who may be good cooperators but bad punishers. Thus, the evolution of sanctions for group-exploiting free-riders is itself a problem. Panchanathan and Boyd (2004) have proposed that it can be solved by 'collective action', implying group-wide norms on what is wrong and right, which appears to cross over to morality, as defined earlier in this section.

Reviewing some of this literature, but with focus on the evolution of *human* altruism/cooperation Boyd and Richerson (2009: 3283) conclude that 'evolutionary thinkers typically explain human cooperation as the resulting from the "three Rs": reputation, reciprocation and retribution', and that 'it seems probable that the three Rs can explain why cooperation is evolutionarily stable'. However, these three factors are not sufficient to explain why it *evolves*:

> The problem is that the three Rs can stabilize *any* behaviour. If everybody agrees that individuals must do *X*, and punish those who do not do *X*, then *X* will be evolutionarily stable as long as the costs of being punished exceed the costs of doing *X*. It is irrelevant whether *X* benefits the group or is socially destructive. It will pay to do *X*. Thus, the three Rs can explain how cooperative behaviours like participating in group defense can be favoured by evolution, but they can also explain anything else. (Boyd and Richerson 2009: 3283)

The only way that human-scale cooperation and altruism can evolve, argue Boyd and Richerson (2009), is through multi-level selection, with a crucial role for cultural adaptation and group selection. Their proposal can be broken down schematically in a four-step process. First, advanced social learning made cumulative cultural evolution possible and increased heritable variation between groups. Second, 'the three Rs' can stabilize different kinds of social behaviours, leading to pronounced differences between groups. Third, competition between groups would favour those with higher cooperative tendencies. Finally, selection within these most successful groups 'favoured genes that gave rise to new, more pro-social motives. Moral systems enforced by systems of sanctions and rewards increased the reproductive success of individuals who functioned well in such environments, and this in turn led to the evolution of other regarding motives like empathy and social emotions like shame' (Boyd and Richerson 2009: 3281–2). Such an account shows not only how 'functional' altruism and coercive social rules can evolve, but also psychological altruism, 'behaviour...motivated by feelings of concern for non-kinsmen' (Boehm 2000a: 213), which is not only culturally learned (*pace* Dawkins 1976). It has been demonstrated convincingly to function as the 'proximal cause' of pro-social acts for a majority of human subjects (Bateson 1991, 2000).

This process of gene-culture co-evolution is quite consistent with Sober and Wilson's (1998, 2000a) general theory of multi-level selection (MLS), which reverses the gene-and-individual centred focus of the traditional accounts. From the perspective of MLS theory, kin selection is a special case of group selection, applying to cases when the group members are closely related. Likewise, models of indirect reciprocity require incentives such as 'reputations' and 'status', as described above, but 'the evolution of an incentive system is itself a multi-level selection problem' (Sober and Wilson 2000b: 260). Finally, while MLS is more general than the cultural group selection model proposed by Boyd and Richerson, it can accommodate the special character of human cooperation and altruism: 'culture allows a form of selection to occur whose elements may be found in the absence of culture. Bees "police" the behaviour of other bees. What is uniquely human is the harnessing of socially shared values' (Sober and Wilson 2000a: 195).

Combining the conclusions of de Waal, Boyd–Richerson, and Sober–Wilson implies that the human-specific levels of intersubjectivity, culture, and morality must have co-evolved during the past 1–2 million years through multi-level selection. What about language? Paraphrasing Sober and Wilson from the final quotation: while some of the elements necessary for the stabilization of cooperation systems can perhaps be found in other species, it is difficult to imagine how systems of shared values and collective action (i.e. fully fledged moral systems) can be established and maintained without the presence of symbolic communication. This is especially so given that early human social groups were characterized by fission-fusion membership and large home ranges, an assumption based both on the character of chimpanzee social groups, and on those of extant hunter-gatherers (Knauft 2000). In the words of Boehm (2000b: 156), 'an ability to communicate with displacement is critical because such communities must continuously track everyone's behavior and group members are often dispersed'. Thus, in order to effectively establish reputations, a communication system with displaced reference would have been required. Such a system, amounting at least to 'protolanguage' would have been even more necessary for reaching consensus on issues of guilt and retribution. The absence of such a system was what allowed the cannibalistic chimpanzees reported by Goodall (1982) to go unpunished.

The following section supports the argument that human intersubjectivity, morality, and language must have co-evolved by considering four currently influential theories focusing on particular aspects of this co-evolutionary process.

18.3 Four theories of the evolution of human sociality

Several theories on the evolution of specifically-human sociality are more or less directly related to language evolution. The following four have been particularly influential. Dunbar (1996b) argued that life in larger groups necessitated a novel mechanism for social bonding, and hence at first *vocal grooming* and then *gossip* emerged in the *Homo* lineage. Deacon (1997) proposed that a *social contract* regulating sex ('marriage') in multi-male/multi-female groups is what propelled our ancestors to higher levels of sociality and symbolic reference. Tomasello (2008) advocated that a cognitive adaptation for *shared intentionality* and a motivational one for *pro-sociality* emerged first, providing an 'infrastructure' for the subsequent evolution of language. Finally, Hrdy (2009) argued that a transition in reproductive and rearing strategy to *alloparenting* (cooperative breeding) radically altered our ancestors' interpersonal relations, and thus provided the basis for adaptations in intersubjectivity and language. Let us compare and evaluate these proposals along the following set of criteria, formulated as five questions:

(1) *Why us and not others?* Does the theory provide an explanation of why a higher level of sociality (and language) evolved in the *Homo* genus, rather than other animals?

(2) *How?* What kind of evolutionary mechanism for the evolution of human-specific sociality is provided or implied?

(3) *When?* Is the timing proposed by the theory consistent with relevant anatomical changes (e.g. bipedalism, reduced canines, reduced sexual dimorphism), attested in the archaeological record?

(4) *What kind of social groups?* Is the theory consistent with anthropological evidence from extant hunter-gatherer societies (as well as technologically advanced ones)?

(5) *Development?* Is the theory consistent with evidence on how the features claimed to be unique for human sociality develop in children?

18.3.1 *Why us and not others?*

Dunbar frames his theory as focusing on the evolution of language. The answer to the *why* question is the following scenario: physical grooming is an important mechanism of social bonding and coalition-building in primates, but it is relatively inefficient, and therefore sets limits on the sizes of primate groups. With life in open territory, larger groups are required (for minimizing risk of predation, extended foraging, and territory defence), but that has negative side effects: more intra-group conflicts. This tension was resolved by the emergence of 'vocal grooming' (chorusing), and eventually 'gossip'. In brief: 'language evolved to service social bonds in a more generic sense by providing a substitute for social grooming' (Dunbar 2009: 14). To the self-posed question 'Why do only humans have language?' Dunbar replies: 'No one else has evolved group sizes large enough to require more than grooming for social bonding' (2009: 30). This, however, is hardly a sufficient explanation. The ecological living conditions of gelada baboons are similar to those envisioned by Dunbar for early humans, and—in partial support for his theory—gelada also live in large terrestrial groups or herds of 200–300 individuals. Interestingly, gelada have evolved enhanced vocal signalling for keeping contact primarily with members of the same 'harem' (a one-male reproductive unit), but not a communication system allowing them to 'gossip'. This shows that the above-mentioned dilemma can be resolved by other means than language and/or large-scale cooperation, e.g. by harem-based social structure and non-symbolic vocalizations.

Deacon's explanation for what led to the uniqueness of human sociality and cognition is that our ancestors lived in the following very unusual conditions:

(a) multi-male/multi-female social groups (for the sake of protection and group hunting), (b) immature infants with slowly maturing brains (in part due to bipedalism), requiring (c) extensive maternal care and paternal provisioning. Together, these conditions constituted an 'evolutionary bottleneck' in which the only groups that survived were those that established a sex contract that required symbolic marking of the social rights and obligations of sex-partners. As stated by Deacon (1997: 401): 'The need to mark these reciprocally altruistic relationships arose as an evolutionary adaptation to the extreme instability of the combination of group hunting/scavenging and male provisioning of mates and offspring.' Thus, Deacon supposes that what spearheaded the process was the evolution of morality and 'symbolic reference', rather than intersubjectivity (social bonding, empathy). Deacon does not consider whether the problem of ensuring (relative) sexual fidelity and male provisioning could not have been at least curtailed by an adaption for strong emotional attachments between sex-partners lasting on average 4–5 years: the time when lactating mothers and children are most vulnerable (Fisher 1992).

Tomasello has for some time argued that the evolution of language must have been preceded by human-specific adaptations for social/cultural life. In an earlier scenario (Tomasello 1999), this prerequisite was the understanding of others as intentional agents. When empirical evidence disproved this, the theory became more social (Tomasello et al. 2005, 2008). Two key adaptations were proposed to have occurred in the hominin line: (a) a capacity for *shared intentionality*, needed for performing actions jointly (e.g. not just for coordinating, but for planning a hunt) and (b) a *prosocial motivation* to share, above all, information. At first, however, almost nothing was offered to explain *why* these capacities would have evolved apart from suggesting that (a) 'evolved in the context of mutualistic collaborative activities' (Tomasello 2008: 170), while for (b) it is necessary 'at some late point to invoke processes of social identification and conformity to account for the sharing motive' (Tomasello 2008: 171). More recently, (a) and (b) have been referred to as *joint intentionality* in a publication offering a more explicit, and somewhat different, version of the envisioned two-step process. Initially, 'a change of ecology...led humans to an interdependent lifestyle, especially collaborative foraging, which resulted in the evolution of new skills and motivation for collaborating with others (joint intentionality), and gave individuals special incentives for helping their partners altruistically as well.' (Tomasello et al. 2012: 685). In other words, Tomasello and collaborators specify the 'mutualism' that led to the initial differentiation of human intersubjectivity to activities such as active scavenging and hunting that simply *require* collaboration, and furthermore suggest that this adaptation was not purely cognitive, but also affective/motivational. The second major step involves extending such 'small-scale collaboration' to whole communities, on the basis of cultural conventions, norms, and institutions, also referred to as 'group-mindedness' or *collective intentionality*. Only at this point, as an implicit third step, it is admitted that 'cultural group selection undoubtedly played a role as well.' (Tomasello et al. 2012: 685).

There is some similarity between the first step of Tomasello et al. (2012) and the account of *Hrdy*, who proposes a very specific answer to the *why* question: what started the cascade of processes that led to increased brain size, human-specific cognitive abilities, and ultimately language was a switch in reproductive and rearing strategy: 'Without doubt, highly complex coevolutionary processes were involved in the evolution of expanded lifespans, prolonged childhoods, and bigger brains. What I want to stress here, however, is that *cooperative breeding was the pre-existing condition* that permitted the evolution of these traits in the hominin line' (Hrdy 2009: 277, emphasis added). Indeed, it is only in our species among the great apes that childcare is extensively shared among group members. While in orang-utans, gorillas, chimpanzees, and even bonobos, mothers are the only ones to hold and nurse infants due to fear of kidnapping from other females, or infanticide by males, other alloparenting primates like marmosets and tamarins are 'unusually altruistic, displaying a curiously human impulse to give' (Hrdy 2009: 96). Thus, the evolution of particularly human intersubjectivity is seen as 'an unprecedented convergence—the evolution of cooperative breeding in a primate already possessing the cognitive capacities...typical of all Great Apes' (Hrdy 2009: 280). Hrdy (2009) repeatedly addresses the issue 'why us and not them', but unlike Dunbar, Deacon, and Tomasello, does not appeal to changes in ecological conditions. While not stated explicitly, the answer seems to be that different species of primates found their respective evolutionarily stable strategies. Our ancestors did not *have* to make the transition to alloparenting which is a very unusual system for mammals (about 3 per cent of mammal species are characterized by cooperative breeding). We simply are the lucky descendants of those who chanced on this route less-travelled, which turned out to be a 'winning strategy'.

18.3.2 *By what kind of evolutionary mechanism?*

Dunbar bases his theory on fairly robust correlations between group size and brain volume in modern human groups and extant apes and monkeys, interpolating the likely group sizes of extinct hominin groups on the basis of cranial volume. The central proposal is that neocortex increased in response to larger groups (the so-called 'social brain hypothesis'): 'Since maintaining coherent groups is cognitively demanding, brain size (or more specifically neocortex volume) will evolve to match the cognitive demands of the species' optimal group size' (Sutcliffe et al. 2012: 151). Dunbar does not explicitly address the kind of selection mechanisms through which such evolution could have taken place, but references to 'mating opportunities' suggest that a standard type of individual selection is assumed: individuals with larger brains, larger numbers of friends, and better vocal grooming reproduced more successfully. However, this is problematic, since 'optimal group size' is not a property that is determined by individual brains, and the communicative signals, even if initially non-symbolic, would need to be shared with both kin and non-kin members of the group. On the other hand, it is conceivable how group selection would have allowed evolution to converge on 'optimal' groups, both in terms of size and the adequate means to bond their members, with within-group selection favouring those most adept for living in such groups. In other words, a multi-level selection process is implied.

Deacon also correlates the evolution of symbolic reference with increase in brain size, above all the prefrontal cortex, responsible for much of 'higher' social cognition and executive function, i.e. voluntarily planned actions. Since at the root of the adaptation proposed by Deacon is not pair-bonding *per se* (which could perhaps be accounted for by direct reciprocity, and resulting in an adaptation for emotional attachment), but symbolically mediated social norms, beneficial for the social group as a whole, a process of group selection is clearly required: groups that found a way to ensure sex-based division of labour and paternal provisioning out-competed those that did not. To the extent that the sex-contract was a cultural invention—which given its symbolic nature would seem to be the case—it could also spread through cultural transmission, implying again a process of cultural group selection.

Tomasello (2008) left the *how* question as open as the *why* question. The original way of dividing shared intentionality and pro-social motivation also had the troublesome implication that motivational/emotional aspects of human intersubjectivity would have evolved only at a (much later) secondary stage, with cultural group selection. The expanded scenario of Tomasello et al. (2012) is quite different. Altruistic motives should evolve during the first step, on the basis of the following process:

[O]bligate collaborative foraging produced interdependence among members of a group, and this makes it in my direct interest to help others who might be my future partners.... I should sacrifice to help potential partners when $sB > C$. In this equation, as in Hamilton's, B represents ultimate reproductive benefits, and these must exceed costs, C, when the benefits are conditioned by the stake, s, I have in the particular partner. (Tomasselo et al. 2012: 679)

Apart from direct experience, s would also be based on reputation or what the authors (somewhat confusingly) refer to as 'social selection . . . a kind of market for collaborative partners such that anyone with poor reputation would be avoided' (Tomasello et al. 2012: 686). In sum, while Tomasello et al. (2012) do not explicitly endorse multi-level selection theory, their overall account, ranging from reproductive benefits for individuals, through 'social selection', to cultural group selection, is fully consistent with it.

For *Hrdy*, the order suggested by Tomasello (2008) is very much reversed, since the transition to alloparenting spearheaded the process and, along with it, the nurturing tendencies of mothers were extended to other members of the group, including fathers but not limited to them. It can be noted that alloparenting relaxes the need for paternal provisioning of their own progeny, allowing food and childcare to be more equally distributed within the group than in Deacon's scenario. Alloparenting was a winning strategy for our ancestors since it allowed for unusually fast rates of reproduction, despite large-brained, slowly maturing, and 'costly' babies: 'Mothers can overshoot their capacities to provide, and fathers can vary, because both sexes evolved in a highly fluid system where alloparents often provided the compensatory assistance' (Hrdy 2009: 167). Hrdy argues that this process can be accounted for by an evolutionary model that generalizes Hamilton's Rule $rB > C$ where r does *not* refer only to genetic relatedness (and hence standard kin selection) since 'once the neural and physiological underpinnings for helping behavior were in place, helpers did not need to be close kin' (Hrdy 2009: 188). Since kin selection can be seen as a special form of group selection (see Section 18.2), this 'generalized kin selection' even more clearly involves multi-level selection, with selection between groups favouring those which have adapted the 'winning strategy'.

18.3.3 When?

On the issue of timing, Dunbar (2009) points to the relatively scarce fossil evidence on a larger thoracic vertebral canal (MacLarnon and Hewitt 1999), which has been interpreted as an index of higher vocal control in *Homo heidelbergensis*. It should be noted, however, that this evidence and interpretation has been seriously questioned (compare Gómez-Olivencia et al. 2007). Together with re-estimated group sizes of hominins, somewhat decreased compared to the original proposal, Dunbar concludes that 'the 0.5 MYA rubicon may mark the appearance of some form of intensely music-like exchanges, with full grammatical language (i.e. language as we know it today) emerging only later—perhaps with the appearance of anatomically modern humans around 200 KYA' (2009: 29). But 0.5 mya is a rather late date for the onset of the process leading to human-specific sociality, given the many earlier adaptations, from *Ardipithecus ramidus* at 4.4 mya (involving reduced canines, reduced sexual dimorphism, and partial bipedalism) to *Homo ergaster/erectus* at 1.8 mya, with basically modern human body anatomy, Achulean bifacial hand-axe technology, and gradual colonization of most of Asia and Europe (Donald 1991).

Similarly to Dunbar, *Deacon* appeals to novel ecological conditions of 'life on the savannah' for what started the process, but places the beginning of the transition to more than 3 mya, with australopithecines. Since for Deacon the transition should begin with 'symbolism' (rather than 'music-like exchanges', as for Dunbar), this is a remarkably early date, without any clear support in the archaeological record. Tomasello et al. (2012) refer to evidence of active collaborative hunting and gathering (corresponding to their first step), coinciding, as they state, with the possible emergence of *Homo heidelbergensis* 0.8 mya. Concerning the second step, in reply to commentaries suggesting a late date coinciding with the Upper Palaeolithic, they propose, with reference to Dunbar's estimates of brain and group size correlations, 'that group members progressed towards critical levels over the middle Pleistocene, with the emergence of *Homo heidelbergensis* between 400,000 and 150,000 years ago'. (Tomasello et al. 2012: 690). It is possible to avoid this apparent inconsistency by assuming that Tomasello et al. meant *Homo sapiens* in the latter case.

Interestingly, *Hrdy* suggests the onset of evolution of human-specific sociality to have occurred between the relatively late dates of Dunbar and Tomasello, and the very early date of Deacon: with *Homo ergaster/erectus* around 1.8 mya. This is based on evidence for changes in diet (including meat), sexual division of labour, larger brains, and longer life-spans. To the extent that *erectus* had made the transition to alloparenting, she argues that the species should be considered 'emotionally modern' (Hrdy 2009: 31). Even so, this was hardly an abrupt transition, especially since the traces of a process of 'self-domestication' can be found in *Ardipithecus ramidus*, with reduced sexual dimorphism and partial bipedalism, as mentioned earlier. This, however, would suggest a co-evolutionary scenario of more immature infants, prolonged childhood, more need for shared care and provisioning, in which alloparenting was not the single initial factor, as suggested by Hrdy, but was itself facilitated by increased altriciality (i.e. very immature babies). For example, in birds, cooperative breeding (alloparenting) has been found to be more likely to evolve in taxa where chicks are helpless rather than in those where they are soon able to survive on their own (Cockburn 2006).

18.3.4 *What kind of social groups?*

Dunbar has made much of group sizes, noting that present-day human social groups fall into three categories—small, medium, and large, corresponding to 'bands', 'cultural lineage groups', and 'tribes'—with respective size ranges of 30–50, 100–200, and 500–2,500 members each. The number that best matches his estimates for 'optimal group size' given human brain size has been approximately 150, but it can be argued that this so-called 'Dunbar's number' has been over-emphasized. In Western societies, it is has been shown that 'the range in network size is vast, with 90% of the adult population knowing anywhere between 250 and 1,710 other people, and half knowing between 400 and 800' (Wellman 2012: 174). On the other hand, most anthropologists emphasize the 'band' of 30–50 people as the most significant group for hunter-gatherers, and it is likely that in such 'societies of intimates' (Givón 1979) that the initial adaptations for human intersubjectivity first occurred.

Hrdy bases her theory extensively on the social practices of extant hunter-gatherer groups. It is, of course, always controversial when extant hunter-gathering societies are used as evidence for evolutionary scenarios. Hrdy is duly cautious, reminding that these should not be viewed as 'living fossils', but rather as the closest models for what the lives of our pre-agricultural ancestors could have been like. It is significant that in culturally, geographically, and environmentally highly distinct hunter-gathering societies, such as Aka, Efe, !Kung San (Central Africa), Himba (Western Africa), Yanomamo (Venezuela), and Agta (Philippines), care is shared between mothers and alloparents, and in some cases fathers. It should be noted that this is related to, but distinct from, the so-called *grandmother hypothesis*, according to which women live longer than female apes after ceasing to ovulate, due to their positive role on the survival of grandchildren (Hawkes 2004). Hrdy observes that human longevity increased for both men and women, and while (maternal) grandmothers typically function as alloparents, other group members do as well: 'Efe babies average 14 different caretakers in the first days of life' (Hrdy 2009: 79).

While Tomasello (2008) had nothing specific to say about the kinds of social groups in which intersubjectivity evolved, this is again rectified by Tomasello et al (2012), where the first step of the process is assumed to have taken place in 'bands'. There is also a clear rapprochement with the theory of alloparenting: 'Further, in this context humans became cooperative breeders, regularly providing child care to offspring who were not their own, and this clearly would have affected emotions and motivations for collaboration and altruism as well (Hrdy 2009).' (Tomasello et al. 2012: 680).

Deacon has rather focused on the family as the primary locus of sharing. This is troublesome, since in hunter-gatherers the distribution of food is not limited to nuclear families but to the whole group, and even beyond (Weissner 2002). Paternal provisioning is far from being a universal phenomenon; as Hrdy (2009: 162) emphasizes: 'Across cultures and between individuals, more variation exists in the form and extent of paternal investment in humans than in all other primates combined.'

18.3.5 *Development*

Since the four theories focus on different aspects of the suite of features defining uniquely human sociality, including intersubjectivity, morality, and language, it is impossible to compare them straightforwardly with respect to developmental evidence. For Dunbar, that would involve the development of vocalization (e.g. babbling), language ('gossip'), and what he refers to as 'levels of intentionality': progressively deeper embedding of mental predicates (Dunbar 2009). For Deacon, it would be the development of symbolic reference, and perhaps moral sense. Tomasello's and Hrdy's accounts are more easily comparable, since they both concern pre-linguistic forms of intersubjectivity: more cognitive for Tomasello, and more emotional for Hrdy. Given these reservations, we can briefly look at what kind of developmental evidence can be adduced in support for each theory.

Dunbar's theory claims that human sociality evolved for the management of intra-group social relations, resulting in expanded neocortex and improved vocalization.

This would imply that to the extent that human infants differ from those of the apes, this should be a side effect of their larger brains, adapted for vocal grooming and higher levels of intentionality. In children, human-specific vocalizations indeed start early in the first year, followed by the emergence of language in the second year of life, while neocortex undergoes extensive expansion first in late childhood (6–11 years), reflected in tests requiring third-order to fifth-order intentionality, e.g. 'I *think* that you *believe* that I *suppose* that we *understand* that Jane *wants*...' (Dunbar 2009: 30).

The thrust of *Deacon*'s explanation is on the evolution of symbols for social roles such as kin terms. While children in Western societies learn some kin terms (*mother, father, brother, sister*) early, it takes quite some time for them to master the complex semantics of kin terms for more distant relations (Haviland and Clark 1974), though corresponding studies for children in traditional societies remain to be carried out.

Tomasello's theory that human sociality evolved through selection for basic pro-social capacities (sharing impulses, joint attention, informative pointing, etc.) finds considerable support in findings that such capacities both develop before language, and are human-specific (Tomasello et al. 2005). While some of these claims have been contested (Leavens et al. 2009), evidence of prolonged childhood compared to apes, and apes failing tasks that require cooperative intentions, where even preverbal children succeed (Tomasello et al. 2012), strongly suggests an extra evolutionary adaptation for intersubjectivity in humanity.

Hrdy's theory is strongly inspired by an updated version of *attachment theory* (Bowlby 1988), where mothers may be special but not unique, and the *infant intersubjectivity* approach in developmental psychology (Trevarthen 1979; Bråten 2007). Growing up in the context of alloparenting, according to Hrdy, the child develops an enhanced understanding of perspective and self-awareness: 'A baby thus had far more incentive to monitor his mother's whereabouts and to maintain visual and vocal contact with her, as well as far more motivation to pay attention to her state of mind, and to the willingness of others who might be available to care for him when his mother was disinclined' (Hrdy 2009: 114). Evolutionarily, the model explicitly assumes a 'self-reinforcing evolutionary process of parents and alloparents who are more sensitive to infantile signals and babies who are better at emitting them' (Hrdy 2009: 220).

In sum, it is characteristic that Dunbar and Deacon pay relatively little attention to developmental evidence, while Tomasello and Hrdy do so extensively. This reflects differences in what the theorists believe the evolutionary mechanisms operated on: while Deacon and Dunbar consider the evolution of human sociality to be based primarily on the selection of adults, for Hrdy what evolved is the whole niche of interactions between mothers, children, and alloparents. Tomasello et al. are indeterminate in this respect, stating that 'traits that are adaptive in adulthood often have ontogenetic pathways that begin in childhood, as long as these early forms are not maladaptive for children' (2012: 689).

18.3.6 *Summary*

The evolutionary theories reviewed in this section all address the five questions outlined at the beginning of this section. Concerning the *why* question, Dunbar and Deacon, and to some extent Tomasello, appeal to specific ecological conditions, and to the need to resolve conflicting tensions. Deacon's and Dunbar's accounts for how these tensions were resolved can be seen as complementary: modern human language is both symbolic and predominantly vocal in its service of social functions such as bonding, gossip, and the maintenance of shared moral norms. However, both Dunbar and Deacon arguably attribute too much importance to language-like communication between adults at the *onset* of the trajectory leading to human-specific sociality, while Hrdy's argument that 'cooperative breeding was the pre-existing condition' for this trajectory is persuasive, as acknowledged by Tomasello et al. (2012). What distinguishes the two theories is that Hrdy emphasizes the primacy of motivational and emotional aspects of sharing (care, food, protection) to cognitive ones, while that of Tomasello does not.

Concerning *how*, it was argued that all four theories rely, explicitly or implicitly, on multi-level selection, including group selection, and in the case of traits subject to cultural transmission ('marriage' and perhaps other social norms such as 'egalitarianism': see Boehm 1999), on *cultural* group selection. This conclusion is likely to be controversial, since the notion of group selection continues to be hotly debated. Still, its outright rejection is no longer possible, as even former opponents seem to be converging toward the notion of multi-level selection (Wilson and Wilson 2007).

Both the differences between the theories, and their complementary nature, become clear when we consider that they may be plotted along a single timeline given some adjusting. Alloparenting can be hypothesized to have begun even before the major changes that happened with *Homo erectus*, and perhaps even to have been one of the crucial factors that led to them. Then, Deacon's 'sex contract' and the co-evolution of morality and symbolic reference could be linked to *erectus*, with larger, more coherent and technologically advanced social groups needed, for example, for long-distance migration. If it is indeed the case that fossilizing adaptations that have been linked to speech such as an enlarged thoracic vertebral canal are not clearly observed until 0.5 MYA, as claimed by Dunbar (2009), this would not be problematic for the present scenario since the origins of sign-use were quite possibly not in the vocal-auditory, but in the bodily-visual channel (Donald 1991; Zlatev 2008). Non-symbolic vocalization would at first have had mostly affiliative functions, but with time could have been reinterpreted symbolically, given the tight synchronization of multi-modal, hand-mouth communication (Brown 2012). This would naturally have set selection pressures for anatomical changes leading to enhanced vocal control. Thus, the origin of multi-modal language can be linked to *Homo heidelbergensis*, and modern-like language with *Homo sapiens*, with language-specific grammars emerging through processes of cultural evolution.

Concerning the kind and size of the relevant social groups in which these evolutionary processes apply, we can again obtain something of a compromise, if we adopt a model of concentric circles for different social networks such as that suggested by Dunbar, to which Sutcliffe et al. (2012) add two even smaller circles: the 'support clique' of 4–5 individuals and the 'sympathy group' of 12–15. These five levels can be characterized with progressively higher reliance on symbolic means for establishing group identity, shared moral values and hence trust and cooperation. The innermost circles, involving immediate family and close friends, are thus the sphere where cooperation/altruism is based most directly on empathy, while identifying and cooperating with the 'clan' of 150 or so people, and the 'tribe' of 500, not to mention still larger circles like 'nation', clearly require moral rules, symbolically mediated shared values, and language. On this reasoning, the middle circle of the 'band' with 30–50 members seems again to play a key role, since this appears as the first generalization 'up' from family and friends. Since this corresponds to the type of group in which alloparenting is assumed to have evolved (and still functions in hunter-gatherers today), this gives further support to Hrdy's theory that the band corresponds most closely to the social niche in which human-specific intersubjectivity first arose, prior to language.

Finally, in terms of *development*, human sociality similarly extends in concentric, Russian-doll-like layers. Bråten and Trevarthen (Bråten 2007: 3) distinguish, schematically, between three such layers: (1) *primary intersubjectivity*, from the first months of life onwards, based on 'direct sympathy with actual others' expressions of feelings in intimate reciprocal subject-subject contact'; (2) *secondary intersubjectivity*, from 9 months, when 'objects of joint attention and emotional referencing are brought into play within trusting relations of companionship...sometimes inviting imitative learning'; and (3) *tertiary intersubjectivity*, based on 'symbolic conversation with actual or virtual companions'. These developmental layers correspond to some extent to the spatial layers discussed above: the first in which the child interacts with mother and alloparents, the second extending to a somewhat wider circle of intimates, including peers, and the third to a virtually open circle, since sharing has become symbolically mediated. While ontogeny does not in general recapitulate phylogeny, there are good reasons to expect a degree of parallelism (Zlatev 2003). Thus, this offers additional support for the proposal of Hrdy that human-specific traits of intersubjectivity evolved first on the level of 'direct sympathy' between child and alloparents, and was subsequently extended to shared intentionality which is not yet dependent on language (as also proposed by Tomasello), and finally to language-mediated intersubjectivity, involving morality.

18.4 Conclusions

We, human beings, are special in the animal world not only for our ability to share languages and to use them cooperatively, but also for sharing communal values of right and wrong, and—at least among great apes—for the degree to which we tend to share material resources and child-care. The argument of this chapter has been that these different kinds of sharing co-evolved. The precise nature of this co-evolutionary process needs to be further investigated, but the discussions of the previous two sections lead to the following conclusions.

The first one is that more mainstream models of evolution based only on individual-level and gene-level selection are insufficient. In order to account for the possibility of human-scale sharing of care, values, and information, i.e. of intersubjectivity, morality, and language, models of multi-level selection, including (cultural) group selection are required. This conclusion is further bolstered by the fact that four of the most influential theories 'on the market' explicitly or implicitly presuppose such a model, at least in part.

The second major conclusion is that the theories of Dunbar, Deacon, Tomasello, and Hrdy were found to be to some extent complementary, rather than in contradiction—especially if they are interpreted somewhat revisionistically. Specific-ally, Hrdy's theory focusing on the evolution of alloparenting was shown to provide the best explanation for the onset of the evolution of human intersubjectivity (as a kind of blend of great ape cognition and tamarin-like altruism), and it was suggested that this could have started along with the transition to bipedalism more than 4 mya. This hypothesis is consistent with Tomasello's theory of shared intentionality and pro-social motivation, after reversing the proposal of Tomasello (2008) for the order in which these two aspects of intersubjectivity evolved, as admitted by Tomasello et al. (2012). Deacon's 'sex contract' can be seen as an important factor (though most likely not as the sole one) for the evolution of morality, understood as a 'system of conflict management based on shared values', and his proposal that this co-evolved with symbolic reference, thus providing an impetus for the evolution of language, is compelling. It was further suggested that this probably coincided with the emergence of *Homo erectus*, and that sign-use was initially multi-modal, but not predominantly vocal, i.e. a form of bodily mimesis (Donald 1991; Zlatev 2008). Finally, Dunbar's theory, specifically on the transition from 'musical' vocal-grooming to vocal 'gossip' can be seen as providing a partial explanation for evolution of *spoken* language with *Homo heidelbergensis* 0.5 mya, though the recruitment of speech may very likely have started earlier. Still, it is characteristic that cultural evolution appears to become cumulative first around this time, with inevitable effects on group differentiation and cultural group selection.

Thus, the co-evolutionary scenario of intersubjectivity, morality, and language that we are led to is, in brief, that intersubjectivity (in an alloparenting context) spear-headed the way, followed by morality and language which evolved co-temporally, in spirals of increasing complexity. However, this linear ordering cannot be strictly maintained, since as morality and language spread culturally, to quote again Boyd and Richerson (2009: 3281–2), they 'increased the reproductive success of individuals who functioned well in such environments, and this in turn led to the evolution of other regarding motives like empathy and social emotions like shame'. Such multi-level selection processes would have applied with respect to individuals who were competent communicators and language users, as well.

Still, there is an important difference between moral systems and language as super-individual, social phenomena, and the 'moral sense' and 'linguistic competence' of individuals. (Confusing language as a social institution and as individual competence is the main fault of the Chomskyan paradigm in linguistics.) There is large individual variation in the latter respects, and there are no clear correlations between levels of moral and linguistic development, either on individual or societal levels. Thus, even if intersubjectivity, morality, and language co-evolved, as here argued, it is possible to disentangle them, and to envision a society with high prescriptive morality, but in which 'regarding motives like empathy and social emotions like shame' are not selected for, but rather the contrary.

Toward the end of her book, Hrdy (2009) alarmingly suggests that current Western societies might be of this type. On the one hand, they are becoming increasingly individualist, consumption-oriented, and alienated: moving further and further away from the conditions necessary both for the evolution of intersubjectivity, and for its development in each successive generation. On the other hand, due to technological and medical advances 'an ever-increasing proportion of the species fails to encounter those conditions but nevertheless survives to reproduce' (Hrdy 2009: 293). The possible outcome is spelled out in the following memorable passage:

If empathy and understanding develop under particular rearing conditions, and if an ever-increasing proportion of the species fails to encounter those conditions but nevertheless survives to reproduce, it won't matter how valuable the underpinnings for collaboration were in the past. Compassion and the quest for emotional connection will fade away as surely as sight in cave-dwelling fish. (Hrdy 2009: 293)

Even if this is a pessimistic assessment of our present situation, it is worth taking seriously. Biological evolution does not plan ahead, but on a cultural and societal level, we are still capable of influencing our future.

19

Forever united: the co-evolution of language and normativity

EHUD LAMM

19.1 Introduction

Language and norms are both fundamental to human society. A social account of language evolution must take into account the normative context in which language acquisition, use, and change occur. However, at the same time, norms in human society are directly affected by language and the linguistic skills of individuals. My aim in this chapter is to explore the evolutionary consequences of this bi-directional interaction. I will discuss how it can help explain central linguistic notions including imperatives, questions, possessives, modal vocabulary, categorization, and performatives, and how it helps explain unique features of human normativity.

Norms delimit or determine appropriate or proper behaviour in a given context, and social life is governed to a large extent by a pervasive normative structure. Loosely speaking, norms can be defined as principles or rules that determine what behaviour is appropriate, required, permissible, or forbidden (see Sripada and Stich 2006).[1] I use the term *normativity* to refer to the capacity to acquire and implement norms. While norms may be acquired by experiencing or observing behaviours that lead to sanctions, they need not be, and in general are not. Moreover, norms enjoy what Sripada and Stich call *independent normativity*: they do not depend on other social institutions nor on sanctions to endow them with their force (see Tomasello 2009). Importantly, norms have motivational consequences: people are motivated to comply with norms they have acquired as ultimate ends and to justify and defend them when the need arises. Sripada and Stich call this type of motivation *intrinsic motivation* and note that violations of norms often lead to punitive attitudes and

---

[1] This characterization should not be understood as committing us to any particular account regarding the way in which norms are stored or represented cognitively.

emotions, such as anger, condemnation, and blame. These two properties indicate the dual nature of social norms: they are social level facts yet they play a fundamental, irreducible role in individual psychology. This is a crucial property of the phenomenology of human normativity. Somewhere along the way, both ontogenetically and phylogenetically, humans come to recognize some reasons as having a normative force that goes beyond that of prudential reasons of the sort that ground instrumental adherence to social conventions, such as driving on the right side of the road (see Bicchieri 2006: 13). A significant aspect of the intrinsic motivation established by a norm is that individuals judge the norm itself as appropriate and employ deontic reasoning to justify it as well as its application in a given context. Many norms are implicit and people obey them unreflectively, of course, but reflection on and attempts to justify norm-governed behaviour as well as of the norms themselves can be induced (Brandom 1994). I take it that an evolutionary account of normativity has to be true to all these phenomenological details. I will argue that the evolutionary interaction between language and normativity helps explain the transition from social enforcement of norms to self-commitment and intrinsic motivation.

Many norm-governed social institutions assist children in the acquisition of language. Moreover, many aspects of language use are normative, for example: (1) symbolization, which involves accepting arbitrary signs as appropriate labels; (2) most pragmatic phenomena, such as speech acts (Dore 1974, 1975), grasping communicative intent, and displaying conversational skills (e.g. turn-taking, handling interruptions); and (3) understanding the normative context of discourse, which can transform questions into commands, requests into demands, and so on (see Labov 1972: 255ff).

Language use is thus clearly affected by the normative background and the normative skills of speakers, yet, reciprocally, norms are affected by language. Acquiring social norms is often affected by linguistic cues (e.g. 'Only women are allowed to go inside.', 'You shouldn't do that!', 'Why did you do that?!') and thus by the explicitly normative vocabulary and categories that are available (e.g. 'must', 'ought', 'may', 'allowed'). Explicit normative or deontic reasoning (and deliberation) is linguistic, not only in adults but in pre-school children (e.g. Harris and Núñez 1996; reviewed in Beller 2009), and through it language affects norm acquisition, maintenance, and enforcement. In addition, various speech acts such as promises commit the speaker to certain permissible and required actions (Austin 1962).

Thus, language affects the normative capacity of individuals and the kinds of norms that can be established, while norms and the normative capacities of individuals affect language acquisition and use. This bi-directional interaction, I will argue, leads to co-evolutionary dynamics that are important for understanding both of these fundamental human abilities. First, however, I will consider how normativity and language are intertwined developmentally.

19.2 Co-developmental evidence

From two to three years of age, children experience a dramatic explosion in linguistic ability as well as a similarly dramatic expansion of normative or deontic performance (Schmidt et al. 2011; Casler et al. 2009; Rakoczy et al. 2008; Cummins 1996; Harris and Núñez 1996). The psychological evidence on deontic reasoning is reviewed in Beller (2009). To explore how normativity and language might have interacted evolutionarily, let's first take a look at how their interactions manifest developmentally and ask how children acquire the competencies underlying the rule-governed employment of language in society. This is the realm of developmental pragmatics.

The following tale illustrates the development of normative pragmatics in a pre-linguistic child and indicates some ways in which normativity in general, normative pragmatics, and language are interrelated. I turn to evolutionary implications in the next section. Each case described below seems *prima facie* to involve normativity of a specific kind, for example the acquisition of norm-governed rituals, paradigmatic social interactions, and social justification of behaviour. The majority of behaviours are prior to full language, and two years of age, most of them much earlier (though I mostly focus on developments between 18 and 23 months of age) and before the regular use of assertion statements and connected discourse.[2]

Like most children, our protagonist, call her Dora, used pointing behaviour by the time she was 12 months old (see Tomasello 2009). This is a form of joint attention and information sharing. Various studies have indicated that preverbal children exhibit a variety of pragmatic behaviours, including requests of various kinds, protests, greetings, transferring objects, showing off, acknowledging, and answering, as well as expressions of social feelings such as sympathy (reviewed in Ninio and Snow 1999). One important context in which these behaviours are exhibited and refined is early games such as peekaboo (Ratner and Bruner 1978).

Even before she was one year old, Dora had learned to use the words 'hi' and 'bye' (interchangeably) when coming and going to day-care. The words are part of a *ritual*, which includes the required answer: 'hi' or 'bye' back. The ritual is later enacted in other situations, for example taking a bag and a hat, saying 'bye', and going to the door at home; waiting for the reply to complete the ritual and then returning to play on the rug. If Dora got no reply, or not the correct reply, she got upset and demanded that the ritual be completed. In general, it is common for first linguistic uses to be situated, local meanings, many of which are ritualized in play (see Bruner 1975a; Ervin-Tripp 1991), while rituals play an important role in the transmission of social norms (Rossano 2012).

Somewhat later Dora started using the word 'up' as an *imperative* when she wanted to be picked up. The verbal command was often combined with the much earlier raising arms *gesture*

---

[2] This description is based on observations of one middle-class child, growing up in California in a Hebrew-English bilingual environment. The examples are roughly in the order of their manifestation. I thank Aya Lamm for assistance in producing this list.

('*pick me up*').[3] Subsequently, raised arms were used for the up command more generally: saying 'daddy up' together with raised arms, to signify daddy get up – not just pick me up. The word 'up' itself served as a command for 'down' as well, even after the word 'down' was acquired. In one episode Dora said 'Up!', and when asked if she meant she wanted down she said 'Yes. [Now] up!'.

When you tickled or otherwise annoyed Dora while introducing a new expression such as 'doom doom doom', Dora immediately said 'No doom doom doom!' to get you to stop. The expression itself could be anything, and need not have had any independent meaning, nor ever be used again. This basic form of *compositionality* ('No X!') appears fairly early, and is used for pragmatic effect. It is not derived from the meaning of assertions.

To help Dora calm down after falling and hurting herself, her parents taught her to *admonish* inanimate objects, like the floor, tables, and doors, by saying 'fuya' ('pfui', an Israeli-Hebrew word which is used to indicate displeasure and disapproval) to the object that 'hit' her. This became a necessary part of calming down after getting hurt (i.e. it became part of a ritual). The admonishing behaviour was used only when the parents were present and depended on other contextual cues. More speculatively, it may be that psychological mechanisms that are involved in detecting 'norm' violations by other individuals also operate when detecting inappropriate 'behaviour' from inanimate objects (and pets, members of other groups, etc.). Normative and modal assessments are similar processes and may be related.

Along with the other children in her day-care class, Dora was taught to use the words 'mine' (initially to indicate/declare possession, but later to express desire to play with a toy laying on the floor etc.) and 'space' (to indicate 'personal space', i.e. that the child doesn't want another child to touch her, or wants to be left alone to play with a toy or with playground equipment). These words function as performatives. It seems that the children 'naturally' want to use them, especially 'mine', and there is a possessive stage where everything is 'mine'. The children also give things to others ('yours'), and can understand a game where you take something from them and say 'mine' (i.e. it belongs to you, not the kid), though such behaviour outside the context of a game would clearly upset them. The possessive form also comes up rather early in Dora's acquisition of syntax and she says 'Mine' as well as 'Dora's' and uses the possessive form with names of other individuals (including 'Daddy's').

The use of 'space' to indicate spatial relationships came much later than the use of the word to indicate a *demand* for personal space. For example, Dora said 'space' when she tried to make her way through a narrow path between two chairs and used 'space' as a form of asking for help with moving obstacles in her path. Somewhat later she learned to use expressions such as 'more space' and so on.

A new set of words Dora acquired is *exclamations*, joke words, and funny sounds used while playing and in other activities. For example: (1) Saying 'Boing!' when something falls, or when throwing something; especially for things that bounce; (2) Saying 'yum yum' for tasty food. It is easy to get a child to realize that these have a different normative status from other words (Dora recognized that her parents smiled when using them, etc.) and the child will not use them in other situations, and will smile when they are used. The words carry weight in interpreting a situation. For example: Dora falls down and is clearly thinking about crying. But the parent says 'Boing!', and

---

[3] The type of learning involved in acquiring the *pick me up* gesture and the role played by normative cues remain open questions (see Marentette and Nicoladis 2012).

Dora accepts the fall as part of a game and may even try to 'fall' again on purpose by attempting to jump. Similarly, she may throw something she knows she is not allowed to throw (a norm violation), say 'Boing!' and smile, indicating a game, and hence that the behaviour is permissible. Dora also learns to 'sing' (without understanding the words or pronouncing them correctly), especially songs with accompanying hand movements such as 'Itsy Bitsy Spider' and 'The wheels on the bus'.

Dora also learned the *prosody of commands* and associated gestures, and used them when giving commands to her parents. These are probably acquired by imitating teachers, possibly via other children. For example: Using the phrase 'Walk away!' with finger pointing the direction, as an order to leave her alone when she wanted to stay longer in the bath. The response from adults is naturally amusement, not compliance.

Until now Dora's linguistic behaviour mostly consisted of one word utterances or speech-acts. Like many other children, Dora's first significant three-word sentence is 'I want this'. Being able to express *desire* opens up a new normative dimension. At around two years: a lot of 'I want...' and 'I need...' and mixing the two (corrected by adults, who attempt to clarify the normative distinction). Even many 'I want, I want, I want...' sentences, where the actual desire is not specified at all, leading the adult to ask 'Do you want X?' and similar interactions. Later (at 26 months): 'want to' coupled with a verb.

At around this point Dora started to exhibit much better *turn-taking behaviour* coupled with explicit vocabulary for declaring and demanding turns: 'my turn', 'daddy's turn', etc.[4] Note the multiple levels interacting here: Turn-taking is governed by norms (e.g. when is it my turn, when am I allowed to do a certain thing); explicit vocabulary, once introduced, is enormously useful for negotiating possibly highly localized turn-taking rules in any domain (e.g. games, shared eating, etc.); and turn-taking skills, that may have been refined and practised in this way, are an important element of more advanced conversation skills (Ninio and Snow 1999).

At around 27 months, Dora reached the stage of incessant *question asking*. The adult is obliged to answer (thereby participating in the question–answer ritual), and the question is asked again and again. 'What's your name? What's your name?' Part of the fun, it seems, is that the adult has to stop what they are doing and answer... Children delight in getting an answer, though it is clearly not the information that they seek, since they ask the same thing again immediately. Many questions of the form 'What's that?' are asked incessantly, e.g. when looking at pictures in a book, or pointing to objects. Even when pointing to blank pages or empty spaces in the book or to text. It seems that most answers are accepted (there are no complaints or tantrums), though the question is often asked repeatedly (and multiple answers are accepted). This appears to be coupled with a tendency to want to read to the adult, i.e. to tell the story from the book, or just to point to elements on the page. This game-like activity involves turn-taking, the rituals of dialogue, the linguistic pragmatics of questioning, the mechanics of questions and answers, and, of course, leads to increased vocabulary (see Tomasello and Todd 1983; Ninio and Bruner 1978).

---

[4] Children are fairly competent at turn-taking by the time they produce their first words but by the time they are five their skills are not yet fully developed (reviewed in Ninio and Snow 1999).

It is at this time that Dora began using *explicitly normative vocabulary*. For example: 'have to take it out' referring to a pit in a fruit that had to be taken out before eating. Explicitly normative vocabulary such as this can be used in commands, requests, questions, or descriptions. Explicitly modal vocabulary, specifically the use of the word 'maybe' also started to appear. This seemed to be used tentatively as if exploring the notion.[5]

While Dora's linguistic and normative skills continue to develop, this tale is enough to illustrate the close developmental interaction between normativity and language capacities, some types of interactions that can occur, and the spectrum of normative dimensions that are involved. It also illustrates how closely language acquisition is tied to norm-governed social institutions such as game playing and social rituals. To summarize, the normative aspects in the behaviours discussed above that are typically marked grammatically or lexically are:

(1) Interjections
(2) Proper names
(3) Imperatives
(4) Possessives
(5) Questions
(6) Explicitly normative vocabulary.

In contrast, the following aspects of normative pragmatics in the behaviours above are not typically explicitly marked grammatically:

(1) Context dependent rituals. Expressions appropriate in specific contexts.
(2) Combined gesture and verbal behaviour, in both song and speech.
(3) Admonishing, conveying disapproval.
(4) Exclamations, joke words, etc.
(5) Pretend play, role-playing, and language games.

Dora's tale gives an idea of how incremental linguistic and normative complexity develops, but it should be noted that the literature suggests that different children exhibit different developmental trajectories and different styles of early speech use (reviewed in Ninio and Snow 1999; see also Dore 1974). Children may be predisposed to display norms and intentions that have arisen due to the evolution of language (and its co-evolution with mind and culture) even before they acquire language. This is particularly to be expected for intentions that have become an entrenched component of human cognition and intentions that play a role in the developmental scaffolding of language. These intentions may be expressed by pre-linguistic children, even though they are not evolutionarily prior to language (see Bruner 1975a, 1975b; Dore 1975, 1978).

---

[5] The deontic/modal distinction as I use it here can be substantially refined but is sufficient for my needs (see Papafragou 1998).

As I noted earlier, somewhere along both the phylogenetic and the developmental progressions, the normative ought, which goes beyond instrumental ought-ness, appears. While I cannot pinpoint the moment of its appearance in the developmental sketch presented above, children's responses to some infractions seem *prima facie* to display rage that is genuinely normative. Children's early displays of normative learning in the absence of explicit instrumental motivation (e.g. Rakoczy et al. 2008) lend credence to the contention that young children already possess some intrinsic normative feelings that go beyond instrumentally learning appropriate behaviours as means for fulfilling desires. The evolutionary account I present in the next section suggests how genuine normative feelings can come to be exhibited by young children who lack full-fledged normative judgement and reasoning. I am not making any general claim about developmental continuity between 'instrumental oughts' and 'normative oughts', however. The normative ought is probably psychologically primitive and of course both kinds of 'oughts' co-exist.

19.3 The co-evolutionary scenario

It is time to discuss how interactions between the linguistic and normative capacities of the sort discussed in the previous sections could affect the evolution of both, and how the vast amount of psycholinguistic evidence about the development of normative pragmatics can help shed light on the evolution of language. This section covers much ground, so here is an outline of the argument that is elaborated in what follows. First, I discuss how innovations and learned behaviours spread in populations and the role played by normative negotiation. Second, how these changes become multi-generational and how this can lead to changes in the innate capacities of individuals, in particular changes in their learning abilities, predispositions, and biases. Finally, I turn to the implications of these processes. I discuss their effect on the evolution of major linguistic categories and I argue that the co-evolution of language and normativity shaped the unique way in which humans self-consciously subject themselves to norms.

19.3.1 *Spread of innovations*

Each of the many kinds of interactions illustrated in the previous sections can affect the direction in which the language and linguistic practices of a community change. Language communities routinely adopt linguistic innovations. Innovations include the introduction of new vocabulary, refinement of the meaning of existing vocabulary, introduction of speech acts, syntactical changes, changes in the tense system, and so on. These innovations, and changes in linguistic practice more generally, are driving forces in the evolution of the language faculty. Two pressures that face innovations are the ability of enough individuals to comprehend them, and ultimately produce them appropriately, on the one hand, and the expressive advantage they provide, on the other. Some innovations will become more prevalent in the community or parts of it because of their social or expressive advantages. As the need to understand the new categories becomes more pervasive, individuals predisposed to acquire them or their linguistic markings more easily have an advantage both socially and because the innovations provide useful expressive and reflective abilities. The ability to adjust to innovations in linguistic practice is of prime importance. This may seem not to be the case today since the current linguistic repertoire is very rich and innovations are primarily small lexical changes that do not radically change the expressiveness of the language, but the introduction of categories such as imperatives, questions, possessives, modal vocabulary, and so on, made tremendous changes to what could be expressed and to what listeners had to be able to interpret. To make these general observations more concrete, I want to sketch a central avenue through which normativity and language interact. The first step of this process involves (a) a *commitment*. An individual takes herself or is taken by others to be committed to something, to have an obligation, to be entitled, and so on. Next, this commitment is (b) *challenged* by other members of the community or by the environment. Two archetypical situations are signs of condemnation or disagreement by the community and recognizing an incompatibility between the commitment and an actual state of affairs. The condemnation is often subtle and even implicit in the behaviours of others; signs include things such as raised eyebrows, minute frowns, growing disinterest, all the way up to gossip and open laughter. Whether the challenge is accepted by the individual or not is itself a normative decision and depends on the authority of the critics and on norms governing the appropriateness of censure. The tension that results from the challenge leads to (c) *reasoning*, which consists of various justificatory moves applying both deontic and non-deontic inferences. These result in (d) a *justification* or *clarification*. The justification can be any behaviour or argument that is produced in order to diffuse the challenge. It should be an appropriate response by the lights of the individual producing it and presentable to others if needed. Note that it need not be a justification in any thick sense of the term; the justification only needs to re-establish the legitimacy or appropriateness of the behaviour or belief that established or expressed the problematic commitment, revise it, or revoke it. The justification may be enough to assuage the normative worry. When it does not, a further stage of (e) *norm(ative) refinement* can occur. This may involve instituting new norms, establishing new normative categories (often implicitly), and so on. This five-step process can repeat indefinitely, each time making use of new elements introduced in previous rounds.

Two elements of this process are important for us. First, the reasoning–justification–refinement pathway is deeply and inherently linguistic. Explicit normative reasoning and belief are of course language-dependent; this is the case even if normative reasoning is a *post hoc* rationalization of emotional responses (e.g. Haidt 2001;

Wheatley and Haidt 2005) or involves self-deceit. Language can, and does, change because of pressures affecting these processes, and meanings are clarified and refined (e.g. by introducing new categories: 'It is not a cat, it is a kitten. You didn't say kitten!'). Mechanisms and technologies of negotiation and clarification are introduced along the way, for example conditionals, subjunctives, and discourse markers such as 'but' and 'however' that improve the ability to engage in conversation. Second, note that the entire process depends on the cognitive abilities of individuals and the normative and linguistic capacities of the society more generally. Thus, the precise way in which the process works changes as language and speakers evolve.

19.3.2 *Evolution of innate capacities and social conventions*

All the processes just enumerated take place in the ontogeny of the individuals taking part in them. They involve learning as well as the institution of new social facts and the introduction of linguistic changes. Social facts, however, transcend the individuals who originate them, and even the entire set of individuals involved. Individuals in society are always already both recipients and exemplars of the normative and linguistic structure of their society and new members acquire current conventions and further perpetuate them. This continuity marks both language (de Saussure 1983 [1915]) and norms (Searle 2010). By biasing individual learning toward particular outcomes, the types of norms that individuals can acquire and apply further increase continuity. More generally, since norms increase social conformity they reduce the probability of large fluctuations and dampen them. Consequently, norms do not simply persist between generations; they in effect establish an inheritance system or channel between generations.

The persistent normative and linguistic environment is the context in which individual evolution takes place. This means that evolutionary change is affected by a directional and persistent pressure, which may lead to varying degrees of genetic assimilation and partial assimilation (Jablonka and Lamb 2005; Dor and Jablonka 2000). These terms refer to evolutionary outcomes in which a behaviour or disposition that was once acquired or learned becomes automatic and innate to a certain degree, allowing individuals to reduce the effort and resources required to learn it and freeing up resources for new learning. This results from traditional natural selection operating on variations in learning ability and predispositions.

A mirror image of genetic assimilation that is also a possible response to the evolutionary pressure is the establishment of social and cultural institutions that will make desired behaviours, norms, and so on, more probable or persistent. It is tempting to think of responses of this kind as assimilation to culture as opposed to assimilation to genes. This *assimilation to culture* will make use of explicit and implicit teaching to youngsters; employ changes to the environment they experience, notably by the use of artefacts such as toys; and institute activities that support, enhance, or induce learning such as game playing (see Sterelny 2003). This is one way in which parenting technologies, in particular forms of alloparenting, may have had great consequences for cognitive evolution (see Hrdy 2009). All these mechanisms involve norms and rely on the normative capacities of individuals. These techniques provide scaffolding for the development of offspring which may result in co-development of the sort discussed in the previous section and bias development toward certain outcomes. Examples of norm-governed scaffolding in language acquisition include the effects of mother–offspring joint attention (Tomasello and Todd 1983) and joint picture-book reading (Ninio and Bruner 1978) on lexical acquisition, and the effects of early games such as peekaboo on the acquisition of dialogue skills (Ratner and Bruner 1978). In a similar fashion, temporal conjunctions are acquired for the purpose of joint planning for play and for social manipulation of peers (Ervin-Tripp 1991). Children need to be receptive to norms to benefit from these social practices. The scaffolded outcomes become prevalent in the society and serve as a stepping stone toward further improvement. In contrast to genetic assimilation which is strictly Darwinian, assimilation to culture depends on cultural innovation which is typically introduced by individuals for the purpose of initiating the young or for some other purposes. It is not based on random variation *per se* and may be the result of deliberation, experimentation, mixing-and-matching, and so on. However, the actual effects of the educational technology are typically uncertain and competition between various approaches undoubtedly occurs. This experimentation can only take place if external selection pressures are not too severe (see Kropotkin 1902). The relaxed selection that is required for this cultural evolution is achieved largely through social support, protection, and division of labour. Once enacted, the developmental scaffolding leads to a second phase of relaxed selection in addition to the relaxed selection that is required for cultural experimentation, this time on the genes that would be involved in ensuring the learned outcome was scaffolding-absent.[6] This permits greater genetic variability in the population which can support further evolution.[7] As they become critical parts of normal cognitive development, the outcomes of both forms of relaxed selection become entrenched and hard to modify (see Deacon 2010).

19.3.3 *Implications*

The co-evolution of the capacities for language and norms through social innovations and assimilation processes helps explain a number of important observations. I focus on (1) why norms are typically generic rules that do not refer to particular

---

[6] As a concrete example consider genes that lead infants to engage in dialogue with their caregiver. If a game involving such dialogues is customary, having the genes becomes less significant.

[7] This is the assimilation-to-culture counterpart of the assimilate–stretch principle which explains how new learned elements may be recruited, when part of a behavioural sequence that formerly depended on learning becomes genetically assimilated (Jablonka and Lamb 2005: 290).

individuals; (2) the evolution of independent normativity and intrinsic motivation; (3) biases in norm acquisition; (4) the implications of the co-evolutionary scenario for the evolution of emotions; and (5) the relationship between normative and modal reasoning.

An important consequence of the fact that normativity evolves through normative negotiation is that norms are typically generic rules or scripts (Bicchieri 2006) that do not refer to particular individuals (e.g. 'he who has the pole can speak', 'one should be respectful of elders'). As a result, normative negotiation and deontic reasoning come to require the ability to represent and express situations from the perspective of interlocutors and third parties. This creates an evolutionary pressure for the ability to represent situations from multiple perspectives.

The need to justify, rationalize, and reflect on normative commitments and emotional responses will be a driving force in the evolution of meta-cognitive abilities. In addition, normative judgements and reasoning will very likely be recruited to serve as prescriptions in domains other than the social. In this way, norms are freed from the demands of social acceptance and come to play a funda-mental role in the private lives of individuals. This and the previous observation help explain the phenomenology of norms discussed in the introduction, in particular their independent normativity and intrinsic motivation.

The pressure for reliable acquisition of norms leads to biases in norm acquisition, which affect the cross-cultural distribution of norms. We should expect some of these biases to manifest themselves as ubiquitous normative categories.[8] Moreover, on the linguistic side, partial assimilation processes, in which innate predispositions evolve to reduce learning costs, may explain the source and prevalence of various linguistic categories and structures, such as pronouns for people, indexicals of various kinds, linguistic categories such as questions, and the prevalent event structure (see Dor and Jablonka 2000). Since categories are introduced and refined constantly, we expect to see the evolution of a capacity for acquiring categories. As experience of the society with categorization advances it is probable that categories will become sharper, since this makes them more useful as well as less prone to elicit conflicts of interpretation. Eventually, categorization as such may require the establishment of sharp boundaries.[9] Learning and modifying the results of previous learning in both domains are funda-mental to the ontogenetic processes, and will be selected for. We would also expect the capacity for innovation in both domains to concomitantly evolve. Language and norms will thus remain learned abilities and not become entirely innate. Consequently,

---

[8] A case in point might be the observation that we find norms regarding murder and incest in all cultures but each culture exhibits local variation in the situations that are considered to be murder or incest.

[9] Cave drawings and figurines often depict beings that are part animal and part human. It is interesting to speculate if this reflects changes in categorization and hence in conceptual thought.

assimilation will, by necessity, be at most partial, leaving ample room for cultural evolution and scaffolding. So while normativity may make use of specific learning mechanisms for identifying behaviours that should serve as candidate norms, and employ mechanisms for generalizing from them, we expect concrete norms to typically not be innate.

I turn to implications for the evolution of emotions. First, many mistakes and misunderstandings manifest themselves as normative infractions. As examples, consider the inappropriate use of a label, such as one carrying problematic connotations, mistakenly issuing a demand rather than a polite request, or simply not listening when you are expected to listen. Being able to acquire the appropriate norms and, just as importantly, to recognize signs such as frowning or grunting that indicate that your behaviour is judged by others as inappropriate, giving you a chance to make amends, are critical skills. There are various ways to respond to norm violations, for both the culprit and the other parties, perhaps the most important of which is diffusing such situations (e.g. through conversational repair) and negotiating refined norms for the future. This normative rigmarole involves many emotional responses (Wilson and O'Gorman 2003). Noticing a violation, as well as being found by others to be a violator, involves emotions such as anger, condemnation, blame, guilt, and shame. There will be an evolutionary pressure for appropriate emotional responses, for greater emotional control, for recognizing emotional cues from others, for rationalizing and reflecting on emotional responses, and for 'emotional engineering' skills, such as displaying appropriate signs of contrition and humility or telling jokes.

Moreover, because of the importance of normative negotiation, we would expect to see emotions becoming more cognitive so that individuals are able, to a degree, to articulate (and thus often further sublimate) their emotional responses. At the same time, we would expect a more or less standardized repertoire of expressions signalling the emotions that arise from recognizing norm violations and strong psychological responses to slight punitive behaviours (i.e. behaviours that are not costly to produce, do not involve violence, etc.). This allows de-escalation of conflicts that are par for the course for norm-governed societies (and that, since norms are variable and changing, cannot be resolved 'evolutionarily' through ritualized behaviour that replaces the conflict altogether). There is also a strong evolutionary pressure for the capacity to quickly and reliably recognize norm- as well as linguistic violations. This favours some level of dedicated processing that does not rely on conscious reflection and may involve recognizing physiological cues in others (e.g. blushing, sweating).[10]

I conclude this section with the possible connection between modal and normative notions. If these are indeed related, as I speculated earlier, then improved normative

---

[10] The model proposed here highlights that deliberation can lead to emotional responses that bypass conscious reasoning providing a middle-ground between sentimentalism and rationalism about morality.

acquisition, assessment, renegotiation, and refinement will play a role in improved coping with the environment, in which epistemic modal reasoning plays a role, and vice versa. This may be particularly significant in complex situations. An important case is the combined social and environmental coping that is part of the manufacture and use of complex tools. Both normative and modal capacities are involved in teaching and learning the possibly multi-person processes of tool making and for handling the epistemic context about the environment and the state of the tool that is needed for successful use of tools. Modal and normative sophistication as well as emotional control, particularly patience, are requirements for a society constructing and making use of complex tools (cf. Stout 2010; Casler et al. 2009; Kenward et al. 2011).

19.4 Predictions

The co-developmental and co-evolutionary interactions suggest a wide range of concrete predictions many of which are confirmed by contemporary psycholinguistics, developmental psychology, cognitive science, anthropology, and evolutionary analysis.

19.4.1 *Language- and norm-acquisition*

Norms play a critical role in the acquisition of language, and language plays a role in the acquisition of many social norms. This provides many opportunities for studying their developmental interactions. Among the predictions that the co-evolutionary scenario suggests are the following:

1. We expect young (pre-school) children to be able to justify their normative behaviour (e.g. to complain if punished unfairly) and explain normative breaches by others. This is indeed the case (see Ingram and Bering 2010; Harris and Núñez 1996).
2. The young age at which children begin expressing possessive sentiments and the prevalence of norms of personal ownership leads us to expect that children's use of the word 'mine' typically occurs before the use of the words 'yours' and 'his' and that the expression 'mine' is first used as a declarative. We can further hypothesize an evolutionary progression from 'mine' (possession, from a first person perspective), possibly even 'my mom' in an allocare context, on to attribution of possession to others ('his'/'hers') that is used when possession is enforced by third parties (which may be unique to humans, see Tomasello 2009: 88), finally paving the way to possessives of a more general form or to norms of possession via partial assimilation. Other pronouns and indexicals can also arise and be utilized in such scenarios. Note that the observation that possessives and the related mental concepts arise at an early normative and linguistic

developmental stage is consistent with the notion of possession being partly genetically assimilated and partly constructed socially, to varying degrees (the disposition can be genetic, social, or both). It should also be noted that various languages have richer systems of possessive classifiers than found, for example, in English (discussed in Evans 2011: ch. 4); however, data on acquisition patterns for most languages used by small populations is very limited and more research is needed. It is also of great interest to examine the developmental trajectory of these norms in children growing up in egalitarian communities, such as the kibbutz.

3. We expect explicitly normative and explicitly modal vocabularies to be related. In particular, we expect the normative vocabulary to be acquired first, or for them to appear at roughly the same time, and for the vocabularies to overlap. This prediction matches cross-linguistic evidence that indicates that both kinds of meaning tend to be expressed using a single class of modal expressions and that modal (i.e. epistemic) meanings are typically acquired later than normative meanings (reviewed in Papafragou 1998). Similar acquisition patterns of words denoting different strengths of commitment within each category further support the hypothesis that normativity and modality are cognitively related (Papafragou 1998). Further confirmation comes from the observation that children's early use of causal vocabulary (i.e. 'because' and 'so') is for justifying commands and requests, while epistemic uses occur later and are less frequent (Kyrantzis et al. 1990), and from the observation that modal expressions such as 'can' and 'will' are acquired for social, hence normative, purposes, in particular for permission requests (Ervin-Tripp 1991).

4. We expect to see some specialization for linguistic norm acquisition and possibly enforcement. We predict that empirical research will show that linguistic behaviour (pragmatics), including intonation and other aspects of prosody, is understood by infants as norm-governed without or with little need for other behavioural cues indication that a norm prevails. In addition, the centrality of normativity in human cognition that is emphasized by the co-evolutionary account suggests that we should expect to find a general tendency or a 'default assumption' in children that observed behaviours should be understood normatively, and dedicated mechanisms for recognizing relevant behaviours and generalizing norms from them. This is indeed the case (Schmidt et al. 2011; Kenward et al. 2011; Casler et al. 2009; Rakoczy et al. 2008).

19.4.2 *Impairments and pathologies*

We expect that impaired normativity will typically be coupled with impaired language. Improvement in language through therapy will lead to improvement in normative capacity and vice versa. Data on language acquisition in the autism spectrum disorders (ASD) can help assess these hypotheses further since both faculties are impaired. As expected, pragmatics are significantly deficient in both high- and low-functioning ASD individuals, as is prosody. Significantly, while the empirical picture is complex it appears that acquisition of grammar, not only pragmatics, is deficient in autistic children. Among the pragmatic skills that are impaired are conversational skills, handling of questions and commands, comprehension and construction of narratives and the use of humour. Pragmatics remain impaired even in children who overcome an ASD diagnosis (reviewed in Eigsti et al. 2011).

19.4.3 *Social evolution, cultural evolution, social institutions*

Here are several predictions regarding social and cultural evolution:

1. We expect that complex language and sophisticated tool use and manufacture have emerged at roughly the same time (see Stout 2010, 2011). Both involve advances in normative capacity. While norms in the rich sense described in the introduction may not be strictly necessary for cumulative cultural evolution, which is required for producing complex tools, normativity and norms contribute to the coordination required for tool manufacture and for the teaching of tool building (including via natural pedagogy, Csibra and Gergely 2009). Modality may also play a significant role in the use and manufacture of complex tools that comprise multiple stages. In addition, normativity will improve the transmissibility of tool culture, including both the preservation and the accumulation of modifications, as well as the regulation of innovation (see Kenward et al. 2011; Casler et al. 2009).

2. We expect to find a tendency for punitive behaviours, in particular avoidance and exclusion, due to linguistic violations. These are behaviours and emotions that are typically related to norm violations (see Sober and Wilson 1998; Sripada and Stich 2006). Congruent with this prediction is the typical use of language for group differentiation and social exclusion.

   We expect the punitive emotional responses that arise when detecting both social norm- and linguistic norm-violations to have physiological manifestations. Similarly, we expect that intentional violation of both kinds of norms will be correlated with physiological manifestations in the transgressor, e.g. blushing, increased heart rate, sweating, etc.

3. Evolution of language and evolution of psychological altruism are intimately related. Human cognition depends on language, and since the hypothesis is that language co-evolved with human normativity, an organism with human cognitive abilities is expected to have a sophisticated normative ability and a rich normative repertoire. Moreover, the importance of scaffolding for language acquisition increases the likelihood that children be predisposed to cooperative

behaviour since this makes scaffolding much easier. This indeed seems to be the case (see Tomasello 2009; Warneken and Tomasello 2009). Human normativity is not merely a prerequisite or a 'modular' add-on, but rather an entrenched and co-evolved part of individual human cognition that played a role throughout its evolution. Its evolution cannot be explained independently of the evolution of language. These considerations have profound implications for debates regarding level of selection needed to explain the evolution of altruism that I cannot develop here. Sripada and Stich (2006: 285) make related claims about normativity and psychological altruism; Knight (2008b) argues that language co-evolved with the rule of law and discusses the evolutionary origin of language in light of various models for the evolution of cooperation.

19.5 Conclusion

The starting point for the discussion in this chapter is that language is a learned, norm-governed, intentional communication system. All of these properties must clearly take part in any attempt to explain the evolution of language. I thus focused my attention on the evolutionary pressures and dynamics that can be found in a society that makes use of learned communication and consists of individuals who have rudimentary susceptibility to social norms (which requires some ability to form expectations, experience surprise, and recognize intentions and mistakes). These are not trivial requirements but they are very far from being equivalent to language or contemporary human normativity. Importantly, they are within the realm of possibility of our closest primate relatives.

I discussed how the evolutionary interaction between language and normativity helps explain the emergence of fundamental aspects of human languages (e.g. imperatives, questions, possessives, modal vocabulary, categorization, performatives) and of human normativity, in particular its entrenched role in human cognition and some aspects of its ontogeny and phenomenology (e.g. independent normativity and intrinsic motivation, the ability to represent situations from multiple perspectives, and the ontogeny of normative categories and vocabulary that result from normative negotiation and metacognition).

It is now accepted by most researchers that cultural evolution is a critical factor in understanding human evolution and that gene-culture co-evolution probably played a significant role in the evolution of the human mind. Society and the social forces it gives rise to, culture with its cognitive and material benefits, and individual human cognition all take part in this evolution. Normativity affects and connects all three realms: norms and the human capacity to acquire and implement them are basic structural elements of human society. They underlie most cultural knowledge and play a part in its transmission between individuals and generations. Finally, the individual mind determines what counts as normative and the phenomenology of normativity, and is itself shaped ontogenetically by developmental scaffolding that is norm-governed. As I tried to show in this chapter, normativity and language, two hallmarks of human cognition, are intimately related. Language acquisition, in particular, is greatly assisted by norm-governed social institutions. These institutions probably had an even greater role than they have today early on in the evolution of language. Human language and normativity transformed and shaped each other during their evolution. They remain closely intertwined in contemporary humans.

19.6 Acknowledgments

Zohar Bronfman assisted in surveying the psycholinguistic literature and provided critical comments on earlier drafts.

20

Why talk?

JEAN-LOUIS DESSALLES

20.1 A fundamental and neglected issue

What is language good for? For a long time, the question has remained not only unanswered, but not even asked. The classic 'reason' invoked to avoid the issue was that language benefited the species as a whole. This way of reasoning is simply wrong (Williams 1966). If information has any value, it is in the interest of no one to give it for free. And if information has no value, why are there ears ready to listen to it? The reason why we talk, and so much, still requires a biological and social explanation.

Many authors consider that language is used for sharing (Corballis and Suddendorf 2007; Győri 1997; Ritt 2004; Pinker and Bloom 1990), exchanging (Carruthers 1996: 231–2), or trading (Pinker 1994: 367) knowledge and information, and that this is the reason why it exists. Another frequently mentioned function of language is that it makes social cooperation possible (Brinck 2004; Carruthers 1996: 231–2; Gärdenfors and Warglien 2006; Nowak and Komarova 2001; Sterelny 2006), but also that it enables behavioural manipulation (Nowak and Komarova 2001; Worden 1998). Some authors consider that its primary role is to teach offspring (Castro et al. 2004; Fitch 2004). Most of these authors would consider that language is immediately *useful*, because it provides increased mastery over the material world, as when individuals go hunting or scavenging (Bickerton 2009; Snowdon 2001). The impact of language on material life seems *obvious* to many authors; most of the scholars above use this adjective. For example:

The adaptive significance of human language is obvious. It pays to talk. Cooperation in hunting, making plans, coordinating activities, task sharing, social bonding, manipulation and deception all benefit from an increase in expressive power. (Nowak and Komarova 2001)

Language also allows [humans] to share knowledge. Each individual can thus learn about the experience of others and avoid repeating their mistakes. . . . It is obvious, then, that language is a good thing to have, both for us as individuals and for our species as a whole. (Ritt 2004: 1–2)

The attribution of 'obviousness' is based on the current ecological success of our species in invading the world these past millennia. The correlation between this ecological feat and the use of language is far from perfect, though. Until the advent of agriculture, the demography of *Homo sapiens* was comparable with that currently documented for great apes (Ray 2003). This means that despite its use of language, our species spent 90 per cent of its existence stagnating at a relatively low level of ecological performance. People intelligent enough to create masterworks like the Lascaux cave paintings were certainly talking like any extant population, but this did not bring them any closer to dominating the material world.

If language does not owe its existence to its practical virtues, what about its social role? Robin Dunbar (1996) famously drew attention to this aspect of language, comparing it with social grooming in apes. But as acknowledged by Dunbar himself, there is more to human conversation than mere bonding signals, as otherwise synchronized grunts would do the job. Language is presented as a tool for enhancing cooperation (Dunbar 1996; Gärdenfors and Warglien 2006) or even as a cooperative activity in its own right. This supposed link with cooperation requires closer examination.

The term 'cooperation', in this context, is used in three ways. It may mean that language is like a *game* in which partners obey definite rules (Grice 1975). This is of little help here, as it does not say much about the function of language. Competitive sports such as tennis are depicted as purely cooperative according to this definition, which misses the point that the main purpose of the players is to defeat their opponent.

The term 'cooperation' is also used in a loose sense, meaning *concerted action*. It is true that the possibility of concerted action is considerably enhanced by the use of language. However, language use does not correlate well with concerted action. Many kinds of collective action, such as hunting, can be performed without language, as numerous animal predators show (Bshary et al. 2006; Boesch 1994). On the other hand, language is mostly used during casual conversation, when there is no material task to perform (see Section 20.2).

When 'cooperation' is used in its strict sense, it means *reciprocal altruism*. Strict cooperation raises the problem of cheating. Cooperative behaviour is vulnerable to invasion by cheats taking advantage of the altruism of others without giving anything in return. This problem applies to language when it is conceptualized as reciprocal altruism. Reciprocity is inherently unstable (Axelrod and Hamilton 1981; Dessalles 1999; Nowak 2006). For some authors, cooperation could be enforced by self-policing in the speaking community, using gossip to build or damage reputations (Dunbar 1996). But this only moves the stability problem one step further, as reputational policing is just cooperation at a higher level.

Contrary to what we would expect from cooperation models, humans need no prompting to talk. On the contrary, talkative individuals abound, making the price of information very low or even negative—as when we make an effort to avoid someone's conversation. As Geoff Miller (2000: 350) puts it:

[Reciprocal cooperation] does not describe the human species as I know it. Watch any group of people conversing, and you will see the exact opposite of the behaviour predicted by the kinship and reciprocity theories of language. People compete to say things. They strive to be heard.... Those who fail to yield the floor to their colleagues are considered selfish, not altruistic. Turn-taking rules have emerged to regulate not who gets to listen, but who gets to talk.

Miller here notes that most judgements about the function of language reflect personal conviction or intuition, not observational data. A notable exception is Robin Dunbar, who pioneered the ethological study of human language. Dunbar's claim that the biological function of language is to contribute to social bonding is fundamental, and the present chapter supports it. However, this does not imply that cooperation plays any role in this process. As I will suggest, conversational moves, far from being cooperative offers, are more like competitive advertising.

In what follows, I will first mention several facts about spontaneous language that show how peculiar a behaviour it is. I will show typical examples illustrating the two main forms that language behaviour takes. These two modes will be presented as fulfilling two functions. As an attempt to explain language uniqueness, I will observe that the classical social primate order has been disrupted at some point in human phylogeny. Language, or something like language, will be shown to be the expected consequence of the new hominin order.

20.2 What is spontaneous language like?

Human language is uniquely pervasive of every aspect of life. Yet although it can be used for coordinating collective action, the primary context, by far, is casual conversation. Human beings devote one third of their waking time, i.e. six hours a day, to language activities (Mehl and Pennebaker 2003). They do so pro-actively, speaking some 16,000 words daily on average (Mehl et al. 2007). An especially talkative individual may utter about 50,000 words a day. This invasion of the acoustic space does not fit with depictions of language as cautious cooperation in which information is bestowed parsimoniously as a valuable gift. Rather it seems to resemble competitive social signalling, as will be suggested in this chapter.

Verbal activities can be classified under two main headings: *conversational narratives* and *argumentative discussion* (Bruner 1986: 11; Dessalles 2009). During narratives, individuals draw attention to current or past events that are described in some detail (Norrick 2000). During discussion, individuals point to inconsistencies or suggest ways of increasing logical consistency (Dessalles 2009). Let us examine these two modes in turn.

20.3 Spontaneous narrative behaviour

Until recently, it remained largely unnoticed that spontaneous narratives constitute a massive phenomenon that may occupy up to 40 per cent of conversational time

(Eggins and Slade 1997). Conversational narratives assume a characteristic form. One person, the narrator, may hold the floor for several minutes, recounting one situated event. 'Situated' means that the four Ws (when, where, what, who) get instantiated. Most narratives are delivered sequentially, in what Deborah Tannen (1984) calls 'story rounds'. In such a round, each story is closely related to the one preceding it.

A fundamental question is: What makes an event narratable? It has been noted that to qualify, an event must be out of the ordinary (Labov and Waletzky 1967; Polanyi 1979). My own work on conversational narratives led me to the conclusion that narratable events must be *unexpected*, every included element contributing to making it seem maximally unexpected (Dessalles 2010c). For instance, recounting that your cousin came to visit you yesterday does not make a story; after all, she might come every day. Likewise, the presence of water in your bathroom is not worth talking about, unless it's a leak or other unexpected event involving water. Conversely, any sufficiently unexpected state of affairs may make a relevant story. This includes events already known to the audience, as unexpectedness can be re-experienced (Norrick 2000: ch. 4). The following example shows a typical narrative (from my own corpus, original in French).

P –I don't know if you heard that . . . these dolls that were sold a few days ago.
D –Oh yeah, no no, completely crooked, or whatever.
P –Crooked, ugly, deformed dolls.
L –E.T.?
D –no no no no
P –Crooked by nature. And then, the point was not . . . they were supposed to be adopted by the little girls, with a certificate of adoption, and . . . it was all the rage, everything disappeared! They didn't . . . The producers weren't able to match the demand, and one mentioned the case of a fellow who went to England to buy one because his daughter unconditionally wanted a doll like this
O –[laughs]
P –and he was unable to find one, [laughs] so for fear that she would get depressed because of that he went abroad to buy it in England!
M –And there were awful struggles!

In this story, unexpectedness comes from the contrast between the ugliness of the dolls and the fact that girls wanted them so intensely. The narrator's emphasis is on both aspects: the ugliness ('Crooked, ugly, deformed') and the girls' craziness about the dolls ('it was all the rage'), aims at amplifying the contrast as much as possible.

Another crucial (but optional) feature of narratable events is that they arouse *emotion*. People systematically attempt to share emotional events with close acquaintances (Rimé 2005). The following conversation, recorded in a Japanese family, retells a past emotional event (original in Japanese; see full excerpt in Dessalles 2011: 119).

T –Once, when Risa was little, her friend came here. [. . .] And there, just over the railroad crossing . . . She had left one hour earlier but she hadn't arrived at her home. And then I got the phone call [from her family] saying that she hadn't arrived yet so something had gone wrong. I began to worry about her so I went to the station. And right there, a girl had just got run over.

[. . .]

T There were a lot of onlookers so I asked them what was going on. And then they said that a girl had been run over and I was like 'Oh my!', you know, I was scared. Then I asked the policeman [whether she was the girl] and then he said he wasn't sure [. . .] so I was afraid it was her. But after that, it turned out to be that she had taken a detour because of the train accident.

The episode, as T experienced it by the time of its occurrence, is emotional by nature, as it deals with the death of a child. Its intensity comes from its unexpectedness: such accidents are rare and usually concern people one does not know. Emotional, unexpected experiences make the best stories. They tend to be shared the very day of their occurrence (Rimé 2005: 90).

Why does *Homo sapiens* feel the urge to share unexpected and emotional experiences? Before considering this issue, let's turn to the other major conversational mode.

20.4 Argumentative discussion

Argumentative discussion makes up the greater share of conversational time. Discussion is what people use language for when they are not telling stories. Unlike narratives, discussions need not deal with situated events. Discussion is nonetheless highly constrained as well.

The fundamental question about spontaneous discussion behaviour is: What makes an issue debatable? The answer is straightforward. Any debatable issue is based on a *contradictory* situation that requires a logical solution (Dessalles 2009). The contradiction may oppose beliefs (epistemic issue) or involve desires (epithymic issue). You may wonder why your colleague is present at work, as you believed she was on holiday in Mexico, and start an epistemic discussion on the topic. You may complain about the fact that the new carpet is red, as you asked for a grey-blue carpet, and start an epithymic discussion to deal with that issue.

The above conversation about the railroad crossing continued with an epistemic discussion (original in Japanese):

S –Was that a suicide?

T –Ummm I guess she just got run over. Since she was merely a junior high school student so I'm not sure. Even if she committed suicide, anyway, she was just a junior high school girl.

S –For a student in junior high school to commit suicide, I guess it means that he or she suffered terrible bullying or was highly addicted to drugs or something.

T –We don't know whether she committed suicide or she got run over, but I found the article about the accident in the next morning's newspaper.

The suicide hypothesis provides a tentative logical explanation for the accident. The mention of bullying and of drugs is another explanatory attempt, this time to make the girl's suicide logically more consistent.

Why does *Homo sapiens* feel the urge to discuss logical issues with conspecifics?

20.5 Conversational moves are social signals

In 1962, the publication of *How to do things with words* (Austin 1962) popularized the idea that language may be just a particular way of performing acts. However, no general theory of action is able to predict that people systematically maximize unexpectedness when retelling an event, or systematically anchor their discussions to some logical inconsistency. As the above examples illustrate, most of our conversational moves are not even related to any material task. Contrary to what uninformed authors have conjectured about the function of language, as we mentioned at the beginning of this chapter, language does not systematically deal with important matters. The fact that little girls are prepared to buy crooked dolls is unlikely to change the survival chances of the people involved in the conversation. Most conversations are about futile matters that have no tangible bearing on the participants' life. If language has a systematic impact, it is not in the material world.

If talking does not boil down to performing tangible acts, perhaps we are talking just because we enjoy doing so! But any biologically relevant behaviour is under the control of the pleasure/displeasure rewarding system. The pleasurable aspect of talking provides no information about the corresponding biological function, beyond the fact that it does exist.

In line with Dunbar's claim about the role of language in establishing and maintaining social bonds, I will propose that human beings choose their friends according to their conversational competence. If we follow this logic, the significance of speech lies not in its tangible effects *per se*, but in the quality signalled by the performer. *Talking is signalling.* By talking in a relevant way, individuals demonstrate their ability to generate unexpectedness and emotion through narratives; and they show off their ability to deal with logical consistency through discussions. This behaviour seems to be universal in our species (Scalise Sugiyama 2001; Dessalles 2011).

If narrative and argumentative skills are what people assess in their actual or potential friends, several pieces of the puzzle fall into place. We can understand why language is competitive signalling, as individuals are in competition to attract friends. We can also understand why conversational topics are often futile, as the immediate utility of words is not what matters. The fact that people are at least as prone to speak as to listen also now makes sense. We also expect both genders to speak equally (Mehl et al. 2007), something that scenarios based on courtship (Miller 2000) or on teaching (Fitch 2004) cannot explain. The importance of generating unexpectedness also accounts for the huge vocabularies found in human languages. Adult human beings can understand tens of thousands of words, a fact that utilitarian theories of language would have a hard time explaining. Since most unexpected situations are rare, a large vocabulary is needed to describe them when they occur; and as we saw in the excerpt about dolls, precise words are also needed to highlight the contrast on which the unexpectedness is based. Lastly, one understands why conversation is not a strictly dyadic process, as we would expect from reciprocal altruism, but is generally collective (Dunbar et al. 1995), as the above excerpts illustrate.

Two points still require an explanation. Why are unexpectedness, emotions, and logical consistency so crucial for human sociality? And why are they apparently not so important in other primate species?

20.6 The demise of the strongest

Primate societies are in part based on the rights of the strongest. Even if primates, especially chimpanzees, are able to form alliances that may slightly alter the rule, even if females seem to have their say on which male will reign over the community, male reproductive success is strongly correlated with the ability to enforce supremacy through physical coercion. In Darwinian terms, the stakes are maximal. A study in the Budongo free-ranging chimpanzee community in Uganda showed that the top-ranking male, or α-male, sired 40 per cent of the next generation born in the group; the β-male fathered 20 per cent of the children and the γ-male 7 per cent (Reynolds 2005).

Imagine you are the γ-male. Moving up through the hierarchy is risky. You have to defeat in battle individuals that in the past proved stronger than you. You will think twice before venturing to challenge them. To help you in this choice, big males engage in displays that allow you to gauge their strength. Now imagine that the rule of the game is slightly changed: you may use a weapon, such as a sharp stick or a big stone, to kill the male next up in rank while he is sleeping or when his back is turned. There is a fantastic payoff for the γ-male to do so: he will get 20 per cent of the Darwinian prize instead of only 7 per cent. For an unknown reason, despite their ability to use tools (but see Gruber et al. 2011) and to throw stones (Osvath 2009), chimpanzees don't kill using surprise. Murder does exist among chimpanzees, but only using bare teeth (Reynolds 2005: 154). Once, for whatever reason, easy killing became possible among our hominin ancestors, the absolute right of the strongest instantaneously became obsolete.

Since the possibility of risk-free killing is universal and systematic in our species, we know for sure that the preceding story did happen at some point in hominin phylogeny. Dating the use of lethal weapons such as stones and sticks is difficult, as it may *not* have resulted in significantly increased violence (Wrangham et al. 2006). Easy murder may be at least as old as *Homo*. Weapon transportation is one of the reasons that have been invoked to explain why hominin bipedal locomotion evolved, despite its poor energetic efficiency (Boehm 1999: 181). If we push the hypothesis to the extreme, the use of weapons to resist (or enable) risk-free killing within the community might be concomitant with the divergence of the hominin lineage. Note that this hypothesis differs from the classical 'man-the-killer' schema (Dart 1953), as we are speaking here of increased *within-group* killing risk. At the other extreme, the fact that easy killing using weapons could have a recent, purely cultural origin can be excluded. Murder and killing threats are ubiquitous and universal in our species (Hill et al. 2007). Considering the Darwinian stakes of resisting coercion and of suppressing competitors, both within and between the sexes, it is unthinkable that weapons were not used for these purposes by our ancestors as they are used in contemporary societies.

The advent of weapons, whenever that occurred, may not have increased the overall level of violence. But it would have had a dramatic impact on the pre-existing social order, leading to a new balance of power. As soon as safe killing is possible, top-ranking individuals become the designated target of subordinates. As a result, we expect an inverted hierarchy (Boehm 1999; Knight, Chapter 17; Knight and Lewis, Chapter 21), in which each individual submits to the group and avoids showing any desire for dominance. We also expect allies to be selected using different criteria. Physical strength is no longer an asset. What, then, should be the qualities of greatest value in a friend?

20.7 From muscle to information displays

Most readers of this book live in integrated societies where police and justice deter potential killers from taking their life. They might forget that in a typical hominin context, the only valid life insurance is to have friends. Individuals must sleep, and they happen to have their back turned to potential murderers. Only friends may offer protection against actual killing and death threats. Those who fail to get appropriate protection from friends are more likely to get intimidated, exploited and even killed by those who have been more successful in the social game.

This new social order turns out to be an efficient one, as human societies are not significantly more violent than primate communities (Wrangham et al. 2006). It's simply that the rules of the game have changed: information has replaced muscle as the principal social asset. In the risk-free killing context of hominin societies, ideal friends must have these qualities:

(Q1)   They anticipate danger and help you avoid being taken by surprise.
(Q2)   They are not themselves a danger to you.
(Q3)   They are ready to share time with you.

These criteria are automatic consequences of the possibility of easy killing: one needs friends to be protected. Any other qualities we may think of, such as being a good cooperator, being courageous, being intelligent, or being efficient in some specific skills such as hunting, are of subordinate importance in comparison with the three qualities above.

In the context that followed the transition to risk-free killing, it became crucial not only to attract friends, but also to be accepted as a friend. The logical consequence is that individuals displayed qualities (Q1)–(Q3). My suggestion is that that the human form of communication, or rather one of its previous forms such as protolanguage (Bickerton 1990), emerged in that context.

How far does language fit this display function? Let's consider narrative behaviour first. As illustrated above, every element in a conversational narrative is designed to make the reported event maximally unexpected and emotional. This property of human narrative is not fortuitous.

Unexpectedness is the only reliable indicator of danger when danger comes from other members of one's own species. Animal species can evolve to delineate and anticipate external danger such as predators. Individuals instinctively know or learn where and when their lives are at risk. But when danger comes from group mates, it cannot be so easily circumscribed. To what extent can one guard against murder? It is difficult for potential murderers to prepare their act without interfering with the normal course of events. Attending to any unexpected modification of the surrounding world is the best available strategy for potential victims to avoid being caught by surprise.

Permanent alertness is not sufficient. To survive in an easy killing context, one must surround oneself with vigilant friends. To appear as ideal friends, individuals of our species, and presumably in earlier hominin species as well, take every opportunity, even the most futile ones, to show off their ability to spot unexpected events. Human infants, by the age of 9 months, begin to point to unexpected things (Carpenter et al. 1998) and then do so systematically through adulthood. Declarative pointing is not known to exist in other species (Tomasello 2006) or is far from being systematic. The closest behaviour is the alarm call, when not directed toward kin (Zuberbühler 2006). Unlike alarm calling, the human propensity to signal unexpectedness is not bound to any specific class of events. Animals are sometimes curious about certain classes of events, but they make no systematic attempts to share their curiosity (Tomasello 2006). This refutes the idea that the communication of information would require special cognitive prerequisites such as some form of 'theory of mind'. If pointing to unexpectedness was advantageous to the pointing individual, animals would do it systematically, even by reflex.

The communication of unexpectedness through narratives or even through pointing gestures matches the display of quality (Q1): in an easy killing context, one is more prone to become acquainted with individuals who are able to spot unexpected states of affairs, rather than with individuals who are blind to novelty, to unusualness, to exceptions, or to coincidences. The former individuals are subjectively perceived as interesting and the latter as boring (Polanyi 1979). According to Rimé (2005: 177):

> Whoever knows about some news, such as an emotional event affecting a third party, holds a key to the extraordinary, since any emotional event by definition involves a dimension of novelty or of unexpectedness. We already discussed the fascination triggered by such events. By communicating information about such an event to others, one gets an opportunity to exert this fascination on them. One is sure, therefore, to elicit their best interest, and to attract to one's own person the greatest attention. And we exist to a very large extent through the attention we receive. (Original in French)

Our unique attraction for unexpected events and for those able to signal them makes perfect sense if language is used to show off one's ability to anticipate danger. It reveals that our ancestors could survive because they chose alert friends and because they demonstrated their own alertness to those friends.

As the railroad crossing example illustrates, the unexpected events that humans share in narratives are often emotional ones. Why are we actively seeking to share our emotions in minute detail with conspecifics? The answer is not straightforward, as emotional communication seems to have only drawbacks. It reveals our weaknesses and it makes us predictable. It is expected to lower our value on the friendship 'market' and to limit our freedom. What we observe is the exact contrary! As Rimé (2005: 130) puts it:

> The more a person confides in another about intimate events, the more the listener will express affection for her. It also works the other way around: those who confide about themselves develop affection for those who listen to them. (Original in French)

There is something paradoxical in the fact that revealing our intimate preferences and sometimes our vulnerability can make us socially attractive. The paradox disappears if one realizes that by sharing our emotions, one displays quality (Q2). Ideal friends, in an easy killing context, should be predictable. This may be the reason why emotion sharing is so prevalent in spontaneous human communication. By sharing emotional events, one makes oneself perfectly readable and predictable to close acquaintances. This behaviour makes sense if it is a way to demonstrate one's reliability and dispel any suspicion that one could be a threat to them.

People not only recount experiences. They also engage in sometimes lengthy discussions. These discussions deal with inconsistencies concerning either beliefs or desires. Elsewhere, I surmised that discussion emerged as an anti-liar device

(Dessalles 1998). There is a danger that individuals distinguish themselves by lying about their supposedly unexpected experiences. One possible protection against a lie is to restrict communication to checkable events. This is presumably the form of communication for which protolanguage was best suited (Dessalles 2008). The other protection against liars consists in checking the consistency of their testimony. In our species, individuals not only take every opportunity to check the logic of what they hear or see, but they do it publicly. The corresponding ability has turned into a fourth quality that ideal friends should have:

(Q4)   Ideal friends are able to detect inconsistencies or to restore consistency.

Conversely, individuals who lack the ability to reason logically are easily deceived and can easily be taken by surprise. Conversational discussions, even when they are about futile topics, would be the manifestation of the tendency to display (Q4). The human capability to deal with displaced reference and with abstract ideas can also be related to the selection pressure created by (Q4) (Dessalles 2008, 2009).

20.8 Discussion

In this chapter, I outlined a scenario in which giving honest information to conspecifics, as humans do in spontaneous conversation, is a profitable strategy, not only for listeners, but primarily for speakers. The scenario has two strong points: it shows how language can be an 'evolutionarily stable strategy' (ESS) (Dessalles 2010b) and it is consistent with the way language is universally used in our species. By contrast, cooperative scenarios fail to explain why most conversational subject matters are futile or inconsequential for addressees' survival. They do not explain either why spontaneous talk is directed almost without discrimination toward several individuals simultaneously, with no expectation of reciprocity (Dunbar et al. 1995). The scenario developed in this chapter also explains several important aspects of language that are not addressed by alternative explanations or that are at odds with them.

- *Inconsequentiality.* The fact that any unexpected situation can be taken as an excuse to prove one's vigilance explains why most conversations are about futile matters.
- *Vocabulary size.* The fact that communication is about unexpected situations, which are by definition rare, contributes to explaining why vocabularies are large and not limited to a few dozen words.
- *No sex difference.* Contrary to models that link language to courtship (Miller 2000), the present model excludes any significant difference in the use of language according to gender, a fact that observation confirms (Mehl et al. 2007).
- *Pro-sociality.* Human beings are known to differ from other primates by their pro-social attitudes towards conspecifics (Warneken and Tomasello 2006).

Instead of attributing this difference to proximal causes such as education or norms (Rachlin 2002; Tomasello 1999), the present model contributes to showing that pro-social attitudes can be beneficial in the easy killing environment that our ancestors experienced for the first time. This explanation is compatible with models of competitive helping (Barclay 2011).

Scenarios of the evolutionary emergence of language are often considered speculative, as if there were a large set of equally likely alternatives to choose from. Indeed, various models have addressed aspects of the problem (some are listed in Johansson, Chapter 5 and in Knight, Chapter 17). However, the present scenario has a rare feature, which is to show how language behaviour (conversation) can be an ESS. Its main hypothesis, the fact that our lineage differs from other species in the possibility of risk-free killing, is a plausible one, as it is known that weapons have been available to hominins for a long time.

As it stands, the model provides a selection pressure for language. However, it does not by itself predict all aspects of language, including syntax and the prevalence of argumentative discussion in conversations. Elsewhere (Dessalles 2009), I tried to delineate and to justify a three-phase evolutionary development for language. In the first phase, communication is bound to the here-and-now. Pointing gestures and isolated words are locally optimal for this function. In a second phase, hominins of our lineage acquire the ability to combine meanings. This second phase is characterized by the use of protolanguage (i.e. syntax-less word strings) (Bickerton 1990) which is locally optimal for an almost-here-almost-now form of communication. The third phase concerns our own species. Our ancestors acquired the ability to oppose mental representations. This opened the way to negation and argumentation, which evolved primarily as an anti-liar device. Syntax (as a way to express logical predicates) and recursion (as a way to determine predicates' arguments) evolved as tools in support of discussion behaviour.

The model offers many testable consequences. The most obvious is the obligatory link between communication and social bonding. Nowadays, this link can be observed in the functioning of social networks on the Web. On social news networks such as Digg or Twitter, social links crucially depend on the freshness and originality of the news (Lerman and Ghosh 2010; Kwak et al. 2010). This emerging collective behaviour might be an indirect consequence of a tendency deeply rooted in our biology, which dates back to the time when human beings became a deadly threat to each other.

The development of the present model was dictated (1) by the urge to find a selection pressure for language (how does speaking benefit speakers?) and (2) with a view to explaining language behaviour *as it is* and not as we might imagine it. Language is a disproportionate behaviour that requires much of our brain resources, much effort to acquire narratable information, and much of our time to tell it.

I submit that this unique biological development, and presumably some other proper features of the human species, can be linked to the use of deadly weapons, a behavioural trait that characterizes *Homo sapiens* and probably some other hominin species. It relies on the hypothesis that teaming up with informative individuals brings additional protection by diminishing the chances of being killed by surprise.

Vocal deception, laughter, and the linguistic significance of reverse dominance

CHRIS KNIGHT AND JEROME LEWIS

> Well, who are you gonna believe, me or your own eyes?
>
> Groucho Marx.[1]

21.1 The problem: how did lying become socially acceptable?

Nonhuman primates have rich conceptual capacities but, from a human standpoint, seem poorly equipped to communicate their thoughts to one another. This applies less to comprehension than to production—particularly vocal production (Pika, Chapter 10; Clay and Zuberbühler, Chapter 11). The human so-called 'speech articulators'—tongue, lips, soft palate, and so forth—have obvious primate counterparts, but in nonhumans are restricted to basic functions such as chewing and breathing (MacNeilage 2008; see Kendon, Chapter 6). When an ape or monkey emits a scream or cry its tongue, for example, plays little or no role (Zuberbühler 2012: 77).

Summing up the situation, Zanna Clay and Klaus Zuberbühler (Chapter 11) conclude that nonhuman primates 'have little control over their articulators', being in this respect 'curiously limited, showing little evidence of cognitive flexibility and creativity'. 'These expressive limitations', as Zuberbühler (2003) has written elsewhere, 'seem to be rooted in at least two deficiencies: a lack of sophisticated control over the articulators in the supra-laryngeal vocal tract and a remarkable shortcoming in social cognition'. In evolutionary debates, the first of these deficiencies tends to be

---

[1] *Duck Soup* (1933), Universal Pictures. Starring Groucho, Harpo, Chico, and Zeppo Marx; written by Bert Kalmer and Harry Ruby; directed by Leo McCarey. Although usually credited to Groucho, the words quoted are actually spoken in the film by Chico.

explained as a genetic defect of some kind—the surprising inability of all but *Homo sapiens* to exert complex motor control over lips, tongue, and other so-called articulators (e.g. Lieberman 1985). Almost all scholars imagine that a mutation conferring cognitive control would have 'obvious' advantages (Bickerton 1990: 156; Lieberman 1992: 23; Nowak and Komarova 2001; Ritt 2004: 1–2; see Dessalles, Chapter 20). At some point during human evolution, it is assumed, one or more genes must have connected cognition with communication, at last establishing full volitional control over the tongue and other articulators.

Yet a moment's reflection should remind us that volitional control cannot quite be the issue. It's not unusual for a mammal to open or close its jaw during the course of a call. Volitional changes in lip configuration are also quite common. The vocal anatomy of big cats—lions, tigers, jaguars, and leopards—corresponds quite closely with that of humans; one might almost imagine that they *could* talk—yet, of course, they don't (Fitch 2002). Most relevant to our discussion, any ancestral hominin must from the outset have possessed volitional control over its tongue—otherwise it would have been unable to taste, masticate, or even safely swallow its food. No ape or monkey has an inflexible tongue. When the animal needs to communicate a thought, however, it leaves the tongue out of it. It is this which needs to be explained.

21.2 Sight versus sound

'Who are you gonna believe, me or your own eyes?', asked Groucho Marx (Blount 2010). The issues can be summed up in no better way. When responding to signals, animals of all species prefer direct sensory evidence over unverifiable claims. The more cognitively manipulable the signal, the lower its chances of being accepted as either reliable or worth responding to—and so the less likely it is to evolve. No better explanation has ever been offered to explain the striking mismatch between the complexity of cognition and that of communication across primate species, with communication generally lagging far behind (Ulbaek 1998). In confirming this pattern, modern Darwinian signal evolution theory (Krebs and Dawkins 1984; Maynard Smith and Harper 1995; Zahavi 1993; Zahavi and Zahavi 1997) backs up Groucho Marx. Mistrusting one another's scheming, Machiavellian minds, primates prefer to rely on the evidence of their own eyes.

When an ape or monkey interprets an incoming signal, its first priority is to evaluate how trustworthy it is. This is easier when the signal is visible. Orofacial expressions, visible invitations to play, requests to be groomed, begging gestures, and so forth don't work over distances. Being reserved for face-to-face encounters, primate orofacial and other visible gestures are observed close-up and in full view of the triggering context (Blount 1990; Tomasello et al. 1994). Since this makes it easier to check veracity, such gestures face reduced pressure to demonstrate *intrinsic* reliability. The signaller is free to bring volition into play, recruiting for communicative purposes—sometimes novel ones—the motor control capacities it already has (Pika, Chapter 10).

So why doesn't the same apply to vocal signalling? What are the overriding evolutionary constraints, apparently acting across primate communication in general, which so strikingly limit flexibility in the use of sound? One possibility is the requirement for reliability. It should be possible to test this. We might expect that when primates vocalize in close proximity to one another there should be reduced pressure to demonstrate reliability. As a consequence, we might then expect quiet vocalizations to be deployed in relatively creative, flexible ways. By contrast, when primates emit long-calls—using sound to communicate across distances—we would expect reverse selection pressures, offering less scope for flexibility.[2]

We can understand the constraints on vocal flexibility by recalling the special communicative virtues of sound. Sound carries over distances, goes round corners, works in the dark—and doesn't require receivers to be facing the right way. Sound can focus attention on an urgent message. On hearing an anti-predator alarm, listeners must respond quickly with a reflex action, accepting the message on trust. When the signal comes from a distant or invisible source, listeners are denied contextual information on which to judge reliability. Cognitive, volitional input is limited because it is not what listeners need. To be safe, nonhuman primates respond preferentially to audible body language which just *cannot* be manipulated or faked (Zahavi and Zahavi 1997). It is this which so tightly constrains the degree of volitional control which field primatologists report (Pika, Chapter 10; Clay and Zuberbühler, Chapter 11). Like the watermark in a banknote, in other words, the relative inflexibility of primate vocal signalling is far from a 'maladaptive trait' or 'deficiency'. In a Darwinian social world, it has positive value: it's how apes and monkeys reassure one another that their signals are not fakes (Zahavi and Zahavi 1997; Knight 1998, 2000, 2002).

So we face a conundrum. How could natural selection have switched from quarantining the primate tongue—excluding it from all but a marginal role in vocal communication—to developing and fine-tuning that same tongue's role as the most important speech articulator of all? Since this development was biologically unprecedented, something quite specific, and remarkable, must have happened. The challenge is to narrow down what it was.

21.3 Theory and ethnography

Language first evolved among hunters and gatherers. To a greater extent than farmers or city-dwellers, extant hunters and gatherers can offer insights into the possible dynamics involved.

---

[2] As if in confirmation, Pika (Chapter 10) points to a study by Crockford and colleagues (2012) indicating that when chimpanzees are spatially close to each other, they use 'alert hoots' which are quiet, intentionally produced, and sensitively adjusted to their audience. When vocalizing over distances, they revert to more hard-to-fake, intrinsically convincing sounds.

Western theoretical linguists may be surprised by the concepts that occupy the minds of hunter-gatherers. Core concepts connect women's blood with the blood of hunted animals, the moon's changing phases, hunting luck, health, fertility, sharing, kinship, and the spirit world. The assumed connections might in principle be expressed in a modern city-dweller's language. But a verbal explanation in, say, English, would take time and effort, with little guarantee of success even then. African hunter-gatherers typically have a single word embracing the entire range of topics—*ekila* among the Mbendjele and Baka, *ekeri* among the Mbuti, *epeme* among the Hadza. If our own cognitive scientists stumble to comprehend the logic, it may be because—as Joseph Henrich and colleagues (2010) point out—our horizons are confined to those of an exotic group, namely people from Western, Educated, Industrialized, Rich, and Democratic (WEIRD) societies. To connect back to the origins of language, we need to break out.

In his groundbreaking book, *Women, Fire and Dangerous Things*, the linguist George Lakoff (1987) warned us not to expect indigenous categories to match the way Western science carves up the world. Hunter-gatherer semantic meanings arise out of metaphors which make sense in the light of *their* reproductive, subsistence, and other strategies, not ours. If cross-cultural uniformities are discernible—if the underlying syntax of hunter-gatherer ritual and myth largely resists historical change (Barnard 1988; Knight et al. 1995; Lévi-Strauss 1970–1981; Watts 2005)—it is not because these patterns are fossilized survivals. Rather, if you're living by hunting and gathering, such cognitive strategies are good ways to respond to and interpret the world. The solutions arrived at by successive generations of hunter-gatherers may be thought of, following Maynard Smith (1982), as optimal responses—evolutionarily stable cognitive and practical strategies—shaped by challenges likely to vary only within a limited range.

In what follows, we focus on ethnographic data from Africa. Following Barnard (1999), we regard hunter-gatherers from this part of the world as offering a better fit to the conditions of modern human social origins than those from other continental regions. A salient point is that most African hunter-gatherer systems of production and exchange—in our view, like those of early modern humans—are 'immediate-return' rather than 'delayed-return' systems (Lewis, Chapter 7), with the implication that wealth cannot be accumulated and the political ethos remains egalitarian. We follow Woodburn (1982, 2005) in viewing 'delayed-return' hunter-gatherer economic systems as complex and derivative, representing relatively recent historical developments.

Restricting ourselves, then, to immediate-return hunter-gatherers in Africa, here are some of the constant and unchanging challenges:

- *The Moon.* Human night vision is weak compared with that of lions (Joubert and Joubert 1997). Immediately following full moon, people across much of rural Africa are especially at risk of being killed and eaten by a lion or other nocturnal predator (Packer et al. 2011). This clarifies why anyone planning an overnight hunting expedition should avoid staying out beyond full moon. When moonlight is absent and the night sky is dark, hunter-gatherers stay close together, attempting to scare away predators by vocalizing as loudly as they can.

- *Blood.* Menstrual blood is a biological signal indicating imminent female fertility. To prevent males from responding by competing for fertile sex, hunter-gatherers across Africa attribute supernatural potency to menstruation in ways that galvanize both sexes into gendered cooperation, successful hunting, childcare, sharing, conservation, and economic abundance (Knight 1991; Power and Aiello 1997; Power 1999; Lewis 2008; compare Testart 1985, 1986).
- *Hunting versus gathering.* Females menstruate and become pregnant; males do not. Women might conceivably climb for honey and hunt big game animals, but in real life they prefer to use their attractions and solidarity to get men to do this for them. In addition to gathering plant foods, women assume responsibility for magically ensnaring large game animals, tying up their spirits while leaving the physical act of killing to men. Women's ability to contribute supernaturally depends on their solidarity and consequent sexual autonomy—their freedom to link legitimate sex with male hunting success and the proper sharing out of meat (Lewis 2002, 2008, 2009).

The moon, menstrual blood, and the facts of sexual difference are natural universals. As hunter-gatherers across sub-Saharan Africa respond to the challenges posed, they generate cultural and symbolic universals. Since the underlying strategies are not arbitrary—since they are optimal and likely to prove evolutionarily stable—they broadly suggest the initial configuration from which hunter-gatherer symbolic and other cultural traditions ultimately derive.

Here, in brief, is our speculative hypothesis:

- Dexterity in the vocal-auditory channel was selected via two main pathways: males developed techniques of vocal mimicry for use in hunting; females with offspring would periodically sing for their lives in defiant/defensive choruses aimed against predators.
- Female coalitions elaborated techniques of choral synchrony to inhibit not only external predators but also threatened outbreaks of human male sexual aggression or other unacceptable behaviour.
- As a result, violence was progressively outlawed as a male strategy for gaining access to females, and a normative order was imposed.
- As men collectively gave way to women's sexual strategies, adult life became structured by rituals which extended the principles of childhood play.
- Rooted in primate play, linguistic creativity had long been a biological potential of the species. That potential was realized as a consequence of these revolutionary new social arrangements.

21.4 From prey into hunter

Evolving hominins, like hunter-gatherers across Africa to this day, had two contrast-ive relations with animals: that of being both hunter and victim (Hart and Sussman 2005). Mbendjele BaYaka living in the forests of northern Congo-Brazzaville regu-larly experience predation and attack by large dangerous animals—particularly leopards, elephants, buffalo, and gorilla. Yet they also hunt these and other animals. The profound psychological reversals involved as predators discover that they are hunted prey and prey animals discover that they are hunters have been of theoretical interest to cognitive anthropologists due to their ubiquity in structuring ritual (Bloch 1992) and their incorporation into cosmological systems (Descola 1993; Viveros de Castros 1998).

Mbendjele men, in common with numerous other hunters across the world,[3] mimic many of their favourite game animals' calls in order to lure them to approach and so kill them more easily. When in the presence of large, dangerous animals, they may try to avoid alerting them by mimicking bird-calls or silently signing—for example by bending over a sapling, pointing leaves in a certain direction or resorting to manual signing in place of speech. In story-telling, they tend to use the charac-teristic sounds of an encounter—the animal calls, thrashings of branches, departures and arrivals—in preference to verbal descriptions of key events.

When Mbendjele hunters use their vocal lures against unsuspecting prey animals, the sounds don't count as symbols. After all, the animal victim on each occasion accepts the fake at face value and is straightforwardly deceived. By contrast, when human hunters re-enact the events in subsequent story-telling, the listeners around the camp fire are not going to be deceived. They'll recognize full well that the 'elephant' or other animal supposedly roaring is no such thing—it's all just make-believe. When vocal signals are accepted and circulated despite being patently false, we may say, following Sperber (1975), that the sounds now qualify as 'symbolic'. With fictional status acceptable, costly signalling constraints no longer apply—leaving signallers to prioritize content and communicative efficiency. Potentially at least, we are on the road toward spoken language.

By way of justification, recall the American philosopher Charles Sanders Peirce (1940), who distinguished between *symbols* (arbitrarily linked with their object), *icons* (similar to their object), and *indices* (physically connected with their object). Only Peirce's third category of sign—his 'index'—is not fake. By primate standards, *both* 'symbol' *and* 'icon' fall into the 'fake' category, since there is no built-in component

---

[3] These practices among traditional people across the world have their modern counterparts. Com-mercially available game calls are widely used in Canada, Europe, and North America to attract wildfowl, turkey, and many other birds; antelope, bear, bobcat, cougar, coyote, deer, elk, fox, jackal, lynx, moose, rabbit, raccoon, wild boar, wolf, and others.

of reliability. But symbolism is more than just fakery. To qualify as a symbol, a fake or replica must meet two further conditions:

(1) Instead of being confused with the original, it must be acknowledged as distinct.
(2) Instead of being rejected on those grounds, it must be accepted and socially circulated.

Now let's return to the Mbendjele. Whenever Mbendjele women go into the forest in search of food, they keep together in as large a group as possible, singing loudly. Why do they do this? According to the women themselves, it's to ward off dangerous animals. When camping in certain parts of the forest, women insist on singing through the night. Each achieves a highly integrated yodelling melody that combines with others sung by neighbours to produce the polyphonic song. The challenge is to listen and attune one's own voice to others in the chorus, accurately timing each note. It could be that such exquisitely synchronized choral singing deters predators by exaggerating the apparent size of the group, rather as synchronized roaring by coalitions of lionesses conveys information about their numerical strength (McComb et al. 1994). Our view is that Mbendjele women's own interpretation of their singing is probably right.

The dangers women sense are particularly acute on dark, moonless nights. At such times during their spirit play rituals, women claim to be hungry. They call on the menfolk to bring them meat, their demands accompanied by sexual humour and teasing. Temporarily defying their husbands, women loudly conduct intimate conversations with the now-invisible moon—acknowledged by all as women's 'biggest husband' (Lewis 2002, 2008). The moon's intimate presence is felt in the form of menstruation (*ama die na uwedi:* 'I am with the moon'), the odour of which, it is said, attracts dangerous animals. As the women sing, calling the forest spirits into being, they sit with limbs and bodies intertwined, forming a tangled, compact mass. The sounds enchant everyone and everything, including most importantly the forest spirits. If the plan is to hunt elephants, special songs (*yelle*) are used to magically ensnare one of these. Women's ability to do this—to 'please the forest'—depends on the level of beauty and synchronicity achieved as they sing. Taking our cue from the Mbendjele, it seems likely that women's choral singing—singing as if one's life depended on it—forms part of the explanation for the evolution of the remarkable vocal abilities underlying and prefiguring human speech (see Merker 2000; Mithen 2005).

We favour our ingroup/outgroup model because we can see no other way of explaining how the reliability constraints obstructing the tongue's involvement in primate vocal communication might have been side-stepped. In the case of both sexes, intentionally deceptive sounds are directed not at Machiavellian insiders capable of mounting resistance but outwards—against animals unable to resist fake versions of their species-specific calls. Whiten and Erdal (2012) explain:

Developing the cognitive niche has allowed human foragers to repeatedly mount.... 'evolutionary surprise attacks' on prey, escalating the arms race between predator and prey such that the latter cannot keep up, through biologically evolving counter-adaptations, with the more rapidly developing, intelligent new forms of assault based on weapons, traps, ambush styles and suites of other clever technological and behavioural innovations.

We would add *vocal deception* to the list of such 'clever innovations'.

21.5 'Rule from below': how female chimpanzees do it

Now let us turn to nonhuman primate social communication. In particular, can we discern anything which prefigures defiant choral singing?

The chimpanzee *waa*-bark is a loud, sharp sound (typically accompanied by threatening gestures such as arm-waving) emitted in response to social disturbance. Jane Goodall (1986: 130) explains:

The *waa*-bark is the comment so often interjected by bystanders during a conflict between others, and usually indicates sympathy for the victim. During a male attack on a female, other females present frequently provide a running commentary of *waa*-barks until the incident is ended. Often, when the victim of aggression becomes suddenly bolder after the event—as when he receives the support of an ally or as the aggressor displays away—his screams change to 'defiant' *waa*-barks.

Interestingly, the *waa*-bark suggests an element of 'normativity' (Lamm, Chapter 19) or even what Knight (2008b) has termed 'the rule of law'.[4]

Franz de Waal (1996: 91–2) describes an incident involving 'Jimoh'—the alpha male holding sway over a large group of chimpanzees in a spacious enclosure at the Yerkes Regional Primate Research Centre. Jimoh had recently discovered one of his favourite females secretively copulating with Socko, an adolescent male:

Socko and the female had wisely disappeared from view, but Jimoh had gone looking for them. Normally, the old male would merely chase off the culprit, but for some reason—perhaps because the female had repeatedly refused to mate with Jimoh himself that day—he this time went full speed after Socko and did not give up. He chased him all around the enclosure— Socko screaming and defecating in fear, Jimoh intent on catching him.

Before he could accomplish his aim, several females close to the scene began to 'woaow' bark. This indignant sound is used in protest against aggressors and intruders. At first the callers looked around to see how the rest of the group was reacting; but when others joined in, particularly the top-ranking female, the intensity of their calls quickly increased until literally everyone's voice was part of a deafening chorus. The scattered beginning almost gave the

---

[4] BaYaka women often make long, loud vocalizations such as '*wuuooo*' or '*wuuaaa*' when they observe violent interactions between members of the camp, especially those provoked by men. In addition to signalling imminent or actual violence, these loud calls get taken up by all the bystanders as a way of reminding participants of the serious potential consequences of what they are doing.

impression that the group was taking a vote. Once the protest had swelled to a chorus, Jimoh broke off his attack with a nervous grin on his face; he got the message. Had he failed to respond, there would no doubt have been concerted female action to end the disturbance.

De Waal comments that it is during such moments that we human observers 'feel most profoundly that there is some moral order upheld by the community'. Christopher Boehm (1999: 166) examined several hundred hours of videotaped recordings of *waa*-barks in the wild, concluding that they tended to be 'given by subordinates expressing hostility to their superiors from a safe distance'. Interestingly, the barks used by females toward badly behaved males are internally redeployed versions of the very same 'mobbing' calls which they use to intimidate external threats such as pythons. Mixed with aggressive *waaas* and various hoots, such noisy vocal 'mobbing' is also heard when neighbouring chimpanzee patrols encounter one another and when hunting parties fend off threats posed by enraged bush pigs or colobus monkeys they are attempting to hunt.

Boehm's analysis (1999: 167, 169) is relevant to our themes because he sees coalitionary *waa*-barking as intrinsically ambivalent:

Clearly, this call (or set of calls) is not dedicated just to the expression of subordinate defiance. What does seem to hold constant, however, is that *waas* invariably express hostility—and that if fear is involved, it is suborned to hostility. When an alpha male begins to display and a subordinate goes *screaming* up a tree, we may interpret this as a submissive act of fear; but when that same subordinate begins to *waa* as the display continues, it is an open, hostile expression of insubordination....

A handful of scattered subordinate protests up in trees can be ignored by a superior as he displays, but an entire group *waa*ing in a context that suggests imminent physical intervention will get his attention. In this sense, *waa*-barks provide a signal by which individuals in various roles can read the political dynamics that are taking place in their group. The subordinates, if they sense enough support, may be emboldened to rebel in deed, rather than by voice alone.

This account of chimpanzee insubordination recalls Steven Pinker (1998: 551) on the subject of human laughter:

No government has the might to control an entire population, so when events happen quickly and people all lose confidence in a regime's authority at the same time, they can overthrow it. This may be the dynamic that brought laughter—that involuntary, disruptive, and contagious signal—into the service of humor. When scattered titters swell into a chorus of hilarity like a nuclear chain reaction, people are acknowledging that they have all noticed the same infirmity in an exalted target. A lone insulter would have risked the reprisals of the target, but a mob of them, unambiguously in cahoots in recognizing the target's foibles, is safe.

In this light, irreverent laughter may testify to the evolutionary importance of humour as a social levelling device (see Woodburn 1982; Lee 1988; Knight 2000; Lewis 2009), helping to sustain those distinctively human levels of in-group trust and mutuality on which linguistic creativity in turn depends.

21.6 Where do hunter-gatherers say it all started?

Western science has problems with the way hunter-gatherers conceptualize their world. Hard as it may be for us to appreciate the reasoning, hunter-gatherers not only across Africa but wherever they are found assume gender segregation as the primordial situation. Myths are not science in the Western sense, but as variations on stable themes, they can be richly informative about long-term historical continuities and processes of cultural change (Gow 2001; Lévi-Strauss 1970–1981). Here is a creation myth, in this case from the Mbendjele hunter-gatherers of the forests of northern Congo-Brazzaville:

In the beginning, the two sexes lived apart. The women caught fish and collected yams while, in a distant part of the forest, men hunted elephants and climbed for honey. Neither sex knew of the other's existence. To make girl babies, the women danced *Ejengi*, a fertility spirit. In the meantime, far away, the men would copulate with *mapombe*—a large hard fruit filled with white cream.

One day, Toli—the men's elder—was walking upstream when he noticed a piece of wild yam floating by. Only humans prepare yams by washing them in a stream. 'Aaa, people must be up there!' Toli thought. He walked on. Eventually, he heard voices. Approaching stealthily, he observed a new type of people dancing *Ejengi*. Babies could be seen falling from the spirit's raffia clothes.

Amazed, Toli returned to the men's camp, recounting all he'd seen. In disbelief, the men insisted on seeing with their own eyes. Next morning they set off, each carrying a parcel of honey. As they approached the women, they heard singing. Surrounding the females as if hunting wild pigs, each grabbed one for himself, beating her with his honeycomb. Struggling at first, the women soon tasted the honey. 'Tasty, ooo so tasty! Who are these people with such sweet things?', they exclaimed. Back at the women's camp, everyone enjoyed sex, the men abandoning their *mapombe* fruit.

Later, the women hid in the forest and secretly danced *Ejengi*. On discovering this, the men seized *Ejengi* for themselves. To this day, by monopolizing *Ejengi*, men have obliged women to come to them for sex in order to have children.

That's the men's version. In the women's, Toli (now a woman) actively leads the men to her camp:

She went to find the men. She entered their camp. When they saw her, the men all got erect penises. She had sex with them and told them about her friends back at her camp. The next morning the men left early, each carrying a parcel of honey. Toli led them all the way to the women's camp.

As the men arrived, the women were hostile at first. On tasting the honey, however, each demanded one man for herself. The men threw away their *mapombe* fruit and everyone had sex.

The women told the men to stay in camp while they looked for yam roots. One man followed them into the forest. He saw the women dancing *Ejengi*, with babies tumbling from the spirit's raffia clothes. He ran back and told the men. They said 'that's something for us men'. Confronting the women, they demanded *Ejengi*. The women gave it to them.

Men claim to have seized *Ejengi* by force. Women deny this, arguing that they made a gift of it. If they could afford to give *Ejengi* away, say the women, they must have been able to keep still better things. Whereas men's edge is superior physical strength—a brute fact—women's claimed superiority is some kind of spirit-power connected with the secrets of pregnancy and reproduction.

The men ambush the women using pig-hunting techniques. Is there no danger that male dominance and aggression—allowed free rein—might culminate in rape? Morna Finnegan (2008, 2013) explores this in her study of gender relations among the Mbendjele and other Central African forest hunter-gatherers. Accepting that the potential for rape is real, she argues that this very fact explains why 'the perpetual motion against dominance must be continually reinvented' (Finnegan 2008: 137). Although Mbendjele men stop well short of endorsing violence against women, they do tend to explore fear and their capacity to inflict physical harm. Women's countervailing solidarity depends, paradoxically, on provoking this threat in order to defeat it.

So decisively do women inhibit male aggression that the contest collapses into laughter and sexual play. The outcome is what Finnegan (2008: 218) terms 'communism in motion'—a never-ending pendulum swinging between male dominance and its celebratory overturn, between brute force on the one hand and, on the other, female collectivized attractiveness and corresponding power asserted through song, ribald laughter, and erotic play. The crucial point is that, finally, men opt to support the women in all this.

The Mbendjele word *massana* means both 'ritual' and 'play'. Women's answer to men's *Ejengi* is *Ngoku*, their own key ritual. Conceptualized as women's communal spirit, *Ngoku* acts out the mythic theme of the primordial 'rule of women'. As the performance begins, little boys run to their fathers and hide away. Men in nearby huts often retreat, some trying to ignore the raucous proceedings by escaping into the forest. As they disappear, the women seize the communal space, subordinating the entire community to their authority.

The female community link arms, charging up and down the length of the camp singing '*Ngoku! Ngoku!*' Older women lead the songs, which consist largely of insults such as '*Doto ba die ebe!*'—'*Old men are no good!*', or '*Mapindi ma mu bola!*'—'*Their testicles are broken!*' In one dance, the women lie on their backs rubbing their thighs together until they become frenzied and are lifted up from behind by an elder *Ngoku* initiate. In another dance, to much laughter, older initiates vividly mimic men attempting sex with the younger ones as they lie in the middle of camp.

Women graphically express erotic desire, which they can safely do only by acting in solidarity to defy male desire. Their teasing occasionally provokes an angry male response. But no man would dare to interrupt the performance; instead he must wait until it's over and then—if he insists—confront his wife. This may prove dangerous: he will quickly be surrounded by other women ridiculing him and supporting her. In addition to being intrinsically enjoyable, *Ngoku* makes it more likely that—as the pendulum swings back—subsequent relations with men will be on women's terms.

Do the men feel angry and humiliated? Not normally. They usually join in good-humouredly, eventually laughing at their wives' hilarious impersonations of themselves. These re-enactments are displayed with such exaggeration and parody as to provoke helpless laughter. Finnegan (2009: 34) comments:

When lines such as 'the penis is no competition' or 'their testicles are broken' are delivered by a line of oiled, painted, dancing women, their sting is somewhat softened.

In waging the battle of the sexes, then, women can afford to go the whole way—to the point of momentarily ruling over men. Lewis (2002: 132) describes the solidarity of each gender group when deployed against its opponent as a system of 'taunt and praise relations'. Men resist women's collective action—retaliating with impressive rituals of their own—but stop short of physical violence, insisting on victory only up to a point. Once satisfied, they draw back, minimizing sexual conflict and letting the pendulum swing back women's way.

To appreciate the significance of this pendulum, it may help if we view it against a wider evolutionary background. On Darwinian theoretical grounds, biologists *expect* male and female strategies to be in conflict (Trivers 1972; Gowaty 1997). The 'ideal male world', as Lucio Vinicius (2010: 145) puts it, 'is a large female harem kept by force'. 'The ideal female world', by contrast, is 'a combination of provisioning husbands, and freedom to choose male partners...'. A harem kept by force may be a male dream, but will always be a nightmare to females needing male commitment and assistance in provisioning their babies. Harems cannot develop among egalitarian ('immediate-return') hunter-gatherers because women are too demanding—they would not allow it. During the course of human evolution, if our line of argument is accepted, the male fantasy of competing for females in harems was roundly defeated. The battle of the sexes was won by the physically weaker side (Knight 1991, 1999, 2008c; Power et al. 2013).

21.7 The evolutionary significance of play

It was the anthropologist Gregory Bateson (1973) who first realized the theoretical significance of *play* for the origins of human symbolic communication. He observed that when young monkeys playfully 'bite' and 'chase' one another, their antics constitute violent aggression—except that the intended meaning is reversed. A 'nip' is an aggressive bite prefaced by the message '*this is play*'. The animal's preliminary play invitation—adoption of a play-face, for example—means, in effect, 'the aggressive actions which follow are not to be mistaken for real'. Each player can now afford to 'lose' for the sake of the game. Turn-taking—each partner's willingness to reverse roles—is as central to the logic of animal play as it is to the dynamics of human gossip and conversation (see Duncan 1972; Enfield and Sidnell, Chapter 8).

As monkeys and apes mature, it is *sex* which most decisively dispels the carefree atmosphere of their earlier years. Former playmates become deadly rivals. Conflict is endemic because in a fight over sex, neither side can afford to lose.

So how was sexual violence contained and transcended in the human case? The Mbendjele origin myth offers a clue. The story culminates in a play-fight. The men fight for the women—by throwing honeycombs at them. The women are happy to lose this particular fight, but insist on winning others—which the men are happy to lose in turn. Ritualized play pervades the very arena which, in other primates—chimpanzees, for example—leads recurrently to sexual violence. Among these and other African hunter-gatherers, sex no longer shuts down play. Instead, play—now scaled up as adult playful ritual—succeeds in transforming and pervading the entire arena of sex (see Knight 1999).

Until now, Darwinian models of human evolution have allowed little scope for play. It's as if play were not serious enough to be taken seriously. Yet when young animals play, they are at their most unpredictable and creative. During bouts of play, cognitive complexity finds direct expression in communicative gestures—suggesting a point of departure for the evolutionary emergence of language (Knight 2000; Lewis 2009). Whereas the vocal signals of young primates tend to be stimulus bound, inflexible, non-symbolic, and limbically controlled, their playful bodily antics are the very opposite. They are strikingly imaginative, unpredictable, incipiently symbolic, and cognitively controlled.

The Mbendjele word *massana*, as we have seen, means both ritual and play. When we adopt a hunter-gatherer perspective on such things, it becomes clear how many of our intellectual difficulties stem from the manner in which Western science carves up the world. We might do better to adopt hunter-gatherer categories and perspectives. From a Mbendjele standpoint, ritual grades imperceptibly into play, which in turn overlaps at many points with language (Lewis 2009; Lewis, Chapter 7). A similar perspective is adopted by Wyman (this volume). Signal evolution theory (Krebs and Dawkins 1984; see Power, Chapter 15) explains the key variable: whether and to what extent the receiver resists, ignores, or positively accepts the signal. Resistance forces signallers to repeat, amplify, and resort to multi-media display. Interest and acceptance has the reverse effect, allowing signals to be reduced to quiet, fast, abbreviated form. Instead of having to repeat the same signal over and over again (as when a chimpanzee emits a pant-hoot or waa-bark), each component of a sequence may contribute novel information. This evolutionary trajectory is the reverse of that leading to copulation screams or pant-hoots, culminating eventually in what biologists term 'conspiratorial whispering' (Krebs and Dawkins 1984), language being the most quiet, fast, and efficient example of all.

There were concrete reasons why it was evolving humans rather than other species who developed speech. In our evolutionary model, mothers with increasingly large-brained babies faced heavier and heavier childcare burdens, prompting them to resort to co-operative childcare (Hrdy 2009). No sooner had they got together to share childcare burdens than something else happened: women began discovering the collective capacity to square up to dominant males (Knight 1991; Power and Aiello 1997). Female-led resistance to dominance and sexual exploitation culminated eventually in 'reverse dominance' (Boehm 1999; Knight, Chapter 17; Power, Chapter 15), outlawing violence or physical threat as a viable reproductive strategy for males. This liberated human creative potential in many ways. Up until this point, play had remained largely restricted to immaturity, since the transition to adulthood invariably brought sex and sexual conflict into the equation. Once sexual violence had been marginalized, imaginative play (as we've seen in the case of *massana* among the Mbendjele) was free to extend without a break into adult life, increasingly embracing it and structuring it—to the point of becoming 'a foundation for hunter-gatherer social existence' (Gray 2009; see Lewis 2009; Whitehead, Chapter 12; Wyman, Chapter 13).

Too rarely do we recognize a human cultural kinship system for what it is—a rule-governed game. So it's important to stress that cultural or fictive kinship—kinship as understood by anthropologists—is just that. In formal terms, hunter-gatherer relationships operate between groups. A common pattern is that I treat my mother's sister *as if* she were my mother, my wife's sister *as if* she were my wife, my sister's children (woman speaking) *as if* they were my children (Morgan 1871; Knight 2008c; Hrdy 2009). If a man wants sex, he cannot simply get his way by raping a woman. In the case of any African hunter-gatherer, the condition of sexual access is that he satisfactorily performs bride-service, proving himself useful to his partner and her kin (Knight 2009).

To the men and women involved, the fictions of cultural kinship as a game appear solid and real (Huizinga 1955). As Wyman (Chapter 13) explains, collaborative pretence is the secret of institutional facts. What applies to sex and family life applies equally to economics and everything else: new entities emerge, *internal* to the particular game being played. Play capitalism, for example—and money, profit, mortgages, and interest seem perfectly real. Play something else and the landscape is dramatically changed (Searle 1995).

To develop our scenario into a testable model, we need to be more concrete. What would 'reverse dominance' look like and through what signals would it be displayed? We can work this out on the basis that its principle is defiance—*female* defiance in particular. Stereotypically 'female' roles must be systematically reversed (see Knight, Chapter 17, for further discussion). We might expect, in other words, roughly what we find among the Mbendjele—women's raucous singing, dancing, laughing, and sexual defiance. Among other things, performers are under pressure to proclaim a patent falsehood, insisting to outsiders that they are *not* what in fact they are. This is important because it suggests the identity of the world's first metaphorical construct. Since any alpha male would be seeking a partner of his own (human) species, of the opposite (female) sex, and currently in her fertile (ovulatory) period, it follows logically that defiant females should convey the opposite on each count, signalling '*wrong* species', '*wrong* sex'—and '*wrong* time' (Knight et al. 1995; Power and Watts 1997, 1999).

A speculative hypothesis, as detailed as this, may seem risky, since it is not difficult to imagine empirical evidence which would disprove it. The model might be falsified by a single example of recent or ancient hunter-gatherer rock art depicting marital sex. To date, none has been found. It's not that sex is prohibited in, say, the cave art of Ice Age Europe—but it has to be species- and/or gender-reversed, with animal brides, metamorphosis into animal shape, vulvas in association with game animals, women dancing with each other, and so forth (Power 2004). Anyone familiar with the initiation rites of African hunters and gatherers—particularly those celebrating a young woman's first menstruation—will be struck by the prominence of similar themes (Lewis-Williams 1981; Watts 2005; Power 2009; Power and Watts 1997, 1999). In the case of the Kalahari Bushmen (Lewis-Williams 1981), the girl at the centre of attention is playfully constructed as a game animal, the eland—and a *Bull* eland at that.

Whether in the Kalahari, the equatorial forests of the Congo or elsewhere across Africa, hunter-gatherer ethnographers have described how reverse dominance in the form of 'women's rule' is momentarily acted out in an atmosphere of sexual teasing, laughter, and gender-bending play. Performed by young and old alike, what westerners term 'rituals' are in fact high-spirited games—reverential but also joyful, playful, and mischievous.

In the Mbendjele creation myth, the battle of the sexes culminates in play. It might have ended in violence—but it doesn't. When a girl first menstruates, that is the moment of greatest risk. The danger is that by signalling her fertility to the world, her body will incite rival males to fight for her. To prevent the violence which might ensue, her relatives choose this as the moment to strike. Turning primate sexual politics upside down, African hunter-gatherer women construct menstrual onset as a celebratory ritual, one of many designed to subordinate sexual passion to the 'rule of law' (Knight 1999, 2008b, 2009; Knight and Power 2012). As the danger is averted— typically to the accompaniment of peals of laughter—the founding principles of hunter-gatherer morality, kinship, ritual, and economics are reinforced and renewed.

21.8 The reversal principle

All this prompts us to suggest a wider evolutionary pattern of mutually reinforcing reversals linking vocal mobbing, song, play, smiling, laughter, ritual—and the earliest beginnings of language. Solutions developed to deal with threats from outsiders, once redeployed internally within the social group, become transformed into their opposite. The common pathway is that a hostile act, when re-enacted under reversed social conditions, assumes a quite different form and conveys a quite different—socially positive—message.

For reversals of this kind to work, there must exist a dividing line between those who are 'in the know' and those who are not. A coalition entails such a boundary, excluding enemies and including friends. Establishing that boundary restructures signals on either side, giving each a dual aspect. A given signal is now threatening or reassuring, negative or positive, true or false—according to one's standpoint outside or inside the coalition. Note also that the inside/outside boundary is likely to fluctuate over time, hardening or dissolving according to the level of perceived threat. A signal expressing fear or alarm may reverse its meaning when repeated over time beyond a certain point. We may equally imagine a former threat display paradoxically serving as a demonstration of affection and trust; a grimace of fear morphing into a display of emotional security and relief; a manipulative falsehood reappearing among insiders as a statement of incontrovertible fact.

Turning to concrete examples, it is widely believed that the distinctively human smile evolved in some such way, originating in the nonhuman primate 'fear grin'—a gesture of tense, nervous submission (van Hooff and Preuschoft 2003). The relaxed human version of this primate facial expression—the good-humoured smile—would then be a fear-grin under reversed social conditions, once the threat originally provoking it had dissolved. The ethologist Eibl-Eibesfeldt (1989: 138) likewise argued that human laughter may be traced back to the rhythmic, hostile 'mobbing' vocalizations of group-living primates seeking to intimidate a common enemy. Laughter in the human case would then be vocal mobbing under reversed social circumstances, the rhythmic chorus now being enjoyed for its own sake once the former threat has unexpectedly dissolved.

Extending the argument, our suggestion in this chapter is that human symbolic culture emerged as coalitionary resistance to dominance culminated in 'reverse dominance' or 'rule from below' by an ungovernable collective (Boehm 1999, 2012; compare Erdal and Whiten 1994, 1996; Whiten and Erdal 2012). To the extent that ordinary primate dominance is sexual, reverse dominance—its logical antithesis—must equally be sexual (Knauft 1991, 2000; Knight 1991, 1999; Power, Chapter 15). As Mbendjele women demonstrate when dancing and singing *Ngoku*, the physically weaker sex *collectively reverses* stereotypically 'female' body language. Women's 'spirit' (*Ngoku*) is coterminous with this defiant reversal. While remaining seductive and sexy, they humorously mimic maleness to clarify that they are not right now yielding to male sexual desire.

21.9 How does vocal mimicry pave the way for grammar?

We have outlined a scenario in which deceptive vocal sounds, in being internally redeployed, begin to function in a quite different way—hinting at spoken language.

But language is more than a repertoire of imitated sounds. How did our ancestors get from a simple repertoire of vocal fakes to the complexities of grammar?

In their ground-breaking volume, *The Genesis of Grammar*, Bernd Heine and Tania Kuteva (2007) invoke 'grammaticalization'—that continuous historical process in which free-standing words develop into grammatical markers, while these in turn become ever more specialized and grammatical. For grammaticalization to start, according to these authors, you need only one thing: licence to innovate. Suppose an early speech community possessed just a few noun-like items such as 'spear', 'dance', or 'fire'. What would stop people from using these *as if they were* verbs? Once you have a noun meaning 'dance', why not use the same word to say 'let's dance'? Only if you were worried about grammar—only if you had the 'noun'-concept already in your head—would this pose any difficulty. Heine and Kuteva insist that categories like 'noun' and 'verb' arise out of usage; they certainly don't need to be hardwired in the human brain from the outset. They also point out that boundaries between categories are not as rigid as some theorists imagine. Over time, as the functions of words diversify, they become subject to subtle changes in the way they can be deployed. Preferences become habits, habits become grammatical rules. Before long, unconsciously and collaboratively, the community will have constructed for itself a fully grammaticalized language (Heine and Kuteva 2012; Hopper 1998; Hopper and Traugott 2003; Hurford 2012; Deutscher 2005; Steels, Chapter 24).

It is important to stress that once unleashed, grammaticalization is rapid:

Once words are sequenced to form linguistic units, grammar emerges naturally and rapidly within a few generations. The emergence of grammar in the first generation of speakers of a Creole attests to the speed of the process. The speed of the emergence of the first grammar at the inception of language is astronomical in comparison to the speed of Darwinian evolution' (Li 2002: 90).

In other words, the initial onset of grammaticalization is likely to have been explosive and revolutionary.

What factors might have blocked grammaticalization in the period before it took off? The age-old obstacle, we are arguing in this chapter, was the requirement for all signals to incorporate a costly component to demonstrate reliability. For as long as humans were restricted to signals of the kind necessary to overcome mistrust, there was no foundation on which grammaticalization could build. There is no fast, efficient, zero-cost way to overcome mistrust. On the other hand, as Steels (Chapter 24) points out, there would be no grammaticalization if efficiency didn't come first. If each meaningful element had to overcome listeners' mistrust, this would rule out efficiency and, by the same token, stop any known process of grammaticalization in its tracks. Roars, screams, pant-hoots, and comparably costly signals are just not the kind of entities that can be reduced, combined, or recursively structured in the manner that grammaticalization requires. For grammar to evolve, then, speakers must first be liberated from primate-style worries about reliability. Listeners must be prepared to give speakers the benefit of the doubt, evaluating 'truth' not signal by signal but on a longer term basis, postponing judgement until the entire utterance or conversation is complete, focusing at each point not on surface meanings but on underlying *communicative intentions*. The liberating freedom to 'lie' depends not only on the speaker: it presupposes encouragement and trust on the audience's part. Narrative can't evolve without this precondition, and neither can grammar. Far from punishing imaginative creativity, sympathetic listeners must go out of their way to reward it, valuing fictions, deviations, and even apparent errors as cues to what speakers may have in mind.

21.10 How the world was turned upside-down

As a constraint on speculation, we have tried to imagine an overarching metaphor—that is, an overarching literal falsehood—of such value to a community that it somehow survived, providing a template from which other valued fictions could be derived (see Lakoff and Johnson 1980; Deutscher 2005). Above all, we have sought to explain why the falsehood was not immediately rejected, as signal evolution theory (Maynard Smith and Harper 1995, 2003; Zahavi and Zahavi 1997) would predict. We have identified a candidate fiction which was collective, essential to the survival of that collective—and aimed at an 'enemy' who might have reason to collude.

These are tight constraints—so tight that in the animal world, they exclude the very possibility of language. Since language exists, the solution must somehow have been found. Returning to the Mbendjele, let's look again at *Ngoku*. Those women fresh from 'singing for their lives' in the forest have now returned back to camp. They redirect their singing toward a different, internal 'enemy'—their own menfolk. They do all they can to express erotic desire while resisting male desire.

At this point, something without evolutionary precedent occurs. The 'enemy' suddenly gives up and joins in. There are good Darwinian reasons why men might accept 'defeat' at the hands of women who are nursing their own genetic offspring (Knight 1999). It is men's willingness to yield which distinguishes them as fully human for the first time. Just as the fear-grin morphs imperceptibly into the smile and vocal mobbing turns into laughter, so women's defiant, boisterous singing and dancing—designed to make sexual violence unthinkable—collapses and reverses, yielding something else. That other thing, we suggest, is language-based human society.

Part V

The Journey Thereafter

Memory, imagination, and the evolution of modern language

SIMONA GINSBURG AND EVA JABLONKA

22.1 Introduction

Characterizing language as an imagination-instructing communication technology positions the question of the evolutionary facilitation and refinement of the capacity for imagination at centre stage (Dor 2011; Clay and Zuberbühler, Chapter 11). We argue that co-developmental and co-evolutionary relations among memory construction, pretend-play, and elementary linguistic communication were crucial for the evolutionary sophistication of instructive communication. Although the question of the selective conditions that could have promoted these co-evolutionary interactions is important, we do not discuss here the possible social and ecological conditions that could have selected for them. We focus on the mutually enabling, reinforcing, and constraining relations among some of the principal processes that had made the evolutionary construction of sophisticated imagination-instructing communication possible.

We start with archaic humans, a loose term including several varieties of *Homo* living at the period beginning half a million years ago. Archaic humans had large brains, reaching up to 1,400 cubic centimetres, a range that overlaps with that of modern humans (Cartmill and Smith 2009; de Sousa and Cunha 2012). The archaeological record suggests that they and their ancestors from the late Acheulian period lived in a complex social cultural niche: the process-standardization of their complex tools suggests they were good imitators, and employed intention-reasoning (Marks et al. 2001; Goren-Inbar 2011; Stout 2011). They lived in bands, and routinely used and tended fire, a 'tool' that was used in many contexts and dramatically altered their lifestyle and their facial morphology (Goren-Inbar 2011; Burton 2009; Wrangham 2009). Some engaged in big game hunting, and cooperated in both its planning and execution (Goren-Inbar 2011; Klein 2009). They colonized large parts of the world, and were able to cope with highly fluctuating environmental conditions (Potts 2007). Moreover, there are indications that red cosmetics (red ochre) were used around 400,000 years ago, suggesting that archaic humans may have performed rituals (Watts, Chapter 16). They also organized their family life in a way that is strikingly different from that of other great apes: humans are the only species of higher apes that practise alloparenting—the care of the young by individuals other than the mother (Hrdy 2009). Hrdy argues convincingly that alloparenting, mainly by female kin, may already have evolved in early hominins, around 1.6 million years ago, and was certainly an important aspect of archaic humans. The emotional profile of these archaic humans had evolved to facilitate their cooperative enterprises which necessitated a good theory of mind, and must have been based on compassionate emotional predispositions as those manifest in very young human infants (Tomasello 2008, 2009). We have suggested that these hominins manifested the social emotions of pride, guilt, shame, and embarrassment, which reinforced cooperative alliances and social coordination (Jablonka et al. 2012). Cultural learning, including natural pedagogy (Csibra and Gergely 2011), probably occurred in many situations and in many ways.

The communication system that enabled the coordination required by such a cooperative and demanding social life-style is assumed to have been fairly well developed, but still far from the fully syntactic symbolic language of modern humans, consisting of a limited vocabulary of modern-word equivalents and their limited combinations (Bickerton 2007, 2009). Such linguistic technology is already instructive, allowing communication beyond the here-and-now of experiential communication, and transcending the constraints of earlier representational-mimetic communication (Donald 1991; see Clay and Zuberbühler, Chapter 11). We argue that such word-based communication entailed a new type of recall—*word-based episodic recall*. Recall and imagination—which consists of reconstructing and recombining representations of past experiences to generate novel ones—became free of the experiential cues that were part of individuals' past experiences. This divorce was fundamental to the process of instructive communication because traces of past private episodes became accessible to recall and imagination-instructing communication, both with others and with oneself. The ability to voluntarily recall a train of episodes gave the individual an insight into others' minds as well as into her own mind. In this chapter we discuss the developmental-evolutionary relations between the emergence of episodic recall and the early stages of instructive linguistic communication, which—we suggest—were mediated through pretend-play.

22.2 The co-evolution of language and memory

Chauncey Wright was the first evolutionist to develop a theory of the evolution of human self-consciousness based on the evolution of semantic memory and language (Wright 1873). He suggested that selection for improved memory led to the ability to recall internal semantic representations that stand for heard or seen communication signs. While in non-human animals representations of communication signs are transient and depend on the temporal persistence of the perceived sign, the evolution of increasingly better memory in the human lineage led to the ability to memorize the communicative signs *as signs*, rather than mere parts of the experienced specific situation. This distinction, Wright argued, resulted in the construction of a new layer of representations mediating between the representations of private episodic past experiences and the associated, transient representation of immediately perceived communication signs. To illustrate this point, he proposed that although the cry 'fox!' may elicit hunting behaviour in both a human hunter and a trained dog, the word is not available to the dog as a memorized sign that it can recall at will even when it is not externally uttered, as it is for the human hunter.

A century after Wright's suggestion that humans, unlike other animals, have distinct (yet co-dependent) systems of mental representation—the experiential-private and the semantic-sign-based—Tulving (1972, 2002) introduced the important distinction between episodic and semantic memory systems: between the recall of episodes of private experiences, which in humans can be incorporated into a sequence constructing one's autobiographical memory, and the recall of semantic knowledge, that is, recall of categories and concepts. What we know about the categorization and discrimination ability of animals suggests that vertebrates are likely to have rich bound experiences in the here-and-now of their lives. However, it is not clear how rich and integrated the *recall* of these experiences is. Although more and more studies of birds, mammals, and even bees show that they display what psychologists call 'episodic-like' recall, the true episodic nature of this recall is debated (reviewed by Crystal 2010). There is no doubt, however, that the communicable semantic representations of animals, which are based on their categorization ability, are scarce compared to those of humans. Although animals do have collective representations of some communication signs, these semantic categories are relatively few in number and most are not jointly identified. It is likely that animals' consequent more modest ability to form links between their few stable semantic representations and their rich but transient episodic representations, does not enable the consolidation of their ephemeral episodic memory and consequently limits their episodic recall.

It is plausible that the evolution of episodic recall in archaic humans was related to their far richer semantic knowledge based on the social complexity of their practices and the manufacturing of sophisticated tools. Both the social life of archaic humans, which required good recall and updating of relationships and social situations, and their cooperative foraging that included the manufacturing of the complex late Acheulean tools (Sterelny 2012), necessitated information sharing, focused attention, causal reasoning, the recognition of functions and goals, patience, tenacity, tolerance of apprentices' and cooperators' mistakes, and executive control (reviewed by Vaesen 2012 with respect to tool-making). A good ability to memorize and recall long sequences of actions was a crucial part of this suite of mental adaptations: it is the persistence of neural representations in working memory that enables the execution of cognitive tasks (Aboitiz et al. 2006, 2010).

We suggest, following and extending Wright's suggestion, that in archaic humans with an already elementary form of instructive communication, it was the accumulation of learned symbols which refer to each other as well as to things, processes, and relations in the external world—the formation of a rich symbolic network—that enabled the *recall* of episodes. Humans have a rich layer of semantic representations linking the partial representations of past (episodic) experiences with the representations of recalled signs (e.g. specific words) referring to aspects of those experiences. This thick, socially learned layer of semantic representations is formed during human development, during the first years of childhood. Facets of episodic representations of private experiences become generalized through joint-identification and linguistic labelling, which enable the formation of semantic-linguistic representations. Modern humans have a large repertoire of constructed linguistic concepts and structures, which interact with their on-line episodic representations, forming, as episodic experiencing occurs, numerous links between these systems of representation. The reactivation of these links enables the later recall of rich episodic experiences. Consequently, the only episodic experiences that can be recalled *as episodes* are those that have been formed through an interaction with linguistic signs of an already existing, rich, semantic network.

Studies of human memory support this view: recollections are elicited only through responses or words that were available at the time of encoding, a phenomenon that explains some important aspects of childhood amnesia (the inability to retrieve episodic memories of events that occurred before 2–4 years). Richardson and Hayne (2007) proposed that memories of episodes that occur very early in life are not translated across stages of development unless they are updated. Their studies suggest that memories maintained in the same representational format in which they were originally encoded; memories of events that occurred before the linguistic phase cannot be recalled and integrated through words and do not form episodic recollections. This, however, does not preclude the possibility that pre-linguistic children's recall is *episodic-like*, and experiments similar to those performed on animals should be performed to assess this possibility.

Once humans used linguistic cues for recall and for the reconstruction of private experiences, a new problem emerged: how can an individual know whether her linguistically constructed private experience has actually occurred, or whether she was told about it and/or imagined it? While at previous evolutionary stages, who *did* what to whom, when, how, and why, was monitored and was the basis of mentalizing, when instructive communication appeared, individuals needed to know, in addition, who *said* what to whom, when, how, and why. The problem of distinguishing between one's own experiences and something one has imagined or has been told about is a difficulty for modern humans (Schacter 2001), and it must have been far more significant during the evolutionary stages before language-based recall was consolidated. 'False memories'—what in children is known as 'source amnesia' (Gopnik 2009)—must have been very common, and could have led to confused causal reasoning, inadequate decision making, and psychological manipulation by others. There must therefore have been strong selection for differentiating between one's own experiences and experiences communicated by others, and this may have led to the developmental stabilization of autobiographical memory that locates an experience within the stream of the individual's biographical history. Hence, once the initial stages have been in place, language affected through both the opportunities and the problems it creates, a further development of semantic memory associated with an integrated sense of agency.

Wright's suggestion, then, that the evolution of memory contributed to the evolution of human language and self-consciousness is certainly part of the story of language evolution. But his account leaves open some important questions. For example, Wright assumed that a special memory system *for signs* had emerged as a result of selection for improved general, largely procedural, memory. But why should improved general memory (which may have evolved for many interrelated reasons, such as increase in group-size and social complexity, ecological fluctuations, and so on) lead to a new sign-based memory system, to a new level of representation? As we pointed out earlier, for a systematic distinction between the sign and the signified to become established, additional factors must have accompanied and interacted with an expanded, general memory. These factors include the material and social technologies of those hominins (Hrdy 2009; Sterelny 2012), a way of communication that was already recursive (Corballis 2011), and the emotional preconditions enabling information-sharing (Tomasello 2008, 2009; Jablonka et al. 2012). In addition, the early developmental conditions that allowed signs to become dissociated from specific experiences, and the conditions that enabled the recombination of signs and the rules for their recombination, need to be considered. We believe that the long childhood of humans and the emergence of children's pretend-play, which is the basis of mature causal and analogical reasoning, were important enabling conditions for the evolution of the human-specific memory system that is part of language.

22.3 Analogical thinking and pretend-play

One of the most important aspects of prolonged childhood is the opportunity it provides for exploration through play. Play behaviour in vertebrates is a very basic trait that promotes learning (Pellegrini and Smith 2004; Bateson 2005); it is the means through which the young construct and practise their budding motor, perceptual, and social skills. Human children engage in play for a very long period, and this is obviously related to their late maturation. A correlation between late maturation and an increase in brain size is characteristic of many mammalian species (Barton and Cappellini 2011), but in humans, childhood is particularly extended, and the rapid growth rate of the brain during the first years of life is far more protracted than that of chimpanzees (Leigh 2004). A recent study suggests that a general increase in neural plasticity in humans is related to their late neural maturation. There is an extreme shift in the timing of synaptic development in the prefrontal cortex in humans, with peak gene expression of neural genes in this area occurring at less than one year in chimpanzees and macaques and at five years in humans (Liu et al. 2012). Children's slowly maturing brain makes them dependent on their parents for a long time and it is during this time that their cognition and emotions are shaped by cultural learning (Tomasello 2008, 2009, 2011).

Hrdy (2009) linked human children's long maturation to their play behaviour. She argued that cooperative alloparenting, which led to more prolonged childhood, enabled children to engage in an extended period of play behaviour, and the advantages accrued through the recruitment of early brain plasticity for learning-through-play led to the evolution of even more slowly developing human brain and to increased brain-size. It is inevitable that as soon as motor and vocal imitation made their appearance in hominins' development, they were practised in children's play.

We suggest that pretend-play, which has precursors in the great apes (Mitchell 2002) had its origins in the intersection between the ability to imitate motor and vocal activities and signs with infants' play behaviour. Pretend-play, or symbolic play, first appears at around 12 months and develops into an increasingly integrated and abstract symbolic scheme for the next 12 months (Hughes 2010). Children, like all mammals, crave play, and, being good and highly motivated imitators already at 12 months, they imitate those around them—parents, alloparents, other children, animals. They also expect others to imitate them, and engage in role reversals, extending reversal to inanimate objects, pretending, for example, that a doll or a teddy-bear is alive and will behave like them (eat, wash, chase, etc.). The early displays of representational play in pre-linguistic children and young bonobos (Mitchell 2002; Lyn et al. 2006), as well as play behaviour in gorillas (Tanner and Byrne 2010), can be seen as the first manifestation of a metaphorical faculty which is later co-opted for language (Modell 2003).

It seems plausible that extensive engagement in mimetic-representational play was selectively advantageous because exercising imitative acts had large effects on all aspects of imitation-based cultural learning, including imitated conventional gestural and vocal signs. When imitated activities are incorporated into different contexts of play, imitated vocalization or gestures can become uncoupled from the specifics of a particular situation, and acquire a general abstract meaning, which can be recognized as a property common to *any* imitated communication sign. This is the crux of William James' suggestion that a greatly enhanced ability to associate-by-similarity is the hallmark of human reasoning, and that language has its origin in the recognition that any sign and any imagined signified have the same sign–signified (abstract) relation. James went on to argue that the recognition of errors, or false (imagined) expectations, make the child recognize and generalize the difference between sign and signified (James 1990 [1890]). It is, however, far more likely that such recognition and abstraction mainly occurs in play situations, especially during pretend-play, which include counterfactuals. Play leads to pleasure and to repetition with variations of the pleasurable activities—especially when it includes several participants— enhancing both causal and metaphorical reasoning.

Advanced stages of pretend-play coincide with the development of language (Lewis et al. 2000; Hughes 2010), and are impaired in autistic children (Rutherford et al. 2007). Child-like manifestations of advanced stages of pretend-play can also be observed in language-instructed apes (Lyn et al. 2006), suggesting that representational play manifesting sensitivity to social interactions is an ancestral, highly plastic trait. As indicated in the framework suggested by Dor and Jablonka (Chapter 2), such culturally learned plastic traits can evolve to become strong dispositions when social-cultural evolution guides the evolutionary process leading to genetic accommodation. We therefore disagree with Carruthers (2002), who proposed that the disposition to engage in pretend-play first appeared only 40,000 years ago, and led to the explosion in human creativity around this time and to fully fledged language. The child-development and ape studies suggest a far earlier origin.

Engagement in pretend-play has several interesting implications that are involved in the scaffolding of the ability to abstract the relations between signifier and signified and to engage in metaphorical reasoning. First, during children's play, actions and their emotional triggers have to be controlled; although the roots of this play-related inhibition are seen in the play behaviour of other vertebrates, pretend-play requires stronger inhibitions because of the expanded range of playfully controlled and explored situations. This inhibition contributes to the control of drives, especially aggression and fear, which is necessary for a highly cooperative lifestyle (Jablonka et al. 2012). Second, words themselves begin to be objects of pretend-play. Words, for children, are fascinating toys, passionate objects of play, just like any other type of local technology, and children crave playing with words and combinations of words when these become available to them. We suggest, therefore, that the language-craving mind that Dor (2011) posits has its roots in children's social pretend-play. Children language-games, with one word or phrase standing for another, provide important scaffolding for the human-specific ability to relate relations, as suggested by Rational Frame Theory advocates (Hayes et al. 2001), and expand language's expressive realm through the use of metaphors. Third, once pretend-play becomes social games, they follow some implicit and explicit rules, thus facilitating socialization and the recognition of norms, including linguistic norms (see Lamm's account, Chapter 19). Gray (2009) highlights this point by putting forward arguments suggesting that among children in hunter-gatherer societies, social play, and especially pretend play, is used to counteract tendencies toward dominance, and is deliberately used for that purpose. Fourth, pretend play fosters causal reasoning, since the pretended acts have consequences which are actively explored by the child in the context of the game (Buchsbaum et al. 2012), and the effects of *pretend-speech-acts* are an important part of this exploration. Fifth, the huge plasticity children manifest through exploratory and pretend-play is responsible for the streamlining of the inventions of adults: what adults had invented with difficulty in the previous generation becomes the playful object of the children in the present one (Avital and Jablonka 2000). We may infer, on the basis of Savage-Rumbaugh's work on language-instructed apes (Savage-Rumbaugh et al. 2001), that such inventions included linguistic innovations.

Language is part of a large suite of human social practices and cognitive-emotional capacities, and its cultural-genetic evolution needs to be understood as part of such an evolving ensemble, where each capacity scaffolds and constructs others and is constructed and scaffolded by them. In this chapter we have focused on the evolution of imagination, and stressed two aspects of it: the emergence of semantic and episodic recall and symbolic play. We argued that the evolution of semantic and episodic memory that enabled the voluntary exercise of imagination evolved in the context of expanded childhood, in particular in the context of children's play.

23

Transmission biases in the cultural evolution of language: towards an explanatory framework

N. J. ENFIELD

23.1 Introduction

In any natural, causal account of linguistic transmission, an important role is played by biases that ultimately regulate the historical, cumulative development and maintenance of language. The existence of transmission biases largely presupposes the evolution of a capacity for cumulative culture in our species, and should ideally give us some insight into that initial phylogenetic transition. In this chapter I draw on the conceptual background of research on transmission biases in cultural diffusion, with an emphasis on the historical evolution of language, and I will point to the need for a coherent conceptual framework within which to explain just why we observe the biases we observe. After sketching a proposal for such a framework, I conclude by pointing toward some lines of research that this opens up.

23.2 Linguistic epidemiology

In the diachronic evolution of language, that is, the diffusion, maintenance, and change of linguistic practices in historical communities, it is often assumed or implied that the unit of analysis is the language system as a whole. But the replication and transmission of whole language systems is not causally conducted at the system level. It is an aggregate outcome of a massive set of much simpler and much smaller concrete speech events that operate on the elements which form part of any language, such as words or pieces of grammar (Hudson 1996). Language systems only exist because populations of linguistic items replicate and circulate in human communities, where these items are directly observable as elements of spoken utterances (Croft

2000; Enfield 2003, 2008). A causal account of language evolution and change focusing on the transmission of linguistic items can be termed an epidemiological account, following Sperber (1985, 1996), and in a similar spirit to Keller (1994) and Croft (2000). In an item-based account, pieces of a language can change independently from other pieces, and they can be plucked out and borrowed from one system to another, as for example when we borrow a word. Of course, the notion of 'item' is an abstraction. An item is always defined by sets of relations. And all sets of relations are embedded in further such sets, and again in further such sets, and so on seemingly without limit, as any grammarian well knows. This is why an item-based account must also ultimately be linked to higher-level linguistic systems. But we must avoid a temptation to think of these coherent systems as organisms with bodies. Languages are not organisms. While, ultimately, we need a causal account for why it sometimes seems like we can treat language systems as if they were distinct and coherent units (e.g. when we write grammars), it is first necessary to define the basic underlying causal anatomy of item-based language transmission. Here I outline the basics of a transmission biases approach to the historical evolution of languages.

23.3 Biased transmission

The diffusion of linguistic items is best understood in terms of a biased transmission model of the distribution of knowledge and practice within human populations and across generations, following a general framework of cultural epidemiology (Sperber 1985, 1996; Boyd and Richerson 1985, 2005; Enfield 2003, 2008). In a biased transmission model, the question of whether fashions of linguistic practice in a population spread, decline, transform, or remain as they are will be determined by the cumulative effect of a range of biases which ultimately serve as filters or pumps in a competition for social uptake.

Linguistic items are not confined to the mind, nor to perceptible performance alone, but are simultaneously manifest in mental and material domains, and in relations between these domains. At any given moment, a human population is abuzz with a mesh of ongoing causal chains that constitute continuous trajectories of production and comprehension of item-level patterns of behaviour. I am referring to all of the situated courses of behaviour in which people carry out goal-directed action by means of words, grammatical constructions, body movements, and other communicative items. These trajectories of behaviour are the contexts in which the natural histories of linguistic items are played out. They constitute causal chains with links from mind (e.g. I know a word), to usage (I utter the word in a communicative act), to mind (my addressee learns or recognizes the word), to usage, to mind, to usage, to mind, to usage, and on. We may call this type of causal trajectory a chain of iterated practice, or a cognitive causal chain (Sperber 2006). See Figure 23.1 for a simplified illustration.

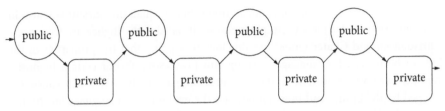

FIGURE 23.1 A chain of iterated practice, or a cognitive causal chain (after Sperber 2006).

Figure 23.1 is not the same as the 'iterated learning' chains presented by Kirby and colleagues (2004, 2008), Christiansen and Chater (2008), among others. Those iterated learning depictions resemble Figure 23.1, but they are not the same. In iterated learning, each arrow from public to private may represent the summary of an entire learning process such as a child's learning of a language. Each link in the chain is effectively a single macro-level state change in ontogeny (e.g. the move from not knowing the language to knowing the language). This is shorthand for a great set of small events and small associated state changes taken together. Learning a language involves not one event but many iterations of exposure and reproduction, and in each occasion of exposure and reproduction there is feedback that comes from others' reactions to our usage of words for communicative goals in context. This feedback plays an essential role in learning. The iterated learning model abstracts away from these details (not without practical reason), while the iterated practice model in Figure 23.1 attempts to capture them directly and explicitly. While iterated learning focuses on the ontogenetic or biographical timescale, iterated practice focuses on the enchronic timescale, that is, the timescale of moves and counter-moves in sequences of human interaction (Enfield 2009a: 10; Enfield 2011: 285–91, 2013: ch. 4). In Figure 23.1, each link in the chain from private–public–private does not represent a generation of individuals in a human population (by contrast with the comparable figure in Christiansen and Chater 2008). It represents one local cycle of instantiation of a practice, such as a single use of a word.

The schema in Figure 23.1 draws our attention to a set of little bridges that a bit of language has to cross if it is to survive a cycled of iterated practice. What are the forces that facilitate the passage across those bridges, and what are the forces that inhibit it? These forces are called transmission biases (following Boyd and Richerson 1985, 2005). This kind of account assumes a standard model of Darwinian evolution (variation of heritable characters in a population), but where the variation is guided in a specific way. As Boyd and Richerson (1985) formulate it, variation of cultural items (including linguistic items) is guided by the properties of human agents. If, for example, a certain way of doing something is easier to learn than some other functionally equivalent way (e.g. doing maths on an abacus versus on a calculator), then this greater ease is likely to increase the frequency of the easier variant in the population, and, all things being equal, this variant will also in turn increase in frequency simply because it is already higher in frequency. Christiansen and Chater (2008) use this idea in arguing that the properties of the human brain, e.g. for language learning and processing, favour certain linguistic variants over others, leading to the view that language is the way it is because it is 'shaped by the brain', and thus not because the evolution of a language faculty has caused the human brain to change in some fundamental way as a result of how language is.

Assuming this model of guided variation, the question then becomes: What are the forces that serve to guide variation in this way, and that operate upon different linguistic variants within a population, ultimately determining whether they become, or remain, conventional in the population? We now consider some of the known biases.

23.4 Some previously described transmission biases

Variants of linguistic behaviour compete for adoption by individuals in human populations. Different researchers have described different biases, sometimes in quite specific terms, sometimes in broader terms. For example, Chater and Christiansen (2009) describe four factors that mostly have to do with properties of the individual human body, especially the brain: (1) perceptuo-motor factors, (2) cognitive limitations on learning and processing, (3) constraints from mental representations, and (4) pragmatic constraints. These factors can affect the likelihood that one linguistic variant is selected over another, though the social mechanisms that are also a necessary part of the process are left implicit by these authors. By contrast, Boyd and Richerson (1985) introduce distinctions that are broader in kind. A direct bias concerns the relationship between the variant and the adopter, and thus it concerns affordances (Gibson 1979). An individual should choose variant A if it is somehow more advantageous than variant B for a proximate function in a given context. Thus, by a direct bias we should choose a linguistic variant that is easier, more efficient, more effective. An indirect bias works with reference to a notion of social identity, assuming that the variant a person selects will be seen by others and that this will lend a certain status to both the adopter (as the kind of person who adopts that variant) and the variant (as a variant that is adopted by that person or someone like that). We adopt variants of behaviours not only for their proximate efficacy but also with some notion of how we will be seen by others when we make that choice. So by an indirect bias we should choose the same turn of phrase, say, as people who we identify with, or want to emulate. Finally, a frequency-dependent bias favours variants that are more frequent.

Similar biases have been described in a vast literature in sociology on the diffusion of innovations (Rogers 2003). Here, we can discern three sets of conditioning or causal factors in the success or failure of a practice. First, *sociometric factors* concern the network structure of demographic groups. Different individuals are differently socially connected, especially in terms of the number of their points of connection to others in a social network, as well as the quality (e.g. intensity) of these connections. A practice is more likely to spread if it is being modelled by someone who is widely connected in a network, simply because he or she will expose a greater number of people to the practice. Gladwell (2000) refers to this as the law of the few. Second, *personality factors* concern differences between individuals in the population that can have consequences for the success or failure of an innovation. Some people are more willing than others to innovate and to adopt others' innovations (early adopters versus laggards). And these differences may correlate with social categories such as age, class, and sub-culture. Some people are better known or better admired in their social milieu and may thus be more likely to be imitated. Third, there is the sheer *utility* of an innovation, more or less what Boyd and Richerson (1985) mean by direct bias, outlined above. The innovation will take off if it is more advantageous to potential adopters.

The biases that we have just reviewed might be seen as a somewhat unstructured, *ad hoc* list. It is clear that they each play an important role in the mechanisms of transmission that drive the circulation of bits of language in human populations. But how to explain them? Where do these biases come from and how are they related to each other? How can we limit this possibility space? Can we motivate these biases by locating them directly in the causal anatomy of transmission? What predictions are possible?

One way to motivate and constrain the possibility space of transmission biases is to develop an explanatory framework that is grounded in the basic structure of iterated practice shown in Figure 23.1. Let us now see how this structure gives us a way of locating and characterizing the biases. This is illustrated in Figure 23.2. If we examine the elements of transmission illustrated in Figure 23.2, we see at the heart of it a repeating, four-stroke cycle of transmission consisting of the following steps:

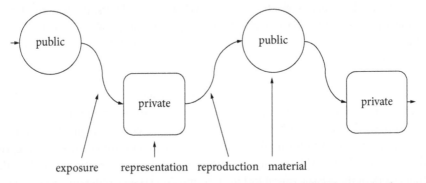

FIGURE 23.2 Loci for transmission in a four-stroke engine model (building on Sperber 1985, 1996, 2006): exposure (world-to-mind transition), representation (mind structure), reproduction (mind-to-world transition), and material (world structure).

(1) *Exposure*, a process of going from public to private, made possible by a mind and body coming into contact with, and perceiving/engaging with, the public instantiation of a bit of language;

(2) *Representation*, the storing and organizing of a private construct based on (1), and the private product of this process (i.e. linguistic competence);

(3) *Reproduction*, a process of going from private to public, made possible in part by an individual's motivation to cause the same public event as in (1).

(4) *Material*, the material instantiation of the result of an event of reproduction of a linguistic item.

(5) Stages (3–4) can then lead to another round by exposing another person to the linguistic item in question (feeding into a new stage (1)).

Each of the four steps is a bridge or existential threshold for any bit of language to succeed or fail in the competition for uptake in a human population. If people aren't exposed to it, it will die. If it is difficult to represent mentally, or if in the course of mental representation it is radically altered, it will die, or effectively die. If people aren't motivated to reproduce it, no further exposure will happen, and with the biological death of those individuals who have mental representations of the practice in question will come the historical death of the practice, as happens for example with language extinction. And if the material realization of the practice is not available to the perception of others, the transmission process will stall. Failure on any of the four loci of transmission causes a break in the chain and may cause the variant to no longer exist.

It is important not to get the impression that a single such chain represents the entire historical trajectory of a linguistic item. It is only the tiniest strand. At any moment, there is a thicket of equivalent chains of iterated practice that keep a linguistic practice alive and evolving in the kind of sizable human population that constitutes a historical linguistic community.

As discussed above, the key question that a biased transmission approach to linguistic epidemiology seeks to answer is: What are the filters, pumps, and transformers in a linguistic item's career? On the present proposal, we can posit four functionally defined loci at which any bias may have an effect. Each locus is defined by the function it serves in accelerating, braking, or altering the transmission of practices in human populations through social-cultural interaction (i.e. at an enchronic level). While there may be a long, if not open, list of possible specific biases, they all should be definable in terms of how they operate upon one or more of the four transmission loci, exhaustively defined by the basic causal structure represented in Figures 23.1 and 23.2 above: exposure (world-to-mind transition), representation (mind structure), reproduction (mind-to-world transition), and material (world structure). Within the framework of these basic causal loci for transmission (1)–(4), different specific biases may affect the transmission of a practice in qualitatively different ways. As sketched above, some of these biases will have to do with facts about social networks; some with individual personality traits; some with properties of human perception, attention, memory, and action; some with culture-specific patterns of linguistic activity; and some with the organization of complex information in cognition. Let us now briefly consider how some of the previously described specific biases fit within the causal framework of these minimal loci for linguistic transmission.

Exposure (relating to the world-to-mind transition) is a locus at which biases can affect the likelihood that a person will come into contact with, and pay attention to, the practice. Following are some of the relevant biases:

- *Connectedness bias.* All people are situated in social networks, but they are situated in different ways. One type of difference between people concerns the number of other people we come into contact with. So-called connectors have a large number of social ties (Granovetter 1973), and so are more likely to be involved in an encounter with an innovation. Those who have few social network connections will have a lower chance of being exposed to a given linguistic practice.
- *Salience bias.* Once one is in the presence of a certain linguistic behaviour one may or may not pay attention to it. Things that stand out are more likely to be attended to. Some things are more likely to be noticed because of the nature of our perception (e.g. a word that is stressed will be more salient than one that is not). Other things are more salient to us because we are on the lookout for them, often because our language encourages or requires it.
- *Identity bias.* Who is the person carrying out the practice when it is encountered? If it is somebody who I want to 'be like' in some way, then I am more likely to pay attention to what the person is doing and how. If it is someone I have no affinity with, or desire to imitate, I will be less likely to inspect their linguistic behaviour. In this way, social identity can play a role in exposure biases, by affecting the extent to which someone will attend, or carefully attend, to the practice when encountered.

Representation (relating to mind structure) is a locus at which biases can affect the likelihood that, or the manner in which, a linguistic practice will be learnt or stored by a person, or how the psychological or otherwise private component of a practice will be structured.

Once we have come into contact with, or at least noticed, a linguistic practice, we can learn it. We form a representation of it, attributing to it some meaning or function, and we incorporate that representation in a framework of existing representations or knowledge. There are effects of the psychological context into which a linguistic practice is embedded. Like any structured domain, knowledge is characterized by structured patterns that include part–whole relations, hierarchical relations, and other sorts of dependency among items in a system—this is especially clear in the case of language. When we learn something, we relate it to other things we know, at the very least because it stood in relation to other things in the context in which we learnt it. As an example, if I learn a new word such as *deplane*, I relate it to other words I already know, both in terms of similarity (*derail, debone, decode*) and association (e.g. the fact that *deplane* is a verb and is used with specific grammatical roles in English sentences). Or, to take an analogy from material culture, if I learn about the possibility of downloadable ringtones I will naturally contextualize this in terms of my existing knowledge of mobile phones and Internet access. Through this context bias I am more readily able to learn and psychologically represent those linguistic items that have an existing place or slot in my current knowledge.

In language, items are structured into conceptual frames, systems of categorization, conceptual metaphors, structural paradigms, and syntagms. While these systems often display a degree of symmetry, consistency, and simplicity, change is always taking place. It is in the nature of systems that when something happens in one place it will have effects in another place. In the densely structured linguistic systems of lexicon and grammar, such system-internal relational perturbations sometimes give rise to a certain 'psychological shakiness', as Sapir (1921) put it, which can lead to reorganization of a system, in the private, mental realm, and then potentially in the public realm.

In the broadest sense of meaning, capturing everything from the arbitrary meanings of words in languages to the affordance-grounded functions of tools (Kockelman 2006), we benefit from what can be called natural meaning. If a word or grammatical expression is compatible with other information, for example by having iconic properties, it is better learnt and remembered. Similarly for technology, if there is a good match between affordances and functions, then we are more likely to understand the practice, it will be easier to learn, and indeed what needs to be stored representationally is reduced because the relevant information can be stored materially (Norman 1991). This kind of content bias pertains to learning, storage, and reduction of load on cognition, thus illustrating some ways in which 'representation' is a functional locus for transmission biases, both in language and in culture more generally.

Reproduction (relating to the mind-to-world transition) is a locus at which biases can affect the likelihood that a person will employ the practice themselves. One way to think of this sense of reproduction is whatever causes a person to turn the private representation of a practice into public action whose production and effects are then perceptible by others.

What motivates us to turn linguistic knowledge into linguistic action? Daily life involves goal-directed behaviour that is motivated by our beliefs and desires (see e.g. Davidson 2006; Searle 1983; Fodor 1987). I may want to get something done for which I need another person's cooperation. One way to secure this is to produce an utterance using some selection of words and grammatical constructions. Depending on my specific goals, I will select certain words and will thereby select against all the other words I could have chosen. This is the competition among words and grammatical forms invoked in Darwin's (1871: 60) quote of Max Müller (1861): 'A struggle for life is constantly going on amongst the words and grammatical forms in each language.'

Boyd and Richerson's content bias fits partly under this rubric. As discussed above, a content bias favours a practice that is more beneficial in some way to the one selecting it. As Boyd and Richerson (1995, 2005) point out, some aspects of these biases are direct, others are indirect. A direct bias is in operation when the benefit concerns the greater functional payoff, or reduced cost, of the practice, in terms of the primary effects it brings about. A direct bias would favour one linguistic strategy if it were lower in cost or greater in benefit than alternative strategies for a comparable function. An *indirect* bias is about the effects of whom you identify with (or against) by virtue of choosing a particular practice. This is one of the central themes of sociolinguistics. Speaking English, I might say *guy* in one context and *bloke* in another. It may be that there is a slight meaning difference between these two words (thus invoking a direct content bias), but these differences may be minimal compared to the effect of identifying myself with certain sub-cultural groups by virtue of this linguistic choice. Clearer examples concern pronunciation: whether I choose to say *working* or *workin'* has more to do with who I identify with (an indirect bias) rather than what meaning I convey (a direct bias). The mechanisms at play will serve to bias a person's motivation for selecting one practice over all the others that he thereby does not select.

The indirect bias is also sometimes described as a model bias. There is an important distinction to be made here depending on the age of the person concerned. How does a child select which variants of a practice to adopt? A conformity bias favours those practices that 'everyone else' adopts (Boyd and Richerson 1985; Gergely and Csibra 2006). Another term for this bias is docility (Simon 1990), that is, an adaptive propensity to do more or less unquestioningly what the other members of your group do. For the infant, this group will tend also to consist of the people to whom one is genetically most closely related. The effect is that linguistic items tend to (but need not) have similar histories as genes.

As a person becomes a full member of a speech community, they will encounter a greater range and number of cultural items (i.e. they continue learning), and they may find themselves therefore with new linguistic choices. This may be because they encounter other ways of saying things than the way 'my people' say things, through their contacts with other groups, for instance in trading, ritual, and other kinds of inter-group social interaction. Different people will have different degrees of mobility, sometimes as a result of personality type, sometimes as a result of gender (men often travel more widely than women), age, or sub-culture. At a later age, there is a greater degree of linguistic choice and therefore greater competition between choices. We may or may not consciously deliberate about such choices. But as adults we may be more aware of the meanings of the different options. Here's where the indirect bias looks more like the model bias exploited in advertising and also active in any other diffusional process as a low-level favouring of those practices, linguistic or otherwise, that are modelled by more admired or charismatic people.

Material (relating to world structure) is a locus at which biases can affect the manner in which a practice will be instantiated in the perceptible world. Materially grounded biases concern the affordances of a cultural item for exposure and reproduction. Material biases can affect exposure biases in some obvious ways. Speech, for instance, as a result of a particular reproduction process (vocalization), has the property of being instantiated in fleeting form. A fact about the material of speech is that it is perceptible at the time of production but then it is gone. But when a reproduction process involving language is carried out through writing, this evanescence is dramatically lessened, and the dynamics of transmission are significantly affected. Outside of language, we see similar contrasts. Forms of activity such as adopting a certain grip for table tennis (for this example, see Boyd and Richerson 1985) are temporally fleeting and are only available for exposure simultaneously with the reproduction process that potentially constitutes the transmission event (photos, etc., aside). The table tennis bat itself, however, has a more persistent physical existence. Material biases concern the specific nature of the 'publication' of cultural practices such that they may continue to play a role in the exposure–reproduction cycle described above under the rubric of iterated practice.

23.5 Conclusion

The purpose of this chapter has been to address the need for an explanatory framework in the study of transmission biases in linguistic epidemiology. A proper account of the diachronic evolution of language must be explicit about the causal anatomy of the process. Previous work has usefully identified and described transmission biases, but one might ask: Why these biases? What other biases might we predict are possible? How many might there be? I submit that we can answer these questions with reference to the basic causal anatomy of social transmission in human populations. Cultural epidemiology is powered by a four-stroke engine, a causal chain from exposure to representation to replication to material instantiation, back to exposure and round again. When we talk about transmission biases, we mean any force that serves as a filter or pump for this process, by virtue of its effects on any of the links in this potentially open-ended chain of iterated practice.

Subsequent research should now turn to the tasks of, firstly, seeing if we can account for all of the currently known and understood biases within this four-stroke engine framework, and secondly, articulating predictions made by the framework such that we may empirically test them. The causal anatomy of biased transmission is central to the question of language evolution in our species because it is intimately connected to our unique capacity for cumulative culture. Culture, including language, could not be historically cumulative without the sustained transmission and diffusion of cultural and linguistic practice. This relates, then, directly to the question of the initial evolution in our species of the capacity for cumulative culture, a capacity that is clearly a prerequisite for language, and that is so strongly pronounced in humans and so weak if present at all in our closest relatives the other apes. We need to consider the known biases, discussed above, in connection with what is known about the cognition and social structure of other species. While we can readily assume that other animals are engaged in goal-directed courses of action, and that they select from among different means for certain ends in both the social and material realms, their selection of means for ends is relatively less flexible than that of humans. We might assume that a chimpanzee, say, will be guided in its selection of a behavioural strategy by a strong content bias, incorporating a basic minimum–maximum payoff logic. But if its repertoire of strategies is, on the whole, not being acquired by learning from others, then transmission biases will have no traction. That said, a topic for research could be to look and see the extent to which other apes possess the cognitive prerequisites for social transmission of the kind described here. While the biggest differences between us and them are known to be in social cognition, they are nevertheless intensely social species with textured social worlds. Many of the key cognitive and sociometric ingredients for biased transmission may have been in place before the evolution of our species, allowing the processes to kick in as soon as culture was being transmitted at all.

23.6 Acknowledgements

I am extremely grateful for comments and suggestions from Dan Dediu, Daniel Dor, Chris Knight, Paul Kockelman, Jack Sidnell, Maggie Tallerman, an anonymous reviewer, and participants at the London conference in 2011. This work is supported by the European Research Council (ERC grant 'Human Sociality and Systems of Language Use', 2010–2014), and the Max Planck Institute for Psycholinguistics, Nijmegen.

24

Breaking down false barriers to understanding

LUC STEELS

The reductionist science tradition has trained us to carve out one aspect of a problem and try to 'solve it' independently of its broader context. But, as current social, economic, and environmental crises show, this 'divide-and-conquer' strategy does not work very well for complex phenomena that are the outcome of many different processes and forces. Clearly, language evolution is such a complex phenomenon and a myopic focus on one aspect is unlikely to give us an adequate explanation. We need to break down barriers caused by focusing exclusively on only one aspect while ignoring (if not downright opposing) other viewpoints. Here I discuss several such barriers, which I believe have hampered the development of language evolution theories. I then focus on how we could use agent-based modelling as a vehicle for going beyond these dichotomies, and propose linguistic selectionism as an overarching theory of (cultural) language evolution.

24.1 False dichotomies

24.1.1 *Synchrony versus diachrony*

A first dichotomy that has a long tradition in linguistics, going back to de Saussure, is between the *synchronic* study of language, i.e. language as a system at a particular point in time, and the *diachronic* study of language, i.e. the cultural evolution of language over time. This dichotomy is unhelpful when developing theories of language evolution. Data from historical linguistics shows that languages have always changed and continue to change in profound ways, including at the level of grammar: new syntactic and semantic categories appear, new types of syntactic structures arise, and new semantic domains may become expressed grammatically. A well-known example of the origins of a new syntactic category concerns the articles. Latin did not feature a system of articles for determination (i.e. for expressing how the referent of a nominal phrase must be accessed given a class of objects delineated by the nominal) but all languages derived from Latin (French, Catalan, etc.) developed such a system. Usually demonstratives (such as that, those, etc.) are the source for the definite articles (Diessel 1999). There are still many languages without articles (such as Japanese), and it is not unreasonable to predict that at some point such languages will develop them. Similar observations can be made for phrase structure. Proto-Indo European had a largely free word order and remarkably little syntactic structure. Words were strung together at the sentence level. Only gradually did hierarchical structure of nominal and verbal phrases appear, leading at each step to further syntactic differentiations, such as the distinction between adjectives and nouns (Van de Velde 2009).

Why are these grammaticalization processes relevant for explaining language evolution? Following Darwin, evolutionary biologists universally adopt the assumption of uniformitarianism, originally introduced by the geologist Charles Lyell. It states that the processes of species change that we can observe today must also have been happening in the past, and so they are available as building blocks for helping to explain the very origins of a species, and going even further back, the origins of life itself (Maynard Smith and Szathmary 1995). So a sharp dichotomy between studies of ongoing species change and studies of the origins of species or life does not exist in biology. The same should be true for language.

The cultural processes that we can observe today in the ongoing evolution of language were most likely also operating at early stages of language evolution, including at the very birth of language. For example, new words come into a language every day and it is not unreasonable to assume that the processes that give rise to new words now are the same as those that gave rise to the very first words. The syntactic potential of verbs undergoes change right under our noses (Hilpert 2013). Syntactic potential determines whether a verb can take as complements that-clauses (as in 'I expect that he will come'), ing-clauses (as in 'He admits stealing the book'), to-infinitives (as in 'I expect to finish the paper today'), or simple noun phrases (as in 'She expects a baby'). The process underlying this expansion or contraction of constructional usage that we observe today was most probably active already at the birth of language, when the very first constructions appeared and spread in the lexicon. We see these processes even more starkly at work when a language is reduced to a much-simplified lexical core out of which a new Creole with complex grammar may spring up (Thomason and Kaufman 1988). It follows that if we want to understand how language originated, and particularly how grammatical structures first appeared in language, we should look to use the same grammaticalization principles and this means that we need to incorporate diachronic studies as a crucial aspect of studies in language evolution (Heine and Kuteva 2007).

24.1.2 *Nature versus culture*

This leads to the next dichotomy. Many researchers participating in debates on language evolution insist on a rather clear-cut division between investigations into the origins of the language faculty, which is usually taken to be a kind of unique event based on a major biological transition, and the cultural evolution of human languages over time, which is taken to be a historical process, only involving superficial change (Fitch 2011b, 2012). Of course, biological evolution sets the constraints within which the cultural process can operate, and it needs to provide the basic cognitive machinery for forming and manipulating complex symbolic structures, motor control, acoustic processing, and so forth. But how specific this machinery needs to be for language (and hence how much weight we need to give to biological evolution) can only be determined after we have worked out in detail what cognitive mechanisms are needed for language and its cultural evolution. We need to seek biological explanations only if our efforts to come up with explanations based on cultural evolution have failed.

Social evolution constitutes a second source of constraints within which cultural evolution (and biological evolution according to the niche construction theory) operates and is particularly important for shaping the kinds of meanings and interaction patterns that are fundamental to language. The requirements of cultural evolution can inform us about what social prerequisites are needed for language. For example, we found that models explaining how lexicons get bootstrapped only work if there is a strong assumption of sociality (Steels 2009). There has to be an attitude of cooperation, an ability to take the perspective of the other, and enough trust to adopt and align to the conventions of others—which raises the fundamental question as to how such a strong form of sociality could have arisen in the first place (Knight et al. 1995; Knight and Lewis, Chapter 21).

So a total picture requires all three types of evolution, whereby increased complexity in one area pushes up complexity in another, resulting in a spiralling process (see Figure 24.1): increased social and ecological complexity requires increased language complexity which in turn requires increased brain capacities, which then further support increased social complexity. Going in the other direction: increased language complexity supports increased social complexity which puts increased pressure on the development of mental processes that in turn again support greater

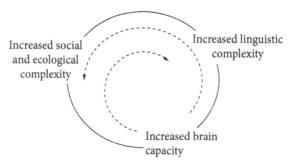

FIGURE 24.1 Biological, social, and cultural evolutions tightly interact, and this interaction leads to a mutual increase in complexity until a viable balance is found.

linguistic complexity. Of course, there are also balancing forces, reducing complexity to keep the language viable for the available needs and mental capacity and to ensure that it remains transmissible across generations.

24.1.3 *Competence versus performance*

The next dichotomy that has informed much linguistic research is a sharp distinction, originally due to Chomsky, but going back much earlier to the work of de Saussure and Bloomfield, between competence and performance. Research on competence is supposed to focus on language independently from the variation that unavoidably arises in actual language use, i.e. in performance. Twentieth-century theoretical linguists declared studies of language performance to be of secondary relevance. However, from the viewpoint of language evolution, this dichotomy stands in the way of explanation. More specifically, it makes it impossible to conceive let alone apply the most powerful explanatory framework we have for evolutionary processes of all kinds, namely selection.

Selectionist theories of evolution (whether biological, social, or cultural) assume a process by which variants are generated (in biological evolution, this happens through genetic mutation, epigenesis, differences in environments during development) and a process by which those variants that are better adapted spread and become dominant (in biological evolution, this happens through factors influencing survival and reproduction). We can apply this to language by introducing variation and selection at the cultural or 'memetic' level (Dawkins 1976; Steels 2011). The variants are variations in categorization and conceptualization and in how these are expressed in language; selection takes place because speakers and hearers maximize communicative success, minimize cognitive effort, and strive for social conformity with their peer group (Mufwene 2001).

That there are variants in language use is empirically attested beyond doubt (Labov 1994). Variation exists owing to different habits of individual speakers, language contact, effects of first language on second language acquisition, accidental errors, and fashion trends in language use. Speakers introduce innovations to express novel concepts or to minimize the cognitive effort of speaking and listening; they can switch register depending on the social context. Selection is brought about by speakers when they decide how to conceptualize and express what they want to say and by hearers when they try to make sense of what is being said and have to decide whether to adopt solutions gleaned from others. Selection drives the population towards increased coherence. Because it integrates relevance, communicative success, and cognitive effort, the language becomes more adapted to the social and communicative needs and the biological and social constraints of its speakers and listeners. This does not mean that purely random factors do not play a role as well (e.g. a particular pronunciation might come into fashion without any adaptive effect), but without selection, language evolution would be a random search process unlikely to lead to the highly efficient communication medium we have today.

A growing number of computational models investigating specific aspects of language have now shown that such a cultural selectionist model can be worked out in sufficient detail to provide possible explanations for many of the features found in human languages, such as parts of speech, agreement, hierarchical structure, case grammar, etc., and there is undoubtedly more to come as the tools for simulating cultural language evolution develop further (Steels 2012). But notice that this approach relies crucially on breaking down the competence–performance barrier. It is indeed through language use and all the errors, deviations, innovations, and inaccuracies that variation is created and maintained in the language and hence that a language is culturally evolvable. Focusing exclusively on competence throws away the data that would show us language evolution at work.

24.1.4 *Processing versus describing*

The competence/performance dichotomy not only ignores language use. It also wants to study language independently of how it is processed. This stance is another obstacle towards the development of a theory of language evolution. If part of the evolution of grammar is due to optimizations in linguistic processing so that more complex utterances can be handled, then we need a theory of language processing in order to study where these optimizations are useful and how they could be achieved. If we want to understand the nature and origins of the language faculty, we need to pay attention to how language is processed. We need to unravel the highly complex mental operations involved in planning what to say, transducing semantic structures to utterances, parsing utterances to reconstruct their semantic structure, interpreting semantic structures with respect to context, and acquiring all the knowledge and processing skills to carry out these processes. It is only when we have such a theory that we can know which processes are necessary and sufficient for language and how these processes differ from those used in other cognitive tasks such as recognizing and parsing sound structures in the environment, planning complex sequences of actions, or forming categories for coping with the natural and social world. Rather than exclusively relying on biological evolution, it is entirely possible that existing cognitive functions became recruited for language, which would imply that the decisive biological prerequisite for language was not one or more highly language-specific genes—but the general capacity for recruiting existing cognitive functions and harnessing them to new purposes (Steels 2007).

24.1.5 *Formalists versus functionalists*

Finally, there is a long tradition of debate in linguistics between so-called formalists and functionalists (Newmeyer 1998). Formalists argue that the grammatical structure of human languages is basically arbitrary—only constrained by properties of the vocal apparatus, the physics of sound, and the cognitive subsystems on which language relies. Functionalists argue that the grammatical structure of language is functionally motivated. For example, they argue that internal agreement in noun phrases (such as for gender and number between articles, adjectives, and nouns in the French noun phrase) is there to signal which constituents belong to which noun phrase and to disambiguate meanings or functions of the noun. For example, 'der Hund'—the dog—is nominative because of 'der' and not because of 'Hund', which can be either nominative or accusative.

Arguments in favour of a formalist view are usually based on examples where languages appear to require systems of expression whose underlying logic is opaque, if not illogical, and on examples where one language has a particular feature (such as an elaborate agreement system) whereas another one does not, suggesting that this feature is of no functional significance. Functionalists counter-argue that languages are not designed in a rational way by committee but arise through an evolutionary and collective process. Hence we cannot expect a clean system but only partial systematicity, often based on recruiting an existing system and adapting it for new purposes. Indeed, this is the case in biological evolution as well, where highly complex apparently irrational designs are abundant. Functionalists also argue that languages are inferential coding systems (Sperber and Wilson 1986), which means that hearers are supposed to use general background knowledge and the context to infer meanings that are not coded explicitly. This means that most features of grammar are not absolutely necessary, but they aid in avoiding misunderstanding and optimize language processing.

The opposition between formalist and functionalist views leads to two approaches to cultural language evolution. When the structure of language is arbitrary, language change can only be explained by random drift without any role for linguistic selection. Language users keep changing their language but the changes are based on random errors that accidentally happen to propagate, or on simplifications and overgeneralizations made during language acquisition (Kirby et al. 2007). The possible changes remain within the (innate) constraints imposed by human cognition but they are not related to the function of language or to an optimization of cognitive effort. On the other hand, when the structure of language is related to its use, a selectionist logic makes more sense: language users prefer those constructs which in one way or another make the language more adapted, for example because they reduce semantic ambiguity by making the argument structure explicit (Steels 2004) or they decrease the complexity of parsing (Hawkins 2004; Steels and Wellens 2006). The debate is reminiscent of that between those emphasizing neutral evolution in biology (Kimura 1983) versus those insisting on the primacy of selection.

24.2 Agent-based modelling

The remainder of this chapter briefly looks at how agent-based models can be used to engage in these various debates. Agent-based models are complementary to macroscopic or aggregate models, which are similar to those developed in population genetics and statistical physics. Macroscopic models mathematically define the aggregate behaviour of language change over time using systems of differential equations (Solé et al. 2010). For example, Nowak et al. (2000) propose a model of lexical diffusion that determines the fraction of a population knowing a word w from terms capturing the average word learning and the population change. The model predicts the S-shaped curve characteristic of lexical diffusion as well as critical thresholds for the survival or death of words.

In contrast, agent-based models define and operationalize the individual behaviour of language users needed for playing language games. An agent-based model is deemed to be successful if the desired aggregate behaviour emerges from the collective activity of the agents. For example, Steels (1995) introduced the Naming Game as a minimal model for lexicon formation and diffusion. The model involves a population in which (artificial) agents take turns being speaker or hearer. When speaking, they select the word that best names an object from their own vocabulary and if the hearer was able to interpret the word correctly (e.g. by pointing to the object named by the speaker), both speaker and hearer increase the score of that word in their respective vocabularies. When the game was not a success, agents repair their vocabularies, either by inventing a new word (if the speaker was missing a word), by adopting a word (if the hearer did not know the word), or by realigning their vocabularies (if there was a mismatch between speaker and hearer). Computer simulations show that this Naming Game model not only explains how a new lexicon can emerge from scratch but also how the S-shaped curve and other lexical diffusion phenomena get generated (Baronchelli et al. 2008). From timid beginnings in the nineties, many agent-based models have now been built, covering a wide range of linguistic phenomena (see Steels 2012, for a recent overview and examples).

Agent-based models are more powerful than macroscopic models for two reasons:

1. They require detailed operational theories of the cognitive processes that are required for handling the linguistic phenomena being studied and theories of the ecological and social conditions that potentially induce these phenomena. For example, if we want to develop an agent-based model of how articles could emerge in a language, we need a theory of how reality is conceptualized for handling quantifiers and a theory of what grammatical processes are needed for parsing, producing, and learning nominal phrases (Pauw and Hilferty 2012). Hence research in agent-based models makes important contributions to the study of language processing and language acquisition.

2. Agent-based models also require a theory as to why the linguistic structures we find in human languages are actually there, for example, why languages may develop articles at all (which they not always do). This point will be illustrated in the present chapter using two examples. The first example is based on the work of Michael Spranger and discusses the origins of parts of speech within the context of spatial language (see Spranger and Steels 2012 for more details). The second example draws on a study of German agreement marking developed by Remi van Trijp (2012a).

24.3 The role of parts of speech

Words in the lexicon belong to certain parts of speech (noun, adjective, adverb, etc.), which constrain the constructions in which a given word may occur. Parts of speech are either defined through the lexicon, signalled by morphology—as in 'slow' (adjective) versus 'slowly' (adverb)—or derivable from the syntactic context. Not all languages distinguish the same parts of speech and there has been cultural evolution towards more and more fine-grained distinctions (Vogel and Comrie 2000). How can we explain the emergence of parts of speech—clearly, one of the major innovations needed to get a grammar off the ground? For a selectionist explanation to apply, we need to show the importance of parts of speech distinctions for making language more reliable and efficient.

From a functionalist point of view, distinctions between parts of speech convey which semantic functions the hearer should use, i.e. what the hearer should do with the predicates introduced by a word. Usually there are a variety of possible functions. We can see this most clearly when we look at the different meanings that can be invoked with the same word stem (and therefore the same predicate). Here are three sentences from German that all invoke the same predicate but suggest different usages:

1. In 'der linke Block' (the left block), the word 'linke' (left) introduces a spatial relation 'left'. The word is used in an adjectival function meaning that the spatial relation should be used to further restrict the set of objects denoted by the noun. The adjectival function is signalled by word order and adjective–noun agreement.
2. In 'links des Blockes' (to the left of the block), the word 'links' (left) is used in a prepositional function, meaning that the spatial relation is to be applied to a landmark denoted by the noun in order to identify a particular region in the scene. The function is signalled by another form of the word stem ('links') and by its position (in front of the noun phrase).
3. In 'der Block links' (the block left), 'links' (left) is used in an adverbial function. The hearer is given a direction (namely to the left) indicating a region in which the object identified by the noun is to be found. The word is now placed after the nominal phrase and there is no agreement.

Each of these sentences gives rise to a different semantic structure and invokes different cognitive operations in the hearer even though the same spatial relation is involved. It is possible to leave it up to the hearer to figure out what semantic function is intended but that increases the risk of misunderstanding and requires more effort from the hearer.

Let us now look at an agent-based experiment testing what the impact is of signalling explicitly semantic functions through grammar. The experiment involves one population of agents that uses a kind of Pidgin German, i.e. a language that uses German words but otherwise has no grammar, so that agents have to infer what semantic function is intended, and a population which has been initialized with a full German grammar that assigns default parts of speech to words and uses morphology and syntactic context to mark semantic functions. The experiment involves language games between robotic agents as shown in Figure 24.2.

The agents are able to extract a world model about the scenes they perceive and play a game of reference in which one robot identifies an object (or a set of objects) in the world and the other robot then points to the object(s) he believes to be the

FIGURE 24.2 Typical experimental set-up for language game experiments exploring how linguistic structures can emerge. Beneath the photograph is the world model constructed by the robots based on what they perceive.

referent. To do such an experiment requires complex cognitive machinery for vision and motor control and for grammatical and semantic processing, a discussion of which falls outside the scope of the present chapter (see Steels 2011 and Steels and Hild 2012 for details).

Of importance for the present discussion are the experimental results shown in Figures 24.3 and 24.4. Figure 24.3 proves that if semantic functions are not made

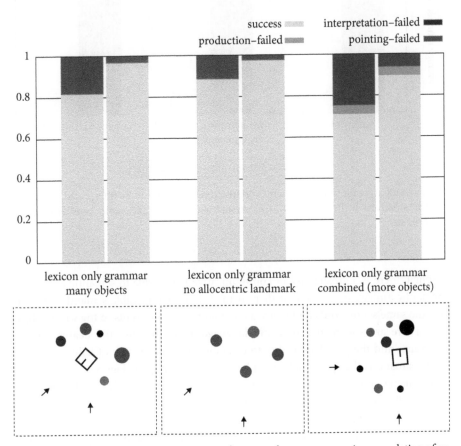

FIGURE 24.3 Average communicative success for 10,000 language games in a population of 10 agents for situations with increased complexity. There is a population without grammar (left column) and one with grammar (right column). The situations either contain many objects and an allocentric landmark (left), fewer objects without such a landmark (middle), or combined situations (right). We see that communicative failure (observable to the speaker because the hearer points to the wrong object) increases as situations become more complex. The difference between the 'Pidgin German' agents and agents using full grammar is significant. For example, Pidgin agents need to consider an average of nine possible interpretations for the middle cases whereas the population with grammar needs to consider basically only one.

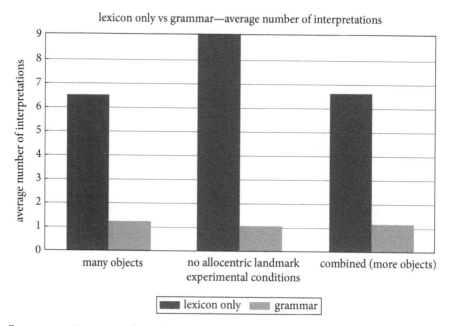

FIGURE 24.4 Average number of semantic structures that have to be interpreted to find out which structure makes sense in the present context for the same conditions as in Figure 24.3.

explicit, there is a greater risk of communicative failure due to semantic ambiguity. Semantic ambiguity means that there is more than one possible semantic structure for the same set of words and hence a risk that the hearer points to the wrong object (s). There are still many successful language games because the hearer can use inference and the perceived reality to disambiguate, but the risk of failure increases if the situations the agents talk about become more complex. Figure 24.4 shows that introducing grammar for signalling semantic functions not only avoids communicative failures but also indeed makes the interpretation process itself more efficient.

So the experiments demonstrate that the use of parts of speech significantly improves the effectiveness of a language. They also help us see how linguistic selection works: agents can assess the performance of the possible choices for achieving some communicative goal and should prefer those choices that increase performance. Concretely, if they have a choice between introducing and grammatically marking parts of speech versus not doing so, they should prefer the former. If this mechanism is coupled with strategies for introducing new parts of speech and ways to syntactically express them, the population gradually arrives at a shared language system that is better adapted (as shown in detail in Spranger and Steels 2012).

24.4 The role of agreement markers

One could argue that the utility of parts of speech is rarely disputed, so let's look at another example where utility is less clear-cut. Many languages feature elaborate agreement systems. For example, German articles and adjectives agree for gender, number, and case with their head nouns. The morphological expression of these features is a deep puzzle because the contemporary German agreement marking system (and most such systems we find in other languages such as Polish) seems very inefficient. The same word form may express many different combinations of features (a phenomenon called syncretism) and thus potentially generate a significant search space in parsing. For example, the article 'der' can signal nominative-singular-masculine, dative-singular-feminine, genitive-singular-feminine, or genitive-plural. This is all the more surprising since earlier versions of the article system (namely those of Old High German) had twice as many forms so that there was less syncretism (Wright 1906). Dative-singular-feminine was expressed as 'deru', genitive-singular-feminine as 'dera', and genitive-plural 'dero'. At first sight, the change to the German article paradigm therefore provides evidence of random drift. Errors, changes brought about by sound shifts, erosion of endings, and overgeneralizations gradually messed up a system that was originally more rational. However, agent-based experiments, as developed in van Trijp (2012a, 2012b), offer convincing counter-evidence that linguistic selection has been at work.

The experiments contrast two populations of agents, one endowed with a reconstruction of the Old High German feature-marking system, the other endowed with its contemporary equivalent (called New High German). Agents play description games about scenes for which they have a shared world model. The descriptions involve various objects and events that involve semantic roles, such as agent or patient. An example utterance is 'Der Frau gaben die Kinder die Zeichnung' ('The children gave the woman the drawing'). One indicator of the performance of the system is the presence of semantic ambiguity, which is measured as the set of possible interpretations left after parsing.

Even though New High German contains half as many forms as Old High German (and is therefore more efficient from the perspective of the size of the inventory), overall semantic ambiguity is hardly affected because there are other cues that can be taken into account. Semantic ambiguity occurs when the same noun phrase can fill multiple possible roles in the sentence, for example when it is not clear whether the noun is nominative or accusative, and hence it can either be the agent or the patient of an action. Word order is not a reliable cue in German, since any constituent can be put in the front position. However, there are three other cues: the morphological markings on the constituents of the noun phrase, subject–verb agreement, and selection restrictions coming from the verb. All three have been incorporated in the model and so the effect of each cue can be determined (see Figure 24.5).

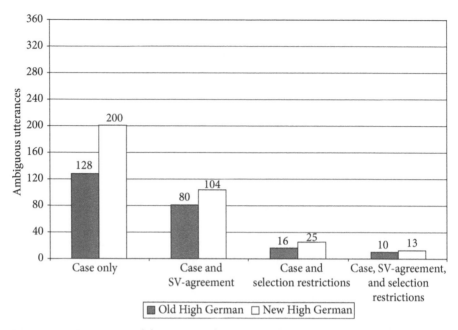

Figure 24.5 Comparison of the amount of semantic ambiguity between Old High German (shaded) and New High German (white) when progressively more cues are considered, from left to right: using only cues from morphological marking, using in addition subject–verb agreement, using morphology and selection restrictions, and finally using all possible cues.

We see that the morphological cues are indeed more reliable in Old High German because there is less syncretism, but if all cues are taken into account a comparable level of semantic ambiguity (in absolute terms) is observed between the two systems. So we can conclude that German speakers have optimized the number of forms in their lexicon by half without significant loss of expressive power.

Computer simulations of the parsing process also show that the size of the search space, which is the number of nodes that needs to be traversed during parsing or production, actually remains constant despite the increased syncretism. This is due to a judicious selection for collapsing those word forms so that no multiplication of hypotheses is required (van Trijp 2012a). Moreover, the articulatory complexity (measured in terms of the articulatory movements needed in the pronunciation of the words) is lowered without compromising—in fact, even optimizing—the acoustic distances between different word forms. We can conclude that the contemporary German agreement marking is not the consequence of random drift. Although there have been phonetic processes (unrelated to function) that have eroded endings and merged forms, only those solutions that lead to a more optimal system from the viewpoint of semantics, morpho-grammar, and phonology have undergone positive selection.

These two agent-based models illustrate how we can explore whether the cultural evolution of language is better explained by linguistic selection or by random drift (i.e. neutral evolution). Although it is certainly the case that languages undergo a constant bombardment of small changes due to accidental errors and deviations in performance or just fashionable trends in pronunciation, word choice, or grammar, we see that these changes are channelled and counteracted by a much more important force that increases or maintains the systematicity and optimality of the overall system. This force is linguistic selection, enacted through the choices speakers and hearers make in producing or interpreting utterances.

References

Abi-Rached, L., Jobin, M.J., Kulkarni, S., et al. (2011). 'The Shaping of Modern Human Immune Systems by Multiregional Admixture with Archaic Humans', *Science* 334: 89–94.

Aboitiz, F. (2012). 'Gestures, Vocalizations and Memory in Language Origins', *Frontiers in Evolutionary Neuroscience* 4: 1–15 (article 2).

Aboitiz, F., Aboitiz, S., and García, R.R. (2010). 'The Phonological Loop: A Key Innovation in Human Evolution', *Current Anthropology* 51(suppl. 1): S55–S65. doi: 10.1086/650525.

Aboitiz, F. and García, R. (2009). 'Merging of Phonological and Gestural Circuits in Early Language Evolution', *Reviews in the Neurosciences* 20: 71–84.

Aboitiz, F., García R.R., Bosman, C., and Brunetti, E. (2006). 'Cortical Memory Mechanisms and Language Origins', *Brain and Language* 98: 40–56. doi:10.1016/j.bandl.2006.01.006.

Aiello, L.C. and Key, C. (2002). 'Energetic Consequences of Being a *Homo Erectus* Female', *American Journal of Human Biology* 14: 551–65.

Aiello, L.C. and Wheeler, P. (1995). 'The Expensive Tissue Hypothesis: The Brain and the Digestive System in Human and Primate Evolution', *Current Anthropology* 36(2): 199–221.

Alcorta C.S. and Sosis, R. (2005). 'Ritual, Emotion, and Sacred Symbols: The Evolution of Religion as an Adaptive Complex', *Human Nature* 16(4): 323–59.

Alemseged, Z., Spoor, F., Kimbel, W.H., Bobe, R., Geraads, D., Reed, D., and Wynn, J.G. (2006). 'A Juvenile Early Hominin Skeleton from Dikika, Ethiopia', *Nature* 443: 296–301.

Alperson-Afil, N., Richter, D., and Goren-Inbar, N. (2007). 'Phantom Hearths and the Use of Fire at Gesher Benot Ya'aqov, Israel', *Paleoanthropology* 2007: 1–15.

Alpert, J. and Lange, R. (1981). 'Lumsden-Wilson Theory of Gene-culture Coevolution', *Proceedings of the National Academy of Sciences USA* 78: 3976–9.

Andreassen, H. (2010). *The Forgotten Cave and the Still Bay: A Technological Lithic Analysis of the Middle Stone Age Layers from Peers Cave, South Africa.* M.A. Thesis. Oslo: University of Oslo.

Andrew, R.J. (1976). 'Use of Formants in the Grunts of Baboons and Other Nonhuman Primates', *Origins and Evolution of Language and Speech Annals of the New York Academy of Sciences* 280: 673–93.

Anton, S. (2003). 'Natural History of *Homo Erectus*', *Yearbook of Physical Anthropology* 46: 126–70.

Apter, M.J. (2008). 'Reversal Theory, Victor Turner, and the Experience of Ritual', in C. Whitehead (ed.), *The Origin of Consciousness in the Social World*. Exeter: Imprint Academic, pp. 184–203.

Arbib, M.A. (2002). 'The Mirror System, Imitation, and the Evolution of Language', in C. Nehaniv and K. Dautenhahn (eds), *Imitation in Animals and Artefacts*. Cambridge, MA: MIT Press, pp. 229–80.

Arbib, M.A. (2005). 'From Monkey-like Action to Human Language: An Evolutionary Framework for Neurolinguistics', *Behavioral and Brain Sciences* 28: 105–67.

Arbib, M.A. (2006a). 'Aphasia, Apraxia and the Evolution of the Language-ready Brain', *Aphasiology* 20: 1125–55.

Arbib, M.A. (2006b). 'The Mirror System and the Linkage of Action and Language', in M.A. Arbib (ed.), *Action to Language via the Mirror Neuron System*. Cambridge: Cambridge University Press, pp. 3–47.

Arbib, M.A. (2008). 'Holophrasis and the Protolanguage Spectrum', *Interaction Studies: Social Behaviour and Communication in Biological and Artificial Systems* 9(1): 154–68.

Arbib, M.A. (2012). *How the Brain Got Language*. Oxford: Oxford University Press.

Arbib, M.A., ed. (2013). *Language, Music, and the Brain: A Mysterious Relationship*. Cambridge, MA: MIT Press.

Arbib, M.A., Liebal, K., and Pika, S. (2008). 'Primate Vocalization, Gesture, and the Evolution of Human Language', *Current Anthropology* 49(6): 1052–75.

Arcadi, A.C. (1996). 'Phrase Structure in Wild Chimpanzee Pant Hoots: Patterns of Production and Interpopulation Variability', *American Journal of Primatology* 39: 159–78.

Arcadi, A.C. (2000). 'Vocal Responsiveness in Male Wild Chimpanzees: Implications for the Evolution of Language', *Journal of Human Evolution* 39: 205–23.

Arensburg, B., Schepartz, L.A., Tillier, A.M., Vandermeersch, B., and Rak, Y. (1990). 'A Reappraisal of the Anatomical Basis for Speech in Middle Palaeolithic Hominids', *American Journal of Physical Anthropology* 83: 137–46.

Arensburg, B., Tillier, A.M., Vandermeersch, B., Duday, H., Schepartz, L.A., and Rak Y. (1989). 'A Middle Palaeolithic Human Hyoid Bone', *Nature* 338: 758–60.

Arnold, K. and Zuberbühler, K. (2006). 'Semantic Combinations in Primate Calls', *Nature* 441: 303.

Arnold, K. and Zuberbühler, K. (2008). 'Meaningful Call Combinations in a Non-human Primate', *Current Biology* 18(5): R202–R203.

Arom, S. (1978). '"Puisque personne ne sait à l'avance ce que tout autre que lui-même va chanter dans la seconde qui suit…". Entretien avec Vincent Dehoux', *Musique en jeu* 32: 67–71.

Arom, S. (1981). '"Un ethnomusicologue chez les Pygmées". Entretien avec A. Jaubert', *La Recherche* 123: 768–73.

Arom, S. (1985). *Polyphonies et polyrythmies d'Afrique Centrale, structure et méthodologie*. 2 vols. Paris: SELAF.

Arthur, W.B. (2007). 'The Structure of Invention', *Research Policy* 36: 274–87.

Atkinson, Q. (2012). 'Response to Comments on "Phonemic diversity supports a serial founder effect model of expansion from Africa"', *Science* 335: 657.

Austin, J.L. (1962). *How to Do Things with Words*. Oxford: Clarendon Press.

Avital, E. and Jablonka, E. (2000). *Animal Traditions: Behavioural Inheritance in Evolution*. Cambridge: Cambridge University Press.

Axelrod, R. and Hamilton, W.D. (1981). 'The Evolution of Cooperation', *Science* 211(4489): 1390–6.

Backwell, L.R. and d'Errico, F. (2001). 'Evidence of Termite Foraging by Swartkrans Early Hominids', *Proceedings of the National Academy of Sciences* 98: 1358–63.

Bahuchet, S. (1992). *Dans la forêt d'Afrique Centrale. Les Pygmées Aka et Baka. Histoire d'une civilisation forestière*. Vol 1. Paris: SELAF/Louvain Peeters.

Bahuchet, S. (1996). 'Fragments pour une histoire de la forêt Africaine et de son peuplement: les données linguistiques et culturelles', in C.M. Hladik, A. Hladik, H. Pagezy, O.F. Linares, G.J.A. Koppert, and A. Froment (eds), *L'alimentation en forêt tropicale: Interactions bioculturelles et perspectives de développement*. Paris: Éditions UNESCO, pp. 97–119.

Bahuchet, S. (2012). 'Changing Language, Remaining Pygmy', *Human Biology* 84(1): 11–43.

Baldwin, J.M. (1894). *Social and Ethical Interpretations of Social Life*. London: Macmillan.

Barclay, P. (2011). 'Competitive Helping Increases with the Size of Biological Markets and Invades Defection', *Journal of Theoretical Biology* 281: 47–55.

Barham, L.S. (2002). 'Systematic Pigment Use in the Middle Pleistocene of South-Central Africa', *Current Anthropology* 31(1): 181–90.

Barham, L. and Mitchell, P. (2008). *The First Africans: African Archaeology from the Earliest Toolmakers to Most Recent Foragers*. Cambridge: Cambridge University Press.

Barnard, A. (1988). 'Structure and Fluidity in Khoisan Religious Ideas', *Journal of Religion in Africa* 18(3): 216–36.

Barnard, A. (1999). 'Modern Hunter-gatherers and Early Symbolic Culture', in R. Dunbar, C. Knight, and C. Power (eds), *The Evolution of Culture: An Interdisciplinary View*. Edinburgh: Edinburgh University Press, pp. 50–68.

Baronchelli, A., Loreto, V., and Steels, L. (2008). 'In-depth Analysis of the Naming Game Dynamics: The Homogeneous Mixing Case', *International Journal of Modern Physics C* 19(5): 785–812.

Baron-Cohen, S. (1995). *Mindblindness: An Essay on Autism and Theory of Mind*. Cambridge, MA: MIT Press.

Barrett, L. and Henzi, S.P. (2001). 'The Utility of Grooming in Baboon Troops', in R. Noe, J.A.R.A.M. van Hooff, and P. Hammerstein (eds), *Economics in Nature: Social Dilemmas, Mate Choice, and Biological Markets*. Cambridge: Cambridge University Press, pp. 119–45.

Barsalou, L.W. (1999). 'Perceptual Symbol Systems', *Behavioral and Brain Sciences* 22, 577–660.

Barton, R.A., and Cappelini, I. (2011). 'Maternal Investment, Life Histories, and the Costs of Brain Growth in Mammals', *Proceedings of the National Academy of Sciences USA* 108: 6169–74.

Bates, E. (1976). *Language and Context: The Acquisition of Pragmatics*. New York: Academic Press.

Bates, E., Benigni, L., Bretherton, I., Camaioni, L., and Volterra, V. (1979). *The Emergence of Symbols: Cognition and Communication in Infancy*. New York: Academic Press.

Bates, T.C., Luciano, M., Medland, S.E., Montgomery, G.W., Wright, M.J., and Martin, N.G. (2011). 'Genetic Variance in a Component of the Language Acquisition Device: ROBO1 Polymorphisms Associated with Phonological Buffer Deficits', *Behavior Genetics* 41: 50–7.

Bateson, C.D. (1991). *The Altruism Question: Toward a Social-Psychological Answer*. Hillsdale, NJ: Lawrence Erlbaum.

Bateson, C.D. (2000). 'Onto Others: A Service…and a disservice', *Journal of Consciousness Studies* 7(1–2): 207–10.

Bateson, G. (1936). *Naven: A Survey of the Problems Suggested by a Composite Picture of the Culture of a New Guinea Tribe Drawn from Three Points of View*. Stanford, CA: Stanford University Press.

Bateson, G. (1973). 'A Theory of Play and Fantasy', *American Psychiatric Association Psychiatric Research Reports* 2, 1955. Reprinted in G. Bateson, *Steps to an Ecology of Mind*. London: Paladin, pp. 150–66.

Bateson, P.P.G. (2005). 'Play and Its Role in the Development of Great Apes and Humans', in A.D. Pellegrini and P.K. Smith (eds), *The Nature of Play: Great Apes and Humans*. New York: Guilford, 13–26.

Bateson, P. and Gluckman, P. (2011). *Plasticity, Robustness, Development and Evolution*. Cambridge: Cambridge University Press.

Bayle, P., Macchiarelli, R., Trinkaus, E., Duarte, C., Mazurier, A., and Zilhão, J. (2010). 'Dental Maturational Sequence and Dental Tissue Proportions in the Early Upper Paleolithic Child from Abrigo Do Lagar Velho, Portugal', *Proceedings of the National Academy of Sciences USA* 107: 1338–42.

Bayly, B. (2010). 'Symmetrical Artefacts, Internal Reward and Language Precursors in the Head', in A.D.M. Smith et al. (eds), *Evolution of Language. Proceedings of Evolang 8, Utrecht*. Singapore: World Scientific Publishing, pp. 19–25.

Beaumont, P. (1973). 'The Ancient Pigment Mines of Southern Africa', *South African Journal of Science* 69: 41–6.

Beaumont, P. (1990a). 'Nooitgedacht 2 and Roseberry Plain', 1, in P. Beaumont and D. Morris (eds), *Guide to Archaeological Sites in the Northern Cape*. Kimberley: McGregor Museum, pp. 4–6.

Beaumont, P. (1990b). 'Kathu', in P. Beaumont and D. Morris (eds), *Guide to Archaeological Sites in the Northern Cape*. Kimberley: McGregor Museum, pp. 75–100.

Beaumont, P. (2004). 'Canteen Koppje', in D. Morris and P. Beaumont (eds), *Archaeology in the Northern Cape: Some Key Sites*. Kimberley: McGregor Museum, pp. 26–30.

Beaumont, P., de Villiers, H., and Vogel, J., (1978). 'Modern Man in Sub-Saharan Africa Prior to 49 000 Years B.P.: A Review and Evaluation with Particular Reference to Border Cave', *South African Journal of Science* 74: 409–19.

Beaumont, P. and Vogel, J. (2006). 'On a Timescale for the Past Million Years of Human History in Central South Africa', *South African Journal of Sciences* 102: 217–28.

Becker, N., Verdu, P., Hewlett, B., and Pavard, S. (2010). 'Can Life History Trade-Offs Explain the Evolution of Short Stature in Human Pygmies? A Response to Migliano et al. 2007', *Human Biology* 82(1): 17–27.

Beckerman, S. and Valentine, P. (2002). 'Introduction', in S. Beckerman and P. Valentine (eds), *Cultures of Multiple Fathers*. Gainesville, FL: University of Florida Press, pp. 1–13.

Bednarik, R. and Beaumont, P. (2010). 'Pleistocene Engravings from Wonderwerk Cave, South Africa', IFRAO Congress, September 2010—*Symposium: Pleistocene Art of Africa (Pre-Acts)*.

Beebe, B. (1982). 'Rhythmic Communication in the Mother-Infant Dyad', in M. Davis (ed.), *Interaction Rhythms: Periodicity in Communicative Behaviour*. New York: Human Sciences Press, pp. 79–100.

Behar, D., Villems, R., Soodyall, H., Blue-Smith, J., Pereira, L., Metspalu, E., Scozzari, R., Makkan, H., Tzur, S., Comas, D., Bertranpetit, J., Qintana-Murci, L., Tyler-Smith, C., Wells, S., and Rosset, S., (2008). 'The Dawn of Human Matrilineal Diversity' *The American Journal of Human Genetics* 82: 1130–40.

Behm-Blancke, G. (1960). 'Altsteinzeitliche Rastplätze im Travertingebiet von Taubac, Weimar, Ehringsdorf', *Alt-Thüringen* 4: 2–246.

Behrensmeyer, A.K. (2008). 'Paleoenvironmental Context of the Pliocene A.L. 333 "First Family" Hominin Locality, Hadar Formation, Ethiopia', in J. Quade and J.G. Wynn (eds), *The Geology of Early Humans in the Horn of Africa*. Geological Society of America Special Paper 446.

Beller, S. (2009). 'Deontic Reasoning Reviewed: Psychological Questions, Empirical Findings, and Current Theories', *Cognitive Processing* 11: 123–32. doi:10.1007/s10339-009-0265-z.

Ben Shalom, D. and Poeppel, D. (2008). 'Functional Anatomical Models of Language: Assembling the Pieces', *Neuroscientist* 14: 119–27.

Berger, P. and Luckmann, T. (1966). *The Social Construction of Reality*. Garden City/New York: Doubleday.

Bergman, T.J., Beehner, J.C., Cheney, D.L., and Seyfarth, R.M. (2003). 'Hierarchical Classification by Rank and Kinship in Baboons', *Science* 302(5648): 1234–6.

Berlin, B. (2005). 'Just Another Fish Story? Size-symbolic Properties of Fish Names', in A. Minelli, G. Ortalli, and G. Sanga (eds), *Animal Names*. Venice: Instituto Veneto di Scienza, Lettre ed. Arti, pp. 9–21.

Berlin, B. (2006). 'The First Congress of Ethnozoological Nomenclature', in R. Ellen (ed.), 'Ethnobiology and the Science of Humankind', *Journal of the Royal Anthropological Institute, Special Issue* 1: 29–54.

Bermejo, M., and Omedes, A. (1999). 'Preliminary Vocal Repertoire and Vocal Communicatino of Wild Bonobos (*Pan paniscus*) at Lilungu (Democratic Republic of Congo)', *Folia Primatologica* 70(6): 328–57.

Berna, F., Goldberg, P., Horwitz, L., Brink, J., Holt, S., Bamford, M., and Chazan, M. (2012). 'Microstratigraphic Evidence of In Situ Fire in the Acheulian Strata of Wonderwerk Cave, Northern Cape Province, South Africa', *Proceedings of the National Academy of Sciences USA* 109(20): E1215–E1220. doi/10.1073/pnas.1117620109.

Berwick, R.C. (2010). 'Invariants and Variation in Biology and Language Evolution', in A.D.M. Smith, M. Schouwstra, B. de Boer, and K. Smith (eds), *Evolution of Language. Proceedings of Evolang 8, Utrecht*. Singapore: World Scientific.

Beuls, K. and Steels, L. (2013). 'Agent-Based Models of Strategies for the Emergence and Evolution of Grammatical Agreement', *PLoS ONE* 8(3): 58960.

Bicchieri, C. (2006). *The Grammar of Society: The Nature and Dynamics of Social Norms*. New York: Cambridge University Press.

Bickerton, D. (1990). *Language and Species*. Chicago: University of Chicago Press.

Bickerton, D. (2002). 'From Protolanguage to Language', in T. Crow (ed.), *The Speciation of Modern Homo Sapiens*. Oxford: Oxford University Press, pp. 103–120.

Bickerton, D. (2003). 'Symbol and Structure: A Comprehensive Framework for Language Evolution', in M.H. Christiansen and S. Kirby (eds), *Language Evolution*. Oxford: Oxford University Press, pp. 77–93.

Bickerton, D. (2007). 'Language Evolution: A Brief Guide for Linguists', *Lingua* 117: 510–26.

Bickerton, D. (2009). *Adam's Tongue: How Humans Made Language, How Language Made Humans*. New York: Hill and Wang.

Bird-David, N. (1999). 'Animism Revisited', *Current Anthropology* 40(Suppl.): S67–S91.

Birdwhistell, R.L. (1963). 'The Kinesic Level in the Investigation of the Emotions', in P.H. Knapp (ed.), *Expression of the Emotions in Man*. New York: International Universities Press, Inc., pp. 123–9.

Birdwhistell, R.L. (1966). 'Some Relations between American Kinesics and Spoken American English', in A.G. Smith (ed.), *Communication and Culture: Readings in the Codes of Human Interaction*. New York: Holt, Rinehart and Winston, pp. 182–9.

Birdwhistell, R.L. (1970). *Kinesics and Context: Essays in Body Motion Communication*. Philadelphia: University of Pennsylvania Press.

Bischoff, J., Williams, R., Rosenbauer, R., Aramburu, A., Arsuaga, J.L., Garcia, N., and Cuenca-Bescós, G., (2007). 'High-resolution U-series Dates from the Sima de los Huesos Hominids Yields 600 $^{+\infty}/_{-66}$ kyrs: Implications for the Evolution of the Early Neanderthal Lineage', *Journal of Archaeological Science* 34: 763–70.

Bishop, D.V.M. (2009). 'Genes, Cognition, and Communication: Insights from Neurodevelopmental Disorders', *Annals of the New York Academy of Sciences* 1156: 1–18.

Blackwell, B. and Schwarcz, H., (1986). 'U-series Analyses of the Lower Travertine at Ehringsdorf, DDR', *Quaternary Research* 25: 215–22.

Blakemore, D. (1987). *Semantic Constraints on Relevance*. Oxford: Blackwell.

Blakemore, D. (2002). *Relevance and Linguistic Meaning*. Cambridge: Cambridge University Press.

Bliss, E.L. (1986). *Multiple Personality, Allied Disorders, and Hypnosis*. Oxford: Oxford University Press.

Bloch, M. (1992). *Prey Into Hunter*. Cambridge: Cambridge University Press.

Blount, B.G. (1990). 'Spatial Expression of Social Relationships Among Captive *Pan Paniscus*: Ontogenetic and Phylogenetic Implications', in S.T. Parker and K.R. Gibson (eds), *'Language' and Intelligence in Monkeys and Apes: Comparative Developmental Perspectives*. Cambridge: Cambridge University Press, pp. 420–32.

Blount, R. (2010). *Hail, Hail, Euphoria!: Presenting the Marx Brothers in Duck Soup, the Greatest War Movie Ever Made*. New York: Harper Collins.

Boehm, C. (1999). *Hierarchy in the Forest: The Evolution of Egalitarian Behavior*. Cambridge, MA: Harvard University Press.

Boehm, C. (2000a). 'Group Selection in the Upper Paleolithic,' *Journal of Consciousness Studies* 7(1–2): 211–15.

Boehm, C. (2000b). 'The Origin of Morality as Social Control,' *Journal of Consciousness Studies* 7(1–2): 149–83.

Boehm, C. (2012). *Moral Origins: The Evolution of Virtue, Altruism, and Shame*. New York: Basic Books.

de Boer, B. (2009). 'Acoustic Analysis of Primate Air Sacs and Their Effect on Vocalization', *Journal of the Acoustical Society of America* 126: 3329–43.

Boesch, C. (1994). 'Hunting Strategies of Gombe and Taï Chimpanzees', in R.W. Wrangham, W.C. McGrew, F.B.M. de Waal, and P.G. Heltne (eds), *Chimpanzee Cultures*. Cambridge, MA: Harvard University Press, pp. 77–91.

Boesch, C. (2007). 'What Makes Us Human (*Homo sapiens*)? The Challenge of Cognitive Cross-species Comparison', *Journal of Comparative Psychology* 3: 227–40.

Boesch, C., Hohmann, G., and Marchandt, L.F., eds (2002). *Behavioral Diversity in Chimpanzees and Bonobos*, Cambridge: Cambridge University Press.

Boivin, N. (2008). *Material Cultures, Material Minds: The Role of Things in Human Thought, Society and Evolution*. Cambridge: Cambridge University Press.

Botha, R. (2000). 'On the Role of Bridge Theories in Accounts of the Evolution of Language', *Language and Communication* 21: 149–60.

Botha, R. (2008). 'Prehistoric Shell Beads as a Window on Language Evolution', *Language and Communication* 28: 197–202.

Botha, R. (2009). 'Theoretical Underpinnings of Inferences about Language Evolution: The Syntax Used at Blombos Cave', in R. Botha and C. Knight (eds), *The Cradle of Language*. Oxford: Oxford University Press, pp. 93–111.

Botha, R. and Knight, C., eds (2009). *The Cradle of Language*. Oxford: Oxford University Press.

Botha, R. and de Swart, H., eds (2009). *Language Evolution: The View from Restricted Linguistic Systems*. Utrecht: LOT.

Bourdieu, P. (1972). *Outline of a Theory of Practice*. Cambridge: Cambridge University Press.

Bourguignon, E. (1973). *Religion, Altered States of Consciousness, and Social Change*. Columbus: Ohio State University Press.

Bouzouggar, A., Barton, N., Vanhaeren, M., d'Errico, F., Collcutt S., Higham, T., Hodge, E., Parfitt, S., Rhodes, E., Schwenninger, J.-L., Stringer, C., Turner, E., Ward, S., Moutmir, A., and Stambouli, A. (2007). '82,000-year-old Shell Beads from North Africa and Implications for the Origins of Modern Human Behavior', *Proceedings of the National Academy of Sciences* 104: 9964–9.

Bowlby, J. (1988). *A Secure Basis: Parent-Child Attachment and Healthy Human Development*. New York: Basic Books.

Bowles, S. (2006). 'Group Competition, Reproductive Leveling, and the Evolution of Altruism', *Science* 314: 1569–72.

Boyd, R. and Richerson, P.J. (1985). *Culture and the Evolutionary Process*. Chicago: University of Chicago Press.

Boyd, R. and Richerson, P.J. (2005). *The Origin and Evolution of Cultures*. New York: Oxford University Press.

Boyd, R. and Richerson, P.J. (2009). 'Culture and the Evolution of Human Cooperation', *Philosophical Transactions of the Royal Society B* 364: 3281–8.

Brandom, R. (1980). 'Asserting', *Journal of Philosophy* 77(11): 766–7.

Brandom, R. (1994). *Making It Explicit: Reasoning, Representing, and Discursive Commitment*. Cambridge, MA: Harvard University Press.

Bråten, S. (2007). 'Introduction', in S. Bråten (ed.), *On Being Moved: From Mirror Neurons to Empathy*. Amsterdam/Philadelphia: Benjamins, pp. 1–17.

Bräuer, G. (2008). 'The Origin of Modern Anatomy: By Speciation or Intraspecific Evolution?', *Evolutionary Anthropology* 17: 22–37.

Bräuer, G., Groden, C., Gröning, F., Kroll, A., Kupcyik, K., Mbua, E., Pommert, A., Schiemann, T. (2004). 'Virtual Study of the Endocranial Morphology of the Matrix-filled Cranium from Eliye Springs, Kenya', *The Anatomical Record Part A: Discoveries in Molecular, Cellular, and Evolutionary Biology* 276A: 113–33.

Brinck, I. (2004). 'Towards an Explanation of the Evolution of Language', in *Coevolution of Language and Theory of Mind*. Interdisciplines: Electronic Conference, <http://www.inter disciplines.org/medias/confs/archives/archive_7.pdf>.

Britten, R. (2002). 'Divergence between Samples of Chimpanzee and Human DNA Sequences is 5%, Counting Indels', *Proceedings of the National Academy of Sciences USA* 21: 13633–5.

Brown, J.E. (2012). 'The Evolution of Symbolic Communication: An Embodied Perspective', Ph.D. Thesis, University of Edinburgh.

Brown, P. (1991). *The Hypnotic Brain: Hypnotherapy and Social Communication*. New Haven, CT: Yale University Press.

Brown, S., Martinez, M.J., and Parsons, L.M. (2006). 'The Neural Basis of Human Dance', *Cerebral Cortex* 16: 1157–67.

Brumm, A., and Moore, M.W. (2005). 'Symbolic Revolutions and the Australian Archaeological Record', *Cambridge Archaeological Journal* 15: 157–75.

Bruner, J.S. (1975a). 'The Ontogenesis of Speech Acts', *Journal of Child Language* 2: 1–19.

Bruner, J.S. (1975b). 'From Communication to Language: A Psychological Perspective', *Cognition* 3: 255–87.

Bruner, J. (1986). *Actual Minds, Possible Worlds*. Cambridge, MA: Harvard University Press.

Bshary, R., Hohner, A., Ait-El-Djoudi, K., and Fricke, H. (2006). 'Interspecific Communicative and Coordinated Hunting between Groupers and Giant Moray Eels in the Red Sea', *PLoS Biology* 4: e431.

Buchsbaum, D., Bridgers, S., Skolnick Weisberg, D., and Gopnik, A. (2012). 'The Power of Possibility: Causal Learning, Counterfactual Reasoning, and Pretend Play', *Philosophical Transactions of the Royal Society B* 367: 2202–12. doi: 10.1098/rstb.2012.0122.

Burkart, J., Hrdy, S., and van Schaik, C. (2009). 'Cooperative Breeding and Human Cognitive Evolution', *Evolutionary Anthropology* 18: 175–86.

Burling, R. (1993). 'Primate Calls, Human Language, and Nonverbal Communication', *Current Anthropology* 34(1): 25–53.

Burling, R. (1999). 'Motivation, Conventionalization and Arbitrariness', in B.J. King (ed.), *The Origins of Language: What Nonhuman Primates Can Tell Us*. Santa Fe: School of American Research Press, pp. 307–50.

Burling, R. (2005). *The Talking Ape: How Language Evolved*. Oxford: Oxford University Press.

Burton, F.D. (2009). *Fire: The Spark that Ignited Human Evolution*. Albuquerque, NM: University of New Mexico Press.

Butterworth, G. and Jarrett, N. (1991). 'What Minds Have in Common is Space: Spatial Mechanisms Serving Joint Visual Attention in Infancy', *British Journal of Developmental Psychology* 9: 55–72.

Butynski, T.M. (1990). 'Comparative Ecology of Blue Monkeys (*Cercopithecus mitis*) in High- and Low-density Subpopulations', *Ecological Monographs* 60: 1–26.

Butzer, K. (1980). 'Comment on Wreshner: Red Ochre and Human Evolution', *Current Anthropology* 21: 635.

Butzer, K. and Vogel, J. (1979). 'Archeo-sedimentological Sequences from the Sub-montane Interior of South Africa: Rose Cottage Cave, Heuningsneskrans, and Bushman Rock Shelter'. Paper presented at Southern African Association of Archaeologists Workshop, *Towards a Better Understanding of the Upper Pleistocene in sub-Saharan Africa*, Stellenbosch, 27–29 June 1979.

Byrne, R.W. and Corp, N. (2004). 'Neocortex Size Predicts Deception Rate in Primates', *Proceedings of the Royal Society of London* B 271: 1693–9.

Byrne, R.W. and Tanner, J.E. (2006). 'Gestural Imitation by a Gorilla: Evidence and Nature of the Phenomenon', *International Journal of Psychology* 6: 215–31.

Byrne, R.W. and Whiten, A., eds (1988). *Machiavellian Intelligence.* Oxford: Oxford University Press.

Calame-Griaule, G. (1986). *Words and the Dogon World.* Philadelphia: Institute for the Study of Human Issues.

Call, J., Hare, B., Carpenter, M., and Tomasello, M. (2004). '"Unwilling" versus "Unable": Chimpanzees' Understanding of Human Intentional Action', *Developmental Science* 7: 488–98.

Call, J. and Tomasello, M. (2005). 'What Do Chimpanzees Know about Seeing Revisited: An Explanation of the Third Kind', in N. Eilan, C. Hoerl, T. McCormack, and J. Roessler (eds), *Issues in Joint Attention.* Oxford: Oxford University Press, pp. 234–53.

Call, J. and Tomasello, M., eds (2007). *The Gestural Communication of Apes and Monkeys.* Mahwah, NJ: Lawrence Erlbaum.

Callaghan, T., Moll, H., Rakoczy, H., Warneken, F., Liszkowski, U., Behne, T., et al. (2011). *Early Social Cognition in Three Cultural Contexts,* Monographs of the Society for Research in Child Development. Boston: Wiley-Blackwell.

Calvo-Merino, B., Glaser, D.E., Grèzes, J., Passingham, R.E., and Haggard, P. (2005). 'Action Observation and Acquired Motor Skills: An fMRI Study with Expert Dancers', *Cerebral Cortex* 15: 1243–9.

Calvo-Merino, B., Grèzes, J., Glaser, D.E., Passingham, R.E., and Haggard, P. (2006). 'Seeing or Doing? Influence of Visual and Motor Familiarity in Action Observation', *Current Biology* 16: 1905–10.

Capasso, L., Michetti, E., and D'Anastasio, R. (2008). 'A *Homo Erectus* Hyoid Bone: Possible Implications for the Origin of the Human Capability for Speech', *Coll Antropol* 32: 1007–11.

Carmody, R., Weintraub, G., and Wrangham, R. (2011). 'Energetic Consequences of Thermal and Nonthermal Food Processing', *Proceedings of the National Academy of Sciences USA* 108: 19199–203.

Caron, F., d'Errico, F., Del Moral, P., Santos, P., and Zilhão, J. (2011). 'The Reality of Neandertal Symbolic Behavior at the Grotte du Renne, Arcy-sur-Cure, France', *PLoS One* 6(6): e21545. doi:10.1371/journal.pone.0021545.

Carpenter, M., Nagell, K., and Tomasello, M. (1998). 'Social Cognition, Joint Attention, and Communicative Competence from 9 to 15 Months of Age', *Monographs of the Society for Research in Child Development* 255(63): 1–143.

Carruthers, P. (1996). *Language, Thought and Consciousness.* Cambridge: Cambridge University Press.

Carruthers, P. (2002). 'Human Creativity: Its Cognitive Basis, Its Evolution, and Its Connection to Childhood Pretence', *The British Journal for the Philosophy of Science* 53: 225–49. doi: 10.1093/bjps/53.2.225.

Cartmill, E.A. and Byrne, R.W. (2007). 'Orangutans Modify Their Gestural Signaling According to Their Audience's Comprehension', *Current Biology* 17: 1345–8.

Cartmill, M. and Smith, F. (2009). *The Human Lineage*. Hoboken, NJ: Wiley-Blackwell.

Casler, K., Terziyan, T., and Greene, K. (2009). 'Toddlers View Artifact Function Normatively', *Cognitive Development* 24: 240–7.

Castoriadis, C. (1998). *The Imaginary Institution of Society*. Cambridge MA: MIT Press.

de Castro, J.M.B., Martinón-Torres, M., Prado, L., Gómez-Robles, A., Rosell, J., López-Polín, L., Arsuaga, J.L., and Carbonell, E. (2010). 'New Immature Hominin Fossil from European Lower Pleistocene Shows the Earliest Evidence of a Modern Human Dental Development Pattern', *Proceedings of the National Academy of Sciences USA* 107: 11739–44.

de Castro, J.M.B., Rosas, A., Carbonell, E., Nicolás, M.E., Rodríguez, J., and Arsuaga, J.L. (1999). 'A Modern Human Pattern of Dental Development in Lower Pleistocene Hominids from Atapuerca-TD6 (Spain)', *Proceedings of the National Academy of Sciences USA* 96: 4210–13.

Castro, L., Medina, A., and Toro, M.A. (2004). 'Hominid Cultural Transmission and the Evolution of Language', *Biology and Philosophy* 19: 721–37.

Cavalli-Sforza, L.L., ed. (1986). *African Pygmies*. London: Academic Press.

Chase, P.G. (1994). 'On Symbols and the Palaeolithic', *Current Anthropology* 35: 627–9.

Chase, P.G. (1999). 'Symbolism as Reference and Symbolism as Culture', in R.I.M Dunbar, C. Knight, and C. Power (eds), *The Evolution of Culture: An Interdisciplinary View*. Edinburgh: Edinburgh University Press, pp. 34–49.

Chater, N., and Christiansen, M.H. (2009). 'Language Acquisition Meets Language Evolution', *Cognitive Science*: 1–27.

Chazan, M. and Horwitz, L.K. (2009). 'Milestones in the Development of Symbolic Behaviour: A Case Study from Wonderwerk Cave, South Africa', *World Archaeology* 41(4): 521–39.

Chazan, M., Ron, H., Matmon, A., Porat, N., Goldberg, P., Yates, R., Avery, M., Sumner, A., Horwitz, L. (2008). 'Radiometric Dating of the Earlier Stone Age Sequence in Excavation 1 at Wonderwerk Cave, South Africa: Preliminary results. *Journal of Human Evolution* 55: 1–11.

Chen, Y-S., Olckers, A., Schurr, T.G., Kogelnik, A.M., Huoponen, K., and Wallace, D.C. (2000). 'Mitochondrial DNA Variation in the South African Kung and Khwe—and their Genetic Relationships to Other African Populations', *American Journal of Human Genetics* 66: 1362–83.

Cheney, D.L. and Seyfarth, R.M. (1981). 'Selective Forces Affecting the Predator Alarm Calls of Vervet Monkeys', *Animal Behaviour* 76: 25–61.

Cheney, D.L. and Seyfarth, R.M. (1988). 'Assessment of Meaning and the Detection of Unreliable Signals in Vervet Monkeys', *Animal Behaviour* 36: 477–86.

Cheney, D.L. and Seyfarth, R.M. (2010). 'Primate Communication and Human Language: Continuities and Discontinuities', in P.M. Kappeler and J.B. Silk (eds), *Mind the Gap: Tracing the Origins of Human Universals*. Berlin/Heidelberg: Springer Verlag, pp. 283–98.

Chiao, J.Y., Li, Z., and Harada, T. (2008). 'Cultural Neuroscience of Consciousness: From Visual Perception to Self-Awareness', in C. Whitehead (ed.), *The Origin of Consciousness in the Social World*. Exeter: Imprint Academic, 58–69.

Chomsky, N. (1968). *Language and Mind*. New York: Harcourt, Brace.

Chomsky, N. (1986). *Knowledge of Language. Its Nature, Origin, and Use*. Westport, CT: Praeger.

Chomsky, N. (1991). 'Linguistics and Cognitive Science: Problems and Mysteries', in A. Kasher (ed.), *The Chomskyan Turn*. Oxford: Blackwell, pp. 26–53.

Chomsky, N. (2000). *New Horizons in the Study of Language and Mind*. Cambridge: Cambridge University Press.

Chomsky, N. (2002). *On Nature and Language*. Cambridge University Press.

Chomsky, N. (2005). 'Three Factors in Language Design', *Linguistic Inquiry* 36(1): 1–22.

Chomsky, N. (2010). 'Some Simple Evo-devo Theses: How True Might They Be for Language?', in R. Larson, V. Déprez, and H. Yamakido (eds), *The Evolution of Human Language*. Cambridge: Cambridge University Press, pp. 54–62.

Chomsky, N. (2012). *The Science of Language. Interviews with James McGilvray*. Cambridge: Cambridge University Press.

Christiansen, M.H. and Chater, N. (2008). 'Language as Shaped by the Brain', *Behavioral and Brain Sciences* 31(5): 489–509.

Christiansen, M.H. and Kirby, S. (2003). 'Language Evolution: the Hardest Problem in Science?', in M.H. Christiansen and S. Kirby (eds), *Language Evolution*. Oxford: Oxford University Press, pp. 1–15.

Churchill, S., Berger, L., Hartstone-Rose, A., and Headman Zondo, B. (2012). 'Body Size in African Middle Pleistocene Homo', in S. Reynolds and A. Gallagher (eds), *African Genesis: Perspectives on Hominin Evolution*. Cambridge: Cambridge University Press, pp. 319–46.

Clark, A. (2006). 'Language, Embodiment and the Cognitive Niche', *Trends in Cognitive Science* 10: 370–4.

Clark, D. (1975). 'Africa in Prehistory: Peripheral or Paramount', *Man* (N.S.) 10: 175–98.

Clark, H. (1996). *Using Language*. Cambridge: Cambridge University Press.

Clark, H.H. and Fox Tree, J.E. (2002). 'Using *Uh* and *Um* in Spontaneous Speaking', *Cognition* 84: 73–111.

Clay, Z., Pika, S., Gruber, T. and Zuberbühler, K. (2011). 'Bonobo Females Use Copulation Calls as Social Signals', *Biology Letters* 7: 513–16.

Clay, Z. and Zuberbühler, K. (2009). 'Food-associated Calling Sequences in Bonobos', *Animal Behaviour* 77: 1387e1396.

Clay, Z. and Zuberbühler, K. (2011a). 'Bonobos Extract Meaning from Call Sequences', *PLoS One* 6: e18786.

Clay, Z. and Zuberbühler, K. (2011b). 'The Structure of Bonobo Copulation Calls in Reproductive and Non-reproductive Sex'. *Ethology* 117: 1158–69.

Clay, Z. and Zuberbühler, K. (2012). 'Communication during Sex among Female Bonobos: Effects of Dominance, Solicitation and Audience', *Scientific Reports* 2: 291.

Cockburn, A. (2006). 'Prevalence of Different Modes of Parental Care in Birds', *Proceedings of the Royal Society of London Biology* 273: 1375–83.

Coltorti, M., Feraud, G., Marzoli, A., Peretto, C., Ton-That, T., Voinchet, P., Bahain, J.-J., Minelli, A., Thun Hohenstein, U. (2005). 'New ^{40}Ar/^{39}Ar, Stratigraphic and Palaeoclimatic Data on the Isernia La Pineta Lower Palaeolithic site, Molise, Italy', *Quarternary International* 131: 11–22.

Conard, N.J. and Niven, L. (2001). 'The Paleolithic Finds from Bollschweil and the Question of Neandertal Mammoth Hunting in the Black Forest', in G. Cavaretta, P. Giola, M. Mussi, and M.R. Palumbo (eds), *The World of Elephants: Proceedings of the First International Congress*. Rome, pp. 194–200.

Condillac, E. Bonnot de (1746). *Essai sur l'origine des connaissances humaines*. Paris: Ch. Houel.

Cooke, H., Malan, B., and Wells, L. (1945). 'Fossil Man in the Lebombo Mountains, South Africa: the "Border Cave", Ingwavuma District, Zululand', *Man* 3: 6–13.

Cooley, C.H. (1902). *Human Nature and the Social Order*. New York: Scribner.

Coqueugniot, H., Hublin, J.J., Veillon, F., Houët, F., and Jacob, T. (2004). 'Early Brain Growth in *Homo Erectus* and Implications for Cognitive Ability', *Nature* 431: 299–302.

Corballis, M.C. (1999). 'The Gestural Origins of Language', *American Scientist* 87: 138–45.

Corballis, M.C. (2002). *From Hand to Mouth: The Origins of Language*. Princeton, NJ: Princeton University Press.

Corballis, M.C. (2011). *The Recursive Mind: The Origins of Human Language, Thought, and Civilization*. Princeton, NJ: Princeton University Press.

Corballis, M.C. and Suddendorf, T. (2007). 'Memory, Time and Language', in C. Pasternak (ed.), *What Makes Us Human*. Oxford: Oneworld, pp. 133–45.

Costall, A. (2004). 'From Darwin to Watson (and Cognitivism) and Back Again: The Principle of Animal-environment Mutuality', *Behavior and Philosophy* 32: 179–95.

Coulson, S., Staurset, S., and Walker, N.J. (2011). 'Ritualized Behavior in the Middle Stone Age: Evidence from Rhino Cave, Tsodilo Hills, Botswana', *PaleoAnthropology*: 18–61.

Cremaschi, M. and Peretto, C. (1988). 'Le Paléolithique inférieur de la plaine du Pô', *L'Anthropologie* 92: 643–82.

Crockford, C. and Boesch, C. (2005). 'Call Combinations in Wild Chimpanzees', *Behaviour* 142: 397–421.

Crockford, C., Herbinger, I., Vigilant, L., and Boesch, C. (2004). 'Wild Chimpanzees Produce Group-specific Calls: A Case for Vocal Learning?', *Ethology* 110(3): 221–43.

Crockford, C., Wittig, R.M., Mundry, R., and Zuberbühler, K. (2012). 'Wild Chimpanzees Inform Ignorant Group Members of Danger', *Current Biology* 22: 142–6.

Croft, W. (2000). *Explaining Language Change: An Evolutionary Approach*. Harlow, Essex: Longman.

Croft, W. (2001). *Radical Construction Grammar*. Oxford: Oxford University Press.

Cross, E.S., Hamilton, A.F. de C., and Grafton, S.T. (2006). 'Building a Motor Simulation de novo: Observation of Dance by Dancers', *NeuroImage* 31: 1257–67.

Cross, I. (2005). 'Music and Meaning, Ambiguity and Evolution', in D. Miell, R. MacDonald, and D. Hargreaves (eds), *Musical Communication*. Oxford: Oxford University Press, pp. 27–43.

Crow, T.J. (2008). 'The "Big Bang" Theory of the Origin of Psychosis and the Faculty of Language', *Schizophrenia Research* 102: 31–52.

Crystal, J.D. (2010). 'Episodic-like Memory in Animals', *Behavioral Brain Research* 215(2): 235–43. doi:10.1016/j.bbr.2010.03.005.

Csibra, G. and Gergely, G. (2009). 'Natural Pedagogy,' *Trends in Cognitive Sciences* 13: 148–53.

Csibra, G. and Gergely, G. (2011). 'Natural Pedagogy As Evolutionary Adaptation', *Philosophical Transactions of the Royal Society B* 36: 1149–57. doi:10.1098/rstb.2010.0319.

Cummins, D.D. (1996). 'Evidence of Deontic Reasoning in 3- and 4-year-old Children', *Memory & Cognition* 24: 823–9.

Currie, G. (2011). 'The Master of the Masek Beds: Handaxes, Art, and the Minds of Early Humans', in E. Schellekens and P. Goldie (eds), *The Aesthetic Mind: Philosophy and Psychology*. Oxford: Oxford University Press, pp. 9–31.

Cysouw, M. and Comrie, B. (2009). 'How Varied Typologically Are the Languages of Africa?', in R. Botha and C. Knight (eds), *The Cradle of Language*. Oxford: Oxford University Press, pp. 189–203.

Dalby, J.T., Gibson, D., Grossi, V., and Schneider, R.D. (1980). 'Lateralized Hand Gestures during Speech', *Journal of Motor Behavior* 12(4): 292–7.

Dart, R.A. (1953). 'The Predatory Transition from Ape to Man', *International Anthropological and Linguistic Review* 1(4).

Darwin, C. (1845). *Journal of Researches into the Natural History and Geology of the Countries Visited During the Voyage Round the World of H.M.S. Beagle*. London: John Murray.

Darwin, C. (1859). *On the Origin of Species by Means of Natural Selection*. London: John Murray.

Darwin, C. (1868). *The Variation of Animals and Plants under Domestication*. London: John Murray.

Darwin, C. (1871). *The Descent of Man, and Selection in Relation to Sex*. London: John Murray.

Darwin, C. (1872). *The Expression of Emotions in Man and Animals*. London: John Murray.

Davidson, D. (1994). 'The Social Aspect of Language', in B. McGuiness and G. Oliveri (eds), *The Philosophy of Michael Dummett*. Dordrecht: Kluwer, pp. 1–16.

Davidson, D. (2006). *The Essential Davidson*. Oxford: Clarendon.

Davidson, I. (2003). 'The Archaeological Evidence of Language Origins: States of Art', in M.H. Christiansen and S. Kirby (eds), *Language Evolution*. Oxford: Oxford University Press.

Davies, R. and Underdown, S. (2006). 'The Neanderthals: a Social Synthesis', *Cambridge Archaeological Journal* 16: 145–64.

Dawkins, R. (1976). *The Selfish Gene*. Oxford: Oxford University Press.

Dawkins, R. (1982). *The Extended Phenotype*. Oxford: Oxford University Press.

Deacon, T.W. (1992a). 'The Human Brain', in S. Jones, R. Martin, and D. Pilbeam (eds), *The Cambridge Encyclopedia of Human Evolution*. Cambridge: Cambridge University Press, pp. 115–23.

Deacon, T.W. (1992b). 'Brain-Language Coevolution', in J.A. Hawkins and M. Gell-Mann (eds), *The Evolution of Human Languages*. Reading, MA: Addison-Wesley.

Deacon, T.W. (1997). *The Symbolic Species: The Co-evolution of Language and the Brain*. New York: Norton.

Deacon, T.W. (2010). 'Colloquium Paper: A Role for Relaxed Selection in the Evolution of the Language Capacity', *Proceedings of the National Academy of Sciences* 107 (May): 9000–6. doi:10.1073/pnas.0914624107.

Dediu, D. (2011). 'Are Languages Really Independent from Genes? If Not, What Would a Genetic Bias Affecting Language Diversity Look Like?', *Human Biology* 83: 279–96.

Dediu, D. and Ladd, D.R. (2007). 'Linguistic Tone Is Related to the Population Frequency of the Adaptive Haplogroups of Two Brain Size Genes, ASPM and Microcephalin', *Proceedings of the National Academy of Sciences USA* 104: 10944–9.

Dediu, D. and Levinson, S.C. (2013). 'On the Antiquity of Language: The Reinterpretation of Neandertal Linguistic Capacities and its Consequences', *Frontiers in Psychology* 4: 397.

DeGusta, D., Gilbert, W.H., and Turner, S.P. (1999). 'Hypoglossal Canal Size and Hominid Speech', *Proceedings of the National Academy of Sciences USA* 96: 1800–4.

Delpeche, F. and Prat, F. (1995). 'Nouvelles observations sur les faunes Acheuléennes de Combe Grenal (Dom, Dordogne)', *Paleo* 7: 123–37.

de Lumley, H. (1966). 'Les fouilles de Terra Amata à Nice', *Bulletin du Musée d'Anthropologie Préhistorique de Monaco* 13: 29–51.

Demars, P.-Y. (1992). 'Les colorants dans le Moustérien du Périgord: l'apport des fouilles de F. Bordes', *Préhistoire Ariegeoise* 47: 185–94.

De Miguel, C. and Henneberg, M. (2001). 'Variation in Hominid Brain Size: How Much is Due to Method? *Homo* 52: 3–58.

Demolin, D. (1993). 'Les rêveurs de la forêt. Polyphonies des Pygmées Efe de l'Itouri (Zaïre)'. *Cahiers de Musiques Traditionnelles* 6 'Polyphonies': 139–51.

Dennell, R.W., Martinón-Torres, M., and de Castro, J.M.B. (2011). 'Hominin Variability, Climatic Instability and Population Demography in Middle Pleistocene Europe', *Quaternary Science Reviews* 30: 1511–24.

Deputte, B.L. and Goustard, M. (1980). 'Copulatory Vocalizations of Female Macaques (*Macaca Fascicularis*): Variability Factors Analysis', *Primates* 21(1): 83–99.

de Ruiter, J.P., Mitterer, H., and Enfield, N.J. (2006). 'Projecting the End of a Speaker's Turn: A Cognitive Cornerstone of Conversation', *Language* 82(3): 515–35.

Descola, P. (1993). 'Les affinités sélectives: alliance, guerre et prédation dans l'ensemble Jivaro', *L'Homme* 126–8: 171–90.

Dessalles, J.-L. (1998). 'Altruism, Status and the Origin of Relevance', in J.R. Hurford, M. Studdert-Kennedy, and C. Knight (eds), *Approaches to the Evolution of Language: Social and Cognitive Bases*. Cambridge: Cambridge University Press, pp. 130–47.

Dessalles, J.-L. (1999). 'Coalition Factor in the Evolution of Non-kin Altruism', *Advances in Complex Systems* 2(2): 143–72.

Dessalles, J.-L. (2008). 'From Metonymy to Syntax in the Communication of Events', *Interaction Studies* 9(1): 51–65.

Dessalles, J.-L. (2009). *Why We Talk—The Evolutionary Origins of Language*. 2nd edn. Oxford: Oxford University Press.

Dessalles, J.-L. (2010a). 'From Metonymy to Syntax in the Communication of Events', in M.A. Arbib and D. Bickerton (eds), *The Emergence of Protolanguage—Holophrasis vs Compositionality*. Amsterdam: John Benjamins, pp. 51–65.

Dessalles, J.-L. (2010b). *Providing Information Can Be a Stable Non-cooperative Evolutionary Strategy*. Paris: Technical Report Telecom ParisTech 2010D025, <http://service.tsi.telecom-paristech.fr/cgi-bin/valipub_download.cgi?dId=223>.

Dessalles, J.-L. (2010c). 'Have You Anything Unexpected to Say? The Human Propensity to Communicate Surprise and its Role in the Emergence of Language', in A.D.M. Smith, M. Schouwstra, B. de Boer, and K. Smith (eds), *The Evolution of Language—Proceedings of the 8th International Conference (Evolang 8—Utrecht)*. Singapore: World Scientific, pp. 99–106.

Dessalles, J.-L. (2011). 'Sharing Cognitive Dissonance as a Way to Reach Social Harmony', *Social Science Information* 50(1): 116–27.

Deutscher, G. (2005). *The Unfolding of Language: The Evolution of Mankind's Greatest Invention*. London: Random House.

Dewey, J. (1938). *Experience and Education*. New York: Touchstone.

Dibble, H. and McPherron, S. (2006). 'The Missing Mousterian', *Current Anthropology* 47: 777–803.

Diderot, D. (1751). 'Lettre sur les sourds et muets (Letter of deaf mutes)', in M. Jourdain (ed.), *Diderot's Early Philosophical Works*. Chicago: Open Court Publishing, 1904, pp. 160–218.

Diessel, H. (1999). *Demonstratives: Form, Function, and Grammaticalization*. Amsterdam: John Benjamins.

Diller, K.C. and Cann, R.L. (2009). 'Evidence Against a Genetic-based Revolution in Language 50,000 Years Ago', in R. Botha and C. Knight (eds), *The Cradle of Language—Studies in the Evolution of Language*. Oxford: Oxford University Press, pp. 135–49.

Diller, K.C. and Cann, R.L. (2012). 'Genetic Influences on Language Evolution: An Evaluation of the Evidence', in M. Tallerman and K.R. Gibson (eds), *The Oxford Handbook of Language Evolution*. Oxford: Oxford University Press, pp. 168–175.

Dilthey, W. (1883–1911). *Selected Writings*, ed. H.P. Rickman. Cambridge: Cambridge University Press, 1976.

Dingemanse, M. and Floyd, S. (2014). 'Conversational Structures in Cross-linguistic Perspective', in N.J. Enfield, P. Kockelman, and J. Sidnell (eds), *The Cambridge Handbook of Linguistic Anthropology*. Cambridge: Cambridge University Press. Forthcoming.

Donald, M. (1991). *Origins of the Modern Mind: Three Stages in the Evolution of Culture and Cognition*. Cambridge, MA: Harvard University Press.

Donald, M. (2001). *A Mind So Rare*. New York: Norton.

Donges, J., Donner, R., Trauth, M., Marwan, N., Schellnhuber, H.-J., and Kurths, J. (2011). 'Nonlinear Detection of Paleoclimate-variability Transitions Possibly Related to Human Evolution', *Proceedings of the National Academy of Sciences USA* 108: 20422–7.

Dor, D. (2011). *Language as a Communication Technology: A Proposal for a New General Linguistic Theory*. <http://people.socsci.tau.ac.il/mu/danield/linguistics-2/language-as-a-communication-technology/>.

Dor, D. and Jablonka, E. (2000). 'From Cultural Selection to Genetic Selection: A Framework for the Evolution of Language', *Selection* 1–3: 33–55.

Dor, D. and Jablonka, E. (2001). 'How Language Changed the Genes: Towards an Explicit Account of the Evolution of Language', in J. Trabant (ed.), *Essays on the Origin of Language*. Berlin: Mouton, pp. 149–75.

Dor, D. and Jablonka, E. (2004). 'Culture and Genes in the Evolution of Human Language', in N. Goren-Inbar and J.D. Speth (eds), *Human Paleoecology in the Levantine Corridor*. Oxford: Oxbow Books, pp. 105–14.

Dor, D. and Jablonka, E. (2010). 'Canalization and Plasticity in the Evolution of Linguistic Communication', in R.K. Larson, V. Deprez, and H. Yamakido (eds), *The Evolution of Human Language*. Cambridge: Cambridge University Press, pp. 135–47.

Dore, J. (1974). 'A Pragmatic Description of Early Language Development', *Journal of Psycholinguistic Research* 3 (October): 343–50. doi:10.1007/BF01068169.

Dore, J. (1975). 'Holophrases, Speech Acts and Language Universals,' *Journal of Child Language* 2: 21–40. doi:10.1017/S0305000900000878.

Dore, J. (1978). 'Conditions for the Acquisition of Speech Acts', in I. Marková (ed.), *The Social Context of Language*. Chichester: Wiley, pp. 87–111.

Duarte, C., Maurício, J., Pettitt, P.B., Souto, P., Trinkaus, E., van der Plicht, H., and Zilhão, J. (1999). 'The Early Upper Paleolithic Human Skeleton from the Abrigo Do Lagar Velho

(Portugal) and Modern Human Emergence in Iberia', *Proceedings of the National Academy of Sciences USA* 96: 7604–9.

DuBrul, E.L. (1977). 'Origins of the Speech Apparatus and Its Reconstruction in Fossils', *Brain and Language* 4: 365–81.

Dugatkin, L.A. (2008). *Principles of Animal Behavior*. New York: Norton.

Dunbar, R.I.M. (1991). 'Functional Significance of Social Grooming in Primates', *Folia Primatologica* 57: 121–31.

Dunbar, R.I.M. (1993). 'Coevolution of Neocortical Size, Group Size and Language in Humans', *Behavioral and Brain Sciences* 16: 681–735.

Dunbar, R.I.M. (1996a). 'Determinants of Group Size in Primates: A General Model', in W.G. Runciman, J. Maynard Smith, and R.I.M. Dunbar (eds), *Evolution of Social Behaviour Patterns in Primates and Man*. Oxford: Oxford University Press, pp. 33–57.

Dunbar, R.I.M. (1996b). *Grooming, Gossip and the Evolution of Language*. London: Faber & Faber.

Dunbar, R.I.M. (1998). 'The Social Brain Hypothesis', *Evolutionary Anthropology* 7: 178–90.

Dunbar, R.I.M. (2003). 'The Social Brain: Mind, Language and Society in Evolutionary Perspective', *Annual Review of Anthropology* 32: 163–81.

Dunbar, R.I.M. (2009). 'Why Only Humans Have Language', in R. Botha and C. Knight (eds), *The Prehistory of Language*. Oxford: Oxford University Press, pp. 12–35.

Dunbar, R.I.M. (2010). 'Deacon's Dilemma: The Problem of Pair-bonding in Human Evolution', in R. Dunbar, C. Gamble, and J. Gowlett (eds), *Social Brain, Distributed Mind*. Oxford, New York: The British Academy, pp. 155–75.

Dunbar, R.I.M., Duncan, N., and Nettle, D. (1995). 'Size and Structure of Freely Forming Conversational Groups', *Human Nature* 6(1): 67–78.

Duncan, S. (1972). 'Some Signals and Rules for Taking Speaking Turns in Conversations', *Journal of Personality and Social Psychology* 24(2): 283–92.

Dunn, J. (1991). 'Young Children's Understanding of Other People: Evidence from Observations within the Family', in D. Frye and C. Moore (eds), *Children's Theories of Mind: Mental States and Social Understanding*. London: Lawrence Erlbaum Associates, pp. 97–114.

Dunn, M., Greenhill, S.J., Levinson, S.C., and Gray, R.D. (2011). 'Evolved Structure of Language Shows Lineage-specific Trends in Word-order Universals', *Nature* 473: 79–82. doi:10.1038/nature09923.

Duranti, A. (1997). *Linguistic Anthropology*. Cambridge: Cambridge University Press.

Duranti, A. and Goodwin, C. (1992). *Rethinking Context: Language as an Interactive Phenomenon*. Cambridge: Cambridge University Press.

Durkheim, É. (1895). *Les règles de la méthode sociologique*. Paris: Alcan.

Durkheim, É. (1964 [1912]). *The Elementary Forms of the Religious Life*. London: Allen & Unwin.

Early, R.L. (2010). 'Social Eavesdropping and the Evolution of Conditional Cooperation and Cheating Strategies', *Philosophical Transaction of the Royal Society Biology* 365: 2675–86.

Eckert, P. (2012). 'Three Waves of Variation Study: The Emergence of Meaning in the Study of Variation', *Annual Review of Anthropology* 41: 87–100.

Eckert, P. and Newmark, R. (1980). 'Central Eskimo Song Duels: A Contextual Analysis of Ritual Ambiguity', *Ethnology*, 19(2): 191–211.

Edwards, C. (2000). 'Children's Play in Cross-cultural Perspective', *Cross-Cultural Research*, 34(4): 318–38.

Eggins, S. and Slade, D. (1997). *Analysing Casual Conversation*. London: Equinox.

Eibl-Eibesfeldt, I. (1989). *Human Ethology*. New York: Aldine de Gruyter.

Eigsti, I.-M., de Marchena, A.B., Schuh, J.M., and Kelley, E. (2011). 'Language Acquisition in Autism Spectrum Disorders: A Developmental Review', *Research in Autism Spectrum Disorders* 5(June): 681–91. doi:10.1016/j.rasd.2010.09.001.

Eisenberg, N. (2000). 'Empathy and Sympathy', in M. Lewis and J.M. Haviland-Jones (eds), *Handbook of Emotion*. 2nd edn. New York: Guilford Press, pp. 677–91.

Ejiri, K. and Masataka, N. (2001). 'Co-occurrence of Preverbal Vocal Behavior and Motor Action in Early Infancy', *Developmental Science* 4: 40–8.

Ekman, P. (1979). 'About Brows: Emotional and Conversational Signals', in M. von Cranach, K. Foppa, W. Lepenies, and D. Ploog (eds), *Human Ethology: Claims and Limits of a New Discipline*. Cambridge: Cambridge University Press, pp. 169–202.

Elman, J., Karmiloff-Smith, A., Bates, E., Johnson, M., Parisi, D., and Plunkett, K. (1996). *Rethinking Innateness: A Connectionist Perspective on Development*. Cambridge, MA: MIT.

Enard, W., Przeworski, M., Fisher, S.E., Lai, C.S.L., Wiebe, V., Kitano, T., Monaco, A.P., and Pääbo, S. (2002). 'Molecular Evolution of FOXP2, a Gene Involved in Speech and Language', *Nature* 418: 869–72.

Endicott, P., Ho, S., and Stringer, C. (2010). 'Using Genetic Evidence to Evaluate Four Palaeoanthropological Hypotheses for the Timing of the Neanderthal and Modern Human Origins', *Journal of Human Evolution* 59: 87–95.

Enfield, N.J. (2003). *Linguistic Epidemiology: Semantics and Grammar of Language Contact in Mainland Southeast Asia*. London: Routledge.

Enfield, N.J. (2005). 'The Body as a Cognitive Artifact in Kinship Representations: Hand Gesture Diagrams by Speakers of Lao', *Current Anthropology* 46(1): 51–81.

Enfield, N.J. (2007). *A Grammar of Lao*. Berlin: Mouton de Gruyter.

Enfield, N.J. (2008). 'Transmission Biases in Linguistic Epidemiology', *Journal of Language Contact THEMA* 2: 295–306.

Enfield, N.J. (2009a). *The Anatomy of Meaning: Speech, Gesture, and Composite Utterances*. Cambridge: Cambridge University Press.

Enfield, N.J. (2009b). 'Everyday Ritual in the Residential World', in G. Senft and E.B. Basso (eds), *Ritual Communication*. Oxford: Berg, pp. 51–80.

Enfield, N.J. (2011). 'Sources of Asymmetry in Human Interaction: Enchrony, Status, Knowledge and Agency', in T. Stivers, L. Mondada, and J. Steensig (eds), *The Morality of Knowledge in Conversation*. Cambridge: Cambridge University Press, pp. 285–312.

Enfield, N.J. (2013). *Relationship Thinking: Agency, Enchrony, and Human Sociality*. New York: Oxford University Press.

Enfield, N.J. and Levinson, S.C. (2006). 'Introduction: Human Sociality as a New Interdisciplinary Field', in N.J. Enfield and S.C. Levinson (eds), *Roots of Human Sociality: Culture, Cognition and Interaction*, Oxford: Berg, pp. 1–35.

Enfield, N.J., Sidnell, J., and Kockelman, P. (2014). *The Cambridge Handbook of Linguistic Anthropology*. Cambridge: Cambridge University Press.

Erdal, D. and Whiten, A. (1994). 'On Human Egalitarianism: An Evolutionary Product of Machiavellian Status Escalation?', *Current Anthropology* 35(2): 175–83.

Erdal, D. and Whiten, A. (1996). 'Egalitarianism and Machiavellian Intelligence in Human Evolution', in P. Mellars and K. Gibson (eds), *Modelling the Early Human Mind*. Cambridge: McDonald Institute Monographs, pp. 139–50.

d'Errico, F. (2003). 'The Invisible Frontier: A Multiple Species Model for the Origin of Behavioral Modernity', *Evolutionary Anthropology* 12: 188–202.

d'Errico, F., Henshilwood, C., Lawson, G., Vanhaeren, M., Tillier, A.-M., Soressi, M., Bresson, F., Maureille, B., Nowell, A., Lakarra, J., Backwell, L., and Julien, M. (2003). 'Archaeological Evidence for the Emergence of Language, Symbolism, and Music—An Alternative Multi-disciplinary Perspective', *Journal of World Prehistory* 17: 1–70.

d'Errico, F., Henshilwood, C.S., Vanhaeren, M., and van Niekerk, K. (2005). '*Nassarius kraussianus* Shell Beads from Blombos Cave: Evidence for Symbolic Behaviour in the Middle Stone Age', *Journal of Human Evolution* 48: 3–24.

d'Errico, F. and Nowell, A. (2000). 'A New Look at the Berekhat Ram Figurine: Implications for the Origins of Symbolism', *Cambridge Archaeological Journal* 10: 123–67.

d'Errico, F. and Soressi, M. (2002). 'Systematic Use of Manganese Pigment by the Pech-de-l'Azé Neandertals: Implications for the Origin of Behavioral Modernity', *Journal of Human Evolution* 42: A13.

d'Errico, F. and Stringer, C. (2011). 'Evolution, Revolution or Saltation Scenario for the Emergence of Modern Culture', *Philosophical Transactions of the Royal Society, Series B.* 366: 1060–9.

d'Errico, F. and Vanhaeren, M. (2009). 'Earliest Personal Ornaments and Their Significance for the Origin of Language Debate', in R. Botha and C. Knight (eds), *The Cradle of Language*. Oxford: Oxford University Press, pp. 16–40.

d'Errico, F., Vanhaeren, M., Henshilwood, C.S., Lawson, G., Maureille, B., Gambier, D., Tillier, A.-M., Soressi, M., and van Niekerk, K. (2009). 'From the Origin of Language to the Diversification of Languages: What Can Archaeology and Palaeoanthropology Say?', in F. d'Errico and J.-M. Hombert (eds), *Becoming Eloquent: Advances in the Emergence of Language, Human Cognition, and Modern Cultures*. Amsterdam: John Benjamins, pp. 13–68.

Ervin-Tripp, S.M. (1991). 'Play in Language Development', in B. Scales, A. Almy, A. Nicolopoulou, and S. M. Ervin-Tripp (eds), *Play and the Social Context of Development in Early Care and Education*. New York: Columbia Teachers College, pp. 84–98.

Evans, C.S. and Marler, P. (1995). 'Language and Animal Communication: Parallels and Contrasts', in H. L. Roitblat and J.-A. Meyers (eds), *Comparative Approaches to Cognitive Science: Complex Adaptive Systems*. Cambridge, MA: MIT Press.

Evans, N. (2011). *Dying Words: Endangered Languages and What They Have to Tell Us*. Wiley-Blackwell.

Evans, N. and Levinson, S.C. (2009). 'The Myth of Language Universals: Language Diversity and Its Importance for Cognitive Science', *Behavioral and Brain Sciences* 32: 429–92.

Evans, P.D., Mekel-Bobrov, N., Vallender, E.J., Hudson, R.R., and Lahn, B.T. (2006). 'Evidence That the Adaptive Allele of the Brain Size Gene Microcephalin Introgressed into *Homo Sapiens* from an Archaic Homo Lineage.' *Proceedings of the National Academy of Sciences USA* 103: 18178–83.

Fagundes, N., Ray, N., Beaumont, M., Neuenschwander, S., Salzano, F., Bonatto, S., and Excoffier, L. (2007). 'Statistical Evaluation of Alternative Models of Human Evolution', *Proceedings of the National Academy of Sciences USA* 104: 17614–19.

Falguères, C., Bahain, J.-J., Pérez-González, A., Mercier, N., Santonja, M., and Dolo, J.-M. (2006). 'The Lower Acheulian Site of Ambrona, Soria (Spain): Ages Derived from a Combined ESR/U-series Model', *Journal of Archaeological Science* 33: 149–57.

Falguères, C., Yokoyama, Y., and Quaegebeur, J.-P. (1991). 'Datation par la resonance de spin électronique (E.S.R.) de sédments quaternaires', *Cahiers du Quaternaires* 16: 39–52.

Falk, D. (1975). 'Comparative Anatomy of the Larynx in Man and the Chimpanzee: Implications for Language in Neanderthal', *American Journal of Physical Anthropology* 43: 123–32.

Farrell, J. and Rabin, M. (1996). 'Cheap talk', *Journal of Economic Perspectives* 10: 110–18.

Fay, J.M. (1989). 'Hand-clapping in Western Lowland Gorillas'. *Mammalia* 53(3): 457–8.

Feblot-Augustins, J. (1993). 'Mobility Strategies in the Late Middle Palaeolithic of Central and Western Europe: Elements of Stability and Variability', *Journal of Archaeology* 12: 211–65.

Fedor, A., Brauer, J., Caplan, D., Friederici, A.D., Gulyás, B., Hagoort, P., Nazir, T., Pléh, C., and Singer, W. (2009). 'What Are the Brain Mechanisms Underlying Syntactic Operations?', in D. Bickerton and E. Szathmary (eds), *Biological Foundations and Origin of Syntax*. Cambridge, MA: MIT Press.

Finnegan, M. (2008). *The Political is Personal: Eros, Ritual Dialogue, and the Speaking Body in Central African Hunter-Gatherer Society*, Ph.D. Thesis, University of Edinburgh.

Finnegan, M. (2009). 'Political Bodies: Some Thoughts on Women's Power among Central African Hunter-Gatherers', *Radical Anthropology* 3: 31–7.

Finnegan, M. (2013). 'The Politics of Eros: Ritual Dialogue and Egalitarianism in Three Central African Hunter-Gatherer Societies', *Journal of the Royal Anthropological Institute* (N.S.) 19: 617–715.

Fisher, H. (1992). *Anatomy of Love: A Natural History of Mating, Marriage, and Why We Stray*. New York: Random House.

Fisher, S.E. and Scharff, C. (2009). 'FOXP2 as a Molecular Window into Speech and Language', *Trends Genet* 25: 166–77.

Fitch, W.T. (2000). 'The Phonetic Potential of Nonhuman Vocal Tracts: Comparative Cineradiographic Observations of Vocalizing Animals', *Phonetica* 57: 205–18.

Fitch, W.T. (2002). 'Comparative Vocal Production and the Evolution of Speech: Reinterpreting the Descent of the Larynx', in A. Wray (ed.), *The Transition to Language*. Oxford: Oxford University Press, pp. 21–45.

Fitch, W.T. (2004). 'Evolving Honest Communication Systems: Kin Selection and "Mother Tongues"', in D.K. Oller and U. Griebel (eds), *The Evolution of Communication Systems: A Comparative Approach*. Cambridge, MA: MIT Press, pp. 275–96.

Fitch, W.T. (2009). 'Fossil Cues to the Evolution of Speech,' in R. Botha and C. Knight (eds), *The Cradle of Language*. Oxford: Oxford University Press, pp. 112–34.

Fitch, W.T. (2010). *The Evolution of Language*. Oxford: Oxford University Press.

Fitch, W.T. (2011a). 'The Evolution of Syntax: An Exaptationist Perspective', *Frontiers in Evolutionary Neuroscience* 3: 9.

Fitch, W.T. (2011b). 'Biological Versus Cultural Evolution: Beyond a False Dichotomy: Comment on *Modeling the Cultural Evolution of Language* by Luc Steels', *Physics of Life Reviews* 8(4): pp. 357–8.

Fitch, W.T. (2012). 'Innateness and Human Language: A Biological Perspective', in M. Tallerman and K.R. Gibson (eds), *The Oxford Handbook of Language Evolution*. Oxford: Oxford University Press, pp. 143–56.

Fitch, W.T., Hauser, M.D., and Chomsky, N. (2005). 'The Evolution of the Language Faculty: Clarifications and Implications', *Cognition* 97(2): 179–210.

Flack, J.C. and de Waal, F.B.M. (2000). 'Any Animal Whatever: Darwinian Building Blocks of Morality in Monkeys and Apes', *Journal of Consciousness Studies* 7(1–2): 1–29.

Floss, H. (2003). 'Did They Meet or Not? Observations on Châtelperronian and Aurignacian Settlement Patterns in Eastern France', in J. Zilhão and F. d'Errico (eds), *The Chronology of the Aurignacian and of the Transitional Technocomplexes. Dating, Stratigraphies, Cultural Implications*. Lisboa: Trabalhos De Arqueologia, pp. 273–87.

Fodor, J.A. (1975). *The Language of Thought*. Cambridge, MA: Harvard University Press.

Fodor, J.A. (1987). *Psychosemantics*. Cambridge, MA: MIT Press.

Ford, C.E. (1993). *Grammar in Interaction: Adverbial Clauses in American English*. Cambridge: Cambridge University Press.

Fossey, D. (1983). *Gorillas In the Mist*. London: Hodder & Stoughton.

Fouts, D.H. (1989). 'Signing Interactions between Mother and Infant Chimpanzees', in P.G. Heltne and L.A. Marquardt (eds), *Understanding Chimpanzees*. Cambridge, MA: Harvard University Press, pp. 242–51.

Fouts, R.S. (1974). 'Language: Origins, Definitions and Chimpanzees', *Journal of Human Evolution* 3: 475–82.

Franciscus, R.G. (2009). 'When Did the Modern Human Pattern of Childbirth Arise? New Insights from an Old Neandertal Pelvis', *Proceedings of the National Academy of Sciences USA* 106: 9125–6.

Fridrich, J. (1976). 'Příspěvek k Problematice Počátků Uměleckého a Estetického Cítění u Paleantropů: ein Beitrag zur Frage nach den Anfängen des Künstlerischen und Ästhetischen Sinns der Urmenschens (Vor-Neandertaler, Neandertaler)', *Pamatky Archeologicke* 68: 5–27.

Fürniss, S. (1993). 'Rigueur et liberté: la polyphonie vocale des Pygmées Aka (Centrafrique)', in C. Meyer (ed.), *Polyphonies de tradition orale. Histoire et traditions vivantes*. Paris: Créaphis, pp. 101–31.

Fürniss, S. (1999). 'La Conception de la musique vocale chez les Aka: Terminologie et combinatoires de paramètres', *Journal des Africanistes* 69(2): 147–62.

Fürniss, S. (2006). 'Aka Polyphony: Music, Theory, Back and Forth', in M. Tenzer (ed.), *Analytical Studies in World Music*. Oxford: Oxford University Press, pp. 163–204.

Fürniss, S. (2007). *Approche Interdisciplinaire des Musiques Pygmées*, Habilitation à diriger des recherches, Université Paris X—Nanterre.

Fürniss, S. and Bahuchet, S. (1995). 'Existe-t-il des Instruments de Musique Pygmées?', in V. Dehoux, S. Fürniss, S. Le Bomin, E. Olivier, H. Rivere, and F. Voisin (eds), *Ndroje Balendro: Musiques, terrains et disciplines. Textes offerts à Simha Arom*. Louvain-Paris: PEETERS (Selaf 359), pp. 67–86.

Fürniss, S. and Olivier, E. (1997). 'Systématique musicale pygmée et bochiman: deux conceptions africaines du contrepoint', *Musurgia. Analyse et pratiques musicales* 4(3): 9–30.

Furuichi, T. (1989). 'Social Interactions and the Life History of Female *Pan Paniscus* in Wamba, Zaire', *International Journal of Primatology* 10(3): 173–97.

Furuichi, T. (2009). 'Factors Underlying Party Size Differences between Chimpanzees and Bonobos: A Review and Hypotheses for Future Study', *Primates* 50(3): 197–209.

Gabora, L. (2003). 'Cultural Focus: A Cognitive Explanation for the Cultural Transition of the Middle/Upper Paleolithic', in *Proceedings of the 25th Annual Meeting of the Cognitive Science Society*. Lawrence Erlbaum Associates.

Gabunia, L., Vekua, A., Lordkipanidze, D., Swisher III, C.C., Ferring, R., Justus, A., Nioradze, M., Tvalchrelidze, M., Antón, S.C., Bosinski, G., Jöris, O., de Lumley, M.-A., Majsuradze, G., and Mouskhelishvili, A. (2000). 'Earliest Pleistocene Hominid Cranial Remains from Dmanisi, Republic of Georgia: Taxonomy, Geological Setting, and Age', *Science* 288: 1019–25.

Galantucci, B. (2005). 'An Experimental Study of the Emergence of Human Communication Systems', *Cognitive Science* 29(5): 737–67.

Gallagher, S. (2008). 'Direct perception in the intersubjective context,' *Consciousness and Cognition* 17: 535–43.

Gallup, G.G. (1994). 'Self-Recognition: Research Strategies and Experimental Design', in S.T. Parker, R.W. Mitchell, and M.L. Boccia (eds), *Self-awareness in Animals and Humans*. Cambridge: Cambridge University Press, pp. 35–50.

Gärdenfors, P. (1995). Cued and detached representations in animal cognition. *Behavioural Processes* 35(1–3): 263–73.

Gärdenfors, P. and Warglien, M. (2006). 'Cooperation, Conceptual Spaces and the Evolution of Semantics', in P. Vogt, Y. Sugita, E. Tuci, and C. Nehaniv (eds), *Symbol Grounding and Beyond*. Berlin: Springer, pp. 16–30.

Gardiner, A. (1932). *The Theory of Speech and Language*. Oxford: Clarendon.

Gardner, R.A. and Gardner, B. (1969). 'Teaching Sign Language to a Chimpanzee', *Science* 165: 664–72.

Gardner, R.A., Gardner, B., and Van Cantford, T.E. (1989). *Teaching Sign Language to Chimpanzees*. Albany, NY: State University of New York Press.

Garfinkel, H. (1967). *Studies in Ethnomethodology*. Englewood Cliffs, NJ: Prentice-Hall.

Gargett, R.H. (1999). 'Middle Palaeolithic Burial is Not a Dead Issue: The View from Qafzeh, Saint-Cesaire, Kebara, Amud, and Dederiyeh', *Journal of Human Evolution* 37: 27–90.

Garrigan, D., Mobasher, Z., Kingan, S.B., Wilder, J.A., and Hammer, M.F. (2005a). 'Deep Haplotype Divergence and Long-range Linkage Disequilibrium at Xp21.1 Provide Evidence that Humans Descend from a Structured Ancestral Population', *Genetics* 170: 1849–56.

Garrigan, D., Mobasher, Z., Severson, T., Wilder, J.A., and Hammer, M. F. (2005b). 'Evidence for Archaic Asian Ancestry on the Human X Chromosome', *Molecular Biology and Evolution* 22: 189–92.

Garvey, C. and Kramer, T. (1989). 'The Language of Social Pretend Play', *Developmental Review* 9(4): 364–82.

Gaskins, S. (2000). 'Children's Daily Activities in a Mayan Village: A Culturally Grounded Description', *Cross-Cultural Research* 34(4): 375–89.

Gaskins, S., Haight, W., and Lancy, D. (2007). 'The Cultural Construction of Play', in A. Göncü and S. Gaskins (eds), *Play and Development: Evolutionary, Sociocultural and Functional Perspectives*. Mahwah, NJ: Lawrence Erlbaum, pp. 179–202.

Gaudzinski-Windheuser, S. and Roebroeks, W. (2011). 'On Neanderthal Subsistence in Last Interglacial Forested Environments in Northern Europe', in N. Conard and J. Richter (eds), *Neanderthal Lifeways, Subsistence and Technology: One Hundred and Fifty Years of Neanderthal Study*. Vertebrate Paleobiology and Paleoanthropology Series, no. 19. Dordrecht: Springer, pp. 61–71.

Gellner, E. (1989). 'Culture, Constraint and Community: Semantic and Coercive Compensations for the Genetic Under-determination of *Homo sapiens sapiens*', in P. Mellars and C. Stringer (eds), *The Human Revolution. Behavioural and Biological Perspectives in the Origins of Modern Humans*. Edinburgh: Edinburgh University Press, pp. 514–25.

Gentilucci, M. and Corballis, M.C. (2006). 'From Manual Gesture to Speech: a Gradual Transition', *Neuroscience and Biobehavioral Reviews* 30: 949–60.

Gentilucci, M. and Dalla Volta, R. (2007). 'The Motor System and the Relationship Between Speech and Gesture', *Gesture* 7(2): 159–77.

Gentilucci, M. and Dalla Volta, R. (2008). 'Spoken Language and Arm Gestures Are Controlled by the Same Motor Control System', *Quarterly Journal of Experimental Psychology*, 61(6): 944–57.

Genty, E., Breuer, T., Hobaiter, C., and Byrne, R.W. (2009). 'Gestural Communication of the Gorilla (*Gorilla gorilla*): Repertoire, Intentionality and Possible Origins', *Animal Cognition* 12(3): 527–46.

Gergely, G. and Csibra, G. (2006). 'Sylvia's Recipe: The Role of Imitation and Pedagogy in the Transmission of Cultural Knowledge', in N.J. Enfield and S.C. Levinson (eds), *Roots of Human Sociality*. London: Berg, pp. 229–55.

German, T.P., Niehaus, J.L., Roarty, M.P., Giesbrecht, B., and Miller, M.B. (2004). 'Neural Correlates of Detecting Pretense: Automatic Engagement of the Intentional Stance under Covert Conditions', *Journal of Cognitive Neuroscience* 16: 1805–17.

Gibson, J. (1979). *The Ecological Approach to Visual Perception*. Boston: Houghton Mifflin.

Gibson, K.R. (2012). 'Language or Protolanguage? A Review of the Ape Language Literature', in M. Tallerman and K.R. Gibson (eds), *The Oxford Handbook of Language Evolution*. Oxford: Oxford University Press, pp. 46–58.

Gil, D. (2011). 'Obligatory vs. Optional Tense-aspect-mood Marking: Areal Patterns and Historical Developments', International Conference on Historical Linguistics, XX. Osaka, Japan, 25–30 July.

Gilbert, M. (1989). *On Social Facts*. Oxford: Princeton University Press.

Gilbert, S.F. and Epel, D. (2009). *Ecological Developmental Biology. Integrating Epigenetics, Medicine, and Evolution*. Sunderland, MA: Sinauer Associates.

Gipper, S. (2011). *Evidentiality and Intersubjectivity in Yurakaré: An Interactional Account*. Nijmegen: Radboud Universiteit Nijmegen.

Givón, T. (1979). *On Understanding Grammar*. New York: Academic Press.

Givón, T. (2009). 'The Adaptive Approach to Grammar', in D. Bickerton and E. Szathmáry (eds), *Biological Foundations and Origin of Syntax*. Cambridge, MA: MIT Press.

Gladwell, M. (2000). *The Tipping Point: How Little Things Can Make a Big Difference*. Boston: Little and Brown.

Glaveanu, V. P. (2011). 'Creativity as Cultural Participation', *Journal for the Theory of Social Behaviour* 41(1): 48–67.

Glezer, I.I. (1958). 'Area Relationships in the Precentral Region in a Comparative-anatomical Series of Primates', *Arkhiv Anatomii, Gistologii i Émbriologii* 2: 26.

Goffman, E. (1959). *The Presentation of Self in Everyday Life.* New York: Doubleday Anchor.

Goffman, E. (1963). *Behavior in Public Places.* New York: The Free Press.

Goffman, E. (1964). 'The Neglected Situation', *American Anthropologist* 66(6, pt.2): 133–6.

Goffman, E. (1967). *Interaction Ritual: Essays in Face-to-face Behavior.* Garden City, NY: Doubleday.

Goffman, E. (1971). *Relations in Public: Microstudies of the Public Order.* New York: Basic Books.

Goffman, E. (1974). *Frame Analysis.* Cambridge, MA: Harvard University Press.

Goldberg, A. (2006). *Constructions at Work: The Nature of Generalization in Language.* New York: Oxford University Press.

Goldin-Meadow, S. (2003). *Hearing Gesture: How our Hands Help Us Think.* Cambridge, MA: Harvard University Press.

Gómez-Olivencia, A., Carretero, J.M., Arsuaga, J.L., Rodríguez-García, L., García-González, R., and Martínez, I. (2007). 'Metric and Morphological Study of the Upper Cervical Spine from the Sima de los Huesos Site (Sierra de Atapuerca, Burgos, Spain)', *Journal of Human Evolution* 53: 6–25.

Göncü, A., Jain, J., and Tuermer, U. (2007). 'Children's Play as Cultural Interpretation', in A. Göncü and S. Gaskins (eds), *Play and Development: Evolutionary, Sociocultural and Functional Perspectives.* Mahwah, NJ: LEA.

Göncü, A., Mistry, J., and Mosier, C. (2000). 'Cultural Variations in the Play of Toddlers', *International Journal of Behavioral Development* 24(3): 321–9.

Goodall, J. (1968). 'A Preliminary Report on Expressive Movements and Communication in the Gombe Stream Chimpanzees', in P.C. Jay (ed.), *Primate Studies in Adaptation and Variability.* New York: Holt, Rinehart and Winston.

Goodall, J. (1982). 'Order without Law', *Journal of Social and Biological Structures* 5: 349–52.

Goodall, J. (1986). *The Chimpanzees of Gombe: Patterns of Behavior.* Cambridge, MA and London: Belknap Press of Harvard University Press.

Goodwin, A. (1929). 'The Middle Stone Age', *Annals of the South African Museum* 29: 95–145.

Goody, J. (1997). *The Domestication of the Savage Mind.* Cambridge: Cambridge University Press.

Gopnik, A. (2009). *The Philosophical Baby.* New York: Farrar, Straus and Giroux.

Gordon, A.D., Green, D.J., and Richmond, B.G. (2008). 'Strong Postcranial Size Dimorphism in Australopithecus Afarensis: Results from Two New Resampling Methods for Multivariate Datasets with Missing Data', *American Journal of Physical Anthropology* 135: 311–28.

Goren-Inbar, N. (2011). 'Culture and Cognition in the Acheulian Industry: A Case Study from Gesher Benot Ya'aqov', *Philosophical Transactions of the Royal Society B* 366 (1567): 1038–49. doi: 10.1098/rstb.2010.0365.

Goren-Inbar, N., Alperson, N., Kislev, M., Simchoni, O., Melamed, Y., Ben-Nun, A., Werker, E., (2004). 'Evidence of Hominin Control of Fire at Gesher Benot Ya'aqov, Israel', *Science* 304: 725–7.

Gouzoules, S., Gouzoules, H., and Marler, P. (1984). 'Rhesus Monkey (*Macaca mulatta*) Screams: Representational Signalling in the Recruitment of Agonistic Aid', *Animal Behaviour* 32(1): 182–93.

Gow, P. (2001). *An Amazonian Myth and Its History*. Oxford: Oxford University Press.

Gowaty, P.A. (1997). 'Sexual Dialectics, Sexual Selection, and Variation in Mating Behavior', in P.A. Gowaty (ed.), *Feminism and Evolutionary Biology: Boundaries, Intersections, and Frontiers*. New York: Chapman and Hall, pp. 351–84.

Grafen, A. (1990a). 'Biological Signals as Handicaps', *Journal of Theoretical Biology* 144: 517–46.

Grafen, A. (1990b). 'Sexual Selection Unhandicapped by the Fisher Process', *Journal of Theoretical Biology* 144: 475–518.

Granovetter, M. (1973). 'The Strength of Weak Ties.' *American Journal of Sociology* 78: 1360–80.

Gratier, M. and Trevarthen, C. (2008). 'Musical Narrative and Motives for Culture in Mother-Infant Vocal Interaction', in C. Whitehead (ed.), *The Origin of Consciousness in the Social World*. Exeter: Imprint Academic, pp. 122–58.

Grauer, V. (2007). 'New Perspectives on the Kalahari Debate: A Tale of Two "Genomes"', *Before Farming* 2(4): article 4.

Grauer, V. (2009). 'Concept, Style and Structure in the Music of the African Pygmies and Bushmen: A Study in Cross-Cultural Analysis', *Ethnomusicology* 53(3): 396–424.

Gray, P. (2009). 'Play as a Foundation for Hunter-gatherer Social Existence', *American Journal of Play* 1(4): 476–522.

Green, R.E., Krause, J., Briggs, A.W., Maricic, T., Stenzel, U., Kircher, M., Patterson, N., et al. (2010). 'A Draft Sequence of the Neandertal Genome', *Science* 328: 710–22.

Green, S. (1975). 'Variations of Vocal Pattern with Social Situation in the Japanese Monkey (*Macaca Fuscata*): A Field Study', in L.A. Rosenblum (ed.), *Primate Behavior, Vol. 4: Developments in Field and Laboratory Research*. New York: Academic Press, pp. 1–107.

Greenhill, S.J., Atkinson, Q.D., Meade, A., and Gray, R.D. (2010). 'The Shape and Tempo of Language Evolution', *Proceedings of the Royal Society B* 277: 2443–50.

Grèzes, J. and Decety, J. (2001). 'Functional Anatomy of Execution, Mental Simulation, Observation, and Verb Generation of Actions: A Meta-analysis', *Human Brain Mapping* 12: 1–19.

Grice, H.P. (1957). 'Meaning', *The Philosophical Review* 66(3): 377–88.

Grice, H.P. (1968). Utterer's Meaning, Sentence Meaning, and Word Meaning, *Foundations of Language*, 4. Reprinted as ch. 6 of Grice, H.P., 1989. *Studies in the Way of Words*. Cambridge, MA: Harvard University Press, 117–137.

Grice, H.P. (1969). 'Utterer's Meanings and Intentions', *Philosophical Review* 78: 147–77.

Grice, H.P. (1975). 'Logic and Conversation', in P. Cole and J.L. Morgan (eds), *Syntax and Semantics, vol. III: Speech Acts*. New York: Academic Press, pp. 41–58. <http://www.sfu.ca/~jeffpell/Cogs300/GriceLogicConvers75.pdf>.

Grossen, M. (2008). 'Methods for Studying Collaborative Creativity: An Original and Adventurous blend', *Thinking Skills and Creativity* 3: 246–9.

Grove, M. and Coward, F. (2008). 'From Individual Neurons to Social Brains', *Cambridge Archaeological Journal* 18: 387–400.

Gruber, T., Muller, M.N., Reynolds, V., Wrangham, R.W., and Zuberbühler, K. (2011). 'Community-specific Evaluation of Tool Affordances in Wild Chimpanzees', *Scientific Reports* 1: 128.

Grün, R. and Beaumont, P. (2001). 'Border Cave Revisited: A Revised ESR Chronology', *Journal of Human Evolution* 40: 467–82.

Grün, R., Brink, J., Spooner, N., Taylor, L., Stringer, C., Franciscus, R., and Murray, A. (1996). 'Direct Dating of Florisbad Hominid', *Nature* 382: 500–1.

Grün, R. and Stringer, C. (2000). 'Tabun Revisited: Revised ESR Chronology and New ESR and U-series Analyses of Dental Material from Tabun C1', *Journal of Human Evolution* 39: 601–12.

Guilford, T. and Dawkins, M.S. (1991). 'Receiver Psychology and the Evolution of Animal Signals', *Animal Behaviour* 42: 1–14.

Gunz, P., Neubauer, S., Maureille, B., and Hublin, J.-J. (2010). 'Brain Development after Birth Differs between Neanderthals and Modern Humans', *Current Biology* 20: R921–R922.

Györi, G. (1997). 'Cognitive Archaeology: A Look at Evolution Outside and Inside Language', in R. Blench and M. Spriggs (eds), *Archaeology and Language I—Theoretical and Methodological Orientations*. London: Routledge, pp. 43–52.

Haak, W., Brandt G., de Jong, H.N., Meyer, C., Ganslmeier, R., Heyd, V., Hawkesworth, C., Pike, A.W., Meller, H., and Alt, K.W. (2008). 'Ancient DNA, Strontium Isotopes, and Osteological Analyses Shed Light on Social and Kinship Organization of the Later Stone Age', *Proceedings of the National Academy of Sciences USA* 105: 18226–31.

Habgood, P.J. and Franklin, N.R. (2008). 'The Revolution that Didn't Arrive: A Review of Pleistocene Sahul', *Journal of Human Evolution* 55: 187–222.

Haesler, S., Wada, K., Nshdejan, A., Morrisey, E.E., Lints, T., Jarvis, E.D., and Scharff, C. (2004). 'FoxP2 Expression in Avian Vocal Learners and Non-learners', *Journal of Neuroscience*, 24: 3164–75.

Haidt, J. (2001). 'The Emotional Dog and its Rational Tail: A Social Intuitionist Approach to Moral Judgment', *Psychological Review* 108: 814.

Haight, W. and Miller, P. (1992). 'The Development of Everyday Pretend: A Longitudinal Study of Mothers' Participation', *Merrill Palmer Quarterly* 38(3): 331–49.

Haight, W., Wang, X., Fung, H., Williams, K., and Mintz, J. (1999). 'Universal, Developmental, and Variable Aspects of Young Children's Play: A Cross-cultural Comparison of Pretending at Home', *Child Development* 70(6): 1477–88.

Hamilton, W.D. (1964). 'The Genetical Evolution of Social Behaviour', *Journal of Theoretical Biology* 7(1): 1–16.

Hardy, A. (1979). *The Spiritual Nature of Man*. Oxford: Clarendon.

Hare, B., Call, J., Agnetta, B., and Tomasello, M. (2000). 'Chimpanzees Know What Conspecifics Do and Do Not See', *Animal Behaviour* 59(4): 771–85.

Hare, B., Call, J., and Tomasello, M. (2001). 'Do Chimpanzees Know What Conspecifics Know?' *Animal Behaviour* 61(1): 139–51.

Hare, B., Call, J., and Tomasello, M. (2006). 'Chimpanzees Deceive a Human Competitor by Hiding', *Cognition* 101(3): 495–514.

Hare, B. and Tan, J. (2011). 'What Cooperative Abilities Did We Inherit as an Ape?' in F. de Waal and P. Ferrari (eds), *The Primate Mind*. Cambridge, MA: Harvard University Press.

Hare, B., Wobber, V., and Wrangham, R. (2012). 'The Self-domestication Hypothesis: Evolution of Bonobo Psychology is Due to Selection Against Aggression', *Animal Behaviour* 83(3): 573–85.

Harmon, E.H. (2006). 'Size and Shape Variation in *Australopithecus Afarensis* Proximal Femora', *Journal of Human Evolution* 51: 217–27.

Harris, P. (2000). *The Work of the Imagination*. Oxford: Blackwell.

Harris, P., Brown, E., Marriott, C., Whittall, S., and Harmer, S. (1991). 'Monsters, Ghosts and Witches: Testing the Limits of the Fantasy–Reality Distinction in Young Children', *British Journal of Developmental Psychology* 9(1): 105–23.

Harris, P. and Kavanaugh, R. (1993). 'Young Children's Understanding of Pretense', *Monographs of the Society for Research in Child Development* 58(1): 1–92.

Harris, P. and Núñez, M. (1996). 'Understanding of Permission Rules by Preschool Children,' *Child Development* 67: 1572–91. doi:10.2307/1131719.

Hart, D. and Sussman, R.W. (2005). *Man the Hunted: Primates, Predators, and Human Evolution*, New York: West View.

Harvati, K., Stringer, C., Grün, R., Aubert, M., Allsworth-Jones, P., and Adebayo Folorunso, C. (2011a). 'The Later Stone Age Calvaria from Iwo Eleru, Nigeria: Morphology and Chronology', *PLoS One* 6: e24024. doi:10.1371/journal.pone.0024024.

Harvati, K., Stringer, C., Karkanas, P. (2011b). 'Multivariate Analysis and Classification of the Apidima 2 Cranium from Mani, Southern Greece', *Journal of Human Evolution* 60: 246–50.

Haspelmath, M., Dryer, M.S., Gil, D., and Comrie, B., eds (2005). *The World Atlas of Language Structures*. Oxford: Oxford University Press.

Hauser, M.D. (1997). *The Evolution of Communication*. Cambridge, MA: MIT.

Hauser, M.D. (1998). 'Functional Referents and Acoustic Similarity: Field Playback Experiments with Rhesus Monkeys', *Animal Behaviour* 55: 1647–58.

Hauser, M.D. (2011a). 'The Illusion of Biological Variation: a Minimalist Approach to the Mind', in M. Piattelli-Palmarini, J. Salaburu, and P. Uriagereka (eds), *Of Minds and Language: A Dialogue with Noam Chomsky in the Basque Country*. Oxford: Oxford University Press.

Hauser, M.D. (2011b). 'Evolingo: The Nature of the Language Faculty', in M. Piattelli-Palmarini, J. Salaburu, and P. Uriagereka (eds), *Of Minds and Language: A Dialogue with Noam Chomsky in the Basque Country*. Oxford: Oxford University Press, pp. 74–84.

Hauser, M.D., Chomsky, N., and Fitch, W.T. (2002). 'The Faculty of Language: What Is It, Who Has It, and How Did It Evolve?', *Science* 298: 1569–79.

Hauser, M.D. and Marler, P. (1993). 'Food-associated Calls in Rhesus Macaques (*Macacca mulatta*): II Costs and Benefits of Call Production and Suppression', *Behavioural Ecology* 4: 206–12.

Hausmann, R. and Brunnacker, K. (1988). 'U-series Dating of Middle European Travertines', in M. Otte (ed.), *L'homme de Néandertal 1. La chronologie*. Liège: University of Liège Press, pp. 45–51.

Haviland, S.E. and Clark, E.V. (1974). '"This Man's Father is My Father's Son": A Study of the Acquisition of English Kin Terms', *Journal of Child Language* 1: 23–47.

Hawkes, K. (2004). 'The Grandmother Effect', *Nature* 428: 128–9.

Hawkes, K. and Bliege Bird, R. (2002). 'Showing Off, Handicap Signalling, and the Evolution of Men's Work', *Evolutionary Anthropology* 11: 58–67.

Hawkes, K., O'Connell, J.F., Blurton Jones, N.G., Alvarez, H., and Charnov, E.L. (1998). 'Grandmothering, Menopause, and the Evolution of Human Life Histories', *Proceedings of the National Academy of Sciences* 95: 1336–9.

Hawkins, J. (2004). *Efficiency and Complexity in Grammars*. Oxford: Oxford University Press.

Hawks, J. and Cochran, G. (2006). 'Dynamics of Adaptive Introgression from Archaic to Modern Humans', *PaleoAnthropology* 2006: 101–15.

Hayashi, M., Raymond, G., and Sidnell, J., eds (2013). *Conversational Repair and Human Understanding*. Cambridge: Cambridge University Press.

Hayes, C. (1951). *The Ape in Our House*. New York: Harper.

Hayes, S.C., Barnes-Holmes, D., and Roche, B., eds (2001). *Relational Frame Theory: A Post-Skinnerian Account of Human Language and Cognition*. New York: Plenum Press.

Head, M. and Gibbard, P. (2005). 'Early-Middle Pleistocene Transitions: An Overview and Recommendation for the Defining Boundary', *London Geological Society, Special Publications* 247: 1–18.

Healy, S.D. and Rowe, C. (2007). 'A Critique of Comparative Studies of Brain Size', *Proceedings of the Royal Society B* 274: 453–64.

Heidegger, M. (1962 [1927]). *Being and Time*. London: SCM Press.

Heim, J., Lautridou, J.-J., Maucorps, J., Puisségur, J.-J., Sommé J., and Thévenin, A. (1982). 'Achenheim: une séquence-type des loess du Pleistocène moyen et supérieur', *Bulletin de l'Association française pour l'étude du quaternaire* 19: 147–59.

Heine, B., Claudi, U., and Hünnemeyer, F. (1991). *Grammaticalization: A Conceptual Framework*. Chicago: University of Chicago Press.

Heine, B. and Kuteva, T. (2002). *World Lexicon of Grammaticalization*. Oxford: Oxford University Press.

Heine, B. and Kuteva, T. (2007). *The Genesis of Grammar: A Reconstruction*. Oxford: Oxford University Press.

Heine, B. and Kuteva, T. (2012). 'Grammaticalization Theory as a Tool for Reconstructing Language Evolution', in M. Tallerman and K.R. Gibson (eds), *The Oxford Handbook of Language Evolution*. Oxford: Oxford University Press, pp. 512–27.

Henrich, J. (2004). 'Demography and Cultural Evolution: How Adaptive Cultural Processes Can Produce Maladaptive Losses—the Tasmanian Case', *American Antiquity* 69: 197–214.

Henrich, J. and Gil-White, F.J. (2001). 'The Evolution of Prestige: Freely Conferred Deference as a Mechanism for Enhancing the Benefits of Cultural Transmission', *Evolution and Human Behavior* 22: 165–96.

Henrich, J., Heine, S.J., and Norenzaya, A. (2010). 'The Weirdest People in the World?', *Behavioural and Brain Sciences*. doi:10.1017/S0140525X0999152X.

Henshilwood, C.S. (2009). 'The Origins of Symbolism, Spirituality, and Shamans: Exploring Middle Stone Age Material Culture in South Africa', in C. Renfrew and I. Morley (eds), *Becoming Human: Innovation in Prehistoric Material and Spiritual Culture*. Cambridge: Cambridge University Press, pp. 29–49.

Henshilwood, C.S. and Dubreuil, B. (2009). 'Reading the Artifacts: Gleaning Language Skills from the Middle Stone Age in Southern Africa', in R. Botha and C. Knight (eds), *The Cradle of Language: Studies in the Evolution of Language*. Oxford: Oxford University Press, pp. 41–61.

Henshilwood, C.S., d'Errico, F., Niekerk, K.L.V., Coquinot, Y., Jacobs, Z., Lauritzen, S.-E., Menu, M., and García-Moreno, R. (2011). 'A 100,000-Year-Old Ochre-Processing Workshop at Blombos Cave, South Africa', *Science* 334(14): 219–22.

Henshilwood, C.S., d'Errico, F., Vanhaeren, M., Niekerk, K. L.v., and Jacobs, Z. (2004). 'Middle Stone Age Shell Beads from South Africa', *Science* 304: 404.

Henshilwood, C.S., d'Errico, F., and Watts, I. (2009). 'Engraved Ochres from Middle Stone Age Levels at Blombos Cave, South Africa', *Journal of Human Evolution* 57: 27–47.

Henshilwood, C.S., d'Errico, F., Yates, R., Jacobs, Z., Tribolo, C., Duller, G., Mercier, N., Sealy, J., Valladas, H., Watts, I., and Wintle, A.G. (2002). 'Emergence of Modern Human Behaviour: Middle Stone Age Engravings from South Africa', *Science* 295: 1278–80.

Henshilwood, C.S. and Marean, C.W. (2003). 'The Origin of Modern Human Behavior: Critique of the Models and Their Test Implications', *Current Anthropology* 44(5): 627–51.

Heritage, J.C. (1984). *Garfinkel and Ethnomethodology*. Cambridge: Polity Press.

Heritage, J.C. (1989). 'Current Developments in Conversation Analysis', in D. Roger and P. Bull (eds), *Conversation: An Interdisciplinary Perspective*. Clevedon: Multilingual Matters, pp. 21–47.

Heritage, J. and Atkinson, J.M. (1984). 'Introduction', in J.M. Atkinson and J. Heritage (eds), *Structures of Social Action: Studies in Conversation Analysis*. Cambridge: Cambridge University Press, pp. 1–15.

Heritage, J. and Raymond, G. (2005). 'The Terms of Agreement: Indexing Epistemic Authority and Subordination in Talk-in-interaction', *Social Psychology Quarterly* 68(1): 15–38.

Herries, A. (2011). 'A Chronological Perspective on the Acheulian and its Transition to the Middle Stone Age in Southern Africa: The Question of the Fauresmith', *International Journal of Evolutionary Biology* 2011: article ID 961401. doi: 10.4061/2011/961401.

Hewes, G.W. (1973). 'Primate Communication and the Gestural Origins of Language', *Current Anthropology* 14: 5–24.

Hewitt, G., MacLarnon, A., and Jones, K.E. (2002). 'The Functions of Laryngeal Air Sacs in Primates: A New Hypothesis', *Folia Primat* 73: 70–94.

Hewlett, B. (1996). 'Cultural Diversity among African Pygmies', in S. Kent (ed.), *Cultural Diversity Among Twentieth-Century Foragers: An African Perspective*. Cambridge: Cambridge University Press, pp. 215–44.

Higham, T., Jacobi, R., Julien, M., David, F., Basell, L., Wood, R., Davies, W., and Ramsey, C.B. (2010). 'Chronology of the Grotte du Renne (France) and Implications for the Context of Ornaments and Human Remains within the Châtelperronian', *Proceedings of the National Academy of Sciences USA* 107: 20234–9.

Hill, K., Hurtado, A.M., and Walker, R.S. (2007). 'High Adult Mortality among Hiwi Hunter-gatherers: Implications for Human Evolution', *Journal of Human Evolution*, 52: 443–54.

Hilpert, M. (2013). *Constructional Change in English*. Cambridge: Cambridge University Press.

Hobaiter, C. and Byrne, R.W. (2011). 'The Gestural Repertoire of the Wild Chimpanzee', *Animal Cognition* 14(5): 747–67.

Hockett, C. (1960). 'The Origin of Speech', *Scientific American* 203: 88–96.

Hodgskiss, T. (2012). 'An Investigation into the Properties of the Ochre from Sibudu, Kwa-Zulu-Natal, South Africa', *Southern African Humanities* 24: 99–120.

Hodgson, D. (2011). 'The First Appearance of Symmetry in the Human Lineage: Where Perception Meets Art', *Symmetry* 3: 37–53. doi:10.3390/sym3010037.

Hohmann, G. and Fruth, B. (1994). 'Structure and Use of Distance Calls in Wild Bonobos (*Pan paniscus*)', *International Journal of Primatology* 15(5): 767–82.

Hohmann, G. and Fruth, B. (2000). 'Use and Function of Genital Contacts among Female Bonobos', *Animal Behavior* 60: 107–20.

Hopkins, W.D., Taglialatela, J.P., and Leavens, D.A. (2007). 'Chimpanzees Differentially Produce Novel Vocalizations to Capture the Attention of a Human', *Animal Behaviour* 73(2): 281–6.

Hopkins, W.D., Taglialatela, J.P., and Leavens, D.A. (2011). 'Do Chimpanzees Have Voluntary Control of Their Facial Expressions and Vocalizations?', in A. Vilain, J.-L. Schwartz, C. Abry, and J. Vauclair (eds), *Primate Communication and Human Language*. Amsterdam and Philadelphia: John Benjamins, pp. 71–88.

Hopper, P.J. (1998). 'Emergent Grammar', in M. Tomasello (ed.), *The New Psychology of Language*. Mahwah, NJ: Lawrence Erlbaum, pp. 155–75.

Hopper, P.J. and Traugott, E.C. (2003). *Grammaticalization*. Cambridge: Cambridge University Press.

Hostetter, A.B. (2011). 'When Do Gestures Communicate? A Meta-analysis', *Psychological Bulletin* 137(2): 297–315.

Houghton, P. (1993). 'Neandertal Supralaryngeal Vocal Tract', *American Journal of Physical Anthropology* 90: 139–46.

Hovers, E., Kimbel, W., and Rak, Y. (2000). 'The Amud 7 Skeleton—Still a Burial. Response to Gargett', *Journal of Human Evolution* 39: 253–60.

Howell, F.C. (1966). 'Observations on the Earlier Phases of the European Lower Paleolithic', *American Anthropologist* 68: 88–201.

Hoyt, M. (1941). *Toto and I*. New York: Lippincott.

Hrdy, S.B. (2009). *Mothers and Others: The Evolutionary Origins of Mutual Understanding*. Cambridge, MA: Belknap Press of Harvard.

Hublin, J.-J. (2009a). 'The Prehistory of Compassion', *Proceedings of the National Academy of Sciences USA* 106: 6429–30.

Hublin, J.-J. (2009b). 'Out of Africa: Modern Human Origins Special Feature: The Origin of Neandertals', *Proceedings of the National Academy of Sciences USA* 106: 16022–7.

Hublin, J.-J. and Roebroeks, W. (2009). 'Ebb and Flow or Regional Extinctions? On the Character of Neandertal Occupation of Northern Environments', *Comptes Rendus Palevol* 8: 503–9.

Hudson, R.A. (1996). *Sociolinguistics*. 2nd edn. Cambridge: Cambridge University Press.

Hughes, F.P. (2010). *Children, Play, and Development*. 4th edn. Thousand Oaks, CA: Sage.

Huizinga, J. (1955). *Homo Ludens: A Study of the Play Element in Culture*. Boston: Beacon Press.

Hurford, J.R. (1999). 'The Evolution of Language and Languages', in R. Dunbar, C. Knight, and C. Power (eds), *The Evolution of Culture: An Interdisciplinary View*. Edinburgh: Edinburgh University Press, pp. 173–93.

Hurford, J.R. (2007). *The Origins of Meaning. Language in the Light of Evolution (I)*. Oxford: Oxford University Press.

Hurford, J.R. (2011). *The Origins of Grammar. Language in the Light of Evolution (II)*. Oxford University Press.

Hutchins, E. (2005). 'Material Anchors for Conceptual Blends', *Journal of Pragmatics* 37: 1555–77.

Huxley, J.S. (1914). 'The Courtship Habits of the Crested Grebe (*Podiceps cristatus*) with an Addition to the Theory of Sexual Selection', *Proceedings of the Zoological Society of London* 35: 491–562.

Ingold, T. (2000). 'Totemism, Animism and the Depiction of Animals', in *The Perception of the Environment*. London: Routledge, pp. 111–31.

Ingram, G.P.D. and Bering, J.M. (2010). 'Children's Tattling: The Reporting of Everyday Norm Violations in Preschool Settings', *Child Development* 81(May): 945–57. doi:10.1111/j.1467-8624.2010.01444.x.

Irvine, J. (1974). 'Strategies of Status Manipulation in the Wolof Greeting', in R. Bauman and J. Sherzer (eds), *Explorations in the Ethnography of Speaking*. Cambridge: Cambridge University Press, pp. 167–99.

Itkonen, E. (1983). *Causality in Linguistic Theory*. London: Croom Helm.

Itkonen, E. (2003). *What is Language? A Study in the Philosophy of Linguistics*. Publications in General Linguistics Series, no. 6. Turku: University of Turku Press.

Iverson, J. and Fagan, M.K. (2004). 'Infant Vocal-motor Coordination: Precursor to the Gesture-speech System?', *Child Development* 75: 1053–66.

Jablonka, E., Ginsburg, S., and Dor, D. (2012). 'The Co-Evolution of Language and the Emotions', *Philosophical Transactions of the Royal Society B* 367: 2152–9. doi:10.1098/rstb.2012.0117

Jablonka, E. and Lamb, M.J. (2005). *Evolution in Four Dimensions: Genetic, Epigenetic, Behavioral, and Symbolic Variation in the History of Life*. Cambridge, MA: MIT Press.

Jackendoff, R. (1990). *Semantic Structures*. Cambridge, MA: MIT Press.

Jackendoff, R. (1999). 'Possible stages in the evolution of the language capacity', *Trends in Cognitive Sciences* 3(7); 272–9.

Jackendoff, R. and Pinker, S. (2005). 'The nature of the language faculty and its implications for evolution of language', *Cognition* 97: 211–25.

Jacobson, L., de Beer, F., Nshimirimana, R., Horwitz, L., and Chazan, M. (2013). 'Neutron Tomographic Assessment of Incisions on Prehistoric Stone Slabs: A Case Study from Wonderwerk Cave, South Africa', *Archaeometry* 55(1): 1–13.

Jakobson, R. (1938). 'Observations sur le classement phonologique des consonnes', Proceedings of the 3rd International Congress of Phonetic Sciences, Ghent.

James, W. (1985 [1902]). *The Varieties of Religious Experience: A Study in Human Nature*. London: Penguin Classics.

James, W. (1990 [1890]). *The Principles of Psychology*. New York: Dover Publications.

Jarvis, E.D. (2007). 'Neural Systems for Vocal Learning in Birds and Humans: A Synopsis', *Journal of Ornithology* 148: S35–S44.

Jefferson, G. (1974). 'Error Correction as an Interactional Resource', *Language in Society* 2: 181–99.

Jennings, S. (1990). *Dramatherapy with Families, Groups and Individuals: Waiting in the Wings*. London: Jessica Kingsley.

Jespersen, O. (1922). *Language: Its Nature, Development and Origin*. New York: Henry Holt and Co.

Jiménez-Arenas, J., Santonja, M., Botella, M., and Palmqvist, P. (2011). 'The Oldest Handaxes in Europe: Fact or Artefact?', *Journal of Archaeological Science* 38: 3340–9.

Joffe, T.H. (1997). 'Social Pressures Have Selected for an Extended Juvenile Period in Primates', *Journal of Human Evolution* 32: 593–605.

Johanson, D.C., Taieb, M., and Coppens, Y. (1982). 'Pliocene Hominids from the Hadar Formation, Ethiopia (1973–1977): Stratigraphic, Chronologic, and Paleoenvironmental

Contexts, with Notes on Hominid Morphology and Systematics', *American Journal of Physical Anthropology* 57: 373–402.

Johansson, S. (2005). *Origins of Language: Constraints on Hypotheses*. Amsterdam: John Benjamins.

Johansson, S. (2011). 'Constraining the Time When Language Evolved', *Linguistic and Philosophical Investigations* 10: 45–59.

Johnson, C. and McBrearty, S. (2010). '500,000 Year Old Blades from the Kapthurin Formation, Kenya', *Journal of Human Evolution* 58: 193–200.

Joubert, D. and Joubert, B. (1997). *The Lions of Savuti: Hunting with the Moon*. Washington: National Geographic Society.

Jungers, W.L., Pokempner, A.A., Kay, R.F., and Cartmill, M. (2003). 'Hypoglossal Canal Size in Living Hominoids and the Evolution of Human Speech', *Human Biology* 75: 473–84.

Jurgens, U. and Alipour, M. (2002). 'A Comparative Study on the Cortico-Hypoglossal Connections in Primates, Using Biotin Dextranamine'. *Neuroscience Letters* 328: 245–8.

Kalish, C. (1998). 'Reasons and Causes: Children's Understanding of Conformity to Social and Physical Laws', *Child Development,* 69(3): 706–20.

Kalish, C. and Sabbagh, M. (2007). 'Conventionality and Cognitive Development: Learning the Right Way to Think', *New Directions in Child and Adolescent Development (Special Issue on Conventionality)* 115: 1–9.

Kalish, C., Weissman, M., and Bernstein, D. (2000). 'Taking Decisions Seriously: Young Children's Understanding of Conventional Truth', *Child Development* 71(5): 1289–1308.

Kaminski, J., Call, J., and Tomasello, M. (2008). 'Chimpanzees Know What Others Know, but Not What They Believe', *Cognition* 109: 224–34.

Kano, T. (1992). *The Last Ape: Pygmy Chimpanzee Behavior and Ecology*. Stanford: Stanford University Press.

Kaplan, F. and Hafner, V. (2006). 'The Challenges of Joint Attention', *Interaction Studies* 7: 135–69.

Kappeler, P.M. and Silk, J.B. (2009). *Mind the Gap: Tracing the Origins of Human Universals*. Berlin, Heidelberg: Springer Verlag.

Karkanas, P., Shahack-Gross, R., Ayalon, A., Bar-Matthews, M., Barkai, R., Frumkin, A., Gopher, A., and Stiner, M. (2007). 'Evidence for Habitual Use of Fire at the End of the Lower Paleolithic: Site-formation Processes at Qesem Cave, Israel', *Journal of Human Evolution* 53: 197–212.

Kazadi, N. (1981). 'Méprises et Admires: L'ambivalance des relations entre les Bacwa (Pygmées) et les Bahemba (Bantu)', *Africa* 51(4): 836–47.

Keller, R. (1994). *On Language Change: The Invisible Hand in Language*. London: Routledge.

Kellog, W.N. and Kellog, L.A. (1933). *The Ape and the Child*. New York: McGraw-Hill.

Kendon, A. (1972). 'Some Relationships between Body Motion and Speech: An Analysis of an Example', in A. Siegman and B. Pope (eds), *Studies in Dyadic Communication*. Elmsford/ New York: Pergamon Press, pp. 177–210.

Kendon, A. (1980). 'Gesticulation and Speech: Two Aspects of the Process of Utterance', in M.R. Key (ed.), *The Relationship of Verbal and Nonverbal Communication*. The Hague: Mouton, pp. 207–27.

Kendon, A. (1990). 'Behavioral Foundations for the Process of Frame-attunement in Face-to-face Interaction', in A. Kendon, *Conducting Interaction*. Cambridge: Cambridge University Press, pp. 239–62.

Kendon, A. (1994). 'Do Gestures Communicate? A Review', *Research on Language and Social Interaction* 27(3): 175–200.

Kendon, A. (2004). *Gesture: Visible Action as Utterance*. Cambridge: Cambridge University Press.

Kendon, A. (2008). 'Review of J. Call and M. Tomasello (eds), *The Gestural Communication of Apes and Monkeys*', *Gesture* 8(3): 375–85.

Kendon, A. (2009). 'Manual Actions, Speech and the Nature of Language', in D. Gambarara and A. Givigliano (eds), *Origine e sviluppo del linguaggio, fra teoria e storia*. Rome: Aracne Editrice, pp. 19–33.

Kendon, A. (2011a). 'Vocalisation, Speech, Gesture and the Language Origins Debate: An Essay Review on Recent Contributions', *Gesture* 11(3): 349–70.

Kendon, A. (2011b). 'Some Modern Considerations for Thinking about Language Evolution: A Discussion of *The Evolution of Language* by Tecumseh Fitch', *Public Journal of Semiotics*, III(1): 79–108.

Kenward, B., Karlsson, M., and Persson J. (2011). 'Over-imitation is Better Explained by Norm Learning than by Distorted Causal Learning,' *Proceedings of the Royal Society B: Biological Sciences* 278: 1239–46. doi:10.1098/rspb.2010.1399.

Keverne, E.B., Martensz, N., and Tuite, B. (1989). 'Beta-endorphin Concentrations in Cerebrospinal Fluid of Monkeys Are Influenced by Grooming Relationships', *Psychoneuroendocrinology* 14: 155–61.

Key, C. and Aiello, L.C. (1999). 'The Evolution of Social Organization', in R.I.M. Dunbar, C. Knight, and C. Power (eds), *The Evolution of Culture*. Edinburgh: Edinburgh University Press, pp. 15–33.

Kimura, D. (1973a). 'Manual Activity during Speaking—I. Right-handers', *Neuropsychologia* 11(1): 48–50.

Kimura, D. (1973b). 'Manual Activity during Speaking—II. Left-handers', *Neuropsychologia*, 11(1): 51–5.

Kimura, M. (1983). *The Neutral Theory of Molecular Evolution*. Cambridge: Cambridge University Press.

King, B. (2004). *The Dynamic Dance: Nonvocal Communication in African Great Apes*. Cambridge, MA: Harvard University Press.

Kirby, S., Cornish, H., and Smith, K. (2008). 'Cumulative Cultural Evolution in the Laboratory: An Experimental Approach to the Origins of Structure in Human Language', *Proceedings of the National Academy of Sciences of America* 105(31): 10681–6.

Kirby, S., Dowman, M., and Griffiths, T. (2007). 'Innateness and Culture in the Evolution of Language', *Proceedings of the National Academy of Sciences* 104(12): 5241–5.

Kirby, S., Smith, K., and Brighton, H. (2004). 'From UG to Universals: Linguistic Adaptation Through Iterated Learning', *Studies in Language* 28(3): 587–607. doi:10.1075/sl.28.3.09kir.

Kisch, S. (2008), 'Deaf Discourse: The Social Construction of Deafness in a Bedouin Community', *Medical Anthropology* 27(3): 283–313.

Kita, S. (2000). 'How Representational Gestures Help Speaking', in D. McNeill (ed.), *Language and Gesture*. Cambridge: Cambridge University Press, pp. 162–85.

Klein, R.G. (1988). 'The Archaeological Significance of Animal Bones from Acheulean Sites in Southern Africa', *The African Archaeological Review* 6: 3–25.

Klein, R.G. (1999). *The Human Career: Human Biological and Cultural Origins*. Chicago: University of Chicago Press.

Klein, R.G. (2008). 'Out of Africa and the Evolution of Human Behavior', *Evolutionary Anthropology* 17: 267–81.

Klein, R.G. (2009). *The Human Career: Human Biological and Cultural Origins*. Chicago: University of Chicago Press.

Klein, R.G., Avery, G., Cruz-Uribe, K., and Steele, T. (2007). 'The Mammalian Fauna Associated with an Archaic Hominin Skullcap and Later Acheulian Artifacts at Elandsfontein, Western Cape Province, South Africa', *Journal of Human Evolution* 52: 164–86.

Klein, R.G. and Edgar, B. (2002). *The Dawn of Human Culture*. New York: John Wiley.

Kline, M.A. and Boyd, R. (2010). 'Population Size Predicts Technological Complexity in Oceania', *Proceedings of the Royal Society B* 277: 2559–64.

Knauft, B.M. (1991). 'Violence and Sociality in Human Evolution', *Current Anthropology* 32(4): 391–428.

Knauft, B.M. (1994). 'Comment on Erdal, D., & Whiten, A., "On Human Egalitarianism: An Evolutionary Product of Machiavellian Status Escalation?"', *Current Anthropology* 35(2): 175–83.

Knauft, B.M. (2000). 'Sex, Symbols and Sociality in the Evolution of Human Morality', *Journal of Consciousness Studies* 7(1–2): 130–8.

Kneblová, V. (1958). 'The Interglacial Flora in Ganovce Travertines in Eastern Slovakia (Czechoslovakia)', *Acta Biologica Cracov* 1: 1–5.

Knight, C. (1987). *Menstruation and the Origins of Culture. A Reconsideration of Lévi-Strauss's Work on Symbolism and Myth*. Ph.D. Thesis. London: University of London.

Knight, C. (1991). *Blood Relations: Menstruation and the Origins of Culture*. New Haven, CT: Yale University Press.

Knight, C. (1997). 'The Wives of the Sun and the Moon', *Journal of the Royal Anthropological Institute* 3: 133–53.

Knight, C. (1998). 'Ritual/Speech Coevolution: A Solution to the Problem of Deception', in J.R. Hurford, M. Studdert-Kennedy, and C. Knight (eds), *Approaches to the Evolution of Language: Social and Cognitive Bases*. Cambridge: Cambridge University Press, pp. 68–91.

Knight, C. (1999). 'Sex and Language as Pretend-play', in R. Dunbar, C. Knight, and C. Power (eds), *The Evolution of Culture. An Interdisciplinary View*. Edinburgh: Edinburgh University Press, pp. 228–47.

Knight, C. (2000). 'Play as Precursor of Phonology and Syntax', in C. Knight, M. Studdert-Kennedy, and J.R. Hurford (eds), *The Evolutionary Emergence of Language: Social Function and the Origins of Linguistic Form*. Cambridge: Cambridge University Press, pp. 99–119.

Knight, C. (2002). 'Language and Revolutionary Consciousness', in A. Wray (ed.), *The Transition to Language*. Oxford: Oxford University Press, pp. 138–60.

Knight, C. (2004). 'Decoding Chomsky', *European Review* 12(4): 581–603.

Knight, C. (2008a). '"Honest Fakes" and Language Origins', *Journal of Consciousness Studies* 15: 236–48.

Knight, C. (2008b). 'Language Co-evolved with the Rule of Law', *Mind & Society* 7: 109–28.

Knight, C. (2008c). 'Early Human Kinship Was Matrilineal', in N.J. Allen, H. Callan, R. Dunbar, and W. James (eds), *Early Human Kinship*. Oxford: Blackwell, pp. 61–82.

Knight, C. (2009). 'Language, Ochre, and the Rule of Law', in R. Botha and C. Knight (eds), *The Cradle of Language: Studies in the Evolution of Language*. Oxford: Oxford University Press, pp. 281–303.

Knight, C. (2010). 'Language, Lies and Lipstick: A Speculative Reconstruction of the African Middle Stone Age "Human Revolution"', in P.M. Kappeler and J.B. Silk (eds), *Mind the Gap*. Berlin: Springer-Verlag, pp. 299–313.

Knight, C. and Power, C. (2012). 'Social Conditions for the Evolutionary Emergence of Language', in M. Tallerman and K. Gibson (eds), *The Oxford Handbook of Language Evolution*. Oxford: Oxford University Press, pp. 346–9.

Knight, C., Power, C., and Watts, I. (1995). 'The Human Symbolic Revolution: A Darwinian Account', *Cambridge Archaeological Journal* 5(1): 75–114.

Kobayashi, H. and Kohshima, S. (2001). 'Unique Morphology of the Human Eye and its Adaptive Meaning: Comparative Studies on External Morphology of the Primate Eye', *Journal of Human Evolution* 40: 419–35.

Kockelman, P. (2006). 'Residence in the World: Affordances, Instruments, Actions, Roles, and Identities', *Semiotica* 162(1–4): 19–71.

Köhler, A. and Lewis, J. (2002). 'Putting Hunter-Gatherer and Farmer Relations in Perspective: A Commentary from Central Africa', in S. Kent (ed.), *Ethnicity, Hunter-Gatherers, and the 'Other': Association or Assimilation in Southern Africa?* Washington: Smithsonian Institute, pp. 276–305.

Kohn, M. (1999). *As We Know It: Coming to Terms with an Evolved Mind*. London: Granta.

Kohn, M. and Mithen, S. (1999). 'Handaxes: Products of Sexual Selection?', *Antiquity* 73: 518–26.

Krause, J., Lalueza-Fox, C., Orlando, L., Enard, W., Green, R.E., Burbano, H.A., Hublin, J.-J., et al. (2007). 'The Derived FOXP2 Variant of Modern Humans Was Shared with Neandertals', *Current Biology* 17: 1908–12.

Krauss, R.M., Chen, Y., and Gottesman, R.F. (2000). 'Lexical Gestures and Lexical Access: A Process Model', in D. McNeill (ed.), *Language and Gesture*. Cambridge: Cambridge University Press, pp. 261–83.

Krebs, J.R. and Dawkins, R. (1984). 'Animal Signals: Mind-reading and Manipulation', in J.R. Krebs and N.B. Davies (eds), *Behavioural Ecology: An Evolutionary Approach*. Oxford: Blackwell, pp. 380–402.

Kropotkin, P.A. (1902). *Mutual Aid: A Factor of Evolution*. London: Heinemann.

Kuhn, S. and Stiner, M. (2007). 'Body Ornamentation as Information Technology: Towards an Understanding of the Significance of Early Beads', in P. Mellars, K. Boyle, O. Bar-Yosef, and C. Stringer (eds), *Rethinking the Human Revolution: New Behavioural and Biological Perspectives on the Origin and Dispersal of Modern Humans*, Cambridge: McDonald Institute Monographs, pp. 45–54.

Kummer, H. (1968). *Social Organization of Hamadryas Baboons*. Chicago: University of Chicago Press.

Kuroda, S.J. (1980). 'Social Behavior of the Pygmy Chimpanzees', *Primates* 21(2): 181–97.

Kwak, H., Lee, C., Park, H., and Moon, S. (2010). 'What is Twitter, a Social Network or a News Media?', in *Proceedings of the 19th International World Wide Web (WWW) Conference*. Raleigh, NC: ACM, pp. 591–600.

Kyrantzis, A., Guo, J., and Ervin-Tripp, S. (1990). 'Pragmatic Conventions Influencing Children's Use of Causal Constructions in Natural Discourse', in *Proceedings of the Sixteenth Annual Meeting of the Berkeley Linguistics Society*: 205–14.

Labov, W. (1972). *Sociolinguistic Patterns*. Philadelphia, PA: University of Pennsylvania Press.

Labov, W. (1994). *Principles of Linguistic Change*. Oxford: Basil Blackwell.

Labov, W. and Waletzky, J. (1967). 'Narrative Analysis: Oral Versions of Personal Experience', in J. Helm (ed.), *Essays On the Verbal and Visual Arts*. Seattle, WA: University of Washington Press, pp. 12–44.

Lachmann, M., Számado, S., and Bergstrom, C.T. (2001). 'Cost and Conflict in Animal Signals and Human Language', *Proceedings of the National Academy of Sciences* 98: 13189–94.

Ladd, D.R., Dediu, D., and Kinsella, A.R. (2008). 'Languages and Genes: Reflections on Biolinguistics and the Nature-Nurture Question', *Biolinguistics* 2: 114–26.

Ladygina-Kohts, N.N. (1935). *Infant Chimpanzee and Human Child: A Classic 1935 Comparative Study of Ape Emotions and Intelligence*. New York: Oxford University Press.

Lai, C.S., Fisher, S.E., Hurst, J.A., Vargha-Khadem, F., and Monaco, A.P. (2001). 'A Forkhead-domain Gene Is Mutated in a Severe Speech and Language Disorder', *Nature* 413: 519–23.

Lakoff, G. (1987). *Women, Fire, and Dangerous Things: What Categories Reveal about the Mind*. Chicago: University of Chicago Press.

Lakoff, G. and Johnson, M. (1980). *Metaphors We Live By*. Chicago: University of Chicago Press.

Lakshminarayanan, V. and Santos, L.R. (2010). 'Evolved Irrationality? Equity and the Origins of Human Economic Behavior', in P.M. Kappeler and J.B. Silk (eds), *Mind the Gap: Tracing the Origins of Human Universals*. Berlin/Heidelberg: Springer Verlag.

Laland, K.N. and Janik, V.M. (2006). 'The Animal Cultures Debate', *Trends in Ecology and Evolution* 21(10): 542–7.

Laland, K.N., Odling-Smee J., and Feldman M.W. (2000). 'Niche Construction, Biological Evolution, and Cultural Change', *Behavioral and Brain Sciences* 23: 131–75.

Lalueza-Fox, C., Rosas, A., Estalrrich, A., Gigli, E., Campos, P.F., García-Tabernero, A., García-Vargas, S., et al. (2011). 'Genetic Evidence for Patrilocal Mating Behavior Among Neandertal Groups', *Proceedings of the National Academy of Sciences USA* 108: 250–3.

Lambrecht, K. (1994). *Information Structure and Sentence Form: Topic, Focus and the Mental Representations of Discourse Referents/Grammatical Relations*. Cambridge: Cambridge University Press.

Lancaster, J.B. (1975). 'Primate Behavior and the Emergence of Human Culture', New York: Holt, Rinehart and Winston.

Lancy, D. (1980). 'Becoming a Blacksmith in Gbarngasuakwelle', *Anthropology & Education Quarterly* 11(4): 266–74.

Lancy, D. (1996). *Playing On the Mother Ground: Cultural Routines for Children's Development*. New York: Guilford Press.

Langacker, R.W. (1987). *Foundations of Cognitive Grammar, vol. 1, Theoretical Prerequisites*. Stanford: Stanford University Press.

Langergraber, K.E., Mitani, J., and Vigilant, L. (2009). 'Kinship and Social Bonds in Female Chimpanzees (*Pan troglodytes*)', *American Journal of Primatology* 71(10): 840–51.

Langergraber, K.E., Pruefer, K., Rowney, C., Boesch, C., Crockford, C., Fawcett, K., Vigilant, L., et al. (2012). 'Generation Times in Wild Chimpanzees and Gorillas Suggest Earlier Divergence Times in Great Ape and Human Evolution', *Proceedings of the National Academy of Sciences of the United States of America* 109(39): 15716–21. doi:10.1073/pnas.1211740109.

Langley, M., Clarkson, C., and Ulm, S. (2008). Behavioural Complexity in Eurasian Neanderthal Populations: A Chronological Perspective. *Cambridge Archaeological Journal* 18: 289–307.

Leavens, D., Racine, T., and Hopkins, D. (2009). 'The Ontogeny and Phylogeny of Non-verbal Deixis', in R. Botha and C. Knight (eds), *The Prehistory of Language*. Oxford: Oxford University Press, pp. 142–65.

Lebel, S., Trinkaus, E., Faure, M., Fernandez, P., Guérin, C., Richter, D., Mercier, N., Valladas, H., and Wagner, G.A. (2001). 'Comparative Morphology and Paleobiology of Middle Pleistocene Human Remains from the Bau de l'Aubesier, Vaucluse, France', *Proceedings of the National Academy of Sciences* 98: 11097–102.

Lebra, T.S. (1976). *Japanese Patterns of Behavior*. Honolulu: University of Hawaii Press.

Lebra, T.S. and Lebra, W.P., eds (1986). *Japanese Culture and Behavior: Selected Readings*. Revised edn. Honolulu: University of Hawaii Press.

Lee, R.B. (1988). 'Reflections on Primitive Communism', in T. Ingold, D. Riches, and J. Woodburn (eds), *Hunters and Gatherers 1: History, Evolution and Social Change*. Chicago: Aldine, pp. 252–68.

Lee, S.-H. and Wolpoff, M. (2003). 'The Pattern of Evolution in Pleistocene Human Brain Size', *Paleobiology* 29: 186–96.

Leigh, S.R. (2004). 'Brain Growth, Life History, and Cognition in Primate and Human Evolution', *American Journal of Primatology* 62: 139–64.

Leigh, S.R. (2006). 'Brain Ontogeny and Life History in *Homo Erectus*', *Journal of Human Evolution* 50: 104–8.

Leimar, O. and Hammerstein, P. (2001). 'Evolution of Cooperation through Indirect Reciprocity', *Proceedings of the Royal Society London Biology* 268: 745–53.

Lemasson, A. (2011). 'What Can Forest Guenons "Tell" Us About the Origin of Language?' in A. Vilain, J.-L. Schwartz, C. Abry, and J. Vauclair (eds), *Primate Communication and Human Language*. Amsterdam: John Benjamins, pp. 39–70.

Le May, M. (1975). 'The Language Capability of Neanderthal Man', *American Journal of Physical Anthropology* 42(1): 9–14.

de León, M.S.P., Golovanova, L., Doronichev, V., Romanova, G., Akazawa, T., Kondo, O., Ishida, H., and Zollikofer, C.P.E. (2008). 'Neanderthal Brain Size at Birth Provides Insights into the Evolution of Human Life History', *Proceedings of the National Academy of Sciences USA* 105: 13764–8.

Lerman, K. and Ghosh, R. (2010). *Information Contagion: An Empirical Study of the Spread of News on Digg and Twitter Social Networks*. Proceedings of 4th International Conference on Weblogs and Social Media.

Leroi-Gourhan, A. (1993). *Gesture and Speech*. Cambridge, MA: MIT.

Levelt, W.J.M. (1983). 'Monitoring and Self-repair in Speech', *Cognition* 14: 41–104.

Levelt, W.J.M. (1989). *Speaking: From Intention to Articulation*. Cambridge, MA: MIT.

Lévi-Strauss, C. (1950). *Introduction to the Work of Marcel Mauss*. London: Routledge.

Lévi-Strauss, C. (1969). *The Elementary Structures of Kinship*. London: Eyre & Spottiswoode.

Lévi-Strauss, C. (1970–1981). *Introduction to a Science of Mythology, Vols. 1–4*. London: Cape.

Levinson, S.C. (2006). 'On the Human "Interaction Engine"', in N.J. Enfield and S.C. Levinson (eds), *Roots of Human Sociality: Culture, Cognition, and Interaction*. Oxford: Berg, pp. 39–69.

Levinson, S.C. and Evans, N. (2010). 'Time for a Sea-change in Linguistics: Response to Comments on "The Myth of Language Universals"', *Lingua* 120: 2733–58.

Levinson, S.C. and Gray, R.D. (2012). 'Tools from Evolutionary Biology Shed New Light on the Diversification of Languages', *Trends in Cognitive Sciences* 16: 167–173.

Levinson, S.C. and Jaisson, P., eds (2006). *Evolution and Culture*. Cambridge, MA: MIT.

Lewis, D. (1969). *Convention: A Philosophical Study*. Cambridge, MA: Harvard University Press.

Lewis, J. (2000). *The Batwa of the Great Lakes Region*. Minority Rights Group Report, London: Minority Rights Group.

Lewis, J. (2002). 'Forest Hunter-Gatherers and their World: A Study of the Mbendjele Yaka Pygmies and their Secular and Religious Activities and Representations', Ph.D. Thesis, University of London.

Lewis, J. (2008). '*Ekila*: Blood, Bodies, and Egalitarian Societies', *Journal of the Royal Anthropological Institute* (N. S.) 14(2): 297–315.

Lewis, J. (2009). 'As Well as Words: Congo Pygmy Hunting, Mimicry, and Play', in R. Botha, and C. Knight (eds), *The Cradle of Language: Studies in the Evolution of Language*. Oxford University Press, Oxford, pp. 236–56.

Lewis, J. (2013). 'A Cross-cultural Perspective on the Significance of Music and Dance on Culture and Society, with Insight from BaYaka Pygmies', in M. Arbib (ed.), *Language, Music and the Brain: A Mysterious Relationship*. Cambridge MA: MIT.

Lewis, J. and Knight, J. (1995). *The Twa of Rwanda: Assessment of the Situation of the Twa and Promotion of Twa Rights in Post-War Rwanda*. IWGIA Document 78. London: World Rainforest Movement/Copenhagen.

Lewis, M. (1994). 'Myself and Me', in S.T. Parker, R.W. Mitchell, and M.L. Boccia (eds), *Self-awareness in Animals and Humans*. Cambridge: Cambridge University Press, pp. 20–34.

Lewis, V., Boucher, J., Lupton, L., and Watson, S. (2000). 'Relationships between Symbolic Play, Functional Play, Verbal and Non-Verbal Ability in Young Children'. *International Journal of Language and Communication Disorders* 35(1): 117–27.

Lewis-Williams, D.J. (1981). *Believing and Seeing: Symbolic Meanings in Southern San Rock Painting*. London: Academic Press.

Li, C.N. (2002). 'Missing Links, Issues and Hypotheses in the Evolutionary Origins of Language', in T. Givón and B.F. Malle (eds), *The Evolution of Language Out of Pre-Language*. Amsterdam: John Benjamins, pp. 83–106.

Liebal, K., Call, J., and Tomasello, M. (2004a). 'Chimpanzee Gesture Sequences', *Primates* 64: 377–96.

Liebal, K., Pika, S., Call, J., and Tomasello, M. (2004b). 'Great Ape Communicators Move in Front of Recipients Before Producing Visual Gestures', *Interaction Studies* 5(2): 199–219.

Lieberman, P. (1968). 'Primate Vocalizations and Human Linguistic Ability', *Journal of the Acoustical Society of America*, 44(6): 1574–84.

Lieberman, P. (1985). 'On the Evolution of Human Syntactic Ability: Its Preadaptive Bases—Motor Control and Speech. *Journal of Human Evolution* 14: 67–75.

Lieberman, P. (1992). 'On the Evolution of Human Language', in J.A. Hawkins and M. Gell-Mann (eds), *The Evolution of Human Languages*, Santa Fe Institute Proceedings Volume XI. Addison-Wesley, pp. 21–47.

Lieberman, P. (1998). 'Speech Evolution: Let Barking Dogs Sleep', *Behavioral and Brain Sciences* 21(4): 520.

Lieberman, P. (2009). 'FOXP2 and Human Cognition', *Cell* 137: 800–2.

Lieberman, P. and Crelin, E. (1971). 'On the Speech of Neanderthal Man', *Linguistic Inquiry* 2: 203–22.

Lindenfors, P. (2005). 'Neocortex Evolution in Primates: the "Social Brain" is for Females', *Biology Letters* 1: 407–10.

Liu, X., Somel, M., Tang, L., et al. (2012). 'Extension of Cortical Synaptic Development Distinguishes Humans from Chimpanzees and Macaques'. *Genome Research* 22(4): 611–22.

Lloyd, B. and Goodwin, R. (1995). 'Let's Pretend—Casting the Characters and Setting the Scene', *British Journal of Developmental Psychology* 13: 261–70.

Lomax, A. (1962). 'Song Structure and Social Structure', *Ethnology* 1(4): 425–51.

Lombard, M. (2007). 'The Gripping Nature of Ochre: The Association of Ochre with Howiesons Poort Adhesives and Later Stone Age Mastics from South Africa', *Journal of Human Evolution* 53: 406–19.

Lorenz, K. (1943). 'Die Angeborenen Formen Möglicher Erfahrung', *Zeitschrift für Tierpsychologie* 5: 235–409.

Lotman, Y. (1990). *Universe of the Mind: A Semiotic Theory of Culture*. New York: Tauris.

Lukes, S. (2007). 'Searle Versus Durkheim', in S. Tsohatzidis (ed.), *Intentional Acts and Institutional Facts: Essays on John Searle's Social Ontology*. Dordrecht: Springer, pp. 191–202.

Lumsden, C.J. and Wilson, E.O. (1981). *Genes, Mind and Culture: The Coevolutionary Process*. Cambridge, MA: Harvard University Press.

Lyn, H., Greenfield, P., and Savage-Rumbaugh, S. (2006). 'The Development of Representational Play in Chimpanzees and Bonobos: Evolutionary Implications, Pretense, and the Role of Interspecies Communication', *Cognitive Development* 21: 199–213.

McBrearty, S. (2007). 'Down with the Revolution', in P. Mellars, K. Boyle, O. Bar-Yosef, and C. Stringer (eds), *Rethinking the Human Revolution: New Behavioural and Biological Perspectives on the Origin and Dispersal of Modern Humans*. Cambridge: McDonald Institute for Archaeological Research, pp. 133–51.

McBrearty, S. and Brooks, A.S. (2000). 'The Revolution that Wasn't: A New Interpretation of the Origins of Modern Human Behavior', *Journal of Human Evolution* 39(5): 453–563.

McComb, K., Packer, C., and Pusey, A. (1994). 'Roaring and Numerical Assessment in Contests between Groups of Female Lions, *Panthera Leo*', *Animal Behaviour* 47: 379–87.

McComb, K. and Semple, S. (2005). 'Coevolution of Vocal Communication and Sociality in Primates', *Biology Letters* 1: 381–5.

McDougall, I., Brown, F., and Fleagle, J. (2005). 'Stratigraphic Placement and Age of Modern Humans from Kibish, Ethiopia', *Nature* 433: 733–6.

McGregor, P.K. (2005). *Animal Communication Networks*. Cambridge, MA: MIT.

McGrew, W.C. (1992). *Chimpanzee Material Culture: Implications for Human Evolution.* Cambridge: Cambridge University Press.

Machin, A. (2009). 'The Role of the Individual Agent in Acheulean Biface Variability: A Multi-factorial Model', *Journal of Social Archaeology* 9: 35–58.

MacLarnon, A.M. and Hewitt, G.P. (1999). 'The Evolution of Human Speech: the Role of Enhanced Breathing Control', *American Journal of Physical Anthropology* 109: 341–63.

MacLarnon, A.M. and Hewitt, G.P. (2004). 'Increased Breathing Control: Another Factor in the Evolution of Human Language', *Evolutionary Anthropology* 13: 181–97.

McNabb, J. (2012). 'The Importance of Conveying Visual Information in Acheulean Society: The Background to the Visual Display Hypothesis', in J. Cole and K. Ruebens (eds), *Lucy to Language: Archaeology of the Social Brain. Papers from the British Academy.* (Seminar Series on Palaeolithic Visual Display. Human Origins—Vol. 1), pp. 1–23.

McNabb, J. and Beaumont, P. (2011). *A Report on the Archaeological Assemblages from Excavations by Peter Beaumont at Canteen Koppie, Northern Cape, South Africa.*, University of Southampton Series in Archaeology no. 4 / BAR International Series, no. 2275. Oxford: Archaeopress.

MacNeilage, P.F. (1998a). 'Evolution of the Mechanism of Language Output: Comparative Neurobiology of Vocal and Manual Communication', in J.R. Hurford, M. Studdert-Kennedy, and C. Knight (eds), *Approaches to the Evolution of Language.* Cambridge: Cambridge University Press, pp. 222–40.

MacNeilage, P.F. (1998b). 'The Frame/Content Theory of Evolution of Speech Production', *Behavioral and Brain Sciences*, 21: 499–546.

MacNeilage, P.F. (2008). *The Origin of Speech.* Oxford: Oxford University Press.

McNeill, D. (1992). *Hand and Mind.* Chicago: Chicago University Press.

McNeill, D. (2005). *Gesture and Thought.* Chicago: Chicago University Press.

McNeill, D. (2012). *How Language Began: Gesture and Speech in Human Evolution.* Cambridge: Cambridge University Press.

McPherron, S.P., Alemseged, Z., Marean, C.W., Wynn, J.G., Reed, D., Geraads, D., Bobe, R., and Béarat, H.A. (2010). 'Evidence for Stone-tool-assisted Consumption of Animal Tissues 3.39 Million Years Ago at Dikika, Ethiopia', *Nature* 466: 857–60.

McWhorter, J. (2008). 'Why Does a Language Undress? Strange Cases in Indonesia', in M. Miestamo, K. Sinnemäki, and F. Karlsson (eds), *Language Complexity: Typology, Contact, Change.* Amsterdam/Philadelphia, PA: John Benjamins Publishing Co., pp. 167–90.

Magnani, L. (2009). *Abductive Cognition: The Epistemological and Eco-cognitive Dimensions of Hypothetical Reasoning.* Berlin: Springer.

Manega, P. (1993). *Geochronology, Geochemistry and Isotopic Study of the Plio-Pleistocene Hominid Sites and the Ngorongoro Volcanic Highland in Northern Tanzania.* Ph.D. Thesis. Denver, CO: University of Colorado.

Mannix, E. and Neale, M.A. (2005). 'What Differences Make a Difference? The Promise and Reality of Diverse Teams in Organizations', *Psychological Science in the Public Interest*, 6: 31–55.

Manzi, G., Magri, D., Milli, S., Palombo, M., Margari, V., Celiberti, V., Barbieri, M., Barbieri, M., Melis, R., Rubini, M., Ruffo, M, Saracino, B., Tzedakis, P., Zarattini, A., and Biddittu, I. (2010). 'The New Chronology of the Ceprano Calvarium (Italy)', *Journal of Human Evolution* 59: 580–5.

Mar, R.A. (2004). 'The Neuropsychology of Narrative: Story Comprehension, Story Production and their Interrelation', *Neuropsychologia* 42: 1414–34.

Marean, C.W. (2011). 'Coastal South Africa and the Coevolution of the Modern Human Lineage and the Coastal Adaptation', in N. Bicho, J. Haws, and L. Davis (eds), *Trekking the Shore: Changing Coastlines and the Antiquity of Coastal Settlement*, Interdisciplinary Contributions to Archaeology, Pt 2. New York: Springer, pp. 421–40.

Marean, C.W., Bar-Matthews, M., Bernatchez, J., Fisher, E., Goldberg, P., Herries, A.I.R., Jacobs, Z., Jerardino, A., Karkanas, P., Minichillo, T., Nilssen, P.J., Thompson, E., Watts, I., Williams, H.M. (2007). 'Early Human Use of Marine Resources and Pigment in South Africa During the Middle Pleistocene', *Nature* 449: 905–8.

Marentette, P. and Nicoladis, E. (2012). 'Does Ontogenetic Ritualization Explain Early Communicative Gestures in Human Infants?', in S. Pika and K. Liebal (eds), *Developments in Primate Gesture Research*. Amsterdam: John Benjamins.

Marks, A.E., Hietala H.J., and Williams J.K. (2001). 'Tool Standardization in the Middle and Upper Palaeolithic: A Closer Look', *Cambridge Archaeological Journal* 11: 17–44.

Marler, P. (1970). 'Vocalizations of East African Monkeys. I. Red Colobus', *Folia Primatologica* 13: 81–91.

Marler, P. (1976). 'Social Organization, Communication and Graded Signals: The Chimpanzee and the Gorilla', in P.P. Bateson and R.A. Hinde (eds), *Growing Points in Ethology*. Cambridge: Cambridge University Press, pp. 239–80.

Marler, P. (1977). 'The Evolution of Communication', in T.S. Sebeok (ed.), *How Animals Communicate*. Bloomington and London: Indiana University Press, pp. 45–70.

Marler, P. and Peters, S. (1982). 'Developmental Overproduction and Selective Attrition: New Processes in the Epigenesis of Birdsong', *Developmental Psychobiology* 15: 369–78.

Marler, P. and Tenaza, R. (1977). 'Signaling Behavior of Apes with Special Reference to Vocalizations', in T.A. Sebeok (ed.), *How Animals Communicate*. Bloomington: Indiana University Press, pp. 965–1033.

Marshack, A. (1976). 'Implications of the Paleolithic Symbolic Evidence for the Origin of Language', *Current Anthropology* 17: 274–84.

Marshack, A. (1981). 'On Paleolithic Ochre and the Early Uses of Color and Symbol', *Current Anthropology* 22(2): 188–91.

Marshall, A.J., Wrangham, R.W., and Arcadi, A.C. (1999). 'Does Learning Affect the Structure of Vocalisations in Chimpanzees?', *Animal Behaviour* 58(4): 825–30.

Martínez, I., Quam, R.M., Rosa, M., Jarabo, P., Lorenzo, C., and Arsuaga, J.L. (2008). 'Auditory Capacities of Human Fossils: A New Approach to the Origin of Speech', *Journal of the Acoustical Society of America* 123: 3606.

Martínez, I., Rosa, M., Arsuaga, J.-L., Jarabo, P., Quam, R., Lorenzo, C., Gracia, A., Carretero, J.-M., de Castro, J.-M.B., and Carbonell, E. (2004). 'Auditory Capacities in Middle Pleistocene Humans from the Sierra de Atapuerca in Spain', *Proceedings of the National Academy of Sciences USA* 101: 9976–81.

Marwick, B. (2003). 'Pleistocene Exchange Networks as Evidence for the Evolution of Language', *Cambridge Archaeological Journal* 13: 67–81.

Mason, R. (1957). 'The Transvaal Middle Stone Age and Statistical Analysis', *South African Archaeological Bulletin* 12: 119–37.

Mason, R. (1962). *The Prehistory of the Transvaal*. Johannesburg: University of Witwatersrand Press.

Mason, R. (1988). *Cave of Hearths, Makapansgat, Transvaal*. Johannesburg: University of Witwatersrand Press.

Mastripieri, D. (1999). 'Primate Social Organization, Gestural Repertoire Size, and Communication Dynamics: A Comparative Study of Macaques', in B.J. King (ed.), *The Origins of Language: What Nonhuman Primates Can Tell Us*. Santa Fe, NM: School for American Research Press, pp. 55–77.

Maynard Smith, J. (1964). 'Group Selection and Kin Selection', *Nature* 201(4924): 1145–7.

Maynard Smith, J. (1982). *Evolution and the Theory of Games*. Cambridge: Cambridge University Press.

Maynard Smith, J. and Harper, D.G.C. (1995). 'Animal Signals: Models and Terminology', *Journal of Theoretical Biology* 177: 305–11.

Maynard Smith, J. and Harper, D.G.C. (2003). *Animal Signals*. Oxford: Oxford University Press.

Maynard Smith, J. and Szathmáry, E. (1995). *The Major Transitions in Evolution*. Oxford: Freeman.

Mayr, E. (1982). *The Growth of Biological Thought*. Cambridge, MA: Belknap Press.

Mead, G.H. (1934). *Mind, Self and Society*, ed. C.W. Morris. Chicago: University of Chicago Press.

Meguerditchian, A., Cochet, H., and Vauclair, J. (2011). 'From Gesture to Language: Ontogenetic and Phylogenetic Perspectives on Gestural Communication and Cerebral Lateralization', in A. Vilain, J.-L. Schwartz, C. Abry, and J. Vauclair (eds), *Primate Communication and Human Language: Vocalization, Gestures, Imitation and Deixis in Humans and Non-Humans*. Amsterdam: John Benjamins, pp. 91–119.

Mehl, M.R. and Pennebaker, J.W. (2003). 'The Sounds of Social Life: A Psychometric Analysis of Students' Daily Social Environments and Natural Conversations', *Journal of Personality and Social Psychology* 84(4): 857–70.

Mehl, M.R., Vazire, S., Ramírez-Esparza, N., Slatcher, R.B., and Pennebaker, J.W. (2007). 'Are Women Really More Talkative than Men?', *Science* 317: 82.

Meillet, A. (1921). *Linguistique historique et linguistique générale*. Paris: Champion.

Meister, I.G., Boroojerdi, B., Foltys, H., Sparing, R., Huber, W., and Topper, R. (2003). 'Motor Cortex Hand Area and Speech: Implications for the Development of Language', *Neuropsychologia* 41(4): 401–6.

Melis, A., Call, J., and Tomasello, M. (2006). 'Chimpanzees (*Pan Troglodytes*) Conceal Visual and Auditory Information from Others', *Journal of Comparative Psychology* 120(2): 154–62.

Mellars, P. (1996). *The Neanderthal Legacy*. Princeton, NJ: Princeton University Press.

Mellars, P. (2005). 'The Impossible Coincidence. A Single-species Model for the Origins of Modern Human Behavior in Europe', *Evolutionary Anthropology* 14: 12–27.

Mellars, P. (2010). 'Neanderthal Symbolism and Ornament Manufacture: The Bursting of a Bubble?', *Proceedings of the National Academy of Sciences USA* 107: 20147–8.

Mellars, P.A., Boyle, K., Bar-Yosef, O., and Stringer, C., eds (2007). *Rethinking the Human Revolution: New Behavioural and Biological Perspectives on the Origin and Dispersal of Modern Humans*. Cambridge: McDonald Institute for Archaeological Research.

Mellars, P.A. and Stringer, C., eds (1989). *The Human Revolution: Behavioural and Biological Perspectives in the Origins of Modern Humans.* Edinburgh: Edinburgh University Press.

Menzel, E.W. (1972). 'Spontaneous Invention of Ladders in a Group of Young Chimpanzees', *Folia Primatologica* 17: 87–106.

Merker, B. (2000). 'Synchronous Chorusing and Human Origins', in N.L. Wallin, B. Merker, and S. Brown (eds), *The Origins of Music: An Introduction to Evolutionary Musicology.* Cambridge, MA: MIT Press, pp. 315–27.

Merleau-Ponty, M. (1945–2012). *Phenomenology of Perception.* New York: Routledge.

Merriam, A.P. (1980). 'Zaïre. 3. Pygmy Music', in S. Sadie (coord.), *The New Grove Dictionary of Music and Musicians,* 20: 623.

Meyer, M.R. (2005). *Functional biology of the Homo erectus axial skeleton from Dmanisi, Georgia.* Ph.D. Thesis. Philadelphia, PA: University of Pennsylvania.

Miles, H.L. (1986). 'Cognitive Development in a Signing Orangutan', *Primate Report* 14: 179–80.

Miles, H.L. (1990). 'The Cognitive Foundations for Reference in a Signing Orangutan', in S.T. Parker and K.R. Gibson (eds), *Language and Intelligence in Monkeys and Apes.* Cambridge: Cambridge University Press, pp. 511–39.

Miller, G.F. (2000). *The Mating Mind.* New York: Doubleday.

Milliken, F.J., Bartel, C.A., and Kurtzberg, T.R. (2003). 'Diversity and Creativity in Work Groups: A Dynamic Perspective on the Affective and Cognitive Processes that Link Diversity and Performance', in P.B. Paulus and B.A. Nijstad (eds), *Group Creativity: Innovation through Collaboration.* Oxford University Press, pp. 32–62.

Mishra, S. (1995). 'Chronology of the Indian Stone Age: The Impact of Recent Absolute and Relative Dating Attempts', *Man and Environment* 20: 11–15.

Mitani, J.C. (1996). 'Comparative Studies of African Ape Vocal Behavior', in W.C. McGrew, L.F. Marchant, and T. Nishida (eds), *Great Ape Societies.* Cambridge: Cambridge University Press, pp. 241–54.

Mitani, J.C. and Amsler, S.J. (2003). 'Social and Spatial Aspects of Male Subgrouping in a Community of Wild Chimpanzees', *Behaviour* 140: 869–84.

Mitani, J.C. and Brandt, K.L. (1994). 'Social Factors Influence the Acoustic Variability in the Long-distance Calls of Male Chimpanzees', *Ethology* 96: 233–52.

Mitani, J.C. and Gros-Louis, J. (1995). 'Species and Sex-Differences in the Screams of Chimpanzees and Bonobos', *International Journal of Primatology* 16(3): 393–411.

Mitani, J.C. and Gros-Louis, J. (1998). 'Chorusing and Convergence in Chimpanzees: Tests of Three Hypotheses', *Behaviour* 135: 1041–64.

Mitani, J.C. and Nishida, T. (1993). 'Contexts and Social Correlates of Long-distance Calling by Male Chimpanzees', *Animal Behaviour* 45: 735–46.

Mitchell, R.W. (1994). 'Multiplicities of Self', in S.T. Parker, R.W. Mitchell, and M.L. Boccia (eds), *Self-awareness in Animals and Humans.* Cambridge: Cambridge University Press, pp. 81–107.

Mitchell, R.W., ed. (2002). *Pretending and Imagination in Animals and Children.* Cambridge: Cambridge University Press.

Mithen, S. (1996). *The Prehistory of the Mind: A Search for the Origins of Art, Science and Religion.* London: Thames & Hudson.

Mithen, S. (1999). 'Symbolism and the Supernatural', in R. Dunbar, C. Knight, and C. Power (eds), *The Evolution of Culture: An Interdisciplinary View*. Edinburgh: Edinburgh University Press, pp. 147–69.

Mithen, S. (2005). *The Singing Neanderthals: The Origins of Music, Language, Mind and Body*. London: Weidenfeld & Nicolson.

Modell, A.H. (2003). *Imagination and the Meaningful Brain*. Cambridge, MA: MIT Press.

Moerman, M. (1988). *Talking Culture: Ethnography and Conversation Analysis*. Philadelphia: University of Pennsylvania Press.

Møller, A.P. (1997). 'Evolutionary Conflicts and Adapted Psychologies', in G.R. Bock and G. Cardew (eds), *Characterizing Human Psychological Adaptations*. CIBA Foundation Symposium 208. Chichester: Wiley, pp. 39–50.

Moncell, M.-H. (2011). 'Technological Behavior and Mobility of Human Groups Deduced from Lithic Assemblages in the Late Middle and Early Late Pleistocene of the Middle Rhône Valley (France)', in N. Conard and J. Richter (eds), *Neanderthal Lifeways, Subsistence and Technology: One Hundred and Fifty Years of Neanderthal Study*. Vertebrate Paleobiology and Paleoanthropology 19. Dordrecht: Springer, pp. 261–87.

Morgan, L.H. (1871). *Systems of Consanguinity and Affinity of the Human Family*. Washington: Smithsonian Institution.

Morin, E. and Laroulandie, V. (2012). 'Presumed Symbolic Use of Diurnal Raptors by Neanderthals', *PLoS One* 7(3): 1–5. doi:10.371/journal.pone.0032856.

Mueller, R.-A. (1996). 'Innateness, autonomy, universality? Neurobiological approaches to language', *Behavioral and Brain Sciences* 19: 611–75.

Mufwene, S.S. (2001). 'Competition and Selection in Language Evolution', *Selection* 3(1): 45–56.

Mufwene, S.S. (2013). 'Language as Technology: Some Questions that Evolutionary Linguistics Should Address', in T. Lohndal (ed.), *In Search of Universal Grammar: From Norse to Zoque*. Amsterdam: John Benjamins, pp. 327–58.

Müller, M. (1861). *Lectures on the Science of Language*. London: Longman, Green.

Nakamura, M. (2000). 'Is Human Conversation More Efficient than Chimpanzee Grooming?', *Human Nature* 11(3): 281–97.

Nelson, K. (1978). 'How Children Represent Knowledge of their World in and out of Language', in R. Siegler (ed.), *Children's Thinking: What Develops*. Hillsdale, NJ: Lawrence Erlbaum Associates, pp. 225–73.

Nelson, K. and Shaw, L.K. (2002). 'Developing a Socially Shared Symbolic System', in J. Byrnes and E. Amseli (eds), *Language, Literacy and Cognitive Development*. Mahwah, NJ: Erlbaum, pp. 27–57.

Nesse, R.M. (2009). 'Social Selection and the Origins of Culture', in M. Schaller, S.J. Heine, A. Norenzayan, T. Yamagishi, and T. Kameda (eds), *Evolution, Culture, and the Human Mind*. Philadelphia, PA: Lawrence Erlbaum Associates, pp. 137–150.

Newbury, D.F. and Monaco, A.P. (2010). 'Genetic Advances in the Study of Speech and Language Disorders', *Neuron* 68: 309–20.

Newmeyer, F.J. (1998). *Language Form and Language Function*. Cambridge, MA: MIT Press.

Newmeyer, F.J. (2003). 'Grammar is Grammar and Usage is Usage', *Language* 79: 682–707.

Ninio, A. and Bruner, J.S. (1978). 'The Achievement and Antecedents of Labelling', *Journal of Child Language* 5: 1–15. doi:10.1017/S0305000900001896.

Ninio, A. and Snow, C.E. (1999). 'The Development of Pragmatics: Learning to Use Language Appropriately', in T.K. Bhatia and W.C. Ritchie (eds), *Handbook of Child Language Acquisition*. New York: Academic Press, pp. 347–83.

Nishida, T., Kano, T., Goodall, J., McGrew, W.C., and Nakamura, M. (1999). 'Ethogram and Ethnography of Mahale Chimpanzees', *Anthropological Science* 107(2): 141–88.

Nishida, T., Mitani, J.C., and Watts, D.P. (2004). 'Variable Grooming Behaviours in Wild Chimpanzees', *Folia Primatologica* 75: 31–6.

Noordzij, M.L., Newman-Norlund, S.E., de Ruiter, J.P., Hagoort, P., Levinson, S.C., and Toni, I. (2010). 'Neural Correlates of Intentional Communication', *Frontiers in Neuroscience* 4: 188.

Norman, D.A. (1991). 'Cognitive Artifacts', in J.M. Carroll (ed.), *Designing Interaction: Psychology at the Human-computer Interface*. Cambridge: Cambridge University Press, pp. 17–38.

Norrick, N.R. (2000). *Conversational Narrative: Storytelling in Everyday Talk*. Amsterdam: John Benjamins Publishing Company.

Nowak, M.A. (2006). 'Five Rules for the Evolution of Cooperation', *Science* 314: 1560–3.

Nowak, M.A. and Komarova, N.L. (2001). 'Towards an Evolutionary Theory of Language', *Trends in Cognitive Sciences* 5(7): 288–95.

Nowak, M.A., Plotkin, J.B., and Jansen, V. A. (2000). 'The Evolution of Syntactic Communication', *Nature* 404: 495–8.

Nowak, M.A. and Sigmund, K. (1998). 'Evolution of Indirect Reciprocity by Image Scoring', *Nature* 393: 573–6.

Nowell, A. and Chang, M. (2009). 'The Case Against Sexual Selection as an Explanation of Handaxe Morphology', *PaleoAnthropology*: 77–88.

Nunn, C.L. (1999). 'The Evolution of Exaggerated Sexual Swellings in Primates and the Graded-Signal Hypothesis. *Animal Behaviour* 58(2): 229–46.

Oakley, K. (1973). 'Fossils Collected by the Earlier Paleolithic Men', in *Mélanges de préhistoire, d'archéocivilization et d'ethnologie offerts à André Varagnac*. Paris: Serpen, pp. 581–4.

O'Connell, J.F., Hawkes, K., and Blurton Jones, N.G. (1999). 'Grandmothering and the Evolution of *Homo erectus*', *Journal of Human Evolution* 36(5): 461–485. doi:10.1006/jhev.1998.0285.

Odling-Smee, F.J. and Laland, K.N. (2009). 'Cultural Niche-construction: Evolution's Cradle of Language', in R. Botha and C. Knight (eds), *The Prehistory of Language*. Oxford: Oxford University Press, pp. 99–121.

Odling-Smee, F.J., Laland, K.N., and Feldman, M.W. (2003). *Niche Construction: The Neglected Process in Evolution. (Monographs in Population Biology 37)*. Princeton, NJ. Princeton University Press.

O'Gorman, R., Wilson, D.S., and Sheldon, K.M. (2008). 'For the Good of the Group? Exploring Group-level Evolutionary Adaptations Using Multilevel Selection Theory', *Group Dynamics-Theory Research and Practice* 12(1): 17–26.

Oller, D.K. and Griebel, U. (2008). *Evolution of Communicative Flexibility*. Cambridge, MA: MIT.

Oloa Biloa, C. (2011). 'La musique des Pygmées Bagyéli (Sud-ouest Cameroun). Etude des conséquences du changement de mode de vie sur le patrimoine musical', Masters Thesis, Université Paris–Ouest-Nanterre.

Opie, K. and Power, C. (2008). 'Grandmothering and Female Coalitions: A Basis for Matrilineal Priority?', in N.J. Allen, H. Callan, R. Dunbar, and W. James (eds), *Early Human Kinship: From Sex to Social Reproduction*. Malden, MA and Oxford: Blackwells, pp. 168–86.

Osvath, M. (2009). 'Spontaneous Planning for Future Stone Throwing by a Male Chimpanzee', *Current Biology* 19(5): R190–R191.

Ouattara, K., Lemasson, A., and Zuberbühler, K. (2009a). 'Campbell's Monkeys Use Affixation to Alter Call Meaning', *PLoS One* 4(11): e7808.

Ouattara, K., Lemasson, A., and Zuberbühler, K. (2009b). 'Campbell's Monkeys Concatenate Vocalizations into Context-specific Call Sequences', *Proceedings of the National Academy of Sciences USA* 106(51): 22026–31.

Ouattara, K., Zuberbühler, K., N'goran, E.K., Gobert, J.-E., and Lemasson, A. (2009c). 'The Alarm Call System of Female Campbell's Monkeys', *Animal Behaviour* 78: 35–44.

Packer, C., Swanson, A., Ikanda D., and Kushnir H. (2011). 'Fear of Darkness, the Full Moon and the Nocturnal Ecology of African Lions.' *PLoS ONE* 6(7): e22285. doi10.1371/journal. pone.0022285.

Packman, S. and Grün, R. (1992). 'TL Analysis of Loess Samples from Achenheim', *Quaternary Science Reviews* 11: 103–7.

Paddayya, K. (1976). 'Excavation of an Acheulian site at Hunsgi, South India', *Current Anthropology* 17: 760–1.

Pagel, M. (2009). 'Human Language as a Culturally Transmitted Replicator', *National Review of Genetics* 10: 405–15.

Palmer, A.R. (2009). 'Animal Asymmetry', *Current Biology* 19(12): R474–R477.

Pan, H. (1994). 'Children's Play in Taiwan', in J. Roopnarine, J. Johnson, and F. Hooper (eds), *Children's Play in Diverse Culture*. Albany: State University of New York Press, pp. 31–50.

Panchanathan, K. and Boyd, R. (2004). 'Indirect Reciprocity Can Stabilize Cooperation without the Second-order Free Rider Problem', *Nature* 432: 499–502.

Papafragou, A. (1998). 'The Acquisition of Modality: Implications for Theories of Semantic Representation', *Mind & Language* 13: 370–399.

Pappu, S., Gunnell, Y., Akhilesh, K., Braucher, R., Taieb, M., Demory, F., and Thouveny, N. (2011). 'Early Pleistocene Presence of Acheulian Hominins in South India', *Science* 331: 1596–9.

Parfitt, S., Ashton, N., Lewis, S., Abel, R., Russell Coope, G., Field, M., Gale, R., Hoare, P., Larkin, N., Lewis, M., Karloukovski, V., Maher, B., Peglar, S., Preece, R., Whittaker, J., and Stringer, C. (2010). 'Early Pleistocene Human Occupation at the Edge of the Boreal Zone in Northwest Europe', *Nature* 466: 229–233.

Parker, S.T. and Milbraith, C. (1994). 'Contributions of Imitation and Role-Playing Games to the Construction of Self in Primates', in S.T. Parker, R.W. Mitchell, and M.L. Boccia (eds), *Self-awareness in Animals and Humans*. Cambridge: Cambridge University Press, pp. 108–28.

Parker, S.T., Mitchell, R.W., and Boccia, M.L. (1994). 'Expanding Dimensions of the Self: Through the Looking Glass and Beyond', in S.T. Parker, R.W. Mitchell, and M.L. Boccia (eds), *Self-awareness in Animals and Humans*. Cambrdige: Cambridge University Press, pp. 3–19.

Parkington, J. (1992). 'Making Sense of Sequence at the Elands Bay Cave, Western Cape, South Africa', in A. Smith and B. Mutti (eds), *Guide to Archaeological Sites in the South-Western Cape*. Cape Town: Southern African Association of Archaeologists, pp. 6–12.

Parnell, R.J. and Buchanan-Smith, H.M. (2001). 'Animal Behaviour: An Unusual Social Display by Gorillas', *Nature* 412: 294.

Patel, A. (2008). *Music, Language and the Brain*. Oxford: Oxford University Press.

Patterson, F. (1978). 'Conversations with a Gorilla', *National Geographic* 134(4): 438–65.

Pauw, S. and Hilferty, J. (2012). 'The Emergence of Quantifiers', in L. Steels (ed.), *Experiments in Cultural Language Evolution*. Amsterdam: John Benjamins, pp. 277–304.

Pawlowski, B., Lowen, C.L., and Dunbar, R.I.M. (1998). 'Neocortex Size, Social Skills and Mating Success in Primates', *Behaviour* 135: 357–68.

Paxton, R., Basile, B.M., Adachi, I., Suzuki, W.A., Wilson, M.E., and Hampton, R.R. (2010). 'Rhesus Monkeys (*Macaca mulatta*) Rapidly Learn to Select Dominant Individuals in Videos of Artificial Social Interactions between Unfamiliar Conspecifics', *Journal of Comparative Psychology* 124(4): 395.

Peirce, C.S. (1940). 'Logic as Semiotic: The Theory of Signs', in J. Buchler (ed.), *The Philosophical Writings of Peirce*. New York: Dover, pp. 98–119.

Pellegrini, A.D. and Smith, P.K., eds (2004). *The Nature of Play: Great Apes and Humans*. New York: Guilford.

Peresani, M., Fiore, I., Gala, M., Romandini, M., and Tagliacozzo, A. (2011). 'Late Neandertals and the Intentional Removal of Feathers as Evidenced from Bird Bone Taphonomy at Fumane Cave 44 ky B.P., Italy', *Proceedings of the National Academy of Sciences USA* 108: 3888–93.

Peretz, I. (2006). 'The Nature of Music from a Biological Perspective', *Cognition* 100: 1–32.

Pérez-Barbería, F.J., Shultz, S., and Dunbar, R.I.M. (2007). 'Evidence for Coevolution of Sociality and Relative Brain Size in Three Orders of Mammals', *Evolution* 61: 2811–21.

Perreault, C. and Mathew, S. (2012). 'Dating the origin of language using phonemic diversity', *PLoS ONE* 7(4): e35289. doi:10.1371/journal.pone.0035289.

Pettitt, P.B. (2011). 'The Living as Symbols, the Dead as Symbols: Problematising the Scale and Pace of Hominin Symbolic Evolution', in C. Henshilwood and F. d'Errico (eds), *Homo Symbolicus. The Dawn of Language, Imagination and Spirituality*. Amsterdam: John Benjamins, pp. 141–62.

Pfefferle, D., Brauch, K., Heistermann, M., Hodges, J.K., and Fischer, J. (2008a). 'Female Barbary Macaque (*Macaca sylvanus*) Copulation Calls Do Not Reveal the Fertile Phase but Influence Mating Outcome', *Proceedings of the Royal Society B- Biological Sciences*, 275 (1634): 571–8.

Pfefferle, D., Heistermann, M., Hodges, J.K., and Fischer, J. (2008b). Male Barbary Macaques Eavesdrop on Mating Outcome: A Playback Study. *Animal Behaviour* 75(6): 1885–91.

Piaget J. (1945). *La Formation du symbole chez l'enfant*. Neuchatel: Delachaux and Niestlé.

Piaget, J. (1979). *Behaviour and Evolution*. London: Routledge.

Piattelli-Palmarini, M. (2010). 'What is Language, That it May Have Evolved, and What is Evolution, That it May Apply to Language', in R.K. Larson, V. Déprez, and H. Yamakido (eds), *The Evolution of Human Language: Biolinguistic Perspectives*. Cambridge: Cambridge University Press.

Pika, S. (2009). 'Our Grooming Cousins: Providing the Link to Declarative Signalling?', *Studies in Communication Sciences* 9(1): 73–102.

Pika, S. and Liebal, K. (2012a). *Developments in Primate Gesture Research*. Amsterdam: John Benjamins.

Pika, S. and Liebal, K. (2012b). 'Introduction: Developments in primate gesture research', in S. Pika and K. Liebal (eds), *Developments in Primate Gesture Research*. Amsterdam: John Benjamins, pp. 1–6.

Pika, S., Liebal, K., Call, J., and Tomasello, M. (2005a). 'The Gestural Communication of Apes', *Gesture* 5(1/2): 41–56.

Pika, S., Liebal, K., and Tomasello, M. (2005b). 'Gestural Communication in Subadult Bonobos (*Pan paniscus*): Gestural Repertoire and Use', *American Journal of Primatology* 65(1): 39–51.

Pika, S., Liebal, K., and Tomasello, M. (2003). 'Gestural Communication in Young Gorillas (*Gorilla gorilla*): Gestural Repertoire, Learning and Use', *American Journal of Primatology* 60(3): 95–111.

Pika, S. and Mitani, J.C. (2006). 'Referential Gesturing in Wild Chimpanzees (*Pan troglodytes*)', *Current Biology* 16(6): 191–2.

Pika, S. and Mitani, J. (2009). 'The Directed Scratch: Evidence for a Referential Gesture in Chimpanzees?', in R. Botha and C. Knight (eds), *The Prehistory of Language*. Oxford: Oxford University Press, pp. 166–80.

Pika, S. and Zuberbühler, K. (2008). 'Social Games between Bonobos and Humans: Evidence for Shared Intentionality?', *American Journal of Primatology* 70(3): 207–10.

Pinker, S. (1994). *The Language Instinct*. London: Penguin.

Pinker, S. (1998). *How the Mind Works*. London: Penguin.

Pinker, S. (2003). 'Language as an Adaptation to the Cognitive Niche', in M. Christiansen and S. Kirby (eds), *Language Evolution: States of the Art*. New York: Oxford University Press.

Pinker, S. and Bloom, P. (1990). 'Natural Language and Natural Selection', *Behavioral and Brain Sciences* 13(4): 707–84.

Plavcan, J.M. (2001). 'Sexual Dimorphism in Primate Evolution', *Yearbook of Physical Anthropology* 44: 25–53.

Ploog, D. (2002). 'Is the Neural Basis of Vocalization Different in Non-human Primates and *Homo Sapiens?*', in T.J. Crow (ed.), *The Speciation of Modern Homo Sapiens*. Oxford: Oxford University Press, pp. 121–35.

Plooij, F.X. (1978). 'Some Basic Traits of Language in Wild Chimpanzees?', in A. Lock (ed.), *Action, Gesture and Symbol*. London: Academic Press, pp. 111–31.

Plooij, F.X. (1979). 'How Wild Chimpanzee Babies Trigger the Onset of Mother-infant play', in M. Bullowa (ed.), *Before Speech*. Cambridge: University Press, pp. 223–43.

Plotkin, H. (2003). *The Imagined World Made Real: Towards a Natural Science of Culture*, New Jersey: Rutgers University Press.

Polanyi, L. (1979). 'So What's the Point?', *Semiotica* 25(3): 207–41.

Pollick, A.S. and de Waal, F.B.M. (2007). 'Ape Gestures and Language Evolution', *Proceedings of the National Academy of Sciences of the United States of America* 104: 8184–9.

Pomerantz, A. (1984). 'Agreeing and Disagreeing with Assessments: Some Features of Preferred/dispreferred Turn Shapes', in J. Maxwell Atkinson and J. Heritage (eds), *Structures of Social Action*. Cambridge: Cambridge University Press, pp. 57–101.

Pomerantz, A. and Heritage, J. (2012). 'Preference', in J. Sidnell and T. Stivers (eds), *The Handbook of Conversation Analysis*. London: Routledge, pp. 210–28.

Porat, N., Chazan, M., Grün, R., Aubert, M., Eisenmann, V., and Horwitz, L. (2010). 'New Radiometric Ages for the Fauresmith Industry from Kathu Pan, Southern Africa:

Implications for the Earlier to Middle Stone Age Transition', *Journal of Archaeological Science* 37: 269–83.

Potts, R. (1998). 'Environmental Hypotheses of Hominin Evolution', *Yearbook of Physical Anthropology* 41: 93–136.

Potts, R. (2007). 'Paleoclimate and Human Evolution', *Evolutionary Anthropology* 16: 1–3. doi: 10.1002/evan.20121.

Potts, R., Behrensmeyer, A., Deino, A., Ditchfield, P., and Clark, J. (2004). 'Small Mid-Pleistocene Hominin Associated with East African Acheulian Technology', *Science* 305: 75–8.

Powell, A., Shennan, S., and Thomas, M.G. (2009). 'Late Pleistocene Demography and the Appearance of Modern Human Behavior', *Science* 324: 1298–1301.

Power, C. (1998). 'Old Wives' Tales: The Gossip Hypothesis and the Reliability of Cheap Signals', in J.R. Hurford, M. Studdert-Kennedy, and C. Knight (eds), *Approaches to the Evolution of Language: Social and Cognitive Bases*. Cambridge: Cambridge University Press, pp. 111–29.

Power, C. (1999). '"Beauty Magic": The Origins of Art', in R. Dunbar, C. Knight, and C. Power (eds), *The Evolution of Culture. An Interdisciplinary View*. Edinburgh, Edinburgh University Press, pp. 92–112.

Power, C. (2000). 'Secret Language Use at Female Initiation: Bounding Gossiping Communities. In C. Knight, M. Studdert-Kennedy, and J. R. Hurford (eds), *The Evolutionary Emergence of Language: Social Function and the Origins of Linguistic Form*. Cambridge: Cambridge University Press, pp. 81–98.

Power, C. (2001). 'Beauty Magic: Deceptive Sexual Signaling and the Evolution of Ritual', Ph.D. Thesis, University of London.

Power, C. (2004). 'Women in Prehistoric Art', in G. Berghaus (ed.), *New Perspectives on Prehistoric Art*. Westport: Praeger, pp. 75–130.

Power, C. (2009). 'Sexual Selection Models for the Emergence of Symbolic Communication: Why They Should Be Reversed', in R. Botha and C. Knight (eds), *The Cradle of Language: Studies in the Evolution of Language*. Oxford: Oxford University Press, pp. 257–80.

Power, C. and Aiello, L.C. (1997). 'Female Proto-symbolic Strategies', in L.D. Hager (ed.), *Women in Human Evolution*. New York: Routledge, pp. 153–71.

Power, C., Sommer, V., and Watts, I. (2013). 'The Seasonality Thermostat: Female Reproductive Synchrony and Male Behaviour in Monkeys, Neanderthals and Modern Humans', *PaleoAnthropology* 2013: 33–60. doi:10.4207/PA.2013.ART79.

Power, C. and Watts, I. (1996). 'Female Strategies and Collective Behaviour: The Archaeology of Earliest *Homo Sapiens Sapiens*', in J. Steele and S. Shennan (eds), *The Archaeology of Human Ancestry*. London and New York: Routledge, pp. 306–30.

Power, C. and Watts, I. (1997). 'The Woman with the Zebra's Penis: Gender, Mutability and Performance', *Journal of the Royal Anthropological Institute* (N.S). 3: 537–60.

Power, C. and Watts, I. (1999). 'First Gender, Wrong Sex', in H. Moore, T. Sanders, and B. Kaare (eds), *Those Who Play with Fire: Gender, Fertility and Transformation in East and Southern Africa*. London/New Brunswick, NJ: Athlone Press, pp. 101–32.

Pradhan, G.R., Engelhardt, A., van Schaik, C.P., and Maestripieri, D. (2006). 'The Evolution of Female Copulation Calls in Primates: A Review and a New Model', *Behavioral Ecology and Sociobiology* 59(3): 333–43.

Premack, A.J. and Premack, D. (1972). 'Teaching Language to an Ape', *Scientific American* 227: 92–9.

Preston, S.D. and de Waal, F.B.M. (2002). 'Empathy: Its Ultimate and Proximate Bases', *Behavioral and Brain Sciences* 25: 1–72.

Quam, R. and Rak, Y. (2008). 'Auditory Ossicles from Southwest Asian Mousterian Sites', *Journal of Human Evolution* 54: 414–33.

Rachlin, H. (2002). 'Altruism and Selfishness', *Behavioral and Brain Sciences* 25: 239–96.

Rakoczy, H. (2006). 'Pretend Play and the Development of Collective Intentionality', *Cognitive Systems Research* 7: 113–27.

Rakoczy, H. (2008). 'Taking Fiction Seriously: Young Children Understand the Normative Structure of Joint Pretend Games', *Developmental Psychology* 44(4): 1195–201.

Rakoczy, H. and Tomasello, M. (2007). 'The Ontogeny of Social Ontology: Steps to Shared Intentionality and Status Functions', in S.L. Tsohatzidis (ed.), *Intentional Acts and Institutional Facts: Essays on John Searle's Social Ontology*. Berlin: Springer Verlag, pp. 227–37.

Rakoczy, H., Warneken, F., and Tomasello, M. (2008). 'The Sources of Normativity: Young Children's Awareness of the Normative Structure of Games.' *Developmental Psychology* 44: 875.

Ramachandran, V.S. and Hubbard, E.M. (2001). 'Synesthesia: A Window into Perception, Thought and Language', *Journal of Consciousness Studies* 8: 3–34.

Rappaport, R.A. (1999). *Ritual and Religion in the Making of Humanity*. Cambridge: Cambridge University Press.

Ratner, N. and Bruner, J.S. (1978). 'Games, Social Exchange and the Acquisition of Language', *Journal of Child Language* 5: 391–401. doi:10.1017/S0305000900002063.

Rawls, J. (1955). 'Two Concepts of Rules', *The Philosophical Review* 64(1): 3–32.

Ray, N. (2003). *Modélisation de la démographie des populations humaines préhistoriques à l'aide de données environnementales et génétiques*. Ph.D. Thesis. Sc. 3448. Geneva: University of Geneva.

Reddy, V. (2001). 'Infant Clowning: The Interpersonal Creation of Humour in Infancy', *Enfance* 3: 247–56.

Reisman, K. (1974). 'Contrapuntal Conversations in an Antiguan Village', in R. Bauman and J. Sherzer (eds), *Explorations in the Ethnography of Speaking*. Cambridge: Cambridge University Press, pp. 110–24.

Reno, P.L., Meindl, R.S., McCollum, M.A., and Lovejoy, C.O. (2003). 'Sexual Dimorphism in *Australopithecus Afarensis* Was Similar to that of Modern Humans', *Proceedings of the National Academy of Sciences* 100: 9404–9.

Reynolds, V. (2005). *The Chimpanzees of the Budongo Forest*. Oxford: Oxford University Press.

Richardson, R. and Hayne, H. (2007). 'You Can't Take It with You: The Translation of Memory Across Development'. *Current Directions in Psychological Science* 16: 223–7. doi: 10.1111/j.1467-8721.2007.00508.x.

Richerson, P.J. and Boyd, R. (2005). *Not by Genes Alone: How Culture Transformed Human Evolution*. Chicago: University of Chicago Press.

Richerson, P.J., Boyd, R., and Bettinger, R.L. (2009). 'Cultural Innovations and Demographic Change', *Human Biology*. 81: 211–35.

Richman, B. (1976). 'Some Vocal Distinctive Features Used By Gelada Monkeys', *Journal of the Acoustical Society of America* 60: 718–24.

Richman, B. (1978). 'The Synchronization of Voices by Gelada Monkeys', *Primates* 19: 569–81.

Richter, D., Dibble, H., Goldberg, P., McPherron, S., Niven, L., Sandgathe, D., Talamo, S., Turq, A. (2013). 'The Late Middle Palaeolithic in Southwest France: New TL Dates for the Sequence of Pech de l'Azé IV', *Quaternary International* 294: 160–7. doi:10.1016/j.quaint.2012.05.028.

Ridley, M. (2003). *Nature Via Nurture: Genes, Experience, and What Makes Us Human*. New York: Harper Collins.

Riel-Salvatore, J. and Clark, G.A. (2001). 'Middle and Upper Paleolithic Burials and the Use of Chronotypology in Contemporary Paleolithic Research', *Current Anthropology* 42: 449–79.

Rifkin, R. (2011). 'Assessing the Efficacy of Red Ochre as a Prehistoric Hide Tanning Ingredient', *Journal of African Archaeology* 9(2): 131–58.

Rightmire, G.P. (1996). 'The Human Cranium from Bodo, Ethiopia: Evidence for Speciation in the Middle Pleistocene', *Journal of Human Evolution* 31: 21–39.

Rightmire, G.P. (2004). 'Brain Size and Encephalization in Early to Mid-Pleistocene *Homo*', *American Journal of Physical Anthropology* 124: 109–23.

Rightmire, G.P. (2009). 'Middle and Later Pleistocene Hominins in Africa and Southwest Asia', *Proceedings of the National Academy of Sciences USA* 106: 16046–50. www.pnas.org_cgi_doi_10.1073_pnas.0903930106.

Rightmire, G.P., Lordkipanidze, D., and Vekua, A. (2006). 'Anatomical Descriptions, Comparative Studies and Evolutionary Significance of the Hominin Skulls from Dmanisi, Republic of Georgia', *Journal of Human Evolution* 50: 115–41.

Rimé, B. (2005). *Le partage social des émotions*. Paris: Presses Universitaires de France.

Rink, W. and Schwarcz, H. (2005). 'Short Contribution: ESR and Uranium Series Dating of Teeth from the Lower Paleolithic Site of Gesher Benot Ya'aqov, Israel: Confirmation of Paleomagnetic Age Indications', *Geoarchaeology* 20: 57–66.

Ritt, N. (2004). *Selfish Sounds and Linguistic Evolution—A Darwinian Approach to Language Change*. Cambridge: Cambridge University Press.

Rizzolatti, G. and Arbib, M. (1998). 'Language within Our Grasp', *Trends in Neurosciences* 21: 188–94.

Rizzolatti, G., Fogassi, L., and Gallese, V. (2006). 'Mirrors in the Mind', *Scientific American* 295 (5): 54–61.

Robbins, P. and Aydede, M. (2009). *The Cambridge Handbook of Situated Cognition*. Cambridge: Cambridge University Press.

Robertson, A.F. (1996). 'The Development of Meaning: Ontogeny and Culture', *Journal of the Royal Anthropological Institute* (N.S.) 2: 591–610.

Robson, S.L. and Wood, B. (2008). 'Hominin Life History: Reconstruction and Evolution', *Journal of Anatomy* 212: 394–425. doi: 10.1111/j.1469-7580.2008.00867.x.

Rodríguez, L., Cabo, L., and Egocheaga, J. (2003). 'Breve nota sobre el hioides Neandertalense de Sidrón (Piloña, Asturias)', in M. Aluja, A. Malgosa, and R. Nogués (eds), *Antropología y Diversidad*. Barcelona: Edicions Bellaterra, vol. 1, pp. 484–93.

Roebroeks, W., Hublin, J.-J., and MacDonald, K. (2011). 'Continuities and Discontinuities in Neandertal Presence: A Closer Look at Northwestern Europe', in N. Ashton, S. Lewis, and

C. Stringer (eds), *The Ancient Human Occupation of Britain*. Developments in Quaternary Science 14. Amsterdam: Elsevier, pp. 113–24.

Roebroeks, W., Sier, M., Nielsen, T., De Loecker, D., Parés, J., Arps, C., and Mücher, H. (2012). 'Use of Red Ochre by Early Neandertals', *Proceedings of the National Academy of Sciences* 109: 1889–94.

Roebroeks, W. and Verpoorte, A. (2009). 'A "Language-free" Explanation for Differences between the European Middle and Upper Paleolithic Record', in R. Botha and C. Knight (eds), *The Cradle of Language*. Oxford: Oxford University Press, pp. 150–66.

Roebroeks, W. and Villa, P. (2011). 'On the Earliest Evidence for Habitual Use of Fire in Europe', *Proceedings of the National Academy of Sciences USA* 108: 5209–14.

Rogers, E.M. (2003). *Diffusion of Innovation*. 5th edn. New York: The Free Press.

Rosenberg, K., Zuné, L., Ruff, C. (2006). 'Body Size, Body Proportions, and Encephalization in a Middle Pleistocene Archaic Human from Northern China', *Proceedings of the National Academy of Sciences USA* 103: 3552–6.

Rossano, F. (2012). 'The Design and Recognition of First Actions in Great Apes', Paper Given at the Conference *Language, Culture, and Mind V*, 28 June 2012, Lisbon.

Rossano, M.J. (2012). 'The Essential Role of Ritual in the Transmission and Reinforcement of Social Norms', *Psychological Bulletin*. doi:10.1037/a0027038.

Rouget, G. (2004). 'L'efficacité musicale: musiquer pour survivre. Le cas des Pygmées', *L'Homme: 'Musique et Anthropologie'* 171–2: 27–52.

Rougier, H., Milota, S., Rodrigo, R., Gherase, M., Sarcina, L., Moldovan, O., Zilhão, J., Constantin, S., Franciscus, R.G., Zollikofer, C.P.E., de León, M.P., and Trinkaus, E. (2007). 'Peştera cu Oase 2 and the Cranial Morphology of Early Modern Europeans', *Proceedings of the National Academy of Sciences USA* 104: 1165–70.

Rowell, T.E. and Hinde, R.A. (1962). 'Vocal Communication by the Rhesus Monkey (*Macaca Mulatta*)', *Proceedings of the Zoological Society of London* 8: 279–94.

Ruff, C. (2002). 'Variation in Human Body Size and Shape', *Annual Review of Anthropology* 31: 211–32.

Ruff, C., Trinkaus, E., and Holliday, T. (1997). 'Body Mass and Encephalization in Pleistocene *Homo*', *Nature* 387: 173–6.

Ruff, C.B., Trinkaus, E., Walker, A., and Larsen, C.S. (1993). 'Postcranial Robusticity in *Homo*. 1: Temporal Trends and Mechanical Interpretation', *American Journal of Physical Anthropology* 91: 21–53.

Rumbaugh, D.M. (1977). *Language Learning by a Chimpanzee: The Lana Project*. New York: Academic Press.

Rumbaugh, D.M., Gill, T.V., and von Glaserfeld, E.C. (1973). 'Reading and Sentence Completion by a Chimpanzee (*Pan*)'. *Science* 182(4113): 731–3.

Rupert, R. (2009). 'Innateness and the Situated Mind', in P. Robbins and M. Aydede (eds), *Cambridge Handbook of Situated Cognition*. Cambridge: Cambridge University Press, pp. 96–116.

Russell, J., Braccini, S., Buehler, N., Kachin, M., Schapiro, S.J., and Hopkins, W.D. (2005). 'Chimpanzees (*Pan troglodytes*) Intentional Communication is not Contingent Upon Food'. *Animal Cognition* 8: 263–72.

Russon, A.E., Kuncoro, P., Ferisa, A., and Handayani, D.P. (2010). 'How Orangutans (*Pongo Pygmaeus*) Innovate for Water', *Journal of Comparative Psychology* 124(1): 14–28.

Rutherford, M.D., Young, G.S., Hepburn, S., and Rogers, S.J. (2007). 'A Longitudinal Study of Pretend Play in Autism', *Journal of Autism and Developmental Disord*ers 37: 1024–39.

Sacks, H. (1992). *Lectures on Conversation*. Oxford: Blackwell.

Sacks, H., Schegloff, E.A., and Jefferson, G. (1974). 'A Simplest Systematics for the Organization of Turn-taking for Conversation', *Language* 50(4): 696–735.

Sahlins, M.D. (1960). 'The Origin of Society', *Scientific American* 203: 76–87.

Salomon, H., Vignaud, C., Coquinot, Y., Beck, L., Stringer, C., Strivay, D., d'Errico, F. (2012). 'Selection and Heating of Colouring Materials in the Mousterian level of Es-Skhul (*c.* 100000 years BP, Mount Carmel, Israel). *Archaeometry* 54: 698–722.

Sampson, G. (1972). 'The Stone Age Industries of the Orange River Scheme and South Africa', *Memoirs of the National Museum Bloemfontein* 6: 1–288.

Sandgathe, D., Dibble, H., Goldberg, P., McPherron, S., Turq, A., Niven, L., and Hodgkins, J. (2011). 'On the Role of Fire in Neandertal Adaptations in Western Europe: Evidence from Pech de l'Azé IV and Roc de Marsal, France', *PaleoAnthropology*: 216–42.

Santonja, M. and Villa, P. (2006). 'The Acheulian of Western Europe', in N. Goren-Inbar and G. Sharon (eds), *Axe Age: Acheulian Toolmaking from Quarry to Discard*. London: Equinox Publishing, pp. 429–78.

Sapir, E. (1921). *Language: An Introduction to the Study of Speech*. New York: Harcourt Brace.

Saucier, D.M. and Elias, L.J. (2001). 'Lateral and Sex Differences in Manual Gesture during Conversation', *Laterality*, 6(3), 239–45.

Saussure, F. de (1983 [1915]). *Course in General Linguistics*. Trans. R. Harris. London: Duckworth.

Savage-Rumbaugh, S.E. and Lewin, R. (1994). *Kanzi: The Ape at the Brink of the Human Mind*. London/New York: Wiley/Doubleday.

Savage-Rumbaugh, E.S., McDonald, K., Sevcic, R.A., Hopkins, W.D., and Rupert, E. (1986). 'Spontaneous Symbol Acquisition and Communicative Use by Pygmy Chimpanzees (*Pan paniscus*)', *Journal of Experimental Psychology: General* 115: 211–35.

Savage-Rumbaugh, E.S., Murphy, J., Sevcic, R.A., Brakke, K.E., Williams, S.L., and Rumbaugh, D.M. (1993). 'Language Comprehension in Ape and Child', *Monographs of the Society for Research in Child Development* 58(3–4): 1–256.

Savage-Rumbaugh, E.S., Shanker, S.G., and Taylor, T.J. (2001). *Apes, Language, and the Human Mind*. New York: Oxford University Press.

Sawyer, K. (2007). *Group Genius: The Creative Power of Collaboration*. New York: Basic Books.

Scalise Sugiyama, M. (2001). 'Narrative Theory and Function: Why Evolution Matters', *Philosophy and Literature* 25(2): 233–50.

Schacter, D. (2001). *The Seven Sins of Memory*. Boston, MA: Houghton Mifflin.

Schaller, G.B. (1963). *The Mountain Gorilla, Ecology and Behavior*. Chicago: University of Chicago Press.

Schaller, G.B. (1964). *The Year of the Gorilla*. Chicago: University of Chicago Press.

Schegloff, E.A. (1968). 'Sequencing in Conversational Openings', *American Anthropologist* 70 (6): 1075–95.

Schegloff, E.A. (2000). 'Overlapping Talk and the Organization of Turn-taking for Conversation', *Language in Society* 29: 1–63.

Schegloff, E.A. (2006). 'Interaction: The Infrastructure for Social Institutions, the Natural Ecological Niche for Language, and the Arena in which Culture is Enacted', in N.J. Enfield and S.C. Levinson (eds), *Roots of Human Sociality: Culture, Cognition, and Interaction* Oxford: Berg, pp. 70–96.

Schegloff, E.A. (2007). *Sequence Organization in Interaction: A Primer in Conversation Analysis*. Cambridge: Cambridge University Press.

Schegloff, E.A., Jefferson, G., and Sacks, H. (1977). 'The Preference for Self-correction in the Organization of Repair in Conversation', *Language* 53(2): 361–82.

Schel, A.M., Townsend, S.W., Machanda, Z., Zuberbühler, K., and Slocombe, K.E. (2013). 'Chimpanzee Alarm Call Production Meets Key Criteria for Intentionality', *PLoS ONE* 8 (10): e76674.

Schiffrin, D. (1988). *Discourse Markers*. Cambridge: Cambridge University Press.

Schmidt, M.F.H., Rakoczy, H., and Tomasello, M. (2011). 'Young Children Attribute Normativity to Novel Actions without Pedagogy or Normative Language', *Developmental Science* 14 (May): 530–9. doi:10.1111/j.1467-7687.2010.01000.x.

Schneider, C., Call, J., and Liebal, K. (2012). 'Onset and Early Use of Gestural Communication in Nonhuman Great Apes', *American Journal of Primatology* 74(2): 102–13.

Schulz, S. and Dunbar, R.I.M. (2007). 'The Evolution of the Social Brain: Anthropoid Primates Contrast with Other Vertebrates', *Proceedings of the Royal Society, London* 274B: 2429–36.

Schütze, C. (1996). *The Empirical Base of Linguistics: Grammaticality Judgments and Linguistic Methodology*. Chicago: University of Chicago Press.

Schütze, C. (2011). 'Linguistic Evidence and Grammatical Theory', *Wiley Interdisciplinary Reviews: Cognitive Science* 2: 206–21. doi:10.1002/wcs.102.

Scott, B. and Ashton, N. (2011). 'The Early Middle Palaeolithic: The European Context', in N. Ashton, S. Lewis, and C. Stringer (eds), *The Ancient Human Occupation of Britain*. Developments in Quaternary Science 14. Amsterdam: Elsevier, pp. 91–112.

Searle, J.R. (1969). *Speech Acts: An Essay in the Philosophy of Language*. Cambridge: Cambridge University Press.

Searle, J.R. (1975). 'The Logical Status of Fictional Discourse', *New Literary History* 6(2): 319–32.

Searle, J.R. (1980). 'Minds, brains, and programs. *Behavioral and Brain Sciences* 3(3): 417–24.

Searle, J.R. (1983). *Intentionality: An Essay in the Philosophy of Mind*. Cambridge: Cambridge University Press.

Searle, J.R. (1995). *The Construction of Social Reality*. New York: The Free Press.

Searle, J.R. (2010). *Making the Social World*. Oxford: Oxford University Press.

Segerdahl, P., Fields, W.M., and Savage-Rumbaugh, E.S. (2005). *Kanzi's Primal Language: The Cultural Initiation of Apes Into Language*. London: Palgrave.

Semaw, S., Rogers, M.J., Quade, J., Renne, P.R., Butler, R.F., Dominguez-Rodrigo, M., Stout, D., Hart, W.S., Pickering, T., and Simpson, S.W. (2003). '2.6-million-year-old Stone Tools and Associated Bones from OGS-6 and OGS-7, Gona, Afar, Ethiopia', *Journal of Human Evolution* 45: 169–77.

Semple, S. (2001). 'Individuality and Male Discrimination of Female Copulation Calls in the Yellow Baboon', *Animal Behaviour* 61(5): 1023–8.

Semple, S. and McComb, K. (2000). 'Perception of Female Reproductive State from Vocal Cues in a Mammal Species', *Proceedings of the Royal Society of London Series B-Biological Sciences* 267(1444): 707–12.

Semple, S., McComb, K., Alberts, S., and Altmann, J. (2002). 'Information Content of Female Copulation Calls in Yellow Baboons, *American Journal of Primatology* 56: 43–56.

Senghas, R.J., Senghas, A., and Pyers, J.E. (2005). 'The Emergence of Nicaraguan Sign Language: Questions of Development, Acquisition and Evolution', in J. Langer, S.T. Parker, and C. Milbrath (eds), *Biology and Knowledge Revisited: From Neurogenesis to Psychogenesis.* Hillsdale, NJ: Lawrence Erlbaum.

Seyfarth, R.M. and Cheney, D.L. (1984). 'Grooming, Alliances and Reciprocal Altruism in Vervet Monkeys', *Nature* 308: 541–2.

Seyfarth, R.M. and Cheney, D.L. (2003). 'Signalers and Receivers in Animal Communication', *Annual Review of Psychology* 54(1): 145–73.

Seyfarth, R.M., Cheney, D.L., Bergman, T., Fischer, J., Zuberbühler, K., and Hammerschmidt, K. (2010). 'The Central Importance of Information in Studies of Animal Communication', *Animal Behaviour* 80(1): 3–8.

Shennan, S. (2001). 'Demography and Cultural Innovation: A Model and its Implications for the Emergence of Modern Human Culture', *Cambridge Archaeological Journal* 11: 5–16.

Shipman, P. (2001). 'What Can You Do with a Bone Fragment?', *Proceedings of the National Academy of Sciences* 98: 1335–7.

Shore, B. (1996). *Culture in Mind: Cognition, Culture and the Problem of Meaning.* New York: Oxford University Press.

Sidnell, J. (2001). 'Conversational Turn-taking in a Caribbean English Creole', *Journal of Pragmatics* 33(8): 1263–90.

Sidnell, J. (2005). *Talk and Practical Epistemology.* Amsterdam: John Benjamins.

Sidnell, J. (2007). 'Comparative Studies in Conversation Analysis', *Annual Review of Anthropology* 36: 229–44.

Sidnell, J., ed. (2009). *Conversation Analysis: Comparative Perspectives.* Cambridge: Cambridge University Press.

Sidnell, J. (2010). *Conversation Analysis: An Introduction.* Chichester: Wiley-Blackwell.

Sidnell, J. (2012). 'Turn Continuation by Self and by Other', *Discourse Processes* 49(3–4): 314–37.

Sidnell, J. and Enfield, N.J. (2012). 'Language Diversity and Social Action', *Current Anthropology* 53(3): 302–33.

Sidnell, J. and Stivers, T., eds (2012). *The Handbook of Conversation Analysis.* Malden, MA: Wiley-Blackwell.

Sigman, M. and Dehaene, S. (2005). 'Parsing a Cognitive Task: A Characterization of the Mind's Bottleneck. *PLoS Biol* 3(2): e37.

Silk, J.B., Kaldor, E., and Boyd, R. (2000). 'Cheap Talk When Interests Conflict', *Animal Behaviour* 59: 423–32.

Simon, H.A. (1990). 'A Mechanism for Social Selection and Successful Altruism', *Science* 250: 1665–8.

Simpson, G.G. (1953). 'The Baldwin Effect', *Evolution* 7: 110–17.

Sims, L. (2006). 'The Solarization of the Moon: Manipulated Knowledge at Stonehenge', *Cambridge Archaeological Journal* 16: 191–207.

Sinha, C. (1988). *Language and Representation: A Socio-Naturalistic Approach to Human Development.* Hemel Hempstead: Harvester-Wheatsheaf.

Sinha, C. (2004). 'The Evolution of Language: From Signals to Symbols to System', in D. Kimbrough Oller and U. Griebel (eds), *Evolution of Communication Systems: A Comparative Approach*. Vienna Series in Theoretical Biology. Cambridge, MA: MIT Press, pp. 217–35.

Sinha, C. (2005). 'Blending out of the Background: Play, Props and Staging in the Material World', *Journal of Pragmatics* 37: 1537–54.

Sinha, C. (2009a). 'Language as a biocultural niche and social institution', in V. Evans and S. Pourcel (eds), *New Directions in Cognitive Linguistics*. Amsterdam: John Benjamins, pp. 289–310.

Sinha, C. (2009b). 'Objects in a storied world: materiality, narrativity and normativity', *Journal of Consciousness Studies* 16(6–8): 167–90.

Sinha, C. and Rodríguez, C. (2008). 'Language and the Signifying Object: From Convention to Imagination', in J. Zlatev, T. Racine, C. Sinha, and E. Itkonen (eds), *The Shared Mind: Perspectives on Intersubjectivity*. Amsterdam: John Benjamins, pp. 358–78.

Slimak, L., Lewis, J., Crégut-Bonnoure, E., Metz, L., Ollivier, V., André, P., Chrzavzez, J., Giraud, Y., Jeannet, M., and Magnin, F. (2010). 'Le Grand Abri aux Puces, a Mousterian Site from the Last Interglacial: Paleogeography, Paleoenvironment, and New Excavation Results', *Journal of Archaeological Science* 37: 2747–61.

Slobin, D. (1996). 'From "thought and language" to "thinking for speaking"', in J.J. Gumperz and S.C. Levinson (eds), *Rethinking Linguistic Relativity*. Cambridge: Cambridge University Press, pp. 70–96.

Slocombe, K.E., Kaller, T., Call, J., and Zuberbühler, K. (2010a). 'Chimpanzees Extract Social Information from Agonistic Screams', *PLoS One* 5(7): e11473.

Slocombe, K.E., Kaller, T., Turman, L., Townsend, S.W., Papworth, S., Squibbs, P., and Zuberbühler, K. (2010b). 'Production of Food-associated Calls in Wild Male Chimpanzees is Dependent on the Composition of the Audience', *Behavioral Ecology and Sociobiology* 64(12): 1959–66.

Slocombe, K.E., Townsend, S.W., and Zuberbühler, K. (2009). 'Wild Chimpanzees (*Pan troglodytes schweinfurthii*) Distinguish between Different Scream Types: Evidence from a Playback Study', *Animal Cognition* 12(3): 441–9.

Slocombe, K.E. and Zuberbühler, K. (2005). 'Agonistic Screams in Wild Chimpanzees (*Pan troglodytes schweinfurthii*) Vary as a Function of Social Role', *Journal of Comparative Psychology* 119(1): 67–77.

Slocombe, K.E. and Zuberbühler, K. (2007). 'Chimpanzees Modify Recruitment Screams as a Function of Audience Composition', *Proceedings of the National Academy of Sciences USA* 104(43): 17228–33.

Slocombe, K.E. and Zuberbühler, K. (2010). 'Vocal Communication in Chimpanzees', in E.V. Lonsdorf, S. Ross, and T. Matsuzawa (eds), *The Mind of the Chimpanzee: Ecological and Empirical Perspectives*. Chicago: University of Chicago Press, pp. 192–207.

Smith, E.D., Englander, Z.A., Lillard, A.S., and Morris, J.P. (2013). 'Cortical Mechanisms of Pretense Observation', *Social Neuroscience* 8(4): 356–68.

Smith, K., Brighton, H., and Kirby, S. (2003). 'Complex Systems in Language Evolution: The Cultural Emergence of Compositional Structure', *Advances in Complex Systems* 6(4): 537–58.

Smith, W.J. (1965). 'Message, Meaning, and Context in Ethology', *American Naturalist* 908: 405–9.

Snowdon, C.T. (2001). 'From Primate Communication to Human Language', in F.B.M. de Waal (ed.), *Tree of Origin: What Primate Behavior Can Tell Us about Human Social Evolution*. Cambridge, MA: Harvard University Press, pp. 193–227.

Sober, E. and Wilson, D.S. (1998). *Unto Others: The Evolution and Psychology of Unselfish Behavior*. Cambridge, MA: Harvard University Press.

Sober, E. and Wilson, D.S. (2000a). 'Summary of Unto Others: The Evolution and Psychology of Unselfish Behavior', *Journal of Consciousness Studies* 7(1–2): 185–206.

Sober, E. and Wilson, D.S. (2000b). 'Morality and "Unto Others"', *Journal of Consciousness Studies* 7(1–2): 257–68.

Soficaru, A., Dobos, A., and Trinkaus, E. (2006). 'Early Modern Humans from the Pestera Muierii, Baia de Fier, Romania', *Proceedings of the National Academy of Sciences USA* 103: 17196–201.

Solé, R., Cormonias-Murtra, B., and Fortuny, J. (2010). 'Diversity, Competition, Extinction: The Ecophysics of Language Change', *Journal of the Royal Society Interface* 7: 1647–64.

Sørensen, B. (2009). 'Energy Use by Eem Neanderthals', *Journal of Archaeological Science* 36: 2201–5.

Soressi, M. and d'Errico, F. (2007). 'Pigments, gravures, parures: les comportements symboliques controversés des Néandertaliens', in B. Vandermeersch and B. Maureille (eds), *Les Néandertaliens: biologie et cultures*. Documents Préhistoriques Series no. 23. Paris: Éditions du CTHS, pp. 297–309.

Sosis, R. (2003). 'Why Aren't We All Hutterites? Costly Signaling Theory and Religious Behavior', *Human Nature* 14(2): 91–127.

Sosis, R. and Alcorta, C. (2003). 'Signaling, Solidarity, and the Sacred: The Evolution of Religious Behavior', *Evolutionary Anthropology* 12: 264–74.

Soto, E., Sesé, C., Pérez-González, A., and Santonja, M. (2001). 'Mammal Fauna with *Elephas (Palaeoloxodon) Antiquus* from the Lower Levels of Ambrona (Soria, Spain)', in G. Cavaretta, P. Gioia, M. Mussi, and M. Palumbo (eds), *The World of Elephants—First International Congress, 16–20 January, Rome*. Rome: Consiglio Nazionale della Ricerche, pp. 607–9.

de Sousa, A. and Cunha, E. (2012). 'Hominins and the Emergence of the Modern Human Brain', in M.A. Hofman and D. Falk (eds), *Progress in Brain Research: Evolution of the Primate Brain. Volume 195: From Neuron to Behavior*. Amsterdam: Elsevier, pp. 293–322.

Sperber, D. (1975). *Rethinking Symbolism*. Cambridge: Cambridge University Press.

Sperber, D. (1985). 'Anthropology and Psychology: Towards an Epidemiology of Representations', *Man* (N.S.) 20: 73–89.

Sperber, D. (1996). *Explaining Culture: A Naturalistic Approach*. London: Blackwell.

Sperber, D. (2005). 'A Pragmatic Perspective on the Evolution of Mindreading, Communication and Language', Paper delivered to the Morris Symposium on the Evolution of Language. New York: Stony Brook.

Sperber, D. (2006). 'Why a Deep Understanding of Cultural Evolution Is Incompatible with Shallow Psychology', in N.J. Enfield and S.C. Levinson (eds), *Roots of Human Sociality: Culture, Cognition, and Interaction*. Oxford: Berg, pp. 431–49.

Sperber, D. and Wilson, D. (1986). *Relevance: Communication and Cognition*. Cambridge, MA: MIT Press.

Speth, J. (2004). 'News Flash: Negative Evidence Convicts Neanderthals of Gross Mental Incompetence', *World Archaeology* 36: 519–26.

Spikins, P.A., Rutherford, H.E., and Needham, A.P. (2010). 'From Hominity to Humanity: Compassion from the Earliest Archaic to Modern Humans', *Time and Mind* 3: 303–25.

Spoctor, M. and Manger, P. (2007). 'The Use of Cranial Variables for the Estimation of Body Mass in Fossil Hominins', *American Journal of Physical Anthropology* 134: 92–105.

Spoor, F., Leakey, M.G., Gathogo, N., Brown, F.H., Antón, S.C., McDougall, I., Kiarie, C., Manthi, F.K., and Leakey, L.N. (2007). 'Implications of New Early *Homo* Fossils from Ileret, East of Lake Turkana, Kenya', *Nature* 448: 688–91.

Spranger, M. and Steels, L. (2012). 'Emergent Functional Grammar for Space', in L. Steels (ed.), *Experiments in Cultural Language Evolution*. Amsterdam: John Benjamins, pp. 207–32.

Sripada, C. and Stich, S. (2006). 'A Framework for the Psychology of Norms', in P. Carruthers, S. Laurence, and S. Stich (eds), *The Innate Mind, Volume 2: Culture and Cognition*. Oxford: Oxford University Press.

Stanford, C.B. (1998). 'The Social Behavior of Chimpanzee and Bonobos—Empirical Evidence and Shifting Assumptions', *Current Anthropology* 39(4): 399–420.

State, M.W. and Šestan, N. (2012). 'The Emerging Biology of Autism Spectrum Disorders', *Science* 337: 1301–3.

Steels, L. (1995). 'A self-organizing Spatial Vocabulary', *Artificial Life Journal* 2(3): pp. 319–32.

Steels, L. (2000). 'Language as a Complex Adaptive System', in M. Schoenauer (ed.), *Proceedings of PPSN VI, Lecture Notes in Computer Science, 1917*. Berlin: Springer-Verlag, pp. 17–26.

Steels, L. (2004). 'Constructivist development of grounded construction grammars', *Proceedings of the 42nd Annual Meeting of the Association for Computational Linguistics*: article 9.

Steels, L. (2007). 'The Recruitment Theory of Language Origins', in C. Lyon, C. Nehaniv, and A. Cangelosi (eds), *Emergence of Communication and Language*. Berlin: Springer Verlag, pp. 129–51.

Steels, L. (2009). 'Is Sociality a Crucial Prerequisite for the Origins of Language?', in R. Botha and C. Knight (eds), *The Prehistory of Language*. Oxford: Oxford University Press, pp. 36–57.

Steels, L. (2011). 'Modeling the Cultural Evolution of Language', *Physics of Life Reviews* 8(4): 330–56.

Steels, L. (2012). 'Self-organization and Selection in Cultural Language Evolution', in L. Steels (ed.), *Experiments in Cultural Language Evolution*. Advances in Interaction Studies 3. Amsterdam/Philadelphia: John Benjamins, pp. 1–37.

Steels, L. and Hild, M., eds (2012). *Language Grounding in Robots*. New York: Springer-Verlag.

Steels, L. and Wellens, P. (2006). 'How grammar emerges to dampen combinatorial search in parsing', in P. Vogt, Y. Suga, E. Tuci, and C. Nehaniv (eds), *Symbol Grounding and Beyond*. LNAI 4211. Berlin: Springer-Verlag, pp. 76–88.

Steguweit, L. (1999). 'Intentionelle Schnittmarken auf Tierknochen von Bilzingsleben: Neue Lasermikroskopische Untersuchungen', *Praehistoria Thuringica* 3: 64–79.

Steklis, H.D. and Harnad, S. (1976). 'From Hand to Mouth: Some Critical Stages in the Evolution of Language', in S. Harnad, H.D. Steklis, and J. Lancaster (eds), *Origins and Evolution of Language and Speech*. New York: New York Academy of Sciences, pp. 445–55.

Sterelny, K. (2003). *Thought in a Hostile World: The Evolution of Human Cognition*. Malden, MA: Blackwell.

Sterelny, K. (2006). 'Language, Modularity and Evolution', in G. Macdonald and D. Papineau (eds), *Teleosemantics*. Oxford: Oxford University Press, pp. 23–41.

Sterelny, K. (2012). *The Evolved Apprentice: How Evolution Made Humans Unique*. Cambridge, MA: MIT.

Stiner, M.C., Barkai, R., and Gopher, A. (2009). 'Cooperative Hunting and Meat Sharing 400–200 kya at Qesem Cave, Israel', *Proceedings of the National Academy of Sciences USA* 106: 13207–12.

Stiner, M.C., Gopher, A., and Barkai, R. (2011). 'Hearth-side Socioeconomics, Hunting and Paleoecology during the Late Lower Paleolithic at Qesem Cave, Israel', *Journal of Human Evolution* 60: 213–33.

Stivers, T., Enfield, N.J., Brown, P., Englert, C., Hayashi, M., Heinemann, T., Hoymann, G., et al. (2009). 'Universals and Cultural Variation in Turn-Taking in Conversation', *Proceedings of the National Academy of Sciences USA* 106(26): 10587–92.

Stivers, T., Mondada, L., and Steensig, J., eds (2011). *The Morality of Knowledge in Conversation*. Cambridge: Cambridge University Press.

Stout, D. (2010). 'Possible Relations between Language and Technology in Human Evolution' in A. Nowell and I. Davidson (eds), *Stone Tools and the Evolution of Human Cognition*. Boulder, CO: University of Colorado Press, pp. 159–84.

Stout, D. (2011). 'Stone Toolmaking and the Evolution of Human Culture and Cognition', *Philosophical Transactions of the Royal Society B* 366(1567): 1050–9. doi: 10.1098/rstb.2010.0369.

Stout, D. and Chaminade, T. (2007). 'The Evolutionary Neuroscience of Tool Making', *Neuropsychologia* 45: 1091–1100.

Stout, D., Toth, N., Schick, K., and Chaminade, T. (2008). 'Neural Correlates of Early Stone Age Toolmaking: Technology, Language and Cognition in Human Evolution', *Philosophical Transactions of the Royal Society B* 363: 1939–49.

Stringer, C. (2002). 'Modern Human Origins: Progress and Prospects', *Philosophical Transactions of the Royal Society B* 357: 563–79.

Stringer, C. (2011). *The Origin of Our Species*. London: Allen Lane.

Stringer, C. (2012). 'The Status of *Homo Heidelbergensis* (Schoetensack 1908)', *Evolutionary Anthropology* 21: 101–7.

Stringer, C.B. and Andrews, P. (1988). 'Genetic and Fossil Evidence for the Origin of Modern Humans', *Science* 239: 1263–8.

Stromswold, K. (2001). 'The Heritability of Language: A Review and Metaanalysis of Twin, Adoption, and Linkage Studies', *Language* 77: 647–723.

Stromswold, K. (2010). 'Genetics and the Evolution of Language: What Genetic Studies Reveal about the Evolution of Language', in R.K. Larson, V. Déprez, and H. Yamakido (eds), *The Evolution of Human Language. Biolinguistic Perspectives*. Cambridge: Cambridge University Press.

Struhsacker, T.T. (1997). *Ecology of an African Rain Forest*. Gainesville, FL: University Presses of Florida.

Sugiyama, Y. (1988). 'Grooming Interactions Among Adult Chimpanzees at Bossou, Guinea, with Special Reference to Social Structure', *International Journal of Primatology* 9(5): 393–407.

Sutcliffe, A., Dunbar, R., Binder, J., and Arrow, H. (2012). 'Relationships and the Social Brain: Integrating Psychological and Evolutionary Perspectives', *British Journal of Psychology* 103: 149–68.

Suwa, G., Kono, R.T., Simpson, S.W., Asfaw, B., Lovejoy, C.O., and White, T.D. (2009). 'Paleobiological Implications of the *Ardipithecus Ramidus* Dentition', *Science* 326: 69, 94–9.

Suzuki, Y. and Nijhout, H.F. (2006). 'Evolution of a Polyphenism by Genetic Accommodation', *Science:* 311: 650–2.

Svoboda, J., Lozek, V., and Vlcek, E. (1996). *Hunters between East and West: The Paleolithic of Moravia*. New York: Plenum Press.

Számadó, S., Hurford, J.R., Bishop, D., Deacon, T.W., d'Errico, F., Fischer, J., Okanoya, K., Szathmáry, E., and White, S.A. (2009). 'What Are the Possible Biological and Genetic Foundations for Syntactic Phenomena?', in D. Bickerton and E. Szathmáry, (eds), *Biological Foundations and Origin of Syntax*. Cambridge MA: MIT.

Tallerman, M. (2007). 'Did our Ancestors Speak a Holistic Protolanguage?', *Lingua* 117: 579–604.

Tallerman, M. (2008). 'Holophrastic Protolanguage: Planning, Processing, Storage, and Retrieval', *Interaction Studies* 9(1): 84–99.

Tallerman, M. (2012). 'Protolanguage', in M. Tallerman and K. Gibson (eds), *The Oxford Handbook of Language Evolution*. Oxford: Oxford University Press, pp. 479–91.

Tallerman, M. and Gibson, K.R. (2012). *The Oxford Handbook of Language Evolution*. Oxford: Oxford University Press.

Tannen, D. (1984). *Conversational Style: Analyzing Talk Among Friends*. Norwood: Ablex Publishing Corporation.

Tanner, J.E. (2004). 'Gestural Phrases and Gestural Exchanges by a Pair of Zoo-living Lowland Gorillas', *Gesture* 4(1): 25–42.

Tanner, J.E. and Byrne, R.W. (2010). 'Triadic and Collaborative Play by Gorillas in Social Games with Objects'. *Animal Cognition* 13(4): 591–607.

Tart, C.T. (2009). *The End of Materialism: How Evidence of the Paranormal is Bringing Science and Spirit Together*. Oakland, CA: Noetic Books and New Harbinger Publications.

Tattersall, I. (1986). 'Species Recognition in Human Paleontology', *Journal of Human Evolution* 15: 165–75.

ten Have, P. (2007). *Doing Conversation Analysis*. London: Sage.

Teschler-Nicola, M., ed. (2006). *Early Modern Humans at the Moravian Gate: The Mladec Caves and their Remains*. Vienna: Springer.

Testart, A. (1985). *Le communisme primitif*. Paris: Éditions de la Maison des sciences de l'homme.

Testart, A. (1986). *Essai sur les fondements de la division sexuelle du travail chez les chasseurs-cueilleurs*. Paris: Éditions de l'École des Hautes Études en Sciences Sociales.

Thaler, L., Arnott, S.R., and Goodale, M.A. (2011). 'Neural Correlates of Natural Human Echolocation in Early and Late Blind Echolocation Experts', *PLoS ONE* 6(5): e20162. doi:10.1371/journal.pone.0020162.

Thieme, H. (1997). 'Lower Paleolithic Hunting Spears from Germany', *Nature* 385: 807–10.

Thierry, B. (2000). 'Darwinian Elements of Morality are not Elements of Morality', *Journal of Consciousness Studies* 7(1–2): 60–2.

Thomason, S. and Kaufman, T. (1988). *Language Contact, Creolization, and Genetic Linguistics.* Berkeley: University of California Press.

Thompson, E., Williams, H., and Minichillo, T. (2010). 'Middle and Late Pleistocene Middle Stone Age Lithic Technology from Pinnacle Point 13B, (Mossel Bay, Western Cape Province, South Africa)', *Journal of Human Evolution* 59: 358–77.

Thompson-Handler, N.T., Malenky, R.K., and Badrian, N. (1984). 'Sexual Behavior of *Pan paniscus*', in R.L. Susman (ed.), *The Pygmy Chimpanzee: Evolutionary Biology and Behavior.* New York: Plenum Press, pp. 347–68.

Tiger, L. and Fox, R. (1966). 'The Zoological Perspective in Social Science', *Man* (N.S.) 1(1): 75–81.

Tinbergen, N. (1952). 'Derived Activities: Their Causation, Biological Significance, Origin and Emancipation During Evolution', *Quarterly Review of Biology* 27: 1–32.

Tinbergen, N. (1959). 'Comparative Studies of the Behaviour of Gulls (*Laridae*): A Progress Report', *Behaviour* 15(1–2): 1–70.

Tobias, P. (1949). 'The Excavation of Mwulu's Cave, Potgietersrust District', *South African Archaeological Bulletin* 4: 2–13.

Tobias, P. (2005). *Into the Past: A Memoir.* Johannesburg: Wits University Press.

Tomasello, M. (1996). 'The Child's Contribution to Culture: A Commentary on Toomela', *Culture and Psychology* 2: 307–18.

Tomasello, M. (1998). *The New Psychology of Language: Cognitive and Functional Approaches to Language Structure.* Mahwah, NJ: Lawrence Erlbaum.

Tomasello, M. (1999). *The Cultural Origins of Human Cognition.* Cambridge, MA: Harvard University Press.

Tomasello, M. (2003a). *Constructing a Language: A Usage-based Approach to Child Language Acquisition.* Cambridge, MA: Harvard University Press.

Tomasello, M. (2003b). 'Different Origins of Symbols and Grammar', in M.H. Christiansen and S. Kirby (eds), *Language Evolution.* Oxford: Oxford University Press, pp. 94–110.

Tomasello, M. (2006). 'Why Don't Apes Point?' in N.J. Enfield and S.C. Levinson (eds), *Roots of Human Sociality: Culture, Cognition and Interaction.* Oxford and New York: Berg, pp. 506–24.

Tomasello, M. (2008). *The Origins of Human Communication.* Cambridge, MA: MIT.

Tomasello, M. (2009). *Why We Cooperate.* Cambridge MA: MIT.

Tomasello, M. (2011). 'Human Culture in Evolutionary Perspective', in M. Gelfand (ed.), *Advances in Culture and Psychology*, New York: Oxford University Press, pp. 5–51.

Tomasello, M., Call, J., and Hare, B. (2003). 'Chimpanzees Understand Psychological States— the Question is which Ones and to what Extent', *Trends in Cognitive Science* 7: 153–6.

Tomasello, M., Call, J., Nagell, K., Olguin, R., and Carpenter, M. (1994). 'The Learning and Use of Gestural Signals by Young Chimpanzees: A Trans-generational Study', *Primates* 35: 137–54.

Tomasello, M., Carpenter, M., Call, J., Behne, T., and Moll, H. (2005). 'Understanding and Sharing Intentions: The Origins of Cultural Cognition', *Behavioral and Brain Sciences*, 28(5): 675–91. doi:10.1017/S0140525X05000129.

Tomasello, M., Hare, B., Lehmann, H., and Call, J. (2007). 'Reliance on Head Versus Eyes in the Gaze Following of Great Apes and Human Infants: The Cooperative Eye Hypothesis', *Journal of Human Evolution* 52: 314–20.

Tomasello, M. and Herrmann, E. (2010). 'Ape and Human Cognition: What's the Difference?', *Current Directions in Psychological Science* 19(1): 3–8.

Tomasello, M., Kruger, A.C., and Ratner, H.H. (1993). 'Cultural Learning', *Behavioral and Brain Sciences* 16: 495–552.

Tomasello, M., Melis, A.P., Tennie, C., Wyman, E., and Herrmann, E. (2012). 'Two Key Steps in the Evolution of Human Cooperation', *Current Anthropology* 53(6): 673–92.

Tomasello, M. and Rakoczy, H. (2003). 'What Makes Human Cognition Unique? From Individual to Shared to Collective Intentionality', *Mind and Language* 18: 121–47.

Tomasello, M. and Todd, J. (1983). 'Joint Attention and Lexical Acquisition Style', *First Language* 4: 197–211. doi:10.1177/014272378300401202.

Tomlin, R.S. (1997). 'Mapping Conceptual Representations into Linguistic Representations: The Role of Attention in Grammar', in J. Nuyts and E. Pedersen (eds), *Language and Conceptualization*. Cambridge: Cambridge University Press, pp. 162–89.

Tooby, J. and Cosmides, L. (1992). 'The Psychological Foundations of Culture', in J. Barkow, L. Cosmides, and J. Tooby (eds), *The Adapted Mind: Evolutionary Psychology and the Generation of Culture*. New York: Oxford University Press, pp. 19–136.

Tooby, J. and Cosmides, L. (1995). 'Foreword', in S. Baron-Cohen, *Mindblindness. An Essay on Autism and Theory of Mind*. Cambridge, MA: MIT Press, pp. xi–xviii.

Townsend, S.W., Deschner, T., and Zuberbühler, K. (2008). 'Female Chimpanzees Use Copulation Calls Flexibly to Prevent Social Competition', *PLoS One* 3(6): 2431.

Townsend, S.W., Deschner, T., and Zuberbühler, K. (2011). 'Copulation Calls in Female Chimpanzees Convey Identity but Do Not Accurately Reflect Fertility', *International Journal of Primatology* 32: 914–23.

Townsend, S.W., Slocombe, K.E., Emery Thompson, M., and Zuberbühler, K. (2007). 'Female-led Infanticide in Wild Chimpanzees', *Current Biology* 17(10): 355.

Townsend, S.W. and Zuberbühler, K. (2009). 'Audience Effects in Chimpanzee Copulation Calls', *Communicative & Integrative Biology* 2(3): 282–4.

Trevarthen, C. (1974). 'Conversations with a Two-Month-Old', *New Scientist* (2 May): 230–5.

Trevarthen, C. (1977). 'Descriptive Analyses of Infant Communicative Behaviour', in H.R. Schaffer (ed.), *Studies in Mother–Infant Interaction*. London and New York: Academic Press, pp. 227–78.

Trevarthen, C. (1979). 'Communication and Cooperation in Early Infancy. A Description of Primary Intersubjectivity', in M. Bullowa (ed.), *Before Speech: The Beginning of Human Communication*. London: Cambridge University Press, pp. 321–47.

Trevarthen, C. (1995). 'The Child's Need to Learn a Culture', *Children and Society* 9: 5–19.

Trevarthen, C. (1998). 'The Concept and Foundations of Infant Intersubjectivity', in S. Bråten (ed.), *Intersubjective Communication and Emotion in Early Ontogeny*. Cambridge: Cambridge University Press, pp. 15–46.

Trevarthen, C. and Hubley, P. (1978). 'Secondary Intersubjectivity: Confidence, Confiding and Acts of Meaning in the First Year', in A. Lock (ed.), *Action, Gesture and Symbol: The Emergence of Language*. London: Academic Press, pp. 183–229.

Tricomi, E., Rangel, A., Camerer, C.F., and O'Doherty, J.P. (2010). 'Neur Inequality-averse Social Preferences', _Nature_ 463: 1089–91.

Trinkaus, E. (2004). 'Eyasi 1 and the Suprainiac Fossa', _American Journal of_ pology 124: 28–32.

Trinkaus, E. (2007). 'European Early Modern Humans and the Fate of the Neandertals', _Proceedings of the National Academy of Sciences USA_ 104: 7367–72.

Trinkaus, E., Moldovan, O., Milota, S., Bîlgăr, A., Sarcina, L., Athreya, S., Bailey, S.E., et al. (2003). 'An Early Modern Human from the Peştera cu Oase, Romania', _Proceedings of the National Academy of Sciences USA_ 100: 11231–6.

Trinkaus, E. and Shipman, P. (1993). _The Neandertals_. London: Pimlico.

Trivers, R.L. (1971). 'The Evolution of Reciprocal Altruism', _Quarterly Review of Biology_ 46: 35–57.

Trivers, R.L. (1972). 'Parental Investment and Sexual Selection', in B. Campbell (ed.), _Sexual Selection and the Descent of Man 1871–1971_. Chicago: Aldine-Atherton, pp. 136–79.

Tryon, C.A. (2010). 'Alternative Explanations for Early Hominin Non-utilitarian Behavior at Wonderwerk Cave, South Africa', _Journal of Taphonomy_ 8: 235–42.

Tsuru, D. (1998). 'Diversity of Spirit Ritual Performances among the Baka Pygmies in Southeastern Cameroon', _African Study Monographs, Supplementary Issue_ 25: 47–84.

Tulving, E. (1972). 'Episodic and Semantic Memory', in E. Tulving and W. Donaldson (eds), _Organization of Memory_. New York: Academic Press, pp. 381–403.

Tulving, E. (2002). 'Episodic Memory: From Mind to Brain', _Annual Review of Psychology_ 53: 1–25.

Turnbull, C. (1966). _Wayward Servants: The Two Worlds of the African Pygmies_. London: Eyre and Spottiswoode.

Turner, V. (1967). _The Forest of Symbols: Aspects of Ndembu Ritual_. Ithaca and London: Cornell University Press.

Turner, V. (1969). _The Ritual Process: Structure and Anti-structure_. Harmondsworth: Penguin.

Turner, V. (1982). _From Ritual to Theatre: The Human Seriousness of Play_. New York: PAJ Publications.

Turner, R. and Whitehead, C. (2008). 'How Collective Representations Can Change the Structure of the Brain', in C. Whitehead (ed.), _The Origin of Consciousness in the Social World_. Exeter: Imprint Academic, pp. 43–57.

Turq, A. (1999). 'Reflections on the Middle Palaeolithic of the Aquitaine Basin', in W. Roebroeks and C. Gamble (eds), _The Middle Palaeolithic Occupation of Europe_. Leiden: Leiden University Press, pp. 107–20.

Tylen, K., Weed, E., Wallentin, M., Roepstorff, A., and Frith, C.D. (2010). 'Language as a Tool for Interacting Minds', _Mind & Language_ 25: 3–29.

Ulbaek, I. (1998). 'The Origin of Language and Cognition', in J.R. Hurford, M. Studdert-Kennedy, and C.D. Knight (eds), _Approaches to the Evolution of Language: Social and Cognitive Bases_. Cambridge: Cambridge University Press, pp. 30–43.

Underhill, D. (2011). 'The Study of the Fauresmith: A Review', _The South African Archaeological Bulletin_ 66: 15–26.

Underhill, D. (2012). _The Fauresmith: The Transition from the Earlier to Middle Stone Ages in Northern South Africa_. Ph.D. Thesis, University of Southampton.

Vaesen, K. (2012). 'The Cognitive Bases of Human Tool Use', *Behavioral and Brain Science* 35 (4): 203–18.

Valensi, P. (2001). 'The Elephants of Terra Amata Open Air Site (Lower Palaeolithic, France)', in G. Cavaretta, P. Gioia, M. Mussi, and M. Palumbo (eds), *The World of Elephants—First International Congress, 16–20 January, Rome*. Rome: Consiglio Nazionale della Ricerche, pp. 260–4.

Van de Velde, F. (2009). 'The Rise of Peripheral Modifiers in the Noun Phrase', in M. Dufresne, F. Dupuis, and E. Vocaj (eds), *Historical Linguistics 2007: Selected Papers from the 18th International Conference on Historical Linguistics, Montreal, 6–11 August 2007*. Amsterdam: John Benjamins, pp. 175–84.

van Hooff, J.A.R.A.M. (1967). 'The Facial Displays of the Catarrhine Monkeys and Apes', in D. Morris (ed.), *Primate Ethology*. London: Weidenfeld & Nicolson, pp. 7–68.

van Hooff, J.A.R.A.M. (1973). 'A Structural Analysis of the Social Behaviour of a Semi-captive Group of Chimpanzees', in M. von Cranach and I. Vine (eds), *Social Communication and Movement: Studies of Interaction and Expression in Man and Chimpanzee*. London and New York: Academic Press, pp. 75–162.

van Hooff, J.A.R.A.M. and Preuschoft, S. (2003). 'Laughter and Smiling: The Intertwining of Nature and Culture', in F.B.M. de Waal and P.L. Tyack (eds), *Animal Social Complexity*. Cambridge, MA: Harvard University Press, pp. 260–87.

Van Lawick-Goodall, J. (1968a). 'The Behavior of Free-ranging Chimpanzees in the Gombe Stream Reserve', *Animal Behaviour Monographs* 1(3): 161–311.

Van Lawick-Goodall, J. (1968b). 'A Preliminary Report on Expressive Movements and Communication in the Gombe Stream Chimpanzees', in P.C. Jay (ed.), *Primates. Studies in Adaptation and Variability*. New York: Holt, Rinehart, and Winston, pp. 313–74.

van Schaik, C.P., Ancrenaz, M., Borgen, G., Galdikas, B.M., Knott, C.D., Singleton, I., et al. (2003). 'Orangutan Cultures and the Evolution of Material Culture', *Science* 299: 102–5.

van Schaik, C.P. and Burkart, J.M. (2010). 'Mind the Gap: Cooperative Breeding and the Evolution of Our Unique Features', in P.M. Kappeler and J.B. Silk (eds), *Mind the Gap: Tracing the Origins of Human Universals*. Berlin/Heidelberg: Springer Verlag.

van Schaik, C.P., Deaner, R.O., and Merrill, M.Y. (1999). 'The Conditions for Tool Use in Primates: Implications for the Evolution of Material Culture', *Journal of Human Evolution* 36: 719–41.

van Schaik, C.P., Isler, K., and Burkart, J. (2012). 'Explaining Brain Size Variation: From Social to Cultural Brain', *Trends in Cognitive Sciences* 16: 277–84.

van Trijp, R. (2012a). 'Not as Awful as it Seems: Explaining German Case through Computational Experiments in Fluid Construction Grammar', *Proceedings of the 13th ACL*, Avignon, pp. 829–39.

van Trijp, R. (2012b). 'Self-Assessing Agents for Explaining Language Change: A Case Study in German', *Proceedings of the 20th European Conference on Artificial Intelligence*, Montpellier.

Vanhaeren, M., d'Errico, F., Stringer, C., James, S.L., Todd, J.A., and Mienis, H.K. (2006). 'Middle Paleolithic Shell Beads in Israel and Algeria', *Science* 312: 1785–8.

Vea, J.J. and Sabater-Pi, J. (1998). 'Spontaneous Pointing Behaviour in the Wild Pygmy Chimpanzee (*Pan paniscus*)', *Folia Primatologica* 69(5): 289–90.

Vekua, A., Lordkipanidze, D., Rightmire, G.P., Agusti, J., Ferring, R., Maisuradze, G., Moush-kelishvili, A., Nioradze, M., Ponce de Leon, M., Tappen, M., Tvalchrelidze, M., and Zolli-kofer, C. (2002). 'A New Skull of Early *Homo* from Dmanisi, Georgia', *Science* 297: 85–9.

Verdu, P., Austerlitz, F., Estoup, A., Vitalis, R., Georges, M., Théry, S., Froment, A., Le Bomin, S., Gessain, A., Hombert, J.-M., Van der Veen, L., Quintana-Murci, L., Bahuchet, S., and Heyer, E. (2009). 'Origins and Genetic Diversity of Pygmy Hunter-gatherers from Western Central Africa', *Current Biology* 19: 312–18.

Vernes, S.C., Newbury, D.F., Abrahams, B.S., Winchester, L., Nicod, J., Groszer, M., Alarcón, M., Oliver, P.L., Davies, K.E., Geschwind, D. H., Monaco, A.P., and Fisher, S.E. (2008). 'A Functional Genetic Link between Distinct Developmental Language Disorders', *New England Journal of Medicine* 359: 2337–45.

Vértes, L. (1959). 'Churinga de Tata (Hongrie)', *Bulletin de la Société préhistorique de France* 56: 604–11.

Villa, P. and Lenoir, M. (2009). 'Hunting and Hunting Weapons of the Lower and Middle Paleolithic of Europe', in J.-J. Hublin and M.P. Richards (eds), *The Evolution of Hominin Diets: Integrating Approaches to the Study of Palaeolithic Subsistence*. Netherlands: Springer, pp. 59–85. doi: 10.1007/978-1-4020-9699-0.

Vinicius, L. (2010). *Modular Evolution: How Natural Selection Produces Biological Complexity*. Cambridge: Cambridge University Press.

Viveiros de Castro, E. (1998). 'Cosmological Deixis and Amerindian Perspectivism', *Journal of the Royal Anthropological Institute* 4(3): 469–88.

Vogel, J. (2001). 'Radiometric Dates for the Middle Stone Age in South Africa', in P. Tobias, M. Raath, J. Moggi-Cecchi, G. Doyle (eds), *Humanity from African Naissance to Coming Millennia*. Florence: Firenze University Press/Johannesburg: Witwatersrand University Press, pp. 261–8.

Vogel, P. and Comrie, B., eds (2000). *Approaches to the Typology of Word Classes*. Berlin: Mouton.

Volman, T. (1981). *The Middle Stone Age in the Southern Cape*. Ph.D. Thesis. Chicago: University of Chicago.

Volman, T. (1984). 'Early Prehistory of Southern Africa', in R. Klein (ed.), *Southern African Prehistory and Paleoenvironments*. Rotterdam: Balkema, pp. 169–220.

Vygotsky, L.S. (1978). 'Mind in Society: The Development of Higher Psychological Processes', Cambridge, MA: Harvard University Press.

Vygotsky, L.S. (1986 [1934]). *Thought and Language*. Cambridge, MA: MIT Press.

de Waal, F.B.M. (1987). 'Tension Regulation and Nonreproductive Functions of Sex in Captive Bonobos', *National Geographic Research* 3(3): 318–35.

de Waal, F.B.M. (1988). 'The Communicative Repertoire of Captive Bonobos (*Pan Paniscus*) Compared to that of Chimpanzees. *Behaviour* 106(3–4): 183–251.

de Waal, F.B.M. (1996). *Good Natured: The Origins of Right and Wrong in Humans and Other Animals*. Cambridge, MA: Harvard University Press.

de Waal, F.B.M. (1997). *Bonobo: The Forgotten Ape*. Berkeley: University of California Press.

de Waal, F.B.M. (2001). *The Ape and the Sushi Master*. London: Allen Lane.

de Waal, F.B.M. (2007). 'The "Russian Doll" Model of Empathy and Imitation', in S. Bråten (ed.), *On Being Moved: From Mirror Neurons to Empathy*. Amsterdam/Philadelphia: Benjamins, pp. 35–48.

Waddington, C.H. (1953). 'Epigenetics and evolution', in R. Brown and J.F. Danielli (eds), *Evolution* (SEB Symposium VII). Cambridge, Cambridge University Press, pp. 186–99.

Waddington, C.H. (1957). *The Strategy of the Genes*. Allen and Unwin, London.

Wadley, L., Hodgskiss, T., and Grant, M. (2009). 'Implications for Complex Cognition from the Hafting of Tools with Compound Adhesives in the Middle Stone Age, South Africa', *Proceedings of the National Academy of Science* 106(24): 9590–4.

Walsh, S., Bramblett, C.A., and Alford, P.L. (1982). 'A Vocabulary of Abnormal Behaviors in Restrictively Reared Chimpanzees', *American Journal of Primatology* 3: 315–19.

Walton, K. (1990). *Mimesis As Make-believe: On the Foundation of the Representational Arts.* Harvard: Harvard University Press.

Warneken, F. and Tomasello, M. (2006). 'Altruistic Helping in Human Infants and Young Chimpanzees', *Science* 311: 1301–3.

Warneken, F. and Tomasello, M. (2009). 'The Roots of Human Altruism', *British Journal of Psychology* 100(August): 455–71. doi:10.1348/000712608X379061.

Watts, D.P. (2000). 'Grooming Between Male Chimpanzees at Ngogo, Kibale National Park, Uganda. I. Partner Number and Diversity and Reciprocity', *International Journal of Primatology* 21: 189–210.

Watts, I. (1998). *The Origins of Symbolic Culture: The Southern African Middle Stone Age and Khoisan Ethnography.* Ph.D. dissertation, University of London.

Watts, I. (1999). 'The Origin of Symbolic Culture', in R. Dunbar, C. Knight, and C. Power (eds), *The Evolution of Culture: A Historical and Scientific Overview*. Edinburgh: Edinburgh University Press, pp. 113–46.

Watts, I. (2002). 'Ochre in the Middle Stone Age of Southern Africa: Ritualized Display or Hide Preservative?', *South African Archaeological Bulletin* 57(175): 1–14.

Watts, I. (2005). '"Time, Too, Grows on the Moon": Some Evidence for Knight's Theory of a Human Universal', in W. James and D. Mills (eds), *The Qualities of Time: Anthropological Approaches*. New York: Berg, pp. 95–118.

Watts, I. (2009). 'Red Ochre, Body Painting and Language: Interpreting the Blombos Ochre', in R. Botha and C. Knight (eds), *The Cradle of Language: Studies in the Evolution of Language*. Oxford: Oxford University Press, pp. 62–92.

Watts, I. (2010). 'The Pigments from Pinnacle Point Cave 13B, Western Cape, South Africa', *Journal of Human Evolution* 59: 392–411.

Weaver, T.D. (2009). 'The Meaning of Neandertal Skeletal Morphology', *Proceedings of the National Academy of Sciences USA* 106: 16028–33.

Weaver, T.D. and Hublin, J.-J. (2009). 'Neandertal Birth Canal Shape and the Evolution of Human Childbirth', *Proceedings of the National Academy of Sciences* 106: 8151–6.

Weaver, T.D., Roseman, C.C., and Stringer, C.B. (2007). 'Were Neandertal and Modern Human Cranial Differences Produced by Natural Selection or Genetic Drift?', *Journal of Human Evolution* 53: 135–45.

Weissner, P. (2002). 'Taking the Risk Out of Risky Transactions: A Forager's Dilemma', in F.K. Salter (ed.), *Risky Transactions: Trust, Kinship and Ethnicity*. New York: Berghahn Books, pp. 21–43.

Wellman, B. (2012). 'Is Dunbar's Number Up?', *British Journal of Psychology* 103: 174–6.

Wenzel, S. (2007). 'Neanderthal Presence and Behaviour in Central and Northwestern Europe during MIS 5e', in F. Sirocko, M. Claussen, M. Sánchez-Goñi, and T. Litt (eds), *The Climate of Past Interglacials*. Developments in Quaternary Sciences 7. Amsterdam: Elsevier, pp. 173–93.

Wernert, P. (1957). 'Stratigraphie paléontologique et préhistorique des sediments quaternaires d'Alsace-Achenheim', *Mémoire du service de la carte géologique de l'Alsace-Lorraine*, Université de Strasbourg.

Wescott, R., Hewes, G., and Stokoe, W.C. (1974). *Language Origins*. Silver Spring, MD: Linstok Press.

West-Eberhard, M.J. (2003). *Developmental Plasticity and Evolution*. Oxford: Oxford University Press.

Wheatley, T. and Haidt, J. (2005). 'Hypnotic Disgust Makes Moral Judgments More Severe', *Psychological Science* 16: 780.

White, M., Ashton, N., Scott, B. (2011). 'The Emergence, Diversity and Significance of the Mode 3 (Prepared Core) Technologies', in N. Ashton, S. Lewis, and C. Stringer (eds), *The Ancient Human Occupation of Britain*. Developments in Quaternary Science 14. Amsterdam: Elsevier, pp. 53–66.

White, T., Asfaw, B., DeGusta, D., Gilbert, H., Richards, G., Suwa, G., and Clark Howell, F. (2003). 'Pleistocene *Homo sapiens* from Middle Awash, Ethiopia', *Nature* 423: 742–7.

Whitehead, C. (1995). *The Uses of Enchantment: The Role of Altered States of Consciousness in Cultural Origins and Change*. M.Sc. dissertation, Department of Anthropology, University College London.

Whitehead, C. (2001). 'Social Mirrors and Shared Experiential Worlds', *Journal of Consciousness Studies* 8(4): 3–36.

Whitehead, C. (2003). *Social Mirrors and the Brain: Including a Functional Imaging Study of Role-Play and Verse*. Ph.D. thesis, Department of Anthropology, University College London.

Whitehead, C. (2008). 'The Neural Correlates of Work and Play', *Journal of Consciousness Studies* 15: 93–121.

Whitehead, C. (2010a). 'Cultural Distortions of Self and Reality-Perception', in C. Whitehead (ed.), *Social Approaches to Consciousness II, Journal of Consciousness Studies* 17(7–8): 95–118.

Whitehead, C. (2010b). 'The Culture Ready Brain', *Social Cognitive and Affective Neuroscience*. doi: 10.1093/scan/nsq036.

Whitehead, C. (2011). 'Altered Consciousness in Society', in E. Cardeña and M. Winkelman (eds), *Altering Consciousness: A Multidisciplinary Perspective*. Santa Barbara, CA: Praeger Publishers, pp. 181–202.

Whitehead, C. (2012). 'Why the Behavioural Sciences Need the Concept of the Culture Ready Brain', *Anthropological Theory* 12(1): 43–71.

Whitehead, C., Marchant, J.L., Craik, D., and Frith, C.D. (2009). 'Neural Correlates of Observing Pretend Play in which One Object is Represented as Another', *Social Cognitive and Affective Neuroscience* 4: 369–78.

Whiten, A. (1999). 'The Evolution of Deep Social Mind in Humans', in M. Corballis and S.E.G. Lea (eds), *The Descent of Mind: Psychological Perspectives on Hominid Evolution*. Oxford: Oxford University Press, pp. 173–93.

Whiten, A. and Erdal, D. (2012). 'The Human Socio-cognitive Niche and its Evolutionary Origins', *Philosophical Transactions of the Royal Society B* 367: 2119–29. doi:10.1098/rstb.2012.0114.

Whiten, A., Goodall, J., McGrew, W.C., Nishida, T., Reynolds, V., Sugiyama, Y., et al. (1999). 'Cultures in Chimpanzees', *Nature* 399(6737): 682–5.

Whiten, A. and van Schaik, C.P. (2007). 'The Evolution of Animal "Cultures" and Social Intelligence', *Philosophical Transactions of the Royal Society B* 362: 603–20.

Wierzbicka, A. (1988). *The Semantics of Grammar*. Amsterdam: John Benjamins.

Wierzbicka, A. (1991). *Cross-cultural Pragmatics: The Semantics of Human Interaction*. Berlin/New York: Mouton.

Wilkins, J. and Chazan, M. (2012). 'Blade Production ~500 Thousand Years Ago at Kathu Pan 1, South Africa: Support for a Multiple Origins Hypothesis for Early Middle Pleistocene Blade Technologies', *Journal of Archaeological Science* 39: 1883–900.

Wilkins, J., Schoville, B., Brown, K., and Chazan, M. (2012). 'Evidence for Early Hafted Hunting Technology', *Science* 338: 942–6.

Wilkinson, R., Leudar, I., and Pika, S. (2012). 'Requesting Behaviours Within Episodes of Active Sharing: A New Look on Chimpanzee Signalling', in S. Pika and K. Liebal (eds), *Developments in Primate Gesture Research*. Amsterdam: John Benjamins, pp. 199–221.

Willems, R.M., Ozyurek, A., and Hagoort, P. (2007). 'When Language Meets Action: The Neural Integration of Gesture and Speech', *Cerebral Cortex*, 17: 2322–33.

Williams, G.C. (1966). *Adaptation and Natural Selection: A Critique of Some Current Evolutionary Thought*. Princeton: Princeton University Press.

Williams, J.M., Pusey, A.E., Carlis, J.V., Farm, B.P., and Goodall, J. (2002), 'Female Competition and Male Territorial Behaviour Influence Female Chimpanzees' Ranging Patterns', *Animal Behaviour* 63: 347–60.

Wilson, D.S. and O'Gorman, R. (2003). 'Emotions and Actions Associated with Norm-breaking Events', *Human Nature* 14: 277–304. doi:10.1007/s12110-003-1007-z.

Wilson, D.S. and Wilson, E.O. (2007). 'Rethinking the Theoretical Foundation of Sociobiology', *Quarterly Review of Biology* 82: 327–48.

Wilson, E.O. (1998). *Consilience: The Unity of Knowledge*. New York: Knopf.

Winnicott, D.W. (1974). *Playing and Reality*. London: Penguin.

Wittgenstein, L. (1953). *Philosophical Investigations*. London: Blackwell.

Wittig, R.M., Crockford, C., Lehmann, J., Whitten, P.L., Seyfarth, R.M., and Cheney, D.L. (2008). 'Focused Grooming Networks and Stress Alleviation in Wild Female Baboons', *Hormones and Behaviour* 54(1): 170–7.

Wolpoff, M. (1996–97). *Human Evolution*. College Custom Series. New York: McGraw-Hill.

Won, Y. J. and Hey, J. (2005). 'Divergence Population Genetics of Chimpanzees', *Molecular Biology and Evolution* 22(2): 297–307.

Wood, B., ed. (2011). *Wiley-Blackwell Encyclopedia of Human Evolution*. Hoboken, NJ: Blackwell Publishing.

Woodburn, J. (1982). 'Egalitarian Societies.' *Man, the Journal of the Royal Anthropological Institute*, 17, no. 3: 431–51.

Woodburn, J. (2005). 'Egalitarian Societies Revisited', in T. Widlok and W.G. Tadesse (eds), *Property and Equality. Volume 1: Ritualisation, Sharing, Egalitarianism*. Oxford and New York: Berghahn, pp. 18–31.

Worden, R. (1998). 'The Evolution of Language from Social Intelligence', in J.R. Hurford, M. Studdert-Kennedy, and C. Knight (eds), *Approaches to the Evolution of Language: Social and Cognitive Bases*. Cambridge: Cambridge University Press, pp. 148–66.

Wrangham, R.W. (1993). 'The Evolution of Sexuality in Chimpanzees and Bonobos', *Human Nature* 4(1): 47–79.

Wrangham, R.W. (2009). *Catching Fire: How Cooking Made Us Human*. New York: Basic Books.

Wrangham, R.W. and Conklin-Brittain, N. (2003). 'Cooking as a Biological Trait', *The online version of Comparative Biochemistry and Physiology Part A: Molecular & Integrative Physiology* 136(1): 35–46.

Wrangham, R.W., Holland Jones, J., Laden, G., Pilbeam, D., and Conklin-Brittain, N. (1999). 'The Raw and the Stolen', *Current Anthropology* 40: 567–94.

Wrangham, R.W., Wilson, M.L., and Muller, M.N. (2006). 'Comparative Rates of Violence in Chimpanzees and Humans', *Primates* 47(1): 14–26.

Wray, A. (1998). 'Protolanguage as a Holistic System for Social Interaction', *Language and Communication* 18: 47–67.

Wray, A. (2002). *Formulaic Language and the Lexicon*. Cambridge: Cambridge University Press.

Wreschner, E. (1983). *Studies in Prehistoric Ochre Technology*. Ph.D. Thesis. Jerusalem: Hebrew University.

Wreschner, E. (1985). 'Evidence and Interpretation of Red Ochre in the Early Prehistoric Sequences', in P. Tobias (ed.), *Hominid Evolution: Past, Present, Future*. New York: Alan Liss, pp. 387–94.

Wright, C. (1873). 'Evolution of Self-Consciousness', *The North American Review* 116(239): 245–310.

Wright, J. (1906). *An Old High German Primer*. 2nd edn. Oxford: Clarendon Press.

Wyman, E. and Rakoczy, H. (2011). 'Social Conventions, Institutions and Human Uniqueness: Lessons from Children and Chimpanzees', in W. Welsch, W. Singer, and A. Wunder (eds), *Interdisciplinary Anthropology: Continuing Evolution of Man*. New York: Springer, pp. 131–56.

Wyman, E., Rakoczy, H., and Tomasello, M. (2009a). 'Normativity and Context in Young Children's Pretend Play', *Cognitive Development* 24: 149–55.

Wyman, E., Rakoczy, H., and Tomasello, M. (2009b). 'Young Children Understand Multiple Pretend Identities in their Object Play', *British Journal of Developmental Psychology* 27(2): 385–404.

Wyman, E. and Tomasello, M. (2007). 'The Ontogenetic Origins of Cooperation', in R. Dunbar and L. Barrett (eds), *The Oxford Handbook of Evolutionary Psychology*. Oxford: Oxford University Press, pp. 227–37.

Wynn, T. (2002). 'Archaeology and Cognitive Evolution', *Behavioral and Brain Sciences* 25: 389–438.

Yamaguchi, N., Kitchener, A.C., Gilissen, E., and Macdonald, D.W. (2009). 'Brain Size of the Lion (*Panthera Leo*) and the Tiger (*P. Tigris*): Implications for Intrageneric Phylogeny,

Intraspecific Differences and the Effects of Captivity', *Biological Journal of the Linnean Society* 98: 85–93.

Yamamoto, S., Yamakoshi, G., Humle, T., and Matsuzawa, T. (2008). 'Invention and Modification of a New Tool Use Behavior: Ant-Fishing in Trees by a Wild Chimpanzee (*Pan Troglodytes Verus*) at Bossou, Guinea', *American Journal of Primatology* 70: 699–702.

Yerkes, R.M. (1943). *Chimpanzees: A Laboratory Colony*. New Haven: Yale University Press.

Young, S. (1992). 'Human Facial Expressions', in S. Jones, R. Martin, and D. Pilbeam (eds), *The Cambridge Encyclopedia of Human Evolution*. Cambridge: Cambridge University Press, pp. 164–5.

Yu, N., Fu, Y.-X., and Li, W.-H. (2002). 'DNA Polymorphism in a Worldwide Sample of Human X Chromosomes', *Molecular Biology and Evolution* 19: 2131–41.

Zahavi, A. (1975). 'Mate Selection—A Selection for a Handicap', *Journal of Theoretical Biology* 53: 205–14.

Zahavi, A. (1993). 'The Fallacy of Conventional Signalling', *Philosophical Transactions of the Royal Society of London* 340: 227–30.

Zahavi, A. (2003). 'Indirect Selection and Individual Selection in Sociobiology: My Personal Views On Theories of Social Behaviour', *Animal Behavior* 65: 859–63.

Zahavi, A. and Zahavi, A. (1997). *The Handicap Principle. A Missing Piece in Darwin's Puzzle*. New York/Oxford: Oxford University Press.

Zietkiewicz, E., Yotova, V., Gehl, D., Wambach, T., Arrieta, I., Batzer, M., Cole, D.E.C., et al. (2003). 'Haplotypes in the Dystrophin DNA Segment Point to a Mosaic Origin of Modern Human Diversity', *American Journal of Human Genetics* 73: 994–1015.

Zilhão, J. (2007). 'The Emergence of Ornaments and Art: An Archaeological Perspective on the Origins of "Behavioural Modernity"', *Journal of Archaeological Research* 15: 1–54.

Zilhão, J. (2011). 'The Emergence of Language, Art and Symbolic Thinking: A Neanderthal Test of Competing Hypotheses', in C. Henshilwood and F. d'Errico (eds), *Homo Symbolicus: The Dawn of Language, Imagination and Spirituality*. Amsterdam: John Benjamins, pp. 111–32.

Zilhão, J., Angelucci, D., Badal-García, E., d'Errico, F., Daniel, F., Dayet, L, Douka, K., Higham, T., Martínez-Sánchez, M., Montes-Bernárdez, R., Murcia-Mascarós, S., Pérez-Sirvent, C., Roldán-García, C., Vanhaeren, M., Villaverde, V., Wood, R., and Zapata, J. (2010). 'Symbolic Use of Marine Shells and Mineral Pigments by Iberian Neandertals', *Proceedings of the National Academy of Sciences* 107: 1023–8.

Zlatev, J. (2003). 'Meaning = Life (+ Culture): An Outline of A Unified Biocultural Theory of Meaning', *Evolution of Communication* 4(2): 253–96.

Zlatev, J. (2008). 'The Coevolution of Intersubjectivity and Bodily Mimesis', in J. Zlatev, T. Racine, C. Sinha, and E. Itkonen (eds), *The Shared Mind: Perspectives on Intersubjectivity*. Amsterdam: John Benjamins, pp. 215–44.

Zlatev, J. and Sinha, C., eds (2008). *The Shared Mind: Perspectives on Intersubjectivity: Converging Evidence in Language and Communication Research*. Amsterdam: John Benjamins.

Zollikofer, C.P.E. and Ponce de Léon, M.S. (2010). 'The Evolution of Hominin Ontogenies', *Seminars in Cell and Developmental Biology* 21: 441–52.

Zuberbühler, K. (2003). 'Referential Signalling in Non-human Primates: Cognitive Precursors and Limitations for the Evolution of Language', *Advances in the Study of Behavior* 33: 265–307.

Zuberbühler, K. (2006). 'Alarm Calls', in K. Brown (ed.), *Encyclopedia of Language and Linguistics*. 2nd edn. Oxford: Elsevier, pp. 143–55.

Zuberbühler, K. (2012). 'Cooperative Breeding and the Evolution of Vocal Flexibility', in M. Tallerman and K.R. Gibson (eds), *Oxford Handbook of Language Evolution*. Oxford: Oxford University Press, pp. 71–81.

Zuberbühler, K., Arnold, K., and Slocombe, K. (2011). 'Living Links to Human Language', in A. Vilain, J.-L. Schwartz, C. Abry, and J. Vauclair (eds), *Primate Communication and Human Language*. Amsterdam: John Benjamins, pp. 13–38.

Zuidema, W.H. (2005). *The Major Transitions in the Evolution of Language*. Ph.D. Thesis. Edinburgh: University of Edinburgh.

Zuidema, W.H and de Boer, B. (2009). 'The Evolution of Combinatorial Phonology', *Journal of Phonetics* 37(2): 125–44.

Index of Authors

Index of Subjects

Oxford Studies in the Evolution of Language

General Editors
Kathleen R. Gibson, *University of Texas at Houston,*
and Maggie Tallerman, *Newcastle University*

Published